JavaScript
The Definitive Guide

JavaScript

The Definitive Guide

Third Edition

David Flanagan

O'REILLY®

Beijing · Cambridge · Köln · Paris · Sebastopol · Taipei · Tokyo

JavaScript: The Definitive Guide, Third Edition
by David Flanagan

Copyright © 1998, 1997, 1996 O'Reilly & Associates, Inc. All rights reserved.
Printed in the United States of America.

Published by O'Reilly & Associates, Inc., 101 Morris Street, Sebastopol, CA 95472.

Editor: Paula Ferguson

Production Editor: Madeleine Newell

Printing History:

August 1996:	Beta Edition.
January 1997:	Second Edition.
June 1998:	Third Edition.

ISBN: 1-56592-392-8   [12/98]

Table of Contents

Preface

This long-overdue third edition of *JavaScript: The Definitive Guide* documents JavaScript 1.2, the version of the language supported by Netscape Navigator 4 and Microsoft Internet Explorer 4. This edition contains a substantial amount of new material: JavaScript 1.2 adds a number of useful and important features to the core language, and the fourth generation web browsers support a variety of exciting new client-side JavaScript features. In addition, the chapters have been overhauled and reorganized, resulting, I believe, in a much better book.

JavaScript 1.2 includes many new features on the client side, notably a new event model, style sheets, and dynamic positioning. Unfortunately, however, the implementations of these features in Navigator 4 and Internet Explorer 4 are almost completely incompatible. Dealing with Dynamic HTML incompatibilities is probably the most difficult (and certainly most annoying) task facing programmers who want to make use of the cutting-edge features of JavaScript 1.2. Chapter 15, *Events and Event Handling*, and Chapter 17, *Dynamic HTML*, discuss these new features and the compatibility issues they raise.

As JavaScript developers, we face a difficult problem: JavaScript continues to evolve more rapidly than it can be documented. This is an exciting time for JavaScript and there are a number of important developments ongoing as I write this. Although the publication schedule for this book won't allow me to cover current developments in this edition, interested readers may want to monitor the progress in these areas:

*   Netscape has released the complete source code to Communicator, nominally an early developer's release of their Version 5 product. This release includes source code for the JavaScript interpreter, and this version of the interpreter contains some features to be found in Version 1.3 of the language. See *http://www.mozilla.org*.

- A group that includes representatives from Netscape and Microsoft, working under the auspices of the World Wide Web Consortium (W3C), is getting close to issuing a Document Object Model (DOM) recommendation. This document would standardize the way that JavaScript interacts with HTML (and XML) documents in Navigator and Internet Explorer. Hopefully, this standard will arrive in time to be supported (compatibly) by the fifth-generation browsers from Netscape and Microsoft. A future version of this DOM will also standardize the event model, further increasing compatibility between conforming browsers. See http://www.w3c.org/DOM/.

- The ECMA-262 standard that specifies the core JavaScript language is expected to be adopted very soon by the International Standards Organization (ISO), making it standard ISO 16262. The current version of this standard specifies a version of core JavaScript that is approximately equal to JavaScript 1.1. Netscape and Microsoft are making proposals, however, for an update to the standard. Such an update would presumably include features added in JavaScript 1.2 and perhaps JavaScript 1.3 as well. At this writing, there is no public information available about this update, but readers can monitor the ECMA web site at http://www.ecma.ch.

Conventions Used in This Book

I use the following formatting conventions in this book:

- **Bold** is occasionally used to refer to particular keys on a computer keyboard or to portions of a user interface, such as the **Back** button or the **Options** menu.

- *Italic* is used for emphasis and to signify the first use of a term. Italic is also used for email addresses, web sites, FTP sites, file and directory names, and newsgroups. Furthermore, italic is used in this book for the names of Java™ classes, to help keep Java class names distinct from JavaScript names.

- `Letter Gothic` is used in all JavaScript code and HTML text listings, and generally for anything that you would type literally when programming.

- `Letter Gothic Oblique` is used for the names of function arguments, and generally as a placeholder to indicate an item that should be replaced with an actual value in your program.

Request for Comments

Please help us at O'Reilly to improve future editions by reporting any errors, inaccuracies, bugs, misleading or confusing statements, and plain old typos that you find anywhere in the book. Email your bug reports and comments to us at:

bookquestions@oreilly.com

Please also let us know what we can do to make the book more useful to you. We take your comments seriously and will try to incorporate reasonable suggestions into future editions of the book.

You can reach us at:

O'Reilly & Associates, Inc.
101 Morris Street
Sebastopol, CA 95472
1-800-998-9938 (in the U.S. or Canada)
1-707-829-0515 (international/local)
1-707-829-0104 (FAX)

Finding the Examples Online

The examples used in this book are available via anonymous FTP on O'Reilly's FTP server. They may be found at:

ftp://ftp.oreilly.com/pub/examples/nutshell/javascript

Acknowledgments

Brendan Eich at Netscape is the originator and chief innovator of JavaScript. I, and many JavaScript developers, owe Brendan a tremendous debt of gratitude for developing JavaScript and for taking the time out of his crazy schedule to answer our questions and even solicit our input. Besides patiently answering my many questions, Brendan also read and provided very helpful comments on the first and third editions of this book.

In addition to Brendan, this book has been blessed by other top-notch technical reviewers, whose comments have gone a long way to making it a stronger, more accurate book. Reviewers for this third edition were Brendan Eich, Waldemar Horwat, and Vidur Apparao at Netscape; Herman Venter at Microsoft; and two independent JavaScript developers, Jay Hodges and Angelo Sirigos.

Dan Shafer of CNET's BUILDER.COM did some preliminary work on the third edition of this book. Although his material was not used in this edition, his ideas and general outline were quite helpful. Norris Boyd and Scott Furman at Netscape also provided useful information for this edition, and Vidur Apparao of Netscape and Scott Issacs of Microsoft each took the time to talk to me about the forthcoming Document Object Model standard. Finally, Dr. Tankred Hirschmann provided challenging insights into the intricacies of JavaScript 1.2 through his web site at *http://www.mpg-ana.uni-potsdam.de/local/js/*.

The second edition of the book benefited greatly from the help and comments of Nick Thompson and Richard Yaker of Netscape; Dr. Shon Katzenberger, Larry Sullivan, and Dave C. Mitchell at Microsoft; and Lynn Rollins of R&B Communications. The first edition was reviewed by Neil Berkman of Bay Networks, and by Andrew Schulman and Terry Allen of O'Reilly & Associates.

This book gains strength from the diversity of editors it has had. Paula Ferguson is the editor of this edition. She's given the book a thorough and much-needed going over, making it easier to read and easier to understand. Frank Willison edited the second edition, and Andrew Schulman edited the first.

David Futato was the production manager for the first two editions of this book, and Madeleine Newell was the production manager and copy editor for this third edition. They were assisted by the whole production team at O'Reilly & Associates. Chris Reilley created the figures for the second edition of the book, and Rob Romano created and updated figures for this third edition. Edie Freedman designed the cover, Kathleen Wilson designed the cover layout, and Nancy Priest and Mary Jane Walsh designed the internal format, which was implemented by Lenny Muellner and Chris Maden. Seth Maislin wrote (and rewrote) the index. Steve Kleinedler proofread this edition, and quality assurance was provided by John Files, Nancy Wolfe Kotary, and Sheryl Avruch.

Finally, my thanks, as always and for so many reasons, to Christie.

David Flanagan
April 1998

1

Introduction to JavaScript

JavaScript is a lightweight interpreted programming language with object-oriented capabilities. The general-purpose core of the language has been embedded in Netscape Navigator, Internet Explorer, and other web browsers and embellished for web programming with the addition of objects that represent the web browser window and its contents. This client-side version of JavaScript allows executable content to be included in web pages—it means that a web page need no longer be static HTML, but can include programs that interact with the user, control the browser, and dynamically create HTML content.

Syntactically, the core JavaScript language resembles C, C++, and Java, with programming constructs such as the `if` statement, the `while` loop, and the `&&` operator. The similarity ends with this syntactic resemblance, however. JavaScript is an untyped language, which means that variables do not need to have a type specified. Objects in JavaScript are more like Perl's associative arrays than they are like structures in C or objects in C++ or Java. The object-oriented inheritance mechanism of JavaScript is like that of the little-known languages Self and NewtonScript, which is quite different from inheritance in C++ and Java. Like Perl, JavaScript is an interpreted language, and it draws inspiration from Perl in a number of places, such as its regular expression and array-handling features.

This chapter is a quick overview of JavaScript; it explains what JavaScript can and cannot do and exposes some myths about the language. It distinguishes the core JavaScript language from embedded and extended versions of the language, such as the client-side JavaScript that is embedded in web browsers and the server-side

JavaScript that is embedded in web servers. (This book documents core and client-side JavaScript.) This chapter also demonstrates real-world web programming with some client-side JavaScript examples.

1.1 JavaScript Myths

JavaScript is the subject of a fair bit of misinformation and confusion. Before proceeding any further with our exploration of JavaScript, it is important that we debunk some common and persistent myths about the language.

1.1.1 JavaScript Is Not Java

One of the most common misconceptions about JavaScript is that it is a simplified version of Java, the programming language from Sun Microsystems. Other than an incomplete syntactic resemblance and the fact that both Java and JavaScript can provide executable content in web browsers, the two languages are entirely unrelated. The similarity of names is purely a marketing ploy (the language was originally called LiveScript and its name was changed to JavaScript at the last minute).

JavaScript and Java do, however, make a good team. The two languages have disjoint sets of capabilities. JavaScript can control browser behavior and content but cannot draw graphics or perform networking. Java has no control over the browser as a whole but can do graphics, networking, and multithreading. Client-side JavaScript can interact with and control Java applets embedded in a web page, and in this sense, JavaScript really can script Java.*

1.1.2 JavaScript Is Not Simple

JavaScript is touted as a scripting language instead of a programming language, the implication being that scripting languages are simpler, that they are programming languages for non-programmers. Indeed, JavaScript appears at first glance to be a fairly simple language, perhaps of the same complexity as BASIC. The language does have a number of features designed to make it more forgiving and easier to use for new and unsophisticated programmers. Non-programmers can use JavaScript for limited, cookbook-style programming tasks.

Beneath its thin veneer of simplicity, however, JavaScript is a full-featured programming language, as complex as any, and more complex than some. Program-

---

* Navigator 3 and later versions support a technology known as LiveConnect, which goes beyond merely interacting with applets and allows much more comprehensive scripting of Java. Chapter 20, *LiveConnect: JavaScript and Java*, describes LiveConnect in detail.

mers who attempt to use JavaScript for non-trivial tasks often find the process frustrating if they do not have a solid understanding of the language. Therefore, this book documents JavaScript comprehensively so that you can develop a sophisticated understanding of the language.

1.2 Versions of JavaScript

The JavaScript language is still evolving, and several different versions of JavaScript are available. The original version of the language, now almost obsolete, is JavaScript 1.0. The next version, JavaScript 1.1, is much more robust and introduces some important new features, such as improved support for arrays. As of this writing, the current version of the language is JavaScript 1.2, which contains a number of new features, like support for regular expressions, the `switch` statement, and the `delete` operator. The upcoming version of the language is expected to be called JavaScript 1.3, and it is likely to have still more new features, such as support for exception handling (an advanced error handling and recovery feature found in languages like C++ and Java).

The name JavaScript is owned by Netscape. Microsoft's implementation of the language is officially known as JScript. Versions of JScript are more or less compatible with the equivalent versions of JavaScript, although JScript skipped a version and went directly from JavaScript 1.0 compatibility to JavaScript 1.2 compatibility.

JavaScript has been standardized by the European Computer Manufacturers Association (ECMA) and is on a fast track for standardization by the International Standards Organization. The relevant standards are ECMA-262, and, when standardized by ISO, ISO-16262. These standards define a language officially known as ECMAScript, which is approximately equivalent to JavaScript 1.1, although not all implementations of JavaScript currently conform to all details of the ECMA standard. The name ECMAScript is universally regarded as ugly and cumbersome and was chosen precisely for this reason: it favors neither Netscape's JavaScript nor Microsoft's JScript. In this book, I use the term ECMA-262 or simply ECMA to refer to the standardized version of the language. As of this writing, proposals for a second, updated version of the standard have been submitted to ECMA by Netscape and Microsoft. The process is still in its early stages, however, and it will be some time before ECMA-262 Version 2 becomes standardized.

In addition to the various versions of the core JavaScript language, variants exist for each context that JavaScript is embedded in. The following sections describe some of these contexts.

1.2.1 Client-Side JavaScript

When a JavaScript interpreter is embedded in a web browser, the result is client-side JavaScript. This is by far the most common variant of JavaScript; when most people refer to JavaScript, they usually mean client-side JavaScript. This book documents client-side JavaScript, along with the core JavaScript language that client-side JavaScript incorporates.

We'll discuss client-side JavaScript and its capabilities in much more detail later in this chapter. In brief, though, client-side JavaScript combines the scripting ability of a JavaScript interpreter with the document object model defined by a web browser. These two distinct technologies combine in a synergistic way, so the result is greater than the sum of its parts: client-side JavaScript enables executable content to be distributed over the web and is at the heart of a new generation of "Dynamic HTML" documents.

As with the core language itself, there are a number of different versions of client-side JavaScript. Different browser versions incorporate different versions of the JavaScript interpreter. Table 1-1 shows the core language version supported by different versions of the two major web browsers.

Table 1–1: Versions of JavaScript Supported by Various Browsers

| | Browser Name | |
Browser Version	Netscape Navigator	Microsoft Internet Explorer
2	JavaScript 1.0	
3	JavaScript 1.1	JavaScript 1.0
4	JavaScript 1.2; not fully ECMA-262 compliant	JavaScript 1.2; ECMA-262 compliant

The differences and incompatibilities between Netscape's and Microsoft's client-side versions of JavaScript are much greater than the differences between their respective implementations of the core language. Still, there is a large subset of client-side JavaScript features that both browsers agree upon. For lack of better names, versions of client-side JavaScript are typically referred to by the version of the core language they are based on. Thus, in many contexts, the term JavaScript 1.2 refers to the version of client-side JavaScript supported by Navigator 4 and Internet Explorer 4. When I use core-language version numbers to refer to client-side versions of JavaScript, I am referring to the compatible subset of features supported by Navigator and Internet Explorer. When I discuss client-side features specific to one browser or the other, I will refer to the browser by name and version number.

Note that Navigator and Internet Explorer are not the only browsers that support client-side JavaScript. For example, Opera 3 (*www.operasoftware.com*), supports client-side JavaScript as well. However, since Navigator and Internet Explorer have the vast majority of market share, they are the only browsers discussed explicitly in this book. Client-side JavaScript implementations in other browsers should conform fairly closely to the implementations in these two browsers.

Similarly, JavaScript is not the only programming language that can be embedded within a web browser. For example, Internet Explorer also supports a language known as VBScript. This variant of Microsoft's Visual Basic language provides many of the same features as JavaScript but can only be used with Microsoft browsers.* The HTML 4.0 specification uses the Tcl programming language as an example of an embedded scripting language in its discussion of the HTML <SCRIPT> tag. While there are no mainstream browsers that support Tcl for this purpose, there is no reason that a browser could not easily support this language.

Readers will notice that this book covers Navigator more thoroughly than Internet Explorer. This bias towards Netscape has steadily declined in each subsequent edition of the book, as Microsoft's implementation of client-side JavaScript has matured and as Internet Explorer has gained market share, but the bias still exists in this edition. The primary reason for the bias is that Netscape invented JavaScript. Until standardization efforts are complete and the language stops evolving so rapidly, Netscape's implementation must naturally be regarded as more definitive and leading-edge than Microsoft's. On the other hand, as we'll see in Chapter 14, *The Document Object Model*, and elsewhere, there are important areas in which Microsoft's implementation of client-side JavaScript is much closer to emerging standards than Netscape's is.

1.2.2 Server-Side JavaScript

Later in this chapter, you'll see how the core JavaScript language has been extended for use in web browsers. Netscape has also taken the core language and extended it in an entirely different way for use in web servers. Netscape initially called their server-side JavaScript product "LiveWire" (not to be confused with LiveConnect, documented in Chapter 20, or with LiveScript, which was the original name for JavaScript), but now they simply refer to it as server-side JavaScript. Microsoft also supports server-side programming with JavaScript in its web server, using its Active Server Pages (ASP) framework. Since this is a simple overview of server-side scripting, we only discuss Netscape's implementation of server-side JavaScript here.

---

* However, NCompass makes a Navigator plugin called ScriptActive that allows VBScript to work in Navigator (*www.ncompasslabs.com*).

Server-side JavaScript provides an alternative to CGI scripts. It goes beyond the CGI model, in fact, because server-side JavaScript code is embedded directly within HTML pages, which allows executable server-side scripts to be directly intermixed with web content. Whenever a document containing server-side JavaScript code is requested by the client, the server executes the script or scripts contained in the document and sends the resulting document (which may be partially static and partially dynamically generated) to the requester. Because execution speed is a very important issue on production web servers, HTML files that contain server-side JavaScript are precompiled to a binary form that can be more efficiently interpreted and sent to the requesting client.

An obvious capability of server-side JavaScript is to dynamically generate HTML to be displayed by the client. Its most powerful features, however, come from the server-side objects it has access to. The File object, for example, allows a server-side script to read and write files on the server. And the Database object allows scripts to perform SQL database queries and updates.

Besides the File and Database objects, server-side JavaScript also provides other powerful objects, including the Request and Client objects. The Request object encapsulates information about the current HTTP request that the server is processing. This object contains any query string or form values that were submitted with the request, for example. The Client object has a longer lifetime than the Request object and allows a server-side JavaScript script to save state across multiple HTTP requests from the same client. Because this object provides such an easy way to save state between requests, writing programs with server-side JavaScript feels much different from writing simple CGI scripts. In fact, the Client object makes it feasible to go beyond writing scripts and create web applications easily.

Because server-side JavaScript is, at least at this point, a proprietary vendor-specific server-side technology, and because it is used by fewer programmers than client-side JavaScript, it is not documented in this book. Nevertheless, the chapters that discuss the core JavaScript language will still be valuable to server-side JavaScript programmers.

1.2.3 Embedded JavaScript

JavaScript is a general-purpose programming language; its use is not restricted to web browsers and web servers. Although web browsers and servers are currently the only highly visible applications that add scripting capabilities by embedding a JavaScript interpreter, there are certainly many other applications in which such a scripting capability would be very useful. Both Netscape and Microsoft have made their JavaScript interpreters available to companies and to programmers that want to embed them in their applications. In addition, Netscape has made the source code of its JavaScript interpreter freely available, along with all the source code to its web browser, on the *www.mozilla.org* web site.

Also, there is a project underway at Netscape to produce a JavaScript implementation written in Java.* Such an implementation would allow virtually any Java program to include JavaScript scripting capabilities quite easily.

Finally, Netscape and Microsoft are not the only players in the embedded JavaScript market. For example, a company named Nombas (*www.nombas.com*) produces and sells its own commercial JavaScript interpreter, designed specifically to be embedded within applications. Also, Ribbit Software Systems (*www.ribbit-soft.com*) produces a commercial JavaScript interpreter and compiler, both written in Java.

We can expect to see more and more applications that use JavaScript as an embedded scripting language. If you are writing scripts for such an application, you'll find the first half of this book, documenting the core language, to be useful. The web-browser specific chapters, however, will probably not be applicable to your scripts.

1.3 Client-Side JavaScript: Executable Content in Web Pages

When a web browser is augmented with a JavaScript interpreter, it allows executable content to be distributed over the Internet in the form of JavaScript scripts. Example 1-1 shows a simple JavaScript program, or script, embedded in a web page.

Example 1-1: A Simple JavaScript Program

```
<HTML>
<BODY>
<SCRIPT LANGUAGE="JavaScript">
document.write("<h2>Table of Factorials</h2>");
for(i = 1, fact = 1; i < 10; i++, fact *= i) {
    document.write(i + "! = " + fact);
    document.write("<br>");
}
</SCRIPT>
</BODY>
</HTML>
```

---

* Flatteringly enough, the codename for this Netscape project is "Rhino."

When loaded into a JavaScript-enabled browser, this script produces the output shown in Figure 1-1.

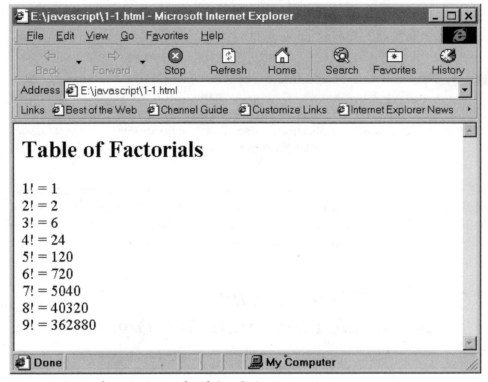

Figure 1–1: A web page generated with JavaScript

As you can see in this example, the `<SCRIPT>` and `</SCRIPT>` tags are used to embed JavaScript code within an HTML file. We'll learn more about the `<SCRIPT>` tag in Chapter 12, *JavaScript in Web Browsers*. The main feature of JavaScript demonstrated by this example is the use of the `document.write()` method.* This method is used to dynamically output HTML text that is parsed and displayed by the web browser; we'll encounter it many more times in this book.

Besides allowing control over the content of web pages, JavaScript allows control over the browser and over the content of the HTML forms that appear in the browser. We'll learn about these capabilities of JavaScript in more detail later in this chapter and in much more detail later in this book.

---

* "Method" is the object-oriented term for function or procedure; you'll see it used throughout this book.

Not only can JavaScript control the content of HTML documents, it can also control the behavior of those documents. That is, a JavaScript program might respond in some way when you enter a value in an input field or click on a image in a document. JavaScript does this by defining "event handlers" for the document— pieces of JavaScript code that are executed when a particular event occurs, such as when the user clicks on a button. Example 1-2 shows the definition of a very simple HTML form that includes an event handler that is executed in response to a button click.

Example 1–2: An HTML Form with a JavaScript Event Handler Defined

```
<FORM>
<INPUT TYPE="button"
      VALUE="Click here"
      onClick="alert('You clicked the button')">
</FORM>
```

Figure 1-2 illustrates the result of clicking the button.

Figure 1–2: The JavaScript response to an event

The onClick attribute shown in Example 1-2 was originally a Netscape extension added to HTML specifically for client-side JavaScript. Now, however, this and other event handler attributes have been standardized in HTML Version 4.0. All JavaScript event handlers are defined with HTML attributes like this one. The value of the onClick attribute is a string of JavaScript code to be executed when the user clicks the button. In this case, the `onClick` event handler calls the `alert()` function. As you can see in Figure 1-2, `alert()` pops up a dialog box to display the specified message.

The examples above highlight only the simplest features of client-side JavaScript. The real power of JavaScript on the client side is that scripts have access to a hierarchy of objects that are based on the content of the web page. For example, client-side JavaScript programs can access and manipulate each of the images that appear in a document and can communicate and interact with Java applets and other objects embedded within an HTML document. Once you have mastered the core JavaScript language, the key to using JavaScript effectively in web pages is learning to use the features of the document object model exposed by the browser.

1.4 Client-Side JavaScript Features

JavaScript is a general-purpose programming language, and, as such, you can write programs in it to perform arbitrary computations. You can write simple scripts, for example, that compute Fibonacci numbers, or search for primes. In the context of the Web and web browsers, however, a more interesting application of the language would be a program that computed the sales tax on an online order, based on information supplied by the user in an HTML form. As mentioned earlier, the real power of JavaScript lies in the browser and document-based objects that the language supports. To give you an idea of JavaScript's potential, the following sections list and explain the important capabilities of client-side JavaScript and the objects it supports.

1.4.1 Control Document Appearance and Content

The JavaScript Document object, through its `write()` method, which we have already seen, allows you to write arbitrary HTML into a document as the document is being parsed by the browser. For example, this allows you to include the current date and time in a document or to display different content on different platforms.

You can also use the Document object to generate documents entirely from scratch. Properties of the Document object allow you to specify colors for the document background, the text, and for the hypertext links within it. What this amounts to is the ability to generate dynamic and conditional HTML documents, a technique that works particularly well in multiframe documents. Indeed, in some cases, dynamic generation of frame content allows a JavaScript program to replace a traditional CGI script entirely.

The new technology of Dynamic HTML is based on the ability to use JavaScript to dynamically modify the contents and appearance of HTML documents. Internet Explorer 4 supports a complete document object model that gives JavaScript access to every single HTML element within a document. In addition, Internet Explorer's DHTML capabilities allow JavaScript to modify the content of any element and to change the appearance of the element dynamically by modifying its style sheet properties.* As you can imagine, this nearly complete power over an HTML document has tremendous dynamic potential. Client-side JavaScript is at the core of this potential.

1.4.2 Control the Browser

Several JavaScript objects allow control over the behavior of the browser. The Window object supports methods to pop up dialog boxes to display simple messages to the user and to get simple input from the user. This object also defines a method to create and open (and close) entirely new browser windows, which can have any specified size and any combination of user controls. This allows you, for example, to open up multiple windows to give the user multiple views of your web site. New browser windows are also useful for temporary display of generated HTML, and, when created without the menubar and other user controls, these windows can serve as dialog boxes for more complex messages or user input.

JavaScript does not define methods that allow you to create and manipulate frames directly within a browser window. However, the ability to generate HTML dynamically allows you to write programmatically the HTML tags that create any desired frame layout.

JavaScript also allows control over which web pages are displayed in the browser. The Location object allows you to download and display the contents of any URL in any window or frame of the browser. The History object allows you to move forward and back within the user's browsing history, simulating the action of the browser's **Forward** and **Back** buttons.

Yet another method of the Window object allows JavaScript to display arbitrary messages to the user in the status line of any browser window.

1.4.3 Interact with HTML Forms

Another important aspect of client-side JavaScript is its ability to interact with HTML forms. This capability is provided by the Form object and the Form element objects it can contain: Button, Checkbox, Hidden, Password, Radio, Reset, Select,

---

* Navigator 4 does not support as complete a DOM, but a future version of Navigator will support the DOM standard now emerging from the W3C standardization process.

Submit, Text, and Textarea objects. These element objects allow you to read and write the values of the input elements in the forms in a document. For example, an online catalog might use an HTML form to allow the user to enter his order and could use JavaScript to read his input from that form in order to compute the cost of the order, the sales tax, and the shipping charge. JavaScript programs like this are, in fact, very common on the Web. We'll see a program shortly that uses an HTML form and JavaScript to allow the user to compute monthly payments on a home mortgage or other loan. JavaScript has an obvious advantage over server-based CGI scripts for applications like these: JavaScript code is executed on the client, so the form's contents don't have to be sent to the server in order for relatively simple computations to be performed.

Another common use of client-side JavaScript with forms is for verification of a form before it is submitted. If client-side JavaScript is able to perform all necessary error checking of a user's input, the CGI script on the server side can be much simpler and, more importantly, there is no round trip to the server to detect and inform the user of the errors. Client-side JavaScript can also perform preprocessing of input data, which can reduce the amount of data that must be transmitted to the server. In some cases, client-side JavaScript can eliminate the need for CGI scripts on the server altogether! (On the other hand, JavaScript and CGI do work well together. For example, a CGI program can dynamically create JavaScript code on the fly, just as it dynamically creates HTML.)

1.4.4 Interact with the User

An important feature of JavaScript is the ability to define event handlers—arbitrary pieces of code to be executed when a particular event occurs. Usually, these events are initiated by the user, when, for example, she moves the mouse over a hypertext link, enters a value in a form, or clicks the **Submit** button in a form. This event-handling capability is a crucial one, because programming with graphical interfaces, such as HTML forms, inherently requires an event-driven model. JavaScript can trigger any kind of action in response to user events. Typical examples might be to display a special message in the status line when the user positions the mouse over a hypertext link or to pop up a confirmation dialog box when the user submits an important form.

1.4.5 Read and Write Client State with Cookies

"Cookie" is Netscape's term for a small amount of state data stored permanently or temporarily by the client. Cookies are transmitted to and from the server and allow a web page or web site to "remember" things about the client—for example, that the user has previously visited the site, or has already registered and obtained a password, or has expressed a preference about the color and layout of web pages. Cookies help you provide the state information that is missing from the stateless HTTP protocol of the Web.

When cookies were invented, they were intended for use exclusively by CGI scripts; although stored on the client, they could only be read or written by the server. The idea was to allow a CGI script to generate and send different HTML to the client depending on the value of a cookie (or cookies). JavaScript changes this because JavaScript programs can read and write cookie values, and as I noted earlier in this chapter, they can dynamically generate HTML based on the value of cookies. The implications of this are subtle. CGI programming is still an important technique in many cases that use cookies. In some cases, however, JavaScript can entirely replace the need for CGI.

1.4.6 Still More Features

In addition to the features I have already mentioned, JavaScript has many other capabilities:

- As of JavaScript 1.1, you can change the image displayed by an <IMG> tag. This allows sophisticated effects, such as having an image change when the mouse passes over it or when the user clicks on a button elsewhere in the browser.

- As of JavaScript 1.1, JavaScript can interact with Java applets and other embedded objects that appear in the browser. JavaScript code can read and write the properties of these applets and objects and can also invoke any methods they define. This feature truly allows JavaScript to script Java.

- As mentioned at the start of this section, JavaScript can perform arbitrary computation. JavaScript has a floating-point data type, arithmetic operators that work with it, and a full complement of standard floating-point mathematical functions.

- The JavaScript Date object simplifies the process of computing and working with dates and times.

- The Document object supports a property that specifies the last modified date for the current document. You can use it to display a timestamp on any document automatically.

- JavaScript has a `window.setTimeout()` method that allows a block of arbitrary JavaScript code to be executed some number of milliseconds in the future. This is useful for building delays or repetitive actions into a JavaScript program. In JavaScript 1.2, `setTimeout()` is augmented by another useful method called `setInterval()`.

- The Navigator object (named after the web browser, of course) has variables that specify the name and version of the browser that is running, as well as variables that identify the platform it is running on. These variables allow scripts to customize their behavior based on browser or platform, so that they can take advantage of extra capabilities supported by some versions or work around bugs that exist on some platforms.

- In client-side JavaScript 1.2, the Screen object provides information about the size and color-depth of the monitor on which the web browser is being displayed.

- As of JavaScript 1.1, the `scroll()` method of the Window object allows JavaScript programs to scroll windows in the X and Y dimensions. In JavaScript 1.2, this method is augmented by a host of others that allow browser windows to be moved and resized.

1.4.7 What JavaScript Can't Do

Client-side JavaScript has an impressive list of capabilities. Note, however, that they are confined to browser-related and HTML-related tasks. Since client-side JavaScript is used in a limited context, it does not have features that would be required for standalone languages:

- JavaScript does not have any graphics capabilities, except for the powerful ability to generate HTML dynamically (including images, tables, frames, forms, fonts, etc.) for the browser to display.

- For security reasons, client-side JavaScript does not allow the reading or writing of files. Obviously, you wouldn't want to allow an untrusted program from any random web site to run on your computer and rearrange your files!

- JavaScript does not support networking of any kind, except that it can cause the browser to download arbitrary URLs and it can send the contents of HTML forms to CGI scripts, email addresses, and Usenet newsgroups.

1.5 JavaScript Security

Early versions of client-side JavaScript were plagued with security problems. In Navigator 2, for example, it was possible to write JavaScript code that could automatically steal the email address of any visitor to the page containing the code. More worrisome was the related capability to send email in the visitor's name, without the visitor's knowledge or approval. This was done by defining an HTML form, with a `mailto:` URL as its `ACTION` attribute and using `POST` as the submission method. With this form defined, JavaScript code could then call the form object's `submit()` method when the page containing the form was first loaded. This automatically generated mail in the visitor's name to any desired address. The mail contained the visitor's email address, which could be stolen for use in Internet marketing, for example. Furthermore, by setting appropriate values within the form, this malicious JavaScript code could send a message in the user's name to any email address.

Fortunately, practically all known security issues in JavaScript have been resolved in Navigator 3. Furthermore, Navigator 4 implements a completely new security model that promises to make client-side JavaScript even more secure. Chapter 21, *JavaScript Security*, contains a complete discussion of security in client-side JavaScript.

1.6 Example: Computing Loan Payments with JavaScript

Example 1-3 is a listing of a complete, non-trivial JavaScript program. The program computes the monthly payment on a home mortgage or other loan, given the amount of the loan, the interest rate, and the repayment period. As you can see, the program consists of an HTML form made interactive with JavaScript code. Figure 1-3 shows what the HTML form looks like when displayed in a web browser. But the figure can only capture a static snapshot of the program. The addition of JavaScript code makes it dynamic: whenever the user changes the amount of the loan, the interest rate, or the number of payments, the JavaScript code recomputes the monthly payment, the total of all payments, and the total interest paid over the lifetime of the loan.

The first half of the example is an HTML form, nicely formatted using an HTML table. Note that several of the form elements define event handlers with `onChange` or `onClick` attributes. The web browser triggers these event handlers when the user changes the input or clicks on the **Compute** button displayed in the form. Note that in each case, the value of the event handler attribute is a string of JavaScript code: `calculate()`. When the event handler is triggered, it executes this code, which causes it to call the function `calculate()`.

The `calculate()` function is defined in the second half of the example, inside `<SCRIPT>` tags. The function reads the user's input from the form, does the math required to compute loan payments, and displays the results of these calculations using the bottom three form elements.

Example 1-3 is a simple one, but it is worth taking the time to look over it carefully. You shouldn't expect to understand all the JavaScript code at this point, but studying this example should give you a good idea of what JavaScript programs

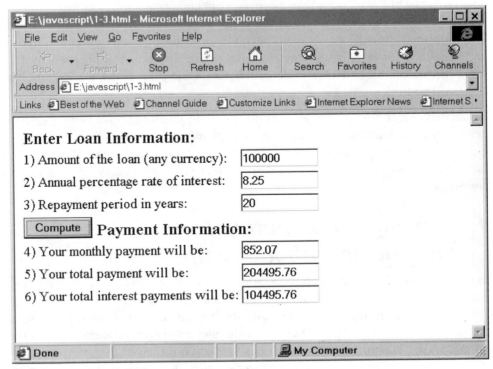

Figure 1-3: A JavaScript loan payment calculator

look like, how event handlers work, and how JavaScript code can be integrated with HTML forms.

Example 1-3: Computing Loan Payments with JavaScript

```
<!--
  This is an HTML form that allows the user to enter data, and allows
  JavaScript to display the results it computes back to the user. The
  form elements are embedded in a table to improve their appearance.
  Note that some of the form elements define "onChange" or "onClick"
  event handlers. These specify strings of JavaScript code to be
  executed when the user enters data or clicks on a button.
-->
<FORM NAME="loandata">
  <TABLE>
    <TR><TD COLSPAN=3><BIG><B>Enter Loan Information:</B></BIG></TD></TR>
    <TR>
      <TD>1)</TD>
      <TD>Amount of the loan (any currency):</TD>
      <TD><INPUT TYPE=text NAME=principal SIZE=12 onChange="calculate()"></TD>
    </TR>
```

Example 1-3: Computing Loan Payments with JavaScript (continued)

```
      <TR>
        <TD>2)</TD>
        <TD>Annual percentage rate of interest:</TD>
        <TD><INPUT TYPE=text NAME=interest SIZE=12 onChange="calculate()"></TD>
      </TR>
      <TR>
        <TD>3)</TD>
        <TD>Repayment period in years:</TD>
        <TD><INPUT TYPE=text NAME=years SIZE=12 onChange="calculate()"></TD>
      </TR>
      <TR><TD COLSPAN=3>
        <BIG><B>
          <INPUT TYPE=button VALUE="Compute" onClick="calculate()">
          Payment Information:
        </B></BIG>
      </TD></TR>
      <TR>
        <TD>4)</TD>
        <TD>Your monthly payment will be:</TD>
        <TD><INPUT TYPE=text NAME=payment SIZE=12></TD>
      </TR>
      <TR>
        <TD>5)</TD>
        <TD>Your total payment will be:</TD>
        <TD><INPUT TYPE=text NAME=total SIZE=12></TD>
      </TR>
      <TR>
        <TD>6)</TD>
        <TD>Your total interest payments will be:</TD>
        <TD><INPUT TYPE=text NAME=totalinterest SIZE=12></TD>
      </TR>
    </TABLE>
</FORM>


<!--
  This is the JavaScript program that makes the example work. Note that
  this script defines the calculate() function called by the event
  handlers in the form.
-->
<SCRIPT LANGUAGE="JavaScript">
function calculate() {
    // Get the user's input from the form. Assume it is all valid.
    // Convert interest from a percentage to a decimal, and convert from
    // an annual rate to a monthly rate. Convert payment period in years
    // to the number of monthly payments.
    var principal = document.loandata.principal.value;
    var interest = document.loandata.interest.value / 100 / 12;
    var payments = document.loandata.years.value * 12;
```

Example 1-3: Computing Loan Payments with JavaScript (continued)

```
    // Now compute the monthly payment figure, using esoteric math.
    var x = Math.pow(1 + interest, payments);
    var monthly = (principal*x*interest)/(x-1);

    // Check that the result is a finite number. If so, display the results
    if (!isNaN(monthly) &&
        (monthly != Number.POSITIVE_INFINITY) &&
        (monthly != Number.NEGATIVE_INFINITY)) {

        document.loandata.payment.value = round(monthly);
        document.loandata.total.value = round(monthly * payments)
        document.loandata.totalinterest.value =
            round((monthly * payments) - principal);
    }
    // Otherwise, the user's input was probably invalid, so don't
    // display anything.
    else {
        document.loandata.payment.value = "";
        document.loandata.total.value = "";
        document.loandata.totalinterest.value = "";
    }
}

// This simple method rounds a number to two decimal places.
function round(x) {
  return Math.round(x*100)/100;
}
</SCRIPT>
```

1.7 Using the Rest of This Book

The rest of this book is in three parts. Part I, which immediately follows this chapter, documents the core JavaScript language. Chapters 2 through 6 begin this section with some bland but necessary reading—these chapters cover the basic information you need to understand when learning a new programming language:

- Chapter 2, *Lexical Structure*, explains the basic structure of the language.

- Chapter 3, *Data Types and Values*, documents the data types supported by JavaScript.

- Chapter 4, *Variables*, covers variables, variable scope, and related topics.

- Chapter 5, *Expressions and Operators*, explains expressions in JavaScript, and documents each of the operators supported by JavaScript. Because JavaScript syntax is modeled on Java, which is, in turn, modeled on C and C++, experienced C, C++, or Java programmers can skim much of this chapter.

- Chapter 6, *Statements*, describes the syntax and usage of each of the JavaScript statements. Again, experienced C, C++, and Java programmers can skim some, but not all, of this chapter.

The next five chapters of this first section become more interesting. They still cover the core of the JavaScript language, but document parts of the language that will not already be familiar to you, even if you already know C or Java. These chapters must be studied carefully if you want to really understand JavaScript:

- Chapter 7, *Functions*, documents how functions are defined, invoked, and manipulated in JavaScript.

- Chapter 8, *Objects*, explains objects, the most important JavaScript data type. This chapter discusses object-oriented programming in JavaScript and explains how you can define your own classes of objects in JavaScript.

- Chapter 9, *Arrays*, describes the creation and use of arrays in JavaScript.

- Chapter 10, *Pattern Matching with Regular Expressions*, explains how to use regular expressions in JavaScript to perform pattern-matching and search-and-replace operations.

- Chapter 11, *Further Topics in JavaScript*, covers advanced topics that have not been covered elsewhere. You can skip this chapter the first time through the book, but the material it contains is important to understand if you want to become a JavaScript expert.

Part II of the book explains client-side JavaScript. The chapters in this part document the web browser objects that are at the heart of client-side JavaScript and provide detailed examples of their use. Any interesting JavaScript program running in a web browser will rely heavily on features specific to the client side:

- Chapter 12, *JavaScript in Web Browsers,* explains the integration of JavaScript with web browsers. It discusses the web browser as a programming environment and explains the various ways in which JavaScript is integrated into web pages for execution on the client side.

- Chapter 13, *Windows and Frames*, documents the most central and important object of client-side JavaScript, the Window object, as well as several important window-related objects.

- Chapter 14, *The Document Object Model,* explains the Document object and related objects that expose the contents of an HTML document to JavaScript code. The document object model is at the core of almost all client-side JavaScript programs.

- Chapter 15, *Events and Event Handling,* covers JavaScript events and event handlers, which are central to all JavaScript programs that interact with the user.

- Chapter 16, *Forms and Form Elements,* documents the Form object, which represents HTML forms. It also documents the various form element objects that appear within HTML forms and shows examples of JavaScript programming using forms.

- Chapter 17, *Dynamic HTML,* explains how JavaScript is used with two of the key technologies of dynamic HTML programming: style sheets and absolute positioning. It also discusses the major incompatibilities between Navigator and Internet Explorer support for DHTML and presents JavaScript code that can be used to work around these incompatibilities.

- Chapter 18, *Saving State with Cookies,* illustrates the use of cookies to save state in web programming.

- Chapter 19, *Compatibility Techniques,* discusses the important issue of compatibility in JavaScript programming. It discusses compatibility between Navigator and Internet Explorer, between different versions of Navigator, and between JavaScript-enabled browsers and browsers that do not support the language.

- Chapter 20, *LiveConnect: JavaScript and Java,* explains how you can use JavaScript to interact with Java classes and objects and even to communicate with and control Java applets. It also covers how you can do the reverse—invoke JavaScript code from Java applets. Because Internet Explorer does not support LiveConnect, most of this chapter is Navigator-specific.

- Chapter 21, *JavaScript Security,* explains the security restrictions built into JavaScript. It also documents the new security model in Navigator 4 that allows these restrictions to be selectively lifted for trusted JavaScript programs that have been digitally signed.

Part III is the reference section that makes up the entire second half of this book. It contains complete documentation for all JavaScript objects, methods, properties, functions, and event handlers, both for core and client-side JavaScript.

1.8 Exploring JavaScript

The way to really learn a new programming language is to write programs with it. As you read through this book, I encourage you to try out JavaScript features as you learn about them. There are a number of techniques that make it easy to experiment with JavaScript.

The most obvious way to explore JavaScript is to write simple scripts. JavaScript has powerful enough features that even simple programs, only a few lines long, can produce complex results. We saw an example that computed factorials at the beginning of this chapter. Suppose you wanted to modify it as follows to display Fibonacci numbers instead:

```
<SCRIPT>
document.write("<h2>Table of Fibonacci Numbers</h2>");
for(i=0,j=1,k=0,fib=1; i<50; i++,fib=j+k,k=j,j=fib) {
    document.write("Fibonacci(" + i + ") = " + fib);
    document.write("<br>");
}
</SCRIPT>
```

This code may be convoluted (and don't worry if you don't yet understand it), but the point is that when you want to experiment with short programs like this, you can simply type them up and try them out in your web browser using a local file: URL. For simple JavaScript experiments like this, you can usually omit the <HTML>, <HEAD>, and <BODY> tags in your HTML file, and you can even omit the LANGUAGE="JavaScript" attribute that you would include in the <SCRIPT> tag of any production code you wrote.

For even simpler experiments with JavaScript, you can sometimes use the javascript: URL pseudo-protocol to evaluate a JavaScript expression and return the result. A JavaScript URL consists of the javascript: protocol specifier followed by arbitrary JavaScript code (with statements separated from one another by semicolons). When the browser loads such a URL, it executes the JavaScript code. The value of the last expression in such a URL is converted to a string, and this string becomes the document specified by the URL. For example, you might type the following JavaScript URLs into the **Location** field of your web browser[*] to test your understanding of some of JavaScript's operators and statements:

```
javascript:5%2
javascript:x = 3; (x < 5)? "x is less": "x is greater"
javascript:d = new Date(); typeof d;
javascript:for(i=0,j=1,k=0,fib=1; i<10; i++,fib=j+k,k=j,j=fib) alert(fib);
```

---

[*] This technique does not work with Internet Explorer 3.

In Navigator, but not Internet Explorer, if you specify the URL `javascript:` by itself, Navigator displays a JavaScript interpreter screen, like that pictured in Figure 1-4. JavaScript code entered into the input field in the lower frame is evaluated and the results are displayed in the upper frame. The figure shows code that pops up a dialog box displaying the name and value of each of the properties of the browser window.

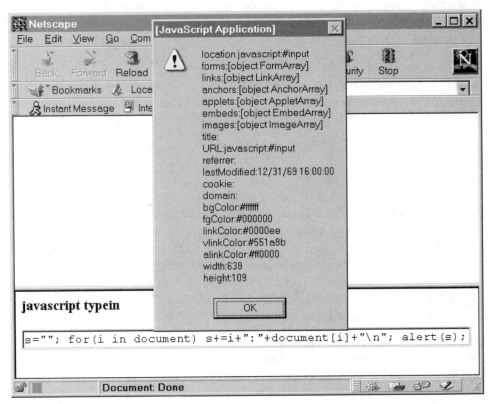

Figure 1-4: The javascript: interpreter screen

The code shown in Figure 1-4 demonstrates some useful techniques for experimenting with JavaScript. First, it shows the use of the `alert()` function to display text. This function pops up a dialog box and displays plain text (i.e., not HTML formatted text) within it. It also demonstrates the `for/in` loop, which loops through all the properties of an object. This is quite useful when trying to discover which objects have what properties. The `for/in` loop is documented in Chapter 6.

While exploring JavaScript, you'll probably write code that doesn't work as you expect it to and want to debug it. The basic debugging technique for JavaScript is like that in many other languages: insert statements into your code to print out the values of relevant variables so that you can try to figure out what is actually happening. As we've seen, you can sometimes use the `document.write()` method to do this. This method doesn't work from within event handlers, however, and has some other shortcomings as well, so it's often easier to use the `alert()` function to display debugging messages in a separate dialog box.

The `for/in` loop mentioned above is also very useful when debugging. You can use it, along with the `alert()` method, to write a function that displays a list of the names and values of all properties of an object, for example. This kind of function can be handy when exploring the language or trying to debug code.

Finally, both Netscape and Microsoft have released debuggers for their versions of client-side JavaScript. You can read about and download these debuggers from:

> http://developer.netscape.com/software/jsdebug.html
> http://msdn.microsoft.com/scripting/debugger/

Good luck with JavaScript, and have fun exploring!

I

Core JavaScript

This part of the book, Chapters 2 through 11, documents the core JavaScript language as it is used in web browsers, web servers, and other embedded JavaScript implementations. This part is meant to be a JavaScript language reference. After you read through it once to learn the language, you may find yourself referring back to it to refresh your memory about some of the trickier points of JavaScript.

2

Lexical Structure

The lexical structure of a programming language is the set of elementary rules that specify how you write programs in the language. It is the lowest-level syntax of a language and specifies such things as what variable names look like, what characters are used for comments, and how one program statement is separated from the next. This short chapter documents the lexical structure of JavaScript.

2.1 Case Sensitivity

JavaScript is a case-sensitive language. This means that language keywords, variables, function names, and any other identifiers must always be typed with a consistent capitalization of letters. The `while` keyword, for example, must be typed "while", and not "While" or "WHILE". Similarly, `online`, `Online`, `OnLine`, and `ONLINE` are four distinct variable names.

Note, however, that HTML is not case-sensitive. Because of its close association with client-side JavaScript, this can be confusing. Many JavaScript objects and properties have the same names as the HTML tags and attributes that they represent. While these tags and attribute names can be typed with any case in HTML, they typically must be all lowercase in JavaScript. For example, the HTML `ONCLICK` event handler attribute is commonly specified as `onClick` or `OnClick` in HTML, but must be referred to as `onclick` in JavaScript code.

While core JavaScript is entirely and exclusively case-sensitive, exceptions to this rule are allowed in client-side JavaScript. In Internet Explorer 3, for example, all client-side objects and properties were case-insensitive. This caused problematic incompatibilities with Navigator, however, so in Internet Explorer 4, client-side objects and properties are case-sensitive. Another example of case insensitivity on the client side is JavaScript style sheets in Navigator 4. JavaScript style sheets (documented in Chapter 17, *Dynamic HTML*) allow style properties to be specified for HTML tags. The client-side objects that represent the collection of tags and their styles are purposely designed so that their property names are case-insensitive. Thus, the following lines of JavaScript code are equivalent in Navigator 4:

```
document.tags.body.color = "red";
document.tags.Body.Color = "red";
document.tags.BODY.COLOR = "red";
```

2.2 Whitespace and Line Breaks

JavaScript ignores spaces, tabs, and newlines that appear between tokens in programs, except those that are part of string constants. A *token* is a keyword, variable name, number, function name, or some other entity in which you would obviously not want to insert a space or a line break. If you place a space or tab or newline within a token, you break it up into two tokens—123 is a single numeric token while 12 3 is two separate tokens (and constitutes a syntax error, incidentally).

Because you can use spaces, tabs, and newlines freely in your program (except in strings and tokens), you are free to format and indent your programs in a neat and consistent way that makes the code easy to read and understand. Note, however, that there is one minor restriction on the placement of line breaks; it is described in the following section.

2.3 Optional Semicolons

Simple statements in JavaScript are generally followed by semicolons (;), just as they are in C, C++, and Java. This serves to separate statements from each other. In JavaScript, however, you are allowed to omit this semicolon if your statements are each placed on a separate line. For example, the following code could be written without semicolons:

```
a = 3;
b = 4;
```

But when formatted as follows, the first semicolon is required:

```
a = 3; b = 4;
```

Omitting semicolons is not a good programming practice; you should get in the habit of using them.

Although JavaScript theoretically allows line breaks between any two tokens, the fact that JavaScript automatically inserts semicolons for you causes some exceptions to this rule. If you break a line of code in such a way that the line before the break appears to be a complete statement, JavaScript thinks you omitted the semicolon and inserts one for you, altering your meaning. Some places you should look out for this are with the `return`, `break`, and `continue` statements. For example, consider the following:

```
return
true;
```

JavaScript assumes you meant:

```
return;
true;
```

However, you probably meant:

```
return true;
```

This is something to watch out for—this code does not cause a syntax error and will fail in a non-obvious way. A similar problem occurs if you write:

```
break
outerloop;
```

JavaScript inserts a semicolon after the `break` keyword, causing a syntax error when it tries to interpret the next line. For similar reasons, the ++ and − postfix operators must always appear on the same line as the expression that they are applied to.

2.4 Comments

JavaScript, like Java, supports both C++ and C-style comments. Any text between a // and the end of a line is treated as a comment and is ignored by JavaScript. Also, any text between the characters /* and */ is treated as a comment. These C-style comments may span multiple lines but may not be nested. The following lines of code are all legal JavaScript comments:

```
// This is a single-line comment.
/* This is also a comment */  // and here is another comment.

/*
 * This is yet another comment.
 * It has multiple lines.
 */
```

The ECMA standard requires JavaScript implementations to allow arbitrary Unicode 2.0 characters to appear within comments.* Navigator 4 does not support Unicode characters, but future versions should. Note that Navigator does support the 8-bit characters of the Western European Latin-1 (ISO8859-1) character set in comments.

In addition to C++ and C-style comments, client-side JavaScript recognizes the HTML comment opening sequence `<!--`. JavaScript treats this as a single-line comment, just as it does the `//` comment. However, JavaScript does not recognize the HTML comment closing sequence `-->`. There is a special reason for recognizing the HTML comment but treating it differently from HTML. In a JavaScript program, if the first line begins with `<!--` and the last line ends with `//-->`, the entire program is contained within an HTML comment and is ignored (instead of formatted and displayed) by browsers that do not support JavaScript. Since the first line begins with `<!--` and the last line begins with `//`, JavaScript ignores both, but does not ignore the lines in between. In this way, it is possible to hide code from web browsers that can't understand it, without hiding it from those that can. Because of the special purpose of the `<!--` comment, you should use it only in the first line of your scripts; other uses would be confusing. See Chapter 19, *Compatibility Techniques*, for further discussion of this and other compatibility techniques.

2.5 Literals

A *literal* is a data value that appears directly in a program. The following are all literals:

```
12
1.2
"hello world"
'Hi'
true
false
null
```

In JavaScript 1.2, more complex kinds of literals are also supported. For example:

```
{ x:1, y:2 }    // An object initializer
[1,2,3,4,5]     // An array initializer
```

---

* Unicode is a character encoding that includes characters from all major contemporary written languages. Unicode characters are two bytes wide, and thus the Unicode standard can represent some 65,000 characters. If you are an English-speaking programmer who does not care about internationalization issues, Unicode support in JavaScript is transparent and irrelevant to you.

Literals are an important part of any programming language, as it is impossible to write a program without them. The various JavaScript literals are described in detail in Chapter 3, *Data Types and Values*.

2.6 Identifiers

An *identifier* is simply a name. In JavaScript, identifiers are used to name variables and functions (both of which are kinds of object properties.) In JavaScript 1.2, they are also used to provide labels for certain loops in JavaScript code. The rules for legal identifier names are the same in JavaScript as they are in Java and many other languages. The first character must be an ASCII letter (lowercase or uppercase), an underscore (_) or a dollar sign ($).* Subsequent characters may be any letter or digit or an underscore or dollar sign. (Numbers are not allowed as the first character so that JavaScript can easily distinguish identifiers from numbers.) These are legal identifiers:

```
i
my_variable_name
v13
_dummy
$str
```

Note that identifiers may contain only ASCII characters. The ECMA specification does not allow other Unicode or Latin-1 characters in JavaScript identifiers.

Finally, identifiers cannot be the same as any of the keywords used for other purposes in JavaScript. The next section lists these special names that are reserved in JavaScript.

2.7 Reserved Words

There are a number of "reserved" words in JavaScript. These are words that you cannot use as identifiers (variable names, function names, and loop labels) in your JavaScript programs. Table 2-1 lists the keywords in JavaScript. These words have special meaning to JavaScript—they are part of the language syntax itself.

---

* Note that dollar signs are not legal in identifiers prior to JavaScript 1.1.

Table 2-1: Reserved JavaScript Keywords

break	do	if	return	var
case	else	import	switch	void
continue	export	in	this	while
default	for	new	typeof	with
delete	function			

Table 2-2 lists other reserved keywords. These words are not used in JavaScript 1.2, but they are reserved by the ECMA standard as possible future extensions to the language.

Table 2-2: Words Reserved for ECMA Extensions

catch	const	enum	finally	throw
class	debugger	extends	super	try

JavaScript also reserves keywords from Java for possible future extensions. Java keywords that are reserved but not yet used by JavaScript are listed in Table 2-3.

Table 2-3: Java Keywords Reserved by JavaScript

abstract	final	int	package	static
boolean	float	interface	private	synchronized
byte	goto	long	protected	throws
char	implements	native	public	transient
double	instanceof	null	short	true
false				

In addition to the reserved words that you may not use as identifier names, there are quite a few other words that you should not use as identifiers. These are the names of properties, methods, and constructors that are already used by JavaScript. If you create variables or functions with these names, you will redefine the existing property or function—something that you should not do unless you are absolutely positive you know exactly what you are doing. Table 2-4 lists a number of these identifiers that you should avoid. This is not an exhaustive list— various versions of JavaScript may define other global properties or functions. In general, you should never give a variable or function the same name as a global variable or function. Also, you should avoid defining any identifiers that begin with two underscores; JavaScript implementations often use identifiers of this form for internal purposes.

Table 2-4: Other Identifiers to Avoid

alert	escape	Math	parseFloat	setTimeout
arguments	eval	menubar	parseInt	status
Array	find	moveBy	personalbar	statusbar
blur	focus	moveTo	print	stop
Boolean	frames	name	prompt	String
callee	Function	NaN	prototype	toolbar
caller	history	netscape	RegExp	top
captureEvents	home	Number	releaseEvents	toString
clearInterval	Infinity	Object	resizeBy	unescape
clearTimeout	innerHeight	open	resizeTo	unwatch
close	innerWidth	opener	routeEvent	valueOf
closed	isFinite	outerHeight	scroll	watch
confirm	isNaN	outerWidth	scrollbars	window
constructor	java	Packages	scrollBy	
Date	length	pageXOffset	scrollTo	
defaultStatus	location	pageYOffset	self	
document	locationbar	parent	setInterval	

3

Data Types and Values

The data types supported by a programming language are perhaps the most fundamental aspect of the language. JavaScript allows you to work with three primitive data types: numbers, strings of text, and boolean truth values. The language also supports two composite data types, objects and arrays, which represent collections of the primitive types. Unlike many languages, JavaScript also supports functions as a data type—this allows JavaScript programs to literally manipulate themselves.

The object data type is a generic one and deserves further comment. As we'll see later, both functions and arrays are specialized types of objects. In addition, JavaScript defines other specialized types of objects with specialized purposes. The Date object represents dates and times, and, in JavaScript 1.2, the RegExp object represents regular expressions, which are used for pattern matching operations. Furthermore, client-side JavaScript introduces a whole slew of specialized object types, such as the Window, Document, and Form objects, as covered in Part II.

The remainder of this chapter discusses each of the basic JavaScript data types in turn: numbers, strings, booleans, functions, objects, and arrays. Later chapters will provide much more detail about functions, objects, and arrays.

3.1 Numbers

Numbers are the most basic data type there is; they require very little explanation. JavaScript differs from programming languages like C and Java in that it does not make a distinction between integer values and floating point values. All numbers in JavaScript are represented as floating-point values. JavaScript represents numbers using the standard 8-byte IEEE floating-point numeric format, which means that it can represent numbers as large as $\pm1.7976931348623157\times10^{308}$ and as small as $\pm5\times10^{-324}$.*

When a number appears directly in a JavaScript program, we call it a numeric literal. JavaScript supports numeric literals in several formats, as described in the following subsections.

3.1.1 Integer Literals

Base-10 integers are represented as sequences of digits that do not begin with the digit zero, or as the digit zero by itself. For example:

```
3
0
10000000
```

Since JavaScript represents all numbers as floating-point values, you can specify extremely large integer literals, but you may lose precision in the trailing digits. All integers between -9007199254740992 (-2^{53}) and 9007199254740992 (2^{53}), inclusive, can be represented exactly. However, most integer manipulations in JavaScript are performed on 32-bit integers, which range from -2^{31} to $2^{31}-1$.

3.1.2 Octal and Hexadecimal Literals

You can also specify integers as octal (base-8) and hexadecimal (base-16) values. An octal value begins with the digit zero, followed by a sequence of digits, each between 0 and 7:

```
0(0-7)*
```

As in C and C++, a hexadecimal literal begins with "0x" or "0X", followed by a string of hexadecimal digits. A hexadecimal digit is one of the digits 0 through 9 or the letters a (or A) through f (or F), which are used to represent values ten through fifteen:

```
0(x|X)(0-9|a-f|A-F)*
```

Examples of octal and hexadecimal integer literals are:

```
026
0377
0xff
0xCAFE911
```

---

* This format should be familiar to Java programmers as the format of the `double` type. It is also the `double` format used in almost all modern implementations of C and C++.

3.1.3 Floating-Point Literals

Floating-point literals can have a decimal point; they use the traditional syntax for scientific notation. A floating-point value is represented as the integral part of the number, followed by a decimal point and the fractional part of the number.

Exponential notation may be represented with additional syntax: the letter e (or E), followed by an optional plus or minus sign, followed by a one-, two-, or three-digit integer exponent. The preceding integral and fractional parts of the number are multiplied by ten to the power of this exponent.

More succinctly, the syntax is:

```
[digits][.digits][(E|e)[(+|-)]digits]
```

Examples:

```
3.14
2345.789
.333333333333333333
6.02e+23
1.4738223E-32
```

3.1.4 Working with Numbers

JavaScript programs work with numbers using the arithmetic operators that the language provides. These include + for addition, − for subtraction, * for multiplication, and / for division. Full details on these and other arithmetic operators can be found in Chapter 5, *Expressions and Operators*.

In addition to these basic arithmetic operations, JavaScript supports more complex mathematical operations through a large number of mathematical functions that are a core part of the language. For convenience, these functions are all stored as properties of a single Math object, so we always use the literal name Math to access them. For example, here's how to compute the sine of the numeric value x:

```
sine_of_x = Math.sin(x);
```

And to compute the square root of a numeric expression:

```
hypot = Math.sqrt(x*x + y*y);
```

See the Math object and subsequent listings in the reference section of this book for full details on all the mathematical functions supported by JavaScript.

There is also one interesting method that you can use with numbers. The toString() method converts a number to a string, using the radix, or base, specified by its argument. For example, to convert a number to hexadecimal, use toString() like this:

```
var x = 33;
var y = x.toString(16);
```

To invoke the toString() method on a number literal, you must use parentheses to prevent the . from being interpreted as a decimal point:

```
var y = (257).toString(16);
```

3.1.5 Special Numeric Values

JavaScript uses several special numeric values. When a floating-point value becomes larger than the largest representable type, the result is a special infinity value, which JavaScript prints as Infinity. Similarly, when a negative value becomes more negative than the most negative representable number, the result is negative infinity, printed as -Infinity.

Another special JavaScript numeric value is returned when a mathematical operation (such as division of zero by zero) yields an undefined result or an error. In this case, the result is the special not-a-number value, printed as NaN. The special not-a-number value has unusual behavior: it does not compare equal to any number, including itself! For this reason, a special function isNaN() is required to test for this value.

As of JavaScript 1.1, there are constants defined (as properties of the Number object) for each of these special numeric values. These constants are listed in Table 3-1.

Table 3-1: Special Numeric Constants

Constant	Meaning
Number.MAX_VALUE	Largest representable number
Number.MIN_VALUE	Most negative representable number
Number.NaN	Special not-a-number value
Number.POSITIVE_INFINITY	Special value to represent infinity
Number.NEGATIVE_INFINITY	Special value to represent negative infinity

The ECMA standard also requires two global properties, Infinity and NaN, that have the same values as Number.POSITIVE_INFINITY and Number.NaN. These properties are implemented in Internet Explorer 4, but not Navigator 4.

3.2 Strings

A *string* is a sequence of letters, digits, punctuation characters, and so on—it is the JavaScript data type for representing text. As you'll see shortly, string literals can be included in your programs by enclosing them in matching pairs of single or double quotation marks. Note that JavaScript does not have a character data type such as char, like C, C++, and Java do. To represent a single character, you simply use a string that has a length of 1.

3.2.1 String Literals

A string is a sequence of zero or more characters enclosed within single or double quotes (' or "). Double-quote characters may be contained within strings delimited by single-quote characters, and single-quote characters may be contained within strings delimited by double quotes. Examples of string literals are:

```
'testing'
"3.14"
'name="myform"'
"Wouldn't you prefer O'Reilly's book?"
```

The ECMA standard requires support for Unicode characters within string literals, just as it requires Unicode support in JavaScript comments. Navigator 4 supports the 8-bit Latin-1 (ISO8859-1) subset of Unicode in string constants but does not provide complete Unicode support. Once Unicode support is added to a future version of the browser, it will be much easier to write internationalized and multilingual programs in JavaScript. Internet Explorer 4 does support Unicode.

Because JavaScript is used to produce output for web pages, you'll be using lots of string literals in your scripts. One thing to be aware of is that HTML makes heavy use of double-quoted strings.* JavaScript code often contains embedded HTML strings and, in addition, JavaScript is often embedded within HTML strings for event handler specifications, so it is a good idea to use single quotes around your

---

* The original versions of HTML required double-quoted strings, though most popular web browsers now allow single-quoted strings as HTML attribute values as well.

JavaScript strings. In the example below, the string "Thank you" is single-quoted within a JavaScript expression, which is double-quoted within an HTML event-handler attribute:

```
<A HREF="" onClick="alert('Thank you')">Click Me</A>
```

On the other hand, when you use single quotes to delimit your strings, you must be careful with English contractions and possessives like "can't" and "O'Reilly's." Since the apostrophe is the same as the single-quote character, you must use the backslash character (\) to escape any apostrophes that appear in single-quoted strings, as explained in the next section.

3.2.2 Escape Sequences in String Literals

The backslash character (\) has a special purpose in JavaScript strings. Combined with the character that follows it, it represents a character that is not otherwise representable within the string, just like in C or C++. For example, \n is an escape sequence that represents a newline character.

Another example, mentioned in the previous section, is the \' escape that represents the single quote (or apostrophe) character. This escape sequence is useful when you need to include an apostrophe in a string literal that is contained within single quotes. You can see why we call these escape sequences—the backslash allows us to escape from the usual interpretation of the single-quote character; instead of using it to mark the end of the string, we use it as an apostrophe.

Table 3-2 lists the JavaScript escape sequences and the characters they represent. Several of the escape sequences are generic ones that can be used to represent any character by specifying its character code in the 8-bit Latin-1 encoding, either as an octal or hexadecimal number. For example, the sequence \251 represents the copyright symbol. The \u escape represents an arbitrary Unicode character specified by four hexadecimal digits. This escape is required by the ECMA standard, but is not yet supported in Navigator 4. Finally, note that if the \ character precedes any character other than those shown in the table, the backslash is simply ignored. For example, "\a" is the same thing as "a".

Table 3-2: JavaScript Escape Sequences

Sequence	Character Represented
\b	Backspace.
\f	Form feed.
\n	Newline.
\r	Carriage return.

Table 3-2: JavaScript Escape Sequences (continued)

Sequence	Character Represented
\t	Tab.
\'	Apostrophe or single quote.
\"	Double quote.
\\	Backslash.
XXX	The character with the Latin-1 encoding specified by the one to three octal digits *XXX*. The octal number must be between 0 and 377. For example: \374.
\x*XX*	The character with the Latin-1 encoding specified by the two hexadecimal digits *XX* between 00 and FF. For example: \x1A.
\u*XXXX*	The Unicode character specified by the four hexadecimal digits *XXXX*. Not supported in Navigator 4.

3.2.3 Working with Strings

One of the built-in features of JavaScript is the ability to concatenate strings. If you use the + operator with numbers, it adds them. But if you use this operator on strings, it joins them by appending the second to the first. For example:

```
msg = "Hello, " + "world";   // Produces the string "Hello, world"
greeting = "Welcome to my home page," + " " + name;
```

To determine the length of a string—the number of characters it contains—you use the length property of the string. If the variable s contains a string, you access its length like this:

```
s.length
```

There are a number of methods you can use to operate on strings. For example, to get the last character of a string s:

```
last_char = s.charAt(s.length - 1)
```

To extract the second, third, and fourth characters from a string s:

```
sub = s.substring(1,4);
```

To find the position of the first letter "a" in a string s:

```
i = s.indexOf('a');
```

There are quite a few other methods you can use to manipulate strings. You'll find full documentation of these methods in the reference section of this book, under the String object and subsequent listings.

As you can tell from the examples above, JavaScript strings, like JavaScript arrays, are indexed starting with zero. That is, the first character in a string is character 0. C, C++, and Java programmers should be perfectly comfortable with this, but programmers used to languages with 1-based arrays and strings may find that it takes some getting used to.

In Navigator 4 (but not Internet Explorer 4), individual characters can be read from strings (but not written into strings) using array notation, so the call to `charAt()` above could also be written like this:

```
last_char = s[s.length - 1];
```

When we discuss the object data type below, you'll see that object properties and methods are used in the same way that string properties and methods are used in the previous examples. This does not mean that strings are a type of object. In fact, strings are a distinct JavaScript data type. They use object syntax for accessing properties and methods, but they are not themselves objects. We'll see just why this is at the end of this chapter.

3.3 Boolean Values

The number and string data types have an infinite number of possible values. The boolean data type, on the other hand, has only two. The two legal boolean values are represented by the literals `true` and `false`. A boolean value represents a "truth value"—it says whether something is true or not.

Boolean values are generally the result of comparisons you make in your JavaScript programs. For example:

```
a == 4
```

This code tests to see if the value of the variable `a` is equal to the number 4. If it is, the result of this comparison is the boolean value `true`. If `a` is not equal to 4, the result of the comparison is `false`.

Boolean values are typically used in JavaScript control structures. For example, the `if/else` statement in JavaScript performs one action if a boolean value is `true` and another action if the value is `false`. You usually combine a comparison that creates a boolean value directly with a statement that uses it. The result looks like this:

```
if (a == 4)
    b = b + 1;
else
    a = a + 1;
```

This code checks if a equals 4. If so, it adds 1 to b; otherwise, it adds 1 to a.

Instead of thinking of the two possible boolean values as true and false, it is sometimes convenient to think of them as "on" (true) and "off" (false) or "yes" (true) and "no" (false). Sometimes it is even useful to consider them equivalent to 1 (true) and 0 (false). (In fact, JavaScript does just this and converts true and false to 1 and 0 when necessary.)

C programmers should note that JavaScript has a distinct boolean data type, unlike C, which simply uses integer values to simulate boolean values. Java programmers should note that although JavaScript has a boolean type, it is not nearly as "pure" as the Java boolean data type—JavaScript boolean values are easily converted to and from other data types, and so in practice, the use of boolean values in JavaScript is much more like their use in C than in Java.

3.4 Functions

A *function* is a piece of JavaScript code that is defined once in a program and can be executed, or invoked, many times by the program. A JavaScript function can be passed arguments, or parameters, specifying the value or values that the function is to operate upon, and a function can return a value. Functions are defined in JavaScript with code like this:

```
function square(x)
{
  return x*x;
}
```

Once a function is defined, you can invoke it by following the function's name with an optional comma-separated list of arguments within parentheses. The following lines are function invocations:

```
y = square(x);
compute_distance(x1, y1, z1, x2, y2, z2)
move()
y = sin(x);
```

An unusual feature of JavaScript is that functions are first-class data values. In many languages, including Java, functions are a syntactic feature of the language—they can be defined and invoked, but they are not data types. The fact that functions are true data types in JavaScript gives a lot of flexibility to the language. It means that functions can be stored in variables, arrays, and objects, and it means that functions can be passed as arguments to other functions. This can quite often be useful. We'll learn more about defining and invoking functions, and also about using them as data values, in Chapter 7, *Functions*.

Since functions are data types just like numbers and strings, they can be assigned to object properties just like other values can. When a function is assigned to a property of an object (described below), it is often referred to as a *method* of that object. In client-side JavaScript, some special methods of certain objects are automatically invoked by the web browser when the user interacts with the browser (by clicking the mouse, for example). These special methods are called *event handlers*. We'll see more about methods in Chapter 8, *Objects*, and about event handlers in Chapter 15, *Events and Event Handling*.

3.4.1 Function Literals

In the preceding section, we saw the definition of a function `square()`. In JavaScript 1.1, a function like this can also be defined by passing the function arguments and body to the `Function()` constructor. For example:

```
var square = new Function("x", "return x*x;");
```

When a function is defined in this way, it is sometimes called an "anonymous" function, since it does not have a name. (The variable `square` holds a reference to the function object, but `square` is not actually the name of the function.)

While the `Function()` constructor is occasionally useful, it has one serious shortcoming: the entire function body must be enclosed in a string, which makes it awkward to define a function with a long body in this way. Furthermore, an invocation of the `Function()` constructor is not really a function literal.

JavaScript 1.2 addresses these issues and defines a true literal syntax for functions. A function literal is defined with the `function` keyword, followed by a parenthesized list of function arguments and the body of the function within curly braces. In other words, a function literal looks just like a function definition, except that it does not have a name. Thus, instead of defining the function `square()` with a function definition:

```
function square(x) { return x*x; }
```

We can define it with a function literal:

```
var square = function(x) { return x*x; }
```

Functions defined in this way are sometimes called "lambda" functions in homage to the LISP programming language, which was one of the first to allow unnamed functions to be embedded as literal data values within a program. Although it is not immediately obvious why one might choose to use function literals in a program, we'll see later that in advanced scripts they can be quite convenient and useful.

3.5 Objects

An *object* is a collection of named pieces of data. These named values are usually referred to as *properties* of the object. (Sometimes they are called "fields" of the object, but this usage can be confusing.) To refer to a property of an object, you refer to the object, followed by a period and the name of the property. For example, if an object named `image` has properties named `width` and `height`, we can refer to those properties like this:

```
image.width
image.height
```

Properties of objects are, in many ways, just like JavaScript variables and can contain any type of data, including arrays, functions, and other objects. Thus, you might see JavaScript code like this:

```
document.myform.button
```

This refers to the `button` property of an object which is itself stored in the `myform` property of an object named `document`.

As mentioned earlier, when a function value is stored in a property of an object, that function is often called a method and the property name becomes the method name. To invoke a method of an object, use the `.` syntax to extract the function value from the object, and then use the `()` syntax to invoke that function. For example, to invoke the `write()` method of the Document object, you can use code like this:

```
document.write("this is a test");
```

Objects in JavaScript have the ability to serve as associative arrays—that is, they can associate arbitrary data values with arbitrary strings. When an object is used in this way, a different syntax is generally required to access the object's properties: a string containing the name of the desired property is enclosed within square brackets. Using this syntax we could access the properties of the `image` object mentioned above with code like this:

```
image["width"]
image["height"]
```

Associative arrays are a powerful data type; they are useful for a number of programming techniques. We'll learn more about objects in their traditional and associative array usages in Chapter 8.

3.5.1 Creating Objects

As we'll see in Chapter 8, objects are created by invoking special *constructor* functions. For example, the following lines all create new objects:

```
var o = new Object();
var now = new Date();
var pattern = new RegExp("\bjava\b", "i");
```

Once you have created an object of your own, you can use and set its properties however you desire:

```
var point = new Object();
point.x = 2.3;
point.y = -1.2;
```

3.5.2 Object Literals

As of JavaScript 1.2, you can create an object and predefine properties for it using a new literal syntax. An object literal (also called an "object initializer") consists of a comma-separated list of colon-separated property/value pairs, all enclosed within curly brackets. Thus, the object `point` in the code above could also be created and initialized with this line:

```
var point = { x:2.3, y:-1.2 };
```

Object literals can also be nested. For example:

```
var rectangle = { upperLeft: { x: 2, y: 2 },
                  lowerRight: { x: 4, y: 4}
                };
```

Finally, the property values used in object literals need not be constant—they can be arbitrary JavaScript expressions:

```
var square = { upperLeft: { x:point.x, y:point.y },
               lowerRight: { x:(point.x + side), y:(point.y+side) }};
```

3.6 Arrays

An *array* is a collection of data values, just as an object is. While each data value contained in an object has a name, each data value in an array has a number, or *index*. In JavaScript, you retrieve a value from an array by enclosing an index within square brackets after the array name. For example, if an array is named a and i is a non-negative integer, a[i] is an element of the array. Array indexes begin with zero. Thus a[2] refers to the *third* element of the array a.

Arrays may contain any type of JavaScript data, including references to other arrays or to objects or functions. For example:

```
document.images[1].width
```

This code refers to the width property of an object stored in the second element of an array stored in the images property of the document object.

Note that the arrays described here differ from the associative arrays described in the previous section. The "regular" arrays we are discussing here are indexed by non-negative integers. Associative arrays are indexed by strings. Also note that JavaScript does not support multidimensional arrays, except as arrays of arrays. Finally, because JavaScript is an untyped language, the elements of an array do not all need to be of the same type, as they do in typed languages like Java. We'll learn more about arrays in Chapter 9, *Arrays*.

3.6.1 Creating Arrays

Arrays can be created with the Array() constructor function. Once created, any number of indexed elements can easily be assigned to the array:

```
var a = new Array();
a[0] = 1.2;
a[1] = "JavaScript";
a[2] = true;
a[3] = { x:1, y:3 };
```

3.6.2 Array Literals

JavaScript 1.2 adds a new literal syntax for creating and initializing arrays. Like object literals, array literals are not available prior to JavaScript 1.2. An array literal (or "array initializer") is a comma-separated list of values contained within square brackets. The values within the brackets are assigned sequentially to array indexes starting with zero. For example, in JavaScript 1.2 the array creation and initialization code above could also be written as:

```
var a = [1.2, "JavaScript", true, { x:1, y:3 }];
```

Like object literals, array literals can be nested:

```
var matrix = [[1,2,3], [4,5,6], [7,8,9]];
```

Also, like object literals, the elements in array literals can be arbitrary expressions and need not be restricted to constants:

```
var base = 1024;
var table = [base, base+1, base+2, base+3];
```

Undefined elements can be included in an array literal by simply omitting a value between commas. For example:

```
var sparseArray = [1,,,,5];
```

Navigator 4 and Internet Explorer 4 differ upon the interpretation of trailing commas at the end of an array literal. Navigator 4 adopts the C-language convention of allowing a trailing comma after the last element of an array literal; it requires two trailing commas to force an undefined element to appear at the end of the array. Internet Explorer 4 creates an undefined element for each trailing comma. Fortunately, this incompatibility is minor and makes very little practical difference.

Finally, note that Navigator 4 has a bug: when an array literal is specified with a number as its single element, that number specifies the length of the array rather than the value of the first element. While this behavior mirrors that of the Array() constructor, it is clearly inappropriate in this context.

3.7 Null

The JavaScript keyword null is a special value that indicates "no value." null is often considered the single legal value of a special data type named Null. Sometimes, however, it is considered to be a special value of object type—a value that represents "no object." In either case, null is a unique value, distinct from all other values. When a variable holds the value null, you know that it does not contain a valid object, array, number, string, or boolean value.

C and C++ programmers should note that null in JavaScript is not the same as 0, as it is in those languages. In certain circumstances, null is converted to 0, but the two are not equivalent.

3.8 Undefined

There is another special value used occasionally by JavaScript. This is the "undefined" value returned when you use a variable that doesn't exist, a variable that has been declared but never had a value assigned to it, or an object property that doesn't exist.

Unlike the null value, there is no undefined keyword for the undefined value. This can make it hard to write JavaScript code that detects this value. The undefined value is not the same as null, but for most practical purposes, you can treat it as if it were. This is because the undefined value compares equal to `null`. Consider the following:

```
my.prop == null
```

This comparison is `true` either if the `my.prop` property doesn't exist or if it does exist but contains the value `null`.

In JavaScript 1.1 and later, you can distinguish between `null` and the undefined value with the `typeof` operator (which is discussed in detail in Chapter 5). This operator returns a string that indicates the data type of any value. When you apply `typeof` to a variable that has not been assigned a value (or to an undefined variable or property), it returns the string "undefined":

```
var new_undefined_variable;
type = typeof new_undefined_variable   // Returns "undefined"
```

On the other hand, when you use `typeof` on `null`, it returns the string "object":

```
type = typeof null;                         // Returns "object"
```

In JavaScript 1.3 (and currently in Internet Explorer 4), you'll be able to use the `===` identity operator to distinguish between `null` and the undefined value. This new operator does not treat the two values as equal. For example, you might test for undefined values like this:

```
// Declare a variable but never give it a value. This way it will
// always be undefined, and we can use it like the null keyword.
var undefined;

if (greeting.text === undefined) greeting.text = "Hello";
```

3.9 The Date Object

The previous sections have described all of the fundamental data types supported by JavaScript. Date and time values are not one of these fundamental types. But JavaScript does provide a type (or *class*) of object that represents dates and times and can be used to manipulate this type of data. A Date object in JavaScript is created with the `new` operator and the `Date()` constructor (the `new` operator will be introduced in Chapter 5, and we'll learn more about object creation in Chapter 8):

```
now = new Date();   // Create an object representing the current date and time.
// Create a Date object representing Christmas.
// Note that months are zero-based, so December is month 11!
xmas = new Date(97, 11, 25);
```

Methods of the Date object allow you to get and set the various date and time values and to convert the Date to a string, using either local time or GMT time. For example:

```
xmas.setYear(xmas.getYear() + 1);    // Change the date to next Christmas.
document.write("Today is: " + now.toLocaleString());
```

In addition, the Date object also defines functions (not methods; they are not invoked through a Date object) to convert a date specified in string or numeric form to an internal millisecond representation that is useful for some kinds of date arithmetic.

You can find full documentation on the Date object and its methods in the reference section of this book. Note that JavaScript 1.2 and the ECMA standard add various new methods to the Date object, primarily for better support of years greater than 1999.

3.10 *Regular Expressions*

JavaScript 1.2 adds support for regular expressions. Regular expressions provide a rich and powerful syntax for describing textual patterns; they are used for pattern matching and for implementing search and replace operations. JavaScript has adopted the Perl programming language syntax for expressing regular expressions.

Regular expressions are represented in JavaScript by the RegExp object and may be created using the RegExp() constructor. Like the Date object, the RegExp object is not one of the fundamental data types of JavaScript, but it is supported by all implementations of core JavaScript (or at least by all implementations of JavaScript 1.2).

Unlike the Date object, however, RegExp objects have a literal syntax and can be encoded directly into JavaScript 1.2 programs. Text between a pair of slashes constitutes a regular expression literal. The second slash in the pair can also be followed by one or more letters, which modify the meaning of the pattern. For example:

```
/^HTML/
/[1-9][0-9]*/
/\bjavascript\b/i
```

The regular expression grammar is fairly complex; it is documented in detail in Chapter 10, *Pattern Matching with Regular Expressions*. At this point, you need only know what a regular expression literal looks like in JavaScript code.

3.11 Primitive Data Type Wrapper Objects

When we discussed strings earlier in this chapter, I pointed out a strange feature of that data type: to operate on strings, you use object notation. For example, a typical operation involving strings might be the following:

```
s = "These are the times that try people's souls.";
last_word = s.substring(s.lastIndexOf(" ")+1, s.length);
```

If you didn't know better, it would appear that s was an object and that you were invoking methods and reading property values of that object.

What's going on? Are strings objects or are they distinct data types? The typeof operator assures us that strings have the data type "string," which is distinct from the object type "object." Why, then, are strings manipulated using object notation?

The truth is that each primitive data type has a corresponding object class defined for it. That is, besides supporting the number, string, and boolean data types, JavaScript also supports Number, String, and Boolean classes. These classes are wrappers around the primitive data types. A *wrapper* contains the same primitive data value but also defines properties and methods that can be used to manipulate that data.

JavaScript can very flexibly convert values from one type to another. When we use a string in an object context—when we try to access a property or method of the string—JavaScript internally creates a String wrapper object for the string value. This String object is used in place of the primitive string value; the object has properties and methods defined, so the use of the primitive value in an object context succeeds. The same is true, of course, for the other primitive types and their corresponding wrapper objects; we just don't use the other types in an object context nearly as often as we use strings in that context.

When we use a string in an object context, note that the String object that is created is a transient one—it is used to allow us to access a property or method and then it is no longer needed, so it is reclaimed by the system. Suppose s is a string and we determine the length of the string with a line like this:

```
len = s.length;
```

In this case, s remains a string; the original string value is not itself changed. A new transient String object is created, which allows us to access the length property, and then the transient object is discarded, with no change to the original value s. If you think that this scheme sounds elegant and bizarrely complex at the same time, you are right. You shouldn't worry, however, because the conversion to a transient object is done quite efficiently within JavaScript.

If we want to use a String object explicitly in our program, we have to create a non-transient one that is not automatically discarded by the system. String objects are created just like other objects, with the `new` operator. For example:

```
s = "hello world";            // A primitive string value
S = new String("Hello World");  // A String object
```

Once we've created a String object S, what can we do with it? Nothing that we cannot do with the corresponding primitive string value. If we use the `typeof` operator, it tells us that S is indeed an object, and not a string value, but except for that case, we'll find that we can't distinguish between a primitive string and the String object. As we've already seen, strings are automatically converted to String objects whenever necessary. It turns out that the reverse is also true. Whenever we use a String object where a primitive string value is expected, JavaScript automatically converts the String to a string. So if we use our String object with the + operator, a transient primitive string value is created so that the string concatenation operation can be performed:

```
msg = S + '!';
```

Bear in mind that everything we've discussed in this section about string values and String objects applies also to number and boolean values and their corresponding Number and Boolean objects. You can learn more about these classes from their respective entries in the reference section of this book. In Chapter 11, *Further Topics in JavaScript*, we'll see more about this primitive type/object duality and about automatic data conversion in JavaScript.

4

Variables

A *variable* is a name associated with a data value; we say that the variable "stores" or "contains" the value. Variables allow you to store and manipulate data in your programs. For example, the following line of JavaScript assigns the value 2 to a variable named i:

```
i = 2;
```

And the following line adds 3 to i and assigns the result to a new variable sum:

```
sum = i + 3;
```

These two lines of code demonstrate just about everything you need to know about variables. However, to fully understand how variables work in JavaScript, you need to master a few more concepts. Unfortunately, these concepts require more than a couple of lines of code to explain! The rest of this chapter explains the typing, declaration, scope, contents, and resolution of variables, and it also explores garbage collection and the variable/property duality.

4.1 *Variable Typing*

An important difference between JavaScript and languages like Java and C is that JavaScript is *untyped*. This means, in part, that a JavaScript variable can hold a value of any data type, unlike a Java or C variable, which can hold only the one particular type of data for which it is declared. For example, it is perfectly legal in JavaScript to assign a number to a variable and later assign a string to it:

```
i = 10;
i = "ten";
```

In C, C++, or Java, these lines of code are illegal.

A feature related to JavaScript's lack of typing is that the language conveniently and automatically converts values from one type to another, as necessary. If you attempt to append a number to a string, for example, JavaScript automatically converts the number to the corresponding string so that it can be appended. We'll see more about data type conversion in section 11.1, "Data Type Conversion."

JavaScript is obviously a simpler language for being untyped. The advantage of typed languages, like C++ and Java, is that they enforce rigorous programming practices, and therefore make it easier to write, maintain, and reuse long, complex programs. Since many JavaScript programs are shorter scripts, this rigor is not necessary and we benefit from the simpler syntax.

4.2 *Variable Declaration*

Before you use a variable in a JavaScript program, you must *declare* it.* Variables are declared with the `var` keyword, like this:

```
var i;
var sum;
```

You can also declare multiple variables with the same `var` keyword:

```
var i, sum;
```

And you can combine variable declaration with variable initialization:

```
var message = "hello";
var i = 0, j = 0, k = 0;
```

If you don't specify an initial value for a variable with the `var` statement, the variable is defined, but its initial value is the special JavaScript undefined value until your code stores a value into it.

Note that the `var` statement can also appear as part of the `for` and `for/in` loops, in order to succinctly declare the loop variable as part of the loop syntax itself. For example:

```
for(var i = 0; i < 10; i++) document.write(i, "<BR>");
for(var i = 0, j=10; i < 10; i++,j--) document.write(i*j, "<BR>");
for(var i in o) document.write(i, "<BR>");
```

The `for` and `for/in` looping constructs are introduced in Chapter 6, *Statements*.

Variables declared with `var` are *permanent*: attempting to delete them with the JavaScript 1.2 `delete` operator causes an error. (This is always true for local variables, but Navigator and Internet Explorer differ as to whether declared global

---

* You *should* declare it, really. We'll see shortly that in one common circumstance, variable declaration is optional.

variables can be deleted or not. It is not clear how this issue will be resolved, but the safest course is to assume that global variables cannot be deleted.) The `delete` operator is introduced in Chapter 5, *Expressions and Operators*.

4.2.1 Repeated and Omitted Declarations

It is legal, and harmless, to declare a variable more than once with the `var` statement. If the repeated declaration has an initializer, it acts as if it were simply an assignment statement.

You can sometimes get away with omitting a `var` statement altogether, but this is not a good habit to get into. When you assign a value to a variable that you haven't declared, JavaScript automatically creates a global variable by that name for you. Within a function, you usually want to create a local variable that is visible only within the body of the function, not a global variable. To be sure you are creating a local variable and not simply assigning a value to a global variable that already exists, you *must* use the `var` statement. (This distinction between local and global variables is explored in more detail in the next section.)

4.3 Variable Scope

The *scope* of a variable is the region of your program in which it is defined. A *global* variable has global scope—it is defined everywhere in your JavaScript code. On the other hand, variables declared within a function are defined only within the body of the function. They are *local* variables and have local scope. Function parameters also count as local variables and are defined only within the body of the function.

Within the body of a function, a local variable takes precedence over a global variable with the same name. If you declare a local variable or function parameter with the same name as a global variable, you effectively "hide" the global variable. For example, the following code prints the word "local":

```
var scope = "global";      // Declare a global variable.
function checkscope() {
    var scope = "local";   // Declare a local variable with the same name.
    document.write(scope); // Use the local variable, not the global one.
}
checkscope();
```

Although you can get away with not using the `var` statement when writing code in the global scope, you must always use `var` to declare local variables. Consider what happens if you don't:

```
    scope = "global";          // Declare a global variable, even without var.
    function checkscope() {
        scope = "local";       // Oops! We just changed the global variable.
        document.write(scope); // Prints "local"
    }
    checkscope();
    document.write(scope);     // This prints "local", too.
```

In general, functions do not know what variables are defined in the global scope or what they are being used for. Thus, if a function uses a global variable instead of a local one, it runs the risk of changing a value that some other part of the program is relying on. Fortunately, avoiding this problem is simple: declare all variables with `var`.

In JavaScript 1.2, function definitions can be nested. Each function has its own local scope, and so it is possible to have several nested layers of local scope. For example:

```
    var scope = "global scope";            // A global variable
    function checkscope() {
        var scope = "local scope";         // A local variable
        function nested() {
            var scope = "nested scope";    // A nested scope of local variables
            document.write(scope);         // Prints "nested scope"
        }
        nested();
    }
    checkscope();
```

4.3.1 No Block Scope

Note that unlike C, C++, and Java, JavaScript does not have block-level scope. All variables declared in a function, no matter where they are declared, are defined *throughout* the function. In the following code, the variables i, j, and k all have the same scope: all three are defined throughout the body of the function. This would not be the case if the code were written in C, C++, or Java:

```
    function test(o) {
        var i = 0;                      // i is defined throughout function.
        if (typeof o == "object") {
            var j = 0;                  // j is defined everywhere, not just block.
            for(var k = 0; k < 10; k++) { // k is defined everywhere, not just loop.
                document.write(k);
            }
            document.write(k);          // k is still defined: prints 10.
        }
        document.write(j);              // j is defined, but may not be initialized.
    }
```

This rule, that all variables declared in a function are defined throughout the function, can cause surprising results. The following code illustrates this:

```
var scope = "global";
function f() {
  alert(scope);          // Displays "undefined", not "global"
  var scope = "local"; // Variable initialized here, but defined everywhere
  alert(scope);          // Displays "local"
}
f();
```

You might think that the first call to alert() would display "global", since the var statement declaring the local variable has not yet been executed. Because of the scope rules, however, this is not what happens. The local variable is defined throughout the body of the function, which means the global variable by the same name is hidden throughout the function. Although the local variable is defined throughout, it is not actually initialized until the var statement is executed. Thus, the function f above is equivalent to the following:

```
function f() {
  var scope;       // Local variable is declared at the start of function.
  alert(scope);    // It exists here, but still has "undefined" value.
  scope = "local"; // Now we initialize it and give it a value.
  alert(scope);    // And here it has a value.
}
```

This example illustrates why it is good programming practice to place all of your variable declarations together at the start of any function.

4.3.2 Undefined Versus Unassigned

The examples in the previous section demonstrate a subtle point in JavaScript programming: there are two different kinds of undefined variables. The first kind of undefined variable is one that has never been declared. An attempt to read the value of such an undeclared variable causes a runtime error. Undeclared variables are undefined because they simply do not exist. As described in the previous section, assigning a value to such an undeclared variable does not cause an error; instead it implicitly declares the variable.

The second kind of undefined variable is one that has been declared but has never had a value assigned to it. If you read the value of one of these variables, you obtain its default value, which is the special undefined value. This type of undefined variable might more usefully be called "unassigned," to distinguish it from the more serious kind of undefined variable that has not even been declared and does not exist.

The following code fragment illustrates some of the differences between truly undefined and merely unassigned variables:

```
var x;       // Declare an unassigned variable. Its value is undefined.
alert(u);    // Using an undeclared variable causes an error.
u = 3;       // Assigning to an undeclared variable creates the variable.
```

4.4 Primitive Types and Reference Types

The next topic we need to consider is the content of variables. We often say that variables "have" or "contain" values. But just what is it they contain? To answer this seemingly simple question, we must look again at the data types supported by JavaScript. The types can be divided into two groups: primitive types and reference types. Numbers, boolean values, and the null and undefined types are primitive. Objects, arrays, and functions are reference types.

A primitive type has a fixed size in memory. For example, a number occupies eight bytes of memory and a boolean value can be represented with only one bit. The number type is the largest of the primitive types. If each JavaScript variable reserves eight bytes of memory, the variable can directly hold any primitive value.*

Reference types are another matter, however. Objects, for example, can be of any length—they do not have a fixed size. The same is true of arrays: an array can have any number of elements. Similarly, a function can contain any amount of JavaScript code. Since these types do not have a fixed size, their values cannot be stored directly in the eight bytes of memory associated with each variable. Instead, the variable stores a *reference* to the value. Typically, this reference is some form of pointer or memory address. It is not the data value itself, but it tells the variable where to look to find the value.

The distinction between primitive and reference types is an important one, because they behave differently. Consider the following code that uses numbers (a primitive type):

```
var a = 3.14;   // Declare and initialize a variable.
var b = a;      // Copy the variable's value to a new variable.
a = 4;          // Modify the value of the original variable.
alert(b)        // Displays 3.14; the copy has not changed.
```

---

* This is an oversimplified explanation and is not intended as a description of an actual JavaScript implementation.

There is nothing surprising with this code. Now consider what happens if we change the code slightly so that it uses arrays (a reference type) instead of numbers:

```
var a = [1,2,3]; // Initialize a variable to refer to an array.
var b = a;       // Copy that reference into a new variable.
a[0] = 99;       // Modify the array using the original reference.
alert(b);        // Display changed array [99,2,3] using new reference.
```

If this result does not seem surprising to you, you're already well familiar with the distinction between primitive and reference types. If it does seem surprising, take a closer look at the second line. Note that the only thing that is being assigned in this statement is the reference to the array value, not the array itself. After that second line of code, we still have only one array object; we just happen to have two references to it.

If the primitive versus reference type distinction is new to you, just try to keep the variable contents in mind. Variables hold the actual values of primitive types, but they hold only references to the values of reference types. The differing behavior of primitive and reference types is explored in more detail in section 11.2, "By Value Versus by Reference."

You may have noticed that I did not specify whether strings are primitive or reference types in JavaScript. Strings are an unusual case. They have variable size, so obviously they cannot be stored directly in fixed-size variables. For efficiency, we would expect JavaScript to copy references to strings, not the contents of strings. On the other hand, strings behave like a primitive type in many ways. The question of whether strings are a primitive or reference type is made more confusing (and perhaps becomes a moot point) by the fact that strings are *immutable*: there is no way to change the contents of a string value. This means that we cannot construct an example like the one shown above that demonstrates that arrays are copied by reference. In the end, it doesn't matter much whether you think of strings as an immutable reference type that behaves like a primitive type or as a primitive type implemented with the internal efficiency of a reference type.

4.5 Garbage Collection

Reference types do not have a fixed size; indeed, some of them can become quite large. As we've already discussed, variables do not directly hold reference values. The value is stored at some other location and the variables merely hold a reference to that location. Now we need to focus briefly on the actual storage for the value.

Since strings, objects, and arrays do not have a fixed size, storage for them must be allocated dynamically, when the size is known. Every time a JavaScript program creates a string, array, or object, the interpreter must allocate memory to store that entity. Whenever memory is dynamically allocated like this, it must eventually be freed up for reuse, or the JavaScript interpreter will use up all the available memory on the system and crash.

In languages like C and C++, memory must be freed manually. It is the programmer's responsibility to keep track of all the objects that are created and to destroy them (freeing their memory) when they are no longer needed. This can be an onerous task and is often the source of bugs.

Instead of requiring manual deallocation, JavaScript relies on a technique called *garbage collection.* The JavaScript interpreter is able to detect when an object will never again be used by the program. When it determines that an object is unreachable (i.e., there is no longer any way to refer to it using the variables in the program), it knows that the object is no longer needed and its memory can be reclaimed. Consider the following lines of code, for example:

```
var s = "hello";          // Allocate memory for a string
var u = s.toUpperCase();  // Create a new string.
s = u;                    // Overwrite reference to original string.
```

After this code runs, the original string "hello" is no longer reachable—there are no references to it in any variables in the program. The system detects this fact and frees up its storage for reuse.

Garbage collection is automatic and invisible to the programmer. You can create all the garbage objects you want and the system will clean up after you! You need to know only enough about garbage collection to trust that it works and not have to wonder about where all the old objects go. For those who aren't satisfied, however, section 11.3, "Garbage Collection," contains further details on the JavaScript garbage collection process.

4.6 *Variables as Properties*

You may have noticed by now that there are a lot of similarities in JavaScript between variables and the properties of objects. They are both assigned the same way, they are used the same way in JavaScript expressions, and so on. Is there really any fundamental difference between the variable i and the property i of an object o? The answer is no. Variables in JavaScript are fundamentally the same as object properties.

4.6.1 The Global Object

When the JavaScript interpreter starts up, one of the first things it does, before executing any JavaScript code, is create a *global object*. The properties of this object are the global variables of JavaScript programs. When you declare a global JavaScript variable, what you are actually doing is defining a property of the global object.

Furthermore, all predefined functions and properties in the JavaScript environment are also properties of the global object. For example, the `parseInt()` function and the Math object are referenced by the `parseInt` and `Math` properties of the global object. In top-level code (i.e., JavaScript code that is not part of a function), you can use the JavaScript keyword `this` to refer to the global object. Within functions, `this` has a different use, which is described in Chapter 7, *Functions*.

In client-side JavaScript, the Window object serves as the global object for all JavaScript code contained in the browser window it represents. This global Window object has a self-referential `window` property that can be used instead of `this` to refer to the global object. The Window object defines the core global properties, such as `parseInt` and `Math`, and also global client-side properties, such as `navigator` and `screen`.

4.6.2 Local Variables: The Call Object

If global variables are properties of the special global object, then what are local variables? They too are properties of an object. This object is known as the *call object*. The call object has a shorter life span than the global object, but it serves the same purpose. While the body of a function is executing, the function arguments and local variables are stored as properties of this call object. The use of an entirely separate object for local variables is what allows JavaScript to keep local variables from overwriting the value of global variables by the same name.

4.6.3 JavaScript Execution Contexts

Each time the JavaScript interpreter begins to execute a function, it creates a new *execution context* for that function. An execution context is, obviously, the context in which any piece of JavaScript code executes. An important part of the context is the object in which variables are defined. Thus, JavaScript code that is not part of any function runs in an execution context that uses the global object for variable definitions. And every JavaScript function runs in its own unique execution context with its own call object in which local variables are defined.

An interesting point to note is that JavaScript implementations may allow multiple global execution contexts, each with a *different* global object. (Although, in this case, each "global" object is not entirely global.) The obvious example of this is client-side JavaScript, in which each separate browser window, or each frame within a window, defines a separate global execution context. Client-side JavaScript code in each frame or window runs in its own execution context and has its own global object. However, these separate client-side global objects have properties that link them to one another. Thus, JavaScript code in one frame might refer to another frame with the expression `parent.frames[1]`, and the global variable `x` in the first frame might be referenced by the expression `parent.frames[0].x` in the second frame.

You don't need to fully understand how separate window and frame execution contexts are linked together in client-side JavaScript right now. We'll cover that topic in detail when we discuss the integration of JavaScript with web browsers in Part II of this book. What you should understand now is that JavaScript is flexible enough that a single JavaScript interpreter can run scripts in different global execution contexts, and that those contexts need not be entirely disjoint—they can refer back and forth to each other.

This last point requires additional consideration. When JavaScript code in one execution context can read and write property values and execute functions that are defined in another execution context, we've reached a level of complexity that requires consideration of security issues. Take client-side JavaScript as an example. Suppose browser window A is running a script or contains information from your local intranet and window B is running a script from some random site out on the Internet. In general, we do not want to allow the code in window B to be able to access the properties of window A. If we allow it to do this, it might be able to read sensitive company information and steal it, for example. Thus, in order to safely run JavaScript code, there must be a security mechanism that prevents access from one execution context to another when such access should not be permitted. We'll return to this topic in Chapter 21, *JavaScript Security*.

4.7 *Variable Scope Revisited*

When we first discussed the notion of variable scope, I based the definition solely on the lexical structure of JavaScript code: global variables have global scope and variables declared in functions have local scope. If one function definition is nested within another, variables declared within that nested function have a nested local scope. Now that we know that global variables are properties of a global object and that local variables are properties of a special call object, we can return to the notion of variable scope and reconceptualize it. This new description of scope offers a very useful way to think about variables in many contexts; it provides a powerful new understanding of how JavaScript works.

Every JavaScript execution context has a *scope chain* associated with it. This scope chain is a list or chain of objects. When JavaScript code needs to look up the value of a variable *x* (a process called *variable name resolution*), it starts by looking at the first object in the chain. If that object has a property named *x*, the value of that property is used. If the first object does not have a property named *x*, JavaScript continues the search with the next object in the chain. If that second object does not have a property named *x*, the search moves on to the next object, and so on.

In top-level JavaScript code (i.e., code not contained within any function definitions), the scope chain consists of a single object, the global object. All variables are looked up in this object. If a variable does not exist, the variable value is undefined. In a (non-nested) function, however, the scope chain consists of two objects. The first is the function's call object and the second is the global object. When the function refers to a variable, the call object (the local scope) is checked first and the global object (the global scope) is checked second. A nested function would have three or more objects in its scope chain. Figure 4-1 illustrates the process of looking up a variable name in the scope chain of a function. We'll have more to say about the scope chain in Chapter 11, *Further Topics in JavaScript.*

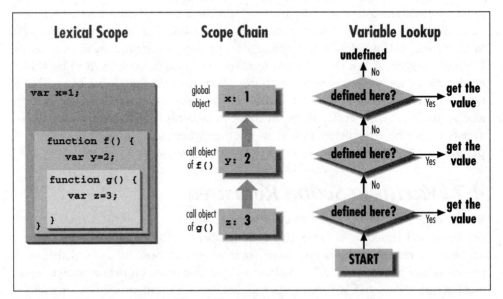

Figure 4–1: The scope chain and variable resolution

5

Expressions and Operators

This chapter explains how expressions and operators work in JavaScript. If you are familiar with C, C++, or Java, you'll notice that the expressions and operators in JavaScript are very similar and you'll be able to skim this chapter quickly. If you are not a C, C++, or Java programmer, this chapter tells you what you need to know about expressions and operators in JavaScript.

5.1 Expressions

An *expression* is a "phrase" of JavaScript that a JavaScript interpreter can *evaluate* to produce a value. The simplest expressions are literals or variable names, like these:

```
1.7                       // A numeric literal
"JavaScript is fun!"      // A string literal
true                      // A Boolean literal
null                      // The literal null value
{ x:2, y:2 }              // An object literal
[2,3,5,7,11,13,17,19]     // An array literal
function(x){return x*x;}  // A function literal
i                         // The variable i
sum                       // The variable sum
```

The value of a constant expression is simply the constant itself. The value of a variable expression is the value that the variable refers to.

These expressions are not particularly interesting. More complex (and interesting) expressions can be created by combining simple expressions. For example, we saw that 1.7 is an expression and i is an expression. The following is also an expression:

```
i + 1.7
```

The value of this expression is determined by adding the values of the two simpler expressions. The + in this example is an *operator* that is used to combine two expressions into a more complex expression. Another operator is −, which is used to combine expressions by subtraction. For example:

```
(i + 1.7) - sum
```

This expression uses the − operator to subtract the value of the sum variable from the value of our previous expression i + 1.7. JavaScript supports a number of other operators besides + and −, as you'll see in the next section.

5.2 Operator Overview

If you are a C, C++, or Java programmer, almost all of the JavaScript operators should already be familiar to you. Table 5-1 summarizes the operators; you can refer to this table for reference. In the table, the column labeled **P** gives the operator precedence, and the column labeled **A** gives the operator associativity, which can be L (left-to-right) or R (right-to-left).

If you do not already understand precedence and associativity, the sections that follow the table explain how to interpret the table and explain what each of the operators does.

Table 5-1: JavaScript Operators

P	A	Operator	Operand Type(s)	Operation Performed
15	L	.	object, property	Property access
	L	[ ]	array, integer	Array index
	L	( )	function, arguments	Function call
14	R	++	number	Pre-or-post increment (unary)
	R	--	number	Pre-or-post decrement (unary)
	R	-	number	Unary minus (negation)
	R	~	integer	Bitwise complement (unary)
	R	!	boolean	Logical complement (unary)
	R	delete [a]	variable	Undefine a property (unary)
	R	new	constructor call	Create new object (unary)

Table 5-1: JavaScript Operators (continued)

P	A	Operator	Operand Type(s)	Operation Performed
	R	`typeof`	any	Return data type (unary)
	R	`void`	any	Return undefined value (unary)
13	L	`*, /, %`	numbers	Multiplication, division, remainder
12	L	`+, -`	numbers	Addition, subtraction
	L	`+`	strings	String concatenation
11	L	`<<`	integers	Left shift
	L	`>>`	integers	Right shift with sign-extension
	L	`>>>`	integers	Right shift with zero extension
10	L	`<, <=`	numbers or strings	Less than, less than or equal
	L	`>, >=`	numbers or strings	Greater than, greater than or equal
9	L	`==`	any	Test for equality
	L	`!=`	any	Test for inequality
	L	`===` [b]	any	Test for identity
	L	`!==` [b]	any	Test for non-identity
8	L	`&`	integers	Bitwise AND
7	L	`^`	integers	Bitwise XOR
6	L	`|`	integers	Bitwise OR
5	L	`&&`	booleans	Logical AND
4	L	`||`	booleans	Logical OR
3	R	`?:`	boolean, any, any	Conditional (ternary) operator
2	R	`=`	variable, any	Assignment
	R	`*=, /=, %=, +=, -=, <<=, >>=, >>>=, &=, ^=, |=`	variable, any	Assignment with operation
1	L	`,`	any	Multiple evaluation

[a] New in JavaScript 1.2
[b] Only supported by Internet Explorer 4

5.2.1 *Number of Operands*

In general, there are three types of operators. Most JavaScript operators, like the +
operator that we saw in the previous section, are *binary operators* that combine
two expressions into a single, more complex expression. That is, they operate on

two operands. JavaScript also supports a number of *unary operators*, which convert a single expression into a single, more complex expression. The – operator in the expression –3 is a unary operator which performs the operation of negation on the operand 3. Finally, JavaScript supports one *ternary operator*, ?:, which combines the value of three expressions into a single expression.

5.2.2 Type of Operands

When constructing JavaScript expressions, you must pay attention to the data types that are being passed to operators and to the data types that are returned. Different operators expect their operands' expressions to evaluate to values of a certain data type. For example, it is not possible to multiply strings, so the expression "a" * "b" is not legal in JavaScript. Note, however, that JavaScript tries to convert expressions to the appropriate type whenever possible, so the expression "3" * "5" is legal. Its value is the number 15, not the string "15".

Furthermore, some operators behave differently depending on the type of the operands. Most notably, the + operator adds numeric operands but concatenates string operands. Also, if passed one string and one number, it converts the number to a string and concatenates the two resulting strings. For example, "1" + 0 yields the string "10".

Finally, note that operators do not always return the same type as their operands. The comparison operators (less than, equal to, greater than, etc.) take operands of various types, but when comparison expressions are evaluated, they always return a boolean result that indicates whether the comparison is true or not. For example, the expression a < 3 returns true if the value of variable a is in fact less than 3. As we'll see, the boolean values returned by comparison operators are used in if statements, while loops, and for loops—JavaScript statements that control the execution of a program based on the results of evaluating expressions that contain comparison operators.

5.2.3 Operator Precedence

In Table 5-1, the column labeled **P** specifies the *precedence* of each operator. Operator precedence controls the order in which operations are performed. Operators with a higher number in the **P** column are performed before those with a lower number.

Consider the following expression:

```
w = x + y*z;
```

The multiplication operator * has a higher precedence than the addition operator +, so the multiplication is performed before the addition. Furthermore, the assignment operator = has the lowest precedence, so the assignment is performed after all the operations on the right-hand side are completed. Operator precedence can be overridden with the explicit use of parentheses. To force the addition to be performed first in the above example, we would write:

```
w = (x + y)*z;
```

In practice, if you are at all unsure about the precedence of your operators, the simplest thing is to use parentheses to make the evaluation order explicit. The only rules that are important to know are: multiplication and division are performed before addition and subtraction, and assignment has very low precedence and is always performed last.

5.2.4 *Operator Associativity*

In Table 5-1, the column labeled **A** specifies the *associativity* of the operator. A value of L specifies left-to-right associativity, and a value of R specifies right-to-left associativity. The associativity of an operator specifies the order in which operations of the same precedence are performed. Left-to-right associativity means that operations are performed from left to right. For example:

```
w = x + y + z;
```

is the same as:

```
w = ((x + y) + z);
```

because the addition operator has left-to-right associativity. On the other hand, the following (almost nonsensical) expressions:

```
x = ~-~y;
w = x = y = z;
q = a?b:c?d:e?f:g;
```

are equivalent to:

```
x = ~(-(~y));
w = (x = (y = z));
q = a?b:(c?d:(e?f:g));
```

because the unary, assignment, and ternary conditional operators have right-to-left associativity.

5.3 *Arithmetic Operators*

Having explained operator precedence, associativity, and other background material, we can start to discuss the operators themselves. This section details the arithmetic operators:

Addition (+)

> The + operator adds numeric operands or concatenates string operands. If one operand is a string, the other is converted to a string and the two strings are then concatenated. Object operands are converted to numbers or strings that can be added or concatenated. The conversion is performed by the valueOf() method and/or the toString() method of the object.

Subtraction (−)

> When − is used as a binary operator, it subtracts its second operand from its first. If used with non-numeric operands, it attempts to convert them to numbers.

Multiplication (*)

> The * operator multiplies its two operands. If used with non-numeric operands, it attempts to convert them to numbers.

Division (/)

> The / operator divides its first operand by its second. If used with non-numeric operands, it attempts to convert them to numbers. If you are a C programmer, you might expect to get an integer result when you divide one integer by another. In JavaScript, however, all numbers are floating-point, so all divisions have floating-point results: 5 / 2 evaluates to 2.5, not 2. Division by zero yields positive or negative infinity, while 0/0 evaluates to the special value NaN.

Modulo (%)

> The % operator computes the first operand modulo the second operand. That is, it returns the remainder when the first operand is divided by the second operand an integral number of times. If used with non-numeric operands, the modulo operator attempts to convert them to numbers. The sign of the result is the same as the sign of the first operand. For example, 5 % 2 evaluates to 1.

> While the modulo operator is typically used with integer operands, it also works for floating-point values. For example, 4.3 % 2.1 == 0.1.

Unary Negation (−)

> When − is used as a unary operator, before a single operand, it performs unary negation. In other words, it converts a positive value to an equivalently negative value, and vice versa. If the operand is not a number, this operator attempts to convert it to one.

Increment (++)

The ++ operator increments (i.e., adds 1 to) its single operand, which must be a variable, an element of an array, or a property of an object. If the value of this variable, element, or property is not a number, the operator attempts first to convert it to one. The precise behavior of this operator depends on its position relative to the operand. When used before the operand, where it is known as the pre-increment operator, it increments the operand and evaluates to the incremented value of that operand. When used after the operand, where it is known as the post-increment operator, it increments its operand, but evaluates to the *unincremented* value of that operand. If the value to be incremented is not a number, it is converted to one by this process.

For example, the following code sets both i and j to 2:

```
i = 1;
j = ++i;
```

But these lines set i to 2 and j to 1:

```
i = 1;
j = i++;
```

This operator, in both of its forms, is most commonly used to increment a counter that controls a loop.

Decrement (−−)

The −− operator decrements (i.e., subtracts 1 from) its single numeric operand, which must be a variable, an element of an array, or a property of an object. If the value of this variable, element, or property is not a number, the operator attempts first to convert it to one. Like the ++ operator, the precise behavior of −− depends on its position relative to the operand. When used before the operand, it decrements and returns the decremented value. When used after the operand, it decrements, but returns the *undecremented* value.

5.4 *Equality and Identity Operators*

This section describes the JavaScript equality and identity operators. These are operators that compare values for equality and identity and return a boolean value (`true` or `false`) depending on the result of the comparison. As we'll see in Chapter 6, *Statements*, they are most commonly used in things like `if` statements and `for` loops to control the flow of program execution.

5.4.1 Equality (==)

The `==` operator returns `true` if its two operands are equal; it returns `false` if they are not equal. The operands may be of any type, and the definition of "equal" depends on the type.

In JavaScript, numbers, strings, and boolean values are compared *by value*. In this case, there are two separate values involved, and the `==` operator checks that these two values are identical. This means that two variables are equal only if they contain the same value. For example, two strings are equal only if they each contain exactly the same characters.

On the other hand, objects, arrays, and functions are compared *by reference*. This means that two variables are equal only if they refer to the same object. Two separate arrays are never equal by the definition of the `==` operator, even if they contain identical elements. For two variables that contain references to objects, arrays, or functions, they are equal only if they refer to the same object, array, or function. If you want to test that two separate objects contain the same properties or that two separate arrays contain the same elements, you'll have to check the properties or elements yourself. (And, if any of the properties or elements are themselves objects or arrays, you'll have to decide which kind of equality you want to test for.)

Two values are compared for equality following these rules:

- If both values have the same type, compare the two values to see if they are equal.

  - If both are strings and contain exactly the same characters in the same positions, they are equal.

  - If both are the same number, they are equal. However, if either or both values are `NaN`, then they are not equal.

  - If both are the boolean value `true` or both are the boolean value `false`, they are equal.

  - If both refer to the same object, array, or function, they are equal. If they refer to different objects (or arrays or functions) they are not equal, even if both objects could be converted to the same primitive value.

  - If both are `null`, or both are undefined, they are equal.

- If one value is `null` and one is undefined, they are equal.

- If the types of the two values differ, attempt to convert them into the same type so they can be compared following the rules above.

  - If one value is a number and the other is a string, convert the string to a number and try the comparison again, using the converted value.

  - If either value is `true`, convert it to 1 and try the comparison again. If either value is `false`, convert it to 0 and try the comparison again.

  - If one value is an object and the other is a number or string, convert the object to a primitive and try the comparison again. An object is converted to a primitive value by either its `toString()` method or its `valueOf()` method. Native JavaScript classes attempt `valueOf()` conversion before `toString()` conversion.

  - Any other combinations of types are not equal.

As an example of testing for equality with type conversion, consider the comparison:

```
"1" == true
```

These two values are in fact equal. The boolean value `true` is first converted to the number 1. Then the string `"1"` is converted to the number 1. Since both numbers are now the same, the comparison returns `true`. Note that when the equality operator in Navigator 3 attempted to convert a string to a number and failed, it displayed an error message noting that the string could not be converted, instead of simply returning `false` as the result of the comparison. This bug has been fixed in Navigator 4.

5.4.1.1 Equality in Navigator 4

Navigator 4 was shipped before the ECMA-262 specification was finalized. When Navigator 4 shipped, the current ECMA draft specified that values were compared for equality without any attempt at type conversion. That is, if two values were of different types, they would never be equal.

This behavior for the equality operator was a change from its behavior in JavaScript 1.0 and JavaScript 1.1, so there was a backwards compatibility problem. To solve this problem, the engineers at Netscape implemented the new, draft behavior only in client-side JavaScript code that explicitly specified that it was JavaScript 1.2 code using the `LANGUAGE` attribute of the `<SCRIPT>` tag. For example, the following code prints "true":

```
<SCRIPT>
// Do a comparison with type conversion.
document.write("1" == 1);
</SCRIPT>
```

while the same code with a LANGUAGE attribute set to JavaScript 1.2 prints "false":

```
<SCRIPT LANGUAGE="JavaScript1.2">
// Do a comparison with type conversion.
document.write("1" == 1);
</SCRIPT>
```

While this was an elegant solution to a difficult compatibility issue, it created a more difficult compatibility issue: when the final version of the ECMA specification reverted to the historical type-conversion behavior of the equality operator, Navigator 4 was left with behavior that did not conform to the final specification.

To summarize, the == operator always behaves as described in the previous section except in client-side JavaScript in Navigator 4, embedded in a <SCRIPT> tag that explicitly specifies JavaScript 1.2 as its LANGUAGE attribute. In this one particular case, equality is computed without type conversion. In all other cases, type conversion is attempted when necessary. Future versions of Navigator will fully revert to the type-converting equality operator and will adopt the identity operator, described shortly, for checking equality without conversion.

5.4.2 Inequality (!=)

The != operator tests for the exact opposite case of the == operator. If two variables are equal to each other, comparing them with the != operator returns false. On the other hand, comparing two objects that are not equal to each other with != returns true. As we'll see, the ! operator computes the boolean NOT operation. This makes it easy to remember that != stands for "not equal to." See the discussion of the == operator for details on how equality is defined for different data types.

Note that in Navigator, the != operator has the same special-case behavior as == does when the LANGUAGE attribute is set to "JavaScript1.2".

5.4.3 Identity (===)

The === identity operator tests for a stricter form of equality than the equality operator (==) does. It evaluates to true only if its two operands have the same value without any type conversion. It follows the comparison rules described for the equality operator but does not perform any of the type conversion that the equality operator does when its operands are of different types. Note that the identity operator does not consider undefined values to be equal to null as the equality operator does.

The identity operator is implemented in Internet Explorer 4. It is expected to be formalized in Version 2 of the ECMA specification and will be included in JavaScript 1.3 and Navigator 5. The behavior of the identity operator is the same as the behavior of the equality operator in Navigator 4, when the `LAN-GUAGE="JavaScript1.2"` attribute is specified.

With the introduction of the identity operator, JavaScript supports =, ==, and === operators. Be sure you understand the difference between the assignment, equality, and identity operators, and be careful, when coding, that you use the right one! Although it is tempting to refer to all three operators as "equals," it may help to keep them distinct if you read "gets" or "is assigned" for =; "is equal to" for ==; and "is identical to" for ===.

5.4.4 Non-identity (!==)

The `!==` non-identity operator tests for the exact opposite case of the === operator. It evaluates to `true` only if its two operands are not identical. That is, it evaluates to `true` if its operands have different types or different values.

5.5 Comparison Operators

This section describes the JavaScript comparison operators. These are operators that compare values of various types and return a boolean value (`true` or `false`) depending on the result of the comparison. As we'll see in Chapter 6, they are most commonly used in things like `if` statements and `while` loops to control the flow of program execution. The comparison operators are:

Less Than (<)
> The < operator evaluates to `true` if its first operand is less than its second operand; otherwise it evaluates to `false`.

Greater Than (>)
> The > operator evaluates to `true` if its first operand is greater than its second operand; otherwise it evaluates to `false`.

Less Than or Equal (<=)
> The <= operator evaluates to `true` if its first operand is less than or equal to its second operand; otherwise it evaluates to `false`.

Greater Than or Equal (>=)
> The >= operator evaluates to `true` if its first operand is greater than or equal to its second operand; otherwise it evaluates to `false`.

The operands of these comparison operators may be of any type. Comparison can only be performed on numbers and strings, however, so operands that are not numbers or strings are converted. If both operands are numbers, or if both convert to numbers, they are compared numerically. If both operands are strings or convert to strings, they are compared in alphabetical order. If one operand is or converts to a string and one is or converts to a number, the operator attempts to convert the string to a number and perform a numerical comparison. If the operands cannot both be successfully converted to numbers or to strings, these operations always result in `false`.

5.6 *String Operators*

As we've discussed in the previous sections, there are several operators that have special effects when their operands are strings.

The + operator concatenates two string operands. That is, it creates a new string that consists of the first string followed by the second. Thus, for example, the following expression evaluates to the string "hello there":

```
"hello" + " " + "there"
```

And the following lines produce the string "22":

```
a = "2"; b = "2";
c = a + b;
```

The <, <=, >, and >= operators compare two strings to determine what order they fall in. The comparison uses alphabetical order. Note, however, that this "alphabetical" order is based on the Unicode character encoding used by JavaScript (or on the ASCII or Latin-1 subsets used by non-internationalized implementations). In this encoding, all capital letters in the Latin alphabet come before (are "less than") all lowercase letters, which can cause unexpected results. It means, for example, that the following expression evaluates to `true`:

```
"Zoo" < "aardvark"
```

The == and != operators work on strings, but, as we've seen, these operators work for all data types, and they do not have any special behavior when used with strings.

The + operator is a special one—it gives priority to string operands over numeric operands. As noted earlier, if either operand to + is a string (or an object), the other operand is converted to a string (or both operands are converted to strings) and concatenated, rather than added. On the other hand, the comparison operators only perform string comparison if *both* operands are strings. If only one operand is a string, JavaScript attempts to convert it to a number. The following lines illustrate:

```
1 + 2           // Addition. Result is 3.
"1" + "2"       // Concatenation. Result is "12".
"1" + 2         // Concatenation; 2 is converted to "2". Result is 12.
11 < 3          // Numeric comparison. Result is false.
"11" < "3"      // String comparison. Result is true.
"11" < 3        // Numeric comparison; "11" converted to 11. Result is false.
"eleven" < 3    // Causes error because "eleven" can't be converted to a number.
```

Finally, it is important to note that when the + operator is used with strings and numbers, it may not be associative. That is, the result may depend on the order in which operations are performed. This can be seen with examples like this:

```
s = 1 + 2 + " blind mice";       // Yields "3 blind mice"
vt = "# of blind mice: " + 1 + 2; // Yields "# of blind mice: 12"
```

The reason for this surprising difference in behavior is that the + operator works from left to right, unless parentheses change this order. Thus the two lines above are equivalent to these:

```
s = (1 + 2) + "blind mice";      // 1st + yields number; 2nd yields string
t = ("# of blind mice: " + 1) + 2;   // Both operations yield strings.
```

5.7 *Logical Operators*

The logical operators are typically used to perform "boolean algebra." They are often used in conjunction with comparison operators to express complex comparisons that involve more than one variable and are frequently used with the `if`, `while`, and `for` statements.

5.7.1 *Logical AND (&&)*

When used with boolean operands, the `&&` operator performs the Boolean AND operation on the two values: it returns `true` if and only if both its first operand *and* its second operand are `true`. Otherwise it returns `false`.

The actual behavior of this operator is somewhat more complicated. It starts by evaluating its first operand, the expression on its left. If the value of this expression can be converted to `false` (for example, if the left operand evaluates to `null`, `0`, `""`, or the undefined value), the operator returns the value of the left-hand expression. Otherwise, it evaluates its second operand, the expression on its right, and returns the value of that expression. (Navigator 2 and 3 had a bug: if the left-hand expression evaluated to `false`, the operator returned `false`, rather than returning the unconverted value of the left-hand expression.)

Note that, depending on the value of the left-hand expression, this operator may or may not evaluate the right-hand expression. You may occasionally see code that purposely exploits this feature of the && operator. For example, the following two lines of JavaScript code have equivalent effects:

```
if (a == b) stop();
(a == b) && stop();
```

While some programmers find this a natural and useful programming idiom, I recommend against using it. The fact that the right-hand side is not guaranteed to be evaluated can be a frequent source of bugs. Consider the following code for example:

```
if ((a == null) && (b++ > 10)) stop();
```

This statement probably does not do what the programmer intended, since the increment operator on the right-hand side is not evaluated whenever the comparison on the left-hand side is false. To avoid this problem, do not use expressions with side effects (assignments, increments, decrements, and function calls) on the right-hand side of && unless you are quite sure you know exactly what you are doing.

Despite the fairly confusing way that this operator actually works, it is easiest, and perfectly safe, to think of it as merely a boolean algebra operator. Although it does not actually return a boolean value, the value it returns can always be converted to a boolean value.

5.7.2 Logical OR (||)

When used with boolean operands, the || operator performs the Boolean OR operation on the two values: it returns true if either the first operand *or* the second operand is true (or both are true). Otherwise, if both operands are false, it returns false.

Although the || operator is most often used simply as a Boolean OR operator, it, like the && operator, has more complex behavior. It starts by evaluating its first operand, the expression on its left. If the value of this expression can be converted to true, it returns the value of the left-hand expression. Otherwise, it evaluates its second operand, the expression on its right, and returns the value of that expression. (There was a bug in this operator in Navigator 2 and Navigator 3: if the left-hand expression evaluated to true, the operator returned true, rather than returning the unconverted value of the left-hand expression.)

As with the && operator, you should avoid right-hand operands that include side-effects, unless you purposely want to make use of the fact that the right-hand expression may not be evaluated.

Even when the || operator is used with operands that are not boolean values, it can still be considered a Boolean OR operator, since its return value, whatever the type, can be converted to a boolean value.

5.7.3 Logical NOT (!)

The ! operator is a unary operator; it is placed before a single operand. Its purpose is to invert the boolean value of its operand. For example, if the variable a has the value true (or is a value that converts to true), !a has the value false. And if the expression p && q evaluates to false (or to a value that converts to false), !(p && q) evaluates to true.

5.8 Bitwise Operators

Despite the fact that all numbers in JavaScript are floating-point, the bitwise operators require numeric operands that have integral values. They operate on these integer operands using a 32-bit integer representation instead of the equivalent floating-point representation. These operators return NaN if used with operands that are not integers or that are too large to fit in a 32-bit integer representation. Four of these operators perform boolean algebra on the individual bits of the operands, behaving as if each bit in each operand were a boolean value and performing similar operations to the logical operators we saw earlier. The other three bitwise operators are used to shift bits left and right.

If you are not familiar with binary numbers and the binary representation of decimal integers, you can skip the operators described in this section. The purpose of these operators is not described here; they are needed for low-level manipulation of binary numbers and are not commonly used in JavaScript programming. The bitwise operators are:

Bitwise And (&)
> The & operator performs a boolean AND operation on each bit of its integer arguments. A bit is set in the result only if the corresponding bit is set in both operands.

Bitwise Or (|)
> The | operator performs a boolean OR operation on each bit of its integer arguments. A bit is set in the result if the corresponding bit is set in one or both of the operands.

Bitwise Xor (^)

> The ^ operator performs a boolean exclusive OR operation on each bit of its integer argument. Exclusive OR means either operand one is true or operand two is true, but not both. A bit is set in the result of this operation if a corresponding bit is set in one (but not both) of the two operands.

Bitwise Not (~)

> The ~ operator is a unary operator that appears before its single integer argument. It operates by reversing all bits in the operand. Because of how signed integers are represented in JavaScript, applying the ~ operator to a value is equivalent to changing its sign and subtracting 1.

Shift Left (<<)

> The << operator moves all bits in its first operand to the left by the number of places specified in the second operand, which should be an integer between 0 and 31 (if it is outside this range, it is treated as modulo 32). For example, in the operation a <<1, the first bit (the ones bit) of a becomes the second bit (the twos bit), the second bit of a becomes the third, etc. A zero is used for the new first bit, and the value of the 32nd bit is lost. Shifting a value left by one position is equivalent to multiplying by 2, shifting two positions is equivalent to multiplying by 4, and so on.

Shift Right with Sign (>>)

> The >> operator moves all bits in its first operand to the right by the number of places specified in the second operand (an integer between 0 and 31). Bits that are shifted off the right are lost. The bits filled in on the left depend on the sign bit of the original operand, in order to preserve the sign of the result. If the first operand is positive, the result has zeroes placed in the high bits; if the first operand is negative, the result has ones placed in the high bits. Shifting a value right one place is equivalent to dividing by two (discarding the remainder), shifting right two places is equivalent to integer division by four, and so on.

Shift Right Zero Fill (>>>)

> The >>> operator is just like the >> operator, except that the bits shifted in on the left are always zero, regardless of the sign of the first operand.

5.9 *Assignment Operators*

As we saw in the discussion of variables in Chapter 4, *Variables*, = is used in JavaScript to assign a value to a variable. For example:

```
i = 0
```

While you might not normally think of such a line of JavaScript as an expression that can be evaluated, it is in fact an expression and, technically speaking, = is an operator.

The = operator expects its left-hand operand to be a variable, the element of an array, or a property of an object. It expects its right-hand operand to be an arbitrary value of any type. The value of an assignment expression is the value of the right-hand operand. As a side effect, the = operator assigns the value on the right to the variable, element, or property on the left, so that future uses of the variable, element, or property refer to the value.

Because = is defined as an operator, you can include it in more complex expressions. For example, you can assign and test a value in the same expression with code like this:

```
(a = b) == 0
```

If you do this, be sure you are clear on the difference between the = and == operators!

The assignment operator has right-to-left associativity, which means that when multiple assignment operators appear in an expression, they are evaluated from right to left. This means that you can write code like the following to assign a single value to multiple variables:

```
i = j = k = 0;
```

Remember that each assignment expression has a value that is the value of the right-hand side. So in the above code, the value of the first assignment (the right-most one) becomes the right-hand side for the second assignment (the middle one) and this value becomes the right-hand side for the last (leftmost) assignment.

5.9.1 Assignment with Operation

Besides the normal = assignment operator, JavaScript supports a number of other assignment operators that provide a shortcut by combining assignment with some other operation. For example, the += operator performs addition and assignment. The following expression:

```
total += sales_tax
```

is equivalent to this one:

```
total = total + sales_tax
```

As you might expect, the += operator works for numbers or strings. For numeric operands, it performs addition and assignment, and for string operands, it performs concatenation and assignment.

Similar operators include −=, *=, &=, and so on. Table 5-2 lists them all. In most simple cases, the expression:

```
a op= b
```

where *op* is an operator, is equivalent to:

```
a = a op b
```

Table 5-2: Assignment Operators

Operator	Example	Equivalent
+=	a += b	a = a + b
−=	a −= b	a = a − b
*=	a *= b	a = a * b
/=	a /= b	a = a / b
%=	a %= b	a = a % b
<<=	a <<= b	a = a << b
>>=	a >>= b	a = a >> b
>>>=	a >>>= b	a = a >>> b
&=	a &= b	a = a & b
|=	a |= b	a = a	b
^=	a ^= b	a = a ^ b

5.10 Miscellaneous Operators

JavaScript supports a number of other miscellaneous operators, described in the following sections.

5.10.1 The Conditional Operator (?:)

The conditional operator is the only ternary operator (three operands) in JavaScript and is sometimes actually called the ternary operator. This operator is sometimes written ?:, although it does not appear quite that way in code. Because this operator has three operands, the first goes before the ?, the second goes between the ? and the :, and the third goes after the :. It is used like this:

```
x > 0 ? x*y : -x*y
```

The first operand of the conditional operator must have a boolean value—usually this is the result of a comparison expression. The second and third operands may have any value. The value returned by the conditional operator depends on the boolean value of the first operand. If that operand is `true`, the value of the conditional expression is the value of the second operand. If the first operand is `false`, the value is the value of the third operand.

While you can achieve similar results using the `if` statement, the `?:` operator is a very handy shortcut in many cases. Here is a typical usage, which checks to be sure that a variable is defined, uses it if so, and provides a default value if not:

```
greeting = "hello " + ((username != null) ? username : "there");
```

This is equivalent to, but more compact than, the following `if` statement:

```
greeting = "hello ";
if (username != null)
    greeting += username;
else
    greeting += "there";
```

5.10.2 The typeof Operator

The `typeof` operator is available as of Navigator 3 and Internet Explorer 3. `typeof` is an unusual operator because it is not represented by punctuation characters but instead by the `typeof` keyword. It is a unary operator that is placed before its single operand, which can be of any type. The value of the `typeof` operator is a string indicating the data type of the operand.[*]

The `typeof` operator evaluates to "number", "string", or "boolean" if its operand is a number, string, or boolean value. It evaluates to "object" for objects, arrays, and (surprisingly) `null`. It evaluates to "function" for function operands, and to "undefined" if the operand is undefined.

`typeof` evaluates to "object" when its operand is a Number, String, or Boolean wrapper object. It also evaluates to "object" for Date and RegExp objects. `typeof` evaluates to an implementation-dependent value for objects that are not part of core JavaScript, but are provided by the context in which JavaScript is embedded. In client-side JavaScript, however, `typeof` evaluates to "object" for all client-side objects just as it does for all core objects.

You might use the `typeof` operator in expressions like these:

```
typeof i
(typeof value == "string") ? "'" + value + "'" : value
```

---

[*] This means that `typeof typeof` *x*, where *x* is any value, always yields the value `"string"`.

Note that you can place parentheses around the operand to `typeof`, which makes `typeof` look like the name of a function rather than an operator keyword:

```
typeof(i)
```

Because `typeof` evaluates to "object" for all object and array types, it is useful only to distinguish objects from other, primitive types. In order to distinguish one object type from another, you must use other techniques. One technique that works for most objects is to inspect the `constructor` property, which should be a reference to the constructor function that was used to create the object. For example, you might use a line like the following to check whether a variable d contains a Date object:

```
if ((typeof d == "object") && (d.constructor == Date)) {
  ...
}
```

5.10.3 Object Creation Operator (new)

As we saw in Chapter 3, *Data Types and Values*, numbers, strings, and boolean values are represented by literals in JavaScript. That is, you just type a string representation into your program and then your program can manipulate that value. As we'll see later, you can use the `function` keyword to define functions that your program can work with. But JavaScript supports two other data types as well—objects and arrays. Object and array values cannot simply be typed into your JavaScript programs; they must be created. You use the `new` operator to do this.

The `new` operator, like `typeof`, is represented by a keyword rather than by special punctuation characters. The `new` operator is a unary operator that appears before its operand. It has the following syntax:

```
new constructor
```

`constructor` must be a function-call expression, or, in other words, it must include an expression that refers to a function, and this function should be followed by an optional argument list in parentheses. As a special case, for the `new` operator only, JavaScript simplifies the grammar by allowing the parentheses to be omitted if there are no arguments in the function call. Here are some examples of using the `new` operator:

```
o = new Object;    // Optional parentheses omitted here
d = new Date();
c = new rectangle(3.0, 4.0, 1.5, 2.75);
obj[i] = new constructors[i]();
```

The new operator works by first creating a new object with no properties defined. Next, it invokes the specified constructor function, passing the specified arguments and also passing the newly created object as the value of the this keyword. The constructor function can then use the this keyword to initialize the new object in any way desired. We'll learn more about the this keyword and about constructor functions in Chapter 8, *Objects*.

The new operator is also used to create arrays, using the new Array() syntax. We'll see more about creating and working with objects and arrays in Chapter 8 and Chapter 9, *Arrays*.

5.10.4 The delete Operator

The delete operator in JavaScript 1.2 deletes or undefines the object property or array element specified as its operand. Any attempt to access a deleted property or element results in the undefined value. Note that not all variables and properties can be deleted. Some built-in core and client-side properties are immune from deletion; attempts to delete them fail silently. Similarly, variables declared with the var statement cannot be deleted; an attempt to do so produces an error.

The delete operator existed prior to JavaScript 1.2, but it did not actually delete properties in JavaScript 1.0 and 1.1. In those versions, it instead set the property to null, which is very different.

Note that delete affects only property values, not objects referred to by those properties. Consider the following code:

```
my.birthday = new Date();    // my.birthday refers to a Date object.
my.baptism = my.birthday;    // my.baptism refers to the same object.
delete my.birthday;          // my.birthday becomes undefined
document.write(my.baptism);  // but my.baptism still refers to the Date.
```

If you are a C++ programmer, note that the delete operator in JavaScript is nothing like the delete operator in C++. In JavaScript, memory deallocation is handled automatically by garbage collection, and you never have to worry about explicitly freeing up memory. Thus, there is no need for a C++-style delete to delete entire objects.

5.10.5 The void Operator

void is a unary operator that can appear before an expression with any value. The purpose of this operator is an unusual one: it always discards its operand value and simply returns an undefined value. One place where you are likely to want to do this is in a javascript: URL. void is useful here if you want to evaluate an expression for its side effects but do not want the browser to display the value of the evaluated expression. Thus, you might use the `void` operator in an HTML tag as follows:

```
<A HREF="javascript:void window.open();">Open New Window</A>
```

Another use for `void` is in comparisons using the identity (`===`) operator, when you want to test for the undefined value. Since there is no special `undefined` keyword in JavaScript, you can only test for an undefined value by comparing it to some other undefined value. The `void` operator allows you to generate the necessary undefined value, with code like this:

```
if (form.greeting === (void 0)) form.greeting = "Hello World!";
```

Note that `void` requires an operand, but that the operand is totally arbitrary. In the code above, we use the literal 0.

The `void` operator is supported in JavaScript 1.1 and later.

5.10.6 The Comma Operator (,)

The comma operator is a simple one. It evaluates its left argument, evaluates its right argument, and then returns the value of its right argument. Thus, this line:

```
i=0, j=1, k=2;
```

is equivalent to:

```
i = 0;
j = 1;
k = 2;
```

This strange operator is useful only in a few limited circumstances, primarily when you need to evaluate several independent expressions with side effects in a situation where only a single expression is allowed. In practice, the comma operator is really only used in conjunction with the `for` loop statement, which we'll see later in Chapter 6.

5.10.7 Array and Object Access Operators

As noted briefly in Chapter 3, you can access elements of an array using square brackets [ ], and you can access elements of an object using a dot (.). Both [] and . are treated as operators in JavaScript.

The . operator expects an object as its left operand and the name of an object property (including method names) as its right operand. This right operand should not be a string or a variable that contains a string, but should be the literal name of the property or method, without quotes of any kind. Here are some examples:

```
document.lastModified
navigator.appName
frames[0].length
document.write("hello world")
```

If the specified property does not exist in the object, JavaScript does not issue an error, but instead simply returns the special undefined value as the value of the expression.

Most operators allow arbitrary expressions for either operand, as long as the type of the operand is suitable. The . operator is an exception: the right-hand operand must be an identifier. Nothing else is allowed.

The [ ] operator allows access to array elements. It also allows access to object properties without the restrictions that the . operator places on the right-hand operand. If the first operand (which goes before the left bracket) refers to an array, the second operand (which goes between the brackets) should be an expression that evaluates to an integer. For example:

```
frames[1]
document.forms[i + j]
document.forms[i].elements[j++]
```

If the first operand to the [ ] operator is a reference to an object, on the other hand, the second operand should be an expression that evaluates to a string that names a property of the object. Note that in this case, the second operand is a string, not a literal name. It should be a constant in quotes or a variable or expression that refers to a string. This works like associative arrays in the Perl and awk programming languages. For example:

```
document["lastModified"]
frames[0]['length']
data["val" + i]
```

The [ ] operator is typically used to access the elements of an array. It is less convenient than the . operator for accessing properties of an object because of the need to quote the name of the property. When an object is used as an associative array, however, and the property names are dynamically generated, the . operator cannot be used and only the [ ] operator will do. This is commonly the case when you use the for/in loop, which is introduced in Chapter 6. For example, the following JavaScript code uses a for/in loop and the [ ] operator to print out the name and value of all of the properties in an object o:

```
for (f in o) {
    document.write('o.' + f + ' = ' + o[f]);
    document.write('<BR>');
}
```

5.10.8 Function Call Operator

The ( ) operator is used to invoke functions in JavaScript. This is an unusual operator in that it does not have a fixed number of operands. The first operand is always the name of a function or an expression that refers to a function. This is followed by the left parenthesis and any number of additional operands, which may be arbitrary expressions, each separated from the next with a comma. The right parenthesis follows the final operand. The ( ) operator evaluates each of its operands and then invokes the function specified by the first operand, with the value of the remaining operands passed as arguments. For example:

```
document.close()
Math.sin(x)
alert("Welcome " + name)
Date.UTC(99, 11, 31, 23, 59, 59)
funcs[i].f(funcs[i].args[0], funcs[i].args[1])
```

6

Statements

As we saw in the last chapter, *expressions* are JavaScript phrases that can be evaluated to yield a value. Operators within an expression may have side effects, but in general, expressions don't do anything. To make something happen, you use a JavaScript *statement*, which is akin to a complete sentence or command.

A JavaScript program is simply a collection of statements. Statements usually end with semicolons. In fact, if you place each statement on a line by itself, you may omit the semicolons. There are circumstances in which you are required to use semicolons, however, so it is a good idea to get in the habit of using them everywhere.

This chapter describes the various statements in JavaScript and explains their syntax.

6.1 Expression Statements

The simplest kinds of statements in JavaScript are expressions that have side effects. We've seen this sort of statement in the section on operators in Chapter 5, *Expressions and Operators*. Assignment statements are one major category of expression statements. For example:

```
s = "Hello " + name;
i *= 3;
```

The increment and decrement operators, ++ and --, are related to assignment statements. These have the side effect of changing a variable value, just as if an assignment had been performed:

```
counter++;
```

Function calls are another major category of expression statements. For example:

```
alert("Welcome, " + name);
window.close();
```

These function calls are expressions, but they also affect the web browser, so they are statements, too. If a function does not have any side effects, there is no sense in calling it, unless it is part of an assignment statement. For example, you wouldn't just compute a cosine and discard the result:

```
Math.cos(x);
```

Instead, you'd compute the value and assign it to a variable for future use:

```
cx = Math.cos(x);
```

6.2 Compound Statements

In Chapter 5, we saw that the comma operator can be used to combine a number of expressions into a single expression. JavaScript also has a way to combine a number of statements into a single statement, or *statement block*. This is done simply by enclosing any number of statements within curly braces. Thus, the following lines act as a single statement and can be used anywhere that JavaScript expects a single statement:

```
{
    x = Math.PI;
    cx = Math.cos(x);
    alert("cos(" + x + ") = " + cx);
}
```

Note that although this statement block acts as a single statement, it does *not* end with a semicolon. The primitive statements within the block end in semicolons, but the block itself does not.

Although combining expressions with the comma operator is an infrequently used technique, combining statements into larger statement blocks is extremely common. As we'll see in the following sections, a number of JavaScript statements themselves contain statements (just as expressions can contain other expressions); these statements are *compound statements*. Formal JavaScript syntax specifies that these compound statements contain a single sub-statement. Using statement blocks, you can place any number of statements within this single allowed sub-statement.

6.3 *if*

The if statement is the fundamental control statement that allows JavaScript to make decisions, or, more precisely, to execute statements conditionally. This statement has two forms. The first is:

```
if (expression)
    statement
```

In this form, the *expression* is evaluated. If the resulting value is true or can be converted to true, *statement* is executed. If the *expression* is false or converts to false, *statement* is not executed. For example:

```
if (username == null)       // If username is null or undefined,
    username = "John Doe";  // define it.
```

Or similarly:

```
// If username is null, undefined, 0, or "", it converts to false, and
// this statement will assign a new value to it.
if (!username) username = "John Doe"
```

Although they look extraneous, the parentheses around the expression are a required part of the syntax for the if statement.

As mentioned above, we can always replace a single statement with a statement block. So the if statement might also look like this:

```
if ((address == null) || (address == "")) {
    address = "undefined";
    alert("Please specify a mailing address.");
}
```

The indentation used in these examples is not mandatory. Extra spaces and tabs are ignored in JavaScript, and since we used semicolons after all the primitive statements, these examples could be written all on one line if we wanted to. Using line breaks and indentation as shown here, however, makes the code easier to read and understand.

The second form of the if statement introduces an else clause that is executed when *expression* is false. Its syntax is:

```
if (expression)
    statement1
else
    statement2
```

In this form of the statement, the *expression* is evaluated, and if it is true, *statement1* is executed; otherwise *statement2* is executed. For example:

```
if (username != null)
    alert("Hello " + username + "\nWelcome to my home page.");
else {
    username = prompt("Welcome!\n What is your name?");
    alert("Hello " + username);
}
```

When you have nested if statements with else clauses, some caution is required to ensure that the else clause goes with the appropriate if statement. Consider the following lines:

```
i = j = 1;
k = 2;
if (i == j)
    if (j == k)
        document.write("i equals k");
else
    document.write("i doesn't equal j");    // WRONG!!
```

In this example, the inner if statement forms the single statement allowed by the syntax of the outer if statement. Unfortunately, it is not clear (except from the hint given by the indentation) which if the else goes with. And in this example, the indenting hint is wrong, because a JavaScript interpreter actually interprets the previous example as:

```
if (i == j) {
    if (j == k)
        document.write("i equals k");
    else
        document.write("i doesn't equal j");    // OOPS!
}
```

The rule in JavaScript (as in most programming languages) is that an `else` clause is part of the nearest `if` statement. To make this example less ambiguous, and easier to read, understand, maintain, and debug, you should use curly braces:

```
if (i == j) {
    if (j == k) {
        document.write("i equals k");
    }
}
else { // What a difference the location of a curly brace makes!
    document.write("i doesn't equal j");
}
```

Although it is not the style used in this book, many programmers make a habit of enclosing the bodies of `if` and `else` statements (as well as other compound statements such as `while` loops) within curly braces, even when the body consists of only a single statement. Doing so consistently can prevent the sort of problems shown above.

6.4 *else if*

We've seen that the `if`/`else` statement is useful for testing a condition and executing one of two pieces of code, depending on the outcome. But what about when we need to execute one of many pieces of code? One way to do this is with an `else if` statement. `else if` is not really a JavaScript statement, but simply a frequently used programming idiom that results when repeated `if`/`else` statements are used:

```
if (n == 1) {
    // Execute code block #1.
}
else if (n == 2) {
    // Execute code block #2.
}
else if (n == 3) {
    // Execute code block #3.
}
else {
    // If all else fails, execute block #4.
}
```

There is nothing special about this code. It is just a series of `if` statements, where each `if` is part of the `else` clause of the previous statement. Using the `else if` idiom is preferable to, and more legible than, writing these statements out in their syntactically equivalent fully nested form:

```
if (n == 1) {
    // Execute code block #1.
}
else {
    if (n == 2) {
        // Execute code block #2.
    }
    else {
        if (n == 3) {
            // Execute code block #3.
        }
        else {
            // If all else fails, execute block #4.
        }
    }
}
```

6.5 *switch*

An if statement causes a branch in the flow of a program's execution. You can use multiple if statements, as in the previous section, to perform a multi-way branch. However, this is not always the best solution, especially when all of the branches depend on the value of a single variable. In this case, it is wasteful to repeatedly check the value of the same variable in multiple if statements.

JavaScript 1.2 provides the more efficient switch statement to handle exactly this situation. The JavaScript switch statement is quite similar to the switch statement in Java or C. The switch keyword is followed by an expression and a block of code, much like the if statement:

```
switch ( expression ) {
   statements
}
```

However, the full syntax of a switch statement is more complex than this. Various locations in the block of code are labeled with the case keyword followed by a value and a colon. When a switch executes, it computes the value of the expression, and then looks for a case label that matches that value. If it finds one, it starts executing the block of code at the first statement following the case label. If it does not find a case label with a matching value, it starts execution at the first statement following a special case default: label. Or, if there is no default: label, it skips the block of code altogether.

switch is a confusing statement to explain; its operation becomes much clearer with an example. The following switch statement is equivalent to the repeated if/else statements shown in the previous section:

```
switch(n) {
  case 1:                    // Start here if n == 1.
    // Execute code block #1.
    break;                   // Stop here.
  case 2:                    // Start here if n == 2.
    // Execute code block #2.
    break;                   // Stop here.
  case 3:                    // Start here if n == 3.
    // Execute code block #3.
    break;                   // Stop here.
  default:                   // If all else fails
    // Execute code block #4.
    break;                   // stop here.
}
```

Note the break keyword used at the end of each case in the code above. The break statement, described later in this chapter, causes execution to jump to the end of a switch statement or loop. The case clauses in a switch statement only specify the *starting point* of the desired code; they do not specify any ending point. In the absence of break statements, a switch statement begins executing its block of code at the case label that matches the value of its *expression* and continues executing statements until it reaches the end of the block. On rare occasions, it is useful to write code like this that falls through from one case label to the next, but 99% of the time you should be very careful to end every case within a switch with a break statement. (When using switch inside a function, however, you may use a return statement instead of a break statement. Both serve to terminate the switch statement and prevent execution from falling through to the next case.)

Here is a more realistic example of the switch statement; it converts a value to a string in a way that depends on the type of the value:

```
function convert(x) {
    switch(typeof x) {
      case 'number':             // Convert the number to a hexadecimal integer.
        return x.toString(16);
      case 'string':             // Return the string enclosed in quotes.
        return '"' + x + '"';
      case 'boolean':            // Convert to TRUE or FALSE, in uppercase.
        return x.toString().toUpperCase();
      default:                   // Convert any other type in the usual way.
        return x.toString()
    }
}
```

There are three important differences between the JavaScript switch statement and the corresponding C and Java statements that inspired it. First, C and Java allow only integers and other integral types as the values of case clauses. As you can see from the code above, however, JavaScript allows strings as the values of case labels. It also allows both integer and floating-point numbers and boolean values. Objects, arrays, and functions are not allowed.

The second difference has to do with typing. Because Java and C are strongly typed languages, all case label values within a single switch must be of the same type. In JavaScript, however, each case label can be of any of the allowed types.

The third difference is that JavaScript is not as strict as C and Java in requiring that the values associated with case labels be constants. Java and C require that the expressions used as the values of case labels must either be constants or constant expressions that can be evaluated at compile time. Expressions that vary at run-time are not allowed. JavaScript is not so strict, in part because the language does not have a strict notion of exactly what constitutes a "constant." The following case labels are legal because they involve only literals and clearly have constant values that can be evaluated at compile time:

```
case 0:
case 60*60*24:
case "hello"
case "hello" + " world":
```

JavaScript also allows case labels like this one:

```
case Number.POSITIVE_INFINITY:
```

The Number.POSITIVE_INFINITY property is read-only, so this expression is also guaranteed to be constant. JavaScript does not allow user-defined variables to be used in case labels, because they are clearly not constants. So, for example, these are illegal:

```
case name:
case n+1:
```

However, JavaScript does allow system properties to be used in case labels. For example:

```
case document.forms.length:
```

This property is not a constant. Depending on the relative position of the JavaScript code and the client-side HTML forms this property refers to, the property may have a different value when the script is compiled than it has when the script is executed. How does the switch statement behave in this case? It is not clear: the switch statement is new to the language. Its behavior is not yet carefully specified and is therefore subject to tweaking in JavaScript 1.3. To be safe, you should only use `case` label expressions that you know are guaranteed to remain constant between the time that the statement is compiled and the time it is executed.

6.6 *while*

Just as the `if` statement is the basic control statement that allows JavaScript to make decisions, the `while` statement is the basic statement that allows JavaScript to perform repetitive actions. It has the following syntax:

```
while (expression)
    statement
```

The `while` statement works by first evaluating the *expression*. If it is `false`, JavaScript moves on to the next statement in the program. If it is `true`, the *statement* that forms the body of the loop is executed and *expression* is evaluated again. Again, if the value of *expression* is `false`, JavaScript moves on to the next statement in the program; otherwise it executes the *statement* again. This cycle continues until *expression* evaluates to `false`, at which point the `while` statement ends and JavaScript moves on. Note that you can create an infinite loop with the syntax `while(true)`.

Usually, you do not want JavaScript to perform exactly the same operation over and over again, so in almost every loop, one or more variables change with each *iteration* of the loop. Since the variables change, the actions performed by executing *statement* may differ each time through the loop. Furthermore, if the changing variable or variables are involved in *expression*, the value of the expression may be different each time through the loop. This is important, otherwise an expression that starts off `true` would never change and the loop would never end! Here is an example `while` loop:

```
count = 0;
while (count < 10) {
    document.write(count + "<br>");
    count++;
}
```

As you can see, the variable `count` starts off at 0 in this example and is incremented each time the body of the loop runs. Once the loop has executed ten times, the expression becomes `false` (i.e., the variable `count` is no longer less than 10), the `while` statement finishes, and JavaScript can move on to the next statement in the program. Most loops have a counter variable like `count`. The variable names `i`, `j`, and `k` are commonly used as a loop counters, though you should use more descriptive names if it makes your code easier to understand.

6.7 do/while

JavaScript 1.2 adds support for the `do/while` statement, which behaves just as it does in languages like C and Java. A `do/while` loop is much like a `while` loop, except that the loop expression is tested at the bottom of the loop rather than at the top. This means that the body of the loop is always executed at least once. The syntax is:

```
do
    statement
while ( expression );
```

The `do` loop is less commonly used than its `while` cousin. This is because, in practice, it is somewhat uncommon to encounter a situation where you are always sure that you want a loop to execute at least once. For example:

```
function printArray(a) {
    if (a.length == 0)
        document.write("Empty Array");
    else {
        var i = 0;
        do {
            document.write(a[i] + "<BR)>";
        } while (++i < a.length);
    }
}
```

There are a couple of differences to notice between the `do` loop and the ordinary `while` loop. First, the `do` loop requires both the `do` keyword to mark the beginning of the loop and the `while` keyword to mark the end and introduce the loop condition. Also, unlike the `while` loop, the `do` loop is terminated with a semicolon. This is because the `do` loop ends with the loop condition, rather than simply ending with a curly brace that marks the end of the loop body.

In most versions of Navigator 4, there is a bug in the behavior of the `continue` statement (see section 6.12, "continue," later in this chapter) when it is used inside a `do/while` loop. For this reason, you should avoid the use of `continue` within `do/while` statements in Navigator 4.

6.8 for

The `for` statement provides a looping construct that is often more convenient than the `while` statement. The `for` statement takes advantage of a pattern common to most loops (including the `while` loop example above). Most loops have a counter variable of some kind. This variable is initialized before the loop starts and then it is tested as part of the *expression* evaluated before each iteration of the loop. Finally, the counter variable is incremented or otherwise updated at the end of the loop body just before the expression is evaluated again.

The initialization, the test, and the update are the three crucial manipulations of a loop variable; the for statement makes these three steps an explicit part of the loop syntax. This makes it especially easy to understand what a for loop is doing and prevents mistakes such as forgetting to initialize or increment the loop variable. The syntax of the for statement is:

```
for(initialize ; test ; increment)
    statement
```

The simplest way to explain what this for loop does is to show the equivalent while loop:*

```
initialize;
while(test) {
    statement
    increment;
}
```

In other words, the *initialize* expression is evaluated once, before the loop begins. To be useful, this is an expression with side effects, usually an assignment. The *test* expression is evaluated before each iteration and controls whether the body of the loop is executed. If the *test* expression is true, the *statement* that is the body of the loop is executed. Finally, the *increment* expression is evaluated. Again, this must be an expression with side effects in order to be useful. Generally, it is an assignment expression or it uses the ++ or −− operators.

The example while loop of the previous section can be rewritten as the following for loop, which counts from 0 to 9:

```
for(count = 0 ; count < 10 ; count++)
    document.write(count + "<br>");
```

Notice how this syntax places all of the important information about the loop variable on a single line, which makes it very clear how the loop executes. Also note that placing the increment expression in the for statement itself simplifies the body of the loop to a single statement; we don't even need to use curly braces to produce a statement block.

---

* As we'll see when we consider the continue statement, this while loop is not an exact equivalent to the for loop.

Loops can become a lot more complex than these simple examples, of course, and sometimes multiple variables change with each iteration of the loop. This situation is the only place that the comma operator is commonly used in JavaScript—it provides a way to combine multiple initialization and increment expressions into a single expression suitable for use in a `for` loop. For example:

```
for(i = 0, j = 10 ; i < 10 ; i++, j--)
    sum += i * j;
```

6.9 *for/in*

The `for` keyword is used in two ways in JavaScript. We've just seen how it is used in the `for` loop. It is also used in the `for/in` statement. This statement is a somewhat different kind of loop with the following syntax:

```
for (variable in object)
    statement
```

variable should be the name of a variable, an element of an array, or a property of an object (i.e., it should be something suitable as the left-hand side of an assignment expression). *object* is the name of an object or an expression that evaluates to an object. As usual, *statement* is a primitive statement or statement block that forms the body of the loop.

You can loop through the elements of an array by simply incrementing an index variable each time through a `while` or `for` loop. The `for/in` statement provides a way to loop through the properties of an object. The body of the `for/in` loop is executed once for each property of *object*. Before the body of the loop is executed, the name of one of the object's properties is assigned to *variable*, as a string. Within the body of the loop, you can use this variable to look up the value of the object's property with the [ ] operator. For example, the following `for/in` loop prints out the name and value of each property of an object:

```
for (prop in my_object) {
    document.write("name: " + prop + "; value: " + my_object[prop], "<br>");
}
```

The `for/in` loop does not specify the order in which the properties of an object are assigned to the variable. There is no way to tell in advance, and the behavior may differ between implementations or versions of JavaScript.

The `for/in` loop does not actually loop through all possible properties of all objects. In the same way that some object properties are flagged to be read-only or permanent (non-deletable), certain properties are flagged to be non-enumerable. These properties are not enumerated by the `for/in` loop. While all user-defined properties are enumerated, many built-in properties, including all built-in methods, are not enumerated. As we'll see in Chapter 8, *Objects*, objects can inherit properties from other objects. Inherited properties that are user-defined are also enumerated by the `for/in` loop.

6.10 Labels

The `case` and `default` labels used in conjunction with the `switch` statement are a special case of a more general label statement. In JavaScript 1.2, any statement may be labeled by preceding it with an identifier name and a colon:

```
identifier: statement
```

The `identifier` can be any legal JavaScript identifier that is not a reserved word. Label names are distinct from variable and function names, so you do not need to worry about name collisions if you give a label the same name as a variable or function. Here is an example of a labeled `while` statement:

```
parser:
  while(token != null) {
      // Code omitted here
  }
```

By labeling a statement, you give it a name that you can use to refer to it elsewhere in your program. You can label any statement, although the only statements that are commonly labeled are loops: `while`, `do/while`, `for`, and `for/in`. By giving a loop a name, you can use `break` and `continue` to exit the loop or to exit a single iteration of the loop.

JavaScript reserves the `goto` keyword, but does not currently have a `goto` statement. If JavaScript ever implements a C-style `goto` statement (which is unlikely), that statement will also rely on labels to enable JavaScript code to jump to arbitrary named statements.

6.11 break

The `break` statement causes the innermost enclosing loop or a `switch` statement to exit immediately. It has a very simple syntax:

```
break;
```

Because it causes a loop or `switch` to exit, this form of the `break` statement is legal only if it appears within one of these statements.

In JavaScript 1.2, the `break` keyword may also be followed by the name of a label:

```
break labelname;
```

Note that *labelname* is simply an identifier; it is not followed by a colon as it would be when defining a labeled statement.

When `break` is used with a label, it jumps to the end of, or terminates, the named statement, which may be any enclosing statement. The named statement need not be a loop or a `switch`; a `break` statement used with a label need not even be contained within a loop or a `switch`. The only restriction on the label of the `break` statement is that it name an *enclosing* statement. The label can name an `if` statement, for example, or even a block of statements grouped within curly braces, for the sole purpose of naming the block with a label.

As discussed in Chapter 2, *Lexical Structure*, a newline is not allowed between the `break` keyword and the labelname. This is an oddity of JavaScript syntax caused by its automatic insertion of omitted semicolons. If you break a line of code between the `break` keyword and the following label, JavaScript assumes you meant to use the simple, unlabeled form of the statement and adds a semicolon for you.

We've already seen examples of the `break` statement within a `switch` statement. In loops, it is typically used to exit prematurely when, for whatever reason, there is no longer any need to complete the loop. When a loop has complex termination conditions, it is often easier to implement some of these conditions with `break` statements, rather than trying to express them all in a single loop expression. The following code searches the elements of an array for a particular value. The loop terminates naturally when it reaches the end of the array; it terminates with a `break` statement if it finds what it is looking for in the array:

```
for(i = 0; i < a.length; i++) {
    if (a[i] == target)
        break;
}
```

You only need the labeled form of the `break` statement when you are using nested loops or `switch` statements and need to break out of a statement that is not the innermost one. The following example shows labeled `for` loops and labeled `break` statements. See if you can figure out what its output will be:

```
outerloop:
  for(var i = 0; i < 10; i++) {
    innerloop:
      for(var j = 0; j < 10; j++) {
        if (j > 3) break;             // Quit the innermost loop.
        if (i == 2) break innerloop;  // Do the same thing.
```

```
            if (i == 4) break outerloop;      // Quit the outer loop.
            document.write("i = " + i + " j = " + j + "<BR>");
        }
    }
    document.write("FINAL i = " + i + " j = " + j + "<BR>");
```

6.12 *continue*

The continue statement is similar to the break statement. Instead of exiting a loop, however, continue restarts a loop in a new iteration. The continue statement has a syntax that is just as simple as the break statement:

```
continue;
```

Or, when used with a label:

```
continue labelname;
```

The continue statement can be used only within the body of a while, for, or for/in loop. Using it anywhere else causes a syntax error.

When the continue statement is executed, the current iteration of the enclosing loop is terminated and the next iteration begins. This means different things for different types of loops:

- In a while loop, the specified *expression* at the beginning of the loop is tested again, and if true, the loop body is executed starting from the top.

- In a do/while loop, execution is supposed to skip to the bottom of the loop, where the loop condition is tested again before restarting the loop at the top. However, Navigator 4 contains a bug that causes the continue statement to jump directly to the top of a do/while loop without testing the loop condition. Therefore, if you plan to use a continue statement in a loop, you should avoid the do/while loop unless you can be certain that your users have browsers without this bug. This is not a serious problem, however, because a do/while loop can always be replaced by an equivalent while loop.

- In a for loop, the *increment* expression is evaluated, and the *test* expression is tested again to determine if another iteration should be done.

- In a for/in loop, the loop starts over with the next property name being assigned to the specified variable.

Note the difference in behavior of the continue statement for the while and for loops—a while loop returns directly to its condition, but a for loop first evaluates its increment expression and then returns to its condition. Previously, in the discussion of the for loop, I explained the behavior of the for loop in terms of an equivalent `while` loop. Because the `continue` statement behaves differently for these two loops, it is not possible to perfectly simulate a `for` loop with a `while` loop.

The following example shows an unlabeled `continue` statement being used to exit the current iteration of a loop when an error occurs:

```
for(i = 0; i < data.length; i++) {
    if (data[i] == null)
        continue;  // Can't proceed with undefined data
    total += data[i];
}
```

Like the `break` statement, the `continue` statement can be used in its labeled form within nested loops when the loop to be restarted is not the immediately enclosing loop. Also, like the `break` statement, line breaks are not allowed between the `continue` statement and its *labelname*.

6.13 *var*

The `var` statement provides a way to explicitly declare a variable or variables. The syntax of this statement is:

```
var name_1 [ = value_1] [ ,..., name_n [= value_n]]
```

The `var` keyword is followed by a comma-separated list of variables to declare; each variable in the list may optionally have an initializer expression that specifies its initial value. For example:

```
var i;
var j = 0;
var p, q;
var greeting = "hello" + name;
var x = 2.34, y = Math.cos(0.75), r, theta;
```

The `var` statement defines each named variable by creating a property with that name in the call object of the enclosing function, or in the global object if the declaration does not appear within a function body. Note that enclosing a `var` statement in a `with` statement (see section 6.16, "with," later in this chapter) does not change this behavior.

If no initial value is specified for a variable with the `var` statement, the variable is defined but its initial value is the special JavaScript undefined value.

Note that the `var` statement can also appear as part of the `for` and `for/in` loops. For example:

```
for(var i = 0; i < 10; i++) document.write(i, "<BR>");
for(var i = 0, j=10; i < 10; i++,j--) document.write(i*j, "<BR>");
for(var i in o) document.write(i, "<BR>");
```

Chapter 4, *Variables*, contains much more information on JavaScript variables and variable declarations.

6.14 *function*

The `function` statement defines a JavaScript function. It has the following syntax:

```
function funcname([arg1 [,arg2 [..., argn]]]) {
    statements
}
```

funcname is the name of the function being defined. This must be an identifier, not a string or an expression. The function name is followed by a comma-separated list of argument names in parentheses. These names can be used within the body of the function to refer to the argument values passed when the function is invoked.

The body of the function is composed of any number of JavaScript statements, contained within curly braces. These statements are not executed when the function is defined. Instead, they are compiled and associated with the new function object for execution when the function is invoked with the ( ) function call operator. Note that the curly braces are a required part of the `function` statement. Unlike statement blocks used with `while` loops and other statements, a function body requires curly braces, even if the body consists of only a single statement.

A function definition creates a new function object and stores that object in a newly created property named *funcname*. Here are some example function definitions:

```
function welcome() { alert("Welcome to my home page!"); }

function print(msg) {
    document.write(msg, "<br>");
}

function hypotenuse(x, y) {
    return Math.sqrt(x*x + y*y);      // return is documented below.
}

function factorial(n) {              // A recursive function
    if (n <= 1) return 1;
```

```
        return n * factorial(n - 1);
    }
```

Technically speaking, the `function` statement is not a statement. Statements cause dynamic behavior in a JavaScript program, while function definitions describe the static structure of a program. Statements are executed at runtime, but functions are defined, on the other hand, when JavaScript code is parsed, or compiled, before it is actually run. When the JavaScript parser encounters a function definition, it parses and stores (without executing) the statements that comprise the body of the function. Then it defines a property (in the global object or in the call object if the function definition is nested in another function) with the same name as the function to hold the function.

The fact that function definitions occur at parse time rather than at runtime causes some surprising effects. Consider the following code:

```
    alert(f(4));    // Displays 16. f() can be called before it is defined.
    var f = 0;      // This statement overwrites the property f.
    function f(x) { // This "statement" defines the function f before either
        return x*x; // of the lines above are executed.
    }
    alert(f);       // Displays 0. f() has been overwritten by the variable f.
```

These unusual results occur because function definition occurs at a different time than variable definition. Fortunately, these situations do not arise very often.

We'll learn more about functions in Chapter 7, *Functions*. Later in this chapter, section 6.16, "with," discusses the behavior of the `function` statement when it is contained in the body of a `with` statement.

6.15 return

As you'll recall, invoking a function with the ( ) operator is an expression. All expressions have values; the `return` statement is used to specify the value returned by a function. This value is the value of the function invocation expression. The syntax of the `return` statement is:

```
    return [ expression ];
```

When the `return` statement is executed, *expression* is evaluated and returned as the value of the function. Execution of the function stops when the `return` statement is executed, even if there are other statements still remaining in the function body. The `return` statement can be used to return a value like this:

```
    function square(x) { return x*x; }
```

The `return` statement may also be used without an *expression* to simply terminate execution of the function without returning a value. For example:

```
function display_object(obj) {
    // First make sure our argument is valid
    // and skip rest of function if it is not.
    if (obj == null) return;

    // Rest of the function goes here...
}
```

If a function executes a `return` statement with no *expression*, or if it returns
because it reaches the end of the function body, the value of the function call
expression is the undefined value.

It is a syntax error to use the `return` statement anywhere except in a function
body.

6.16 *with*

In Chapter 4, we discussed variable scope and the scope chain—a list of objects
that are searched in order, to perform variable name resolution. The `with` statement is used to temporarily modify the scope chain. It has the following syntax:

```
with (object)
    statement
```

This statement effectively adds *object* to the front of the scope chain, executes
the *statement*, and then restores the scope chain to its original state.

In practice, you can use the `with` statement to save yourself a lot of typing. In
client-side JavaScript, for example, it is common to work with deeply nested object
hierarchies. For example, you may have to type expressions like this one to access
elements of an HTML form:

```
frames[1].document.forms[0].address_field.value
```

If you need to access this form a number of times, you can use the `with` statement
to add the form to the scope chain:

```
with(frames[1].document.forms[0]) {
    // Access form elements directly here. For example:
    name.value = "";
    address.value = "";
    email.value = "";
}
```

This reduces the amount of typing you have to do—you no longer need to prefix
each form property name with `frames[1].document.forms[0]`. That object is

temporarily part of the scope chain and is automatically searched when JavaScript needs to resolve an identifier like `address_field`.

Despite its occasional convenience, the use of the `with` statement is frowned upon. JavaScript code that uses `with` is difficult to optimize, and may therefore run more slowly than the equivalent code written without the `with`. Furthermore, function definitions and variable initializations within the body of a `with` statement can have surprising and counterintuitive behavior.* For these reasons, therefore, it is recommended that you avoid the `with` statement.

Note that there are other, perfectly legitimate ways to save yourself typing. The `with` example above could be rewritten as follows:

```
var form = frames[1].document.forms[0];
form.name.value = "";
form.address.value = "";
form.email.value = "";
```

6.17 import and export

In Navigator 4, `import` and `export` are a pair of statements that are used together to make properties of one execution context available within another context. `export` makes a specified list of variables or functions defined in one execution context (i.e., in one client-side window, frame, or layer) available for import into another execution context. The `import` statement copies the value of an exported variable or function from its source context and assigns it to a property with the same name in the importing execution context.

Like the `var` statement, `import` can define either global or local variables. If an `import` statement appears in top-level code, it stores the imported value or values in properties of the global object. If an `import` statement appears within a function, however, it stores the imported values in local variables—in properties of the function's call object.

The `import` and `export` statements are not supported by Internet Explorer 4.

The code below shows a simple client-side example of the `import` and `export` statements.† The example contains two scripts. Note that the first is contained within a `<LAYER>` tag, which causes it to run in its own context with its own global object, as if it were in a separate window or frame. The `export` statement

---

* This behavior, and the reasons behind it, are too complicated to explain here.

† You are not expected to understand the details of this code if you have not already done a lot of client-side JavaScript programming. Two distinct execution contexts are required to demonstrate the `import` and `export` statements and we can only obtain these distinct contexts by resorting to a client-side example.

makes the function defined in this layer available to any other context (window, frame, or layer) that chooses to import it. This is exactly what the next script (not in a layer) does:

```
<!-- This layer displays some black text on a yellow background -->
<!-- and defines and exports a function to move itself around. -->
<LAYER name="layer1" bgColor="yellow">
I am a layer
<SCRIPT LANGUAGE="JavaScript1.2">
// Here is a function that sets my position.
function move(x,y) { this.x = x; this.y = y; }
// Make this function available to anyone that wants it.
export move;
</SCRIPT>
</LAYER>

<SCRIPT LANGUAGE="JavaScript1.2">
// This script imports all functions defined by the layer.
import document.layer1.*;

// Then it performs an animation by repeatedly calling the move()
// function that it has imported. Note that it can just say move()
// instead of the more cumbersome document.layer1.move().
var x = 0; y = 0;
setInterval(function() { move(x, y); x = (x + 5)%200; y = (y+5)%200; },
           100);
</SCRIPT>
```

import and export work correctly only in Navigator 4 when the LANGUAGE attribute of the <SCRIPT> tag is explicitly set to "JavaScript1.2". This is unfortunate, because, as we've seen in Chapter 5, specifying this value for the LANGUAGE attribute causes the == and != operators to behave in a way that does not conform to the ECMA specification.

In the example above, the import and export statements merely allow us to type move() instead of document.layer1.move(). As we'll see in Chapter 21, *JavaScript Security*, however, there is a much more important reason to use this pair of statements: to selectively override the security restriction that prevents an unsigned script from reading the properties of a signed script. The statements allow signed modules of code to be used by unsigned (or differently signed) web pages, as long as the signed modules export the properties and functions that are safe to export and the unsigned pages import the functions and properties they need to use. Chapter 21 includes more detailed discussion on the import and export statements.

6.18 The Empty Statement

One final legal statement in JavaScript is the empty statement. It looks like this:

```
;
```

Executing the empty statement obviously has no effect and performs no action. You might think that there would be little reason ever to use such a statement, but it turns out that the empty statement is occasionally useful when you want to create a loop that has an empty body. For example:

```
// Initialize an array a.
for(i=0; i < a.length; a[i++] = 0) ;
```

Note that the accidental inclusion of a semicolon after the right parenthesis of a for loop, while loop, or if statement can cause frustrating bugs that are difficult to detect. For example, the following code probably does not do what the author intended:

```
if ((a == 0) || (b == 0));     // Oops!  This line does nothing...
    o = null;                  // ... and this line is always executed.
```

When you intentionally use the empty statement, it is a good idea to comment your code in a way that makes it clear that you are doing it on purpose. For example:

```
for(i=0; i < a.length; a[i++] = 0) /* empty */ ;
```

6.19 Defining Modules

JavaScript 1.3 is expected, but not guaranteed, to include a package statement, modeled after the package statement of Java. This statement will make it easier to define reusable modules of JavaScript code. This forthcoming package statement will be tightly integrated with and will increase the utility of the import and export statements of JavaScript 1.2.

6.20 Exception Handling

Another innovation expected in JavaScript 1.3 is exception handling. Exception handling is a powerful and general-purpose system for error handling and recovery, used by a number of object-oriented languages, including Java and C++. Although the details of exception handling in JavaScript 1.3 are not finalized as this book goes to press, both Netscape and Microsoft plan to add this feature to the language, and the two companies have agreed to cooperate in its design and development so that they do not ship incompatible versions.

Although JavaScript exception handling is not yet finalized, chances are good that it will be quite similar to the Java exception handling model. With Java exception handling, when a function wants to signal that an error or exception of some sort has occurred, it throws an exception. It does this with the `throw` statement. The exception it throws is simply an object that contains whatever information is necessary for someone else to report or recover from the error. When an exception is thrown, the flow of control tries to find an appropriate exception handler to catch the exception and take appropriate steps to handle it. Depending on the nature of the exception, the appropriate action might be to ignore the exception, to try to work around it, or even to exit the program. If you want to define an exception handler to catch any exceptions thrown by a block of code, you enclose that code in a `try` statement. The `try` statement is followed by a `catch` statement that defines a block of code to be executed if an exception is thrown within the `try` block or within any functions called by the `try` block.

6.21 *Summary of JavaScript Statements*

This chapter has introduced each of the statements of the JavaScript language. Table 6-1 summarizes these statements, their syntax, and their purpose.

Table 6-1: JavaScript Statement Syntax

Statement	Syntax	Purpose
`break`	`break ;` `break `*`label`*` ;` [a]	Exit from the innermost loop or `switch` statement or from the statement named by *`label`*.
`case` [a]	`case `*`constant-expression`*` :`	Label a statement within a `switch` statement.
`continue`	`continue;` `continue `*`label`*` ;` [a]	Restart the innermost loop or the loop named by *`label`*.
`default` [a]	`default :`	Label the default statement within a `switch` statement.

`do/while` [a]	`do`
	   `statement`
	`while `(*`expression`*) `;`
		An alternative to the `while` loop.

`empty`	`;`	Do nothing.
`export` [a]	`export `*`expression`*` [ ,` *`expression`*` . . . ] ;`	Make the specified functions and variables accessible in other windows or execution contexts.

Table 6-1: JavaScript Statement Syntax (continued)

Statement	Syntax	Purpose
`for`	`for (initialize ; test ; increment) statement`	An easy-to-use loop.
`for/in`	`for (variable in object) statement`	Loop through properties of an object.
`function`	`function funcname([arg1 [ ..., argn]]) { statements }`	Declare a function.
`if/else`	`if (expression) statement1 [ else statement2 ]`	Conditionally execute code.
`import` [a]	`import expression [ , expression ... ] ; import expression.*;`	Import the named functions and variables into the current execution context.
label [a]	`identifier : statement`	Give `statement` the name `identifier`.
`return`	`return [expression] ;`	Return from a function or return the value of `expression` from a function.
`switch` [a]	`switch ( expression ) { statements }`	Multi-way branch to statements labeled with `case` or `default`.
`var`	`var name_1 [ = value_1 ] [ ..., name_n [ = value_n]] ;`	Declare and initialize variables.
`while`	`while (expression) statement`	A basic loop construct.
`with`	`with (object) statement`	Extend the current scope chain.

[a] New in JavaScript 1.2

7

Functions

Functions are an important and complex part of the JavaScript language. This chapter examines functions from several points of view. First, we discuss functions from the syntactic standpoint, explaining how they are defined and invoked. Second, we cover functions as a data type, with examples of the useful programming techniques that are made possible by treating functions as data. Finally, we consider the topic of variable scope within the body of a function and examine some of the useful function-related properties that are available to an executing function. This includes a discussion of how to write JavaScript functions that accept an arbitrary number of arguments.

This chapter focuses on defining and invoking user-defined JavaScript functions. It is also important to remember that JavaScript supports quite a few built-in functions, such as `eval()`, `parseInt()`, and the `sort()` method of the Array class. Client-side JavaScript defines others, such as `document.write()` and `alert()`. Built-in functions in JavaScript can be used in exactly the same ways as user-defined functions. You can find more information about the built-in functions mentioned here in the reference section of this book.

Functions and objects are intertwined in JavaScript. For this reason, we defer discussion of some features of functions until Chapter 8, *Objects*.

7.1 Defining and Invoking Functions

As we saw in Chapter 6, *Statements*, the most common way to define a function is with the `function` statement. This consists of the `function` keyword, which is followed by:

- The name of the function

- An optional comma-separated list of parameter names in parentheses

- The JavaScript statements that comprise the body of the function, contained within curly braces

Example 7-1 shows the definition of several functions. Although these functions are short and very simple, they all contain each of the elements listed above. Note that functions may be defined to expect varying numbers of arguments, and that they may or may not contain a `return` statement. The `return` statement was introduced in Chapter 6; it causes the function to stop executing and return the value of its expression (if any) to the caller. If a function does not contain a `return` statement, it simply executes each statement in the function body and returns the undefined value to the caller.

Example 7-1: Defining JavaScript Functions

```
// A short-cut function, sometimes useful instead of document.write()
// This function has no return statement, so it returns no value.
function print(msg)
{
    document.write(msg, "<BR>");
}


// A function that computes and returns the distance between two points
function distance(x1, y1, x2, y2)
{
    var dx = x2 - x1;
    var dy = y2 - y1;
    return Math.sqrt(dx*dx + dy*dy);
}


// A recursive function (one that calls itself) that computes factorials
// Recall that x! is the product of x and all positive integers less than it.
function factorial(x)
{
    if (x <= 1)
        return 1;
    return x * factorial(x-1);
}
```

Once a function has been defined, it may be invoked with the `( )` operator, introduced in Chapter 5, *Expressions and Operators*. Recall that the parentheses appear after the name of the function, and that an optional comma-separated list of argument values (or expressions) appears within the parentheses. The functions defined in Example 7-1 could be invoked with code like the following:

```
print("Hello, " + name);
print("Welcome to my home page!");
total_dist = distance(0,0,2,1) + distance(2,1,3,5);
print("The probability of that is: " + factorial(39)/factorial(52));
```

When you invoke a function, each of the expressions you specify between the parentheses is evaluated and the resulting value is used as an argument of the function. These values are assigned to the parameters named when the function was defined, and the function operates on its parameters by referring to them by name. Note that these parameter variables are only defined while the function is being executed; they do not persist once the function returns.

Since JavaScript is an untyped language, you are not expected to specify a data type for function parameters, and JavaScript does not check whether you have passed the type of data that the function expects. If the data type of an argument is important, you can test it yourself with the typeof operator. JavaScript does not check whether you have passed the correct number of arguments, either. If you pass more arguments than the function expects, the extra values are simply ignored. If you pass fewer than expected, some of the parameters are given the undefined value—which, in many circumstances, causes your function to behave incorrectly. Later in this chapter, we'll see a technique you can use to test whether the correct number of arguments have been passed to a function.

Note that the print() function does not contain a return statement. This means that it always returns the undefined value and cannot meaningfully be used as part of a larger expression. The distance() and factorial() functions, on the other hand, can be used as parts of larger expressions, as is shown in the previous examples.

7.1.1 Nested Functions

Prior to JavaScript 1.2, function definition was only allowed at the top level. In JavaScript 1.0 and JavaScript 1.1, the function statement cannot appear within other function definitions, within loops or if/else statements, or within with statements. In JavaScript 1.2, however, function definitions may appear anywhere, including nested within other functions. For example:

```
function hypotenuse(a, b) {
    function square(x) { return x*x; }
    return Math.sqrt(square(a) + square(b));
}
```

While allowing function definitions everywhere increases the flexibility of JavaScript, it also increases the complexity of what we mean by the term "function." JavaScript uses lexical, or static, scoping, which means that functions are executed using the scope chain that was in effect when they were defined, not the scope chain in effect when they are executed. The implementation of this kind of scoping requires the introduction of a "closure," which is an object that combines a function definition with a scope chain. You do not need to understand this now. We'll discuss nested functions, lexical scoping, and closures in more detail in Chapter 11, *Further Topics in JavaScript.*

7.1.2 The Function() Constructor

The `function` statement is not the only way to define a new function. In JavaScript 1.1, you can also use the `Function()` constructor and the `new` operator. (We saw the `new` operator in Chapter 5 and we'll learn more about constructors in Chapter 8.) Here is an example of creating a function in this way:

```
var f = new Function("x", "y", "return x*y;");
```

This line of code creates a new function that is more or less equivalent to a function defined with the familiar syntax:

```
function f(x, y) { return x*y; }
```

The `Function()` constructor expects any number of string arguments. The last argument is the body of the function—it can contain arbitrary JavaScript statements, separated from each other by semicolons. All other arguments to the constructor are strings that specify the names of the parameters to the function being defined. If you are defining a function that takes no arguments, you simply pass a single string—the function body—to the constructor.

Notice that the `Function()` constructor is not passed any argument that specifies a name for the function it creates. When you convert such an unnamed function to a string, the name "anonymous" is used. For this reason, functions created with the `Function()` constructor are sometimes called "anonymous functions."

You might well wonder what the point of the `Function()` constructor is. Why not simply define all functions with the `function` statement? One reason is that `Function()` allows us to build and compile functions dynamically; it does not restrict us to the precompiled function bodies of the `function` statement. The flip side of this is that the `Function()` constructor has to compile a function each time it is called. Therefore, you probably do not want to call this constructor within the body of a loop or within a frequently used function.

Another reason to use the `Function()` constructor is that it is sometimes convenient, and even elegant, to be able to define a function as part of a JavaScript expression, rather than as a statement. We'll see examples of this later in the chapter. In JavaScript 1.2, when you want to define a function in an expression rather than a statement, a function literal is an even more elegant choice than the `Function()` constructor. We'll consider function literals next.

7.1.3 *Function Literals*

JavaScript 1.2 introduces function literals, which are a third way to create functions. As discussed in Chapter 3, *Data Types and Values*, a function literal is an expression that creates an unnamed lambda function. The syntax for a function literal is much like that of the `function` statement, except that it is used as an expression rather than as a statement and no function name is specified. The following three lines of code define three more or less identical functions using the `function` statement, the `Function()` constructor, and a function literal:

```
function f(x) { return x*x; }           // function statement
var f = new Function("x", "return x*x;");  // Function() constructor
var f = function(x) { return x*x; };    // function literal
```

Keep in mind that the `function` statement is available in all versions of JavaScript, the `Function()` constructor is available only in JavaScript 1.1 and later, and function literals are available only in JavaScript 1.2 and later. Note that we said that the functions defined by the code above are "more or less" equivalent. There are some differences between these three techniques for function definition, which we'll consider in section 11.7, "The Function Constructor and Function Literals."

Function literals are useful in much the same way as functions created with the `Function()` constructor. Because they are created by JavaScript expressions rather than statements, they can be used in more flexible ways and are particularly suited for functions that are used only once and need not be named. For example, the function specified by a function literal expression can be stored into a variable, passed to another function, or even invoked directly:

```
a[0] = function(x) { return x*x; };    // Define a function and store it.
a.sort(function(a,b){return a-b;});    // Define a function; pass it to another.
var tensquared = (function(x) {return x*x;})(10);   // Define and invoke.
```

Like the `Function()` constructor, function literals create unnamed functions and do not automatically store those functions into properties. Function literals have an important advantage over the `Function()` constructor, however. The body of a function created by `Function()` must be specified in a string, and it can be awkward to express long, complex function bodies in this way. The body of a function literal, however, uses standard JavaScript syntax.

7.2 *Functions as Data*

The most important features of functions are that they can be defined and invoked, as shown in the previous section. Function definition and invocation are syntactic features of JavaScript and of most other programming languages. In JavaScript, however, functions are not only syntax but also data. In some languages, like Java, functions are part of a program but cannot be manipulated by the program—you cannot, for example, pass one function as an argument to another function in Java. Other languages, like C and C++, are more flexible. While a function defined in C is not actually a data value, function pointers can be manipulated by the program, and it is possible to pass these function pointers to other functions and to assign them to variables.

JavaScript goes even further than C. Functions in JavaScript are data, and thus can be treated like any other data value—assigned to variables, stored in the properties of objects or the elements of arrays, passed to functions, and so on.

To understand how functions are JavaScript data as well as JavaScript syntax, consider this function definition:

```
function square(x) { return x*x; }
```

This definition creates a new function object and assigns it to the variable `square`. The name of a function is really immaterial—it is simply the name of a variable that holds the function. The function can be assigned to another variable and it still works the same way:

```
a = square(4);    // a contains the number 16.
b = square;       // Now b refers to the same function as square does.
c = b(5);         // c contains the number 25.
```

Functions can also be assigned to object properties rather than global variables. When we do this, we call them methods:

```
o = new Object;
o.square = new Function("x", "return x*x");  // Note Function() constructor.
y = o.square(16);                            // y equals 256.
```

Functions don't even require names at all, as when we assign them to array elements:

```
a = new Array(10);
a[0] = function(x) { return x*x; }  // Note function literal.
a[1] = 20;
a[2] = a[0](a[1]);                  // a[2] contains 400.
```

The function invocation syntax in this last example looks strange, but is still a legal use of the JavaScript ( ) operator!

Example 7-2 is a detailed example of the things that can be done when functions are used as data. It demonstrates how functions can be passed as arguments to other functions, and also how they can be stored in associative arrays (which were introduced in Chapter 3 and are explained in detail in Chapter 8.) This example may be a little tricky, but the comments explain what is going on; it is worth studying carefully.

Example 7-2: Using Functions as Data

```
// We define some simple functions here.
function add(x,y) { return x + y; }
function subtract(x,y) { return x - y; }
function multiply(x,y) { return x * y; }
function divide(x,y) { return x / y; }

// Here's a function that takes one of the above functions
// as an argument and invokes it on two operands.
function operate(operator, operand1, operand2)
{
    return operator(operand1, operand2);
}

// We could invoke this function like this to compute the value (2+3) + (4*5):
var i = operate(add, operate(add, 2, 3), operate(multiply, 4, 5));

// For the sake of example, we implement the functions again, this time
// using function literals. We store the functions in an associative array.
var operators = new Object();
operators["add"] = function(x,y) { return x+y; };
operators["subtract"] = function(x,y) { return x-y; };
operators["multiply"] = function(x,y) { return x*y; };
operators["divide"] = function(x,y) { return x/y; };
operators["pow"] = Math.pow;   // works for predefined functions too.

// This function takes the name of an operator, looks up that operator
// in the array, and then invokes it on the supplied operands. Note
// the syntax used to invoke the operator function.
function operate2(op_name, operand1, operand2)
{
    if (operators[op_name] == null) return "unknown operator";
    else return operators[op_name](operand1, operand2);
}

// We could invoke this function as follows to compute
// the value ("hello" + " " + "world"):
var j = operate2("add", "hello", operate2("add", " ", "world"))
```

Example 7-2: Using Functions as Data (continued)

```
// Using the predefined Math.pow() function
var k = operate2("pow", 10, 2)
```

If the preceding example does not convince you of the utility of being able to pass functions as arguments to other functions and otherwise treat functions as data values, consider the `Array.sort()` function. This function sorts the elements of an array. Because there are many possible orders to sort by (numerical order, alphabetical order, date order, ascending, descending, and so on), the `sort()` function optionally takes another function as an argument to tell it how to perform the sort. This function has a very simple job—it takes two elements of the array, compares them, and then returns a value that specifies which element comes first. This function argument makes the `Array.sort()` method perfectly general and infinitely flexible—it can sort any type of data into any conceivable order!

7.3 Function Scope: The Call Object

As described in Chapter 4, *Variables*, the body of a JavaScript function executes in a local scope that differs from the global scope. This new scope is created by adding the call object to the front of the scope chain. Since the call object is part of the scope chain, any properties of this object are accessible as variables within the body of the function. Local variables declared with the `var` statement are created as properties of this object; the parameters of the function are also made available as properties of the object.

In addition to local variables and parameters, the call object also defines one special property named `arguments`. This property refers to another special object known as the arguments object, which is discussed in the next section. Because the `arguments` property is a property of the call object, it has exactly the same status as local variables and function parameters. For this reason, the identifier `arguments` should be considered a reserved word and not be used as a variable or parameter name.

7.4 Function Arguments: The Arguments Object

Within the body of a function, the identifier `arguments` always has special meaning. As described above, `arguments` is a special property of the call object that refers to an object known as the *arguments object*. This arguments object is quite a bit more interesting than the call object that refers to it. The object has a couple of useful properties that we'll describe below, and in addition to this, it doubles as an array. As you might expect, the elements of this `arguments[]` array hold the argument values that were passed to the function.

Although a JavaScript function is defined with a fixed number of named arguments, it can be passed any number of arguments when it is invoked. The `arguments[]` array allows full access to these argument values, even when some are unnamed. Suppose you define a function f that expects to be passed one argument x. If you invoke this function with two arguments, the first argument is accessible within the function by the parameter name x or as `arguments[0]`. The second argument is accessible only as `arguments[1]`. Furthermore, like all arrays, `arguments` has a `length` property that specifies the number of elements it contains. Thus, within the body of our function f, invoked with two arguments, `arguments.length` has the value 2.

The `arguments[]` array is useful in a number of ways. The following example shows how you can use it to check that a function is invoked with the correct number of arguments, since JavaScript doesn't do this for you:

```
function f(x, y, z)
{
    // First, check that the right number of arguments were passed.
    if (arguments.length != 3) {
        alert("function f called with " + arguments.length +
            "arguments, but it expects 3 arguments.");
        return null;
    }
    // Now do the actual function...
}
```

The `arguments[]` array also opens up an important possibility for JavaScript functions: they can be written so that they work with any number of arguments. Here's an example that shows how you can write a simple `max()` function that accepts any number of arguments and returns the value of the largest argument it is passed:

```
function max()
{
    var m = Number.NEGATIVE_INFINITY;

    // Loop through all the arguments, looking for, and
    // remembering, the biggest.
    for(var i = 0; i < arguments.length; i++)
        if (arguments[i] > m) m = arguments[i];
    // Return the biggest.
    return m;
```

```
}

    var largest = max(1, 10, 100, 2, 3, 1000, 4, 5, 10000, 6);
```

You can also use the `arguments[]` array to write functions that expect a fixed number of named arguments followed by an arbitrary number of unnamed arguments.

In Navigator 4, you may notice a strange fact if you invoke the `toString()` method of the arguments object of a function. Calling this method returns the string "[object Call]", which indicates that the arguments object is of type Call. This is because the JavaScript implementation in Navigator 4 unifies the call object and the arguments object into a single object (of class Call). The `arguments` property of the call object is actually a reference back to the unified call/arguments object. Despite this unification of the two objects, the Navigator 4 implementation takes several steps to make it appear as if there were really two separate objects. The unification of the objects is an implementation detail that may well change in future implementations—it is not something that you should attempt to rely on. It is best just to consider the call and arguments objects to be separate and distinct.

In addition to its array elements and `length` property, the arguments object defines two other properties, `callee` and `caller`.

7.4.1 The callee Property

The `callee` property of the arguments object refers to the function that is currently being executed. This is useful, for example, to allow unnamed functions to invoke themselves recursively. For example, here is an unnamed function literal that computes factorials:

```
function(x) {
    if (x > 1) return x * arguments.callee(x-1);
    return x;
}
```

The `callee` property is new in JavaScript 1.2; it is not available in previous versions of the language.

7.4.2 The caller Property

The `caller` property of the arguments object refers to the calling context from which the current function was invoked. Note, though, that `arguments.caller` does not refer to the function that invoked the current one; instead, it refers to the arguments object of the function that invoked the current one. To refer to the calling function, we must therefore use `arguments.caller.callee`.

You can use the `caller` property to write a debugging function that prints a stack trace. In order to do this, though, you need to be aware of a bug in Navigator 4. You might expect that a function called from the top level would have `arguments.caller` set to `null` or to the undefined value. In Navigator 4, however, such a function has `arguments.caller` set to the `arguments` object. Thus, when you write a function to follow the `caller` property up the stack of arguments objects, you need a technique to detect when you've reached the top level or you'll enter an infinite loop. Example 7-3 shows the stack trace function.

Example 7-3: Function That Prints a Stack Trace

```
// This function returns the name of a given function. It does this by
// converting the function to a string, then using a regular expression
// to extract the function name from the resulting code.
function funcname(f) {
    var s = f.toString().match(/function (\w*)/)[1];
    if ((s == null) || (s.length == 0)) return "anonymous";
    return s;
}


// This function returns a string that contains a "stack trace."
function stacktrace() {
    var s = "";  // This is the string we'll return.
    // Loop through the stack of functions, using the caller property of
    // one arguments object to refer to the next arguments object on the
    // stack.
    for(var a = arguments.caller; a != null; a = a.caller) {
        // Add the name of the current function to the return value.
        s += funcname(a.callee) + "\n";

        // Because of a bug in Navigator 4.0, we need this line to break.
        // a.caller will equal a rather than null when we reach the end
        // of the stack. The following line works around this.
        if (a.caller == a) break;
    }
    return s;
}
```

You can use the `arguments.caller` property in Navigator 3, but in that implementation of JavaScript, it refers directly to the calling function rather than to the arguments object of the calling function. For this reason, it is not possible to write a stack trace function that works in Navigator 3. In effect, you should consider the `caller` property of the arguments object to be new in Navigator 4. The `caller` property has not yet been standardized, and it creates difficulties for program optimization, so it is possible that it will be deprecated or removed in future versions of the language.

7.5 *Function Properties and Methods*

We've seen that functions can be used as data values in JavaScript programs and we've seen that they can be created with the Function() constructor. These are sure signs that functions are actually represented by a type of JavaScript object, the Function object. Since functions are objects, they have properties and methods, just like the String and Date objects, for example. Now that we've discussed the call and arguments objects that are used in the context of function invocation, we turn to the Function object itself.

7.5.1 *The length and arity Properties*

As we've seen, within the body of a function, the length property of the argu-ments array specifies the number of arguments that were passed to the function. The length property of a function itself, however, has a different meaning. This property returns the number of arguments that the function *expects* to be passed— that is, the number of parameters it declares in its parameter list. Recall that a func-tion can be invoked with any number of arguments, which it can retrieve through the arguments array, regardless of the number of parameters it declares. The length property of the Function object specifies exactly how many declared parameters a function has. Note that unlike arguments.length, this length prop-erty is available both inside and outside of the function body.

The length property of the Function object is available in JavaScript 1.1 and later. In Navigator 4, a bug prevents this property from working correctly unless the LANGUAGE attribute of the <SCRIPT> tag is explicitly set to "JavaScript1.2".

In Navigator 4, the Function object has a new property, named arity, that has the same value and meaning as the length property. In Navigator 4 and later, the arity property is preferred over length (length is deprecated), to avoid confu-sion with the length property of arrays. Note that the arity property suffers from the same bug as the length property; it only functions correctly in Navigator 4 if the LANGUAGE attribute is set to "JavaScript1.2".

Example 7-4 shows how the arity property of a Function object can be used to verify that a function is invoked with the right number of arguments. Note the use of the caller and callee properties of the arguments object.

Example 7–4: Function to Verify Correct Number of Arguments

```
function checkargs() {
    // arguments.caller.callee is the Function object that called us.
    // Its arity property is the number of arguments that were expected.
    var expected = arguments.caller.callee.arity;
```

Example 7–4: Function to Verify Correct Number of Arguments (continued)

```
    // arguments.caller is the arguments object of the function that
    // called us. Its length property is the number of actual args passed.
    var passed = arguments.caller.length;

    // If they don't match, do some fancy regular expression work to get
    // the name of the calling function, and display a warning.
    if (passed != expected) {
      var funcname = arguments.caller.callee.toString().match(/function (\w*)/)[1];
      alert("WARNING:\n" +
          funcname + "() " + "was invoked with wrong number of arguments!\n" +
          "Expected " + expected + " arguments, but passed " + passed);
    }
}

// Here is a test function that uses checkargs().
function f(x,y,z) { checkargs(); return x+y+z; }
f(1,2,3);        // Passed the right number of arguments
f(1,2);          // Passed too few arguments; checkargs() displays a warning.
```

7.5.2 The arguments and caller Properties

The Function object has its own `arguments` and `caller` properties. They are left over from JavaScript 1.0, when there was no arguments object, and they are now deprecated. In old JavaScript code, you may still find these properties being used, however. Because they are properties of the function itself and are not part of the local scope, they have to be prefixed by the name of the function. So, in JavaScript 1.0, for example, a function `f` could refer to its arguments array as `f.arguments`. This syntax still works in JavaScript 1.2, but its use is discouraged.

7.5.3 The prototype Property

Every function has a `prototype` property that refers to a predefined *prototype object*. This prototype object comes into play when the function is used as a constructor with the `new` operator; it has a very important role to play in the process of defining new object types. We'll explore this property in detail in Chapter 8.

7.5.4 Defining Your Own Function Properties

By adding your own properties to a Function object, you can simulate C-style static variables. A static variable is used only within a function; its value persists across function invocations. For example, suppose we want to write a function that returns a unique identifier whenever it is invoked. The function must never return the same value twice. In order to manage this, the function needs to keep track of the values it has already returned, and this information must persist across function invocations. We could store this information in a global variable, but that is unnecessary because the information is used only by the function itself. It is better to store the information in a property of the function object. Here is an example that returns a unique integer whenever it is called:

```
// Create and initialize the "static" variable.
// Function declarations are processed before code is executed, so
// we really can do this assignment before the function declaration.
uniqueInteger.counter = 0;

// Here's the function. It returns a different value each time
// it is called and uses a "static" property of itself to keep track
// of the last value it returned.
function uniqueInteger() {
  // Increment and return our "static" variable.
  return uniqueInteger.counter++;
}
```

7.5.5 The apply() and call() Methods

Navigator 4 adds a new method, apply(), to the Function object. This method allows you to invoke a function as if it were a method of some other object. (Note that we have not discussed methods yet; you may find this section more understandable once you have read Chapter 8.) The first argument to apply() is the object on which the function is to be invoked; this argument becomes the value of the this keyword within the body of the function. The second argument to apply() is an optional array of arguments to be passed to the function. So, to invoke the function f() with two arguments, as if it were a method of the object o, you can use code like the following:

```
f.apply(o, [1,2]);
```

This is similar to the following lines of code:

```
o.m = f;
o.m(1,2);
delete o.m;
```

You can also use apply() to run the default Object toString() method for an object that overrides it with a more specialized method of its own (you are not expected to understand this example until you have read Chapter 8):

```
Object.prototype.toString.apply(o);
```

Navigator 4 introduced the apply() method and Navigator 5 is expected to add a similar method named call(), which behaves just like apply(), except that the arguments to be passed to the function are passed as an argument list rather than as an array. Thus, the following two lines of code should be equivalent in Navigator 5:

```
f.apply(o, [1,2]);    // Arguments passed in an array
f.call(o, 1, 2);      // Arguments passed directly in an argument list
```

8

Objects

Chapter 3, *Data Types and Values*, explained that objects are one of the fundamental data types in JavaScript. They are also one of the most important. This chapter describes JavaScript objects in detail. Basic usage of objects, described in the first section below, is straightforward, but as we'll see in later sections, objects have more complex uses and behaviors.

8.1 Objects and Properties

A primitive data type holds a single data value: a single number, a single string, or a single boolean. Objects, on the other hand, are compound types: they aggregate multiple data values into single units and allow us to store and retrieve those values by name. Another way to explain this is to say that an object is a collection of *properties*, each of which has a name and a value.

8.1.1 Creating Objects

Objects are created with the new operator. This operator must be followed by the name of a constructor function that serves to initialize the object. For example, we can create an empty object (an object with no properties) like this:

```
var o = new Object();
```

JavaScript supports other built-in constructor functions that initialize newly created objects in other, less trivial, ways. For example, we saw in Chapter 7, *Functions*, that we can create a function object with the Function() constructor:

```
var square = new Function("x", "return x*x;");
```

Later in this chapter, we'll see that it is possible to define custom constructor methods to initialize newly created objects in any way you desire.

In JavaScript 1.2, object literals provide another way to create new objects. As we saw in Chapter 3, an object literal allows us to embed an object description literally in JavaScript code in much the same way that we embed textual data into JavaScript code as quoted strings. An object literal consists of a comma-separated list of property specifications enclosed within curly braces. Each property specification in an object literal consists of the property name followed by a colon and the property value. For example:

```
var circle = { x:0, y:0, radius:2 }
var homer = {
            name: "Homer Simpson",
            age: 34,
            married: true,
            occupation: "plant operator",
            email: homer@simpsons.com
        };
```

8.1.2 Accessing Object Properties

You normally use the . operator to access the value of an object's properties. The value on the left of the . should be a reference to an object (usually just the name of the variable that contains the object reference). The value on the right of the . should be the name of the property. This must be an identifier, not a string or an expression. For example, you refer to the property p in object o with o.p. Or, you refer to the property radius in the object circle with circle.radius. Object properties work a lot like variables: you can store values in them and read values from them. For example:

```
// Create an object. Store a reference to it in a variable.
var book = new Object();

// Set a property in the object.
book.title = "JavaScript: The Definitive Guide"

// Set some more properties. Note the nested objects.
book.chapter1 = new Object();
book.chapter1.title = "Introduction";
book.chapter1.pages = 25;
book.chapter2 = { title: "Lexical Structure", pages: 10 };

// Read some property values from the object.
alert("Outline: " + book.title + "\n\t" +
    "Chapter 1 " + book.chapter1.title + "\n\t" +
    "Chapter 2 " + book.chapter2.title);
```

An important point to notice about this example is that you can create a new property of an object simply by assigning a value to it. Although we usually declare variables with the `var` keyword, there is no need (and no way) to do so with object properties. Furthermore, once you have created an object property by assigning a value to it, you can change the value of the property at any time, simply by assigning a new value:

```
book.title = "JavaScript: The Rhino Book"
```

8.1.3 Undefined Object Properties

If you attempt to read the value of a property that does not exist (in other words, a property that has never had a value assigned to it), you end up retrieving the special JavaScript undefined value (introduced in Chapter 3).

In JavaScript 1.2, you can use the `delete` operator to delete the property of an object:

```
delete book.chapter2;
```

Prior to JavaScript 1.2, there was no way to delete a property. In JavaScript 1.0 and JavaScript 1.1, the `delete` operator simply sets a property to `null`, something that you can more simply do with an assignment statement:

```
book.chapter2 = null;
```

You can even set a property to the undefined value by assigning it the value of some nonexistent property:

```
book.chapter2 = book.no_such_property;
```

Or, in JavaScript 1.1, you can use the `void` operator to generate an undefined value in a more elegant way:

```
book.chapter2 = void 0;
```

Note, however, that setting a property to the undefined value is not the same as actually deleting it: the property still exists, it just contains an undefined value. The JavaScript 1.2 `delete` operator is the only way to truly remove a property from an object. The `for/in` loop demonstrates this difference: it enumerates properties that have been set to the undefined value, but it does not enumerate deleted properties.

8.1.4 Enumerating Object Properties

The `for/in` loop discussed in Chapter 6, *Statements*, provides a way to loop through, or enumerate, the properties of an object. This can be useful when debugging scripts or when working with objects that may have arbitrary properties whose names you do not know in advance. The following code shows a function you can use to list the property names of an object:

```
function listPropertyNames(obj) {
  var names = "";
  for(var i in obj) names += i + "\n";
  alert(names);
}
```

Note that the `for/in` loop does not enumerate properties in any specific order, and although it enumerates all user-defined properties, it does not enumerate certain predefined properties and methods.

8.2 Constructors

We saw above that you can create and initialize a new object in JavaScript by using the `new` operator in conjunction with a predefined constructor function like `Object()`, `Date()`, or `Function()`. There are many instances in which these predefined constructors and the built-in object types they create are useful. However, in object-oriented programming, it is also very common to work with custom object types defined by your program. For example, if you are writing a program that manipulates rectangles, you might want to represent rectangles with a special type, or *class*, of object. Each object of this rectangle class would have a `width` property and a `height` property, since they are the essential defining characteristics of rectangles.

To create objects with properties such as `width` and `height` already defined, we need to write a *constructor* to create and initialize these properties in a new object. A constructor is a JavaScript function with two special features:

- It is invoked through the `new` operator.

- It is passed a reference to a newly created, empty object as the value of the special `this` keyword, and it is responsible for performing appropriate initialization for that new object.

Example 8-1 shows how the constructor function for a rectangle object might be defined and invoked.

Example 8-1: A Rectangle Object Constructor Function

```
// Define the constructor.
// Note how it initializes the object referred to by "this".
function Rectangle(w, h)
{
    this.width = w;
    this.height = h;
}
```

Example 8-1: A Rectangle Object Constructor Function (continued)

```
// Invoke the constructor to create two rectangle objects.
// Notice that we pass the width and height to the constructor, so it
// can initialize each new object appropriately.
var rect1 = new Rectangle(2, 4);
var rect2 = new Rectangle(8.5, 11);
```

Notice how the constructor uses its arguments to initialize properties of the object referred to by the `this` keyword. Keep in mind that a constructor function simply initializes the specified object; it does not have to return that object.

We have defined a class of objects simply by defining an appropriate constructor function—all objects created with the `Rectangle()` constructor are now guaranteed to have initialized `width` and `height` properties. This means that we can write programs that rely on this fact and treat all Rectangle objects uniformly. Because every constructor defines a class of objects, it is stylistically important to give a constructor function a name that indicates the class of objects it creates. Creating a rectangle with `new Rectangle(1,2)` is a lot more intuitive than with `new init_rect(1,2)`, for example.

Constructor functions typically do not have return values. They initialize the object passed as the value of `this` and return nothing. However, a constructor is allowed to return an object value, and, if it does so, that returned object becomes the value of the `new` expression. In this case, the object that was the value of `this` is simply discarded.

8.3 *Methods*

A *method* is nothing more than a JavaScript function that is invoked through an object. Recall that functions are data values and that there is nothing special about the name they are defined with—a function can be assigned to any variable, or even to any property of an object. If we have a function `f` and an object `o`, we can define a method named `m` with the following line:

```
o.m = f;
```

Having defined the method `m()` of the object `o`, we invoke it like this:

```
o.m();
```

Or, if `m()` expects two arguments, we might invoke it like this:

```
o.m(x, x+2);
```

Methods have one very important property: the object a method is invoked through becomes the value of the this keyword within the body of the method. For example, when we invoke o.m( ), the body of the method can refer to the object o with the this keyword.

The discussion of the this keyword should begin to make it clear why we use methods at all. Any function that is used as a method is effectively passed an extra argument—the object through which it is invoked. Typically, a method performs some sort of operation on that object, so the method invocation syntax is a particularly elegant way to express the fact that a function is operating on an object. Compare the following two lines of code:

```
rect.setSize(x, y);
setRectSize(rect, x, y);
```

The two lines may perform exactly the same operation on the object rect, but the method invocation syntax shown first more clearly indicates the idea that it is the object rect that is the primary focus, or target, of the operation. (If the first line does not seem a more natural syntax to you, you are probably new to object-oriented programming. With a little experience, you will learn to love it!)

While it is useful to think of functions and methods differently, there is not actually as much difference between them as there initially appears to be. Recall that functions are values stored in variables and that variables are nothing more than properties of a global object. Thus, when you invoke a function, you are actually invoking a method of the global object. Within such a function, the this keyword refers to the global object. Thus, there is no technical difference between functions and methods. The real difference lies in design and intent: methods are written to operate somehow on the this object, while functions usually stand alone and do not use the this object.

The typical usage of methods is more clearly illustrated through an example. Example 8-2 returns to the Rectangle objects of Example 8-1 and shows how a method that operates on Rectangle objects can be defined and invoked.

Example 8-2: Defining and Invoking a Method

```
// This function uses the this keyword, so it doesn't make sense to
// invoke it by itself; it needs instead to be made a method of some
// object that has "width" and "height" properties defined.
function compute_area()
{
    return this.width * this.height;
}


// Create a new Rectangle object, using the constructor defined earlier.
var page = new Rectangle(8.5, 11);
```

Example 8-2: Defining and Invoking a Method (continued)

```
// Define a method by assigning the function to a property of the object.
page.area = compute_area;

// Invoke the new method like this:
var a = page.area();     // a = 8.5*11 = 93.5
```

There is a shortcoming that is evident in Example 8-2: before you can invoke the
area() method for the rect object, you must assign that method to a property of
the object. While we can invoke the area() method on the particular object
named page, we can't invoke it on any other Rectangle objects without first
assigning the method to them. This quickly becomes tedious. Example 8-3 defines
some additional Rectangle methods and shows how they can automatically be
assigned to all Rectangle objects with a constructor function.

Example 8-3: Defining Methods in a Constructor

```
// First, define some functions that will be used as methods.
function Rectangle_area() { return this.width * this.height; }
function Rectangle_perimeter() { return 2*this.width + 2*this.height; }
function Rectangle_set_size(w,h) { this.width = w; this.height = h; }
function Rectangle_enlarge() { this.width *= 2; this.height *= 2; }
function Rectangle_shrink() { this.width /= 2; this.height /= 2; }

// Then define a constructor method for our Rectangle objects.
// The constructor initializes properties and also assigns methods.
function Rectangle(w, h)
{
    // Initialize object properties.
    this.width = w;
    this.height = h;

    // Define methods for the object.
    this.area = Rectangle_area;
    this.perimeter = Rectangle_perimeter;
    this.set_size = Rectangle_set_size;
    this.enlarge = Rectangle_enlarge;
    this.shrink = Rectangle_shrink;
}
// Now, when we create a rectangle, we can immediately invoke methods on it:
var r = new Rectangle(2,2);
var a = r.area();
r.enlarge();
var p = r.perimeter();
```

The technique shown in Example 8-3 also has a shortcoming. In this example, the `Rectangle()` constructor sets seven properties of each and every Rectangle object it initializes, even though five of those properties have constant values that are the same for every rectangle. Each property takes up memory space; by adding methods to our Rectangle class, we've more than tripled the memory requirements of each Rectangle object. Fortunately, JavaScript 1.1 introduced a solution to this problem: it allowed an object to inherit properties from a prototype object. The next section describes this technique in detail.

8.4 Prototypes and Inheritance

We've seen how inefficient it can be to use a constructor to assign methods to the objects it initializes. When we do this, each and every object in the class has identical copies of the same method properties. In JavaScript 1.1 and later, there is a much more efficient way to specify methods, constants, and other properties that are shared by all objects in a class.

JavaScript 1.1 introduced the notion of a *prototype object*. Every object has a prototype; an object inherits all of the properties of its prototype. This means that all of the properties of the prototype object appear to be properties of the objects that inherit them. To specify the prototype object for a class of objects, we set the value of the `prototype` property of the constructor function to the appropriate object. Then, when a new object is initialized with the constructor, JavaScript automatically uses the specified object as the prototype for the newly created object.

A constructor defines a class of objects and initializes properties, such as `width` and `height`, that are the state variables for the class. The prototype object is associated with the constructor, so each member of the class inherits exactly the same set of properties from the prototype. This means that the prototype object is an ideal place for methods and other constant properties.

Note that inheritance occurs automatically as part of the process of looking up a property value. Properties are *not* copied from the prototype object into new objects; they merely appear as if they were properties of those objects. This has two important implications. First, the use of prototype objects can dramatically decrease the amount of memory required by each object, since it can inherit many of its properties. The second implication is that an object inherits properties even if they are added to its prototype *after* the object is created.

Each class has one prototype object, with one set of properties. But there are potentially many instances of a class, each of which inherits those prototype properties. Because one prototype property can be inherited by many objects,

JavaScript must enforce a fundamental asymmetry between reading and writing property values. When you read property p of an object o, JavaScript first checks to see if o has a property named p. If it does not, it next checks to see if the prototype object of o has a property named p. This is what makes prototype-based inheritance work.

When you write the value of a property, on the other hand, JavaScript does not use the prototype object. To see why, consider what would happen if it did: suppose you try to set the value of the property o.p when the object o does not have a property named p. Further suppose that JavaScript goes ahead and looks up the property p in the prototype object of o and allows you to set the property of the prototype. Now you have changed the value of p for a whole class of objects—not at all what you intended.

Therefore, property inheritance occurs only when you read property values, not when you write them. If you set the property p in an object o that inherits that property from its prototype, what happens is that you create a new property p directly in o. Now that o has its own property named p, it no longer inherits the value of p from its prototype. When you read the value of p, JavaScript first looks at the properties of o. Since it finds p defined in o, it doesn't need to search the prototype object and never finds the value of p defined there. We sometimes say that the property p in o "shadows" or "hides" the property p in the prototype object. Prototype inheritance can be a confusing topic. Figure 8-1 illustrates the concepts we've discussed here.

Because prototype properties are shared by all objects of a class, it generally makes sense to use them only to define properties that are the same for all objects within the class. This makes prototypes ideal for defining methods. Other properties with constant values (such as mathematical constants) are also suitable for definition with prototype properties. If your class defines a property with a very commonly used default value, you might define this property and its default value in a prototype object. Then, the few objects that want to deviate from the default value can create their own private, unshared copies of the property and define their own non-default values.

Let's move from an abstract discussion of prototype inheritance to a concrete example. Suppose we define a `Circle()` constructor function to create objects that represent circles. The prototype object for this class is `Circle.prototype`, so we can define a constant available to all Circle objects like this:

```
Circle.prototype.pi = 3.14159;
```

The prototype object of a constructor is created automatically by JavaScript. In most versions of JavaScript, every function is automatically given an empty prototype object, just in case it is used as a constructor. In Navigator 3, however, the

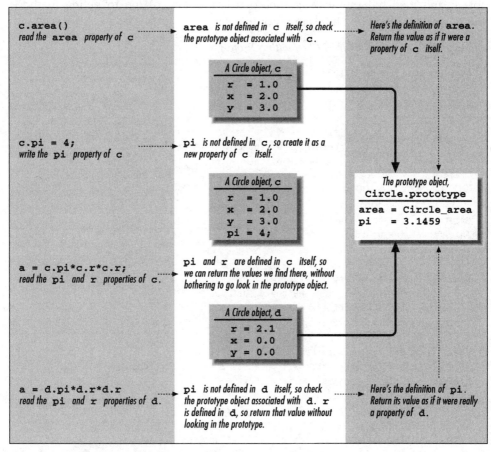

Figure 8-1: Objects and prototypes

prototype object is not created until the function is used as a constructor for the first time. What this means is that for compatibility with Navigator 3, you should create at least one object of a class before you use the prototype object to assign methods and constants to objects of that class. So, if we have defined a Circle() constructor, but not yet used it to create any Circle objects, we'd define the constant property pi like this:

```
// First create and discard a dummy Circle object.
// This forces Navigator 3 to create the prototype object.
new Circle();

// Now we can set properties in the prototype.
Circle.prototype.pi = 3.14159;
```

Example 8-4 shows our Circle example fully fleshed out. The code defines a Circle class by first defining a Circle() constructor to initialize each individual object, and then by setting properties of `Circle.prototype` to define methods and constants shared by all instances of the class.

Example 8–4: Defining a Circle Class with a Prototype Object

```
// Define a constructor method for our class.
// Use it to initialize properties that will be different for
// each individual circle object.
function Circle(x, y, r)
{
    this.x = x;   // The X-coordinate of the center of the  circle
    this.y = y;   // The Y-coordinate of the center of the circle
    this.r = r;   // The radius of the circle
}

// Create and discard an initial Circle object.
// This forces the prototype object to be created in Navigator 3.
new Circle(0,0,0);

// Define a constant: a property that will be shared by
// all circle objects. Actually, we could just use Math.PI,
// but we do it this way for the sake of example.
Circle.prototype.pi = 3.14159;

// Define a method to compute the circumference of the circle.
// First declare a function, then assign it to a prototype property.
// Note the use of the constant defined above.
function Circle_circumference() { return 2 * this.pi * this.r; }
Circle.prototype.circumference = Circle_circumference;

// Define another method. This time we use the Function()
// constructor to define the function and assign it to a prototype
// property all in one step.
Circle.prototype.area = new Function("return this.pi * this.r * this.r;");

// The Circle class is defined.
// Now we can create an instance and invoke its methods.
var c = new Circle(0.0, 0.0, 1.0);
var a = c.area();
var p = c.circumference();
```

8.4.1 Prototypes and Built-In Classes

It is not only user-defined classes that have prototype objects. Built-in classes, such as String and Date, have prototype objects too, and you can assign values to them. (This does not work in IE 3, however).

For example, the following code defines a new method that is available for all String objects:

```
// Returns true if the last character is c
String.prototype.endsWith = function(c) {
    return (c == this.charAt(this.length-1))
}
```

Having defined the new `endsWith()` method in the String prototype object, we can use it like this:

```
var message = "hello world";
message.endsWith('h')        // Returns false
message.endsWith('d')        // Returns true
```

8.5 Object-Oriented JavaScript

Although JavaScript supports a data type we call an object, it does not have a formal notion of a class. This makes it quite different from classic object-oriented languages such as C++ and Java. The common conception about object-oriented programming languages is that they are strongly typed and support class-based inheritance. By these criteria, it is easy to dismiss JavaScript as not being a true object-oriented language. On the other hand, we've seen that JavaScript certainly makes heavy use of objects, and we've seen that it has its own type of prototype-based inheritance. The truth is that JavaScript is a true object-oriented language. It draws inspiration from a number of other (relatively obscure) object-oriented languages that use prototype-based inheritance instead of class-based inheritance.

Although JavaScript is not a class-based object-oriented language, it does a good job of simulating the features of class-based languages like Java and C++. I've been using the term class informally throughout this chapter. This section more formally explores the parallels between JavaScript and true class-based inheritance languages like Java and C++.

Let's start by defining some basic terminology. An *object*, as we've already seen, is a data structure that contains various pieces of named data and may also contain various methods to operate on those pieces of data. An object groups related data values and methods into a single convenient package, which generally makes programming easier by increasing the modularity and reusability of code. Objects in JavaScript may have any number of properties, and properties may be added to an object dynamically. This is not the case in strictly typed languages like Java and C++. In those languages, each object has a predefined set of properties (or fields, as they are often called), where each property is of a predefined type. When we are using JavaScript objects to simulate object-oriented programming techniques, we generally define in advance the set of properties for each object and the type of data that each property holds.

In Java and C++, a *class* defines the structure of an object. It is the class that specifies exactly what fields an object contains, and what types of data each holds. It is also the class that defines the methods that operate on an object. JavaScript does not have a formal notion of a class, but, as we've seen, it approximates classes with its constructors and their prototype objects.

In both JavaScript and class-based object-oriented languages, there may be multiple objects of the same class. We often say that an object is an *instance* of its class. Thus, there may be many instances of any class. Sometimes we use the term *instantiate* to describe the process of creating an object (an instance of a class).

In Java, it is a common programming convention to name classes with an initial capital letter and to name objects with lower case letters. This convention helps keep classes and objects distinct from each other in our code; it is a useful convention to follow in JavaScript programming as well. In previous sections, for example, we've defined the `Circle` and `Rectangle` classes and have created instances of those classes named `c` and `rect`.

The members of a Java class may be of four basic types: instance variables, instance methods, static or class variables, and static or class methods. In the following sections, we'll explore the differences between these types of members and show how they are simulated in JavaScript.

8.5.1 Instance Variables

Every object has its own separate copies of its *instance variables*. In other words, if there are ten objects of a given class, there are ten copies of each instance variable. In our Circle class, for example, every circle object has a property r that specifies the radius of the circle. In this case r is an instance variable. Since each object has its own copy of instance variables, these variables are accessed through individual objects. If c is an object that is an instance of the Circle class, for example, we refer to its radius as:

```
c.r
```

By default, any object property in JavaScript is an instance variable. To truly simulate object-oriented programming, however, we will say that instance variables in JavaScript are those properties that are created and/or initialized in an object by the constructor function.

8.5.2 Instance Methods

An *instance method* is much like an instance variable, except that it is a method rather than a data value. (In Java, functions and methods are not data, as they are in JavaScript, so this distinction is more clear). Instance methods are invoked on a particular object, or instance. The `area()` method of our Circle class is an instance method. It is invoked on a Circle object c like this:

```
a = c.area();
```

Instance methods use the `this` keyword to refer to the object or instance they are operating on. An instance method can be invoked for any instance of a class, but this does not mean that each object contains its own private copy of the method as it does with instance variables. Instead, each instance method is shared by all instances of a class. In JavaScript, we define an instance method for a class by setting a property in the constructor's prototype object to a function value. This way, all objects created by that constructor share a reference to the function and can invoke it using the method invocation syntax shown above. (In JavaScript 1.0, which does not support prototype objects, instance methods can be defined in a constructor function as instance variables are; this is less efficient, though.)

8.5.3 Class Variables

A *class variable* (or *static variable*) in Java is a variable that is associated with a class itself, rather than with each instance of a class. No matter how many instances of the class are created, there is only one copy of each class variable. Just as instance variables are accessed through an instance of a class, class variables are accessed through the class itself. `Number.MAX_VALUE` is an example of a class variable in JavaScript: the `MAX_VALUE` property is accessed through the `Number` class. Because there is only one copy of each class variable, class variables are essentially global variables. What is nice about them, however, is that they are associated with a class and they have a logical niche, a position in the JavaScript name space, where they are not likely to be overwritten by other variables with the same name. As is probably clear, we simulate a class variable in JavaScript simply by defining a property of the constructor function itself. For example, to create a class variable `Circle.PI` to store the mathematical constant *pi*, we can do the following:

```
Circle.PI = 3.14;
```

8.5.4 Class Methods

Finally, we come to class methods. A *class method* (or *static method*) is a method associated with a class rather than with an instance of a class. Class methods are invoked through the class, rather than through a particular instance of the class. The `Date.parse()` method (which you can look up in the reference section) is a class method. You always invoke it through the `Date` constructor object, rather than through a particular instance of the Date class.

Because class methods are not invoked through a particular object, they cannot meaningfully use the `this` keyword—`this` refers to the object that an instance method is invoked for. Like class variables, class methods are global. Because they do not operate on a particular object, static methods can often more easily be thought of as functions that happen to be invoked through a class. Again, associating these functions with a class gives them a convenient niche in the JavaScript name space and prevents name space collisions. To define a class method in JavaScript, we simply make the appropriate function a property of the constructor.

8.5.5 Example: The Circle Class

Example 8-5 is a reimplementation of our Circle class that contains examples of each of these four basic types of members.

Example 8–5: Defining Circle Instance and Class Variables and Methods

```
function Circle(radius) {    // The constructor defines the class itself.
    // r is an instance variable; defined and initialized in the constructor.
    this.r = radius;
}

// Circle.PI is a class variable--it is a property of the constructor function.
Circle.PI = 3.14159;

// Here is a function that computes a circle area.
function Circle_area() { return Circle.PI * this.r * this.r; }


// Here we make the function into an instance method by assigning it
// to the prototype object of the constructor. Remember that, for
// compatibility with Navigator 3, we have to create and discard
// one object before the prototype object exists.
new Circle(0);
Circle.prototype.area = Circle_area;

// Here's another function. It takes two circle objects as arguments and
// returns the one that is larger (has the larger radius).
function Circle_max(a,b) {
```

Example 8–5: Defining Circle Instance and Class Variables and Methods (continued)

```
    if (a.r > b.r) return a;
    else return b;
}


// Since this function compares two circle objects, it doesn't make sense as
// an instance method operating on a single circle object. But we don't want
// it to be a standalone function either, so we make it into a class method
// by assigning it to the constructor function:
Circle.max = Circle_max;

// Here is some code that uses each of these fields:
var c = new Circle(1.0);     // Create an instance of the Circle class.
c.r = 2.2;                   // Set the r instance variable.
var a = c.area();            // Invoke the area() instance method.
var x = Math.exp(Circle.PI); // Use the PI class variable in our own computation.
var d = new Circle(1.2);     // Create another Circle instance.
var bigger = Circle.max(c,d); // Use the max() class method.
```

8.5.6 Example: Complex Numbers

Example 8-6 is another example, somewhat more formal than the last, of defining a class of objects in JavaScript. The code and the comments are worth careful study. Note that this example uses the function literal syntax of JavaScript 1.2. Because it requires this version of the language, it does not bother with the Navigator 3 compatibility technique of invoking the constructor once before assigning to its prototype object.

Example 8–6: A Complex Number Class

```
/*
 * Complex.js:
 * This file defines a Complex class to represent complex numbers.
 * Recall that a complex number is the sum of a real number and an
 * imaginary number, and that the imaginary number i is the
 * square-root of -1.
 */


/*
 * The first step in defining a class is defining the constructor
 * function of the class. This constructor should initialize any
 * instance properties of the object. These are the essential
 * "state variables" that make each instance of the class different.
 */
function Complex(real, imaginary) {
    this.x = real;       // The real part of the number
    this.y = imaginary;  // The imaginary part of the number
```

Example 8-6: A Complex Number Class (continued)

```
}

/*
 * The second step in defining a class is defining its instance
 * methods (and possibly other properties) in the prototype object
 * of the constructor. Any properties defined in this object will
 * be inherited by all instances of the class. Note that instance
 * methods operate implicitly on the "this" keyword. For many methods
 * no other arguments are needed.
 */

// Return the magnitude of a complex number. This is defined
// as its distance from the origin (0,0) of the complex plane.
Complex.prototype.magnitude = function() {
    return Math.sqrt(this.x*this.x + this.y*this.y);
};

// Return a complex number that is the negative of this one.
Complex.prototype.negative = function() {
    return new Complex(-this.x, -this.y);
};

// Convert a Complex object to a string in a useful way.
// This is invoked when a Complex object is used as a string.
Complex.prototype.toString = function() {
    return "{" + this.x + "," + this.y + "}";
};

// Return the real portion of a complex number. This function
// is invoked when a Complex object is treated as a primitive value.
Complex.prototype.valueOf = function() { return this.x; }

/*
 * The third step in defining a class is to define class methods,
 * constants, and any needed class variables as properties of the
 * constructor function itself (instead of as properties of the
 * prototype object of the constructor). Note that static methods
 * do not use the "this" keyword: they operate only on their arguments.
 */

// Add two complex numbers and return the result.
Complex.add = function (a, b) {
    return new Complex(a.x + b.x, a.y + b.y);
};

// Subtract one complex number from another.
Complex.subtract = function (a, b) {
    return new Complex(a.x - b.x, a.y - b.y);
```

Example 8-6: A Complex Number Class (continued)

```
};

// Multiply two complex numbers and return the product.
Complex.multiply = function(a, b) {
    return new Complex(a.x * b.x - a.y * b.y,
                       a.x * b.y + a.y * b.x);
};

// Here are some useful predefined complex numbers.
// They are defined as Class variables, where they can be used as
// "constants." (Note, though that they are not actually read-only.)
Complex.zero = new Complex(0,0);
Complex.one = new Complex(1,0);
Complex.i = new Complex(0,1);
```

8.5.7 Superclasses and Subclasses

In Java, C++, and other class-based object-oriented languages, there is an explicit concept of the *class hierarchy*. Every class can have a *superclass* from which it inherits properties and methods. Any class can be extended, or subclassed, so that the resulting *subclass* inherits its behavior. As we've seen, JavaScript supports prototype inheritance instead of class-based inheritance. Still, JavaScript analogies to the class hierarchy can be drawn. In JavaScript, the Object class is the most generic, and all other classes are specialized versions, or subclasses, of it. Another way to say this is that Object is the superclass of all the built-in classes. All classes inherit a few basic methods (described later in this chapter) from Object.

We've learned that objects inherit properties from the prototype object of their constructor. How do they also inherit properties from the Object class? Remember that the prototype object is itself an object; it is created with the Object() constructor. This means that the prototype object itself inherits properties from Object.prototype! So, an object of class Complex inherits properties from the Complex.prototype object, which itself inherits properties from Object.prototype. Thus, the Complex object inherits properties of both objects. When you look up a property in a Complex object, the object itself is searched first. If the property is not found, the Complex.prototype object is searched next. Finally, if the property is not found in that object, the Object.prototype object is searched.

Note that because the Complex prototype object is searched before the Object prototype object, properties of Complex.prototype hide any properties with the same name in Object.prototype. For example, in the class definition shown in Example 8-6, we define a toString() method in the Complex.prototype object.

`Object.prototype` also defines a method with this name, but Complex objects never see it because the definition of `toString()` in `Complex.prototype` is found first.

The classes we've shown in this chapter are all direct subclasses of Object. This is typical of JavaScript programming; there is not usually any need to produce a more complex class hierarchy. When necessary, however, it is possible to subclass any other class. For example, suppose we want to produce a subclass of Complex in order to add some more methods. To do this, we simply have to make sure that the prototype object of the new class is itself an instance of Complex, so that it inherits all the properties of `Complex.prototype`:

```
// This is the constructor for the subclass.
function MoreComplex(real, imaginary) {
    this.x = real;
    this.y = imaginary;
}

// We force its prototype to be a Complex object. This means that
// instances of our new class inherit from MoreComplex.prototype
// which inherits from Complex.prototype, which inherits from
// Object.prototype.
MoreComplex.prototype = new Complex(0,0);

// Now add a new method or other new features to this subclass.
MoreComplex.prototype.swap = function() {
    var tmp = this.x;
    this.x = this.y;
    this.y = tmp;
}
```

There is one subtle shortcoming to the subclassing technique shown here. Since we explicitly set `MoreComplex.prototype` to an object of our own creation, we overwrite the prototype object provided by JavaScript and discard the `construc-tor` property we are given. This `constructor` property, described later in the chapter, is supposed to refer to the constructor function that created the object. A `MoreComplex` object, however, inherits the `constructor` property of its super-class, rather than having one of their own. One solution is to set this property explicitly:

```
MoreComplex.prototype.constructor = MoreComplex;
```

Unfortunately, a bug in some versions of Navigator makes the `constructor` prop-erty read-only and prevents it from being set in this way.

An advanced technique (available only in Navigator 4) that overcomes this prob-lem is to accept the prototype object assigned to the `MoreComplex` constructor, but to tweak it so that it inherits properties from `Complex.prototype` instead of from `Object.prototype`. To do this, we replace this line of code:

```
MoreComplex.prototype = new Complex(0,0);
```

with this line:

```
MoreComplex.prototype.__proto__ = Complex.prototype;
```

Since this new line does not overwrite the prototype object assigned to the `More-Complex()` constructor, we retain the correct value of the `constructor` property. You are not expected to understand how setting the `__proto__` property tweaks the inheritance chain and makes this subclass work; see section 11.4, "More About Prototypes," for an explanation. You should be aware, however, that the `__proto__` property has not been standardized, and there is a chance that it will change or be deprecated in future versions of the language.

8.6 *Objects as Associative Arrays*

We've seen the `.` operator used to access the properties of an object. It is also possible to use the `[ ]` operator, more commonly used with arrays, to access these properties. Thus, the following two JavaScript expressions have the same value:

```
object.property
object["property"]
```

The important difference to note between these two syntaxes is that in the first, the property name is an identifier, and in the second, the property name is a string. We'll see why this is so important shortly.

In C, C++, Java, and similar strongly typed languages, an object can have only a fixed number of properties, and the names of these properties must be defined in advance. Since JavaScript is a loosely typed language, this rule does not apply—a program can create any number of properties in any object. When you use the `.` operator to access a property of an object, however, the name of the property is expressed as an identifier. Identifiers must be typed literally into your JavaScript program—they are not a data type, so they cannot be manipulated by the program.

On the other hand, when you access a property of an object with the `[ ]` array notation, the name of the property is expressed as a string. Strings are JavaScript data types, so they can be manipulated and created while a program is running. So, for example, you could write the following code in JavaScript:

```
var addr = "";
for(i = 0; i < 4; i++) {
```

```
        addr += customer["address" + i]
    }
```

This code reads and concatenates the address0, address1, address2, and address3 properties of the customer object.

The code fragment above demonstrates the flexibility of using array notation to access properties of an object with string expressions. We could have written that example using the . notation, but there are cases where only the array notation will do. Suppose, for example, that you are writing a program that uses network resources to compute the current value of the user's stock market investments. The program allows the user to type in the name of each stock she owns, as well as the number of shares of each stock. You might use an object named portfolio to hold this information. The object has one property for each stock. The name of the property is the name of the stock and the property value is the number of shares of that stock. So, for example, if a user holds 50 shares of stock in Netscape Communications Corporation, the portfolio.nscp property has the value 50.

Part of this program needs to have a loop that prompts the user to enter the name of a stock she owns, and then asks her to enter the number of shares she owns of that stock. Inside the loop, you'd have code something like the following:

```
    var stock_name = get_stock_name_from_user();
    var shares = get_number_of_shares();
    portfolio[stock_name] = shares;
```

Since the user enters stock names at runtime, there is no way that you can know the property names ahead of time. Since you can't know the property names when you write the program, there is no way you can use the . operator to access the properties of the portfolio object. You can use the [] operator, however, because it uses a string value (which is dynamic and can change at runtime), rather than an identifier (which is static and must be hardcoded in the program), to name the property.

When an object is used this fashion, it is often called an *associative array*—a data structure that allows you to dynamically associate arbitrary data values with arbitrary strings. JavaScript objects are actually implemented internally as associative arrays. The . notation for accessing properties makes them seem like the static objects of C++ and Java, and they work perfectly well in that capacity. But they also have the powerful ability to associate values with arbitrary strings. In this respect, JavaScript objects are much more like Perl arrays than C++ or Java objects.

Chapter 6 introduced the for/in loop. The real power of this JavaScript statement becomes clear when we consider its use with associative arrays. To return to the stock portfolio example, we might use the following code after the user has entered her portfolio and we are computing its current total value:

```
var value = 0;
for (stock in portfolio) {  // For each stock in the portfolio
    // get the per share value and multiply it by the number of shares.
    value += get_share_value(stock) * portfolio[stock];
}
```

We cannot write this code without the for/in loop because the names of the stocks aren't known in advance. This is the only way to extract those property names from the associative array (or JavaScript object) named portfolio.

8.7 Object Properties and Methods

All objects in JavaScript inherit from the Object class. While more specialized classes, like the built-in String class and or a user-defined Complex class, define properties and methods of their own, all objects, whatever their class, also support the properties and methods defined by the Object class. Because of their universality, these properties and methods are of particular interest.

8.7.1 The constructor Property

Starting with JavaScript 1.1, every object has a constructor property that refers to the constructor function that was used to initialize the object. For example, if I create an object o with the Complex() constructor, the property o.constructor refers to Complex:

```
var o = new Complex(1,2);
o.constructor == Complex;              // Evaluates to true
```

Each Complex object (or object of whatever type) does not have its own unique constructor property, of course; instead, this property is inherited from the prototype object. As discussed earlier in the chapter, JavaScript creates a prototype object for each constructor function we define and assigns that object to the prototype property of the constructor. What I did not reveal earlier in the chapter, however, is that the prototype object is not initially empty. When created, it includes a constructor property that refers to the constructor function. That is, for any function f, f.prototype.constructor is always equal to f.

Since the constructor function defines the class of an object, the constructor property can be a powerful tool for determining the type of any given object. For example, you might use code like the following to determine the type of an unknown object:

```
if ((typeof n == "object") && (n.constructor == Number))
    // Then do something with the Number object...
```

The existence of the constructor property is not always guaranteed, however. The author of a class might replace the prototype object of a constructor with an entirely new object, for example, and the new object might not have a valid constructor property.

8.7.2 The toString() Method

The toString() method takes no arguments; it returns a string that somehow represents the type and/or value of the object it is invoked on. JavaScript invokes this method of an object whenever it needs to convert the object to a string. This occurs, for example, when you use the + operator to concatenate a string with an object or when you pass an object to a method like alert() or document.write().

The default toString() method is not very informative. For example, the following lines of code simply cause the browser to display the string "[object Object]":

```
c = new Circle(1, 0, 0);
document.write(c);
```

Because this default method does not display much useful information, many classes define their own versions of toString(). For example, when an array is converted to a string, we obtain a list of the array elements, themselves each converted to a string, and when a function is converted to a string, we obtain the source code for the function.

The idea behind toString() is that each class of objects has its own particular string representation, so it should define an appropriate toString() method to convert objects to that string form. Thus, when you define a class, you should define a custom toString() method for it so that instances of the class can be converted to meaningful strings. The string should contain information about the object being converted, as this is very useful for debugging purposes. If the string conversion is chosen carefully, it can also be useful in programs themselves.

The code below shows a toString() method we might define for the Circle class of Example 8-5:

```
Circle.prototype.toString = function () {
    return "[Circle of radius " + this.r + ", centered at ("
        + this.x + ", " + this.y + ").]";
}
```

With this `toString()` method defined, a typical Circle object might be converted to the string "[Circle of radius 1, centered at (0,0).]".

If you look back at Example 8-6, you'll see that it defines a `toString()` method for our `Complex` class of complex numbers.

One interesting feature of the default `toString()` method defined by the `Object` class is that it reveals some internal type information about built-in objects. This default `toString()` method always returns a string of the form "[object *class*]", where *class* is the class of the object. This *class* might be a built-in object type like "Object," "Array," or "Function." In client-side JavaScript, it might be a client-side type like "Window," "Form," and so on. Thus, we can use this default `toString()` method to inspect the type of an unknown object, which is a technique I often find useful when debugging. The trick, though, is to invoke the `toString()` method of the Object class rather than the more specialized methods defined by classes like Array and Function. In JavaScript 1.2, you can invoke the default `toString()` method on an object o like this:

```
Object.prototype.toString.apply(o);
```

As you can see, this line of code invokes the `toString()` method defined by the Object class, instead of invoking whatever customized method was defined for the object o.

8.7.3 The toString() and toSource() Methods

There is an exception to the behavior described above for the default `toString()` method. In Navigator 4, when the LANGUAGE attribute of the <SCRIPT> tag is explicitly set to "JavaScript1.2", the default `toString()` method returns a string that lists all the properties of the object, along with their values, using object literal syntax. Consider the `Complex` class defined in Example 8-6, for example. If this class did not define a custom `toString()` method, Complex objects would be converted to the string "[object Object]". In the special case where the LANGUAGE attribute is set, however, the default `toString()` method would return a much more interesting result. Consider this client-side code:

```
<SCRIPT LANGUAGE="JavaScript1.2">
  var c = new Complex(1,2);
  alert(Object.prototype.toString.apply(c));
</SCRIPT>
```

This code displays the string "{x:1,y:2}".

The Navigator 4 special case behavior of `toString()` when the LANGUAGE attribute is explicitly set to "JavaScript1.2" is actually quite powerful. Note that the return value of `toString()` is always a legal object literal string, suitable to be passed to the eval() function. Also note that this version of toString() recursively converts nested objects to strings. Thus, we can make complete copies of trees of objects with code like this:

```
var treecopy = eval(tree.toString());
```

Despite the power of this variation on toString(), this behavior violates the ECMA specification. Thus, in JavaScript 1.3, we can expect toString() to return to its original behavior. In addition, we can expect every object to support a toSource() method that will convert it to a string in legal JavaScript literal syntax. While it is common for classes to provide their own definition of toString(), toSource() is a method that should not be overridden; it works best if left as is.

8.7.4 *The valueOf() Method*

The valueOf() method is much like the toString() method, but it is called when JavaScript needs to convert an object to some primitive type other than a string, typically a number. The function should return a number, boolean, or function that somehow represents the value of the object referred to by the this keyword.

By definition, objects are not primitive values, so most objects do not have a primitive equivalent. Thus, the valueOf() method defined by the Object class performs no conversion and simply returns the object that it is invoked on. Classes like Number and Boolean have obvious primitive equivalents, so they override the valueOf() method to return appropriate primitive values. This is the reason that Number and Boolean objects can behave so much like their equivalent primitive values.

Occasionally, you may define a class that has some reasonable primitive equivalent. In this case, you may want to define a custom valueOf() method for the class. If you refer back to Example 8-6, you'll see that we defined a valueOf() method for the Complex class. This method simply returned the real part of the complex number. Thus, when a Complex object is used in a numeric context, it behaves as if it were a real number without its imaginary component. Consider the following code:

```
var a = new Complex(5,4);
var b = new Complex(2,1);
var c = Complex.subtract(a,b);    // c is the complex number {3,3}.
var d = a - b;                    // d is the number 3.
```

One note of caution about defining a valueOf() method: the valueOf() method can, in some circumstances, take priority over the toString() method when converting an object to a string. Thus, when you define a valueOf() method for a class, you may need to be more explicit about calling the toString() method when you want to force an object of that class to be converted to a string. To continue with the Complex example:

```
alert("c = " + c);            // Uses valueOf(). Displays "c = 3";
alert("c = " + c.toString()); // Displays "c = {3,3}";
```

One reason for this problem with the valueOf() method affecting the conversion of an object to a string is that valueOf() is overburdened: it is called to convert an object to some other type, but there is no indication of the desired type. In some circumstances, Navigator 4 does actually pass an argument to valueOf(). This argument, if specified, is a string, such as "number", "boolean", or "function", that specifies the type of the desired conversion. In other circumstances, however, valueOf() is called with no argument, and in this case, the method itself must decide what its most natural return format is. Currently, the type argument to valueOf() is implemented only in Navigator 4, and it is not clear whether it will be standardized by ECMA and adopted by Internet Explorer.

8.7.5 *The watch() and unwatch() Methods*

JavaScript 1.2 in Navigator 4 introduces two new methods that are useful primarily for debugging. The watch() method sets a watchpoint for a named property of an object, and unwatch() removes the watchpoint. Note that watch() and unwatch() are methods that you call, not methods that you override in class definitions, like toString() and valueOf().

You invoke watch() for a particular object. The method takes two arguments: the name of the property to be watched and a handler function that is invoked any time the value of that property changes. This handler function can take any action you want when the property changes; for example, it might use the client-side alert() method to notify you of the change. The return value of the handler function becomes the new value of the property, so the function even has the power to veto or override the new value of the property.

The handler function is passed three arguments: the name of the property being changed, its original value, and the new value being proposed for it. The actual value set on the property is whatever value the handler returns. So, for example, to make all properties of an object read-only, you could use a handler and the watch() method like this:

```
// This handler function vetoes any changes to a property.
function readOnlyHandler(propertyName, originalValue, proposedValue) {
    if (proposedValue != originalValue)
        alert("Property " + propertyName + " is read only.");
    return originalValue;
}
```

```
// Now we can use watch() and the handler to make all properties of an
// object read-only.
for(i in o) o.watch(i, readOnlyHandler);
```

For debugging purposes, you might want to use watch() to notify you when a global variable changes. Note that invoking watch() as a function rather than a method is equivalent to invoking it as a method of the global object where global variables are stored. The following code demonstrates this:

```
function watchHandler(varname, original, proposed) {
    alert("Variable " + varname + " has been changed.\n" +
          "Original value: " + original + "\n" +
          "New value: " + proposed);
    return proposed;
}


var x;  // The variable we want to watch
watch('x', watchHandler);
```

As a final example, suppose we are defining a new class that has a property that must always contain an uppercase string. We can enforce this constraint with an appropriate watch() handler set in the constructor function. Note that we've specified the handler function with an unnamed function literal directly in the argument list to watch():

```
function Person(firstname, lastname) {
    this.watch('lastname',
               function(name, original, proposed) {
                   if (typeof proposed != "string") return original;
                   return proposed.toUpperCase();
               });
    this.firstname = firstname;
    this.lastname = lastname;
}
```

The unwatch() method simply undoes the effect of watch(). It is passed a single string argument that specifies a property name and cancels any previous watch() call in effect for that property.

9

Arrays

Chapter 8, *Objects*, documented the JavaScript object type—a data structure that contains named pieces of data. This chapter documents the array type—a data structure that contains numbered pieces of data. Note that the arrays we'll be discussing in this chapter are different than the associative arrays described in the previous chapter. Associative arrays associate values with strings. The arrays described in this chapter are just regular numeric arrays—they associate values with numbers (with non-negative integers, to be precise).

Throughout this book, we often treat objects and arrays as if they were distinct data types. This is a useful and reasonable simplification; you can treat objects and arrays as separate types for most of your JavaScript programming. To fully understand the behavior of objects and arrays, however, you have to know the truth: an array is nothing more than an object with a thin layer of extra functionality. We see this when we use the `typeof` operator: applied to an array value, it returns the string "object".

This chapter documents basic array syntax, array programming techniques, and methods that operate on arrays. Note that arrays changed fairly dramatically between JavaScript 1.0 and JavaScript 1.1. In JavaScript 1.0, arrays were identical to objects and had only rudimentary functionality. In JavaScript 1.1, some basic new features and robust support were added—arrays became much more useful and usable. Most of this chapter, therefore, applies only to JavaScript 1.1 and later. A section at the end of the chapter summarizes the shortcomings of arrays prior to JavaScript 1.1.

9.1 Arrays and Array Elements

An array is a data type that contains or stores numbered pieces of data. Each numbered datum is called an *element* of the array, and the number assigned to an element is called its *index*. Because JavaScript is an untyped language, an element of an array may be of any type, and different elements of the same array may be of different types. Array elements may even contain other arrays; this allows you to create data structures that are arrays of arrays.

9.1.1 Creating Arrays

In JavaScript 1.1 and later, arrays are created with the `Array()` constructor and the `new` operator. You can invoke the `Array()` constructor in three distinct ways. The first is to call it with no arguments:

```
var a = new Array();
```

This method creates an empty array with no elements.

The second method of invoking the `Array()` constructor allows you to explicitly specify values for the first *n* elements of an array:

```
var a = new Array(5, 4, 3, 2, 1, "testing, testing");
```

In this form, the constructor takes a list of arguments. Each argument specifies an element value and may be of any type. Elements are assigned to the array starting with element 0. The `length` property of the array is set to the number of arguments passed to the constructor.

The third way to invoke the `Array()` constructor is to call it with a single numeric argument, which specifies a length:

```
var a = new Array(10);
```

This technique creates an array with the specified number of elements (each of which has the undefined value). It also sets the `length` property of the array to the value specified.

Note that this third constructor syntax overrides the second syntax shown above: if you pass a single numeric argument, you specify an array length, not a single element value. There is one exception, however. In Navigator 4 and later, if you specify the `LANGUAGE="JavaScript1.2"` attribute in your `<SCRIPT>` tag, JavaScript does not recognize this third form of the constructor. In this case, passing a single numeric argument to `Array()` simply creates an array with a length of one and initializes its single element to the specified value. This behavior is not part of the ECMA standard and will presumably remain a special case in Navigator for scripts that explicitly specify JavaScript 1.2.

Finally, JavaScript 1.2 introduces array literals, which provide another way to create arrays. An array literal allows us to embed an array value directly into a JavaScript program in the same way that we define a string literal by placing the string text between quotation marks. To create an array literal, simply place a comma-separated list of values between square brackets. For example:

```
var primes = [2, 3, 5, 7, 11];
var a = ['a', true, 4.78];
```

Array literals can contain object literals or other array literals:

```
var b = [[1,{x:1, y:2}], [2, {x:3, y:4}]];
```

9.1.2 Reading and Writing Array Elements

You access an element of an array using the [ ] operator. A reference to the array should appear to the left of the brackets. An arbitrary expression that has a non-negative integer value should be inside the brackets. You can use this syntax to both read and write the value of an element of an array. Thus, the following are all legal JavaScript:

```
value = a[0];
a[1] = 3.14;
i = 2;
a[i] = 3;
a[i + 1] = "hello";
a[a[i]] = a[0];
```

In some languages, the first element of an array is at index 1. In JavaScript, as well as in C, C++, and Java, however, the first element of an array is at index 0.

As we saw in Chapter 8, the [ ] operator can also be used to access object properties:

```
my['salary'] *= 2;
```

This is a clue that tells us that objects and arrays are fundamentally the same thing.

9.1.3 Adding New Elements to an Array

In languages like C and Java, an array has a fixed number of elements that must be specified when you create the array. This is not the case in JavaScript—an array can have any number of elements and you can change the number of elements at any time.

To add a new element to an array, simply assign a value to it:

```
a[10] = 10;
```

Arrays in JavaScript are *sparse*. This means that array indexes need not fall into a contiguous range of numbers; memory is allocated only for those array elements that are actually stored in the array. Thus, when you execute the following lines of code, JavaScript allocates memory only for array indexes 0 and 10,000 and not for the 9,999 indexes between:

```
a[0] = 1;
a[10000] = "this is element 10,000";
```

Note that array elements can also be added to objects:

```
var c = new Circle(1,2,3);
c[0] = "this is an array element of an object!"
```

However, as we'll see later, merely adding array elements to an object does not make it an array. Arrays created with the `Array()` constructor or an array literal have some special features that objects do not share.

9.1.4 Array Length

All arrays, whether created with the `Array()` constructor or defined with an array literal, have a special `length` property that specifies how many elements the array contains. More precisely, since arrays can have undefined elements, the `length` property is *always* one larger than the largest element number in the array. Unlike regular object properties, the `length` property of an array is automatically updated to maintain this invariant when new elements are added to the array. The following code illustrates:

```
var a = new Array();    // a.length == 0  (no elements defined)
a = new Array(10);      // a.length == 10 (empty elements 0-9 defined)
a = new Array(1,2,3);   // a.length == 3  (elements 0-2 defined)
a = [4, 5];             // a.length == 2  (elements 0 and 1 defined)
a[5] = -1;              // a.length == 6  (elements 0, 1, and 5 defined)
a[49] = 0;              // a.length == 50 (elements 0, 1, 5, and 49 defined)
```

Probably the most common use of the `length` property of an array is to allow us to loop through the elements of an array:

```
var fruits = ["mango", "banana", "cherry", "pear"];
for(var i = 0; i < fruits.length; i++)
    alert(fruits[i]);
```

This example assumes, of course, that elements of the array are contiguous and begin at element 0. If this were not the case, we would want to test that each array element was defined before using it:

```
for(var i = 0; i < fruits.length; i++)
    if (fruits[i]) alert(fruits[i]);
```

The length property of an array is a read/write value. If you set length to a value smaller than its current value, the array is truncated to the new length; any elements that no longer fit are discarded and their values are lost. If you make length larger than its current value, new, undefined elements are added at the end of the array to increase it to the newly specified size.

Truncating an array by setting its length property is the only way that you can actually remove elements from an array. If you use the delete operator to delete an array element, that element becomes undefined, but the length property does not change.

Note that although objects can be assigned array elements, they do not have a length property. The length property, with its special behavior, is one of the features that give arrays a distinct identity in JavaScript 1.1 and later.

9.1.5 Multidimensional Arrays

JavaScript does not support true multidimensional arrays, but it does allow you to approximate them quite nicely with arrays of arrays. To access a data element in an array of arrays, simply use the [ ] operator twice. For example, suppose the variable matrix is an array of arrays of numbers. Every element matrix[x] is an array of numbers. To access a particular number within this array, you would write matrix[x][y].

9.2 Array Methods

In addition to the [ ] operator, arrays can also be manipulated through various methods provided by the Array class. The following sections introduce these methods. Many of the methods were inspired in part by the Perl programming language; Perl programmers may find them comfortingly familiar. As usual, this is an overview only; complete details can be found in the reference section. Also, note that none of these methods are available prior to JavaScript 1.1, and some have been introduced in JavaScript 1.2.

9.2.1 join()

The `Array.join()` method, defined in JavaScript 1.1, converts all the elements of an array to a string and concatenates them. You can specify an optional string that is used to separate the elements in the resulting string. If no separator string is specified, a comma is used. For example, the following lines of code produce the string "1,2,3":

```
var a = [1, 2, 3];  // Create a new array with these three elements.
s = a.join();       // s == "1,2,3"
```

The following invocation specifies the optional separator to produce a slightly different result:

```
s = a.join(", ");   // s == "1, 2, 3". Note the space after the comma.
```

The `Array.join()` method is the inverse of the `String.split()` method, which creates an array by breaking a string up into pieces.

9.2.2 reverse()

The `Array.reverse()` method (defined in JavaScript 1.1) reverses the order of the elements of an array. It does this in place—in other words, it doesn't create a new array with the elements rearranged, but instead rearranges them in the already existing array. For example, the following code, which uses the `reverse()` and the `join()` methods, produces the string "3,2,1":

```
a = new Array(1,2,3);  // a[0] = 1; a[1] = 2; a[2] = 3;
a.reverse();           // now a[0] = 3; a[1] = 2; a[2] = 1;
s = a.join();          // s == "3,2,1"
```

9.2.3 sort()

Another JavaScript 1.1 array method is `Array.sort()`, which sorts the elements of an array. Like the `reverse()` method, it does this in place. When `sort()` is called with no arguments, it sorts the array elements in alphabetical order (temporarily converting them to strings to perform the comparison, if necessary):

```
a = new Array("banana", "cherry", "apple");
a.sort();
s = a.join(", ");  // s == "apple, banana, cherry".
```

To sort an array into some order other than alphabetical, you must pass a comparison function as an argument to `sort()`. This function has the job of deciding which of its two arguments should appear first in the sorted array. If the first argument should appear before the second, the comparison function should return a number less than zero. If the first argument should appear after the second in the sorted array, the function should return a number greater than zero. And if the two values are equivalent (i.e., their order is irrelevant), the comparison function should return 0. So, for example, to sort array elements into numerical, rather than alphabetical order, you might do the following:

```
var a = [33, 4, 1111, 222];
a.sort();               // Alphabetical order:  1111, 222, 33, 4
a.sort(function(a,b) {  // Numerical order: 4, 33, 222, 1111
        return a-b;
     });
```

Note the convenient use of a function literal, or lambda function, in the code above. Since the comparison function is used only once, there is no need to give it a name. In JavaScript 1.1, you could use an anonymous function created with the Function() constructor here.

As another example of sorting array items, you might perform a case-insensitive alphabetical sort on an array of strings by passing a comparison function that converts both of its arguments to lowercase (with the toLowerCase() method) before comparing them. You can probably think of other comparison functions that sort numbers into various esoteric orders: reverse numerical order, odd numbers before even numbers, etc. The possibilities become more interesting, of course, when the array elements you are comparing are objects, rather than simple types like numbers or strings.

9.2.4 concat()

The Array.concat() method, new in JavaScript 1.2, creates and returns an array that contains the elements of the original array that concat() was invoked on, followed by each of the arguments to concat(). If any of these arguments is itself an array, it is flattened and its elements are added to the returned array. Note, however, that concat() does not recursively flatten arrays of arrays. Here are some examples:

```
var a = [1,2,3];
a.concat(4, 5)          // Returns [1,2,3,4,5]
a.concat([4,5]);        // Returns [1,2,3,4,5]
a.concat([4,5],[6,7])   // Returns [1,2,3,4,5,6,7]
a.concat(4, [5,[6,7]])  // Returns [1,2,3,4,5,[6,7]]
```

9.2.5 slice()

The `Array.slice()` method, also new in JavaScript 1.2, returns a slice, or sub-array, of the specified array. Its two arguments specify the start and end of the slice to be returned. The returned array contains the element specified by the first argument and contains all subsequent elements up to, but not including, the element specified by the second argument. If only one argument is specified, the returned array contains all elements from the start position to the end of the array. If either argument is negative, it specifies an array element relative to the last element in the array. An argument of -1, for example, specifies the last element in the array, and an argument of -3 specifies the third from last element of the array. Here are some examples:

```
var a = [1,2,3,4,5];
a.slice(0,3);     // Returns [1,2,3]
a.slice(3);       // Returns [4,5]
a.slice(1,-1);    // Returns [2,3,4]
a.slice(-3,-2);   // Returns [3]. Buggy in IE 4: returns [1,2,3]
```

9.2.6 splice()

The `Array.splice()` method (new in Navigator 4, but not supported by Internet Explorer 4) is a general-purpose method for inserting or removing elements from an array. `splice()` modifies the array in place; it does not return a new array as `slice()` and `concat()` do. Note that `splice()` and `slice()` have very similar names but perform substantially different operations.

`splice()` can delete elements from an array, insert new elements into an array, or perform both operations at the same time. Array elements that appear after the insertion or deletion are moved as necessary so that they remain contiguous with the rest of the array. The first argument to `splice()` specifies the array position at which the insertion and/or deletion is to begin. The second argument specifies the number of elements that should be deleted from (spliced out of) the array. If this second argument is omitted, all array elements from the start element to the end of the array are removed. `splice()` returns an array of the deleted elements, or an empty array if no elements were deleted.

There is a bug in Navigator 4, however: if one element is deleted, Navigator 4 returns the element, not an array; and if no elements are deleted, Navigator 4 returns nothing instead of the empty array. For example:

```
var a = [1,2,3,4,5,6,7,8]
a.splice(4);    // Returns [5,6,7,8]. a is [1,2,3,4].
a.splice(1,2);  // Returns [2,3]. a is [1,4]
a.splice(1,1);  // Should return [4]. Nav 4 returns 4.  a is [1]
```

The first two arguments to splice() specify which array elements are to be deleted. These arguments may be followed by any number of additional arguments that specify elements to be inserted into the array starting at the position specified by the first argument. For example:

```
a = [1,2,3,4,5]
a.splice(2,0,'a','b');  // Should return []. Nav 4 returns nothing...
                        // ...modifies a to  [1,2,'a','b',3,4,5].
a.splice(2,2,[1,2],3);  // Returns ['a','b']. a is [1,2,[1,2],3,3,4,5].
```

Note that, unlike concat(), splice() does not flatten array arguments that it inserts. That is, if it is passed an array to insert, it inserts the array itself, not the elements of that array.

9.2.7 *push() and pop()*

push() and pop() are a pair of methods, new in Navigator 4 but not supported by Internet Explorer 4, that allows us to work with arrays as if they were stacks. The push() method appends one or more new elements to the end of an array and returns the last value it appends. The pop() method does the reverse: it deletes the last element of an array, decrements the array length, and returns the value that it removed. Note that both of these methods modify the array in place rather than producing a modified copy of the array. The combination of push() and pop() allows us to use a JavaScript array to implement a first in, last out (FILO) stack. For example:

```
var stack = [];         // stack: []
stack.push(1, 2);       // stack: [1,2]      Returns 2
stack.pop();            // stack: [1]        Returns 2
stack.push(3);          // stack: [1,3]      Returns 3
stack.pop();            // stack: [1]        Returns 3
stack.push([4,5]);      // stack: [1,[4,5]]  Returns [4,5]
stack.pop()             // stack: [1]        Returns [4,5]
stack.pop();            // stack: []         Returns 1
```

9.2.8 *unshift() and shift()*

unshift() and shift() are another pair of methods that are new in Navigator 4 and not defined by Internet Explorer 4. They behave much like push() and pop(), except that they insert and remove elements from the beginning of an array, rather than from the end. unshift() adds an element or elements to the beginning of the array, shifts the existing array elements up to higher indexes to make room, and returns the new length of the array. `shift()` removes and returns the first element of the array, shifting all subsequent elements down one place to occupy the newly vacant space at the start of the array. For example:

```
var a = [];           // a:[]
a.unshift(1);         // a:[1]             Returns: 1
a.unshift(22);        // a:[22,1]          Returns: 2
a.shift();            // a:[1]             Returns: 22
a.unshift(3,[4,5]);   // a:[3,[4,5],1]     Returns: 3
a.shift();            // a:[[4,5],1]       Returns: 3
a.shift();            // a:[1]             Returns: [4,5]
a.shift();            // a:[]              Returns: 1
```

Note the possibly surprising behavior of `unshift()` when invoked with multiple arguments. Instead of being inserted into the array one at a time, arguments are inserted all at once (as with the `splice()` method). This means that they appear in the resulting array in the same order in which they appeared in the argument list. Had the elements been inserted one at a time, their order would have been reversed.

9.2.9 *toString() and toSource()*

An array, like any JavaScript object, has a `toString()` method. For an array, this method converts each of its elements to a string (calling the `toString()` methods of its elements, if necessary) and outputs a comma-separated list of those strings. Note that the output does not include square brackets or any other sort of delimiter around the array value. For example:

```
[1,2,3].toString()          // Yields '1,2,3'
["a", "b", "c"].toString()  // Yields 'a,b,c'
[1, [2,'c']].toString()     // Yields '1,2,c'
```

Note that `toString()` returns the same string as the `join()` method does when it is invoked with no arguments.

There is one exception to the behavior described above. In Navigator 4, when the `LANGUAGE` attribute of `<SCRIPT>` is set to "JavaScript1.2", `toString()` behaves in a more complex way. In this case, it converts arrays to strings that include square brackets, so that the resulting strings are valid array literal expressions. These strings are valid JavaScript code and can be passed to the `eval()` function. So, if we ran the code shown above in an environment that explicitly specifies JavaScript 1.2 behavior, we would obtain results with slight, but important, differences:

```
[1,2,3].toString()          // Yields '[1, 2, 3]'
["a", "b", "c"].toString()  // Yields '["a", "b", "c"]'
[1, [2,'c']].toString()     // Yields '[1, [2, "c"]]'
```

The reason for this special case behavior for JavaScript 1.2 in Navigator 4 is that the JavaScript implementors at Netscape were attempting to anticipate the ECMA specification. Unfortunately, the draft specification changed after Navigator 4 had already been released. The final version of the specification sticks to the original behavior of toString(), so the special case behavior for JavaScript 1.2 is non-conforming. Still, it is quite useful. For JavaScript 1.3, Navigator will revert to the original behavior of toString() and make the special-case behavior available through a new method named toSource().

9.3 *Arrays in JavaScript 1.0*

In JavaScript 1.0, support for arrays was very rudimentary. It consisted of little more than the JavaScript syntax that allowed us to refer to object properties with the array [ ] operator. In JavaScript 1.0, there were no Array() constructor and array methods. User-defined arrays did not have a length property, although built-in client-side arrays, such as forms[], did have this property.

In JavaScript 1.1 and later, arrays are objects with special behavior that makes them more array-like. In JavaScript 1.0, none of this special behavior was implemented, so arrays were exactly the same thing as objects. This was made very clear by the fact that the only way to create an array in JavaScript 1.0 was with the Object() constructor:

```
fruits = new Object();
fruits[0] = "apple";
fruits[1] = "banana";
```

Despite the lack of array-specific features, we could still simulate arrays in JavaScript 1.0 by using the [ ] operator to access numeric property names of objects. Unfortunately, however, the use of arrays in JavaScript 1.0 was complicated by a serious design flaw. In this early version of the language, named object properties and numbered array elements shared the same set of internal slots. Named properties were assigned the next available slot number, and numbered array elements corresponded directly to slot numbers. Thus, in JavaScript 1.0, properties and array elements were not independent and could actually overwrite each other. The following code illustrates the problem:

```
p = new Object(); // Arrays in JavaScript 1.0 share "slots."
p.name = "david"; // Sets slot 0. p.name == p[0] == "david"
p[0] = "frank";    // Overwrites the property. p.name == "frank"
```

The fact that object properties and array elements overlapped in JavaScript 1.0 meant that you had to be very careful when using both in an object. The best policy was to treat objects either as pure objects with only named properties or as pure arrays with only numbered elements. If you needed to keep track of how many elements an array contained, the easiest way to do so was in a separate variable that you updated whenever the size of the array changed. A common technique was to begin your arrays at slot 1 and reserve slot 0 for the array length. For example, you can still find array constructor functions like the following in old JavaScript code:

```
function EmptyArray(length) {
    this.size = length;  // Sets slot 0 in JavaScript 1.0
    this[0] = length;    // Sets slot 0 in other versions
    // Slots 1 and up are used for actual array elements.
    for(var i = 1; i <= length; i++) this[i] = 0;
}
```

10

In this chapter:
- *Defining Regular Expressions*
- *String Methods for Pattern Matching*
- *The RegExp Object*
- *RegExp Methods for Pattern Matching*
- *RegExp Instance Properties*
- *RegExp Class Properties*

Pattern Matching with Regular Expressions

A *regular expression* is an object that describes a pattern of characters. The JavaScript RegExp and String objects define methods that use regular expression patterns to perform powerful pattern matching and textual search-and-replace functions.*

This chapter defines the syntax that regular expressions use to describe textual patterns. It also describes the String and RegExp methods and properties used in conjunction with regular expressions. Note that regular expressions and the methods that use them are new in JavaScript 1.2. None of the features described in this chapter is available in earlier versions of the language.

10.1 Defining Regular Expressions

In JavaScript, regular expressions are represented by a RegExp object. RegExp objects may be created with the `RegExp()` constructor, of course, but they may also be created literally with a special language syntax added in JavaScript 1.2. Just as string literals are specified as characters within quotation marks, regular expression literals are specified as characters within a pair of slash (/) characters. Thus, your JavaScript code may contain lines like the following:

```
var pattern = /s$/;
```

This line creates a new RegExp object and assigns it to the variable `pattern`. This particular RegExp object matches any string that ends with the letter "s". (We'll talk

---

* The term "regular expression" is an obscure one that dates back many years. The syntax used to describe a textual pattern is indeed a type of expression. However, as we'll see, that syntax is far from regular! A regular expression is sometimes called a "regexp" or even an "RE."

about the grammar for defining patterns shortly.) This regular expression could have equivalently been defined with the RegExp() constructor like this:

```
var pattern = new RegExp("s$");
```

Creating a RegExp object, either literally or with the RegExp() constructor, is the easy part. The more difficult task is describing the desired pattern of characters using regular expression syntax. JavaScript adopts a fairly complete subset of the regular expression syntax used by Perl, so if you are an experienced Perl programmer, you already know how to describe patterns in JavaScript.*

Regular expression pattern specifications consist of a series of characters. Most characters, including all alphanumeric characters, simply describe characters to be matched literally. Thus, the regular expression /java/ matches any string that contains the substring "java". Other characters in regular expressions are not matched literally, but have special significance. The regular expression /s$/ contains two characters. The first, "s", matches itself literally. The second, "$", is a special metacharacter that matches the end of a string. Thus, this regular expression matches any string that contains the letter "s" as its last character.

The following sections describe the various characters and metacharacters used in JavaScript regular expressions. Note, however, that a complete tutorial on regular expression grammar is beyond the scope of this book. For complete details of the syntax, consult a book on Perl, such as *Programming Perl*, by Larry Wall, Tom Christiansen, and Randal L. Schwartz (O'Reilly). *Mastering Regular Expressions*, by Jeffrey E.F. Friedl (O'Reilly) is another excellent source of information on regular expressions.

10.1.1 Literal Characters

As we've seen, all alphabetic characters and digits match themselves literally in regular expressions. JavaScript regular expression syntax also supports certain non-alphabetic characters through escape sequences that begin with a backslash (\). For example, the sequence "\n" matches a literal newline character in a string. A number of punctuation characters have special meanings in regular expressions. I'll be introducing these characters and their meanings in the sections that follow. If you want to include the special punctuation characters literally in a regular expression, you must precede them with a \. Table 10-1 lists these characters.

---

* JavaScript 1.2 adopts Perl 4 regular expressions. JavaScript 1.3 will probably extend regular expression support to include Perl 5 regular expression features.

Table 10-1: Regular Expression Literal Characters

Character	Matches
Alphanumeric character	Itself.
\f	Form feed.
\n	Newline.
\r	Carriage return.
\t	Tab.
\v	Vertical tab.
\/	A literal /.
\\	A literal \.
\.	A literal .
*	A literal *.
\+	A literal +.
\?	A literal ?.
|	A literal |.
\(	A literal (.
\)	A literal).
\[	A literal [.
\]	A literal].
\{	A literal {.
\}	A literal }.
\xxx.	The ASCII character specified by the octal number *xxx*.
\xnn	The ASCII character specified by the hexadecimal number *nn*.
\cX	The control character ^X. For example, \cI is equivalent to \t and \cJ is equivalent to \n.

10.1.2 Character Classes

Individual literal characters can be combined into *character classes* by placing them within square brackets. A character class matches any one character that is contained within it. Thus, the regular expression /[abc]/ matches any one of the letters "a", "b", or "c". Negated character classes can also be defined—these match any character except those contained within the brackets. A negated character class is specified by placing a caret (^) as the first character inside the left bracket. The regexp /[^abc]/ matches any one character other than "a", "b", or "c".

Character classes can use a hyphen to indicate a range of characters. The set of lowercase letters is /[a-z]/, while the set of all alphanumeric characters is /[a-zA-Z0-9]/.

Because certain character classes are commonly used, the JavaScript regular expression syntax includes special characters and escape sequences to represent these common classes. For example, \s matches the space character, the tab character, and any other whitespace character, and \S matches any character that is *not* whitespace. Table 10-2 lists these characters and summarizes character class syntax.

Note that these special character class escapes can be used within square brackets. \s matches any whitespace character and \d matches any digit, so /[\s\d]/ matches any one whitespace character or digit. Note that there is one special case. As we'll see below, the \b escape has a special meaning. When used within a character class, however, it represents the backspace character. Thus, to represent a backspace character literally in a regular expression, use the character class with one element: /[\b]/.

Table 10-2: Regular Expression Character Classes

Character	Matches
[...]	Any one character between the brackets.
[^...]	Any one character not between the brackets.
.	Any character except newline. Equivalent to [^\n].
\w	Any word character. Equivalent to [a-zA-Z0-9_].
\W	Any non-word character. Equivalent to [^a-zA-Z0-9_].
\s	Any whitespace character. Equivalent to [\t\n\r\f\v].
\S	Any non-whitespace character. Equivalent to [^ \t\n\r\f\v]. Note that \w and \S are not the same thing.
\d	Any digit. Equivalent to [0-9].
\D	Any character other than a digit. Equivalent to [^0-9].
[\b]	A literal backspace (special case).

10.1.3 Repetition

With the regular expression syntax we have learned so far, we can describe a two digit number as /\d\d/ and a four digit number as /\d\d\d\d/. But we don't have any way to describe a number that can have any number of digits or a string of three letters followed by an optional digit. These more complex patterns use regular expression syntax that specifies how many times an element of a regular expression may be repeated.

The characters that specify repetition always follow the pattern they are being applied to. Because certain types of repetition are quite commonly used, there are special characters to represent these cases. For example, + matches one or more occurrences of the previous pattern. Table 10-3 summarizes the repetition syntax. The following lines show some examples:

```
/\d{2,4}/     // Match between 2 and 4 digits.
/\w{3}\d?/    // Match exactly three word characters and an optional digit.
/\s+java\s+/  // Match "java" with one or more spaces before and after.
/[^"]*/       // Match zero or more non-quote characters.
```

Table 10-3: Regular Expression Repetition Characters

Character	Meaning
{n,m}	Match the previous item at least *n* times but no more than *m* times.
{n,}	Match the previous item *n* or more times.
{n}	Match exactly *n* occurrences of the previous item.
?	Match zero or one occurrences of the previous item. That is, the previous item is optional. Equivalent to {0,1}.
+	Match one or more occurrences of the previous item. Equivalent to {1,}.
*	Match zero or more occurrences of the previous item. Equivalent to {0,}.

10.1.4 *Alternation, Grouping, and References*

The regular expression grammar includes special characters for specifying alternatives, for grouping subexpressions, and for referring to previous subexpressions. The | character separates alternatives. For example, /ab|cd|ef/ matches the string "ab" or the string "cd" or the string "ef". And /\d{3}|[a-z]{4}/ matches either three digits or four lowercase letters.

Parentheses have several purposes in regular expressions. Primarily, they group separate items into a single subexpression, so that the items can be treated as a single unit by *, +, ?, and so on. For example, /java(script)?/ matches "java" followed by the optional "script". And /(ab|cd)+|ef)/ matches either the string "ef", or one or more repetitions of either of the strings "ab" or "cd".

A secondary purpose of parentheses in regular expressions is to define subpatterns within the complete pattern. When a regular expression is successfully matched against a target string, it is possible to extract the portions of the target string that matched any particular parenthesized subpattern. (We'll see how these matching substrings are obtained later in the chapter.) For example, suppose we are looking for one or more lowercase letters followed by one or more digits. We might use the pattern /[a-z]+\d+/. But suppose we only really care about the digits at the end of each match. If we put that part of the pattern in parentheses (/[a-z]+(\d+)/), we can extract the digits from any matches we find, as explained later.

Another use of parenthesized subexpressions is to allow us to refer back to a subexpression later in the same regular expression. This is done by following a \ character by a digit or digits. The digits refer to the position of the parenthesized subexpression within the regular expression. For example, \1 refers back to the first subexpression and \3 refers to the third. Note that because subexpressions can be nested within others, it is the position of the left parenthesis that is counted. In the following regular expression, for example, the nested subexpression is specified as \2:

```
/([Jj]ava([Ss]cript))\sis\s(fun\w*)/
```

A reference to a previous subexpression of a regular expression does *not* refer to the pattern for that subexpression, but rather to the text that matched the pattern. Thus, references are not simply shorthand that prevent you from having to type repetitive portions of a regular expression. Instead, they enforce a constraint that separate portions of a string contain exactly the same characters. For example, the following regular expression matches any characters that are within single or double quotes. However, it does not require the opening and closing quotes to match (i.e., both single quotes or both double quotes):

```
/['"][^'"]*['"]/
```

To require the quotes to match, we can use a reference:

```
/(['"])[^'"]*\1/
```

The \1 matches whatever the first parenthesized subexpression matched. In this example, it enforces the constraint that the closing quote match the opening quote. Note that if a backslash is followed by a number larger than the number of parenthesized subexpressions, it is interpreted as an octal escape character instead of a reference. You can avoid this ambiguity by always using a full three characters for your escapes. For example, use $ instead of \44.

Later in this chapter, we'll see that a similar kind of reference can also be used in regular expression search-and-replace operations. Table 10-4 summarizes the regular expression alternation, grouping, and referencing operators.

Table 10–4: Regular Expression Alternation, Grouping, and Reference Characters

Character	Meaning
|	Alternation. Match either the subexpressions to the left or the subexpression to the right.
(...)	Grouping. Group several items into a single unit that can be used with *, +, ?, |, and so on, and remember the characters that match this group for use with later references.
\n	Match the same characters that were matched when group number *n* was first matched. Groups are subexpressions within (possibly nested) parentheses. Group numbers are assigned by counting left parentheses from left to right.

10.1.5 Specifying Match Position

We've seen that many elements of a regular expression match a single character in a string. For example, \s matches a single character of whitespace. Other regular expression elements match the zero-width spaces between characters instead of actual characters. \b for example, matches a word boundary—it matches the boundary between a \w word character and a \W non-word character. Elements like \b do not specify any characters to be used in a matched string; what they do specify, however, is legal positions at which a match can occur. Sometimes these elements are called regular expression anchors, because they anchor the pattern to a specific position in the search string. The most commonly used anchor elements are ^, which ties the pattern to the beginning of the string, and $, which anchors the pattern to the end of the string.

For example, to match the word "JavaScript" on a line by itself, we could use the regular expression /^JavaScript$/. If we wanted to search for "Java" used as a word by itself (not as a prefix as it is in "JavaScript"), we might try the pattern /\sJava\s/, which requires a space before and after the word. But there are two problems with this. First, it does not match "Java" if that word appears at the beginning or the end of a string, but only if it appears with space on either side. Second, when this pattern does find a match, the matched string it returns has leading and trailing spaces, which is not quite what we want. So instead of matching actual space characters with \s, we instead match (or anchor to) word boundaries with \b. The resulting expression is /\bJava\b/. Table 10-5 summarizes regular expression anchors.

Table 10–5: Regular Expression Anchor Characters

Character	Meaning
^	Match the beginning of the string, and, in multiline searches, the beginning of a line.
$	Match the end of the string, and, in multiline searches, the end of a line.
\b	Match a word boundary. That is, match the position between a \w character and a \W character. (Note, however, that [\b] matches backspace.)
\B	Match a position that is not a word boundary.

10.1.6 Attributes

There is one final element of the regular expression grammar. Regular expression attributes specify high-level pattern-matching rules. Unlike the rest of regular expression syntax, attributes are specified outside of the / characters: instead of appearing within the slashes, they appear following the second slash. JavaScript 1.2 supports two attributes. The i attribute specifies that pattern matching should be case-insensitive. The g attribute specifies that pattern matching should be global—that is, that all matches within the searched string should be found. Both attributes may be combined to perform a global case-insensitive match.

For example, to do a case-insensitive search for the first occurrence of the word "java" (or "Java", "JAVA", etc.), we could use the case-insensitive regular expression /\bjava\b/i. And to find all occurrences of the word in a string, we would add the g attribute: /\bjava\b/gi.

Table 10-6 summarizes these regular expression attributes. Note that we'll see more about the g attribute later in this chapter when we consider the String and RegExp methods used to actually perform matches.

Table 10–6: Regular Expression Attributes

Character	Meaning
i	Perform case-insensitive matching.
g	Perform a global match. That is, find all matches rather than stopping after the first match.

In addition to the g and i attributes, there is another attribute-like feature of regular expressions. If you set the static multiline property of the RegExp constructor to true, pattern matching is performed in multiline mode. In this mode, the ^ and $ anchor characters match not only the start and end of the search string, but also match the start and end of any lines within the search string. For example, the pattern /Java$/ matches "Java", but does not normally match "Java\nis fun". However, it does match if we first set the multiline property:

```
RegExp.multiline = true;
```

In JavaScript 1.2, setting this multiline property is the only way to perform searches in multiline mode. In JavaScript 1.3, there will probably be a new m attribute that can be used like the g and i attributes to indicate that a regular expression should be run in multiline mode.

Finally, note that client-side JavaScript sets the multiline property to true when it invokes an event handler for a TextArea object and then sets the property back to false when the event handler exits. For this reason, you cannot rely on the value of multiline remaining true. Thus, in client-side JavaScript, if you want to perform a pattern match in multiline mode, you must set the multiline property explicitly and not rely on its value remaining unchanged from some previous invocation.

10.1.7 Regular Expressions in JavaScript 1.3

JavaScript 1.2 implements Perl 4 regular expressions. In JavaScript 1.3, regular expression support is expected to be expanded to include support for several important features from Perl 5. A number of the features use the extension syntax from Perl 5, which begins with "(?". The expected new features include:

- Single-line and multi-line pattern-matching modes, with s and m attributes to select these modes.

- Repetition with minimal matching, specified with a question mark following the repetition character. For example, *? will specify zero or more repetitions but will match as few characters as possible, instead of as many as possible.

- Anchors specified by generic lookahead patterns. For example, (?=[A-Z]) matches a position right before a capital letter, and (?![A-Z]) matches a position that is not right before a capital letter. Neither pattern actually matches any characters itself.

- Parentheses for grouping but not referencing. A left parenthesis followed by ?: will serve to group a subexpression without creating a numbered reference to the text matched by that subexpression.

Because these new JavaScript 1.3 features will be based on Perl 5, you can find complete information in a Perl reference manual.

10.2 String Methods for Pattern Matching

Until now, we've been discussing the grammar used to create regular expressions, but we haven't examined how those regular expressions can actually be used in JavaScript code. In this section, we discuss methods of the String object that use regular expressions to perform pattern matching and search-and-replace operations. In the sections that follow this one, we'll continue the discussion of pattern matching with JavaScript regular expressions by discussing the RegExp object and its methods and properties. Note that the discussion that follows is merely an overview of the various methods and properties related to regular expressions. As usual, complete details can be found in the reference section of this book.

Strings support four methods that make use of regular expressions. The simplest is search(). This method takes a regular expression argument and returns the character position of the start of the first matching substring or -1 if there is no match. search() does not support global searches—it ignores the g attribute of its regular expression argument. For example, the following call returns 4:

```
"JavaScript".search(/script/i);
```

The replace() method performs a search-and-replace operation. It takes a regular expression as its first argument and a replacement string as its second argument. It searches the string it is called on for matches with the specified pattern. If the regular expression has the g attribute set, the method replaces all matches in the string with the replacement string, otherwise it replaces only the first match it finds. For example, we could use replace() as follows to provide uniform capitalization of the word "JavaScript" throughout a string of text:

```
// No matter how it is capitalized, replace it with the correct capitalization.
text.replace(/javascript/gi, "JavaScript");
```

replace() is more powerful than this, however. Recall that parenthesized subexpressions of a regular expression are numbered from left to right, and that the regular expression remembers the text that each subexpression matches. If a $ followed by a digit appears in the replacement string, replace() replaces those two characters with the text that matched the specified subexpression. This is a very useful feature. We can use it, for example, to replace straight quotes in a string with curly quotes, simulated with ASCII characters:

```
// A quote is a quotation mark followed by any number of
// non-quotation-mark characters (which we remember) followed
// by another quotation mark.
var quote = /"([^"]*)"/g;
// Replace the straight quotation marks with "curly quotes,"
```

```
// and leave the contents of the quote (stored in $1) unchanged.
text.replace(quote, "``$1''");
```

The `match()` method is the most general of the String regular expression methods. It takes a regular expression as its only argument and returns an array that contains the results of the match. If the regular expression has the g attribute, the method returns an array of all matches that appear in the string. For example:

```
"1 plus 2 equals 3".match(/\d+/g)  // returns ["1", "2", "3"]
```

On the other hand, if the regular expression does not have the g attribute, `match()` does not do a global search; it simply searches for the first match. However, `match()` returns an array even when it does not perform a global search. In this case, the first element of the array is the matching string and any remaining elements are the parenthesized subexpressions of the regular expression. Thus, if `match()` returns an array a, a[0] contains the complete match, a[1] contains the substring that matched the first parenthesized expression, and so on. To draw a parallel with the `replace()` method, a[*n*] holds the contents of $*n*.

For example, consider parsing a URL with the following code:

```
var url = /(\w+):\/\/([\w.]+)\/(\S*)/;
var text = "Visit my home page at http://www.isp.com/~david";
var result = text.match(url);
if (result != null) {
    var fullurl = result[0];   // Contains "http://www.isp.com/~david"
    var protocol = result[1];  // Contains "http"
    var host = result[2];      // Contains "www.isp.com"
    var path = result[3];      // Contains "~david"
}
```

Finally, there is one more feature of the `match()` method that you should know about. The array it returns has a `length` property, as all arrays do. When `match()` is invoked on a non-global regular expression, however, the returned array also has two other properties: the `index` property, which contains the character position within the string at which the match begins, and the `input` property, which is a copy of the target string. So in the code above, `result.index` would be equal to 21, since the matched URL begins at character position 21 in the text. And the `result.input` property would hold the same string that the `text` variable does.

The last of the regular expression methods of the String object is `split()`. This method breaks the string it is called on into an array of substrings, using the argument as a separator. For example:

```
"123,456,789".split(",");  // Returns ["123","456","789"]
```

The `split()` method exists in JavaScript 1.1, but in JavaScript 1.2 it has been extended so that we can specify a regular expression as its argument. This makes the method more powerful. For example, we can now specify a separator character that allows an arbitrary amount of whitespace on either side:

```
"1,2, 3 , 4 ,5".split(/\s*,\s*/); // Returns ["1","2","3","4","5"]
```

10.3 *The RegExp Object*

As mentioned at the beginning of this chapter, regular expressions are represented as RegExp objects. In addition to the `RegExp()` constructor, RegExp objects support three methods and a number of properties. An unusual feature of the RegExp class is that it defines both class (or static) properties and instance properties. That is, it defines global properties that belong to the `RegExp()` constructor and other properties that belong to individual RegExp objects. RegExp pattern matching methods and properties are described in later sections.

The `RegExp()` constructor takes one or two string arguments and creates a new regular expression object. The first argument to this constructor is a string that contains the body of the regular expression—the text that would appear within slashes in a regular expression literal. Note that both string literals and regular expressions use the \ character for escape sequences, so when you pass a regular expression to `RegExp()` as a string literal, you must replace all \ characters with \\. The second argument to `RegExp()` is optional. If supplied, it indicates the regular expression attributes. In JavaScript 1.2, it should be "g", "i", or "gi". For example:

```
// Find all five digit numbers in a string. Note the double \\ in this case.
var zipcode = new RegExp("\\d{5}", "g");
```

The `RegExp()` constructor is useful when a regular expression is being created dynamically, and, thus, cannot be represented with the regular expression literal syntax. For example, to search for a string entered by the user, a regular expression must be created at runtime with `RegExp()`.

Each RegExp object has a `compile()` method. You can use this when you want to change the contents of a RegExp object, rather than discarding the object and creating a new one. `compile()` takes the same arguments as the `RegExp()` constructor does:

```
// Change the zipcode pattern to optionally accept 9 digit codes.
zipcode.compile("\\d{5}(-\\d{4})?", "g");
```

10.4 RegExp Methods for Pattern Matching

RegExp objects define two methods that perform pattern-matching operations; they behave similarly to the String methods described earlier. The `test()` method is the simpler method of the two. It takes a string and returns `true` if the string contains a match with the regular expression:

```
var pattern = "/java/i";
pattern.test("JavaScript");  // Returns true
```

The other RegExp pattern-matching method is `exec()`. It is similar to the String `match()` method described above, except that it is a RegExp method that takes a string, rather than a String method that takes a RegExp. The `exec()` method executes a regular expression on the specified string. That is, it searches the string for a match. If it finds none, it returns `null`. If it does find one, however, it returns an array just like the array returned by the `match()` method for non-global searches. Element 0 of the array contains the string that matched the regular expression, and any subsequent array elements contain the substrings that matched any parenthesized subexpressions. Furthermore, the `index` property contains the character position at which the match occurred, and the `input` property refers to the string that was searched.

Unlike the `match()` method, `exec()` returns the same type of result, whether or not the regular expression has the global g attribute. Recall that the `match()` method returns an array of matches when passed a global regular expression. The `exec()` method, by contrast, always returns a single match and provides complete information about that match. When `exec()` is used with a global RegExp object, it sets the `lastIndex` property of that object to the character immediately following the matched substring. When `exec()` is invoked a second time for the same RegExp, it begins its search at the character position indicated by the `lastIndex` property. If `exec()` does not find a match, it resets `lastIndex` to 0. (You can also set `lastIndex` to 0 at any time, which you should do any time you quit a search before you find the last match in one string and begin searching another string with the same RegExp object.) This special behavior allows us to call `exec()` repeatedly in order to loop through all regular expression matches in a string. For example:

```
var pattern = /Java/g;
var text = "JavaScript is more fun than Java!";
var result;
while((result = pattern.exec(text)) != null) {
    alert("Matched '" + result[0] + "' at position " + result.index);
}
```

Finally, note that there is one quirky feature of RegExp objects and the exec() method that you may occasionally see used. RegExp objects may themselves be invoked as functions, and doing so is exactly the same as invoking the exec() method. Thus, for any RegExp p and string s, p.exec(s) is equivalent to p(s).

The test() method behaves the same way as the exec() method when invoked for a global regular expression: it begins searching the specified string at the position specified by lastIndex, and if it finds a match, it sets lastIndex to the position of the character immediately following the match. Thus, we can loop through a string using the test() method just as we can with the exec() method.

The String methods search(), replace(), and match() do not use the lastIndex property as exec() and test() do. In fact, the String methods simply reset lastIndex() to 0. If you use exec() or test() with a global pattern and are searching multiple strings, you must either find all matches in each string, so that lastIndex is automatically reset to zero (this happens when the last search fails), or you must explicitly set the lastIndex property to 0 yourself. If you forget to do this, you may start searching a new string at some arbitrary position within the string rather than from the beginning. Finally, remember that this special lastIndex behavior occurs only for global regular expressions. exec() and test() ignore the lastIndex property of RegExp objects that do not have the g attribute.

10.5 RegExp Instance Properties

Each RegExp object has four properties. The source property is a read-only string that contains the text of the regular expression. The global property is a read-only boolean value that specifies whether the regular expression has the g attribute. The ignoreCase property is a read-only boolean value that specifies whether the regular expression has the i attribute. The fourth property is the lastIndex property, a read-write integer. For global patterns, this property stores the position in the string at which the next search is to begin. It is used by the exec() and test() methods, as described in the previous section.

10.6 RegExp Class Properties

Regular expressions have class (or static) properties—properties of the RegExp() constructor itself—that are more interesting than the instance properties described above. Whenever you perform pattern matching with the String search(), replace(), or match() methods, or with the RegExp exec() and test() methods, these static properties of the RegExp constructor are set, providing further information about the match. Note, however, that as static properties, these values are global and, therefore, transient—any other regular expression operation over-writes them. Also, in client-side JavaScript, the value of the static `input` and `multiline` properties may be modified when JavaScript enters an event handler. The static properties and their values are listed in Table 10-7.

Table 10–7: Static RegExp Properties

Property	Description
leftContext	The text to the left of the most recent match.
rightContext	The text to the right of the most recent match.
lastMatch	The most recently matched text.
lastParen	The text matched by the last parenthesized subexpression of the most recent match.
$1, $2, ..., $9	These properties hold the text matched by the first nine parenthesized subexpressions of the most recent match.
input	The string to search, if no string is passed to exec() or test().
multiline	A boolean value that specifies whether the string being searched should be treated as a single line or as multiple lines separated by newline characters.

For example, if we match the pattern `/java(script)/i` against the string "I like JavaScript!", `RegExp.leftContext` is "I like " and `RegExp.rightContext` is "!". The `lastMatch` property is "JavaScript". The `lastParen` and $1 properties both have the value "Script". Properties $2 through $9 are undefined. Note that the values of the $1 through $9 properties are also available as array elements of the value returned by the `exec()` method. The values of `leftContext`, `rightContext`, `lastMatch`, and `lastParen` can be derived from the `exec()` return value.

Two of these RegExp static properties deserve additional comment. One is the `multiline` property mentioned earlier in this chapter. If set to `true`, the ^ and $ characters match the beginning and end of lines, as well as the beginning and end of a string. Recall that in client-side JavaScript, this property is set to `true` and reset to `false` by certain event handlers, so if you want multiline behavior, you should set it every time you perform a pattern match.

The other static RegExp property worthy of note is `input`. This is a read/write string. If you do not pass a string to the `exec()` or `test()` method, it uses the value of this `input` property instead. This can be useful when repeating a global search over a string: you can just set the `input` property once and then call `exec()` multiple times without having to pass the search string each time. In client-side JavaScript, the event handlers of the Text, TextArea, Select, and Anchor objects set this `input` property to the text string that they contain. This allows a simple shortcut for certain event handlers, but it also means that you cannot rely on the `input` property to retain the value you give it.

As a convenience to Perl programmers, JavaScript defines alternate names for the static RegExp properties. For example, you can use `$`` instead of `leftContext`. Note, however, that since the `` ` `` character isn't legal in JavaScript identifiers, you have to use this property name with array syntax: `RegExp["$`"]`. The complete list of alternative names is listed in the reference section. Using these property names is discouraged, however, as they typically make your code harder to read and understand.

10.6.1 Dynamic Scoping of RegExp Properties

As you may recall from discussions in Chapter 4, *Variables*, and Chapter 7, *Functions*, JavaScript uses static scoping. This means that JavaScript functions are executed in the scope in which they were defined, not in the scope from which they are executed. Consider the case of a client-side JavaScript program that uses two frames within a web browser window. If JavaScript code running in the bottom frame invokes a function defined in the top frame, that function runs in the top frame, not the bottom frame. That is, when the function uses a global variable, the value of that variable is looked up in the global object associated with the top frame.

The static properties of the RegExp object are an exception to this rule. Following the example of Perl, these properties are dynamically scoped rather than statically scoped. If JavaScript code in the bottom frame of our two-frame example calls a function in the top frame, and if that function performs a pattern-matching operation, the properties of the RegExp object in the bottom frame are updated, not the properties of the RegExp object of the top frame.

When we look at this behavior, as we just have, in terms of dynamic versus static scoping, it seems to be a strange special case. However, if you think about typical uses of regular expressions in client-side JavaScript, it makes more sense. Suppose a pattern-matching function is defined in the `<HEAD>` section of an HTML document and is used from each of several frames defined by the document. If the RegExp properties were statically scoped, the results stored in these properties by an invocation of the function from one frame might be immediately overwritten by an invocation of the function from another frame. This is an especially difficult problem if each frame runs its JavaScript code in an independent thread. Dynamic scoping avoids this problem: results generated by a frame are always stored in that frame and cannot be accidentally overwritten by any other frame.

11

Further Topics in JavaScript

This chapter covers miscellaneous JavaScript topics that would have bogged down previous chapters had they been covered earlier. Now that you have read through the preceding chapters and are experienced with the core JavaScript language, you are prepared to tackle the more advanced and detailed concepts presented here. You may prefer, however, to move on to other chapters and learn about the specifics of client-side JavaScript before returning to this chapter.

11.1 Data Type Conversion

We've seen that JavaScript is an untyped language (or, perhaps more accurately, a loosely typed or dynamically typed language). This means, for example, that we don't have to specify the data type of a variable when we declare it. The fact that JavaScript is untyped gives it the flexibility and simplicity that are desirable for a scripting language (although those features come at the expense of rigor, which is important for the longer, more complex programs often written in stricter languages like C and Java). An important feature of JavaScript's flexible treatment of data types is the automatic type conversions it performs. For example, if you pass a number to the document.write() method, JavaScript automatically converts that value into its equivalent string representation. Similarly, if you test a string value in the condition of an if statement, JavaScript automatically converts that string to a boolean value—to false if the string is empty and to true otherwise.

The basic rule is that when a value of one type is used in a context that requires a value of some other type, JavaScript automatically attempts to convert the value as needed. So, for example, if a number is used in a "boolean context," it is converted to a boolean. If an object is used in a "string context," it is converted to a string. If a string is used in a numeric context, JavaScript attempts to convert it to a number. Table 11-1 summarizes each of these conversions—it shows the conversion that is performed when a particular type of value is used in a particular context.

Table 11-1: Automatic Data Type Conversions

Value	Used as a			
	String	Number	Boolean	Object
Non-empty string	-	Numeric value of string or NaN	`true`	String object
Empty string	-	0	`false`	String object
`0`	`"0"`	-	`false`	Number object
NaN	`"NaN"`	-	`false`	Number object
Infinity	`"Infinity"`	-	`true`	Number object
Negative infinity	`"-Infinity"`	-	`true`	Number object
Any other number	String value of number	-	`true`	Number object
`true`	`"true"`	1	-	Boolean object
`false`	`"false"`	0	-	Boolean object
Object	`toString()` or `valueOf()` or error	`valueOf()` or `toString()` or error	`true`	-
Array	Comma-separated list of elements	Non-portable; see note below	Non-portable; see note below	-

Table 11-1: Automatic Data Type Conversions (continued)

Value	Used as a			
	String	**Number**	**Boolean**	**Object**
Function	Implementation-dependent function listing	NaN	true	-
null	"null"	0	false	error
Undefined value	"undefined"	NaN	false	error

The ECMA-262 specification does not explicitly address array-to-number conversion. Indirectly, however, it implies that all arrays should be converted to NaN unless they have only a single element that is a number or can be converted to a number. In this case, the array is converted to whatever number its single element converts to. This is the behavior of Internet Explorer 4. Navigator 3 and 4 have different behavior, however: when an array is used in a numeric context, it is converted to its length.* An empty array converts to 0, an array with one element to 1, and an array with 10 elements to 10. Because of this non-portability, you should never rely on implicit array-to-number conversion.

The ECMA-262 specification does not explicitly address array-to-boolean conversion either. It does say, however, that all (non-null) object values convert to true. Since arrays are objects, this implies that all arrays should convert to true. This is the behavior of IE 4. Navigator 3 and 4 have a different behavior, however: they convert all non-empty arrays to true and convert all empty (zero length) arrays to false.† Because of this incompatibility, you should not rely on implicit array-to-boolean conversion. When you need to test an array, be explicit. For example:

```
if (a) ...  // Relies on implicit conversion to boolean; non-portable
if (a != null) ...              // Do this for IE behavior
if ((a != null) && (a.length > 0)) ... // or this for Navigator behavior.
```

---

* Navigator 5 will likely change to conform to the specification and match the IE 4 behavior.

† Navigator 5 will likely change to conform to the specification and match the IE 4 behavior.

11.1.1 Object-to-Primitive Conversion

Table 11-1 specifies how an object is converted when used in a string context: JavaScript first attempts to call its toString() method. If this method does not exist or does not return an appropriate value, JavaScript next tries the valueOf() method. The table also shows how an object is converted when used in a numeric context: by reversing the algorithm and trying valueOf() before toString().

However, there are a couple of places in JavaScript where the context is ambiguous. The + operator and the comparison operators (<, <=, >, and >=) operate on both numbers and strings. When an object is used with one of these operators, it is not clear from the table how it is converted. In both cases, JavaScript attempts the conversion first with valueOf() and then with toString(). There is one exception: when a Date object is used with the + operator, conversion is attempted first with the toString() method. This exception exists because Date has both toString() and valueOf() methods. When a Date is used with +, you almost always want to perform a string concatenation. But when using a Date with the comparison operators, you almost always want to perform a numeric comparison to determine which of two times is earlier than the other.

Most objects do not have valueOf() methods or do not have valueOf() methods that return useful results. When you use an object with the + operator, you most often get string concatenation rather than addition. When you use an object with a comparison operator, you most often get string comparison rather than numeric comparison. An object that defines a custom valueOf() method may behave differently. If you define a valueOf() method that returns a number, you can use arithmetic and other operators with your object, but adding your object to a string may not behave as you expect: the toString() method is no longer called, and a string representation of the number returned by valueOf() is concatenated to the string. Finally, remember that valueOf() is not called toNumber(): strictly speaking, its job is to convert an object to a reasonable primitive value, so some objects may have valueOf() methods that return strings.

11.1.2 Explicit Type Conversions

Table 11-1 lists the automatic data type conversions that JavaScript performs. It is also possible to convert values from one type to another explicitly. JavaScript does not define a cast operator as C, C++, and Java do, but it does provide similar facilities for converting data values.

As of JavaScript 1.1 (and the ECMA-262 standard), Number(), Boolean(), String(), and Object() may be called as functions as well as being invoked as constructors. When invoked in this way, one of these functions attempts to convert its argument to the appropriate type. For example, you could convert any value x to a string with `String(x)` and convert any value y to an object with `Object(y)`.

Because of JavaScript's tendency to automatically convert data to whatever type is required, explicit conversions using these functions are usually unnecessary. They are occasionally helpful, however, and can also be used to make your code clearer and more precise.

11.1.3 *Converting Numbers to Strings*

The number-to-string conversion is probably the one most often performed in JavaScript. Although it usually happens automatically, there are a couple of useful ways to perform this conversion explicitly. Perhaps the simplest is to add the empty string to a number. This forces the number to be converted (because it is used in a string context) and concatenated with nothing:

```
string_value = number + "";
```

Another technique for converting numbers to strings is with the `toString()` method, as we saw above:

```
string_value = number.toString();
```

The `toString()` method of the Number object (numbers are converted to Number objects so that this method can be called) takes an optional argument that specifies a radix, or base, for the conversion. If you do not specify the argument, the conversion is done in base 10. But you can also convert numbers in other bases (between 2 and 16) as well. For example:

```
binary_string = n.toString(2);
octal_string = "0" + n.toString(8);
hex_string = "0x" + n.toString(16);
```

A shortcoming of JavaScript is that there is no built-in way to convert a number to a string and specify the number of decimal places to be included. This can make it a little difficult to display numbers that have traditional formats, such as numbers that represent monetary values. In fact, JavaScript lacks any kind of numeric formatting function, so it is not possible to specify whether or not exponential notation should be used, whether leading zeros should be displayed, and so on.

11.1.4 *Converting Strings to Numbers*

We've seen that strings that represent numbers are automatically converted to actual numbers when used in a numeric context. We can make this conversion explicit by choosing the numeric context we use. Just as we can convert a number to a string by adding the empty string to it, we can convert a string to a number by subtracting zero from it:

```
numeric_value = string_value - 0;
```

We can't add zero, of course, because in that case the + operator is interpreted as the string concatenation operator.

The trouble with this sort of string-to-number conversion is that it is overly strict. It works only with base-10 numbers and only when the string contains nothing but leading spaces and numbers with no trailing characters, not even trailing spaces. To allow more flexible conversions, you can use the parseInt() and parse- Float() functions. These convert and return any number at the beginning of a string, ignoring any trailing non-numbers. parseInt() only parses integers, while parseFloat() parses both integers and floating-point numbers. If a number begins with 0, parseInt() interprets it as an octal number. If it begins with 0x or 0X, parseInt() interprets it as a hexadecimal number.

```
parseInt("3 blind mice");        // Returns 3
parseFloat("3.14 meters");       // Returns 3.14
parseInt("12.34");               // Returns 12
parseInt("077");                 // Returns 63 (7*8 + 7)
parseInt("0xFF");                // Returns 255
```

parseInt() can even take a second argument, which specifies the radix (base) of the number to be parsed. Legal values are between 2 and 36. For example:

```
parseInt("11", 2);               // Returns 3 (1*2 + 1)
parseInt("ff", 16);              // Returns 255 (15*16 + 15)
parseInt("zz", 36);              // Returns 1295 (35*36 + 35)
```

If parseInt() or parseFloat() cannot convert the specified string to a number, it returns NaN (except in JavaScript 1.0, where it unfortunately returns 0):

```
parseInt("eleven");              // Returns NaN
parseFloat("$72.47");            // Returns NaN
```

11.2 By Value Versus by Reference

In JavaScript, as in all programming languages, there are three important ways that you can manipulate a data value. First, you can copy it, for example, by assigning it to a new variable. Second, you can pass it as an argument to a function or method. Third, you can compare it with another value to see if the two values are equal. To understand any programming language, you must understand how these three operations are performed in that language.

There are two fundamentally distinct ways to manipulate data values. These techniques are called "by value" and "by reference." When a value is manipulated by value, it is the *value* of the datum that matters. In an assignment, a copy of the actual value is made and that copy is stored in a variable, object property, or array element; the copy and the original are two totally independent values that are stored separately. When a datum is passed by value to a function, a copy of the datum is passed to the function; if the function modifies the value, the change affects only the function's copy of the datum—it does not affect the original datum. Finally, when a datum is compared by value to another datum, the two distinct pieces of data must represent exactly the same value (which usually means that a byte-by-byte comparison finds them to be equal).

The other way of manipulating a value is by reference. With this technique, there is only one actual copy of the value; references to that value are manipulated.* If a value is manipulated by reference, variables do not hold that value directly; they only hold references to it. It is these references that are copied, passed, and compared. So, in an assignment made by reference, it is the reference to the value that is assigned, not a copy of the value and not the value itself. After the assignment, the new variable contains the same reference to the value that the original variable contains. Both references are equally valid and both can be used to manipulate the value—if the value is changed through one reference, that change also appears through the original reference. The situation is similar when a value is passed to a function by reference. A reference to the value is passed to the function and the function can use that reference to modify the value itself; any such modifications are visible outside the function. Finally, when a value is compared to another by reference, the two references are compared to see if they refer to the same unique copy of a value; references to two distinct values that happen to be equivalent (i.e., consist of the same bytes) are not treated as equal.

These are two very different ways of manipulating values, and they have very important implications that you should understand. Table 11-2 summarizes these implications. This discussion of manipulating data by value and by reference has been a general one: the distinctions apply to all programming languages. The sections that follow explain how these distinctions apply specifically to JavaScript—they discuss which data types are manipulated by value and which are manipulated by reference.

---

* C programmers and anyone else familiar with the concept of pointers should understand the idea of a reference in this context. Note, however, that JavaScript does not support pointers.

Table 11-2: By Value Versus by Reference

	By Value	**By Reference**
Copy	The value is actually copied; there are two distinct, independent copies.	Only a reference to the value is copied. If the value is modified through the new reference, that change is also visible through the original reference.
Pass	A distinct copy of the value is passed to the function; changes to it have no effect outside the function.	A reference to the value is passed to the function. If the function modifies the value through the passed reference, the modification is visible outside the function.
Compare	Two distinct values are compared (often byte by byte) to see if they are the same value.	Two references are compared to see if they refer to the same value. Two references to distinct values are not equal, even if the two values consist of the same bytes.

11.2.1 *Primitive Types and Reference Types*

The basic rule in JavaScript is this: primitive types are manipulated by value, and reference types, as the name suggests, are manipulated by reference. Numbers and booleans are primitive types in JavaScript—primitive because they consist of nothing more than a small, fixed number of bytes that are easily manipulated at the low (primitive) levels of the JavaScript interpreter. Objects, on the other hand, are reference types. Arrays and functions, which are specialized types of objects, are therefore also reference types. These data types can contain arbitrary numbers of properties or elements, so they cannot be as easily manipulated as fixed-size primitive values can. Since object and array values can become quite large, it doesn't make sense to manipulate these types by value, as this could involve the inefficient copying and comparing of large amounts of memory.

What about strings? A string can have an arbitrary length, so it would seem that strings should be reference types. In fact, though, they are usually considered to be primitive types in JavaScript simply because they are not objects. Strings don't actually fit into the primitive versus reference type dichotomy. We'll have more to say about strings and their behavior a little later.

The best way to explore the differences between data manipulation by value and data manipulation by reference is through example. Study the following examples carefully, paying attention to the comments. Example 11-1 copies, passes, and compares numbers. Since numbers are primitive types, this illustrates data manipulation by value.

Example 11–1: Copying, Passing, and Comparing by Value

```
// First we illustrate copy by value.
var n = 1;          // Variable n holds the value 1.
var m = n;          // Copy by value: variable m holds a distinct value 1.

// Here's a function we'll use to illustrate pass-by-value.
// As we'll see, the function doesn't work the way we'd like it to.
function add_to_total(total, x)
{
    total = total + x;  // This line only changes the internal copy of total.
}

// Now call the function, passing the numbers contained in n and m by value.
// The value of n is copied, and that copied value is named total within the
// function. The function adds a copy of m to that copy of n. But adding
// something to a copy of n doesn't affect the original value of n outside
// of the function. So calling this function doesn't accomplish anything.
add_to_total(n, m);

// Now, we'll look at comparison by value.
// In the line of code below, the literal 1 is clearly a distinct numeric
// value encoded in the program. We compare it to the value held in variable
// n. In comparison by value, the bytes of the two numbers are checked to
// see if they are the same.
if (n == 1) m = 2;   // n contains the same value as the literal 1; m is now 2.
```

Now, consider Example 11-2. This example copies, passes, and compares an object. Since objects are reference types, these manipulations are performed by reference. The example uses Date objects, which you can read about in the reference section of this book, if necessary.

Example 11–2: Copying, Passing, and Comparing by Reference

```
// Here we create an object representing the date of Christmas, 1996.
// The variable xmas contains a reference to the object, not the object itself.
var xmas = new Date(96, 11, 25);

// When we copy by reference, we get a new reference to the original object.
var solstice = xmas; // Both variables now refer to the same object value.

// Here we change the object through our new reference to it.
solstice.setDate(21);

// The change is visible through the original reference, as well.
xmas.getDate();       // Returns 21, not the original value of 25.
```

Example 11-2: Copying, Passing, and Comparing by Reference (continued)

```
// The same is true when objects and arrays are passed to functions.
// The following function adds a value to each element of an array.
// A reference to the array is passed to the function, not a copy of the array.
// Therefore, the function can change the contents of the array through
// the reference, and those changes will be visible when the function returns.
function add_to_totals(totals, x)
{
    totals[0] = totals[0] + x;
    totals[1] = totals[1] + x;
    totals[2] = totals[2] + x;
}


// Finally, we'll examine comparison by value.
// When we compare the two variables defined above, we find they are
// equal, because they refer to the same object, even though we were trying
// to make them refer to different dates:
(xmas == solstice)           // Evaluates to true

// The two variables defined below refer to two distinct objects, both
// of which represent exactly the same date.
var xmas = new Date(96, 11, 25);
var solstice_plus_4 = new Date(96, 11, 25);

// But, by the rules of "compare by reference," distinct objects not equal!
(xmas != solstice_plus_4)    // Evaluates to true
```

Before we leave the topic of manipulating objects and arrays by reference, a point of nomenclature needs to be cleared up. The phrase "pass by reference" can have several meanings. To some readers, the phrase refers to a function invocation technique that allows a function to assign new values to its arguments and to have those modified values visible outside the function. This is not the way the term is used in this book. Here, we mean simply that a reference to an object or array is passed to a function, not the object itself. A function can use the reference to modify properties of the object or elements of the array. But if the function overwrites the reference with a reference to a new object or array, that modification is not visible outside of the function. Readers familiar with the other meaning of this term may prefer to say that objects and arrays are passed by value, but the value that is passed is actually a reference rather than the object itself. Example 11-3 illustrates this issue.

Example 11-3: References Themselves Are Passed by Value

```
// This is another version of the add_to_totals() function. It doesn't
// work, though, because instead of changing the array itself, it tries to
// change the reference to the array.
```

Example 11-3: References Themselves Are Passed by Value (continued)

```
function add_to_totals2(totals, x)
{
    newtotals = new Array(3);
    newtotals[0] = totals[0] + x;
    newtotals[1] = totals[1] + x;
    newtotals[2] = totals[2] + x;
    totals = newtotals;  // This line has no effect outside of the function.
}
```

11.2.2 Copying and Passing Strings

As mentioned earlier, JavaScript strings don't fit neatly into the primitive type versus reference type dichotomy. Since strings are not objects, it is natural to assume that they are primitive. If they are primitive types, then by the rules given above, they should be manipulated by value. But since strings can be arbitrarily long, it would seem inefficient to copy, pass, and compare them byte by byte. Therefore, it would also be natural to assume that strings are implemented as reference types.

Instead of making assumptions about strings, suppose we write some JavaScript code to experiment with string manipulation. If strings are copied and passed by reference, we should be able to modify the contents of a string through the reference stored in another variable or passed to a function.

When we set out to write the code to perform this experiment, however, we run into a major stumbling block: there is no way to modify the contents of a string. The charAt() method returns the character at a given position in a string, but there is no corresponding setCharAt() method. This is not an oversight. JavaScript strings are intentionally *immutable*—that is, there is no JavaScript syntax, method, or property that allows you to change the characters in a string.

Since strings are immutable, our original question is moot: there is no way to tell if strings are passed by value or by reference. We can assume that, for efficiency, JavaScript is implemented so that strings are passed by reference, but in actuality it doesn't matter, since it has no practical bearing on the code we write.

11.2.3 Comparing Strings

Despite the fact that we cannot determine whether strings are copied and passed by value or by reference, we can write JavaScript code to determine whether they are compared by value or by reference. Example 11-4 shows the code we might use to make this determination.

Example 11-4: Are Strings Compared by Value or by Reference?

```
// Determining whether strings are compared by value or reference is easy.
// We compare two clearly distinct strings that happen to contain the same
// characters. If they are compared by value they will be equal, but if they
// are compared by reference, they will not be equal:
var s1 = "hello";
var s2 = "hell" + "o";
if (s1 == s2) document.write("Strings compared by value");
```

This experiment demonstrates that strings are compared by value. This may be surprising to some programmers. In C, C++, and Java, strings are reference types and are compared by reference. If you want to compare the actual contents of two strings, you must use a special method or function. JavaScript, however, is a higher-level language and recognizes that when you compare strings you most often want to compare them by value. Thus, despite the fact that, for efficiency, JavaScript strings are (presumably) copied and passed by reference, they are compared by value.

11.2.4 By Value Versus by Reference: Summary

Table 11-3 summarizes the way that the various JavaScript types are manipulated.

Table 11-3: Data Type Manipulation in JavaScript

Type	Copied by	Passed by	Compared by
Number	value	value	value
Boolean	value	value	value
String	immutable	immutable	value
Object	reference	reference	reference
Array	reference	reference	reference
Function	reference	reference	reference

11.3 Garbage Collection

As explained in Chapter 4, *Variables*, JavaScript uses "garbage collection" to reclaim the memory occupied by strings, objects, arrays, and functions that are no longer in use. This frees you, the programmer, from having to explicitly deallocate memory yourself and is an important part of what makes JavaScript programming easier than, say, C programming.

A key feature of garbage collection is that the garbage collector must be able to determine when it is safe to reclaim memory. Obviously, it must never reclaim values that are still in use and should only collect values that are no longer reachable: values that cannot be referred to through any of the variables, object properties, or array elements in the program. If you are the curious type, you may be wondering just how a garbage collector distinguishes between garbage to be collected and values that are still being used or that could potentially be used. The following sections explain some of the gory details.

11.3.1 Mark and Sweep Garbage Collection

The computer science literature on garbage collection is large and technical; the actual operation of the garbage collector is really an implementation-specific detail that may vary in different implementations of the language. Still, almost all serious garbage collectors use some variation on a basic garbage collection algorithm known as "mark and sweep." The JavaScript implementations in Navigator 4 and later and in Internet Explorer 3 and later use this algorithm.

A mark and sweep garbage collector periodically traverses the list of all variables in the JavaScript environment, and marks any values referred to by these variables. If any referenced values are objects or arrays, it recursively marks the object properties and array elements. By recursively traversing this tree or graph of values, the garbage collector is able to find (and mark) every single value that is still reachable. It follows, then that any unmarked values are garbage.

Once a mark and sweep garbage collector has finished marking all reachable values, it begins its sweep phase. During this phase, it looks through the list of all values in the environment and deallocates any that are not marked. Classic mark and sweep garbage collectors do a complete mark and a complete sweep all at once, which causes a noticeable slowdown in the system during garbage collection. More sophisticated variations on the algorithm make the process relatively efficient and perform collection in the background without disrupting system performance.

As I mentioned above, as of Navigator 4 and Internet Explorer 3, the JavaScript garbage collectors are based on the mark and sweep algorithm. Navigator 3 uses a somewhat simpler garbage collection scheme that has some shortcomings. Navigator 2 uses a very simple garbage collection technique that has some serious flaws. If you are writing code to be compatible with either of these browsers, the following sections explain the shortcomings of the garbage collectors in those browsers.

11.3.2 Garbage Collection by Reference Counting

In Navigator 3, garbage collection is performed by reference counting. This means that every object (whether a user object created by JavaScript code or a built-in HTML object created by the browser) keeps track of how many references there are to it. Recall that objects are assigned by reference in JavaScript, rather than having their complete value copied.

When an object is created and a reference to it is stored in a variable, the object's reference count is 1. When the reference to the object is copied and stored in another variable, the reference count is incremented to 2. When one of the two variables that holds these references is overwritten with some new value, the object's reference count is decremented back to 1. If the reference count reaches zero, there are no more references to the object. Since there are no references to copy, there can never again be a reference to the object in the program. Therefore, JavaScript knows that it is safe to destroy the object and garbage collect the memory associated with it.

Unfortunately, there are shortcomings to using reference counting as a garbage collection scheme. In fact, some people don't even consider reference counting to be true garbage collection and reserve that term for better algorithms, such as mark and sweep garbage collection. Reference counting is a very simple form of garbage collection, it is easy to implement, and it works fine in many situations. There is an important situation, however, in which reference counting cannot correctly detect and collect all garbage, and you need to be aware of it.

The basic flaw with reference counting has to do with cyclical references. If object A contains a reference to object B and object B contains a reference to object A, a cycle of references exists. A cycle would also exist, for example, if A referred to B, B referred to C, and C referred back to A. In cycles such as these, there is always a reference from within the cycle to every element in the cycle. Thus, even if none of the elements of the cycle have any remaining outside references, their reference counts will never drop below one and they can never be garbage collected. The entire cycle may be garbage if there is no way to refer to any of these objects from a program, but because they all refer to each other, a reference counting garbage collector cannot detect and free this unused memory.

This problem with cycles is the price that must be paid for a simple garbage collection scheme. The only way to prevent this problem is by manual intervention. If you create a cycle of objects, you must recognize this fact and take steps to ensure that the objects are garbage collected when they are no longer needed. To allow a cycle of objects to be garbage collected, you must break the cycle. You can do this by picking one of the objects in the cycle and setting the property of it that refers to the next object to null. For example, suppose that A, B, and C are objects that each have a next property, and the value of this property is set so that these objects refer to each other and form a cycle. When these objects are no longer in use, you can break the cycle by setting A.next to null. This means that object B no longer has a reference from A, so its reference count can drop to zero and it can be garbage collected. Once it has been garbage collected, it will no longer refer to C, so C's reference count can drop to zero and it can be garbage collected. Once C is garbage collected, A can finally be garbage collected.

Note, of course, that none of this can happen if A, B, and C are stored in global variables in a window that is still open, because those variables A, B, and C still refer to the objects. If these were local variables in a function and you broke their cycle before the function returned, they could be garbage collected. But if they are stored in global variables, they remain referenced until the window that contains them closes. In this case, if you want to force them to be garbage collected, you must break the cycle and set all the variables to null:

```
A.next = null;    // Break the cycle.
A = B = C = null;    // Remove the last remaining external references.
```

11.3.3 Per-Page Memory Management in Navigator 2

The garbage collection scheme in Navigator 2 is even simpler than the one in Navigator 3, and, unfortunately, it is inadequate for the needs of JavaScript programs that use multiple windows and frames. In Navigator 2, all objects created by JavaScript code running in any particular window allocate memory from a pool of memory owned by the window. Then, when the window is destroyed or when the document (containing the JavaScript program) displayed in the window is unloaded, the entire pool of memory is freed at once. No memory is freed until then.

With this garbage collection scheme, all memory allocated by the JavaScript running in a window can be freed in a single stroke. It is a simple and efficient scheme to implement. Unfortunately, it suffers from two major drawbacks.

First, if an object is created in one window and a reference to that object is stored in a variable in a second window, that object is destroyed when the first window moves on to a new page, despite the fact that there is still an active reference to it from the other window. If this other window attempts to use this reference to the destroyed object, an error results, possibly crashing the browser! This is an especially pernicious problem because doing something as simple as assigning a string can cause it to happen. Consider the following code:

```
newwin = window.open("", "temp_window");
newwin.defaultStatus = "temporary browser window".
```

The defaultStatus property is set to a string owned by the original window. If that window is closed, the string is destroyed and the next reference to default-Status goes looking for a nonexistent string.

The second problem with this scheme is that if a window never unloads, the memory associated with it is never freed. For a page that runs some JavaScript once and then is static, this is not a problem. But consider a page that performs a status-bar animation, for example. If it updates the status bar several times a second for a long time, the memory consumed by that page grows and grows. Another example occurs with the use of frames. One frame might serve as a navigation window, with controls that allow a user to easily browse a large site in other frames or other windows. These other frames and windows may load and unload pages frequently, freeing memory. But the navigation frame itself remains the same, and the memory associated with it is not freed. Depending on how the event handlers are written, there is a good chance that each time the user interacts with the navigation controls some new string or object is created. Since no memory is ever freed, eventually the browser will run out of memory and may well crash.

It is possible to compensate, somewhat, for these memory management problems in Navigator 2. For the problem of memory not being released until the page is unloaded, the solution is simply to be careful about how much memory your scripts consume. If your page loops a lot or does a repetitive animation, look very carefully at the code that is executed over and over and minimize the number of objects created on each iteration. Similarly, if you write a script that the user may use frequently without ever unloading, be sure to keep careful tabs on your memory usage. Note that string manipulation is a big memory sink—each time you call a method on a string object, a new string object is generally created for the result. The same is true for string concatenation with the + operator.

For the problem of dangling references from one window to destroyed objects that were owned by another, one solution is to avoid programs that rely on inter-window references. Another solution is to be sure to make copies of all strings and other objects that are passed from one window to another. Suppose that in window 1, you want to set the defaultStatus property of window 2, as we saw earlier. If you do this directly with code in window 1, window 2 contains a reference to an object owned by window 1. But if you call a function in window 2 to do the assignment and make sure that the function makes a copy of the object, the object assigned in window 2 is owned by window 2. You could, for example, define the following function in window 2:

```
function set_string_property(name, value)
{
    // Assign a property to this window, using associative array notation.
    // We add the empty string to the value to force JavaScript to make
    // a copy. If this function is called from another window, we won't
    // own the value string, but by making a copy, we do own the result.
    self[name] = value + "";
}
```

With this function defined, you can then set the property from window 1 with a line like the following:

```
window2.set_string_property("defaultStatus", "temporary browser window");
```

11.4 More About Prototypes

As we saw in Chapter 8, *Objects*, JavaScript constructor functions have a `proto-type` property that refers to the prototype object inherited by instances of the class it defines. That is, if `Complex()` is a constructor function, `Complex.prototype` refers to the prototype object for the class. Every object created by the `Complex()` constructor automatically inherits properties from this prototype object.

In fact, every object has an internal property that refers to the object from which it inherits properties, if there is one. When a constructor creates an object, it initializes this internal property using the value of its own (non-internal) `prototype` property.

In Navigator 4, this internal property has been exposed, and given the name `__proto__`. Note, however, that it is not clear whether this property will be standardized or whether it will ever be supported by Internet Explorer. The `__proto__` property allows for some interesting tricks. For example, it allows us to explicitly initialize inheritance chains:

```
var o = { x:1, y:2, z:3 };          // o inherits from Object.prototype.
var p = { x:1, y:2, __proto__:o };  // p inherits from o.
var q = { x:1, __proto__:p };       // q inherits from p.
```

This code creates an object q that inherits a property y from the object p and inherits the property z from object o.

A more interesting example of what is possible with the `__proto__` property is given in Example 11-5. It shows an `instanceOf()` method that checks whether a given object is an instance of a given class. More precisely, passed an object and a constructor, it follows the `__proto__` chain of the object to see if it inherits from the object referred to by the `prototype` property of the constructor. If so, the object is an instance of the class defined by the constructor and the function returns `true`. Otherwise, the function returns `false`.*

Example 11–5: An instanceOf() Method Using __proto__

```
// Return true if object o is an instance of class (constructor) c.
function instanceOf(o, c) {
    var p = o.__proto__;
    while(p != null) {
        if (p == c.prototype) return true;
        p = p.__proto__;
    }
    return false;
}
```

11.5 Working with the Scope Chain

As we discussed in Chapter 4, when JavaScript has to look up the value of a variable, it sequentially checks each of the objects in the scope chain to see if the variable is defined as a property of that object. In top-level code, the scope chain consists of a single object: the global object. In a non-nested function, the first object in the scope chain is the call object of the function, where local variables and function arguments are defined, and the second object is the global object. In a nested function, several distinct call objects may appear in the scope chain before the global object.

Scope chains can actually be quite substantial. As we'll see in Chapter 15, *Events and Event Handling*, for example, event handler functions are scoped to the hierarchy of containing HTML elements. The function that is invoked when the user clicks on an HTML button has a scope chain that consists of its own call object, the object that represents the button, the object that represents the form, the object that represents the HTML document, and finally, the global object.

One point to notice about a scope chain is that it is a chain, not an array, and each element in the chain is linked to the next. Navigator 4 exposes the previously internal property that links the objects in a scope chain to each other. This new `__parent__` property, like the `__proto__` property, has not been standardized, and its addition to the language can impose performance penalties on the JavaScript interpreter, so it is not clear whether it will ever be supported by

---

* Note that JavaScript 1.3 may well provide a built-in `instanceof` operator, which would make this (non-portable) example obsolete.

Internet Explorer. Every object has a `__parent__` property which, by default, refers to the global object. We can use this property to alter the scope chain in which a function executes, for example:

```
var x = "global";
function f() { return x; }
f();                              // Returns "global"
var o = { x:"defined in o" };     // Create an object.
o.__parent__ = f.__parent__;      // Insert it into the scope chain.
f.__parent__ = o;
f();                              // Now f() returns "defined in o".
```

Modifying the `__parent__` property of a function directly is a very heavy-handed way to alter its scope chain. We'll see a more elegant way in the next section.

11.6 *Lexical Scoping and the Closure Object*

Functions in JavaScript are lexically scoped rather than dynamically scoped. This means that they run in the scope in which they are defined, not the scope from which they are executed. Prior to JavaScript 1.2, functions could only be defined in the global scope, and lexical scoping was not much of an issue: all functions were executed in the same, global scope (with the call object of the function chained to that global scope).

In JavaScript 1.2, however, functions can be defined anywhere, and tricky issues of scope arise. For example, consider a function g defined within a function f. g is always executed in the scope of f. Its scope chain includes three objects: its own call object, the call object of f( ), and the global object. It is interesting that this is always true, even when g( ) is invoked as f.g( ) from outside the body of f. This means that the call object for f( ) is kept around, as part of the scope chain for g( ), even when f( ) is not executing! The following code demonstrates this:

```
var x = "global";
function f() {
    var x = "local";
    function g() {
        alert(x);
    }
}
// Displays "undefined". f() has not been invoked yet, so
// while the local variable x exists in its call object, it has not
// yet had a value assigned to it.
f.g();
// Calling f() initializes the variable.
f();
```

```
// Now when we invoke the nested function we obtain the value of
// f's local variable
f.g();  // displays "local"
```

That example may seem a little strange, but it can get stranger. The following code includes a function that returns a function. Each time it is called, it creates and returns a function. The function created is always the same, but the scope it is created in differs slightly on each invocation (the value of the arguments to the outer function differ on each occasion.) If we save the returned functions in an array and then invoke each one, we'll see that each returns a different value. Since each function consists of identical JavaScript code and each is invoked from exactly the same scope, the only factor that could be causing the differing return values is the scope in which the functions were defined.

```
// This function returns a function each time it is called.
// The scope in which the function is defined differs for each call.
function makefunc(x) {
  return function() { return x; }
}

// Call makefunc() several times, and save results in an array:
a = [makefunc(0), makefunc(1), makefunc(2)];

// Now call these functions and display their values.
// Although the body of each function is the same, the scope is
// different, and each call returns a different value:
alert(a[0]());  // Displays 0
alert(a[1]());  // Displays 1
alert(a[2]());  // Displays 2
```

The results of this code may be surprising. Still, they are the results expected from a strict application of the lexical scoping rule: a function is executed in the scope in which it was defined. That scope includes the state of local variables and arguments. Even though local variables and function arguments are transient, their state is frozen and becomes part of the lexical scope of any functions defined while they are in effect.

How does lexical scoping work? The code samples above demonstrate that the body of a function alone is not enough to determine the result of executing it: the scope also plays an important role. In fact, the scope is so important that whenever a function is defined outside of the global scope, it cannot be used alone: it must be bundled with its definition scope. In computer science terminology, the combination of a function body with its definition scope is called a "closure." Any nested function in JavaScript 1.2 is actually implemented with a closure. Although it has not been standardized, Navigator 4 exposes closures as instances of the Closure class. In the example above, if you were to investigate the type of the array elements, you would find that they are not actually function objects, but instead are Closure objects:

```
alert(typeof a[0]);   // Displays "function"
alert(a[0]);          // Displays "[object Closure]"
```

A Closure object appears to be a function (since it can be invoked like a function) to the `typeof` operator. But when converted to a string, a Closure object betrays its true nature by displaying the name of its class rather than the body of its function. (This is not behavior that should be relied on in future versions of the language, however.)

A Closure object combines a function and a scope by storing the function as its `__proto__` property and the scope as its `__parent__` property. This has a couple of implications. First, the Closure object inherits all the properties of the function object. This includes the internal property of the function object that contains the executable code for the function. Therefore, a Closure object can be invoked just like a function, even though it is not actually a function. The second implication is that when Closure is invoked, it always runs in its definition scope, because that scope is specified explicitly by its `__parent__` property. Thus, a Closure object links a function and its scope directly together. Continuing with the example above, we can investigate these two properties of a Closure object with code like this:

```
alert(a[0].__proto__);   // Displays the function body
alert(a[0].__parent__);  // Displays "[object Call]"
```

Besides confirming the values of the `__parent__` and `__proto__` properties of a Closure object, this code reveals that Navigator 4 exposes the call object of a function as an object of class Call.

Most of the time, we can just rely on the lexical scoping of JavaScript, and we don't have to think about the `__parent__` property and Closure objects. However, we can use the `__parent__` property and Closures in some interesting ways. Consider the following code:

```
var x = "x is a global variable";
var o = { x: "x is a property of o" };
var p = { x: "x is a property of p"};
function f() { alert(x); }
```

The function f is defined in the global scope, so if we run it, it displays the message "x is a global variable". If we want to force f to run in the scope of the object o, we can explicitly set its `__parent__` property:

```
f.__parent__ = o;
f(); // Now displays "x is a property of o"
```

As I mentioned when I first introduced the property, setting the __parent__ of a function directly is a heavy-handed and inelegant way to modify its scope chain. What if we wanted to to be able to run f in the scope of objects o *and* p? Instead of modifying the function directly, it is more elegant (and perhaps more portable to future versions of JavaScript) to use a Closure object:

```
f_in_o = new Closure(f, o);
f_in_p = new Closure(f, p);
f();       // Displays "x is a global variable"
f_in_o(); // Displays "x is a property of o"
f_in_p(); // Displays "x is a property of p"
```

11.7 *The Function Constructor and Function Literals*

As we saw in Chapter 7, *Functions*, there are two ways to define functions other than the basic function statement. As of JavaScript 1.1, functions can be defined using the Function() constructor, and in JavaScript 1.2, they can be defined with function literals. You should be aware of some important differences between these two techniques.

First, the Function() constructor allows JavaScript code to be dynamically created and compiled at runtime. Function literals, however, are a static part of program structure, just as function statements are.

Second, as a corollary of the first difference, the Function() constructor parses the function body and creates a new function object each time it is called. If the call to the constructor appears within a loop or within a frequently called function, this can be inefficient. On the other hand, a function literal or nested function that appears within a loop or function is not recompiled each time it is encountered. Nor is a different function object created each time a function literal is encountered (a new Closure object may need to be created, however).

The third difference between the Function() constructor and function literals is that functions created with the Function() constructor do not use static scoping; instead, they are always compiled as if they were top-level functions, as the following code demonstrates:

```
var y = "global"
function constructFunction() {
  var y = "local"
  return new Function("return y"); // Does not capture the local scope!
}
```

```
// This line displays "global", because the function returned by the
// Function() constructor does not use the local scope. Had a function
// literal been used instead, this line would have displayed "local".
alert(constructFunction()());        // Displays "global"
```

II

Client-Side JavaScript

This part of the book, Chapters 12 through 21, documents JavaScript as it is implemented in web browsers. These chapters introduce a host of new JavaScript objects that represent the web browser and the contents of HTML documents. Many examples show typical uses of these client-side objects. You will find it helpful to study these examples carefully.

12

JavaScript in Web Browsers

The first part of this book described the core JavaScript language. Now we move on to JavaScript as used within web browsers, commonly called client-side JavaScript.* Most of the examples we've seen until now, while legal JavaScript code, had no particular context—they were JavaScript fragments that ran in no specified environment. This chapter provides that context. It begins with a conceptual introduction to the web browser programming environment and to basic client-side JavaScript concepts. Next, it discusses how we actually embed JavaScript code within HTML documents so that it can run in a web browser. Finally, the chapter goes into detail about how JavaScript programs are executed in a web browser.

12.1 The Web Browser Environment

To understand client-side JavaScript, you must understand the conceptual framework of the programming environment provided by a web browser. The following sections introduce three important features of that programming environment:

- The Window object that serves as the global object and global execution context for client-side JavaScript code

- The client-side object hierarchy

- The event-driven programming model

---

* The term "client-side JavaScript" is left over from the days when JavaScript was used in only two places: web browsers (clients) and web servers. As JavaScript is adopted as a scripting language in more and more places, the term "client-side" will no longer make much sense because it doesn't specify the client-side of *what.* Nevertheless, we'll continue to use the term in this book.

12.1.1 The Window as Global Execution Context

The primary task of a web browser is to display HTML documents in a window. In client-side JavaScript, the Document object represents an HTML document, and the Window object represents the window (or frame) that displays the document. While the Document and the Window objects are both important to client-side JavaScript, the Window object is more important. This is for one substantial reason: the Window object is the global object in client-side programming.

Recall from Chapter 4, *Variables*, that in every implementation of JavaScript there is always a global object at the head of the scope chain; the properties of this global object are global variables. In client-side JavaScript, the Window object is the global object. The Window object defines a number of properties and methods that allow us to manipulate the web browser window. It also defines properties that refer to other important objects, such as the `document` property for the Document object. Finally, the Window object has two self-referential properties, `window` and `self`. You can use either of these global variables to refer directly to the Window object.

Since the Window object is the global object in client-side JavaScript, all global variables are defined as properties of the window. For example, the following two lines of code perform essentially the same function:

```
var answer = 42;     // Declare and initialize a global variable.
window.answer = 42;  // Create a new property of the Window object.
```

The Window object represents a web browser window or a frame within a window. To client-side JavaScript, top-level windows and frames are essentially equivalent. It is common to write JavaScript applications that use multiple frames and possible, if less common, to write applications that use multiple windows. Each window or frame involved in an application has a unique Window object and defines a unique execution context for client-side JavaScript code. In other words, a global variable declared by JavaScript code in one frame is not a global variable within a second frame. However, the second frame *can* access a global variable of the first frame; we'll see how when we consider these issues in more detail in Chapter 13, *Windows and Frames*.

12.1.2 The Client-Side Object Hierarchy

We've seen that the Window object is the key object in client-side JavaScript. All other client-side objects are connected to this object. For example, every Window object contains a `document` property that refers to the Document object associated with the window and a `location` property that refers to the Location object associated with the window. A window object also contains a `frames[]` array that refers to the Window objects that represent the frames of the original window. Thus, `document` represents the Document object of the current window, and `frames[1].document` refers to the Document object of the second child frame of the current window.

An object referenced through the current window or through some other Window object may itself refer to other objects. For example, every Document object has a `forms[]` array containing Form objects that represent any HTML forms appearing in the document. To refer to one of these forms, you might write:

```
self.document.forms[0]
```

To continue with the same example, each Form object has an `elements[]` array containing objects that represent the various HTML form elements (input fields, buttons, etc.) that appear within the form. In extreme cases, you can write code that refers to an object at the end of a whole chain of objects, ending up with expressions as complex as this one:

```
parent.frames[0].document.forms[0].elements[3].options[2].text
```

We've seen that the Window object is the global object at the head of the scope chain and that all client-side objects in JavaScript are accessible as properties of other objects. What this means is that there is a hierarchy of JavaScript objects with the Window object at its root. Figure 12-1 shows this hierarchy. Study this figure carefully; understanding the hierarchy and the objects it contains is crucial to successful client-side JavaScript programming.

Note that Figure 12-1 shows just the object properties that refer to other objects. Most of the objects shown in the diagram have quite a few more properties than those shown. The notation "1.1" in the figure indicates properties that were added in JavaScript 1.1. Later chapters document the objects shown in the object hierarchy diagram and demonstrate common JavaScript programming techniques that employ those objects. You may find it useful to refer back to this figure while reading these chapters.

12.1.3 The Event-Driven Programming Model

In the old days, computer programs often ran in batch mode. This meant that they read in a batch of data, did some computation on that data, and then wrote out the results. Later, with timesharing and text-based terminals, limited kinds of interactivity became possible—the program could ask the user for input, and the user could type in data. The computer could then process the data and display the results on screen.

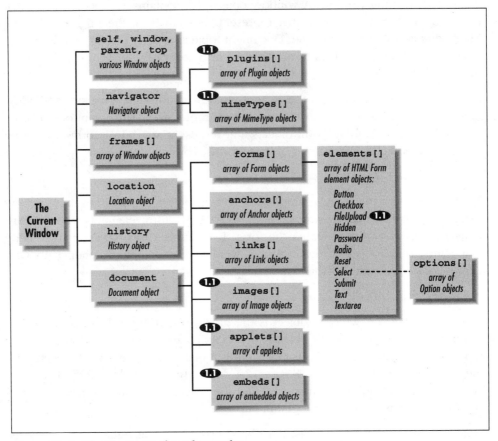

Figure 12–1: The JavaScript object hierarchy

Nowadays, with graphical displays and pointing devices like mice, the situation is different. Programs are generally event driven; they respond to asynchronous user input in the form of mouse clicks and keystrokes in a way that depends on the position of the mouse pointer. A web browser is just such a graphical environment. An HTML document contains an embedded GUI (graphical user interface), so client-side JavaScript uses the event-driven programming model.

It is perfectly possible to write a static JavaScript program that does not accept user input and does exactly the same thing every time. Sometimes this sort of program is useful. More often, however, we want to write dynamic programs that interact with the user. To do this, we must be able to respond to user input.

In client-side JavaScript, the web browser notifies our programs of user input by generating *events*. There are various types of events, such as keystroke events, mouse motion events, and so on. When an event occurs, the web browser attempts to invoke an appropriate *event handler* function to respond to the event. Thus, to write dynamic, interactive client-side JavaScript programs, we must define appropriate event handlers and register them with the system, so that the browser can invoke them at appropriate times.

If you are not already accustomed to the event-driven programming model, it can take a little getting used to. In the old model, you would write a single, monolithic block of code that followed some well-defined flow of control and ran to completion from beginning to end. Event-driven programming stands this model on its head. In event-driven programming, you write a number of independent (but mutually interacting) event handlers. You do not invoke these handlers directly, but allow the system to invoke them at the appropriate times. Since they are triggered by the user's input, the handlers will be invoked at unpredictable, asynchronous times. Much of the time your program is not running at all, but merely sitting waiting for the system to invoke one of its event handlers.

The next section explains how JavaScript code is embedded within HTML files. It shows how we can define both static blocks of code that run synchronously from start to finish and also event handlers that are invoked asynchronously by the system. We'll also discuss events and event handling in much greater detail in Chapter 15, *Events and Event Handling*.

12.2 Embedding JavaScript in HTML

If JavaScript is to be integrated into a web browser, an obvious requirement is that JavaScript code be embedded into the documents that web browsers display. There are actually seven ways that JavaScript code can be embedded into HTML documents:

- Between a pair of `<SCRIPT>` and `</SCRIPT>` tags

- From an external file specified by the `SRC` or `ARCHIVE` attributes of a `<SCRIPT>` tag

- In an event handler, specified as the value of an HTML attribute such as `onClick` or `onMouseOver`

- As the body of a URL that uses the special `javascript:` protocol

- In a style sheet, between `<STYLE TYPE="text/javascript">` and `</STYLE>` tags

- In a JavaScript entity, as the value of an HTML attribute

- In a conditional comment that comments out HTML text unless a given JavaScript expression evaluates to `true`

The following sections document each of these seven JavaScript embedding techniques in more detail. Together, they explain all the ways to include JavaScript in web pages—that is, they explain the allowed structure of JavaScript programs on the client side.

12.2.1 *The <SCRIPT> Tag*

Client-side JavaScript scripts are part of an HTML file and are usually coded within the `<SCRIPT>` and `</SCRIPT>` tags. You may place any number of JavaScript statements between these tags; they are executed in order of appearance, as part of the document loading process. `<SCRIPT>` tags may appear in either the `<HEAD>` or `<BODY>` of an HTML document.

A single HTML document may contain any number of non-overlapping pairs of `<SCRIPT>` and `</SCRIPT>` tags. These multiple, separate scripts are executed in the order in which they appear within the document. While separate scripts within a single file are executed at different times during the loading and parsing of the HTML file, they constitute part of the same JavaScript program: functions and variables defined in one script are available to all scripts that follow in the same file.* For example, you can have the following script somewhere in an HTML page:

```
<SCRIPT>var x = 1;</SCRIPT>
```

Later on in the same HTML page, you can refer to x, even though it's in a different script block. The context that matters is the HTML page, not the script block:

```
<SCRIPT>document.write(x);</SCRIPT>
```

Example 12-1 shows a sample HTML file that includes a simple JavaScript program. Note the difference between this example and many of the code fragments shown earlier in the book: this one is integrated with an HTML file and has a clear context in which it runs. Note also the use of a LANGUAGE attribute in the `<SCRIPT>` tag. This is explained in the next section.

Example 12-1: A Simple JavaScript Program in an HTML File

```
<HTML>
<HEAD>
<TITLE>Today's Date</TITLE>
    <SCRIPT LANGUAGE="JavaScript">
```

---

* In Navigator 4, the exception to this rule is that scripts located in their own layers (within `<LAYER>` tags, for example) run in their own contexts.

Example 12-1: A Simple JavaScript Program in an HTML File (continued)

```
    // Define a function for use later on.
    function print_todays_date()
    {
        var d = new Date();  // Today's date and time
        document.write(d.toLocaleString());
    }
    </SCRIPT>
</HEAD>
<BODY>
<HR>The date and time are:<BR><B>
    <SCRIPT LANGUAGE="JavaScript">
    // Now call the function we defined above.
    print_todays_date();
    </SCRIPT>
</B><HR>
</BODY>
</HTML>
```

12.2.1.1 The LANGUAGE attribute

The <SCRIPT> tag has an optional LANGUAGE attribute that specifies the scripting language used for the script. This attribute is necessary because there is more than one version of JavaScript and there is more than one scripting language that can be embedded between <SCRIPT> and </SCRIPT> tags. By specifying which language a script is written in, you tell a browser whether it should attempt to interpret the script, or whether the script is written in a language that the browser doesn't understand, and should therefore be ignored.

If you are writing JavaScript code, use the LANGUAGE attribute as follows:

```
<SCRIPT LANGUAGE="JavaScript">
    // JavaScript code goes here.
</SCRIPT>
```

On the other hand, if you are writing a script in Microsoft's VBScript language[*] you should use the attribute like this:

```
<SCRIPT LANGUAGE="VBScript">
    ' VBScript code goes here (' is a comment character like // in JavaScript)
</SCRIPT>
```

When you specify the LANGUAGE="JavaScript" attribute for a script, any JavaScript-enabled browser will run the script, while browsers that understand the

---

[*] The language is actually called Visual Basic Scripting Edition. Obviously, it is a version of Microsoft's Visual Basic language. The only browser that supports VBScript is Internet Explorer. VBScript interfaces with HTML objects in the same way that JavaScript does, but the core language itself has a different syntax than JavaScript.

<SCRIPT> tag but do not understand JavaScript will ignore the script. But the LAN-GUAGE attribute can be used to specify more than just the scripting language in use: it can also specify the version of the language. For example, if you specify LANGUAGE="JavaScript1.1", only browsers that support JavaScript 1.1 (or later) will run the script; other browsers (such as Navigator 2) will ignore it. Similarly, if you specify a LANGUAGE attribute of "JavaScript1.2", only JavaScript 1.2 browsers (such as Navigator 4) will run the script.

The use of the string "JavaScript1.2" in the LANGUAGE attribute deserves special mention. When Navigator 4 was being prepared for release, it appeared that the emerging ECMA-262 standard would require some incompatible changes to certain features of the language. To prevent these incompatible changes from breaking existing scripts, the designers of JavaScript at Netscape took the sensible precaution of implementing the changes only when "JavaScript1.2" was explicitly specified in the LANGUAGE attribute. This ensured that only code written explicitly for the new platform would get the new behavior. JavaScript code written for previous browsers would still get the old-style behavior it expected.

Unfortunately, the ECMA standard was not finalized before Navigator 4 was released, and after the release, the proposed incompatible changes to the language were removed from the standard. Thus, specifying a LANGUAGE attribute of "JavaScript1.2" makes Navigator 4 behave in ways that are not compatible with previous browsers and not compatible with the ECMA specification. For this reason, you may want to avoid specifying "JavaScript1.2" as a value for the LANGUAGE attribute.

JavaScript is, and is likely to remain, the *default* scripting language for the Web. If you omit the LANGUAGE attribute, both Navigator and Internet Explorer default to the value "JavaScript". Nonetheless, because there are now multiple scripting languages available, it is a good habit to always use the LANGUAGE attribute to specify exactly what language (or what version) your scripts are written in.

12.2.1.2 The </SCRIPT> tag

You may at some point find yourself writing a script that writes a script into some other browser window or frame.* If you do this, you'll need to write out a </SCRIPT> tag to terminate the script you are writing. You must be careful, though—the HTML parser doesn't know about quoted strings, so if you write out a string that contains the characters "</SCRIPT>", the HTML parser terminates the currently running script.

---

* This happens more often than you might think; one commonly used feature of JavaScript is the ability to dynamically generate HTML and JavaScript content for display in other browser windows and frames.

To avoid this problem, simply break the tag up into pieces and write it out using an expression like `"</" + "SCRIPT>"`:

```
<SCRIPT>
f1.document.write("<SCRIPT>");
f1.document.write("document.write('<H2>This is the quoted script</H2>')");
f1.document.write("</" + "SCRIPT>");
</SCRIPT>
```

Alternatively, you can escape the / in `</SCRIPT>` with a backslash:

```
f1.document.write("<\/SCRIPT>");
```

12.2.2 Including JavaScript Files

As of JavaScript 1.1, the `<SCRIPT>` tag supports a `SRC` attribute. The value of this attribute specifies the URL of a file of JavaScript code. It is used like this:

```
<SCRIPT SRC="../../javascript/util.js"></SCRIPT>
```

A JavaScript file is just that—pure JavaScript, without `<SCRIPT>` tags or any other HTML. A JavaScript file typically has a *.js* extension, and should be exported by a web server with MIME-type `application/x-javascript`. This last point is important; your web server may require special configuration in order to success-fully use JavaScript files in this way.

The `<SCRIPT>` tag with the `SRC` attribute specified behaves exactly as if the con-tents of the specified JavaScript file appeared directly between the `<SCRIPT>` and `</SCRIPT>` tags. Any code that does appear between the open and close `<SCRIPT>` tags is ignored by browsers that support the `SRC` attribute (although it is still executed by browsers like Navigator 2 that do not recognize the tag). Note that the closing `</SCRIPT>` tag is required even when the `SRC` attribute is specified and there is no JavaScript between the `<SCRIPT>` and `</SCRIPT>` tags.

There are a number of advantages to using the `SRC` tag:

- It simplifies your HTML files by allowing you to remove large blocks of JavaScript code from them.

- When you have a function or other JavaScript code used by several different HTML files, you can keep it in a single file and read it into each HTML file that needs it. This reduces disk usage and makes code maintenance much easier.

- When JavaScript functions are used by more than one page, placing them in a separate JavaScript file allows them to be cached by the browser, making them load more quickly. When JavaScript code is shared by multiple pages, the time savings of caching more than outweigh the small delay required for the browser to open a separate network connection to download the JavaScript file the first time it is requested.

- Because the SRC attribute takes an arbitrary URL as its value, a JavaScript program or web page from one web server can employ code (such as subroutine libraries) exported by other web servers.

12.2.2.1 The ARCHIVE attribute

In Navigator 4 and Internet Explorer 4, the SRC attribute of the <SCRIPT> tag is complemented by the ARCHIVE attribute. ARCHIVE specifies a JAR (Java archive) file that contains a number of compressed JavaScript files (and may also contain other auxiliary files, such as digital signatures). If your program uses a number of JavaScript files, it can be more efficient to combine them into a single compressed JAR file that can be loaded over the network. Note that the ARCHIVE attribute specifies only the name of the archive, not the name of the individual *.js* file that you want to use within it. Thus, the ARCHIVE attribute must be used with the SRC attribute. For example:

```
<SCRIPT ARCHIVE="utils.jar" SRC="animation.js"></SCRIPT>
```

A JAR archive file is simply a common ZIP file with some additional manifest information added. Netscape provides a free tool that allows developers to create JAR archives. One of the most important uses of archives is attaching digital signatures to scripts. We'll talk more about this, and about creating and using JAR archives, in Chapter 21, *JavaScript Security*.

12.2.3 Event Handlers

JavaScript code in a <SCRIPT> is executed once, when the HTML file that contains it is read into the web browser. A program that uses only this sort of static script cannot respond dynamically to the user. More dynamic programs define event handlers that are automatically invoked by the web browser when certain events occur—for example, when the user clicks on a button within a form. Because events in client-side JavaScript originate from HTML objects (like buttons), event handlers are defined as attributes of those objects.

In order to allow us to define JavaScript event handlers as part of HTML object definitions, JavaScript extends HTML* by adding new event handler attributes to various HTML tags. For example, to define an event handler that is invoked when the user clicks on a checkbox in a form, you specify the handler code as an attribute of the HTML tag that defines the checkbox:

```
<INPUT
    TYPE="checkbox"
```

---

* These event handler extensions to HTML have now been recognized and standardized by the HTML 4.0 standard.

```
          NAME="opts"
          VALUE="ignore-case"
          onClick="ignore_case = this.checked;"
    >
```

What's of interest to us here is the `onClick` attribute.* The string value of the `onClick` attribute may contain one or more JavaScript statements. If there is more than one statement, the statements must be separated from each other with semi-colons. When the specified event—in this case, a click—occurs on the checkbox, the JavaScript code within the string is executed.

While you can include any number of JavaScript statements within an event handler definition, a common technique when more than one or two simple statements are required is to define the body of an event handler as a function between `<SCRIPT>` and `</SCRIPT>` tags. Then you can simply invoke this function from the event handler. This keeps most of your actual JavaScript code within scripts and reduces the need to mingle JavaScript and HTML.

We'll cover events and event handlers in much more detail in Chapter 15.

12.2.3.1 Event handlers in <SCRIPT> tags

In Internet Explorer, but not in Navigator, there is an alternative syntax for defining event handlers. It involves using new `FOR` and `EVENT` attributes to the `<SCRIPT>` tag to specify code that constitutes an event handler for a named object and a named event. Using this Internet Explorer technique, we could rewrite the checkbox example shown earlier like this:

```
    <INPUT TYPE="checkbox" NAME="opts" VALUE="ignore-case">
    <SCRIPT FOR="opts" EVENT="onClick">
        ignore_case = this.checked;
    </SCRIPT>
```

Note that the value of the `FOR` attribute must be an object name assigned with the `NAME` attribute when the object is defined. And the value of the `EVENT` attribute is the name of the event handler (but not the name of the event itself).

There is a certain elegance to specifying event handlers in this way—it avoids the need to add new JavaScript-specific attributes to all HTML objects. However, this technique for defining event handlers is typically of more use to VBScript programmers than to JavaScript programmers, and since it is not supported by Navigator, its use is not recommended.

---

* All event handler attribute names begin with "on." The mixed-case capitalization of `onClick` is a common convention for JavaScript event handlers defined in HTML files. HTML element and attribute names are case-insensitive, but writing "onClick" rather than "ONCLICK" sets off the handlers from standard HTML tags, which are, by convention, shown in all capitals.

12.2.4 JavaScript in URLs

Another way that JavaScript code can be included on the client side is in a URL following the `javascript:` pseudo-protocol specifier. This special protocol type specifies that the body of the URL is arbitrary JavaScript code to be run by the JavaScript interpreter. If the JavaScript code in a `javascript:` URL contains multiple statements, the statements must be separated from one another by semicolons. Such a URL might look like this:

```
javascript:var now = new Date(); "<h1>The time is:</h1>" + now;
```

When the browser loads one of these JavaScript URLs, it executes the JavaScript code contained in the URL and displays the document referred to by the URL. This document is the string value of the last JavaScript statement in the URL. The string is formatted and displayed just like any other document loaded into the browser.

More commonly, a JavaScript URL contains JavaScript statements that perform actions but return no value. For example:

```
javascript:alert("Hello World!")
```

When this sort of URL is loaded, the browser executes the JavaScript code, but because there is no value to display as the new document, it does not modify the currently displayed document.

Note that as of JavaScript 1.1, you can use the `void` operator to force an expression to have no value. This is useful when you want to execute an assignment statement, for example, but do not want to display the assigned value in the browser window. (Recall that assignment statements are also expressions, and that they evaluate to the value of the right-hand side of the assignment.)

A `javascript:` URL can be used anywhere you'd use a regular URL. In Navigator, one important way to use this syntax is to type it directly into the **Location** field of your browser, where it allows you to test arbitrary JavaScript code without having to get out your editor and create an HTML file containing the code.

In fact, Navigator takes this idea even further. As described in Chapter 1, *Introduction to JavaScript*, if you enter the URL `javascript:` alone, with no JavaScript code following it, Navigator displays a JavaScript interpreter page that allows you to sequentially enter and execute lines of code. Unfortunately, neither of these techniques works in Internet Explorer.

`javascript:` URLs can also be used in other contexts. You might use one as the target of a hypertext link, for example. When the user clicks on the link, the specified JavaScript code is executed. Or, if you specify a `javascript:` URL as the value of the `ACTION` attribute of a `<FORM>` tag, the JavaScript code in the URL is executed when the user submits the form. In these contexts, the `javascript:` URL is essentially a substitute for an event handler. Event handlers and `javascript:` URLs can often be used interchangeably—which you choose is a stylistic matter.

There are a few circumstances where a `javascript:` URL can be used with objects that do not support event handlers. For example, the `<AREA>` tag does not support an `onClick` event handler on Windows platforms in Navigator 3 (though it does in Navigator 4). So, if you want to execute JavaScript code when the user clicks on a client-side image map prior to Navigator 4, you must use a `javascript:` URL.

12.2.5 *JavaScript Style Sheet Syntax*

In Navigator 4, JavaScript code may appear in a style sheet, between the tag `<STYLE TYPE="text/javascript">` and the tag `</STYLE>`. Any such JavaScript code should appear in the `<HEAD>` of an HTML document; its purpose should be to define a style sheet by setting properties of the `tags`, `classes`, and `ids` attributes. JavaScript style sheet (JSS) syntax is an alternative to standard cascading style sheet (CSS) syntax. For example, the following style sheet uses JavaScript code to specify that all `<H1>` headings in a document should appear in bold red text:

```
<STYLE TYPE="text/javascript">
  tags.H1.fontstyle="bold";
  tags.H1.color = "red";
</STYLE>
```

Although JavaScript code in a `STYLE` tag should only be used to defined style sheets, in practice it can be used (or abused) for any purpose, like a `<SCRIPT>` tag. The only difference between `<STYLE>` code and `<SCRIPT>` code is that JavaScript code in a `<STYLE>` tag is scoped to the Document object rather than the Window object. That is, when it looks up variables, it finds properties (such as `tags`) of the Document object before it finds properties of the Window object. Because this is the only difference, it is also possible to define style sheet syntax with a `<SCRIPT>` tag. Note, however, that we must explicitly specify that the `tags` and other objects are properties of the Document object:

```
<SCRIPT LANGUAGE="javascript">
  document.tags.H1.fontstyle="bold";
  document.tags.H1.color = "red";
</SCRIPT>
```

Note that because JSS syntax is not supported by Internet Explorer and is not likely to be adopted as a standard, its use is discouraged. In general, you should use standard CSS syntax wherever possible. We'll see more about cascading style sheet and JavaScript style sheet syntax in Chapter 17, *Dynamic HTML.*

12.2.6 *JavaScript Entities*

In Navigator 3 and later, JavaScript code may appear in HTML attribute values in a special form known as a *JavaScript entity*. Recall that an HTML entity is a sequence of characters like < that represents a special character like <. A JavaScript entity is similar. It has the following syntax:

```
&{ JavaScript-statements };
```

The entity may contain any number of JavaScript statements, which must be separated from one another by semicolons. It must begin with an ampersand and an open curly bracket and end with a close curly bracket and a semicolon.

Whenever an entity is encountered in HTML, it is replaced with its value. The value of a JavaScript entity is the value of the last JavaScript statement or expression within the entity, converted to a string.

In general, entities can be used anywhere within HTML code. JavaScript entities, however, may appear only within the values of HTML attributes. These entities allow you, in effect, to write conditional HTML. Typical usage might look like this:

```
<BODY BGCOLOR="&{favorite_color();};">
<INPUT TYPE="text" NAME="lastname" VALUE="&{defaults.lastname};">
```

12.2.7 *Conditional Comments*

In Navigator 4 and later, a JavaScript entity may be used with a modified HTML comment syntax to produce a *conditional comment*. If the JavaScript expression embedded in the entity evaluates to `true`, the comment is ignored and the body of the comment (typically HTML text) is processed as usual. If the expression evaluates to `false` (or is not evaluated by a browser that doesn't understand this special comment syntax), the comment behaves as normal and the contents of the comment are ignored.

Conditional comments allow you to write JavaScript code that runs only on platforms that can support it. The code below, for example, runs only if the `navigator.platform` property (new in JavaScript 1.2) is equal to the string "win95" (i.e., if the code is running on a Windows 95 browser):

```
<!--&{navigator.platform == "win95"};
  <SCRIPT>
    ... // JavaScript code goes here.
  </SCRIPT>
-->
```

Unfortunately, since conditional comments are not supported by Internet Explorer 4, their utility is somewhat limited.

12.3 Execution of JavaScript Programs

The previous section discussed the mechanics of integrating JavaScript code into an HTML file. Now we move on to discuss exactly how that integrated JavaScript code is executed by the JavaScript interpreter. The following sections explain how different forms of JavaScript code are executed. While some of this material is fairly obvious, there are a number of important details that are not so obvious.

12.3.1 Scripts

JavaScript statements that appear between `<SCRIPT>` and `</SCRIPT>` tags are executed in order of appearance, and when more than one script appears in a file, those scripts are executed in the order in which they appear. The same rules apply to scripts included from separate files with the `SRC` attribute. This much is obvious.

The detail that is not so obvious but that is important to remember is that execution of scripts occurs as part of the web browser's HTML parsing process. Thus, if a script appears in the `<HEAD>` section of an HTML document, none of the `<BODY>` section of the document has been defined yet. This means that the JavaScript objects that represent the contents of the document body, such as Form and Link, have not been created yet and cannot be manipulated by that code.

Your scripts should not attempt to manipulate objects that haven't been created yet. For example, you can't write a script that manipulates the contents of an HTML form if the script appears before the form in the HTML file. Some other, similar rules apply on a case-by-case basis. For example, there are properties of the Document object that may be set only from a script in the `<HEAD>` section of an HTML document before Navigator has begun to parse the document content in the `<BODY>` section. Any special rules of this sort are documented in the reference entry for the affected object or property.

Since scripts are executed while the HTML document that contains them is being parsed and displayed, they should not take too long to run. An HTML document cannot be fully displayed until all scripts it contains have finished executing. If a script performs some computationally intensive task that takes a long time to run, the user may become frustrated waiting for the document to be displayed. Thus, if you need to perform a lot of computation with JavaScript, you should define a function to do the computation and invoke that function from an event handler when the user requests it rather than doing the computation when the document is first loaded.

As noted earlier, scripts that use the SRC attribute to read in external JavaScript files are executed just like scripts that include their code directly in the file. What this means is that the HTML parser and the JavaScript interpreter must both stop and wait for the external JavaScript file to be downloaded—scripts cannot be downloaded in parallel, as embedded images can. Downloading an external file of JavaScript code, even over a relatively fast modem connection, can cause noticeable delays in the loading and execution of a web page. Of course, once the JavaScript code is cached locally, this problem effectively disappears.

As we discussed in the previous section, Navigator 4 allows JavaScript code to be included in a style sheet within a pair of <STYLE> and </STYLE> tags. The JavaScript statements within a style sheet execute just like JavaScript statements within a <SCRIPT>, except that the scope chain is modified so that variables are looked up as properties of the Document object before they are looked up as properties of the Window object. This means that JavaScript style sheets can refer to the tags, classes, and ids properties of the Document object as if they were global variables, instead of using expressions like document.tags.

In Navigator 2, there is a notable bug relating to execution of scripts: whenever the web browser is resized, all the scripts within it are reinterpreted.

12.3.2 Functions

Remember that defining a function is not the same as executing it. It is perfectly safe to define a function that manipulates objects that haven't been created yet. You simply must take care that the function is not executed or invoked until the necessary variables, objects, and so on, all exist. I said earlier that you can't write a script to manipulate an HTML form if the script appears before the form in the HTML file. You can, however, write a script that defines a function to manipulate the form, regardless of the relative location of the script and form. In fact, this is a common thing to do. Many JavaScript programs start off with a script at the beginning of the file that does nothing more than define functions that are used further down in the HTML file.

It is also common to write JavaScript programs that use scripts simply to define functions that are later invoked through event handlers. As we'll see in the next section, you must take care in this case to ensure two things: that all functions are defined before any event handler attempts to invoke them, and that event handlers and the functions they invoke do not attempt to use objects that have not been defined yet.

12.3.3 Event Handlers

As we've seen, defining an event handler creates a JavaScript function. These event handler functions are defined as part of the HTML parsing process, but like functions defined directly by scripts, event handlers are not executed immediately. Event handler execution is asynchronous. Since events generally occur when the user interacts with HTML objects, there is no way to predict when an event handler will be invoked.

Event handlers share an important restriction with scripts: they should not take a long time to execute. As we've seen, scripts should run quickly because the HTML parser cannot continue parsing until the script finishes executing. Event handlers, on the other hand, should not take long to run because the user cannot interact with your program until the program has finished handling the event. If an event handler performs some time-consuming operation, it may appear to the user that the program has hung, frozen up, or crashed.

If for some reason you must perform a long operation in an event handler, be sure that the user has explicitly requested that operation and then be sure to notify him that there will be a wait. As we'll see in Chapter 13, you can notify the user by posting an `alert()` dialog box or by displaying text in the browser's status line. Also, if your program requires a lot of background processing, you can schedule a function to be called repeatedly during idle time with the `setTimeout()` method.

It is important to understand that event handlers may be invoked before a web page is fully loaded and parsed. This is easier to understand if you imagine a slow network connection—even a half-loaded document may display hypertext links and form elements that the user can interact with, thereby causing event handlers to be invoked before the second half of the document is loaded.

The fact that event handlers can be invoked before a document is fully loaded has two important implications. First, if your event handler invokes a function, you must be sure that the function is already defined before the handler calls it. One way to guarantee this is to define all your functions in the `<HEAD>` section of an HTML document. This section of a document is always completely parsed (and any functions in it defined) before the `<BODY>` section of the document is parsed. Since all objects that define event handlers must themselves be defined in the `<BODY>` section, functions in the `<HEAD>` section are guaranteed to be defined before any event handlers are invoked.

The second implication is that you must be sure that your event handler does not attempt to manipulate HTML objects that have not yet been parsed and created. An event handler can always safely manipulate its own object, of course, and also any objects that are defined before it in the HTML file. One strategy is simply to define your web page user interface in such a way that event handlers refer only to objects defined previously. For example, if you define a form that uses event handlers only on the **Submit** and **Reset** buttons, you just need to place these buttons at the bottom of the form (which is where good user-interface style says they should go anyway).

In more complex programs, you may not be able to ensure that event handlers only manipulate objects defined before them, so you need to take extra care with these programs. If an event handler only manipulates objects defined within the same form, it is pretty unlikely that you'll ever have problems. When you manipulate objects in other forms or in other frames, however, this starts to be a real concern. One technique is to test for the existence of the object you want to manipulate before you manipulate it. You can do this simply by comparing it (and any parent objects) to `null`. For example:

```
<SCRIPT>
function set_name_other_frame(name)
{
    if (parent.frames[1] == null) return;   // Other frame not defined yet
    if (!parent.frames[1].document) return; // Document not loaded in it yet
    if (!parent.frames[1].document.myform) return;     // Form not defined yet
    if (!parent.frames[1].document.myform.name) return; // Field not defined

    parent.frames[1].document.myform.name.value = name;
}
</SCRIPT>

<INPUT TYPE="text" NAME="lastname"
       onChange="set_name_other_frame(this.value)";
>
```

Another technique that an event handler can use to ensure that all required objects are defined involves the `onLoad` event handler. This event handler is defined in the `<BODY>` or `<FRAMESET>` tag of an HTML file and is invoked when the document or frameset is fully loaded. If you set a flag within the `onLoad` event handler, other event handlers can test this flag to see if they can safely run, with the knowledge that the document is fully loaded and all objects it contains are defined. For example:

```
<BODY onLoad="window.loaded = true;">
  <FORM>
    <INPUT TYPE="button" VALUE="Press Me"
           onClick="if (window.loaded != true) return; doit();"
    >
  </FORM>
</BODY>
```

12.3.3.1 onLoad() and onUnload() event handlers

The onLoad event handler and its partner the onUnload handler are worth a special mention in the context of the execution order of JavaScript programs. Both of these event handlers are defined in the <BODY> or <FRAMESET> tag of an HTML file. (No HTML file can legally contain both these tags.) The onLoad handler is executed when the document or frameset is fully loaded, which means that all images have been downloaded and displayed, all subframes have loaded, any Java applets and plugins (Navigator) have started running, and so on. The onUnload handler is executed just before the page is unloaded, which occurs when the browser is about to move on to a new page. Be aware that when you are working with multiple frames, there is no guarantee of the order in which the onLoad event handler is invoked for the various frames, except that the handler for the parent frame is invoked after the handlers of all its children frames (although this is buggy and doesn't always work correctly in Navigator 2).

The onLoad event handler lets you perform initialization for your web page, while the onUnload event handler lets you undo any lingering effects of the initialization or perform any other necessary cleanup on your page. For example, onLoad could set the Window.defaultStatus property to display a special message in the browser's status bar. Then the onUnload handler would restore the defaultStatus property to its default (the empty string), so that the message does not persist on other pages.

Note that the onUnload event handler should not run any kind of time-consuming operation, nor should it pop up a dialog box. It exists simply to perform a quick cleanup operation; running it should not slow down or impede the transition to a new page.

12.3.4 JavaScript URLs

JavaScript code in a javascript: URL is not executed when the document containing the URL is loaded. It is not interpreted until the browser tries to load the document that the URL refers to. This may be when a user types in a JavaScript URL, or, more likely, when a user follows a link, clicks on a client-side image map, or submits a form. javascript: URLs are usually equivalent to event handlers, and as with event handlers, the code in those URLs can be executed before a document is fully loaded. Thus, you must take the same precautions with javascript: URLs that you take with event handlers to ensure that they do not attempt to reference objects (or functions) that are not yet defined.

12.3.5 JavaScript Entities and Conditional Comments

A JavaScript entity, whether used as the value of an HTML attribute or as part of a conditional comment, must be evaluated as part of the process of HTML parsing. In fact, since the JavaScript code in an entity produces a value that becomes part of the HTML itself, the HTML parsing process is dependent on the JavaScript interpreter in this case. JavaScript entities can always be replaced by more cumbersome scripts that write the affected HTML tags dynamically. Take the following line of HTML:

```
<INPUT TYPE="text" NAME="lastname" VALUE="&{defaults.lastname};">
```

This can be replaced with these lines:

```
<SCRIPT>
  document.write('<INPUT TYPE="text" NAME="lastname" VALUE="' +
                 defaults.lastname +
                 '">');
</SCRIPT>
```

Similarly, any conditional comment can be replaced by a script that dynamically outputs the HTML content within the comment only if the entity evaluates to true. For all intents and purposes, JavaScript entities and conditional comments are executed just like their equivalent scripts.

12.3.6 Window and Variable Lifetime

A final topic in our investigation of how client-side JavaScript programs run is the issue of variable lifetime. We've seen that the Window object is the global object for client-side JavaScript and all global variables are properties of the Window object. What happens to Window objects and the variables they contain when the web browser moves from one web page to another?

A Window object that represents a top-level browser window exists as long as that window exists. A reference to the Window object remains valid regardless of how many web pages the window loads and unloads. The Window object is valid as long as the top-level window is open.*

A Window object that represents a frame remains valid as long as that frame remains within the frame or window that contains it. If the containing frame or window loads a new document, the frames it originally contained are destroyed in the process of loading that new document.

---

* A Window object may not actually be destroyed when its window is closed. If there are still references to the Window object from other windows, the object is not garbage collected. However, a reference to a window that has been closed is of very little practical use.

All this points to the fact that Window objects, whether they represent top-level windows or frames, are fairly persistent. The lifetime of a Window object may be longer than that of the web pages that it contains and displays and longer than the lifetime of the scripts contained in the web pages it displays.

When a web page that contains a script is unloaded because the user has pointed the browser to a new page, the script is unloaded along with the page that contains it. (If the script were not unloaded, a browser might soon be overflowing with various lingering scripts!) But what about the variables defined by the script? Since these variables are actually properties of the Window object that contained the script, you might think that they would remain defined. On the other hand, leaving them defined seems dangerous—a new script that was loaded wouldn't be starting with a clean slate, and in fact, it could never know what sorts of properties (and therefore variables) were already defined.

In fact, all user-defined properties (which includes all variables) are erased whenever a web page is unloaded. The scripts in a freshly loaded document start with no variables defined and no properties in their Window object, except for the standard core and client-side JavaScript properties defined by the system. What this means is that the lifetime of scripts and of the variables they define is the same as the lifetime of the document that contains the scripts. This is potentially much shorter than the lifetime of the window or frame that displays the document containing the scripts. There are important security reasons why this must be so.

The point to remember is that the scripts you write and the variables and functions they define do not and cannot persist across web pages. The programming environment (i.e., the global object) is wiped clean when the browser moves from one web page to another. Every web page begins execution with a clean slate.

13

Windows and Frames

Chapter 12, *JavaScript in Web Browsers*, described the Window object and the central role it plays in client-side JavaScript. We've seen that the Window object serves as the global object for client-side JavaScript programs, and as illustrated in Figure 12-1, it is also the root of the client-side object hierarchy.

Besides these special roles, the Window object is an important object in its own right. Every web browser window and every frame within every window is represented by a Window object. The Window object defines quite a few properties and methods that are important in client-side JavaScript programming. This chapter explores those properties and methods and demonstrates some important techniques for programming with windows and frames. Note that because the Window object is so central to client-side programming, this chapter is quite long. Don't feel you have to master all this material at once—you may find it easier to study this chapter in several shorter chunks!

13.1 Window Overview

We begin this chapter with an overview of some of the most commonly used properties and methods of the Window object. Later sections of the chapter explain this material in more detail. As usual, the reference section contains complete coverage of Window object properties and methods.

The most important properties of the Window object are:

`closed`
A boolean value that is `true` only if the window has been closed.

`defaultStatus, status`
These properties specify the text that appears in the status line of the browser.

`document`
A reference to the Document object that represents the HTML document displayed in the window. The Document object is covered in detail in Chapter 14, *The Document Object Model*.

`frames[]`
An array of Window objects that represent the frames (if any) within the window.

`history`
A reference to the History object that represents the user's browsing history for the window.

`innerHeight, innerWidth, outerHeight, outerWidth`
The inner and outer dimensions of the window; not available in Internet Explorer 4.

`location`
A reference to the Location object that represents the URL of the document displayed in the window. Setting this property causes the browser to load a new document.

`locationbar, menubar, personalbar, scrollbars, statusbar, toolbar`
References to Bar objects that specify the visibility of the various parts of the Navigator window; not available in IE 4.

`name`
The name of the window. Can be used with the `TARGET` attribute of the HTML <A> tag, for example.

`opener`
A reference to the Window object that opened this one, or `null` if this window was opened by the user.

`pageXOffset, pageYOffset`
The amounts that the document has been scrolled to the right and down within the window; not available in IE 4.

parent

    If the current window is a frame, a reference to the frame of the window that contains it.

self

    A self-referential property; a reference to the current Window object. A synonym for window.

top

    If the current window is a frame, a reference to the Window object of the top-level window that contains the frame. Note that top is different from parent for frames nested within other frames.

window

    A self-referential property; a reference to the current Window object. A synonym for self.

The Window object also supports a number of important methods:

alert(), confirm(), prompt()

    Display simple dialog boxes to the user, and, for confirm() and prompt(), get the user's response.

close()

    Close the window.

find(), home(), print(), stop()

    Duplicate the functionality of buttons in the Navigator button bar; these methods not available in IE 4.

focus(), blur()

    Request or relinquish keyboard focus for the window; these methods not available in IE 3.

moveBy(), moveTo()

    Move the window.

resizeBy(), resizeTo()

    Resize the window.

scrollBy(), scrollTo()

    Scroll the document displayed within the window.

setInterval(), clearInterval()

    Schedule or cancel a function to be repeatedly invoked with a specified delay between invocations.

```
setTimeout(), clearTimeout()
```
Schedule or cancel a function to be invoked once after a specified number of milliseconds

As you can see from these lists, the Window object provides quite a bit of functionality. The remainder of this chapter explores much of that functionality in more detail.

13.2 Simple Dialogs

Three commonly used Window methods are `alert()`, `confirm()`, and `prompt()`. These methods pop up simple dialog boxes. `alert()` displays a message to the user. `confirm()` asks the user to click an **Ok** or **Cancel** button to confirm or cancel an operation. And `prompt()` asks the user to enter a string. Sample dialogs produced by these three methods are shown in Figure 13-1.

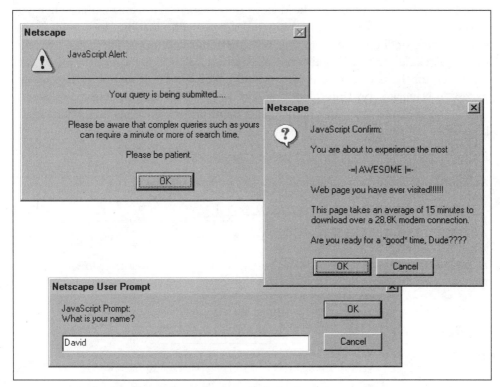

Figure 13-1: alert(), confirm(), and prompt() dialog boxes

Note that the text displayed by these dialog boxes is plain text, not HTML-formatted text. The only formatting you can do is with spaces, newlines, and various punctuation characters. Adjusting the layout generally requires trial and error. Bear in mind, though, that the dialogs look different on different platforms and in different browsers, so you can't always count on your formatting to look right on all possible browsers.

Note that the word "JavaScript" appears in the titlebar or upper left corner of all dialog boxes produced by alert(), confirm(), and prompt(). Although it is annoying, there is no way to get rid of it; it is there to prevent you from writing Trojan horse code that spoofs system dialogs and tricks users into entering their passwords or doing other things that they shouldn't do. (Note that Internet Explorer includes the words "Internet Explorer" in the titlebar of its dialogs, which is not as strong a measure to prevent Trojan horses.)

The confirm() and prompt() methods block—that is, those methods do not return until the user dismisses the dialogs they display. This means that when you pop one up, your code stops running and the currently loading document, if any, stops loading until the user responds with the requested input. There is no alternative to blocking for these methods—their return value is the user's input, so they must wait for the user before they can return. The alert() method is also modal, except in Navigator on Unix platforms. On these platforms, JavaScript displays the dialog and then moves on to the next statement. In practice, this minor incompatibility does not cause many problems.

Example 13-1 shows some typical uses of these methods.

Example 13-1: Using the alert(), confirm(), and prompt() Methods

```
// Here's a function that uses the alert() method to tell the user
// that form submission will take some time, and that the user should
// be patient. It would be suitable for use in the onSubmit event handler
// of an HTML form.
// Note that all formatting is done with spaces, newlines, and underscores.
function warn_on_submit()
{
    alert("\n_____\n\n" +
          "                 Your query is being submitted...\n"     +
          "_____\n\n"   +
          "Please be aware that complex queries such as yours\n"    +
          "     can require a minute or more of search time.\n\n"   +
          "                    Please be patient.");
}

// Here is a use of the confirm() method to ask if the user really
// wants to visit a web page that takes a long time to download. Note that
// the return value of the method indicates the user response. Based
```

Example 13-1: Using the alert(), confirm(), and prompt() Methods (continued)

```
// on this response, we reroute the browser to an appropriate page.

var msg = "\nYou are about to experience the most\n\n" +
          "              -=| AWESOME |=-\n\n" +
          "Web page you have ever visited!!!!!!\n\n" +
          "This page takes an average of 15 minutes to\n" +
          "download over a 28.8K modem connection.\n\n" +
          "Are you ready for a *good* time, Dude????";

if (confirm(msg))
    location.replace("awesome_page.html");
else
    location.replace("lame_page.html");

// Here's some very simple code that uses the prompt() method to get
// a user's name, and then uses that name in dynamically generated HTML.
n = prompt("What is your name?", "");
document.write("<hr><h1>Welcome to my home page, " + n + "</h1><hr>");
```

13.3 The Status Line

There is a *status line* at the bottom of every browser window (except for those we explicitly create without one). This is a location where the browser can display messages to the user. When the user moves the mouse over a hypertext link, for example, the browser displays the URL that the link points to. And when the user moves the mouse over a browser control button, the browser displays a simple "context help" message that explains the purpose of the button. You can also make use of this status line in your own programs—its contents are controlled by two properties of the Window object: status and defaultStatus.

I've just said that browsers display the URL of a hypertext link when the user passes the mouse pointer over the link. This is generally the case, but in your excursions through the web, you may have found some links that don't behave this way—links that display some text other than the link's URL. This is done with the status property of the Window object and the onMouseOver event handler of hypertext links:

```
<!-- Here's how you set the status line in a hyperlink.
  -- Note that the event handler *must* return true for this to work. -->
Lost? Dazed and confused? Visit the
<A HREF="sitemap.html" onMouseOver="status='Go to Site Map'; return true;">
  Site Map
</A>
```

```
<!-- You can do the same thing for client-side image maps.-->
<IMG SRC="images/imgmap1.gif" USEMAP="#map1">
<MAP NAME="map1">
  <AREA COORDS="0,0,50,20" HREF="info.html"
    onMouseover="status='Visit our Information Center'; return true;">
  <AREA COORDS="0,20,50,40" HREF="order.html"
    onMouseOver="status='Place an order'; return true;">
  <AREA COORDS="0,40,50,60" HREF="help.html"
    onMouseOver="status='Get help fast!'; return true;">
</MAP>
```

The onMouseOver event handler in the previous example must return true. This tells the browser that it should not perform its own default action for the event—that is, it should not display the URL of the link in the status line. If you forget to return true, the browser overwrites whatever message the handler displays in the status line with its own URL. Don't worry if you do not fully understand the event handler in this example. We'll explain events in Chapter 15, *Events and Event Handling*.

When the user moves the mouse pointer over a hyperlink, the browser displays the URL for the link and then erases it when the mouse moves off the hyperlink. The same is true when you use an onMouseOver event handler to set the Window status property—your custom message is displayed while the mouse is over the hyperlink, and then it is erased when the mouse moves off the link. Or that is the way it is supposed to work, anyway. In the Windows version of Navigator 3 (but not the Mac or X11 versions), the status line is not automatically cleared when you set the status property from an onMouseOver event handler. To force it to be erased, you can use the onMouseOut event handler, like this:

```
<A HREF="sitemap.html"
  onMouseOver="status='Go to Site Map'; return true;"
  onMouseOut="status='';">
Site Map
</A>
```

The status property is intended for exactly the sort of transient message we saw above. Sometimes, though, you want to display a message that is not so transient in the status line—for example, you might display a welcome message to users visiting your web page or a simple line of help text for novice visitors. To do this, you set the defaultStatus property of the Window—this property specifies the default text displayed in the status line. That text is temporarily replaced with URLs, context help messages, or other transient text when the mouse pointer is over hyperlinks or browser control buttons, but once the mouse moves off those areas, the default text is restored.

You might use the `defaultStatus` property like this to provide a friendly and helpful message to real beginners:

```
<SCRIPT>
defaultStatus = "Welcome!  Click on underlined blue text to navigate.";
</SCRIPT>
```

If your web page contains an HTML form, you might change the `defaultStatus` property as the user enters data in the form in order to display step-by-step instructions for completing it.

13.4 Timeouts and Intervals

The `setTimeout()` method of the Window object schedules a piece of JavaScript code to be run at some specified time in the future. The `clearTimeout()` method can be used to cancel the execution of that code. `setTimeout()` is commonly used to perform animations or other kinds of repetitive actions. If a function runs and then uses `setTimeout()` to schedule itself to be called again, we get a process that repeats without any user intervention. JavaScript 1.2 has added the `setInterval()` and `clearInterval()` methods, which are like `setTimeout()` and `clearTimeout()`, except that they automatically reschedule the code to run repeatedly; there is no need for the code to reschedule itself.

The `setTimeout()` method is commonly used in conjunction with the `status` or `defaultStatus` properties to animate some kind of message in the status bar of the browser. In general, animations involving the status bar are gaudy and you should shun them! There are a few status bar animation techniques, however, which can be useful and in good taste. Example 13-2 shows such a tasteful status bar animation. It displays the current time in the status bar and updates that time once a minute. Because the update only occurs once a minute, this animation does not produce a constant flickering distraction at the bottom of the browser window like so many others do.

Note the use of the `onLoad` event handler to perform the first call to the `display_time_in_status_line()` method. This event handler is invoked once when the HTML document is fully loaded into the browser. After this first call, the method uses `setTimeout()` to schedule itself to be called every 60 seconds so that it can update the displayed time. The `onLoad` event handler is specified here as an attribute of the `<BODY>` tag.

Example 13-2: A Digital Clock in the Status Line

```
<HTML>
<HEAD>
<SCRIPT>
// This function displays the time in the status line.
// Invoke it once to activate the clock; it will call itself from then on.
function display_time_in_status_line()
{
    var d = new Date();                 // Get current time.
    var h = d.getHours();               // Extract hours: 0 to 23.
    var m = d.getMinutes();             // Extract minutes: 0 to 59.
    var ampm = (h >= 12)?"PM":"AM";     // Is it am or pm?
    if (h > 12) h -= 12;                // Convert 24-hour format to 12-hour.
    if (h == 0) h = 12;                 // Convert 0 o'clock to midnight.
    if (m < 10) m = "0" + m;            // Convert 0 minutes to 00 minutes, etc.
    var t = h + ':' + m + ' ' + ampm;   // Put it all together.

    defaultStatus = t;                  // Display it in the status line.

    // Arrange to do it all again in 1 minute.
    setTimeout("display_time_in_status_line()", 60000); // 60000 ms is 1 minute.
}
</SCRIPT>
</HEAD>
<!-- Don't bother starting the clock till everything is loaded. The
  -- status line will be busy with other messages during loading, anyway. -->
<BODY onLoad="display_time_in_status_line();">
<!-- The HTML document contents go here. -->
</BODY>
</HTML>
```

In JavaScript 1.2, Example 13-2 could be written using setInterval() instead of
setTimeout(). In this case, the setTimeout() call would be removed from the
display_time_in_status_line() method, and the onLoad event handler would
be changed to call setInterval() to schedule an invocation of that method that
automatically repeats once every 60,000 milliseconds.

13.5 *The Navigator Object*

The Window.navigator property refers to a Navigator object that contains information about the web browser as a whole (such as the version and the list of data
formats it can display). The Navigator object is named after Netscape Navigator,
but it is also supported by Internet Explorer. IE also supports clientInformation
as a vendor-neutral synonym for navigator. Unfortunately, Navigator 4 does not
support this property.

The Navigator object has six main properties that provide version information about the browser that is running:

appName

> The simple name of the web browser.

appVersion

> The version number and/or other version information for the browser.

userAgent

> The string that the browser sends in its USER-AGENT HTTP header. This property typically contains all the information in both appName and appVersion.

appCodeName

> The code name of the browser. Navigator uses this property for the code name "Mozilla," but, in general, this property does not provide any information not provided by other Navigator properties.

platform

> The hardware platform on which the browser is running. This property is new in JavaScript 1.2.

language

> The language this version of the browser supports. This is typically a standard two-letter language code, such as "en" for English or "fr" for French. This property is new in Navigator 4. IE 4 defines similar userLanguage and systemLanguage properties instead.

The following lines of JavaScript code display each of these Navigator object properties in a dialog box. Figure 13-2 shows the dialogs displayed when the code is run on typical versions of Navigator 4 and Internet Explorer 4:

```
var browser = "BROWSER INFORMATION:\n";
for(var propname in navigator) {
    browser += propname + ": " + navigator[propname] + "\n"
}
alert(browser);
```

As you can see from Figure 13-2, the properties of the Navigator object have values that are sometimes more complex than we are interested in. We are often only interested in the first digit of the appVersion property, for example. When using the Navigator object to test browser information, we often use methods like parseInt() and String.indexOf() to extract only the information we want. Example 13-3 shows some code that does this: it processes the properties of the Navigator object and stores them in an object named browser. These properties, in their processed form, are easier to use than the raw navigator properties. The general term for code like this is a "sniffer," and you can find more complex and general-purpose sniffer code on the Internet. For many purposes, however, something as simple as that shown in Example 13-3 works just fine.

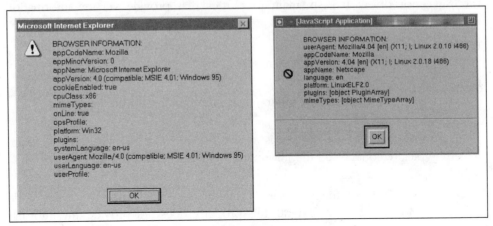

Figure 13–2: Navigator object properties for two different browsers

Example 13–3: Determining Browser Vendor and Version

```
/*
 * File: browser.js
 * Include with: <SCRIPT SRC="browser.js"></SCRIPT>
 *
 * A simple "sniffer" that determines browser version and vendor.
 * It creates an object named "browser" that is easier to use than
 * the "navigator" object.
 */
// Create the browser object.
var browser = new Object();

// Figure out the browser major version.
browser.version = parseInt(navigator.appVersion);

// Now figure out if the browser is from one of the two
// major browser vendors. Start by assuming it is not.
browser.isNavigator = false;
browser.isIE = false;
if (navigator.appName.indexOf("Netscape") != -1)
    browser.isNavigator = true;
else if (navigator.appName.indexOf("Microsoft") != -1)
    browser.isIE = true;
```

13.5.1 The MimeType and Plugin Objects

As you probably noticed, Figure 13-2 shows that the Navigator object has properties other than those we have discussed so far. Many of these properties are incompatible extensions in Internet Explorer and are not discussed here. If you want to make use of the properties, be sure that you first use code like that in Example 13-3 to ensure that your code is running in Internet Explorer 4 or later. Two properties, `mimeTypes` and `plugins`, do bear further discussion, however. These properties are supported in Navigator 3 and later. In IE 4, the properties are defined for compatibility but are not truly supported: the arrays they refer to are always empty.

The `navigator.mimeTypes[]` property is an array of MimeType objects, each of which describes one MIME data format (`text/html` and `image/gif`, for example) that the web browser can display (either directly, with an external helper application, or with a plugin). The MimeType object itself contains properties that describe the data format.

The `mimeTypes[]` array is indexed numerically, but it is also an associative array, indexed by the name of the MIME type. Thus, you can easily check for support of a given data format on the browser:

```
// Check to see if the browser can display MPEG files.
var show_movie = (navigator.mimeTypes["video/mpeg"] != null);
```

The `navigator.plugins[]` property is an array of Plugin objects, each of which represents one plugin module that has been installed in the browser. The properties of the Plugin object provide various details about the plugin. The Plugin object also contains array elements, which are MimeType objects describing each of the data formats supported by that particular plugin. Note that this array is different than the `navigator.mimeTypes[]` array described earlier.

You can use the `plugins[]` property as an associative array, just as you can the `mimeTypes[]` property. This lets you check for the existence of a particular plugin without having to loop through the array numerically and check every element:

```
// Check to see if the browser has the Shockwave plugin installed.
var shocked = (navigator.plugins["Shockwave"] != null);
```

13.5.2 Navigator Methods

In addition to its properties, the Navigator object defines methods that provide further information about the browser. In JavaScript 1.1 and later, the `javaEnabled()` method returns `true` if the browser supports Java and if Java support is enabled; otherwise it returns `false`. Navigator 4 adds the `preference()` method, which allows signed scripts to query and set user preferences.

13.6 The Screen Object

In JavaScript 1.2, the `screen` property of a Window object refers to a Screen object. This Screen object provides information about the size of the user's display and the number of colors available. The `width` and `height` properties specify the size of the display in pixels. The `availWidth` and `availHeight` properties specify the display size that is actually available: they exclude the space required by features like the Windows 95 taskbar. You can use these properties to help you decide what size images to include in a document, for example, or in a program that creates multiple browser windows, what size windows to create.

The `colorDepth` property specifies the base-2 logarithm of the number of colors that can be displayed. Often, this value is the same as the number of bits per pixel used by the display. For example, an 8-bit display can display 256 colors, and if all of these colors were available for use by the browser, the `screen.colorDepth` property would be 8. In some circumstances, however, the browser may restrict itself to a subset of the available colors, and you might find a `screen.colorDepth` value that is lower than the bits-per-pixel value of the screen. If you have several versions of an image that were defined using different numbers of colors, you can test this `colorDepth` property to decide which version to include in a document.

13.7 Window Control Methods

The Window object defines several methods that allow high-level control of the window itself. The following sections explore how these methods allow us to open and close windows, to control window position and size, to request and relinquish keyboard focus, and to scroll the contents of a window. We conclude with an example that demonstrates several of these features.

13.7.1 Opening Windows

You can open a new web browser window with the `open()` method of the Window object. This method takes four optional arguments and returns a Window object that represents the newly opened window. The first argument to `open()` is the URL of the document to display in the new window. If this argument is omitted (or is `null` or the empty string), the window will be empty.

The second argument to `open()` is the name of the window. As we'll discuss later in the chapter, this name can be useful as the value of the `TARGET` attribute of a `<FORM>` or `<A>` tag. If you specify the name of a window that already exists, `open()` simply uses that existing window rather than opening a new one.

The third optional argument to open() is a list of features that specify the window size and GUI decorations. If you omit this argument, the new window is given a default size and has a full set of standard features: a menubar, status line, toolbar, and so on. On the other hand, if you specify this argument, you can explicitly specify the size of the window and the set of features it includes. For example, to open a small resizeable browser window with a status bar but no menubar, toolbar, or locationbar, you could use the following line of JavaScript:

```
var w = window.open("smallwin.html", "smallwin",
                    "width=400,height=350,status=yes,resizeable=yes");
```

Note that when you specify this third argument, any features you do not explicitly specify are omitted. The reference section documents the full set of available features and their names.

The fourth argument to open() is useful only when the second argument names an already existing window. This fourth argument is a boolean value that specifies whether the URL specified as the first argument should replace the current entry in the window's browsing history (true) or create a new entry in the window's browsing history (false), which is the default behavior.

The return value of the open() method is the Window object that represents the newly created window. You can use this Window object in your JavaScript code to refer to the new window, just as you use the implicit Window object window to refer to the window within which your code is running. But what about the reverse situation? What if JavaScript code in the new window wants to refer back to the window that opened it? In JavaScript 1.1 and later, the opener property of a window refers to the window from which it was opened. If the window was created by the user instead of by JavaScript code, the opener property is null.

An important point about the open() method is that it is almost always invoked as window.open(), even though window refers to the global object and should therefore be entirely optional. The reason that window is specified explicitly is that the Document object also has an open() method, so specifying window.open() helps to make it very clear what we are trying to do. This is not only a helpful habit; it is required in some circumstances, because, as we'll learn in Chapter 15, event handlers execute in the scope of the object that defines them. When the event handler of an HTML button executes, for example, the scope chain includes the Button object, the Form object that contains the button, the Document object that contains the form, and, finally, the Window object that contains the document. Thus, if such an event handler refers merely to the open() method, this identifier ends up being resolved in the Document object, and the event handler opens a new document rather than opening a new window!

We'll see an example of the open() method in Example 13-4.

13.7.2 Closing Windows

Just as the open() method opens a new window, the close() method closes one. If we've created a Window object *w*, we can close it with:

```
w.close();
```

JavaScript code running within that window itself could close it with:

```
window.close();
```

Again, note the explicit use of the window identifier to disambiguate the close() method of the Window object from the close() method of the Document object.

You can only automatically close windows that your own JavaScript code has created. If you attempt to close any other window, the user is presented with a dialog box that asks him to confirm (or cancel) that request to close the window. This prevents inconsiderate web sites from closing your main browsing window.

In JavaScript 1.1 and later, a Window object continues to exist after the window it represents has been closed. You should not attempt to use any of its properties or methods, however, except to test the closed property. This property is true if the window has been closed. Remember that the user can close any window at any time, so to avoid errors, it is a good idea to check periodically that the window you are trying to use is still open. We'll see an example of doing just this in Example 13-4.

13.7.3 Window Geometry

In JavaScript 1.2, moveTo() moves the upper-left corner of the window to the specified coordinates. Similarly, moveBy() moves the window a specified number of pixels left or right and up or down. resizeTo() and resizeBy() resize the window by an absolute or relative amount; they are also new in JavaScript 1.2. Note that in Navigator 4, there are some security restrictions on how you can move and resize windows. We'll see more about this in Chapter 21, *JavaScript Security*, but basically, you are not allowed to move a window off screen or to make it too small. This is so that you can't create a hidden window that the user might forget about.

13.7.4 Keyboard Focus

The focus() and blur() methods also provide high-level control over a window. Calling focus() requests that the system give keyboard focus to the window and blur() relinquishes keyboard focus. These methods are defined in JavaScript 1.1 and later.

13.7.5 Scrolling

Window also contains some methods that control the scrollbars of the window, rather than the window itself. scrollBy() scrolls the document displayed in the window by a specified number of pixels left or right and up or down. scrollTo() scrolls the document to an absolute position. It moves the document so that the specified document coordinates are displayed in the upper-left corner of the document area within the window. These two methods are defined in JavaScript 1.2. In JavaScript 1.1, the scroll() method performs the same function as the JavaScript 1.2 scrollTo() method. scrollTo() is the preferred method, but scroll() remains for backwards compatibility.

In JavaScript 1.2, the elements of the anchors[] array of the Document object are Anchor objects. Each Anchor object has x and y properties that specify the location of the anchor within the document. Thus, you can use these values in conjunction with the scrollTo() method to scroll to known locations within the document.

13.7.6 Window Methods Example

Example 13-4 demonstrates the Window open(), close(), and moveTo() methods and several other window programming techniques that we've discussed. It creates a new window and then uses setInterval() to repeatedly call a function that moves it around the screen. It determines the size of the screen with the Screen object and then uses this information to make the window "bounce" when it reaches any edge of the screen.

Example 13–4: Moving a Window

```
<script>
// Here are the initial values for our animation.
var x = 0, y = 0, w=200, h=200;   // Window position and size
var dx = 5, dy = 5;               // Window velocity
var interval = 100;               // Milliseconds between updates

// Create the window that we're going to move around.
// The javascript: URL is simply a way to display a short document.
// The final argument specifies the window size.
var win = window.open('javascript:"<H1>BOUNCE!</H1>"', "",
                      "width=" + w + ",height=" + h);

// Set the initial position of the window.
win.moveTo(x,y);

// Use setInterval() to call the bounce() method every interval
// milliseconds. Store the return value so that we can stop the
// animation by passing it to clearInterval().
```

Example 13-4: Moving a Window (continued)

```
var intervalID  = window.setInterval("bounce()", interval);

// This function moves the window by (dx, dy) every interval ms.
// It bounces whenever the window reaches the edge of the screen.
function bounce() {
    // If the user closed the window, stop the animation.
    if (win.closed) {
        clearInterval(intervalID);
        return;
    }

    // Have we reached the right or left edge?
    if ((x+dx > (screen.availWidth - w)) || (x+dx < 0)) dx = -dx;

    // Have we reached the bottom or top edge?
    if ((y+dy > (screen.availHeight - h)) || (y+dy < 0)) dy = -dy;

    // Update the current position of the window.
    x += dx;
    y += dy;

    // Finally, move the window to the new position.
    win.moveTo(x,y);
}
</script>

<!-- Clicking this button stops the animation! -->
<FORM>
<INPUT TYPE=button VALUE="Stop"
       onClick="clearInterval(intervalID); win.close();">
</FORM>
```

13.8 *The Location Object*

The location property of a window is a reference to a Location object—a representation of the URL of the document currently being displayed in that window. The href property of the Location object is a string that contains the complete text of the URL. Other properties of this object, such as protocol, host, pathname, and search, specify the various individual parts of the URL.

This search property of the Location object is an interesting one. It contains any portion of a URL following (and including) a question mark. This is often some sort of query string. In general, the question mark syntax in a URL is a technique for embedding arguments in the URL. While these arguments are usually intended for CGI scripts run on a server, there is no reason why they cannot also be used in JavaScript-enabled pages. Example 13-5 shows the definition of a general-purpose getArgs() function that you can use to extract arguments from the search property of a URL. It also shows how this getArgs() method could have been used to set initial values of the bouncing window animation parameters in Example 13-4.

Example 13–5: Extracting Arguments from a URL

```
/*
 * This function parses comma-separated name=value argument pairs from
 * the query string of the URL. It stores the name=value pairs in
 * properties of an object and returns that object.
 */
function getArgs() {
    var args = new Object();
    var query = location.search.substring(1);   // Get query string.
    var pairs = query.split(",");                // Break at comma.
    for(var i = 0; i < pairs.length; i++) {
        var pos = pairs[i].indexOf('=');         // Look for "name=value".
        if (pos == -1) continue;                 // If not found, skip.
        var argname = pairs[i].substring(0,pos); // Extract the name.
        var value = pairs[i].substring(pos+1);   // Extract the value.
        args[argname] = unescape(value);         // Store as a property.
    }
    return args;                                 // Return the object.
}


/*
 * We could have used getArgs() in the previous bouncing window example
 * to parse optional animation parameters from the URL.
 */
var args = getArgs();                   // Get arguments.
if (args.x) x = parseInt(args.x);       // If arguments are defined...
if (args.y) y = parseInt(args.y);       // ... override default values.
if (args.w) w = parseInt(args.w);
if (args.h) h = parseInt(args.h);
if (args.dx) dx = parseInt(args.dx);
if (args.dy) dy = parseInt(args.dy);
if (args.interval) interval = parseInt(args.interval);
```

In addition to its properties, the Location object can be used as if it were itself a primitive string value. If you read the value of a Location object, you get the same string as you would if you read the href property of the object (because the Location object has a suitable toString() method). What is far more interesting, though, is that you can assign a new URL string to the location property of a window. Assigning a URL to the Location object like this has a very important side effect: it causes the browser to load and display the contents of the URL you assign. For example, you might assign a URL to the `location` property like this:

```
// If Java isn't enabled, go to a page that displays a message
// saying that you can't run this page without Java.
if (!navigator.javaEnabled())
    location = "needsjava.html";
```

As you can imagine, making the browser load specified web pages into windows is a very important programming technique. While you might expect there to be a method you can call to make the browser display a new web page, assigning a URL to the `location` property of a window is the supported technique to accomplish this.

Although the Location object does not have a method that serves the same function as assigning a URL directly to the `location` property of a window, this object does support two methods (added in JavaScript 1.1). The `reload()` method reloads the currently displayed page from the web server. The `replace()` method loads and displays a URL that you specify. But invoking this method for a given URL is different than assigning that URL to the `location` property of a window. When you call `replace()`, the specified URL replaces the current one in the browser's history list rather than creating a new entry in that history list. Therefore, if you use `replace()` to overwrite one document with a new one, the **Back** button does not take the user back to the original document, as it does if you load the new document by assigning to the `location` property. For web sites that use frames and display a lot of temporary pages (perhaps generated by a CGI script), using `replace()` is often useful. By not storing temporary pages in the history list, the **Back** button becomes more useful to the user.

Finally, don't confuse the `location` property of the Window object, which refers to a Location object, with the `location` property of the Document object, which is simply a read-only string with none of the special features of the Location object. `Document.location` is a synonym for `Document.URL`, which in Navigator 3 is the preferred name for this property (because it avoids the potential confusion). In most cases, `document.location` is the same as `location.href`. When there is a server redirect, however, `document.location` contains the actual URL as loaded, and `location.href` contains the URL as originally requested.

13.9 *The History Object*

The `history` property of the Window object refers to a History object for the window. The History object is an array of the URLs in the browsing history of the window or frame. For a top-level Navigator window, the History object is a representation of the contents of the browser's **Go** menu.

A user's browsing session history is private information, so, for security reasons, there are heavy restrictions on how the History object can be used. In Navigator 4, the elements of the `history` array are accessible to signed scripts. In other versions of Navigator and in Internet Explorer, the elements of the array are never accessible, and the History object is less useful.

The History object supports three methods, which can be used by unsigned scripts in all versions of Navigator and Internet Explorer. The `back()` and `forward()` methods perform the same action as clicking on the **Back** and **Forward** browser buttons. The third method, `go()`, suffers from bugs in Navigator 2 and 3 and has incompatible behavior in Internet Explorer 3; it is best avoided.

Example 13-6 shows how you might use the `back()` and `forward()` methods of the History object and the Location object to add a navigation bar to a framed web site. Figure 13-3 shows what a navigation bar looks like. Note that the example uses JavaScript with multiple frames, which is something we will discuss shortly. It also contains a simple HTML form and uses JavaScript to read and write values from the form. This is covered in detail in Chapter 16, *Forms and Form Elements*.

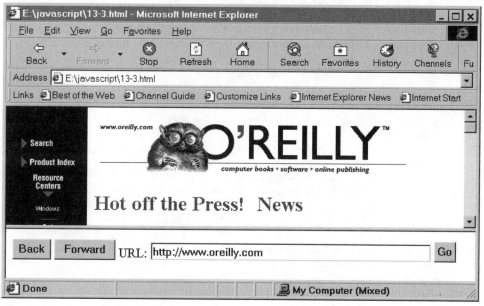

Figure 13-3: A navigation bar

Example 13-6: A Navigation Bar Using the History and Location Objects

```
<!-- This file implements a navigation bar, designed to go in a frame at
       the bottom of a window. Include it in a frameset like the following:

           <frameset rows="*,75">
           <frame src="about:blank">
           <frame src="navigation.html">
           </frameset>
-->


<SCRIPT>
// The function is invoked by the Back button in our navigation bar.
function go_back()
{
    // First, clear the URL entry field in our form.
    document.navbar.url.value = "";

    // Then use the History object of the main frame to go back.
    parent.frames[0].history.back();

    // Wait a second, and then update the URL entry field in the form
    // from the location.href property of the main frame. The wait seems
    // to be necessary to allow the location.href property to get in sync.
    setTimeout("document.navbar.url.value = parent.frames[0].location.href;",
               1000);
}


// This function is invoked by the Forward button in the navigation bar.
// It works just like the one above.
function go_forward()
{
    document.navbar.url.value = "";
    parent.frames[0].history.forward();
    setTimeout("document.navbar.url.value = parent.frames[0].location.href;",
               1000);
}


// This function is invoked by the Go button in the navigation bar, and also
// when the form is submitted (when the user hits the Return key).
function go_to()
{
    // Just set the location property of the main frame to the URL
    // that the user typed in.
    parent.frames[0].location = document.navbar.url.value;
}
</SCRIPT>


<!-- Here's the form, with event handlers that invoke the functions above. -->
<FORM NAME="navbar" onSubmit="go_to(); return false">
```

Example 13-6: A Navigation Bar Using the History and Location Objects (continued)

```
<INPUT TYPE="button" VALUE="Back"  onClick="go_back();">
<INPUT TYPE="button" VALUE="Forward"  onClick="go_forward()">
URL:
<INPUT TYPE="text" NAME="url" SIZE=50>
<INPUT TYPE="button" VALUE="Go" onClick="go_to()">
</FORM>
```

13.10 *Multiple Windows and Frames*

Most of the client-side JavaScript examples we've seen so far have involved only a
single window or frame. In the real world, most interesting JavaScript applications
involve multiple windows or frames. Recall that frames within a window are represented by Window objects; JavaScript makes little distinction between windows
and frames. In the most interesting applications, there is JavaScript code that runs
independently in each of several windows. The next section explains how the
JavaScript code in each window can interact and cooperate with each of the other
windows and with the scripts running in each of these windows.

13.10.1 *Relationships Between Frames*

We've already seen that the open() method of the Window object returns a new
Window object representing the newly created window. We've also seen that this
new window has an opener property that refers back to the original window. In
this way, the two windows can refer to each other, and each can read properties
and invoke methods of the other. The same thing is possible with frames. Any
frame in a window can refer to any other frame through the use of the frames[],
parent, and top properties of the Window object.

Every window has a frames property. This property refers to an array of Window
objects, each of which represents a frame contained within the window. (If a window does not have any frames, the frames[] array is empty and frames.length
is zero.) Thus, a window (or frame) can refer to its first subframe as frames[0],
its second subframe as frames[1], and so on. Similarly, JavaScript code running
in a window can refer to the third subframe of its second frame like this:

```
frames[1].frames[2]
```

Every window also has a parent property, which refers to the Window object in
which it is contained. Thus, the first frame within a window might refer to its sibling frame (the second frame within the window) like this:

```
parent.frames[1]
```

If a window is a top-level window and not a frame, `parent` simply refers to the window itself:

```
parent == self;  // For any top-level window
```

If a frame is contained within another frame that is contained within a top-level window, that frame can refer to the top-level window as `parent.parent`. The `top` property is a general-case shortcut, however: no matter how deeply a frame is nested, its `top` property refers to the top-level containing window. If a Window object represents a top-level window, `top` simply refers to the window itself. For frames that are direct children of a top-level window, the `top` property is the same as the `parent` property.

Figure 13-4 illustrates these relationships between frames and shows how code running in any one frame can refer to any other frame through the use of the `frames`, `parent`, and `top` properties. With this understanding of the relationships between windows, you may want to revisit Example 13-6, paying particular attention this time to the way the second frame refers to the `history` and `location` properties of the first.

13.10.2 *Window and Frame Names*

The second, optional argument to the `open()` method discussed earlier is a name for the newly created window. When you create a frame with the HTML `<FRAME>` tag, you can specify a name with the `NAME` attribute. An important reason to specify names for windows and frames is that those names can be used as the value of the `TARGET` attribute of the `<A>`, `<MAP>`, and `<FORM>` tags. This tells the browser where you want the results of activating a link, clicking on an image map, or submitting a form to be displayed.

For example, if you have two windows, one named `table_of_contents` and the other named `mainwin`, you might have HTML like the following in the `table_of_contents` window:

```
<A HREF="chapter01.html" TARGET="mainwin">
Chapter 1, Introduction
</A>
```

When the user clicks on this hyperlink, the browser loads the specified URL, but instead of displaying the URL in the same window as the link, it displays it in the window named `mainwin`. If there is no window with the name `mainwin`, clicking the link creates a new window with that name and loads the specified URL into it.

The `TARGET` and `NAME` attributes are part of HTML and operate without the intervention of JavaScript, but there are also JavaScript-related reasons to give names

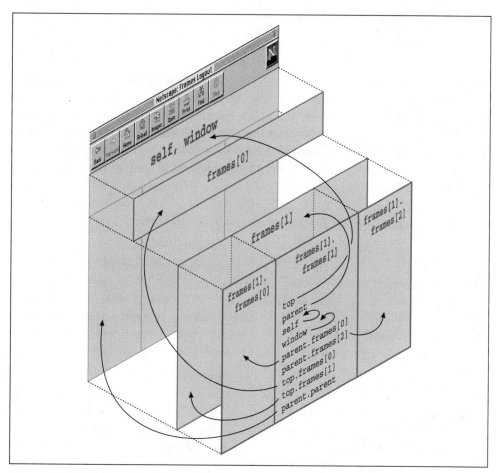

Figure 13–4: Relationships between frames

to your frames. We've seen that every Window object has a `frames[]` array that contains references to each of its frames. This array contains all frames in a window (or frame) whether or not they have names. If a frame is given a name, however, a reference to that frame is also stored in a new property of the parent Window object. The name of that new property is the same as the name of the frame. Therefore, you might create a frame with HTML like this:

```
<FRAME NAME="table_of_contents" SRC="toc.html">
```

Now you can refer to that frame from another, sibling frame with:

```
parent.table_of_contents
```

This makes your code easier to read and understand than using (and relying on) a hardcoded array index, as you'd have to do with an unnamed frame:

```
parent.frames[1]
```

The `name` property of any Window object contains the name of that window. In JavaScript 1.0, this property is read-only. In JavaScript 1.1, however, you can set this property, thereby changing the name of a window or a frame. One common reason to do this is to set the name of the initial browser window. When Navigator starts up, the initial window has no name, so it cannot be used with the `TARGET` attribute. If you set the `name` property of the window, however, you can then use that name in `TARGET` attributes.

13.10.3 *JavaScript in Interacting Windows*

Recall what we learned in Chapter 12: the Window object serves as the global object for client-side JavaScript code, and the window serves as the execution context for all JavaScript code it contains. This holds true for frames as well: every frame is an independent JavaScript execution context. Because every Window object is its own global object, each window defines its own namespace and its own set of "global" variables. When viewed from the perspective of multiple frames or windows, global variables do not seem all that global, after all!

Although each window and frame defines an independent JavaScript execution context, this does not mean that JavaScript code running in one window is isolated from code running in other windows. Code running in one frame has a different Window object at the top of its scope chain than code running in another frame. However, the code from both frames is executed by the same JavaScript interpreter, in the same JavaScript environment. As we've seen, one frame can refer to any other frame by using the `frames`, `parent`, and `top` properties. So, although JavaScript code in different frames is executed with different scope chains, this does not prevent the code in one frame from referring to, and using, the variables and functions defined by code in another frame.

For example, suppose code in frame A defines a variable `i`:

```
var i = 3;
```

That variable is nothing more than a property of the global object—a property of the Window object. Code in frame A could refer to the variable explicitly as such a property with either of these two expressions:

```
window.i
self.i
```

Now suppose that frame A has a sibling frame B that wants to set the value of the variable `i` defined by the code in frame A. If frame B just sets a variable `i`, it merely succeeds in creating a new property of its own Window object. So instead, it must explicitly refer to the property i in its sibling frame with code like this:

```
parent.frames[0].i = 4;
```

Recall that the function keyword that defines functions declares a variable just like the var keyword does. If JavaScript code in frame A declares a function f, that function is defined only within frame A. Code in frame A can invoke f like this:

```
f();
```

Code in frame B, however, must refer to f as a property of the Window object of frame A:

```
parent.frames[0].f();
```

If the code in frame B needs to use this function frequently, it might assign the function to a variable of frame B so that it can more conveniently refer to the function:

```
var f = parent.frames[0].f;
```

Now code in frame B can invoke the function as f(), just as code in frame A does.

When you share functions between frames or windows like this, it is very important to keep the rules of lexical scoping in mind. A function is executed in the scope in which it was defined, not in the scope from which it is invoked. Thus, to continue with the example above, if the function f refers to global variables, these variables are looked up as properties of frame A, even when the function is invoked from frame B.*

If you don't pay careful attention to this, you can end up with programs that behave in unexpected and confusing ways. For example, suppose you define the following function in the <HEAD> section of a multiframe document, with the idea that it will help with debugging:

```
function debug(msg) {
    alert("Debugging message from frame: " + name + "\n" + msg);
}
```

The JavaScript code in each of your frames can refer to this function as top.debug(). Whenever this function is invoked, however, it looks up the variable name in the context of the top-level window in which the function is defined,

---

* If you have read Chapter 11, *Further Topics in JavaScript*, you can probably think of a way to use the Closure() constructor of Navigator 4 to define a version of the function f that executes in the scope of frame B.

rather than the context of the frame from which it is invoked. Thus, the debugging messages always carry the name of the top-level window, rather than the name of the frame that sent the message, as was intended.

Remember that constructors are also functions, so when you define a class of objects with a constructor function and an associated prototype object, that class is only defined for a single window. Recall the Complex class we defined in Chapter 8, *Objects*, and consider the following multiframed HTML document:

```
<HEAD>
<SCRIPT SRC="Complex.js"></SCRIPT>
</HEAD>
<FRAMESET ROWS="50%,50%">
  <FRAME NAME="frame1" SRC="frame1.html">
  <FRAME NAME="frame2" SRC="frame2.html">
</FRAMESET>
```

JavaScript code in the files *frame1.html* and *frame2.html* cannot create a Complex object with an expression like this:

```
var c = new Complex(1,2);  // Won't work from either frame
```

Instead, code in these files must explicitly refer to the constructor function:

```
var c = new top.Complex(3,4);
```

Alternatively, code in either frame can define its own variable to refer more conveniently to the constructor function:

```
var Complex = top.Complex;
var c = new Complex(1,2);
```

Unlike user-defined constructors, predefined constructors are automatically predefined in all windows. Note, however, that each window has an independent copy of the constructor and an independent copy of the constructor's prototype object. For example, each window has its own copy of the String() constructor and the String.prototype object. So, if you write a new method for manipulating JavaScript strings and make it a method of the String class by assigning it to the String.prototype object in the current window, all strings in that window can use the new method. However, the new method is not accessible to strings defined in other windows. Note that it does not matter which window holds a reference to the string, only which window the string was actually created in.

13.10.4 Example: Colored Frames

Example 13-7, a frame set that defines a grid of nine frames, demonstrates some of the techniques we've been discussing in this chapter. The <HEAD> section of the

frame set includes a <SCRIPT> that defines a JavaScript function named set-
color(). The onLoad event handler of the <FRAMESET> tag invokes setcolor()
once for each of the nine frames.

setcolor() is passed a Window object as its argument. It generates a random
color and uses it as the new value of the bgColor property of the Document
object. (We'll see more about the Document object and its properties in Chapter
14.) Finally, setcolor() uses the setTimeout() method to schedule itself to be
called again in one second. This call to setTimeout() is the most interesting part
of the example. Notice especially how it uses the parent and name properties of
Window objects.

Example 13-7: A Frame Color Animation

```
<HEAD>
<TITLE>Colored Frames</TITLE>
<SCRIPT>
function setcolor(w) {
    // Generate a random color.
    var r = (Math.random() * 256).toString(16);
    var g = (Math.random() * 256).toString(16);
    var b = (Math.random() * 256).toString(16);
    var colorString = "#" + r + g + b;

    // Set the frame background to the random color.
    w.document.bgColor = colorString;

    // Schedule another call to this method in one second.
    // Since we call the setTimeout() method of the frame, the string
    // will be executed in that context, so we must prefix properties
    // of the top-level window with "parent."
    w.setTimeout('parent.setcolor(parent.' + w.name + ')', 1000);

    // We could also have done the same thing more simply like this.
    // setTimeout('setcolor(' + w.name + ')', 1000);
}
</SCRIPT>
</HEAD>
<FRAMESET rows="33%,33%,34%" cols="33%,33%,34%"
  onLoad="for(var i = 0; i < 9; i++) setcolor(frames[i]);">
<FRAME NAME="f1" SRC="javascript:''"><FRAME NAME="f2" SRC="javascript:''">
<FRAME NAME="f3" SRC="javascript:''"><FRAME NAME="f4" SRC="javascript:''">
<FRAME NAME="f5" SRC="javascript:''"><FRAME NAME="f6" SRC="javascript:''">
<FRAME NAME="f7" SRC="javascript:''"><FRAME NAME="f8" SRC="javascript:''">
<FRAME NAME="f9" SRC="javascript:''">
</FRAMESET>
```

14

The Document
Object Model

If the Window object, which represents a window or a frame, is the central object in client-side JavaScript, the Document object, which represents the contents of a window or frame, runs a close second. This object is probably the most commonly used object in client-side JavaScript. The Document object has properties that specify information about the document displayed in the browser: its URL, its last-modified date, the URL of the document that linked to it, the colors in which it is displayed, and so on. The Document object also has methods that allow JavaScript programs to dynamically output text into a document and to dynamically create new documents from scratch. Finally, several properties of the Document object are arrays that represent the forms, images, links, anchors, and applets contained in the document. These arrays and the objects they contain are very important in JavaScript programming; they are described in their own sections later in this chapter.

With the introduction of Internet Explorer 4, the Document object becomes the root node in what is known as the document object model (DOM). The DOM is an evolving standard that specifies how a scripting language, like JavaScript, can access and manipulate the detailed structure of an HTML* document. This chapter begins with an overview of the DOM and of the standardization effort that is currently underway. It then covers those Document object properties, methods, and arrays (and the objects contained in the arrays) that are already solid de facto standards. The chapter concludes with a look at the future of DOM standardization.

---

* Or an Extensible Markup Language (XML) document.

14.1 The DOM: An Overview

Every Window object has a `document` property. This property refers to a Document object that represents the document (typically an HTML document) displayed in the window. The Document object provides several properties, such as `bgColor` and `lastModified`, that supply information about the document as a whole. It also defines a `write()` method that allows JavaScript code to dynamically add HTML text to a document while the document is being parsed. This much is relatively straightforward.

I mentioned earlier that the Document object is the most commonly used object in client-side JavaScript. Client-side JavaScript exists to turn static HTML documents into interactive programs—it is the Document object that gives JavaScript interactive access to the contents of otherwise static documents. The Document object has a number of properties that refer to arrays of interesting objects that JavaScript can operate on. The `forms[]` array, for instance, contains Form objects that represent all the HTML forms in the document. And the `images[]` and `applets[]` arrays contain objects that represent the images and applets in the document. Much of this chapter discusses the objects contained by these arrays: they open up a world of possibilities for client-side JavaScript programs.

The Document object has evolved since the first JavaScript-enabled web browsers were introduced. For example, JavaScript 1.1 introduced the `images[]` array and the Image objects that it contains. These objects allowed JavaScript programs to dynamically change images within a document, producing a wave of new special effects within web pages.

This evolution continues. As described here, only a few HTML elements such as forms and links are singled out for special treatment by the Document object. The goal is to replace this special-case Document object with a comprehensive document object model that allows JavaScript or any other scripting language complete access to the elements, attributes, and text of any HTML or XML document.

Internet Explorer 4 implements such a document object model, but Navigator 4 does not. The incompatibility between these two browsers lends urgency to the current standardization effort, under the auspices of the World Wide Web Consortium (W3C), that aims to create a common DOM that both browsers can support. Both Netscape and Microsoft have pledged to support the standard that emerges from the process; hopefully, we'll see the results of the W3C standardization effort in the next generation (Version 5) of the two browsers.

In the meantime, the existing properties, methods, and arrays of the Document object have been enshrined as "Level 0" of the DOM standard. The bulk of this chapter documents that base level of standard document functionality. At the end of the chapter, I'll discuss the expected features of the Level 1 DOM standard and look further out to plans for Level 2 and beyond.

Note that the DOM implemented by Internet Explorer 4 is similar to the emerging Level 1 standard. Experimenting with the DOM features in IE 4 is perhaps the best way to familiarize yourself with the general concepts and overall structure of the standard. However, since the IE 4 DOM will not actually be compatible with the W3C standard, and because it is not supported by Navigator (still the majority browser), it is not documented in this book. You can learn more about the IE 4 DOM from the following Microsoft web site:

http://www.microsoft.com/msdn/sdk/inetsdk/help/dhtml/doc_object/doc_object.htm

14.1.1 Document Object Naming

Before we begin our discussion of the Document object and its arrays—the de facto Level 0 DOM—there is one general principle that you'll find it helpful to be aware of. As you'll see, every <FORM> element in an HTML document creates a numbered element in the forms[] array of the Document object. Similarly, every <APPLET> element creates an element of the applets[] array. The same applies for <A>, <IMG>, and <EMBED> tags.

In addition to these arrays, however, if any of these tags is given a NAME attribute, the value of that attribute is used as the name of a Document object property. The value of that property is the object that represents the tag. So, for example, suppose an HTML document contains the following form:

```
<FORM NAME="f1">
<INPUT TYPE="button" VALUE="Push Me">
</FORM>
```

Your JavaScript code can refer to the resulting Form object with either of the following two expressions:

```
document.forms[0]  // Refer to the form by position within the document.
document.f1        // Refer to the form by name.
```

As you might imagine, it is convenient to give names to frequently used document objects so that you can refer to them more easily in your scripts. We'll see this technique used a number of times in this and later chapters. Note, however, that there is a flaw: by allowing the creation of arbitrary new properties of the Document object, the designers of JavaScript have opened up the possibility of name collisions with new properties they add to the object in future versions of the

DOM. Thus, in the Level 1 DOM, it is likely that named HTML elements will become properties of some object referred to by the Document object but will not be properties of the Document object itself. While this should help prevent the name collision problem, backwards compatibility will be maintained for the HTML elements that are covered by the Level 0 DOM.

14.1.2 Document Objects and Events

For an HTML document to be interactive, the document and the elements within it must respond to user events. We discussed events and event handlers briefly in Chapter 12, *JavaScript in Web Browsers*, and have seen several examples that use simple event handlers. We'll see many more examples of event handlers in this chapter, because it is nigh to impossible to write an interesting client-side JavaScript program that works with document objects without relying heavily on event handlers.

Unfortunately, a complete discussion of events and event handlers must be deferred until Chapter 15, *Events and Event Handling*. For now, it is sufficient to remember that event handlers are defined by attributes like `onClick` and `onMouseOver` of HTML elements. The values of these attributes should be strings of JavaScript code. This code is executed whenever the specified event occurs on the HTML element.

14.2 Document Properties

The Document object defines the following properties:

`alinkColor`
> The color of a link while it is activated (i.e., while the user is clicking on it). Corresponds to the `ALINK` attribute of the `<BODY>` tag.

`anchors[]`
> An array of Anchor objects that represent the anchors in the document.

`applets[]`
> An array of objects that represent the applets in the document.

`bgColor`
> The background color of the document. Corresponds to the `BGCOLOR` property of the `<BODY>` tag.

cookie

> A special property that allows JavaScript programs to read and write HTTP cookies. See Chapter 18, *Saving State with Cookies*, for details.

domain

> A property that allows mutually trusted web servers within the same Internet domain to collaboratively relax certain security restrictions on interactions between their web pages. See Chapter 21, *JavaScript Security*.

embeds[]

> An array of objects that represent the embedded objects (i.e., plugins and ActiveX controls) in the document.

fgColor

> The default text color of the document. Corresponds to the TEXT attribute of the <BODY> tag.

forms[]

> An array of Form objects that represent the <FORM> elements in the document.

images[]

> An array of Image objects that represent the <IMG> elements in the document.

lastModified

> A string that contains the modification date of the document.

linkColor

> The color of unvisited links in the document. Corresponds to the LINK attribute of the <BODY> tag.

links[]

> An array of Link objects that represent the hypertext links in the document.

location

> A deprecated synonym for the URL property. This property exists only for compatibility with JavaScript 1.0.

referrer

> The URL of the document that contained the link that the user clicked on to get to the current document, if any.

title

> The text between the <TITLE> and </TITLE> tags for this document.

URL

> A string specifying the URL from which the document was loaded. The value of this property is the same as the location.href property of the Window object, except when a server redirect has occurred.

vlinkColor

> The color of visited links in the document. Corresponds to the VLINK attribute of the <BODY> tag.

The color properties of the Document object are read/write properties, but they can only be set before the <BODY> tag is parsed. You can set them dynamically with JavaScript code in the <HEAD> section of a document or you can set them statically as attributes of the <BODY> tag, but you cannot set them elsewhere. The exception to this rule is the bgColor property. You can set this property at any time; doing so causes the background color of the browser window to change.*

Each of these color properties has a string value. To set a color, you can use one of the predefined color names listed at:

http://developer.netscape.com/docs/manuals/communicator/jsguide4/colors.htm

You can also specify the color as red, green, and blue color values, expressed as a string of six hexadecimal digits in the form *#RRGGBB*. If you recall, Example 13-7 sets the bgColor property to a color string expressed in this fashion.

Other than bgColor, the color properties of the Document object merely expose attributes of the <BODY> tag and are basically uninteresting. Furthermore, with the introduction of style sheets, properties and attributes like these become somewhat obsolete.

Several of the other Document properties are more interesting than the color properties, however. For example, the following code shows how you can use the lastModified, title, and URL properties to include an automatic timestamp within a document. This allows users to judge how up-to-date (or out-of-date) a document is. This code uses the write() method, which is described shortly:

```
<HR><FONT SIZE=1>
Document: <I><SCRIPT>document.write(document.title);</SCRIPT></I><BR>
URL: <I><SCRIPT>document.write(document.URL);</SCRIPT></I><BR>
Last Update: <I><SCRIPT>document.write(document.lastModified);</SCRIPT></I>
</FONT>
```

referrer is another interesting property. One possible use is to save this value in a hidden field of a form on your web page. When the user submits the form (for whatever reason your page contains the form in the first place), you can save this referrer data on the server. This allows you to analyze the links that refer to your page, and you can also track the percentage of hits that come through various links. Another use of this property is a trick to prevent unauthorized links to your page from working correctly. For example, suppose you only want to allow other

---

* There is a bug in Navigator 3 on Unix platforms such that changing the background color can make the contents of the page disappear (usually until the window is scrolled or otherwise redrawn).

sites to link to the top-level home page on your site. You can use the `referrer` property in conjunction with the `location` property of the Window object, to redirect any links from outside the site to the top-level home page:

```
<SCRIPT>
// If linked from somewhere offsite, go to home page first.
if (document.referrer == "" || document.referrer.indexOf("mysite.com") == -1)
    window.location = "http://home.mysite.com";
</SCRIPT>
```

Don't consider this trick to be any kind of serious security measure, of course. One obvious flaw is that it doesn't work for browsers that don't support JavaScript or for users who have disabled JavaScript.

14.3 Dynamically Generated Documents

The Document object defines four methods that allow JavaScript programs to dynamically add HTML text to a document that is being parsed. These methods also allow JavaScript to dynamically create entire new documents from scratch. The `write()`, `writeln()`, `open()`, and `close()` methods are documented in the following sections.

14.3.1 The write() Method

One of the most important features of the Document object (and perhaps of client-side JavaScript in general) is the `write()` method, which allows you to dynamically generate web page content from your JavaScript programs. There are several ways this method can be used. The most obvious is to use it within a script to output HTML into the document that is currently being parsed: this is the way it was used in the previous section to display the value of the `lastModified` property within a web page.

Be aware that you can only output HTML to the current document while that document is being parsed. That is, you can only call `document.write()` from within `<SCRIPT>` tags because these scripts are executed as part of the document parsing process. In particular, if you call `document.write()` from an event handler, you will end up overwriting the current document (including its event handlers), instead of appending text to it.

Although you cannot usefully write to the current document from an event handler, there is no reason why you can't write to a document in another window or frame—doing so can be a useful technique with multiwindow or multiframe web sites. For example, JavaScript code in one frame of a multiframe site might display a message in another frame with code like this:

```
<SCRIPT>
parent.frames[0].document.open();
parent.frames[0].document.write("<HR>Hello from your sibling frame!<HR>");
parent.frames[0].document.close();
</SCRIPT>
```

To create a new document, we first call the `open()` method of the Document object, then call `write()` any number of times to output the contents of the document, and finally call the `close()` method of the Document object to indicate that we have finished. This last step is important—if you forget to close the document, the browser does not stop the "document loading" animation it displays. Also, the browser may buffer the HTML you have written; it is not required to display the buffered output until you explicitly end the document by calling `close()`.

In contrast to the `close()` call, which is required, the `open()` call is optional. If you call the `write()` method on a document that has already been closed, JavaScript implicitly opens a new HTML document, as if you had called the `open()` method. This explains what happens when you call `document.write()` from an event handler within the same document—JavaScript opens a new document. In the process, however, the current document (and its contents, including scripts and event handlers) is discarded. In Navigator 3 and later, this causes surprising programming difficulties and unexpected error messages. In Navigator 2, it can actually cause the browser to crash. As a general rule of thumb, a document should never call `write()` on itself from within an event handler.

A couple of final notes about the `write()` method. First, many people do not realize that the `write()` method can take more than one argument. When you pass multiple arguments, they are output one after another, just as if they had been concatenated. So instead of writing:

```
document.write('Hello, ' + username + " Welcome to my home page!");
```

you can equivalently write:

```
document.write('Hello, ', username, " Welcome to my home page!");
```

The second point to note about the `write()` method is that the Document object also supports a `writeln()` method, which is identical to the `write()` method in every way except that it appends a newline after outputting its arguments. Since HTML ignores line breaks, this newline character usually doesn't make a difference, but as we'll see in a bit, the `writeln()` method can be convenient when working with non-HTML documents.

Example 14-1 shows how you might create a complex dialog box with the Window `open()` method and the methods of the Document object. This example registers an `onerror` event handler function for the window; the function is invoked when a JavaScript error occurs. (We'll discuss `onerror` in Chapter 15. Here, we're just using it for the sake of example.) The error handler function creates a new window and uses the Document object methods to create an HTML form within the window. The form allows the user to see details about the error that occurred, and to email a bug report to the author of the JavaScript code. Figure 14-1 shows a sample window.

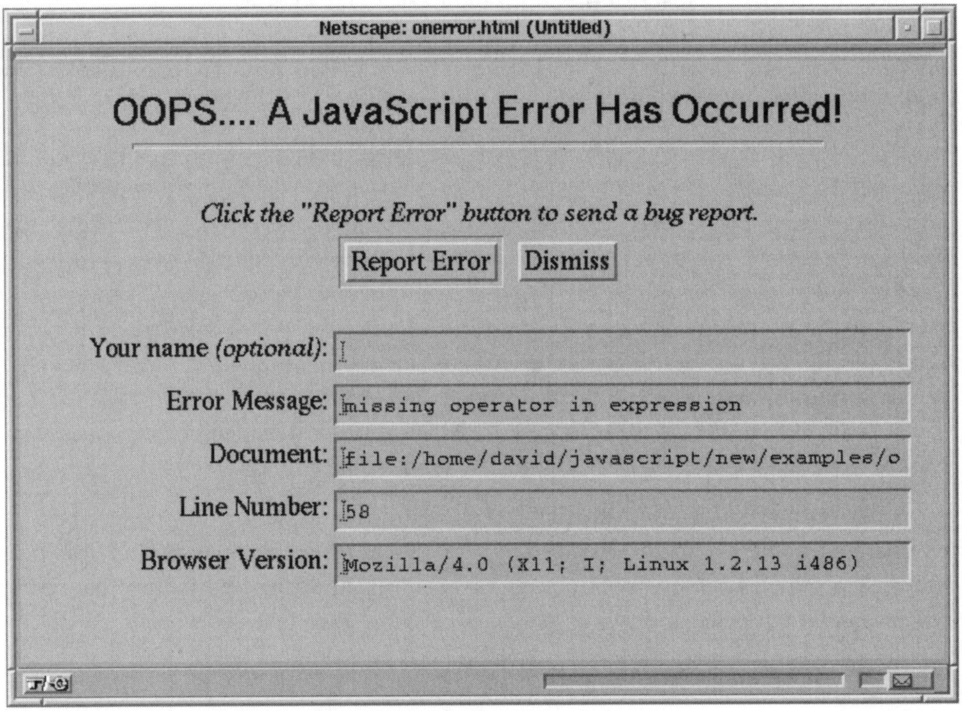

Figure 14-1: Using a browser window as a dialog box

Example 14-1: Dynamically Creating a Dialog Window

```
<SCRIPT>
// A variable we use to ensure that each error window we create is unique.
var error_count = 0;

// Set this variable to your email address.
var email = "myname@mydomain.com";

// Define the error handler. It generates an HTML form so
// the user can report the error to the author.
function report_error(msg, url, line)
{
    var w = window.open("",                    // URL (none specified)
```

Example 14–1: Dynamically Creating a Dialog Window (continued)

```
                    "error"+error_count++, // Name (force it to be unique)
                    "resizable,status,width=625,height=400"); // Features
var d = w.document;   // We use this variable to save typing!

// Output an HTML document, including a form, into the new window.
d.write('<DIV align=center>');
d.write('<FONT SIZE=7 FACE="helvetica"><B>');
d.write('OOPS.... A JavaScript Error Has Occurred!');
d.write('</B></FONT><BR><HR SIZE=4 WIDTH="80%">');
d.write('<FORM ACTION="mailto:' + email + '" METHOD=post');
d.write(' ENCTYPE="text/plain">');
d.write('<FONT SIZE=3>');
d.write('<I>Click the "Report Error" button to send a bug report.</I><BR>');
d.write('<INPUT TYPE="submit" VALUE="Report Error">  ');
d.write('<INPUT TYPE="button" VALUE="Dismiss" onClick="self.close()">');
d.write('</DIV><DIV align=right>');
d.write('<BR>Your name <I>(optional)</I>: ');
d.write('<INPUT SIZE=42 NAME="name" VALUE="">');
d.write('<BR>Error Message: ');
d.write('<INPUT SIZE=42 NAME="message" VALUE="' + msg + '">');
d.write('<BR>Document: <INPUT SIZE=42 NAME="url" VALUE="' + url + '">');
d.write('<BR>Line Number: <INPUT SIZE=42 NAME="line" VALUE="' + line +'">');
d.write('<BR>Browser Version: ');
d.write('<INPUT SIZE=42 NAME="version" VALUE="'+navigator.userAgent + '">');
d.write('</DIV></FONT>');
d.write('</FORM>');
// Remember to close the document when we're done.
d.close();

// Return true from this error handler, so that JavaScript does not
// display its own error dialog.
return true;
}


// Before the event handler can take effect, we have to register it
// for a particular window.
self.onerror = report_error;
</SCRIPT>

<SCRIPT>
// The following line of code purposely causes an error as a test.
self = null;
</SCRIPT>
```

14.3.2 Non-HTML Documents

When you call the Document open() method with no arguments, it opens a new HTML document. Remember, though, that web browsers can display a number of other data formats besides HTML text. When you want to dynamically create and display a document using some other data format, you call the open() method with a single argument, which is the MIME type you desire.*

The MIME type for HTML is text/html. The most common format besides HTML is plain text, with a MIME type of text/plain. If you want to use the write() method to output text that uses newlines, spaces, and tab characters for formatting, you should open the document by passing the string "text/plain" to the open() method. Example 14-2 shows one way you might do this. It implements a debug() function that you can use to output plain-text debugging messages from your scripts into a separate window that appears when needed. Figure 14-2 shows what the resulting window looks like.

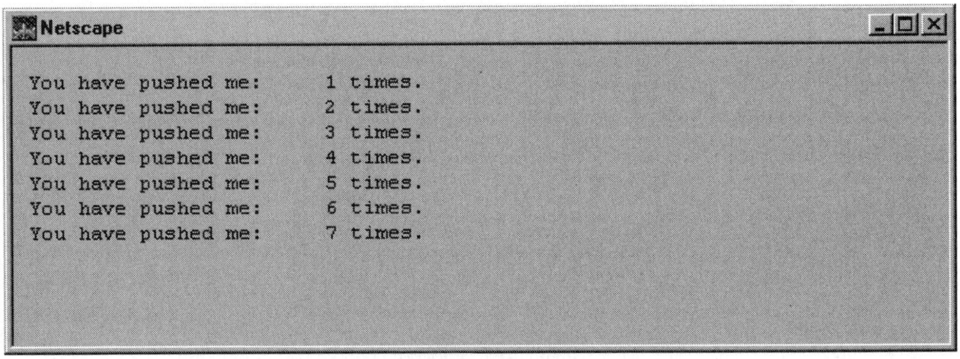

Figure 14-2: A window for plain-text debugging output

Example 14-2: Creating a Plain-Text Document

```
<SCRIPT>
var _console = null;

function debug(msg)
{
    // Open a window the first time we are called, or after an existing
    // console window has been closed.
    if ((_console == null) || (_console.closed)) {
        _console = window.open("","console","width=600,height=300,resizable");
        // Open a document in the window to display plain text.
        _console.document.open("text/plain");
    }
```

---

* This technique does not work in Internet Explorer 3.

Example 14-2: Creating a Plain-Text Document (continued)

```
    _console.document.writeln(msg);
}
</SCRIPT>

<!-- Here's an example of using this script. -->
<SCRIPT>var n = 0;</SCRIPT>
<FORM>
<INPUT TYPE="button" VALUE="Push Me"
       onClick="debug('You have pushed me:\t' + ++n + ' times.');">
</FORM>
```

14.4 Forms

The forms[] array of the Document object contains Form objects that represent any <FORM> elements in the document. Because HTML forms contain push buttons, text input fields, and the other input elements that usually comprise the GUI of a web application, the Form object is a very important one in client-side JavaScript. The Form object has an elements[] property that contains objects that represent the HTML input elements contained within the form. These element objects allow JavaScript programs to set default values in the form and to read the user's input from the form. They are also important sites for the event handlers that add interactivity to a program.

Because forms and their elements are such a large and important part of client-side JavaScript programming, they deserve a chapter of their own. We will return to the forms[] array and the Form object in Chapter 16, *Forms and Form Elements*.

14.5 Images

The images[] property of the Document object is an array of Image elements, each representing one of the inline images, created with an <IMG> tag, that is contained in the document. The images[] array and the Image object were added in JavaScript 1.1. While web browsers have always been able to display images with the <IMG> tag, the addition of the Image object was a major step forward—it allowed programs to dynamically manipulate those images.

14.5.1 Image Replacement with the src Property

The main feature of the Image object is that its src property is read/write. You can read this property to obtain the URL from which an image was loaded and, more importantly, you can set the src property to make the browser load and display a new image in the same space. For this to work, the new image must have the same width and height as the original one.

The ability to dynamically replace one image in a static HTML document with another image opens the door to any number of special effects, from animation, to images that change when clicked on, to digital clocks that update themselves in real time. With a bit of thought, you can probably imagine many more potential uses for this technique. To make the image replacement technique viable, the animations or other special effects need to be responsive. This means that we need some way to ensure that the necessary images are loaded into the browser's cache.

14.5.2 Off-Screen Images and Caching

To force an image to be cached, we create an off-screen image and load the desired image into it. Then, when the image is required on screen, we know it can be loaded quickly from the cache, rather than loaded slowly over the network. Example 14-3 shows code that performs a simple animation using this technique.

Example 14–3: An Animation Using Image Replacement

```
<!-- The image that will be animated. Give it a name for convenience. -->
<IMG SRC="images/0.gif" NAME=animation>

<SCRIPT>
// Create a bunch of off-screen images, and get them started
// loading the images we're going to animate.
var images = new Array(10);
for(var i = 0; i < 10; i++) {
    images[i] = new Image();                // Create an Image object.
    images[i].src = "images/" + i + ".gif"; // Tell it what URL to load.
}

// Later, when we want to perform our animation, we can use these URLs,
// knowing that they've been loaded into the cache. Note that we perform
// the animation by assigning the URL, not the Image object itself.
// Also note that we call the image by name, rather than as document.images[0].
function animate()
{
    document.animation.src = images[frame].src;
    frame = (frame + 1)%10;
    timeout_id = setTimeout("animate()", 250);  // Display next frame later.
}
var frame = 0;        // Keep track of what frame of the animation we're on.
var timeout_id = null; // This allows us to stop the animation.
</SCRIPT>
```

Example 14-3: An Animation Using Image Replacement (continued)

```
<FORM>                  <!-- Buttons to control the animation. -->
  <INPUT TYPE=button VALUE="Start"
         onClick="if (timeout_id == null) animate()">
  <INPUT TYPE=button VALUE="Stop"
         onClick="if (timeout_id) clearTimeout(timeout_id); timeout_id=null;">
</FORM>
```

Example 14-3 demonstrates the important steps involved in creating an off-screen image for image caching. The first step is to create an Image object with the Image() constructor. The second step is to assign the URL of the desired image to the src property of the newly created Image object. Doing so causes the browser to start loading the contents of the specified URL, which, unless caching is turned off, causes the image to be loaded into the cache, even though it is not displayed anywhere.

A confusing detail about the use of off-screen Image objects is that they themselves are not directly used for anything. To perform image replacement with an off-screen Image object, you do *not* assign the Image object directly into the images[] array of the Document object. Instead, you simply set the src property of the desired on-screen image to the URL of the desired image. If this URL has previously been loaded by an off-screen image, the desired image should be in the cache and the on-screen image replacement happens quickly. The off-screen image object is used to force the image to be loaded, but there isn't anything else that you can do with it.

14.5.3 Image Event Handlers

In Example 14-3, our animation does not begin until the user clicks the **Start** button, which allows plenty of time for our images to be loaded into the cache. But what about the more common case in which we want to begin an animation automatically as soon as all the necessary images are loaded? It turns out that images, whether created on screen with an <IMG> tag or off screen with the Image() constructor, have an onLoad event handler that is invoked when the image is fully loaded. Example 14-4 is an update to the previous example and shows how we could automatically start the animation as soon as the images are loaded.

Example 14-4: An Animation Using the onLoad Event Handler

```
<!-- The image that will be animated. Give it a name for convenience. -->
<IMG SRC="images/0.gif" NAME=animation>

<SCRIPT>
// Count how many images have been loaded. When we reach 10, start animating.
function count_images() {  if (++num_loaded_images == 10) animate(); }
var num_loaded_images = 0;
```

Example 14-4: An Animation Using the onLoad Event Handler (continued)

```
// Create the off-screen images and assign the image URLs.
// Also assign an event handler so we can count how many images have been
// loaded. Note that we assign the handler before the URL, because otherwise
// the image might finish loading (e.g., if it is already cached) before
// we assign the handler, and then we'll lose count of how many have loaded!
var images = new Array(10);
for(var i = 0; i < 10; i++) {
    images[i] = new Image();                 // Create an Image object.
    images[i].onload = count_images;         // Assign the event handler.
    images[i].src = "images/" + i + ".gif";  // Tell it what URL to load.
}

function animate()  // The function that does the animation.
{
    document.animation.src = images[frame].src;
    frame = (frame + 1)%10;
    timeout_id = setTimeout("animate()", 250);  // Display next frame later.
}
var frame = 0;        // Keep track of what frame of the animation we're on.
var timeout_id = null; // This allows us to stop the animation.
</SCRIPT>

<!-- Buttons to control the animation. Note that we don't let the user
  -- start the animation before all the images are loaded. -->
<FORM>
  <INPUT TYPE=button VALUE="Start"
         onClick="if (timeout_id==null && num_loaded_images==10) animate()">
  <INPUT TYPE=button VALUE="Stop"
         onClick="if (timeout_id) clearTimeout(timeout_id); timeout_id=null;">
</FORM>
```

In addition to the onLoad event handler, the Image object supports two others. The onError event handler is invoked when an error occurs during image loading, such as when the specified URL refers to corrupt image data. The onAbort() handler is invoked if the user cancels the image load (for example, by clicking the **Stop** button in the browser) before it has finished. For any image, one (and only one) of these handlers is called.

In addition to these handlers, each Image object also has a complete property. This property is false while the image is loading; it is changed to true once the image has loaded or once the browser has stopped trying to load it. That is, the complete property becomes true after one of the three possible event handlers is invoked.

14.5.4 Other Image Properties

The Image object has a few other properties as well. Most of them are read-only properties that simply mirror attributes of the <IMG> tag that created the image. The width, height, border, hspace, and vspace properties are read-only integers that specify the size of the image, the width of its border, and the size of its horizontal and vertical margins. These properties are set by the attributes of the IMG tag that share their names.

The lowsrc property of the Image object mirrors the LOWSRC attribute of the IMG tag. It specifies the URL of an optional image to display when the page is viewed on a low-resolution device. The lowsrc property is a read/write string, like src, but unlike the src property, setting lowsrc does not cause the browser to load and display the newly specified, low resolution image. If you want to perform an animation, or some other special effect, that works with low-resolution images as well as high-resolution ones, always remember to update the lowsrc property before you set the src property. If the browser is running on a low-resolution device when you set the src literal, it loads the new lowsrc image instead.

14.5.5 Image Replacement Example

Because image replacement is such a versatile technique, we'll end our discussion of the Image object with an extended example. Example 14-5 defines a ToggleButton class that uses image replacement to simulate a graphical checkbox. Because this class uses images that we provide, we can use bolder graphics than those plain old graphics used by the standard HTML Checkbox object. Figure 14-3 shows how these toggle button graphics could appear on a web page. This is a complex, real-world example and is worth studying carefully.

Example 14–5: Implementing a ToggleButton with Image Replacement

```
<SCRIPT LANGUAGE="JavaScript1.1">
// This is the constructor function for our new ToggleButton class.
// Calling it creates a ToggleButton object and outputs the required
// <A> and <IMG> tags into the specified document at the current location.
// Therefore, don't call it for the current document from an event handler.
// Arguments:
//    document: The Document object the buttons will be created in.
//    checked:  A boolean that says whether the button is initially checked.
//    label:    An optional string that specifies text to appear after the button.
//    onclick:  An optional function to be called when the toggle button is
//              clicked. It will be passed a boolean indicating the new
//              state of the button. You can also pass a string, which will
//              be converted to a function which is passed a boolean argument
//              named "state".
function ToggleButton(document, checked, label, onclick)
```

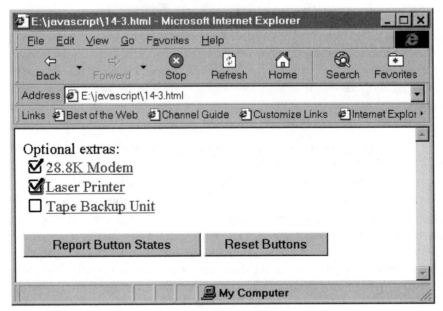

Figure 14-3: ToggleButtons implemented with image replacement

Example 14-5: Implementing a ToggleButton with Image Replacement (continued)

```
{
    // First time called, document will be false. Ignore this call.
    if (document == null) return;

    // The first time we are called (and only the first time) we have
    // to do some special stuff. First, now that the prototype object
    // is created, we can set up our methods.
    // Second, we've got to load the images that we'll be using.
    // Doing this will get the images in the cache for when we need them.
    if (!ToggleButton.prototype.over) {
        // Initialize the prototype object to create our methods.
        ToggleButton.prototype.over = _ToggleButton_over;
        ToggleButton.prototype.out = _ToggleButton_out;
        ToggleButton.prototype.click = _ToggleButton_click;

        // Now create an array of image objects, and assign URLs to them.
        // The URLs of the images are configurable, and are stored in an
        // array property of the constructor function itself. They will be
        // initialized below. Because of a bug in Navigator, we've got
        // to maintain references to these images, so we store the array
        // in a property of the constructor rather than using a local variable.
        ToggleButton.images = new Array(4);
        for(var i = 0; i < 4; i++) {
            ToggleButton.images[i] = new Image(ToggleButton.width,
```

Example 14–5: Implementing a ToggleButton with Image Replacement (continued)

```
                                                    ToggleButton.height);
        ToggleButton.images[i].src = ToggleButton.imagenames[i];
    }
}

// Save some of the arguments we were passed.
this.document = document;
this.checked = checked;

// Remember that the mouse is not currently on top of us.
this.highlighted = false;

// Save the onclick argument to be called when the button is clicked.
// If it is not already a function, attempt to convert it
// to a function that is passed a single argument, named state.
this.onclick = onclick;
if (typeof this.onclick == "string")
    this.onclick = new Function("state", this.onclick);

// Figure out what entry in the document.images[] array the images
// for this checkbox will be stored at.
var index = document.images.length;

// Now output the HTML code for this checkbox. Use <A> and <IMG> tags.
// The event handlers we output here are confusing, but crucial to the
// operation of this class. The "_tb" property is defined below, as
// are the over(), out(), and click() methods.
document.write(' <A HREF ="" ' +
  'onMouseOver="document.images[' + index + ']._tb.over();return true;" '+
  'onMouseOut="document.images[' + index + ']._tb.out()" '+
  'onClick="document.images[' + index + ']._tb.click(); return false;">');
document.write('<IMG SRC="' + ToggleButton.imagenames[this.checked+0] +'"'+
              ' WIDTH=' + ToggleButton.width +
              ' HEIGHT=' + ToggleButton.height +
              ' BORDER=0 HSPACE=0 VSPACE=0 ALIGN="absmiddle">');
if (label) document.write(label);
document.write('</A>');

// Now that we've output the <IMG> tag, save a reference to the
// Image object that it created in the ToggleButton object.
this.image = document.images[index];

// And also make a link in the other direction: from the Image object
// to this ToggleButton object. Do this by defining a "_tb" property
// in the Image object.
this.image._tb = this;
}
```

Example 14-5: Implementing a ToggleButton with Image Replacement (continued)

```
// This becomes the over() method.
function _ToggleButton_over()
{
    // Change the image, and remember that we're highlighted.
    this.image.src = ToggleButton.imagenames[this.checked + 2];
    this.highlighted = true;
}


// This becomes the out() method.
function _ToggleButton_out()
{
    // Change the image, and remember that we're not highlighted.
    this.image.src = ToggleButton.imagenames[this.checked + 0];
    this.highlighted = false;
}


// This becomes the click() method.
function _ToggleButton_click()
{
    // Toggle the state of the button, change the image, and call the
    // onclick method, if it was specified for this ToggleButton.
    this.checked = !this.checked;
    this.image.src = ToggleButton.imagenames[this.checked+this.highlighted*2];
    if (this.onclick) this.onclick(this.checked);
}


// Initialize static class properties that describe the checkbox images. These
// are just defaults. Programs can override them by assigning new values.
// But they should only be overridden *before* any ToggleButtons are created.
ToggleButton.imagenames = new Array(4);          // Create an array.
ToggleButton.imagenames[0] = "togglebutton0.gif"; // The unchecked box
ToggleButton.imagenames[1] = "togglebutton1.gif"; // The box with a check mark
ToggleButton.imagenames[2] = "togglebutton2.gif"; // Unchecked but highlighted
ToggleButton.imagenames[3] = "togglebutton3.gif"; // Checked and highlighted
ToggleButton.width = ToggleButton.height = 25;    // Size of all images
</SCRIPT>

<!-- Here's how we might use the ToggleButton class. -->
Optional extras:<BR>
<SCRIPT LANGUAGE="JavaScript1.1">
// Create the buttons.
var tb1 = new ToggleButton(document, true, "28.8K Modem<BR>");
var tb2 = new ToggleButton(document, false, "Laser Printer<BR>");
var tb3 = new ToggleButton(document, false, "Tape Backup Unit<BR>");
</SCRIPT>

<!-- Here's how we can use the ToggleButton objects from event handlers. -->
<FORM>
```

Example 14-5: Implementing a ToggleButton with Image Replacement (continued)

```
<INPUT TYPE="button" VALUE="Report Button States"
       onClick="alert(tb1.checked + '\n' + tb2.checked + '\n' + tb3.checked)">
<INPUT TYPE="button" VALUE="Reset Buttons"
       onClick="if (tb1.checked) tb1.click();
                if (tb2.checked) tb2.click();
                if (tb3.checked) tb3.click();">
</FORM>
```

14.6 Links

The links[] array of the Document object contains Link objects that represent each of the hypertext links in a document. Recall that HTML hypertext links are coded with the HREF attribute of the <A> tag. In JavaScript 1.1 and later, the <AREA> tag in a client-side image map also creates a Link object in the Document links[] array.

The Link object represents the URL of the hypertext link and contains all of the properties that the Location object (introduced in Chapter 13, *Windows and Frames*) does. For example, the href property of a Link object contains the complete text of the URL that it is linked to, while the hostname property contains only the hostname portion of that URL. See the reference section for a complete list of these URL-related properties.

Example 14-6 shows a function that generates a list of all links in a document. Note the use of the Document write() and close() methods to dynamically generate a document, as discussed earlier in the chapter.

Example 14-6: Listing the Links in a Document

```
/*
 * FILE: listlinks.js
 * List all links in the specified document in a new window.
 */
function listlinks(d) {
    var newwin = window.open("", "linklist",
                    "menubar,scrollbars,resizable,width=600,height=300");

    for (var i = 0; i < d.links.length; i++) {
        newwin.document.write('<A HREF="' + d.links[i].href + '">')
        newwin.document.write(d.links[i].href);
        newwin.document.writeln("</A><BR>");
    }
    newwin.document.close();
}
```

In Navigator 4, this example could be enhanced to use the new text property of the Link object. This property contains the text that appears between the <A> and </A> tags of the hypertext link. The text property is not supported in Internet Explorer 4; in that browser, you use innerText or innerHTML instead. Hopefully, the Level 1 DOM will resolve this incompatibility by specifying a standard property name.

14.6.1 Links, Web Crawlers, and JavaScript Security

One obvious use of the Link object and the links[] array is to write a web crawler program. This program runs in one browser window or frame and reads web pages into another window or frame (by setting the location property of the Window object). For each page it reads in, it looks through the links[] array and recursively follows them. If carefully written (so it doesn't get caught in infinite recursion or start going in circles), such a program can be used, for example, to generate a list of all web pages that are accessible from a given starting page. This can be quite useful in web site maintenance.

Don't expect to crawl the entire Internet using these techniques, however. For security reasons, JavaScript does not allow an unsigned script in one window or frame to read the properties (such as document.links) of another window or frame unless both windows are displaying documents that came from the same web server. This restriction prevents important security breaches: imagine that an employee at a large security-conscious company is browsing the Internet through a corporate firewall and is also using his browser to browse proprietary company information on the corporate intranet. Without the security restriction we've described, an untrusted script from some random Internet site could snoop on what was going on in the other window. The authors of the snooping script might not be able to glean much useful information from the links[] array of the proprietary documents, but this would nevertheless be a serious breach of security.

The web crawler program we've described is not a threat to Internet security or privacy, but unfortunately, it is still subject to the general security restrictions of JavaScript, which prevent it from crawling very far beyond the site from which it was loaded. (When the crawler loads a page from a different site, it appears as if that page simply has no links on it.) See Chapter 21 for a complete discussion of JavaScript security, including a description of how to avoid this security restriction with signed scripts.

14.6.2 Link Event Handlers

The Link object supports a number of interesting event handlers. We already saw the onMouseOver event handler in Example 14-6, where it was used with both <A> and <AREA> to change the message in the browser's status line when the mouse moved over the link. The onClick event handler is invoked when the user clicks on a hypertext link. In JavaScript 1.1 and later, if this event handler returns false, the browser doesn't follow the link as it would otherwise. As of JavaScript 1.1, both the <A> and <AREA> tags support an onMouseOut event handler. This is simply the opposite of the onMouseOver handler—it is run when the mouse pointer moves off a hypertext link. If you used onMouseOver to display a message in the status line, you can use onMouseOut to clear it.

The event handling model has become much more general in JavaScript 1.2 and links support quite a few other event handlers. See Chapter 15 for details.

Finally, it is worth mentioning that href and the other URL properties of the Link object are read/write. Thus, you can write a JavaScript program that dynamically modifies the destinations of hypertext links! Here is a frivolous piece of JavaScript-enhanced HTML that uses a Link event handler to write to the href property and create a random hypertext link:

```
<A HREF="about:"
    onMouseOver="status = 'Take a chance... Click me.'; return true;"
    onMouseOut="status = ''"
    onClick="this.href =
            document.links[Math.floor(Math.random()*document.links.length)]"
>
Random Link
</A>
```

This example demonstrates all the features of the Link object that we've considered: the links[] array, the use of Link event handlers, and the dynamic setting of the destination of a Link. Note that the example sets the href property of the Link, but doesn't bother to read the href property of the link it randomly chooses. Instead, it relies on the toString() method of the Link object to return the URL.

14.7 Anchors

The anchors[] array of the Document object contains Anchor objects that represent named locations in the HTML document that are marked with the <A> tag and its NAME attribute. The anchors[] array has existed since JavaScript 1.0, but the Anchor object is new in Navigator 4. In previous versions, the elements of the anchors[] array were all undefined, and only the length property was useful.

The Anchor object is a simple one. The only standard property it defines is name, which is the value of the HTML NAME attribute. As with the Link object, the text that appears between the <A> and </A> tags of the anchor is specified by the text property in Navigator 4 and by the innerText property in Internet Explorer 4. (The Level 1 DOM should standardize the name for this property.) Furthermore, in Navigator 4, every Anchor object also has x and y properties, which specify the document coordinates of the anchor. These can be used with the scrollTo() method of the Window object, for example.

Example 14-7 shows a function that creates a navigation window for a specified document. It displays the text (or innerText) or name of all anchors in the document. The anchor text or name is displayed within hypertext links—clicking on any anchor causes the document to scroll to display that anchor. The code in this example is particularly useful if you write your HTML documents so that all section headings are enclosed in anchors. For example:

```
<A NAME="sect14.6"><H2>The Anchor Object</H2></A>
```

Example 14-7: Listing All Anchors

```
/*
 * FILE: listanchors.js
 * The function listanchors() is passed a document as its argument, and
 * opens a new window to serve as a "navigation window" for that
 * document. The new window displays a list of all anchors in the document.
 * Clicking on any anchor in the list causes the document to scroll to
 * the position of that anchor.
 */

// First, figure out what browser we're running in.
// Assume Navigator, but check for IE. We assume version 4 of either.
listanchors.nav = true;
if (navigator.appName.indexOf("Microsoft") != -1) listanchors.nav = false;

// Now define the function. Pass the document that is to have its anchors
// listed as the sole argument. Call it once the document is fully (or
// mostly) parsed, not at the beginning of the document.
function listanchors(d) {
    // Open the new window.
    var newwin = window.open("", "navwin",
                            "menubar=yes,scrollbars=yes,resizable=yes," +
                            "width=600,height=300");

    // Give it a title.
    newwin.document.writeln("<H1>Navigation Window:<BR>" +
                            document.title + "</H1>");
    // List all anchors.
    for(var i = 0; i < d.anchors.length; i++) {
```

Example 14-7: Listing All Anchors (continued)

```
            // For each anchor object, determine the text to display.
            // First, try to get the text between <A> and </A> using a
            // browser-dependent property. If none, use the name instead.
            var text;
            var a = d.anchors[i];
            if (listanchors.nav) text = a.text;  // Navigator 4
            else text = a.innerText;             // Internet Explorer 4
            if ((text == null) || (text == '')) text = a.name;

            // Now output that text as a link. Note the use of the location
            // property of the original window.
            newwin.document.write('<A HREF="#' + a.name + '"' +
                                  ' onClick="opener.location.hash=\'' + a.name +
                                  '\'; return false;">');
            newwin.document.write(text);
            newwin.document.writeln('</A><BR>');
        }
        newwin.document.close();    // Never forget to close the document!
    }
```

14.8 Applets and Embedded Data

The applets[] array of the Document object contains objects that represent the applets embedded in the document with the <APPLET> tag. An applet is a portable, secure Java program that is loaded over the Internet and executed by the web browser; both Navigator and Internet Explorer support Java. Similarly, the embeds[] array contains objects that represent data embedded in the document with the <EMBED> tag. Embedded data can take many forms (audio, video, spreadsheets, etc.). The browser must have an appropriate viewer installed or available so that it can display the data to the user. In Navigator, special modules known as "plugins" are responsible for displaying embedded data. In Internet Explorer, embedded data is displayed by ActiveX controls. Both plugins and ActiveX controls can be automatically downloaded from the network and installed as needed.

As of Navigator 3 and Internet Explorer 3, both browsers allow JavaScript to invoke public methods and read and write the public properties of Java applets. (As we'll see in Chapter 20, *LiveConnect: JavaScript and Java*, Navigator also supports much richer bidirectional interactions between JavaScript and Java.) All applets have a few standard public methods that they inherit from their super-classes, but the most interesting methods and properties vary on a case-by-case basis. If you are the author of the applet that you want to control from JavaScript, you already know what public methods and properties it defines. If you are not the author, you should consult the applet's documentation to determine what you can do with it.

Here's how you might embed a Java applet in a web page with the <APPLET> tag and then invoke the start() and stop() methods of that applet from JavaScript event handlers:

```
<APPLET NAME="animation" CODE="Animation.class" WIDTH=500 HEIGHT=200>
</APPLET>
<FORM>
<INPUT TYPE=button VALUE="Start" onclick="document.animation.start()">
<INPUT TYPE=button VALUE="Stop" onclick="document.animation.stop()">
</FORM>
```

All applets define these two methods. If we assume that the applet performs some kind of animation, we can further assume that the two HTML buttons invoke event handlers that tell the applet to start and stop the animation. Note that we've used the NAME attribute of the <APPLET> tag, so we can refer to the applet by name, rather than as a numbered element of the applets[] array.

This example does not fully demonstrate the power of JavaScript to script Java applets: the Java methods invoked from the JavaScript event handlers are passed no arguments and return no values. In fact, JavaScript can pass numbers, strings, and boolean values as arguments to Java methods and can accept numbers, strings, and boolean return values from those functions. (As we'll see in Chapter 20, Navigator can also pass and return JavaScript and Java objects to and from Java methods.) The automatic conversion of data between JavaScript and Java allows for fairly rich interactions. For example, an applet might implement a method that returns a string of JavaScript code. JavaScript could then use the eval() method to evaluate that code.

Applets can also implement methods that don't operate on the applet itself, but instead simply serve as conduits between JavaScript and the Java environment. For instance, an applet might define a method that invokes the System.getProperty() method for a given string argument. This would allow JavaScript to look up the value of Java system properties and determine, for example, the version of Java that is supported by the browser.

While the elements of the applets[] array all represent Java applets, the elements of the embeds[] array tend to be more diverse, and few generalizations can be made about them. The properties and methods of these objects depend upon the particular plugin or ActiveX control that is used to display the embedded data. You should consult the vendor-specific documentation for the plugin or ActiveX control you are using. If it supports any kind of scripting from JavaScript, the documentation should say so, and it should describe the properties and methods that you can use from JavaScript. For example, the documentation for the LiveVideo plugin from Netscape says that the LiveVideo object in the `embeds[]` array supports four methods: `play()`, `stop()`, `rewind()`, and `seek()`. With this information, you can write simple scripts that control how the plugin displays the movie you have embedded on the web page. Note that while some vendors may produce plugins and ActiveX controls with the same API, this is not always the case. Scripting embedded objects usually involves platform-specific JavaScript code.

14.9 The Future of the DOM

As I noted at the beginning of this chapter, the World Wide Web Consortium is working to standardize a way for programming languages to interact with HTML documents. Both Netscape and Microsoft have committed to fully supporting the eventual W3C Document Object Model (DOM) standard. The standardization committee has defined several levels of the DOM. Level 0 is the current de facto standard supported by Navigator and Internet Explorer. Level 1 is the current focus of standardization efforts: it will define an API that allows programs to read and write the text, elements, and attributes of HTML and XML documents. We can expect that Navigator 5 and Internet Explorer 5 will support the Level 1 DOM standard and will do so in compatible ways, which will be a real boon for JavaScript programmers.

Future levels (Levels 2 and 3) of the DOM will be standardized later. Plans for these levels are not yet as clear as they are for Level 1. However, we do know that these future levels will define APIs for reading and manipulating style sheets, and will standardize the event model that client-side JavaScript relies so heavily on. It is not clear yet whether the fifth-generation web browsers will have compatible models for style sheets and events. Beyond style sheets and events, a future level will standardize a security model and may even move beyond the Document object and standardize APIs for interacting with the document context—in other words, the Window object in which the document appears.

14.9.1 The Level 1 DOM

The standardization efforts for the Level 1 DOM are progressing rapidly, but as this book goes to press, the current draft of the standard is not yet stable enough to begin to provide actual JavaScript code samples of how you might use it in a fifth-generation web browser. Nevertheless, the goals and structure of the Level 1 standard are clear, and it is possible to give a complete overview of the standard that is emerging. You can find the latest information on DOM standardization at *http://www.w3.org/DOM*.

The Level 1 DOM exposes the complete content of the document: its text, its HTML elements, and the attribute names and values of those elements. The document is represented as a tree of objects, where each object represents either a string of text or an HTML tag and its attributes. The root node of any such tree is presumably an object that represents the <HTML> element. This node has children representing the document <HEAD> and <BODY>. The head node may have a child representing the <TITLE> element, and the body may have many children. The first child of the body node might, for example, be an object representing an <H1> element, and this node might have an object that represents a string of text as its sole child. In this way, any HTML document, no matter how complex, can be represented as a tree of objects. The Level 1 DOM provides an API to traverse the tree and to manipulate its nodes.

In the JavaScript binding to the DOM, each HTML element is represented as an object, and its attributes are represented by properties. In most cases, the property names are lowercase or mixed-case versions of the attribute names. For example, the NAME attribute is represented by the name property, and the BGCOLOR attribute is represented by the bgColor property. When the name of an attribute is a reserved word in JavaScript, the property name will have "html" prepended. For example, the FOR attribute will be represented by the htmlFor property. Some objects, such as the object that represents <TABLE> elements, will support convenience methods that make it easier to manipulate those elements.

Because these HTML objects form a tree, each one has an array of child nodes and a property that refers to the parent node. These properties are enough to allow you to traverse the tree in any way you want and find any node within the tree. Each node will probably also support convenience methods that make traversal simpler. There will also be some high-level way to look up any node that has a unique NAME or ID attribute, and there will probably be a convenient way to obtain a list of all elements of a certain type, such as a list of all <H1> objects.

The Level 1 DOM does not just support traversal and examination of the document tree and of document content: it also allows modifications. There will be functions or constructors to create new HTML objects and each node will support functions to insert, delete, and replace child nodes. Thus, it will be possible to build an entire HTML document, piece by piece, from scratch. And it will be possible to insert, delete, edit, or replace any string of text or any element anywhere in the document. When such changes are made, the web browser will typically have to dynamically reformat, or reflow, the document.

The Level 1 DOM will be similar to, but incompatible with, the DOM implemented by Internet Explorer 4. One major incompatibility is that IE does not include text nodes in its tree of HTML elements. Instead, each HTML object in the tree has properties that specify the text it contains. Also, the DOM standard may not support the `document.all[]` collection that features prominently in the IE 4 DOM. In addition to these major incompatibilities, there will be some property name differences, a few of which may be significant. Nevertheless, the IE DOM is the closest thing currently available to the future standard, so if you want to gain experience with the general features and capabilities of a DOM, you may want to begin experimenting now with the IE 4 model.

15

Events and
Event Handling

As we saw in Chapter 12, *JavaScript in Web Browsers*, interactive JavaScript programs use an event-driven programming model. Most interesting JavaScript programs rely heavily on their event handlers. We've already seen a number of JavaScript examples that use event handlers. This chapter fills in all the missing details about events and event handlers.

15.1 Event Types

Client-side JavaScript supports quite a few different types of events. Different types of events are generated under different circumstances. The event generated when the user clicks on a button is different than the event generated when the browser loads a new document, for example. Different objects may also generate events differently under the same or similar circumstances. Thus, a mouse click on a button generates an onClick event, while a mouse click on a text element generates no event at all.

Event types are distinguished from each other primarily by the event handlers that they trigger. Table 15-1 lists the various types of event handlers, the circumstances under which they are triggered, and the client-side objects that support them.

Note that a number of the client-side objects listed in the third column of the table are form element objects, which we will discuss in Chapter 16, *Forms and Form Elements*. When the table refers to button elements, it means the Button, Checkbox, Radio, Reset, and Submit objects. When it refers to text elements, it means the Text, Textarea, Password, and FileUpload objects.

Table 15–1: Event Handlers and the Objects That Support Them

Handler	Triggered when	Supported by
onAbort[a]	Loading interrupted.	Image
onBlur	Element loses input focus.	Text elements, Window,[a] all other elements[a]
onChange	User selects or deselects an item or enters text and moves input focus to another element.	Select, text input elements
onClick	User clicks once. Return `false` to cancel default action (i.e., follow link, reset, submit).	Link, button elements
onDblClick[b c d]	User clicks twice.	Document, Link, Image, button elements
onError[a]	Error occurs while loading an image.	Image
onFocus	Element given input focus.	Text elements, Window,[a] all other form elements[a]
onKeyDown[b]	Key pressed by user. Return `false` to cancel.	Document,[c] Image,[c] Link,[c] text elements
onKeyPress[b]	Key pressed by user; a combination of `onKeyDown` and `onKeyUp`. Return `false` to cancel.	Document,[c] Image,[c] Link,[c] text elements
onKeyUp[b]	Key released by user.	Document,[c] Image,[c] Link,[c] text elements
onLoad	Document or image finishes loading.	Window, Image[a]
onMouseDown[b]	User presses mouse button. Return `false` to cancel.	Document, Link, Image, button elements[c]
onMouseOut[a]	Mouse moves off element.	Link, Image,[b c] Layer[b]
onMouseOver	Mouse moves over element. For links, return `true` to prevent URL from appearing in the status bar.	Link, Image,[b c] Layer[b]
onMouseUp[b]	User releases mouse button. Return `false` to cancel.	Document, Link, Image, button elements[c]
onReset[a]	Form reset requested. Return `false` to prevent reset.	Form
onResize[b]	Window is resized.	Window

Table 15-1: Event Handlers and the Objects That Support Them (continued)

Handler	Triggered when	Supported by
onSubmit[a]	Form submission requested. Return `false` to prevent submission.	Form
onUnload	Document is unloaded.	Window

[a] New in JavaScript 1.1
[b] New in JavaScript 1.2
[c] Does not work on Navigator 4 Unix platforms
[d] Does not work on Navigator 4 Macintosh platforms

Internet Explorer 4 supports practically every event type on practically every HTML object. For this reason, Table 15-1 attempts to present the least common denominator: the set of events that you can count on to work in both Internet Explorer and Navigator. As you can see from the table footnotes, however, there are quite a few platform dependencies for Navigator in this list of supported events. This is a direct result of the difficulties of integrating the diverse event handling models of the various supported operating systems. These difficulties cause confusion over the "official" list of supported event handlers, and this confusion is reflected even in the official documentation from Netscape, which has never been able to present a complete, definitive statement of exactly which event handlers are supported for which objects on which platforms. Therefore, this table should not be considered the final word on the matter; you should be sure to verify that the events you require work on all of your target platforms.

15.1.1 Event Handler Return Values

In many cases, an event handler uses its return value to indicate the disposition of the event. For example, if you use the `onSubmit` event handler of a Form object to perform form validation and discover that the user has not filled in all the fields, you can return `false` from the handler to prevent the form from actually being submitted. More commonly, if you use the `onMouseOver` event handler of a Link to display a special message in the status line, you should return `true` from the event handler to prevent the browser from automatically overwriting your message with the URL of the link. For event handlers that support return values, the second column of Table 15-1 indicates the meaning of the return value. Note that for historical reasons, there is no consistency in the return values: in some cases you have to return `true` and in others you must return `false`.

15.2 Event Handlers as HTML Attributes

As we've seen in many examples prior to this chapter, event handlers are expressed as the values of HTML attributes. So, for example, the onLoad event handler can be specified with the onLoad attribute of the <BODY> tag, and the onReset event handler can be specified with the onReset attribute of the <FORM> tag. Originally extensions to HTML, these event handler attributes have been made official by the HTML 4.0 standard.

The value of an event handler attribute is an arbitrary string of JavaScript code. If the handler consists of multiple JavaScript statements, the statements must be separated from each other by semicolons. When an event handler requires multiple statements, however, it is usually easier to define them in the body of a function, and then use the HTML event handler attribute to invoke that function.

15.2.1 Scope of Event Handlers

Event handlers are very much like functions except for a subtle but important difference: they execute using a different scope than that used by normal functions. Recall from the discussion in Chapter 4, *Variables*, that the scope of a function is defined by a scope chain, or list of objects, that is searched in turn for variable definitions. When a variable x is looked up or resolved in a normal function, JavaScript first looks for a local variable or argument by checking the call object of the function for a property of that name. If no such property is found, JavaScript proceeds to the next object in the scope chain: the global object. It checks the properties of the global object to see if the variable is a global variable.

Event handlers have a more complex scope chain than this. The head of the scope chain is the call object, and any arguments passed to the event handler are defined here, as are any local variables declared in the body of the event handler. The next object in an event handler's scope chain isn't the global object, however; it is the object that triggered the event handler. So, for example, suppose you use an <INPUT> tag to define a Button object in an HTML form, and then use the onClick attribute to define an event handler. If the code for the event handler uses a variable named form, that variable is resolved to the form property of the Button object.

The scope chain of an event handler does not stop with the object that defines the handler: it proceeds up the containment hierarchy. For the onClick event handler described above, the scope chain begins with the call object of the handler function. Then it proceeds to the Button object, as we've discussed. After that, it continues on to the Form object that contains the button, the Document object that contains the form, and finally the Window object (the global object) that contains the document. The same is true for an event handler on any object in the document object model: variables are looked up first in the object that triggered the event handler and then, recursively, in the objects that contain that object.

When I introduced the `open()` method of the Window object, I said that it was important to invoke this method using the expression `window.open()`, rather than `open()`, as you would do for other "global" methods, such as `alert()` and `set-Timeout()`, defined by the Window object. The reason for this is that the Document object also defines a method named `open()`. If you call `open()` from an event handler without qualifying it with a reference to a window, the identifier `open` is resolved in the Document object rather than in the Window object. For the same reason, it is important that you don't add a property named `window` to any HTML object that might become part of the scope chain for an event handler.

15.3 Event Handlers as JavaScript Properties

Although event handlers are most often defined as the values of HTML attributes, this is not the only way to define them. In JavaScript 1.1 and later, you can also explicitly define event handlers as functions, and then assign those functions to JavaScript properties of the HTML object. For example, consider the following HTML button:

```
<INPUT TYPE="button" NAME="b1" VALUE="Press Me">
```

An event handler for this button could be expressed in HTML like this:

```
<INPUT TYPE="button" NAME="b1" VALUE="Press Me"
        onClick="alert('Thanks!');">
```

Or, alternatively, it could be expressed in JavaScript code like the following:

```
document.b1.onclick = function() { alert('Thanks!'); }
```

Each client-side JavaScript object that represents an HTML element has properties that correspond to the event handler attributes of that HTML element. If you assign a function to one of these properties, that function is used as an event handler and is invoked automatically by the system whenever the appropriate event occurs. HTML event handler attributes are case-insensitive and are conventionally expressed in mixed case: `onClick`, for example. By contrast, JavaScript event handler properties are case-sensitive and must be expressed exclusively in lowercase: `onclick`, `ondblclick`, `onload`, `onmouseover`, and so on.

There are a couple of advantages to expressing event handlers as JavaScript properties. First, it reduces the intermingling of HTML and JavaScript, promoting modularity and cleaner, more maintainable code. This will become even more important as the DOM standard emerges and we are able to create HTML elements dynamically from JavaScript code. The second advantage is that the functions need not be fixed. Unlike HTML attributes, which are a static part of the document and can only be set when the document is created, JavaScript properties can be changed at any time. In complex interactive programs, it can sometimes be useful to change dynamically the event handlers registered for HTML elements.

15.3.1 Explicitly Invoking Event Handlers

Even when event handlers are defined as HTML attributes, they become accessible to JavaScript code through the corresponding JavaScript object properties. So, if you define an event handler with the `onMouseOver` attribute of an `<A>` tag, you can refer to that handler function in your JavaScript code through the `onmouseover` attribute of the appropriate Link object.

What this means is that JavaScript code can invoke event handler functions directly. For example, if we've used the `onSubmit` attribute of a `<FORM>` tag to define a form validation function and we want to validate the form at some point before the user attempts to submit it, we can use the `onsubmit` property of the Form object to invoke the event handler function.

This technique of explicitly invoking event handlers is not as useful as it might at first appear. Invoking an event handler is not a way to simulate what happens when the event actually occurs. If we invoke the `onclick` method of a Link object, for example, it does not make the browser follow the link and load a new document. It merely executes whatever function we've defined as the value of that property. To make the browser load a new document, we'd have to set the `location` property of the Window object, as we saw in Chapter 13, *Windows and Frames*. The same is true, for example, of the `onsubmit` method of a Form object or the `onclick` method of a Submit object: invoking the method runs the event handler function but does not cause the form to be submitted. To actually submit the form, we call the `submit()` method of the Form object: this method makes the browser behave as if the user had just clicked on the **Submit** button.

15.3.2 Scope of Event Handler Functions

We saw above that event handlers defined as HTML attributes execute with a special scope chain. This is not the case for event handlers defined as functions.

JavaScript uses static scoping, so, as always, functions execute in the scope in which they were defined. Consider the following line of JavaScript, which sets an event handler property to a function defined in the global scope:

```
document.b1.onclick = function() { alert('Thanks!'); }
```

When this function is executed (no matter what context it is invoked from), its scope chain consists of its own call object and the global object. The Button, Form, and Document objects are *not* part of the scope chain.

For the event handler shown here, the scope chain really doesn't matter, since the only identifier involved is a property (alert) of the global object. However, in more sophisticated programs, the difference in scope chains could have a profound effect. This is a subtle issue that you must be aware of when defining event handlers.

If you want to define an event handler function in JavaScript but you want it to execute in the scope of the object for which it is defined, you must resort to the JavaScript 1.2 Closure object,* which was introduced in Chapter 11, *Further Topics in JavaScript.* For example:

```
document.b1.onclick =
    new Closure(function() { alert("You clicked: " + name); },
                document.b1);
```

15.4 Special Event Types

In addition to the event handlers listed in Table 15-1, client-side JavaScript defines a couple of other event types. Although these "events" do not follow the standard model that true events do, they are still an important part of the overall event-based programming model that client-side JavaScript relies on. The following sections discuss timer events and error events.

15.4.1 Timer Events

As we saw in Chapter 13, you can use the setTimeout() and setInterval() methods to arrange for JavaScript code to be executed at some point in the future. What you are doing when you call either of these methods is essentially registering a handler to be invoked by the system when a particular event occurs. In this case, however, the event of interest is the passage of a specified amount of time.

We will not cover the setTimeout() and setInterval() methods again here. Refer to Chapter 13 or the reference section to refresh your memory. It is important that you conceptualize these methods as part of the event-driven programming model.

---

* The Closure object is supported by Navigator 4 but not Internet Explorer 4.

15.4.2 Error Events

Table 15-1 lists an onError event handler for the Image object. This handler is invoked if an error occurs while the image is being loaded into the browser. The Window object also has an error handler function, which we will discuss here. By assigning a function to the onerror property of a Window object, you specify an error handler function that is invoked whenever a JavaScript error occurs within that window.

Again, this error handler is part of the overall event-based programming model. Like any event handler, it is a function that you register with the system (by assigning it to a specified property). The system invokes the function whenever a certain event (in this case an error) occurs. The onerror error handler is unlike regular event handlers in a couple of ways, however. First, it cannot be specified as an HTML attribute: there is no generic HTML onError attribute that you can specify. Second, when the system invokes the onerror error handler, it passes arguments that are not passed to other event handlers.

Three arguments are passed to an error handler. The first is a message describing the error that occurred. This is something like "missing operator in expression" or "self is read-only" or "myname is not defined." The second argument is a string that contains the URL of the document containing the JavaScript code that caused the error. The third argument is the line number within the document where the error occurred. An error handler can use these arguments for any purpose it desires. A typical error handler might display the error message to the user, log it somewhere, or force the error to be ignored. Recall that Example 14-1 used the onerror handler to display the error details to the user and allow the user to submit a bug report containing those details.

In addition to the three arguments, the return value of the onerror handler is significant. By default, the system displays its own error dialog box when a JavaScript error occurs. If the onerror handler returns true, it tells the system that the handler has handled the error and that no further action is necessary—in other words, the system should not display its own error dialog. So, for example, if you do not want your users to be pestered by error messages, no matter how buggy the code you write is, you could use a line of code like this at the start of all your JavaScript programs:

```
self.onerror = function() { return true; }
```

Of course, doing this will make it very difficult for users to give you feedback when your programs fail silently without producing error messages.

15.5 Fourth-Generation Event Model

The picture of events and event handlers that I have described so far is the core client-side event model, and except for some variations in which objects support which events, it is consistent in both Navigator and Internet Explorer. In the fourth-generation browsers from both Netscape and Microsoft, this core event model is extended to include some useful and important features. Unfortunately, although not surprisingly, the extended event models adopted by Navigator 4 and Internet Explorer 4 are almost entirely incompatible.

The DOM standardization efforts underway at the W3C will eventually standardize this event model, but it is not clear whether this will happen in time for the fifth generation of web browsers. In the meantime, the following sections outline the extended event features of Navigator 4 and Internet Explorer 4. Because the models are incompatible and neither one is likely to be compatible with the eventual standard, the details here and in the reference section are purposely left somewhat sketchy. You can obtain complete information about these vendor-specific extensions from the Netscape and Microsoft developer web sites. However, I suggest that, as much as possible, you stick to the core event model and refrain from relying on the extended features until a compatible standard emerges.

15.5.1 The Event Object

One serious hole in the core event model is that there is no way to obtain details about an event that has occurred. When the `onMouseDown` event handler is invoked, for example, we might like to know which mouse button the user pressed. Under the core model, we have no way to obtain this type of information. The solution is to create an object for every event that occurs and to set properties of this object to specify the details, like which mouse button was clicked, which key was pressed, what the position of the mouse pointer was, what modifier keys were held down, and so on.

Both Navigator 4 and Internet Explorer 4 define an Event object, but because Netscape and Microsoft defined their event models independently of each other, the properties of the object are almost completely different in the two browsers. Table 15-2 summarizes the situation.

Table 15–2: Event Object Properties for Navigator 4 and Internet Explorer 4

Feature	Navigator 4	Internet Explorer 4
Event type	`type` property, a string that contains the event type name.	`type` property, a string that contains the event type name.
Event source	`target` property.	`srcElement` property.
Mouse button	`which` property: 1, 2, or 3.	`button` property: 1, 2, or 3.

Table 15-2: Event Object Properties for Navigator 4 and Internet Explorer 4 (continued)

Feature	Navigator 4	Internet Explorer 4
Key	`which` property holds Unicode character code (not a string).	`keyCode` property holds Unicode character code (not a string).
Modifier keys	`modifiers` property is a bitmask containing the `Event.ALT_MASK`, `Event.CONTROL_MASK`, `Event.META_MASK`, and `Event.SHIFT_MASK` flags.	`altKey`, `ctrlKey`, and `shiftKey` properties contain individual boolean values.
Mouse position	`pageX` and `pageY` properties specify coordinates relative to the web page; `screenX`, `screenY` specify coordinates relative to the screen.	`clientX` and `clientY` properties specify coordinates relative to the web page; `screenX`, `screenY` specify coordinates relative to the screen.

In addition to the differences in Event object properties, the way the Event object is made available to event handlers differs dramatically between the two browsers. In Navigator 4, the event object is passed as an argument to the event handler. In IE 4, the Event object is stored in the global variable named `event`. In Navigator 4, event handlers defined as HTML attributes are implicitly defined as functions with an argument named `event`, so in practice, HTML-specified event handlers in both Navigator and IE can simply refer to the Event object with the identifier `event`. In Navigator, this refers to the (implicit) function argument, and in IE, it refers to a global variable. When defining event handlers as JavaScript functions, however, some vendor-dependent code is required. For example:

```
function myHandler(e) {
    // If we're running in IE, then we don't get passed the event object
    // in argument e, so we've got to put it there ourselves!
    if (navigator.appName.indexOf("Microsoft") != -1) e = window.event;

    // Now we can go ahead and work with the event object in e.
    // Using its properties also requires vendor-dependent code, of course.
}
```

Earlier in this chapter, we discussed the equivalence of event handlers specified in HTML and those specified as JavaScript properties. Now that we have discussed the Event object, we can digress and have the final word on this equivalence. In Navigator 4, defining an HTML event handler attribute for object o to x is equivalent to setting the corresponding JavaScript event handler property to:

```
new Closure(function(event) { x }, o)
```

15.5.2 Event Propagation

Another important feature of the extended event models in the fourth-generation browsers is that they define a notion of event propagation. Event propagation means that events do not simply occur on an object and then die out; instead they propagate and can be handled on other objects. When used in conjunction with the Event object, event propagation can be useful. For example, instead of registering a bunch of different event handlers on each and every element within an HTML form, you might prefer to simply register a few general-purpose event handlers on some top-level object like Document. If the events that occur within the form propagate to the Document object, they can be handled there in a convenient centralized way.

Unfortunately, the Netscape and Microsoft implementations of event propagation could not be more different from each other if they had actively tried to be incompatible. Netscape's model is called "event capturing": the Window and Document objects have new methods that allow them to request a chance to handle events before they are handled by the source elements. The events then trickle from the top (window or document) back down the containment hierarchy to the source element. Microsoft's model, on the other hand, is called "event bubbling": events bubble from the original source element up the containment hierarchy until they are dealt with by a handler that explicitly specifies that they should bubble no further. The only island of compatibility between these divergent models is that under both models, certain events can be propagated to the Window or Document objects for centralized processing. The routes by which the events are propagated to those objects differ considerably, however.

The W3C working group has not yet turned its attention to the event model in a serious way, so it is not at all clear what form of event propagation model will arise from their standardization efforts. Both the event bubbling and the event capturing models have strong precedents in the history of GUI event handling schemes. An ideal, perhaps, would be a default event bubbling scheme that could optionally be overridden by event capturing when that was required. In any case, these two models are described in somewhat more detail in the following sections.

15.5.2.1 Event capturing in Navigator 4

In Navigator 4, the Window, Document, and Layer objects may request the opportunity to preview certain types of events before they are processed by the elements that generated them. Such a request is made with the new captureEvents() function (actually a method of Window, Document, and Layer). The argument to this method is a bitmask composed of constants defined as static properties of the Event constructor. So, for example, if a program wants all mouse down and mouse up events to be routed to the Window object before being han-

dled by the object for which they were intended, it can call captureEvents()
like this:

```
window.captureEvents(Event.MOUSEDOWN | Event.MOUSEUP);
```

Having made this request to receive the events, the program then has to register
event handlers for those events:

```
window.onmousedown = function(event) { ... };
window.onmouseup = function(event) { ... };
```

When one of these capturing event handlers receives an event, it gets to decide
what should happen to it next. In some programs, a captured event is handled
and propagates no further. In other circumstances, however, the program wants to
pass the event along. If you pass the event to the routeEvent() method (of the
Window, Document, and Layer objects), the method passes the event to the next
Window, Document, or Layer object that has used captureEvents() to specify
interest in that type of event. Or, if there is no other capturing object to route the
event to, it is routed to its original source object and the appropriate event handler
of that object is invoked. An alternative to calling routeEvent() is to simply pass
the Event object to the handleEvent() method of the object that you want the
event delivered to. The handleEvent() method passes the event to the appropriate event handler of that object.

15.5.2.2 *Event bubbling in Internet Explorer 4*

The Internet Explorer event propagation model stands the Navigator model on its
head. Instead of capturing events at the top of the HTML object hierarchy and
them routing them downwards to the source object, event handling in IE 4 always
begins at the source object and bubbles up through the object hierarchy. For
example, if a mouse down event occurs on a button in IE 4, the button's
onmousedown event handler is invoked. Next, the onmousedown handler of the
Form object is invoked (the Form object doesn't even support such a handler in
Navigator 4). After that, the onmousedown handlers of the Document and then the
Window object are invoked. Any of these event handlers can prevent the event
from bubbling any higher by setting the cancelBubble property of the Event
object (stored in the global variable event, remember) to true.

Since IE 4 includes all HTML elements in its DOM, it can support event handlers
on all the elements. This means that when the mouse moves over a paragraph of
text, a mouseover event is generated and the onmouseover handler of the <P> element is invoked. Then, the event propagates up through all containing HTML elements to the Document and Window objects.

There is a catch to this event bubbling model, however: not all types of events bubble. To understand this, we need to make a distinction between "raw" input events and "semantic" events. A raw input event is one that simply reports a keyboard or mouse event. These include mouse down, mouse up, mouse over, mouse out, key down, key up, key press, focus, and blur. Semantic events, on the other hand, interpret user input and impose some meaning on it. For example, the click event does not simply report a single mouse event. It reports a button click—a coordinated series of mouse events that occur over a button object. Similarly, the reset and submit events of the Form object are semantic events: they attach higher-level meaning to the user's input actions.

Event bubbling rules follow this division between event categories. Input events bubble up the HTML containment hierarchy, while semantic events do not. It is quite useful to have input events bubble, particularly when any HTML element can generate these events. For example, when the user clicks the mouse over a paragraph of text, the <P> tag of that paragraph may have no interest in those mouse events, but the <TD> table cell element that contains the paragraph of text may have a onmousedown event handler registered to detect mouse button presses that occur within the cell. Event bubbling is crucial to make this sort of scenario work. You can probably see why event bubbling will be a required part of the event model that will emerge from the future DOM standard.

The fact that semantic events do not bubble is justified because the source element that defines the meaning of the semantic event is, of course, the one best suited to process that event. For example, there is no place more logical to handle a form submission event than on the Form object itself. On the other hand, it is unfortunate that these events do not bubble because there is still a possible economy to be gained by centralizing the event handling system. For example, a document with multiple forms might want to define a single form validation event handler on the document object and allow all submission events to bubble up to that level. Under IE's implementation, this is not possible.

15.6 Example: An Event Monitor

We conclude this chapter with an example. Example 15-1 defines an HTML document that contains a Link, an Image, and a Form that uses one of every type of form element. (We'll learn more about forms and their elements in Chapter 16.) The example defines a general-purpose event handler and then uses another JavaScript function to register this event handler function on all possible event handler properties of the Link, Image, Form, and form element objects. In this way, it creates an event handling diagnostic tool. The event handler function itself outputs event details (using the Event object and vendor-specific code) to a separate window. Using this program, you can experiment with events, check whether a given event is generated by a given object, and see which fields of the Event object are defined for that event. You may find this script to be a useful debugging aid when writing programs that do a lot of event handling.

Example 15–1: An Event Monitoring Tool

```
<!-- This form contains one of everything. -->
<FORM NAME="form" ACTION="javascript:void(0)">
<INPUT NAME="button" TYPE=button VALUE="Button"><BR>
<INPUT NAME="reset" TYPE=reset><BR>
<INPUT NAME="submit" TYPE=submit><BR>
<INPUT NAME="radio" TYPE=radio> Radio Button<BR>
<INPUT NAME="checkbox" TYPE=checkbox> Checkbox<BR>

Select 1: <SELECT NAME="menu">
<OPTION>Option 1</OPTION><OPTION>Option 2</OPTION><OPTION>Option 3</OPTION>
</SELECT>

Select any: <SELECT MULTIPLE NAME="list">
<OPTION>Option 1</OPTION><OPTION>Option 2</OPTION><OPTION>Option 3</OPTION>
</SELECT><BR>

Text: <INPUT NAME="text" TYPE=text><BR>
Password: <INPUT NAME="password" TYPE=password><BR>
File: <INPUT NAME="fileupload" TYPE=file><BR>
Textarea: <TEXTAREA NAME="textarea" ROWS=2 COLS=20></TEXTAREA><BR>
</FORM>

<!-- Here are a couple more objects that support event handlers. -->
Link: <A HREF="javascript:void(0)">This is a link</A><BR>
Image: <IMG SRC="testimage.gif">

<SCRIPT>
// Create a new window for our event handler to display event details in.
var ewin = window.open("", "EventTester",
                       "width=300,height=600,scrollbars,resizable,menubar");

// Figure out whether this is Navigator or IE. Assume version 4.
var isNav = (navigator.appName.indexOf("Netscape") != -1);
var isIE = (navigator.appName.indexOf("Microsoft") != -1);

// This general purpose event handler displays details about the event
// in the window we created above. It has vendor-dependent sections
// to deal with the differences in the Event object.
// Because events often arrive in rapid bursts (such as key down/key up
// pairs), this handler takes precautions to prevent these events from
// overwriting each other. It uses setTimeout() and removeTimeout() to
```

Example 15–1: An Event Monitoring Tool (continued)

```
// arrange that the Document object not be closed until a second has passed
// without the arrival of any straggling events. Any events that arrive
// within that one-second window will be appended to the end of the document
// instead of overwriting the document.
function handler(e) {
  var d = ewin.document;        // Shorthand
  if (!handler.docopen) {       // If the document is not already open
      d.open("text/plain");     // ...open it as plain text.
      handler.docopen = true;
  }

  // If we're in Navigator, report event details in this way.
  if (isNav) {
    d.writeln("Type: " + e.type);
    if (e.target) d.writeln("Target: " +
                            Object.prototype.toString.apply(e.target));
    if (e.target.name) d.writeln("Target name: " + e.target.name);
    if (e.x || e.y) d.writeln("X: " + e.x + " Y: " + e.y);
    if (e.which) d.writeln("which: " + e.which);
    if (e.modifiers) d.writeln("modifiers: " + e.modifiers);
  }

  // If we're in Internet Explorer, first copy the event from the
  // global event variable, then report its details. Finally, set
  // the cancelBubble property so it doesn't bubble and get reported
  // multiple times.
  if (isIE) {
    e = window.event;    // Grab the event.
    d.writeln("Type: " + e.type);
    if (e.srcElement && e.srcElement.name)
        d.writeln("srcElement name: " + e.srcElement.name);
    if (e.clientX || e.clientY)
        d.writeln("X: " + e.clientX + " Y: " + e.clientY);
    if (e.button) d.writeln("button: " + e.button);
    if (e.keyCode) d.writeln("keyCode: " + e.keyCode);
    if (e.altKey) d.writeln("altKey");
    if (e.ctrlKey) d.writeln("ctrlKey");
    if (e.shiftKey) d.writeln("shiftKey");

    // We've reported this event, and don't want our container to
    // report it too, so don't let it bubble up any further.
    e.cancelBubble = true;
  }
  d.writeln();  // Put a blank line between events.

  // Arrange to close the document a second from now, resetting any timer
  // set by a previous event.
  if (handler.timeoutid) ewin.clearTimeout(handler.timeoutid);
```

Example 15-1: An Event Monitoring Tool (continued)

```
    handler.timeoutid =
        setTimeout("ewin.document.close(); handler.docopen=false;",
                    1000);
}


// This function registers the event handler defined above on all possible
// event handlers for the specified object. Note that when using this
// program as a diagnostic tool, you may find that you get too many
// annoying blur, focus, mouseover, and mouseout events. If so, simply
// comment those event handlers out here.
function addhandlers(o) {
    o.onabort = handler;        o.onblur = handler;
    o.onchange = handler;       o.onclick = handler;
    o.ondblclick = handler;     o.onerror = handler;
    o.onfocus = handler;        o.onkeydown = handler;
    o.onkeypress = handler;     o.onkeyup = handler;
    o.onload = handler;         o.onmousedown = handler;
    o.onmouseout = handler;     o.onmouseover = handler;
    o.onmouseup = handler;      o.onmove = handler;
    o.onreset = handler;        o.onresize = handler;
    o.onselect = handler;       o.onsubmit = handler;
    o.onunload = handler;
}


// Now use addhandlers() to register all event handlers on all
// objects of interest in the document.
addhandlers(window);
addhandlers(document);

// Add handlers to all links.
for(var d = 0; d < document.links.length; d++)
    addhandlers(document.links[d]);

// Add handlers to all images.
for(var d = 0; d < document.images.length; d++)
    addhandlers(document.images[d]);

// Add handlers on all forms and all form elements.
for(var d = 0; d < document.forms.length; d++) {
    addhandlers(document.forms[d]);
    for(var e = 0; e < document.forms[d].elements.length; e++)
        addhandlers(document.forms[d].elements[e]);
}
</SCRIPT>
```

16

Forms and
Form Elements

As we've seen in examples throughout this book, the use of HTML forms is basic to almost all web programs, whether they are implemented with CGI, JavaScript, or a combination of the two. This chapter explains the details of programming with forms in JavaScript. It is assumed that you already are somewhat familiar with the creation of HTML forms and with the input elements that they contain. If not, you may want to refer to a good book on HTML.* The reference section of this book lists the HTML syntax along with the JavaScript syntax for forms and form elements; you may find these useful for quick reference.

If you are already familiar with CGI programming using HTML forms, you may find that things are done differently when forms are used with JavaScript. In the CGI model, a form with the input data it contains is submitted to the web server all at once. The emphasis is on processing a complete batch of input data and dynamically producing a new web page in response. With JavaScript, the programming model is quite different. In JavaScript programs, the emphasis is not on form submission and processing but instead on event handling. A form and all input elements in it have event handlers that JavaScript can use to respond to user interactions within the form. If the user clicks on a checkbox, for example, a JavaScript program can receive notification through an event handler and might respond by changing the value displayed in some other element of the form.

With CGI programs, an HTML form isn't useful unless it has a **Submit** button (or unless it has only a single text input field and allows the user to press the **Return** key as a shortcut for submission). With JavaScript, on the other hand, a **Submit**

---

* Such as *HTML: The Definitive Guide*, by Chuck Musciano and Bill Kennedy (O'Reilly).

button is never necessary (unless the JavaScript program is working with a cooperating CGI program, of course). With JavaScript, a form can have any number of push buttons with event handlers that perform any number of actions when clicked. In previous chapters, we've seen some of the possible actions that such buttons can trigger: replacing one image with another, using the `location` property to load and display a new web page, opening a new browser window, and dynamically generating a new HTML document in another window or frame. As we'll see later in this section, a JavaScript event handler can even trigger a form to be submitted.

As we've seen in examples throughout this book, event handlers are almost always the central element of any interesting JavaScript program. And the most commonly used event handlers (excluding the event handlers of the Link object) are those used with forms or form elements. This chapter introduces the JavaScript Form object and the various JavaScript objects that represent form elements. It concludes with an example that illustrates how you can use JavaScript to validate user input on the client before submitting it to a CGI program running on the web server.

As discussed in Chapter 14, *The Document Object Model,* work is ongoing to standardize a document object model. Once such a standard DOM is in place, you will be able to use it to create and modify HTML forms on the fly. Until then, however, forms can be created only by static HTML elements. (The exception, as we'll see, is the Option object; this object can be dynamically added to and removed from a Select element.)

16.1 The Form Object

The JavaScript Form object represents an HTML form. Forms are always found as elements of the `forms[]` array, which is a property of the Document object. Forms appear in this array in the order in which they appear within the document. Thus, `document.forms[0]` refers to the first form in a document. You can refer to the last form in a document with:

```
document.forms[document.forms.length-1]
```

The most interesting property of the Form object is the `elements[]` array, which contains JavaScript objects (of various types) that represent the various input elements of the form. Again, elements appear in this array in the same order as they appear in the document. So `document.forms[1].elements[2]` refers to the third element of the second form in the document of the current window.

The remaining properties of the Form object are of less importance. They are `action`, `encoding`, `method`, and `target`; they correspond directly to the `ACTION`, `ENCODING`, `METHOD`, and `TARGET` attributes of the `<FORM>` tag. These properties and attributes are all used to control how form data is submitted to the web server and where the results are displayed; they are therefore only useful when the form is actually submitted to a CGI script. See the reference section for an explanation of the properties, or see a book on HTML or CGI programming* for a thorough discussion of the attributes. What is worth noting here is that these Form properties are all read/write strings, so a JavaScript program can dynamically set their values in order to change the way the form is submitted.†

In the days before JavaScript, a form was submitted with a special-purpose **Submit** button and form elements had their values reset with a special-purpose **Reset** button. The JavaScript Form object supports two methods, `submit()` and (as of JavaScript 1.1) `reset()`, that serve the same purpose. Invoking the `submit()` method of a Form submits the form, exactly as if the user had clicked on a **Submit** button, while invoking `reset()` resets the form elements, exactly as if the user had clicked on a **Reset** button.

To accompany the `submit()` and `reset()` methods, the Form object provides the `onSubmit` event handler to detect form submission and (as of JavaScript 1.1) the `onReset` event handler to detect form resets. The `onSubmit` handler is invoked just before the form is submitted; it can cancel the submission by returning `false`. This provides an opportunity for a JavaScript program to check the user's input for errors in order to avoid submitting incomplete or invalid data over the network to a CGI program. We'll see an example of such error checking at the end of this chapter.

The `onReset` event handler is similar to the `onSubmit` handler. It is invoked just before the form is reset, and it can prevent the form elements from being reset by returning `false`. This allows a JavaScript program to ask for confirmation of the reset, which can be a good idea when the form is long or detailed. You might request this sort of confirmation with an event handler like the following:

```
<FORM...
    onReset="return confirm('Really erase ALL data and start over?')"
>
```

---

* Such as *CGI Programming on the World Wide Web*, by Shishir Gundavaram (O'Reilly).

† You can set these properties in Internet Explorer 3, but the values you specify are ignored.

16.2 Form Elements

As noted previously, every Form object has an `elements[]` property, which is an array of the JavaScript objects that represent the input elements contained in the form. There are many possible HTML form elements and corresponding JavaScript objects. They are listed in Table 16-1.

Table 16-1: HTML Form Elements

Object	HTML Tag	type Property	Description and Events
Button	`<INPUT TYPE=button>`	"button"	A push button; `onClick`.
Checkbox	`<INPUT TYPE=checkbox>`	"checkbox"	A toggle button without radio button behavior; `onClick`.
FileUpload	`<INPUT TYPE=file>`	"file"	An input field for entering the name of a file to upload to the web server; `onChange`.
Hidden	`<INPUT TYPE=hidden>`	"hidden"	Data submitted with the form but not visible to the user; no event handlers.
Option	`<OPTION>`	none	A single item within a Select object; event handlers are on the Select object, not on individual Option objects.
Password	`<INPUT TYPE=password>`	"password"	An input field for password entry—typed characters are not visible; `onChange`.
Radio	`<INPUT TYPE=radio>`	"radio"	A toggle button with radio behavior—only one selected at a time; `onClick`.
Reset	`<INPUT TYPE=reset>`	"reset"	A push button that resets a form; `onClick`.
Select	`<SELECT>`	"select-one"	A list or drop-down menu from which one item may be selected; `onChange`. See also Option object.
Select	`<SELECT MULTIPLE>`	"select-multiple"	A list from which multiple items may be selected; `onChange`. See also Option object.

Table 16–1: HTML Form Elements (continued)

Object	HTML Tag	type Property	Description and Events
Submit	`<INPUT TYPE=submit>`	"submit"	A push button that submits a form; `onClick`.
Text	`<INPUT TYPE=text>`	"text"	A single-line text entry field; `onChange`.
Textarea	`<TEXTAREA>`	"textarea"	A multiline text entry field; `onChange`.

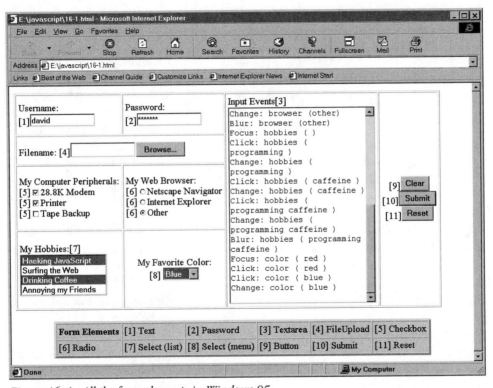

Figure 16–1: All the form elements in Windows 95

Possible HTML form elements and corresponding JavaScript objects are pictured in Figure 16-1. The HTML (and JavaScript) code that generated that figure is listed in Example 16-1. For comparison, Figure 16-2 shows the same form elements as they appear in a different operating system. You can find out more about these JavaScript objects in the reference section of this book, but you may want to refer to an HTML book for complete details on the HTML tags and attributes used to create the form elements.

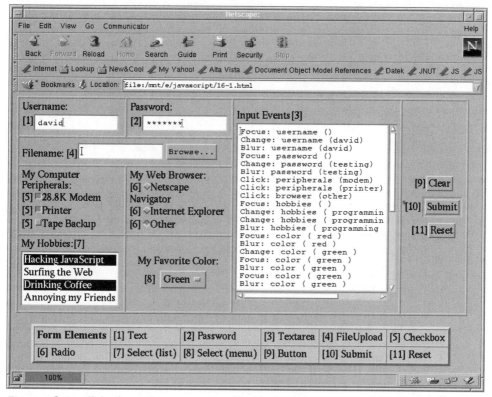

Figure 16–2: All the form elements in Unix

Example 16–1: An HTML Form Containing All Form Elements

```
<FORM NAME="everything">  <!-- A one-of-everything HTML form... -->
 <TABLE BORDER CELLPADDING=5>    <!-- ...in a big HTML table. -->
   <TR>
     <TD>Username:<BR>[1]<INPUT TYPE=text NAME="username" SIZE=15></TD>
     <TD>Password:<BR>[2]<INPUT TYPE=password NAME="password" SIZE=15></TD>
     <TD ROWSPAN=4>Input Events[3]<BR>
       <TEXTAREA NAME="textarea" ROWS=20 COLS=28></TEXTAREA></TD>
     <TD ROWSPAN=4 ALIGN=center VALIGN=center>
       [9]<INPUT TYPE=button VALUE="Clear" NAME="clearbutton"><BR>
       [10]<INPUT TYPE=submit NAME="submitbutton" VALUE="Submit"><BR>
       [11]<INPUT TYPE=reset NAME="resetbutton" VALUE="Reset"></TD></TR>
   <TR>
     <TD COLSPAN=2>Filename: [4]<INPUT TYPE=file NAME="file" SIZE=15></TD></TR>
   <TR>
     <TD>My Computer Peripherals:<BR>
       [5]<INPUT TYPE=checkbox NAME="peripherals" VALUE="modem">28.8K Modem<BR>
       [5]<INPUT TYPE=checkbox NAME="peripherals" VALUE="printer">Printer<BR>
       [5]<INPUT TYPE=checkbox NAME="peripherals" VALUE="tape">Tape Backup</TD>
     <TD>My Web Browser:<BR>
```

Example 16-1: An HTML Form Containing All Form Elements (continued)

```
      [6]<INPUT TYPE=radio NAME="browser" VALUE="nn">Netscape Navigator<BR>
      [6]<INPUT TYPE=radio NAME="browser" VALUE="ie">Internet Explorer<BR>
      [6]<INPUT TYPE=radio NAME="browser" VALUE="other">Other</TD></TR>
  <TR>
    <TD>My Hobbies:[7]<BR>
      <SELECT multiple NAME="hobbies" SIZE=4>
        <OPTION VALUE="programming">Hacking JavaScript
        <OPTION VALUE="surfing">Surfing the Web
        <OPTION VALUE="caffeine">Drinking Coffee
        <OPTION VALUE="annoying">Annoying my Friends
      </SELECT></TD>
    <TD align=center valign=center>My Favorite Color:<BR>[8]
      <SELECT NAME="color">
        <OPTION VALUE="red">Red        <OPTION VALUE="green">Green
        <OPTION VALUE="blue">Blue       <OPTION VALUE="white">White
        <OPTION VALUE="violet">Violet  <OPTION VALUE="peach">Peach
      </SELECT></TD></TR>
 </TABLE>
</FORM>

<DIV ALIGN=center>        <!-- Another table--the key to the one above. -->
  <TABLE BORDER=4 BGCOLOR=pink CELLSPACING=1 CELLPADDING=4>
    <TR>
      <TD ALIGN=center><B>Form Elements</B></TD>
      <TD>[1] Text</TD>  <TD>[2] Password</TD>  <TD>[3] Textarea</TD>
      <TD>[4] FileUpload</TD> <TD>[5] Checkbox</TD></TR>
    <TR>
      <TD>[6] Radio</TD>  <TD>[7] Select (list)</TD>
      <TD>[8] Select (menu)</TD>  <TD>[9] Button</TD>
      <TD>[10] Submit</TD>  <TD>[11] Reset</TD></TR>
  </TABLE>
</DIV>

<SCRIPT LANGUAGE="JavaScript1.1">
// This generic function appends details of an event to the big Textarea
// element in the form above. It will be called from various event handlers.
function report(element, event)
{
    var t = element.form.textarea;
    var elmtname = element.name;
    if ((element.type == "select-one") || (element.type == "select-multiple")){
        value = " ";
        for(var i = 0; i < element.options.length; i++)
            if (element.options[i].selected)
                value += element.options[i].value + " ";
    }
    else if (element.type == "textarea") value = "...";
    else value = element.value;
```

Example 16–1: An HTML Form Containing All Form Elements (continued)

```
    var msg = event + ": " + elmtname + ' (' + value + ')\n';
    t.value = t.value + msg;
}


// This function adds a bunch of event handlers to every element in a form.
// It doesn't bother checking to see if the element supports the event handler,
// it just adds them all. Note that the event handlers call report() above.
function addhandlers(f)
{
    var click_handler = new Function("report(this, 'Click')");
    var change_handler = new Function("report(this, 'Change')");
    var focus_handler = new Function("report(this, 'Focus')");
    var blur_handler = new Function("report(this, 'Blur')");
    var select_handler = new Function("report(this, 'Select')");

    for(var i = 0; i < f.elements.length; i++) {
        var e = f.elements[i];
        e.onclick = click_handler;
        e.onchange = change_handler;
        e.onfocus = focus_handler;
        e.onblur = blur_handler;
        e.onselect = select_handler;
    }

    // Special case handlers for the buttons:
    f.clearbutton.onclick =
        new Function("this.form.textarea.value=''; report(this, 'Click');");
    f.submitbutton.onclick =
        new Function("report(this, 'Click'); return false");
    f.resetbutton.onclick =
        new Function("this.form.reset(); report(this, 'Click'); return false");
}
// Activate our form by adding all possible event handlers!
addhandlers(document.everything);
</SCRIPT>
```

The specific details about the JavaScript form element objects can be found on their respective reference pages. However, there are some features that all form element objects share. One obvious similarity is that (almost) all form element objects define event handlers that are invoked when the user interacts with the elements. The important ones are usually called onClick or onChange, depending on the type of object. The primary event handlers supported by each form element are listed in the fourth column of Table 16-1. In addition to the event handlers listed in the table, recall from Chapter 15, *Events and Event Handling*, that as of JavaScript 1.1 all form elements have `onblur` and `onfocus` handlers. Also, as of JavaScript 1.2, some form elements support other handlers, such as `onkeypress` and `onmousedown`.

As of JavaScript 1.1, every form element object has a `type` property that identifies what type of element it is. The third column of Table 16-1 specifies the value of this property for each object. The `elements[]` array of the Form object contains various types of form element objects; the `type` property allows you to loop through the `elements[]` array and operate on the form objects it contains in ways that depend on their type. We'll see this done in Example 16-2, later in the chapter.

Every form element object also has a `form` property. This is simply a reference to the Form object that contains the element. This property provides a useful way for a form element object to refer to another form element from its event handlers. Within a form element event handler, the `this` keyword refers to the element object itself. This means that `this.form` always refers to the containing form. Therefore, an event handler of a form element can refer to a sibling object in the same form with an expression like this:

```
this.form.elements[4]
```

16.3 Naming Forms and Form Elements

Every form element has a `NAME` attribute that must be set in its HTML tag if the form is to be submitted to a CGI script. While form submission is not generally of interest to JavaScript programs, there is another useful reason to specify this `NAME` tag, as you'll see shortly.

In addition, the `<FORM>` tag itself has a `NAME` attribute that you can set. This attribute has nothing to do with form submission. It exists for the convenience of JavaScript programmers. If the `NAME` attribute is defined in a `<FORM>` tag, when the Form object is created for that form, it is stored as an element in the `forms[]` array of the Document object, as usual, and it is also stored in its own personal property of the Document object. The name of this newly defined property is the value of the `NAME` attribute. Say you define a form with HTML like this:

```
<FORM NAME="questionnaire">
    ...
</FORM>
```

Then you can refer to that form as:

```
document.questionnaire
```

Often, you'll find this more convenient than the array notation:

```
document.forms[2]
```

Note that `<IMG>`, `<APPLET>`, `<EMBED>`, and other HTML tags also have `NAME` attributes that work the same as the `NAME` attribute of `<FORM>`. But with forms, this style of naming goes a step further because all elements contained within a form have `NAME` attributes. When you give a form element a `NAME` attribute, you create a new property of the Form object that refers to that element. The name of this property is the value of the attribute. Thus, you can refer to an element named "zipcode" in a form named "address" as:

```
document.address.zipcode
```

With reasonably chosen names, this syntax is much more elegant than the alternative, which relies on hardcoded array indices:

```
document.forms[1].elements[4]
```

CGI programming requires that grouped Checkbox and Radio elements within an HTML form all be given the same name. For example, if a form contains a number of Radio buttons that allow the user to indicate her favorite web browser, each of these buttons might be given the name "favorite". The `VALUE` property of one of the buttons might be "nn", while the `VALUE` of another might be "ie". When the form is submitted, a string like "favorite=opera" is sent to indicate the user's selection. Using the same name for multiple elements is not a problem in this case because only one of those elements can be selected at a time, so only one value can be submitted with that name.

When more than one element in a form has the same `NAME` attribute, JavaScript simply places those elements into an array with the specified name. So, if the Radio objects in the example above are part of our form named "questionnaire", you can refer to them with expressions like these:

```
document.questionnaire.favorite[0]
document.questionnaire.favorite[1]
```

Now that we know how to name form elements and refer to named elements, we can discuss how to use JavaScript to set default values in form elements and read the user's input from form elements.

16.4 Form Element Values

In addition to its `name` property, every form element has a `value` property. When a form is submitted, the user's input data is passed to the web server in the form of name/value pairs. The `name` and `value` properties specify the name under which each element's data is submitted and the value submitted for that element.

The value property is a read/write string for every form element object. The initial value of the value property is usually specified, logically enough, by the VALUE attribute of the HTML tag that defined the form element. For some objects, however, the initial value is specified in some other way.

Different form elements use the value property in different ways, some more intuitive than others. For Text and TextArea objects, the value property is simply the string contained in the input field. Setting the value property for one of these objects changes the text that the input field displays. For Button, Reset, and Submit objects, however, the value property is the text that is displayed by the push button. Although the property is read/write, changing it does not change the text that appears in the button (at least not on all platforms). Also, the value of a Button or Reset object is never actually submitted with the form that contains the object. (The value of a Submit object is submitted only when the Submit object is the one that caused the form to be submitted. This allows a CGI script to determine how the form was submitted in cases where there is more than one way to do so.)

The value property for Checkbox and Radio objects is also a little bit tricky. Since these objects represent toggle buttons in an HTML form, you might expect the value property to indicate the state of the button—in other words, to be a boolean value that indicates whether the toggle button is checked or not. In fact, it is the checked property of these objects that indicates their state. The value property, as always, is the string value that is submitted with the form if the Checkbox or Radio object is checked when the form is submitted. It should be set to some string that is meaningful to the CGI script that receives the form submission.

The Select object is another unusual case. It displays a list or drop-down menu of options and allows the user to select one or more of them. These options are specified not by the <SELECT> tag but by separate <OPTION> tags. As a result, the Select object does not have a value property; it is an exception to the rule that every form element object has a property by this name. Since the VALUE attribute belongs to the <OPTION> tag, the value property belongs to the Option object. You might expect that the value property of the Option object, like that of the Text and Button objects, specifies the text that is displayed to the user in the list or drop-down menu, but this is not how it is done. The text displayed for an Option object is meant to be a verbose, human-readable string, which is not ideal for processing by a CGI script. The text property of the Option object specifies the string that the user sees, while the value property specifies the shorter string that is submitted to the CGI script.

16.4.1 The Select and Option objects

While we are discussing the Select and Option objects, it is worth mentioning that these objects differ in a number of ways from other form element objects. First, the Option object is not itself a form element—it is an object contained by a Select object. The Select object is the only form element object that contains other objects. They are contained in its `options[]` array, so you may end up referring to individual Option objects with very long expressions, like the following:

```
document.forms[0].elements[1].options[2]
```

The second unique feature of Option is that, as of JavaScript 1.1, these objects can be created dynamically at runtime. Option objects are created with the `Option()` constructor function and can be added to the `options[]` array of a Select object by simple assignment. This `options[]` property has several special behaviors: if you decrease the value of `options.length`, options are deleted from the end of the list or menu displayed by the Select object. Similarly, if you set one of the entries in the `options[]` array to `null`, that option is removed from the list or menu and the elements following it in the array are moved to fill the newly vacated array element. For full details, see the reference section.

16.5 Form Verification Example

We'll close our discussion of forms with an extended example that demonstrates several of the concepts we've been talking about. Example 16-2 shows how you might use the `onSubmit` event handler of the Form object to perform input validation so that you can notify the user and prevent the form from being submitted when it contains missing or invalid data. After studying this example, you may want to turn back to Example 1-3, the forms programming example we began this book with. The code of that example will probably make more sense now that you are a JavaScript expert!

Example 16-2 defines a `verify()` function suitable for use as a generic form validator. It checks for required fields that are empty. In addition, it can check that a numeric value is in fact numeric and also falls within a specified numeric range. This `verify()` function relies on the `type` property of a form element to determine which kind of element it is. The function also relies on additional user-defined properties to distinguish optional fields from required fields and to specify the allowed ranges for numeric fields. Note how the function reads the `value` property of an input field and uses the `name` property of a field when reporting errors. Figure 16-3 shows an example form that uses this verification scheme, with the error message that is displayed when the user attempts to submit the form before correctly filling it in.

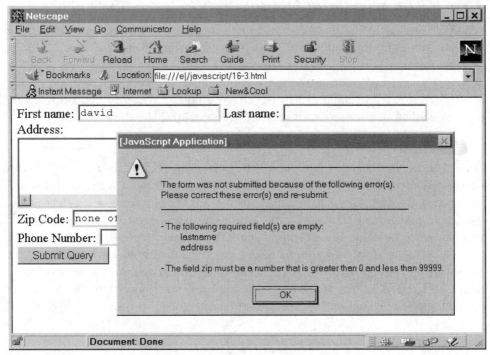

Figure 16–3: A form that failed validation

Example 16–2: Performing Form Validation

```
<SCRIPT LANGUAGE="JavaScript1.1">
// A utility function that returns true if a string contains only
// whitespace characters.
function isblank(s)
{
    for(var i = 0; i < s.length; i++) {
        var c = s.charAt(i);
        if ((c != ' ') && (c != '\n') && (c != '\t')) return false;
    }
    return true;
}


// This is the function that performs form verification. It will be invoked
// from the onSubmit() event handler. The handler should return whatever
// value this function returns.
function verify(f)
{
    var msg;
    var empty_fields = "";
    var errors = "";
```

Example 16-2: Performing Form Validation (continued)

```
// Loop through the elements of the form, looking for all
// text and textarea elements that don't have an "optional" property
// defined. Then, check for fields that are empty and make a list of them.
// Also, if any of these elements have a "min" or a "max" property defined,
// then verify that they are numbers and that they are in the right range.
// Put together error messages for fields that are wrong.
for(var i = 0; i < f.length; i++) {
    var e = f.elements[i];
    if (((e.type == "text") || (e.type == "textarea")) && !e.optional) {
        // first check if the field is empty
        if ((e.value == null) || (e.value == "") || isblank(e.value)) {
            empty_fields += "\n            " + e.name;
            continue;
        }


        // Now check for fields that are supposed to be numeric.
        if (e.numeric || (e.min != null) || (e.max != null)) {
            var v = parseFloat(e.value);
            if (isNaN(v) ||
                ((e.min != null) && (v < e.min)) ||
                ((e.max != null) && (v > e.max))) {
                errors += "- The field " + e.name + " must be a number";
                if (e.min != null)
                    errors += " that is greater than " + e.min;
                if (e.max != null && e.min != null)
                    errors += " and less than " + e.max;
                else if (e.max != null)
                    errors += " that is less than " + e.max;
                errors += ".\n";
            }
        }
    }
}

// Now, if there were any errors, display the messages, and
// return false to prevent the form from being submitted.
// Otherwise return true.
if (!empty_fields && !errors) return true;

msg  = "_____\n\n"
msg += "The form was not submitted because of the following error(s).\n";
msg += "Please correct these error(s) and re-submit.\n";
msg += "_____\n\n"

if (empty_fields) {
    msg += "- The following required field(s) are empty:"
            + empty_fields + "\n";
    if (errors) msg += "\n";
```

Example 16-2: Performing Form Validation (continued)

```
    }
    msg += errors;
    alert(msg);
    return false;
}
</SCRIPT>


<!------------------------------------------------------------------------
    Here's a sample form to test our verification with. Note that we
    call verify() from the onSubmit() event handler, and return whatever
    value it returns. Also note that we use the onSubmit() handler as
    an opportunity to set properties on the form objects that verify()
    will use in the verification process.
------------------------------------------------------------------------->
<FORM onSubmit="
    this.firstname.optional = true;
    this.phonenumber.optional = true;
    this.zip.min = 0;
    this.zip.max = 99999;
    return verify(this);
">

First name: <INPUT TYPE=text NAME="firstname">
Last name: <INPUT TYPE=text NAME="lastname"><BR>
Address:<BR><TEXTAREA NAME="address" ROWS=4 COLS=40></TEXTAREA><BR>
Zip Code: <INPUT TYPE=text NAME="zip"><BR>
Phone Number: <INPUT TYPE=text NAME="phonenumber"><BR>
<INPUT TYPE=submit>
</FORM>
```

17

Dynamic HTML

Dynamic HTML, or DHTML, is a loosely defined term for a suite of fourth-generation browser technologies that enable HTML documents to be more dynamic and interactive than was previously possible. The major new technologies of DHTML are the emerging Document Object Model (DOM) standard described in Chapter 14, *The Document Object Model*; the extended event model described in Chapter 15, *Events and Event Handling*; cascading style sheets (CSS); and, most importantly, the capability for absolute positioning of HTML elements.

This chapter describes the last two of these new technologies. The CSS standard from the World Wide Web Consortium (W3C) specifies how document style attributes (e.g., fonts, colors, margins) can be specified for HTML documents. Both Navigator 4 and Internet Explorer 4 support the CSS standard and allow JavaScript programs to access and manipulate styles. Both browsers also support an extension to the CSS standard known as CSS-Positioning (CSS-P)* that allows absolute positioning. Absolute positioning is really the heart of DHTML: it allows any HTML element to be positioned, under program control, at a specific location in a web page. Furthermore, it allows JavaScript programs to change dynamically the location of absolutely positioned elements. As you can imagine, this opens the door to a whole world of animations and other special effects.

Despite the fact that both Navigator 4 and Internet Explorer 4 support the CSS and CSS-P standards, browser incompatibilities are still the major stumbling block in DHTML programming. The CSS and CSS-P standards specify HTML extensions that allow the addition of style and position information to HTML documents, but neither standard defines an API for accessing and manipulating style and position

---

* At the time of this writing, the CSS-P extensions have been merged into the current working draft of the CSS-2 standard. For the purposes of this discussion, it is useful to be able to talk specifically about the positioning styles, so I will continue to refer to CSS-P here.

information dynamically. The DOM standard will eventually (probably in Level 2) standardize a "style sheet object model" API, but until then, we are stuck with two totally incompatible APIs, one each from Netscape and Microsoft.

In practice, you have two choices with regard to DHTML programming. You can program specifically for one browser or the other, or you can carefully select DHTML features available in both browsers and encapsulate this functionality in a compatibility layer that performs the appropriate vendor-specific DHTML operations. After we discuss style sheets and absolute positioning for the two browsers, we conclude the chapter with an example that does just that. It defines a DynEl (Dynamic Element) class that can be used in either Navigator 4 or IE 4.

Because of the severe incompatibilities between the Netscape and Microsoft versions, DHTML must be considered an immature technology. The material in this chapter should be considered an overview. I will not provide detailed documentation on the incompatible vendor-specific APIs that will be superseded by eventual standards and become obsolete. If you really need to create cutting edge dynamic web pages and want to push either of the vendor-specific APIs to its limit, you should consult vendor-specific documentation, such as the material available on the Netscape and Microsoft developer web sites. You should also consider investing in book that covers DHTML comprehensively, such as the forthcoming *Dynamic HTML: The Definitive Reference*, by Danny Goodman (O'Reilly).

17.1 Style Sheets

Style sheets enable the separation of document style (fonts, colors, margins, etc.) from document structure (headings, paragraphs, lists, etc.). The introduction of style sheets is an important step forward in the evolution of the Web. While the topic of styles and style sheets is very important to web page designers, it is of somewhat less interest to JavaScript programmers. We discuss style sheets here primarily because the CSS-P positioning standard is an extension of the CSS style sheet standard.

This section begins with a quick overview of the CSS standard and then discusses the Navigator 4 and IE 4 APIs for working with style sheets in JavaScript.

17.1.1 Cascading Style Sheets

CSS styles are specified as a semicolon-separated list of name/value attribute pairs, where each name and value are separated by colons. This list of styles is associated with the HTML tag to which it applies or with a class name or identifier name. With a class name, the styles apply to any HTML tags that use that class name as their CLASS attribute. With an identifier name, the styles apply to the unique HTML tag that has that identifier as the value of its ID attribute.

A collection of one or more of these style specifications constitutes a style sheet. A style sheet can be linked from an external file with the <LINK> tag, or it can appear literally in an HTML document between a pair of <STYLE> and </STYLE> tags. If a set of styles is to apply to only a single HTML element, the styles can be specified as inline styles using the element's STYLE attribute.

Example 17-1 is an HTML file that defines and uses a style sheet. Note that styles are defined for element types and for specific CLASS and ID attribute values. The HTML text that follows the style sheet definition uses these styles in various ways, and it also defines an inline style with the STYLE attribute. This example is meant as an overview (or review) of CSS syntax and capabilities. Full coverage of CSS is beyond the scope of this book. You can find the complete CSS specification at the W3C web site (*http://www.w3.org*),* and you can also find information on style sheets in *HTML: The Definitive Guide*, by Chuck Musciano and Bill Kennedy (O'Reilly).

Example 17–1: Defining and Using Cascading Style Sheets

```
<STYLE TYPE="text/css">
/* Specify that headings display in blue italic text. */
H1, H2 { color: blue; font-style: italic }

/*
 * Any element of CLASS="WARNING" displays in bold on an
 * indented yellow background with a fat red border.
 */
.WARNING {
        font-weight: bold;
        background-color: yellow;
        margin-left: 1in;
        margin-right: 1in;
        border-color: red;
        border-width: 8;
        border-style: solid
}

/*
 * A H1 or H2 heading within an element with CLASS="WARNING"
 * should be centered, in addition to appearing in blue italics.
 */
.WARNING H1, .WARNING H2 { text-align: center }
```

---

* The W3C actually issues recommendations, but they carry substantial weight and serve the same purpose as specifications. As of this writing, the current CSS recommendation is version 1 (CSS-1) and the next version (CSS-2) is under development.

Example 17-1: Defining and Using Cascading Style Sheets (continued)

```
/* The single element with ID="P23" displays in centered uppercase. */
#P23 {
        text-align: center;
        text-transform: uppercase;
}
</STYLE>

<H1>Cascading Style Sheets Demo</H1>

<DIV CLASS="WARNING">
<H2>Warning</H2>
This is a warning!
Notice how it grabs your attention with its bold text and bright colors.
Also notice that the heading is centered and in blue italics.
</DIV>

<P ID="P23">
This paragraph is centered<BR>
and appears in uppercase letters.<BR>
<SPAN STYLE="text-transform: none">
Here we explicitly use an inline style to override the uppercase letters.
</SPAN>
</P>
```

17.1.2 Styles in Navigator

Navigator 4 provides a relatively simple and elegant mapping between CSS syntax and JavaScript syntax. It defines `tags`, `classes`, and `ids` properties of the Document object that give access to the style properties of HTML tags, and to any defined style classes or IDs. For example, you could set the color of <H1> elements with a line like this:

```
document.tags.H1.color = "red";
```

The style properties you can set in this way correspond directly to the style properties defined by CSS. Many CSS properties contain the hyphen character, however, which is not legal in JavaScript identifiers (because it is interpreted as a minus sign). Therefore, the JavaScript style property names are written without hyphens, using mixed case. For example, the CSS `background-color` property becomes `backgroundColor` when accessing it from JavaScript in Navigator 4. Similarly, the identifier `float` is reserved in JavaScript, so the CSS `float` property is named `align` in JavaScript 1.2.

You can use the `tags`, `classes`, and `ids` properties to read style values at any time. You can also write style values at any time, but the styles do not take effect unless you set the style properties in the <HEAD> section of the document before any text has been formatted. Setting style properties in the <BODY> section of the document does not cause any immediate change, although the changed styles do appear if the user resizes the window, causing the document to be reformatted.

Although Navigator 4 exposes style sheets through the `tags`, `classes`, and `ids` properties, it does not provide any access to inline styles specified through explicit `STYLE` attributes of HTML elements. One important reason for this is that the Navigator 4 DOM does not provide access to most of the HTML elements on which the `STYLE` attribute could be used.

Example 17-2 shows how you can define styles using JavaScript syntax. It defines a stylesheet identical to the one defined in Example 17-1, although this example omits the HTML text that uses the styles. Note that the style sheet definition appears within a <STYLE> tag with its `TYPE` attribute set to `"text/javascript"`. As explained in Chapter 12, *JavaScript in Web Browsers,* JavaScript code that appears in <STYLE> tags like this runs just like code in <SCRIPT> tags, except that it has the Document object in its scope chain before the Window object. This means that we can use the Document properties `tags`, `classes`, and `ids` as if they were global variables. Also note the use of the `contextual()` method of the Document object. This method returns a style object that represents the specified contextual style. In this case, it is used to return a styles object that we can use to specify the styles for <H1> and <H2> elements that are contained within an element with a CLASS attribute of "WARNING".

Example 17-2: Specifying Styles with JavaScript Syntax

```
<STYLE TYPE="text/javascript">
// This is regular JavaScript code, running in the scope of the Document.

/* Specify that headings display in blue italic text. */
tags.H1.color = tags.H2.color = "blue";
tags.H1.fontStyle = tags.H2.fontStyle = "italic";

/*
 * Any element of CLASS="WARNING" displays in bold on an
 * indented yellow background with a fat red border.
 */
classes.WARNING.all.fontWeight = "bold"
classes.WARNING.all.backgroundColor = "yellow";
classes.WARNING.all.marginLeft = "1in";
classes.WARNING.all.marginRight = "1in";
classes.WARNING.all.borderWidth = "8px";
classes.WARNING.all.borderStyle = "solid";
```

Example 17-2: Specifying Styles with JavaScript Syntax (continued)

```
classes.WARNING.all.borderColor = "red";

/*
 * A H1 or H2 heading within an element with CLASS="WARNING"
 * should be centered, in addition to appearing in blue italics.
 */
contextual(classes.WARNING.all, tags.H1).textAlign = "center";
contextual(classes.WARNING.all, tags.H2).textAlign = "center";

/* The single element with ID="P23" displays in centered uppercase. */
ids.P23.textAlign = "center";
ids.P23.textTransform = "uppercase";
</STYLE>

<SCRIPT>
// We can also specify styles in regular SCRIPT tags, but here we
// have to explicitly specify the Document object. Also, it is only
// meaningful to write style properties in the HEAD of the document
// before any text has been formatted and output.
document.ids.P23.color = "green";

// Style objects behave just like other objects, and we can read
// style properties from them.
var style = document.classes.WARNING.all, s = "";
for (i in style) s += i + ": " + style[i] + "\n";
alert(s);
</SCRIPT>
```

17.1.3 Styles in Internet Explorer

Internet Explorer 4 supports an entirely different JavaScript API for working with style sheets. The only similarity between its model and the Navigator 4 model is in the property names used. Like Navigator, IE converts CSS property names that contain hyphens to unhyphenated, mixed-case JavaScript property names. So, for example, the CSS property text-decoration is named textDecoration in both Navigator and IE.

Internet Explorer 4 allows JavaScript access to styles and style sheets, but with an API that is harder to use than Navigator's. In IE, style sheets are contained in the styleSheets[] array of the Document object. Each element of this array is a StyleSheet object, which contains a rules[] array and an addRule() method. With the array, you can access the CSS rules in source order; with the method, you can define new style rules within the stylesheet. Unfortunately, these techniques are awkward because they rely on knowledge about the source order of style rules. The IE API mirrors CSS syntax, whereas the Navigator API mirrors the more fundamental CSS structure. While the Navigator API provides a viable alternative to CSS for defining styles, the IE API is useful only to access and modify already defined style rules.

Internet Explorer more than makes up for the awkwardness of its API for accessing style sheets by providing access to inline styles, a feature that Navigator lacks. Recall that the IE 4 DOM exposes all HTML elements within a document. Every such element has a `style` property that refers to a Style object on which you can set any style properties you want. Even better is the fact that IE 4 automatically redraws and, if necessary, reformats the document after you change a style property. This means that any changes you make to an element's style take effect immediately.

Example 17-3 displays some HTML that uses the styles defined in the cascading style sheet of Example 17-1. It uses JavaScript to animate the color of an element by dynamically changing its inline style. Note that, for brevity, this example does not repeat the CSS style sheet definitions of the earlier example.

Example 17-3: Dynamic Inline Styles in Internet Explorer

```
<!-- Here's some HTML.  We're going to animate the color of the named H1. -->
<DIV CLASS="WARNING">
<H2 ID="WARNING1" STYLE="color:red; text-align:center">Red Alert!</H2>
The Web server is on fire!
</DIV>

<SCRIPT>
// Animate the color of the element with ID="WARNING1", by
// setting properties of its style object every half second.
var colors = ["red", "orange", "black"];  // Cycle through these colors.
var nextcolor = 0;

// Invoke this function to change to the next color.
function changecolor() {
    document.all.WARNING1.style.color = colors[nextcolor++];
    nextcolor = nextcolor % colors.length;
}

// Arrange to call changecolor() every half second.
setInterval("changecolor()", 500);
</SCRIPT>
```

17.2 Dynamic Positioning

A proposed extension to the CSS standard, known as CSS-P, defines CSS properties that you can use to specify the precise pixel position, as well as the size, visibility, and stacking order, of any HTML element. This absolute positioning allows a web page designer absolute control over the layout of her pages.

While absolute positioning is very interesting to web page designers, it is of less interest to JavaScript programmers. What programmers are interested in is *dynamic* positioning: the ability to move arbitrary HTML elements around on the screen to produce animations or other special effects. Once again, although both Navigator 4 and Internet Explorer 4 implement CSS-P, the JavaScript APIs they provide to interact with CSS-P properties differ and, more importantly, are incompatible. The following sections explain how absolute positioning with CSS-P works and then move on to discuss how Interet Explorer and Navigator allow us to use JavaScript to transform absolute positioning into dynamic positioning.

17.2.1 Absolute Positioning with CSS-P

The CSS-P proposal allows absolute positioning of HTML elements simply by defining a few more CSS properties that can be set. The most important property is position. If this property is set to absolute, it means that the affected element is subject to absolute positioning, rather than being automatically positioned based on its natural location in the HTML text. (The position property can also be set to relative, which means that the element should be offset from its natural position. While relative positioning is sometimes useful, we do not discuss it here.)

By setting the CSS position property for an element, you indicate that the element is to be positioned. Next, you specify where it is to be positioned by setting the left and top properties. You can also set the visibility property to be visible or hidden and set the z-index property to an integer that specifies the stacking order of the element. (The stacking order determines which of two or more overlapping elements appears on top.)

Since each absolutely positioned element is positioned independently from any others, it doesn't make sense to use the CSS-P properties in tag-based or class-based styles. You can use them in an ID-based style, but it is often easier to simply use them as inline styles with the STYLE tag. For example, here is some HTML we can use to position some text and an image at an absolute position on the screen:

```
<SPAN STYLE="position:absolute; left:100px; top:200px;">
A positioned image: <IMG SRC="image.gif" WIDTH=50 HEIGHT=50>
</SPAN>
```

Note the use of the <SPAN> tag to combine the text and image to be positioned into a single element.* Images are commonly used with absolute positioning. Although CSS-P specifies that any element can be positioned, Navigator 4 incorrectly allows only container elements (i.e., elements that have both an opening tag and a closing tag) to be positioned. Thus, in Navigator 4, non-container elements like <IMG> cannot be positioned directly and must be included within a <SPAN>, <DIV>, <A>, or some other container element.

17.2.2 *Dynamic Positioning with Internet Explorer*

As we've seen, Internet Explorer 4 allows JavaScript to access and dynamically modify the inline style of any HTML element with the `style` property. Thus, to dynamically modify the absolute positioning of an element in IE, all you need to do is to change the value of the appropriate properties. You can move an element by setting its `left` and `top` properties, you can hide or show an element by setting its `visibility` property, and you can change the stacking order of an element by setting its `zOrder` property.

One point to note is that the values of the `left` and `top` properties are strings that include measurement units. So, for example, you might set the *x*-coordinate of the element with `ID="P23"` using code like this:

```
document.all.P23.style.left = "2.25in";
```

Often when you are dynamically changing the pixel coordinates of an element, it is easier to use the `pixelLeft` and `pixelTop` properties—these properties are set to numeric values instead of string values and are implicitly measured in pixel units.

In addition to dynamically changing the position of an element, you may at times want to dynamically change the content of an element. This is not done with style properties. Instead, you set the `innerHTML` property of the element itself. Suppose, for example, that your document contains a <H1> element with its `ID` attribute set to "sect1". You could use the following code to change the color and the content of that element:

```
document.all.sect1.style.color = "red";
document.all.sect1.innerHTML = "New, <I>Improved</I> Heading";
```

---

* The new <SPAN> tag allows sequential span of HTML elements to be grouped into a single element that can be assigned a single name, a single style, and so on. <SPAN> is like <DIV> in this regard, except that it does not force a line break.

17.2.3 *Dynamic Positioning with Navigator Layers*

Dynamic positioning with Navigator 4 is a more complicated affair. Navigator 4 does not support a full object model, so it does not allow JavaScript programs to refer to arbitrary HTML elements. It cannot, therefore, allow access to the inline styles of arbitrary elements. Instead, it defines a special Layer object. Any element that is absolutely positioned (that is, any element that has its position style set to absolute) is placed in a separate layer from the rest of the document. This layer can be independently positioned, hidden, shown, lowered below or raised above other layers, and so on.

Each independently positioned layer in a document is represented by a Layer object, and not surprisingly, the layers[] array of the Document object contains the complete set of Layer objects in a document. (Layer objects appear in this array in the same order as they appear in the document). Additionally, any layer that is given a name with the ID attribute can be accessed by name. For example, if a layer specifies ID="L2", you can refer to it in Navigator as document.L2 or as document.layers["L2"].

A layer is something like a separate window or frame. Although the Layer object is not the same as the Window object, it does have a document property, just as windows and frames do. The document property of a Layer object refers to a Document object: each layer has its own totally independent HTML document. Layers can even be nested; we might output some HTML text into a nested layer with code like this:

```
document.layers[1].document.layers[0].document.write("Layers are Fun!");
document.layers[1].document.layers[0].document.close();
```

Although we cannot directly set the style properties of an absolutely positioned element, the Layer object provides properties and methods that we can use to dynamically position layers. The properties of the Layer object are similar to, but not the same as, the properties of the Internet Explorer 4 Style object that we use for dynamic positioning in that browser. The left and top properties of the Layer object specify the numeric position of the layer; setting these properties of a Layer is like setting the pixelLeft and pixelTop properties of an element's inline style in IE 4. The visibility property of a Layer specifies whether the contents of the layer should be visible or not. It should be set to one of the strings "show" or "hide" (not "visible" or "hidden" as in CSS-P and IE 4). The Layer object also supports a zIndex property that works exactly as the IE 4 Style object's zIndex property works.

The Layer object even supports a couple of properties that are not related to dynamic positioning. The `background.src` property specifies a background image for the layer, and the `bgColor` property specifies a background color for the layer. These properties correspond to the `background` and `backgroundColor` style properties in IE 4.

In addition to its properties, the Layer object also offers a number of convenient methods. `moveBy()` and `moveTo()` move a layer by a relative amount or to an absolute position. `moveAbove()` and `moveBelow()` set the `zIndex` of a layer relative to that of some other Layer.

Because every layer contains an independent document, you can dynamically update the contents of the layer with the `open()`, `write()`, and `close()` methods of the Document object, as we saw in Chapter 14. In addition, the `src` property of a Layer specifies the URL of the document that it displays. By setting this property, you can force the browser to load an entirely new document for display in the layer. The `load()` method is similar: it loads a new URL and changes the layer's width at the same time. Because layers often contain dynamically generated content, you may find it convenient to use `javascript:` URLs with the `src` property and `load()` method.

For compatibility, this chapter discusses dynamic positioning with CSS-P. We've seen that Navigator 4 automatically creates a Layer object for any element that has its `position` style property set to `absolute`. However, Navigator also allows layers to be created in other, less compatible, ways. For example, Navigator defines an HTML <LAYER> tag that allows layers to be defined directly in HTML. <LAYER> was not included in the recent HTML 4 standard, however, so it is not likely to become a standard HTML element. Nothing can be done with the <LAYER> tag that cannot be accomplished with style sheets.

However, Navigator 4 does support a `Layer()` constructor that allows Layer objects to be created dynamically, as needed within a program. For example, a sophisticated use of layers would be to simulate a miniature window system within a browser window. In Navigator 4, new windows (new layers) can be created as necessary with the `Layer()` constructor. This will not be possible with CSS-P until a full-featured DOM allows new HTML elements to be inserted directly into an existing document.

17.3 Example: Portable Dynamic Elements

Because of the incompatibilities between Navigator and Internet Explorer, many DHTML programmers program for either one browser or the other. The only viable alternative is to somehow encapsulate the common DHTML features of both browsers and define a portable API for using those common features.

Example 17-4 does just that: it defines a class named DynEl that represents a dynamic element. The DynEl class defines various methods that allow you to portably move the element, show and hide the element, and set the stacking order of the element. In addition to these positioning capabilities, the DynEl class also defines methods that provide portable access to other DHTML techniques. The setBody() method changes the content of the dynamic element, causing it to be immediately redrawn. The addEventHandler() method adds an event handler to the dynamic element.

This is a long and moderately complex example that you may find useful in your own DHMTL programs. It will repay careful study. The first thing you should note is that the example defines two entirely different sets of DynEl methods, depending on which browser is in use. To understand the setBody() and addEventHandler() methods, you may want to review the material in Chapter 14 and Chapter 15.

Example 17-5 is a simple JavaScript program that makes use of the DynEl class. It performs some interesting animations and makes use of many DynEl methods.

Example 17–4: Portable Dynamic HTML Elements with the DynEl Class

```
/*
 * File: DynEl.js
 * Include with: <SCRIPT SRC="DynEl.js"></SCRIPT>
 *
 * This file defines the DynEl class, which provides a portable API
 * to many Dynamic HTML features.
 */


/*
 * This is the constructor function for DynEl objects.
 * The arguments are the following:
 *    window: The Window object in which the dynamic element is to appear
 *    id:     The HTML ID for the dynamic element. Must be unique.
 *    body:   HTML text that constitutes the body of the dynamic element
 *    left:   The optional initial X-coordinate of the element
 *    top:    The optional initial Y-coordinate of the element
 *    width:  The optional width of the element
 *
 * This constructor outputs a style sheet into the current document.
 * This means that it can only be called from the <HEAD> of the document
 * before any text has been output for display.
 */
function DynEl(window, id, body, left, top, width) {
    // Remember some arguments for later.
    this.window = window;
    this.id = id;
    this.body = body;
```

Example 17-4: Portable Dynamic HTML Elements with the DynEl Class (continued)

```
    // Output a CSS-P style sheet for this element.
    var d = window.document;
    d.writeln('<STYLE TYPE="text/css">');
    d.write('#' + id + ' {position:absolute;');
    if (left) d.write('left:' + left + ';');
    if (top) d.write('top:' + top + ';');
    if (width) d.write('width:' + width + ';');
    d.writeln('}');
    d.writeln('</STYLE>');
}


/*
 * Now we define a bunch of methods for the DynEl class.
 * We define one set of methods if we are running in Navigator, and
 * another set of methods if we are running in Internet Explorer.
 * Note that the APIs of the methods are the same in both cases; it
 * is only the method bodies that change. In this way, we define
 * a portable API to the common DHTML functionality of the two browsers.
 */

// First, define the Navigator methods.
if (navigator.appName.indexOf("Netscape") != -1) {

    /*
     * This function outputs the dynamic element itself into the document.
     * It must be called before any other methods of the DynEl object can
     * be used.
     */
    DynEl.prototype.output = function() {
        var d = this.window.document;  // Shortcut variable: saves typing

        // Output the element within a <DIV> tag.  Specify the element id.
        d.writeln('<DIV ID="' + this.id + '">');
        d.writeln(this.body);
        d.writeln("</DIV>");

        // Now, for convenience, save a reference to the Layer object
        // created by this dynamic element.
        this.layer = d[this.id];
    }

    // Here are methods for moving, hiding, stacking, and otherwise
    // manipulating the dynamic element.
    DynEl.prototype.moveTo = function(x,y) { this.layer.moveTo(x,y); }
    DynEl.prototype.moveBy = function(x,y) { this.layer.moveBy(x,y); }
    DynEl.prototype.show = function() { this.layer.visibility = "show"; }
    DynEl.prototype.hide = function() { this.layer.visibility = "hide"; }
    DynEl.prototype.setStackingOrder = function(z) { this.layer.zIndex = z; }
```

```
DynEl.prototype.setBgColor = function(color) {
    this.layer.bgColor = color;
}
DynEl.prototype.setBgImage = function(image) {
    this.layer.background.src = image;
}


// These methods query the position, size, and other properties
// of the dynamic element.
DynEl.prototype.getX = function() { return this.layer.left; }
DynEl.prototype.getY = function() { return this.layer.top; }
DynEl.prototype.getWidth = function() { return this.layer.width; }
DynEl.prototype.getHeight = function() { return this.layer.height; }
DynEl.prototype.getStackingOrder = function() { return this.layer.zIndex; }
DynEl.prototype.isVisible = function() {
    return this.layer.visibility == "show";
}


/*
 * This method allows us to dynamically change the contents of
 * the dynamic element. The argument or arguments should be HTML
 * strings which become the new body of the element.
 */
DynEl.prototype.setBody = function() {
    for(var i = 0; i < arguments.length; i++)
        this.layer.document.writeln(arguments[i]);
    this.layer.document.close();
}


/*
 * This method registers a handler for the named event on the
 * element. The event name argument should be the name of an
 * event handler property, such as "onmousedown" or "onkeypress".
 * The handler is a function that takes whatever action is necessary.
 * Because Navigator and IE do not have compatible Event objects,
 * all event details are passed as arguments to the handler function.
 * When invoked, the handler will be passed the following nine arguments:
 *    1) A reference to the DynEl object
 *    2) A string containing the event type
 *    3) The X-coordinate of the mouse, relative to the DynEl
 *    4) The Y-coordinate of the mouse.
 *    5) The mouse button that was clicked (if any)
 *    6) The Unicode code of the key that was pressed (if any)
 *    7) A boolean specifying whether the Shift key was down
 *    8) A boolean specifying whether the Control key was down
 *    9) A boolean specifying whether the Alt key was down
 * Event handlers that are not interested in all these arguments do
 * not have to declare them all in their argument lists, of course.
```

Example 17-4: Portable Dynamic HTML Elements with the DynEl Class (continued)

```
    */
    DynEl.prototype.addEventHandler = function(eventname, handler) {
        // Arrange to capture events on this layer.
        this.layer.captureEvents(DynEl._eventmasks[eventname]);
        var dynel = this;  // Current DynEl for use in the nested function.
        // Define an event handler that will invoke the specified handler,
        // and pass it the nine arguments specified above.
        this.layer[eventname] = function(event) {
            return handler(dynel, event.type, event.x, event.y,
                           event.which, event.which,
                           ((event.modifiers & Event.SHIFT_MASK) != 0),
                           ((event.modifiers & Event.CTRL_MASK) != 0),
                           ((event.modifiers & Event.ALT_MASK) != 0));
        }
    }


    /*
     * This method unregisters the named event handler. It should be
     * called with a single string argument such as "onmouseover".
     */
    DynEl.prototype.removeEventHandler = function(eventname) {
        this.layer.releaseEvents(DynEl._eventmasks[eventname]);
        delete this.layer[eventname];
    }


    /*
     * This array is used internally by the two methods above to map
     * from event name to event type.
     */
    DynEl._eventmasks = {
      onabort:Event.ABORT, onblur:Event.BLUR, onchange:Event.CHANGE,
      onclick:Event.CLICK, ondblclick:Event.DBLCLICK,
      ondragdrop:Event.DRAGDROP, onerror:Event.ERROR,
      onfocus:Event.FOCUS, onkeydown:Event.KEYDOWN,
      onkeypress:Event.KEYPRESS, onkeyup:Event.KEYUP, onload:Event.LOAD,
      onmousedown:Event.MOUSEDOWN, onmousemove:Event.MOUSEMOVE,
      onmouseout:Event.MOUSEOUT, onmouseover:Event.MOUSEOVER,
      onmouseup:Event.MOUSEUP, onmove:Event.MOVE, onreset:Event.RESET,
      onresize:Event.RESIZE, onselect:Event.SELECT, onsubmit:Event.SUBMIT,
      onunload:Event.UNLOAD
    };
}


/*
 * Now define methods for Internet Explorer.
 * These methods have identical APIs to the ones defined for Netscape
 * above. Therefore, we will not repeat all the comments above.
 */
```

Example 17-4: Portable Dynamic HTML Elements with the DynEl Class (continued)

```
if (navigator.appName.indexOf("Microsoft") != -1) {

    // The all-important output() method
    DynEl.prototype.output = function() {
        var d = this.window.document;  // Shortcut variable: saves typing

        // Output the element within a <DIV> tag.  Specify the element id.
        d.writeln('<DIV ID="' + this.id + '">');
        d.writeln(this.body);
        d.writeln("</DIV>");

        // Now, for convenience, save references to the <DIV> element
        // we've created, and to its associated Style element.
        // These will be used throughout the methods that follow.
        this.element = d.all[this.id];
        this.style = this.element.style;
    }

    // Methods to move the dynamic object
    DynEl.prototype.moveTo = function(x,y) {
        this.style.pixelLeft = x;
        this.style.pixelTop = y;
    }
    DynEl.prototype.moveBy = function(x,y) {
        this.style.pixelLeft += x;
        this.style.pixelTop += y;
    }

    // Methods to set other attributes of the dynamic object
    DynEl.prototype.show = function() { this.style.visibility = "visible"; }
    DynEl.prototype.hide = function() { this.style.visibility = "hidden"; }
    DynEl.prototype.setStackingOrder = function(z) { this.style.zIndex = z; }
    DynEl.prototype.setBgColor = function(color) {
        this.style.backgroundColor = color;
    }
    DynEl.prototype.setBgImage = function(image) {
        this.style.backgroundImage = image;
    }

    // Methods to query the dynamic object
    DynEl.prototype.getX = function() { return this.style.pixelLeft; }
    DynEl.prototype.getY = function() { return this.style.pixelTop; }
    DynEl.prototype.getWidth = function() { return this.style.width; }
    DynEl.prototype.getHeight = function() { return this.style.height; }
    DynEl.prototype.getStackingOrder = function() { return this.style.zIndex; }
    DynEl.prototype.isVisible = function() {
        return this.style.visibility == "visible";
    }
```

Example 17–4: Portable Dynamic HTML Elements with the DynEl Class (continued)

```
    // Change the contents of the dynamic element.
    DynEl.prototype.setBody = function() {
        var body = "";
        for(var i = 0; i < arguments.length; i++) {
            body += arguments[i] + "\n";
        }
        this.element.innerHTML = body;
    }


    // Define an event handler.
    DynEl.prototype.addEventHandler = function(eventname, handler) {
        var dynel = this;  // Current DynEl for use in the nested function
        // Set an IE4 event handler that invokes the specified handler
        // with the appropriate nine arguments.
        this.element[eventname] = function() {
            var e = dynel.window.event;
            e.cancelBubble = true;
            return handler(dynel, e.type, e.x, e.y,
                            e.button, e.keyCode,
                            e.shiftKey, e.ctrlKey, e.altKey);
        }
    }


    // Remove an event handler.
    DynEl.prototype.removeEventHandler = function(eventname) {
        delete this.element[eventname];
    }
}
```

Example 17–5: Using the DynEl Class

```
<HEAD>
<SCRIPT>
// DynEl.js requires a Version 4 browser, and will cause errors if
// loaded by a Version 3 browser. If the browser version isn't high
// enough, the following code issues a warning, and suppresses any errors
// that occur when DynEl.js is loaded.
function suppressErrors() { return true; }
if (parseInt(navigator.appVersion) < 4) {
    alert("This program requires a version 4 browser!");
    onerror = suppressErrors;
}
</SCRIPT>
<SCRIPT SRC="DynEl.js"></SCRIPT>

<SCRIPT>
// Here are a couple of messages we're going to animate.
var msg1 = '<H1 STYLE="font-size:48pt">Nervous?</H1>'
```

Example 17–5: Using the DynEl Class (continued)

```
var msg2 = '<H1 STYLE="color:red;font-size:48pt">Drink More Coffee!</H1>'

// Create the two DynEl objects that we'll use in the program.
// These must be created in the <HEAD> of the document, because
// the DynEl() constructor outputs a style sheet.
var dynel1 = new DynEl(window, "d1", msg1, 100, 200);
var dynel2 = new DynEl(window, "d2", "Catch Me<BR>If You Can", 0,0,120);
</SCRIPT>
</HEAD>

<BODY>
<SCRIPT>
// Now in the <BODY> of the document, we've got to call the output() method
// of each DynEl object. This method outputs the HTML body of the dynamic
// element and links it to the appropriate style sheet defined in the
// <HEAD>. You must call output() *before* any other DynEl methods!
dynel1.output();
dynel2.output();

// This is the function that is going to animate the first DynEl
// It uses moveTo() to jiggle the dynamic element around.
// Also, it occasionally changes the message that the element displays.
// And it occasionally hides, then shows, the dynamic element.
function randomwalk() {
    var dx = (Math.random()-.5)*10;        // Pick random numbers.
    var dy = (Math.random()-.5)*10;
    dynel1.moveTo(100+dx, 200+dy);         // Move the element.

    var x = Math.random();                 // Pick another number.
    if (x < .1) dynel1.setBody(msg1);      // Change the element body.
    else if (dx < .2) dynel1.setBody(msg2);  // Change the element body.
    else if (dx < .3) {
        dynel1.hide();                     // Hide the element and...
        setTimeout("dynel1.show()", 1000); // ...show it again in 1 sec.
    }
}

// Now call the animation function 10 times a second.
setInterval("randomwalk()", 100);

// We register some event handlers on the second DynEl object.
// If you click the mouse over the top of the dynamic element, this first
// event handler will change it to tell you that you won the game.
// Note, however, that the next event handler makes it very difficult
// to move the mouse over the top of the dynamic element.
dynel2.addEventHandler("onmousedown", function(d) {d.setBody("You Win!");});

// Whenever the mouse moves over the DynEl, this handler moves it to some
```

Example 17–5: Using the DynEl Class (continued)

```
// other random place, and gives it a random background color. This makes
// it hard to click on. If you hold down the shift key when you move the
// mouse, however, this handler will not move the element, and you can
// move over it and click on it. Note, though, that this does not work
// in Navigator 4, because that browser does not include modifier key
// information in its mouseover events. Note that event handlers
// registered on DynEl objects are passed nine arguments.
dynel2.addEventHandler("onmouseover",
        function(d,type,x,y,button,key,shift,ctrl,alt) {
            // If shift key is down, do nothing.  Only works in IE.
            if (shift) return;
            // Move the element to a random position.
            d.moveTo(Math.random()*400, Math.random()*400);
            // And give it a random background color.
            var r = (Math.floor(Math.random()*240+16)).toString(16);
            var g = (Math.floor(Math.random()*240+16)).toString(16);
            var b = (Math.floor(Math.random()*240+16)).toString(16);
            d.setBgColor("#"+r+g+b);
        });
</SCRIPT>
</BODY>
```

18

In this chapter:
• *An Overview of Cookies*
• *Storing Cookies*
• *Reading Cookies*
• *Cookie Example*

Saving State with Cookies

The Document object contains a property named `cookie` that was not discussed in Chapter 14, *The Document Object Model*. On the surface, this property appears to be a simple string value; however, the `cookie` property controls a very important feature of the web browser and is important enough to warrant a complete chapter of its own.

18.1 An Overview of Cookies

A *cookie* is a small amount of named data stored by the web browser and associated with a particular web page or web site.* Cookies serve to give the web browser a memory, so that it can use data that was input on one page in another page, or so it can recall user preferences or other state variables when the user leaves a page and returns. Cookies were originally designed for CGI programming, and at the lowest level, are implemented as an extension to the HTTP protocol. Cookie data is automatically transmitted between web browser and web server, so CGI scripts on the server can read and write cookie values that are stored on the client. As we'll see, JavaScript can also manipulate cookies using the `cookie` property of the Document object.

`cookie` is a string property that allows you to read, create, modify, and delete the cookie or cookies that apply to the current web page. Although `cookie` appears at first to be a normal read/write string property, it has more complex behavior than

---

* The name "cookie" does not have a lot of significance, but is not used without precedent. In the obscure annals of computing history, the term "cookie" or "magic cookie" has been used to refer to a small chunk of data, particularly a chunk of privileged or secret data, akin to a password, that proves identity or permits access. In JavaScript, cookies are used to save state and can serve to establish a kind of identity for a web browser. Cookies in JavaScript do not use any kind of cryptography, however, and are not secure in any way.

this. When you read the value of `cookie`, you get a string that contains the names and values of all the cookies that apply to the document. You create, modify, or delete a cookie by setting the value of the `cookie` property. Later sections of this chapter explain in detail how this works. To use the `cookie` property effectively, however, you need to know more about cookies and how they work.

Each cookie has four optional attributes that control its lifetime, visibility, and security. The first attribute is *expires*, which specifies cookie lifetime. Cookies are transient by default—the values they store last for the duration of the web browser session but are lost when the user exits the browser. If you want a cookie to last beyond a single browsing session, you use its *expires* attribute to specify an expiration date—this causes the browser to save the cookie in a local file so that it can read it back in the next time the user visits the web page. Once the expiration date has past, the cookie is automatically deleted from the cookie file.

The second attribute of a cookie is *path*, which specifies the web pages with which a cookie is associated. By default, a cookie is associated with, and accessible to, the web page that created it and any other web pages in the same directory or any subdirectories of that directory. If the web page *http://www.acme.com/catalog/index.html* creates a cookie, for example, that cookie is also visible to *http://www.acme.com/catalog/order.html* and *http://www.acme.com/catalog/widgets/index.html*, but it is not visible to *http://www.acme.com/about.html*.

This default visibility behavior is often exactly what you want. Sometimes, though, you'll want to use cookie values throughout a multipage web site, regardless of which page creates the cookie. For instance, if the user enters his mailing address in a form on one page, you may want to save that address to use as the default the next time he returns to the page and also to use it as the default in another entirely unrelated form on another page where he is asked to enter a billing address. To allow this, you specify a *path* for the cookie. Then, any web page from the same web server that contains that path in its URL can share the cookies. For example, if a cookie set by *http://www.acme.com/catalog/widgets/index.html* has its path set to "/catalog", that cookie is also visible to *http://www.acme.com/catalog/order.html*. Or, if the path is set to "/", the cookie is visible to any page on the *www.acme.com* web server.

By default, cookies are only accessible to pages on the same web server from which they were set. Large web sites may want cookies to be shared across multiple web servers, however. For example, the server at *order.acme.com* may need to read cookie values set from *catalog.acme.com*. This is where the third cookie attribute, *domain*, comes in. If a cookie created by a page on *catalog.acme.com* sets its *path* attribute to "/" and its *domain* attribute to "acme.com", that cookie is available to all web pages on *catalog.acme.com* and to all web pages on *orders.acme.com* or to any other server in the *acme.com* domain. If the *domain* attribute is not set for a cookie, the default is the hostname of the web server that serves the page. Note that you cannot set the domain of a cookie to a domain other than the domain of your server.

The fourth and final attribute of cookies is a boolean attribute named *secure* that specifies how cookie values are transmitted over the network. By default, cookies are insecure, which means that they are transmitted over a normal, insecure HTTP connection. If a cookie is marked secure, however, it is transmitted only when the browser and server are connected via HTTPS or another secure protocol.

Note that the *expires*, *path*, *domain*, and *secure* attributes of a cookie are not JavaScript object properties. We'll see later in the chapter how you set these attributes of a cookie.

If you are interested in the complete technical details on how cookies work, see *http://www.netscape.com/newsref/std/cookie_spec.html*. This document is the official specification for HTTP cookies; it contains low-level details that are more suitable to CGI programming than to JavaScript programming. The following sections discuss how you can set and query cookie values in JavaScript and how you can specify the *expires*, *path*, *domain*, and *secure* attributes of a cookie.

18.2 Storing Cookies

To associate a transient cookie value with the current document, simply set the `cookie` property to a string of the form:

```
name=value
```

For example:

```
document.cookie = "version=" + escape(document.lastModified);
```

The next time you read the `cookie` property, the name/value pair you stored is included in the list of cookies for the document. Cookie values may not include semicolons, commas, or whitespace. For this reason, you may want to use the JavaScript `escape()` function to encode the value before storing it in the cookie. If you do this, you'll have to use the corresponding `unescape()` function when you read the cookie value.

A cookie written as described above lasts for the current web browsing session but is lost when the user exits the browser. To create a cookie that can last across browser sessions, include an expiration date by setting the *expires* attribute. You can do this by setting the `cookie` property to a string of the form:

```
name=value; expires=date
```

When setting an expiration date like this, `date` should be a date specification in the format written by `Date.toGMTString()`. For example, to create a cookie that persists for a year, you can use code like this:

```
var nextyear = new Date();
nextyear.setFullYear(nextyear.getFullYear() + 1);
document.cookie = "version=" + document.lastModified +
                  "; expires=" + nextyear.toGMTString();
```

Similarly, you can set the *path*, *domain*, and *secure* attributes of a cookie by appending strings of the following form to the cookie value before that value is written to the `cookie` property:

```
; path=path
; domain=domain
; secure
```

To change the value of a cookie, set its value again, using the same name and the new value. Use whatever values are appropriate for *expires*, *path*, and the other attributes.

To delete a cookie, set it again using the same name, an arbitrary value, and an expiration date that has already passed. Note that the browser is not required to immediately delete expired cookies, so a cookie may remain in the browser's cookie file past its expiration date.

18.2.1 Cookie Limitations

Cookies are intended for infrequent storage of small amounts of data. They are not intended as a general-purpose communication or data-transfer mechanism, so you should use them in moderation. Web browsers are not required to retain more than 300 cookies total, nor more than 20 cookies per web server (for the entire server, not just for your page or site on the server), nor to retain more than 4 kilobytes of data per cookie (both name and value count towards this 4-kilobyte limit). The most restrictive of these is the 20 cookies per server limit, so it is not a good idea to use a separate cookie for each variable you want to save. Instead, you should try to store multiple state variables within a single named cookie.

18.3 Reading Cookies

When you use the `cookie` property in a JavaScript expression, the value it returns is a string that contains all the cookies that apply to the current document.* The string is a list of *name=value* pairs separated by semicolons, where *name* is the name of a cookie and *value* is its string value. This value does not include any of the attributes that may have been set for the cookie. To determine the value of the named cookie you are interested in, you can use the `String.indexOf()` and `String.substring()` methods, or you may find it easier to use `String.split()` to break the string into individual cookies.

Once you have extracted the value of a cookie from the `cookie` property, you must interpret that value based on whatever format or encoding was used by the creator of that cookie. For example, the cookie might store multiple pieces of information in colon-separated fields. In this case, you would have to use appropriate string methods to extract the various fields of information. Don't forget to use the `unescape()` function on the cookie value if it was encoded using the `escape()` function.

The following code shows how you might read the `cookie` property, extract a single cookie from it, and use the value of that cookie:

```
// Read the cookie property. This returns all cookies for this document.
var allcookies = document.cookie;

// Look for the start of the cookie named "version".
var pos = allcookies.indexOf("version=");

// If we find a cookie by that name, extract and use its value.
if (pos != -1) {
    var start = pos + 8;                        // Start of cookie value
    var end = allcookies.indexOf(";", start);   // End of cookie value
    if (end == -1) end = allcookies.length;
    var value = allcookies.substring(start, end); // Extract the value.
    value = unescape(value);                    // Decode it.

    // Now that we have the cookie value, we can use it.
    // In this case, the cookie was previously set to the modification
    // date of the document, so we can use it to see if the document has
    // changed since the user last visited.
    if (value != document.lastModified)
        alert("This document has changed since you were last here");
}
```

---

* In Internet Explorer 3, the `cookie` property only works for Document objects that were retrieved using the HTTP protocol. Documents retrieved from the local file system or via other protocols, such as FTP, cannot have cookies associated with them.

Note that the string returned when you read the value of the cookie property does not contain any information about the various cookie attributes. The cookie property allows you to set those attributes, but it does not allow you to read them.

18.4 Cookie Example

Example 18-1 brings together all the aspects of cookies we have discussed. First, the example defines a Cookie class. When you create a Cookie object, you specify a Document object, a name for the cookie, and, optionally, an expiration time, a path, a domain, and a boolean value that indicates whether the cookie should be secure. After creating a Cookie object, you can set arbitrary string properties on this object; the values of these properties are the values stored in the cookie.

The Cookie class defines three methods. The store() method loops through all of the user-defined properties of the Cookie object and concatenates their names and values into a single string that serves as the value of the cookie. The load() method of a Cookie object reads the cookie property of the Document object to obtain the values of all the cookies for the document. It searches this string to find the value of the named cookie and then parses this value into individual names and values, which it stores as properties of the Cookie object. Finally, the remove() method of the Cookie object deletes the specified cookie from the document.

After defining the Cookie class, Example 18-1 demonstrates a useful and elegant way to use cookies. The code is somewhat complicated but is worth studying carefully. You may want to start with the test program at the end of the example; it shows a typical usage of the Cookie class.

Example 18-1: A Utility Class for Working with Cookies

```
<SCRIPT LANGUAGE="JavaScript1.1">

// The constructor function: creates a cookie object for the specified
// document, with a specified name and optional attributes.
// Arguments:
//    document: The Document object that the cookie is stored for. Required.
//    name:     A string that specifies a name for the cookie. Required.
//    hours:    An optional number that specifies the number of hours from now
//              that the cookie should expire.
//    path:     An optional string that specifies the cookie path attribute.
//    domain:   An optional string that specifies the cookie domain attribute.
//    secure:   An optional Boolean value that, if true, requests a secure cookie.
//
function Cookie(document, name, hours, path, domain, secure)
{
```

Example 18-1: A Utility Class for Working with Cookies (continued)

```
    // All the predefined properties of this object begin with '$'
    // to distinguish them from other properties which are the values to
    // be stored in the cookie.
    this.$document = document;
    this.$name = name;
    if (hours)
        this.$expiration = new Date((new Date()).getTime() + hours*3600000);
    else this.$expiration = null;
    if (path) this.$path = path; else this.$path = null;
    if (domain) this.$domain = domain; else this.$domain = null;
    if (secure) this.$secure = true; else this.$secure = false;
}


// This function is the store() method of the Cookie object.
function _Cookie_store()
{
    // First, loop through the properties of the Cookie object and
    // put together the value of the cookie. Since cookies use the
    // equals sign and semicolons as separators, we'll use colons
    // and ampersands for the individual state variables we store
    // within a single cookie value. Note that we escape the value
    // of each state variable, in case it contains punctuation or other
    // illegal characters.
    var cookieval = "";
    for(var prop in this) {
        // Ignore properties with names that begin with '$' and also methods.
        if ((prop.charAt(0) == '$') || ((typeof this[prop]) == 'function'))
            continue;
        if (cookieval != "") cookieval += '&';
        cookieval += prop + ':' + escape(this[prop]);
    }

    // Now that we have the value of the cookie, put together the
    // complete cookie string, which includes the name and the various
    // attributes specified when the Cookie object was created.
    var cookie = this.$name + '=' + cookieval;
    if (this.$expiration)
        cookie += '; expires=' + this.$expiration.toGMTString();
    if (this.$path) cookie += '; path=' + this.$path;
    if (this.$domain) cookie += '; domain=' + this.$domain;
    if (this.$secure) cookie += '; secure';

    // Now store the cookie by setting the magic Document.cookie property.
    this.$document.cookie = cookie;
}
```

Example 18-1: A Utility Class for Working with Cookies (continued)

```
// This function is the load() method of the Cookie object.
function _Cookie_load()
{
    // First, get a list of all cookies that pertain to this document.
    // We do this by reading the magic Document.cookie property.
    var allcookies = this.$document.cookie;
    if (allcookies == "") return false;

    // Now extract just the named cookie from that list.
    var start = allcookies.indexOf(this.$name + '=');
    if (start == -1) return false;   // Cookie not defined for this page.
    start += this.$name.length + 1;  // Skip name and equals sign.
    var end = allcookies.indexOf(';', start);
    if (end == -1) end = allcookies.length;
    var cookieval = allcookies.substring(start, end);

    // Now that we've extracted the value of the named cookie, we've
    // got to break that value down into individual state variable
    // names and values. The name/value pairs are separated from each
    // other by ampersands, and the individual names and values are
    // separated from each other by colons. We use the split method
    // to parse everything.
    var a = cookieval.split('&');    // Break it into array of name/value pairs.
    for(var i=0; i < a.length; i++)  // Break each pair into an array.
        a[i] = a[i].split(':');

    // Now that we've parsed the cookie value, set all the names and values
    // of the state variables in this Cookie object. Note that we unescape()
    // the property value, because we called escape() when we stored it.
    for(var i = 0; i < a.length; i++) {
        this[a[i][0]] = unescape(a[i][1]);
    }

    // We're done, so return the success code.
    return true;
}


// This function is the remove() method of the Cookie object.
function _Cookie_remove()
{
    var cookie;
    cookie = this.$name + '=';
    if (this.$path) cookie += '; path=' + this.$path;
    if (this.$domain) cookie += '; domain=' + this.$domain;
    cookie += '; expires=Fri, 02-Jan-1970 00:00:00 GMT';

    this.$document.cookie = cookie;
}
```

Example 18-1: A Utility Class for Working with Cookies (continued)

```
// Create a dummy Cookie object, so we can use the prototype object to make
// the functions above into methods.
new Cookie();
Cookie.prototype.store = _Cookie_store;
Cookie.prototype.load = _Cookie_load;
Cookie.prototype.remove = _Cookie_remove;


//=================================================================
//   The code above is the definition of the Cookie class.
//   The code below is a sample use of that class.
//=================================================================


// Create the cookie we'll use to save state for this web page.
// Since we're using the default path, this cookie will be accessible
// to all web pages in the same directory as this file or "below" it.
// Therefore, it should have a name that is unique among those pages.
// Note that we set the expiration to 10 days in the future.
var visitordata = new Cookie(document, "name_color_count_state", 240);

// First, try to read data stored in the cookie. If the cookie is not
// defined, or if it doesn't contain the data we need, then query the
// user for that data.
if (!visitordata.load() || !visitordata.name || !visitordata.color) {
    visitordata.name = prompt("What is your name:", "");
    visitordata.color = prompt("What is your favorite color:", "");
}

// Keep track of how many times this user has visited the page:
if (visitordata.visits == null) visitordata.visits = 0;
visitordata.visits++;

// Store the cookie values, even if they were already stored, so that the
// expiration date will be reset to 10 days from this most recent visit.
// Also, store them again to save the updated visits state variable.
visitordata.store();

// Now we can use the state variables we read:
document.write('<FONT SIZE=7 COLOR="' + visitordata.color + '">' +
               'Welcome, ' + visitordata.name + '!' +
               '</FONT>' +
               '<P>You have visited ' + visitordata.visits + ' times.');
</SCRIPT>

<FORM>
<INPUT TYPE="button" VALUE="Forget My Name" onClick="visitordata.remove();">
</FORM>
```

19

Compatibility Techniques

JavaScript, like Java, is one of a new breed of "platform-independent" languages. That is, you can develop a program in JavaScript and expect to run it unchanged in a JavaScript-enabled web browser running on any type of computer with any type of operating system. Though this is the ideal, we live in an imperfect world and have not yet reached that state of perfection.

There are, and probably always will be, compatibility problems that we JavaScript programmers must bear in mind. The one fact that we must always remember is that it is a heterogeneous network out there. Your JavaScript programs will be run possibly on many different platforms, using three or more versions of browsers from at least two different vendors. This can be difficult to keep in mind for those of us who come from the non-portable past, when programs were developed on a platform-specific basis. Remember: it doesn't matter what platform you develop a program on. It may work fine on that platform, but the real test is whether it works fine (or fails gracefully) on *all* platforms on which it is used.

The compatibility issues fall into two broad categories: platform-specific, browser-specific, and version-specific features on one hand, and bugs and language-level incompatibilities, including the incompatibility of JavaScript with non-JavaScript browsers, on the other. This chapter discusses techniques for coping with compatibility issues in both of these areas. If you've worked your way through all the previous chapters in this book, you are probably an expert JavaScript programmer and you may already be writing serious JavaScript programs. Don't release those programs on the Internet (or onto a heterogeneous intranet) before you've read this chapter, though!

19.1 Platform and Browser Compatibility

When developing production-quality JavaScript code, testing and knowledge of platform-specific, vendor-specific, and version-specific incompatibilities are your chief allies. If you know, for example, that Navigator 2 on Macintosh platforms always gets the time wrong by about an hour, you can take steps to deal with this. If you know that Windows platforms do not automatically clear your setting of the status line when the mouse moves off a hypertext link, you can provide an appropriate event handler to explicitly clear the status line. If you know that Internet Explorer 4 and Navigator 4 support vastly different Dynamic HTML models, you can write pages that use the appropriate mechanism depending on the browser in use.

Knowledge of existing incompatibilities is crucial to writing compatible code. Unfortunately, the task of producing a definitive listing of all known vendor, version, and platform incompatibilities would be enormous and has apparently never even been seriously attempted. You may find some assistance on the Internet, but you will have to rely primarily on your own experience and testing. Once you have identified an area of incompatibility, however, there are a number of basic approaches you can take to coping with it, as described in the following sections.

19.1.1 The Least-Common-Denominator Approach

One technique for dealing with incompatibilities is to avoid them like the plague. For example, the Date object is notoriously buggy in Navigator 2. If you want Navigator 2 users to be able to use your programs, you can simply avoid relying upon the Date object altogether.

As another example, Navigator 3 and Internet Explorer 3 both support the `opener` property of the Window object, but Navigator 2 does not. The least-common-denominator approach says that you should not use this property if compatibility with Navigator 2 is a goal. Instead, you can create an equivalent property of your own whenever you open a new window:

```
newwin = window.open("", "new", "width=500, height=300");
newwin.creator = self;
```

If you consistently set a `creator` property for each new window you create, you can rely on it instead of the non-portable `opener` property. (Another alternative, as we'll see later, is to give up on compatibility with Navigator 2 and require a browser that supports JavaScript 1.1 or later, as all such browsers support the `opener` property.)

With this technique, you use only features that are known to work on all your target platforms. It doesn't allow you to write cutting-edge programs or push the envelope, but it results in very portable, safe programs that can serve a lot of important functions.

19.1.2 Defensive Coding

With the defensive coding approach to compatibility, you write code that contains platform-independent workarounds for platform-specific incompatibilities. For example, if you set the status property of a Window object from the onMouseOver event handler to display a custom message in the status line, the status line is cleared when you move the mouse off the hyperlink, except in Windows versions of Navigator 2 and 3. To correct for this, you might just get into the habit of including an onMouseOut event handler to clear the status line.

To return to the example of the opener property from the previous section, the defensive coding approach to compatibility does not discard the property altogether but does insert a workaround to take care of platforms that do not support the property:

```
newwin = window.open("", "new", "width=500, height=300");
if (!newwin.opener) newwin.opener = self;
```

Note how we tested for the existence of the opener property. The same technique works to test for the existence of methods. For example, the split() method of the String object only exists for JavaScript 1.1 implementations. Using defensive coding, we would write our own version of this function that works for JavaScript 1.0 and JavaScript 1.1. But, for efficiency, we'd like to use the fast, built-in method on those platforms that do support it. Our platform-independent code to split() a string might end up looking like this:

```
if (s.split)              // If method exists, use it.
    a = s.split(":");
else                      // Otherwise, use our alternative implementation.
    a = mysplit(s, ":");
```

19.1.3 Platform-Specific Workarounds

When the least-common denominator and defensive coding approaches to incompatibilities won't work, you may find yourself having to create platform-specific workarounds. Recall from Chapter 13, *Windows and Frames*, that the navigator property of the Window object provides information about the vendor and version of the browser and the platform it is running on. You can use this information to insert platform-specific code into your program. You might use this approach to distinguish between Navigator and Internet Explorer when working with Dynamic HTML, for example. This is exactly what I did in developing the portable DynEl class in Chapter 17, *Dynamic HTML*.

Another example of a platform-specific workaround might involve the `bgColor` property of the Document object. On Windows and Macintosh platforms, you can set this property at runtime to change the background color of a document. Unfortunately, when you do this on Unix versions of Navigator 2 and 3, the color changes, but the document contents temporarily disappear. If you wanted to create a special effect using a changing background color, you could use the Navigator object to test for Unix platforms and simply skip the special effect for those platforms. The code could look like this:

```
// Check whether we're running Navigator 2 or 3 on a Unix platform.
var nobg = (parseInt(navigator.appVersion) < 4) &&
           (navigator.appName.indexOf("Netscape") != -1) &&
           (navigator.appVersion.indexOf("X11") != -1);

// If we're not, then go ahead and animate the page background color.
if (!nobg) animate_bg_color();
```

19.1.4 Compatibility Through Server-Side Scripts

Another approach to compatibility is possible if your web application includes the use of server-side scripts, such as CGI scripts or server-side JavaScript. A script on the server side can inspect the `User-Agent` field of the HTTP request header. This allows it to determine exactly what browser the user is running. With this knowledge, it can generate customized JavaScript code that is known to work correctly on that browser. Or, if the server-side script detects that the user's browser is one that does not support JavaScript, it can generate web pages that do not require JavaScript at all. An important drawback to this approach is that a server-side script cannot detect when a user has disabled JavaScript support in his browser.

Note that the topics of CGI programming and server-side scripting in general are beyond the scope of this book.

19.1.5 Ignore the Problem

An important question to ask when considering any incompatibility is "how important is it?" If the incompatibility is a minor or cosmetic one, affects a browser or platform that is not widely used, or only affects an out-of-date version of a browser, you might simply decide to ignore the problem and let the users affected by it cope with it on their own.

For example, earlier I suggested defining an `onMouseOut` event handler to correct for the fact that Navigator 2 and 3 for Windows do not correctly clear the status line. Unfortunately, the `onMouseOut` event handler is not supported in Navigator 2, so this workaround won't work for that platform. If you expect your application to have a lot of users who use Navigator 2 on Windows and you think that it is really important to get that status line cleared, you'll have to develop some other workaround. You could use `setTimeout()` in your `onMouseOver` event handler to arrange for the status line to be cleared in two seconds. But this solution brings problems with it: what if the mouse is still over the hypertext link and the status line shouldn't be cleared in two seconds? In this case, a simpler approach might be to simply ignore the problem. This can easily be justified because Navigator 2 is by now out of date; any users still relying on it should be encouraged to upgrade.

19.1.6 *Fail Gracefully*

Finally, there are some incompatibilities that cannot be ignored and cannot be worked around. In this case, your program should work correctly on all platforms, browsers, and versions that provide the needed features and should fail gracefully on all others. Failing gracefully means recognizing that the required features are not available and informing the user that she will not be able to use your JavaScript program.

For example, the image replacement technique we saw during the discussion of images in Chapter 14, *The Document Object Model*, does not work in Navigator 2 or Internet Explorer 3 and there is really no workaround that can simulate it. Therefore, we should not even attempt to run the program on those platforms; instead, we should politely notify the user of the incompatibility.

Failing gracefully can be harder than it sounds. Much of the rest of this chapter explains techniques for doing so.

19.2 *Language Version Compatibility*

The previous section discussed general compatibility techniques that are useful for coping with incompatibilities between different versions of browsers from different vendors running on different platforms. This section addresses a different compatibility concern: how to use new features of the JavaScript language in a way that does not cause errors on browsers that do not support those features. Our goals are simple: we need to prevent JavaScript code from being interpreted by browsers that don't understand it, and we need to display special messages on those browsers that inform users that their browsers cannot run the scripts.

19.2.1 *The LANGUAGE Attribute*

The first goal is easy. As we saw in Chapter 12, *JavaScript in Web Browsers*, we can prevent a browser from attempting to run code that it cannot understand by setting the `LANGUAGE` attribute of the `<SCRIPT>` tag appropriately. For example, the following `<SCRIPT>` tag specifies that the code it contains uses features of JavaScript 1.1, so that browsers that do not support that version of the scripting language should not attempt to run it:

```
<SCRIPT LANGUAGE="JavaScript1.1">
    // JavaScript 1.1 code goes here.
</SCRIPT>
```

Note that the use of the `LANGUAGE` attribute is a general technique. When set to the string "JavaScript1.2", the attribute prevents JavaScript 1.0 or 1.1 browsers from attempting to run the code. Presumably, the next generation of browsers will allow the `LANGUAGE` attribute to be set to "JavaScript1.3", to prevent interpretation by browsers that do not support the new features of JavaScript 1.3.

Unfortunately, the generalizability of the `LANGUAGE` attribute is marred by the fact that specifying `LANGUAGE="JavaScript1.2"` causes Navigator to behave in ways that are incompatible with the ECMA-262 standard. For example, as we saw in Chapter 5, *Expressions and Operators*, setting the `LANGUAGE` attribute to this value causes the `==` operator to perform equality comparisons without doing any type conversions. And as we saw in Chapter 8, *Objects*, specifying "JavaScript1.2" also causes the `toString()` method to behave quite differently. Unless you explicitly want these new, incompatible behaviors, or unless you can carefully avoid all incompatible features, you should avoid the use of `LANGUAGE="JavaScript1.2"`.

19.2.2 *Explicit Version Testing*

The `LANGUAGE` attribute provides at least a partial solution to the problem of language version compatibility, but it only solves half of the problem. We also need to be able to fail gracefully for browsers that do not support the desired version of JavaScript. If we require JavaScript 1.1, we'd like to be able to notify users of JavaScript 1.0 browsers that they cannot use the page. Example 19-1 shows how we can do this.

Example 19–1: A Message for Browsers That Do Not Support JavaScript 1.1

```
<!-- Set a variable to determine what version of JavaScript we support. -->
<!-- This technique can be extended to any number of language versions. -->
<SCRIPT LANGUAGE="JavaScript"> var _version = 1.0; </SCRIPT>
<SCRIPT LANGUAGE="JavaScript1.1"> _version = 1.1; </SCRIPT>
<SCRIPT LANGUAGE="JavaScript1.2"> _version = 1.2; </SCRIPT>
```

Example 19–1: A Message for Browsers That Do Not Support JavaScript 1.1 (continued)

```
<!-- Run this code on any JavaScript-enabled browser. -->
<!-- If the version is not high enough, display a message. -->
<SCRIPT LANGUAGE="JavaScript">
  if (_version < 1.1) {
    document.write('<HR><H1>This Page Requires JavaScript 1.1</H1>');
    document.write('Your JavaScript 1.0 browser cannot run this page.<HR>');
  }
</SCRIPT>


<!-- Now run the actual program only on JavaScript 1.1 browsers. -->
<SCRIPT LANGUAGE="JavaScript1.1">
    // The actual JavaScript 1.1 code goes here.
</SCRIPT>
```

19.2.3 Suppressing Version-Related Errors

Example 19-1 showed how we can write JavaScript 1.1 code that JavaScript 1.0 browsers do not attempt to execute. What if we wanted to write JavaScript 1.2 code that JavaScript 1.1 browsers do not attempt to execute? We could use the LANGUAGE attribute to explicitly specify "JavaScript1.2", but as discussed earlier, this causes Navigator to behave incompatibly. Unfortunately, JavaScript 1.2 adds a lot of new syntax to the language. If you write code that uses a switch statement, an object initializer, or a function literal and then run that code on a JavaScript 1.1 browser, you'll cause runtime syntax errors.

One way to work around this problem is simply to suppress any errors that occur on JavaScript 1.1 browsers. Example 19-2 shows how this can be done.

Example 19–2: Suppressing Version-Related Errors

```
<!-- Check whether JavaScript 1.2 is supported. -->
<SCRIPT LANGUAGE="JavaScript1.2">var _js12_ = 1.2</SCRIPT>


<!-- Now avoid the problems with JavaScript 1.2 on Navigator by running -->
<!-- the following code on any browser that supports JavaScript 1.1. If -->
<!-- the browser does not support JavaScript 1.2, however, we'll display -->
<!-- an error message and suppress any syntax errors that occur. -->
<SCRIPT LANGUAGE="JavaScript1.1">
// If JavaScript 1.2 is not supported, fail gracefully.
if (!_js12_) {
    alert("This program requires a browser with JavaScript 1.2 support");
    window.onerror = new Function("return true;");
}


// Now proceed with the JavaScript 1.2 code.
</SCRIPT>
```

19.2.4 Conditional Comments

If your program is only going to be used on Navigator platforms with Navigator 4 and later, you can use conditional comments. As you may recall from Chapter 12, a conditional comment is the combination of an HTML comment and a JavaScript entity. If the JavaScript code contained within the entity evaluates to `true`, the HTML comment tags are ignored and the contents of the comment are parsed as if the comment tags were not there. On the other hand, if the JavaScript code evaluates to `false`, the comment behaves like a regular comment and its contents are ignored. Needless to say, browsers that do not support conditional comments always treat them as comments and ignore their contents.

If you only want to support Navigator, you can use a conditional comment as another way to require a version of the browser that supports JavaScript 1.2 without using the problematic `LANGUAGE="JavaScript1.2"` attribute:

```
<!-- The following code only runs on Navigator versions 4 and later. -->
<!--&{parseInt(navigator.appVersion) >= 4};
<SCRIPT>
    // Code that requires Navigator and JavaScript 1.2 goes here.
</SCRIPT>
-->
```

Internet Explorer 4 also supports conditional comments, in an entirely different form. Conditional comments in IE are inspired by the C preprocessor and are used within JavaScript code; they are not HTML comments. For example, IE 4 only runs the following code if it is running on a Macintosh system:

```
@if (@_mac == true)                 // If we're not running on a Mac, then
   alert("Running on a Macintosh"); // ignore code till @else.
@else                               // Otherwise, ignore code till @end.
   alert("Not running on a Macintosh");
@end                                // End of conditional comment.
```

Note that the special conditional comment statements all begin with @. Other IE 4 conditional statements include `@else` and `@elif`. The Microsoft JScript documentation contains a complete list of the predefined variables (such as `@_mac`) that can be used by the `@if` and `@elif` conditional statements. Note that the code above causes a runtime error in Navigator, IE 3, or any other browser that does not support this conditional comment syntax.

19.2.5 Loading a New Page for Compatibility

Another approach to version compatibility is to load a web page that requires a specific level of JavaScript support only after it has been determined whether the browser provides that level of support. Example 19-3 shows how this might be done with a short script that tests whether JavaScript 1.2 is supported. If the browser supports this version, the script uses the `Location.replace()` method to load in a new web page that requires JavaScript 1.2. If JavaScript 1.2 is not supported, the script displays a message saying that it is required.

Example 19–3: A Web Page to Test for JavaScript Compatibility

```
<HEAD>
<SCRIPT LANGUAGE="JavaScript1.2">
// If JavaScript 1.2 is supported, extract a new URL from the portion of
// our URL following the question mark, and load that new URL in.
location.replace(location.search.substring(1));

// Enter a really long, empty, loop so that the body of this document
// doesn't get displayed while the new document is loading.
for(var i = 0; i < 10000000; i++);
</SCRIPT>
</HEAD>
<BODY>
<HR SIZE=4>
<H1>This Page Requires JavaScript 1.2</H1>
Your browser cannot run this page. Please upgrade to a browser that
supports JavaScript 1.2, such as Netscape Navigator 4 or Internet
Explorer 4.
<HR SIZE=4>
</BODY>
```

The most interesting thing about this example is that it is a generic one—the name of the JavaScript 1.2 file to be loaded is encoded in the search portion of the original URL; that file is loaded only if JavaScript 1.2 is supported. Thus, if the file in this example has the name `testjs12.html`, you can use it in URLs like the one shown in this hyperlink:

```
<A HREF="http://my.isp.net/~david/utils/testjs12.html?../js/cooljs12.html">
Visit my cool JavaScript 1.2 page!
</A>
```

The other thing to note about Example 19-3 is that calling `Location.replace()` starts a new page loading but does not immediately stop the current page from loading. Therefore, the JavaScript code in this example enters an long, empty loop after it calls `replace()`. This prevents the rest of the document from being parsed and displayed, so that users of JavaScript 1.2 browsers do not see the message intended for users of browsers that do not support JavaScript 1.2.

Finally, note that the technique shown in Example 19-3 is useful not only to distinguish one version of JavaScript from another, but also to distinguish between browsers that support JavaScript and those that do not. The next section discusses other compatibility techniques that are useful with non-JavaScript browsers.

19.3 Compatibility with Non-JavaScript Browsers

The previous section discussed compatibility with browsers that do not support a particular version of JavaScript. This section considers compatibility with browsers that do not support JavaScript at all. These are either browsers that have no JavaScript capability or browsers in which the user has disabled JavaScript (which some users do because of security concerns). Because there are still a number of such browsers, you should design your web pages to fail gracefully when read into browsers that do not understand JavaScript. There are two parts to doing this: first, you must take care to ensure that your JavaScript code does not appear as if it were HTML text, and second, you should arrange to display a message informing the visitor that his browser cannot correctly handle the page.

19.3.1 Hiding Scripts from Old Browsers

Web browsers that support JavaScript execute the JavaScript statements that appear between the <SCRIPT> and </SCRIPT> tags. Browsers that don't support JavaScript but that recognize the <SCRIPT> tag simply ignore everything between <SCRIPT> and </SCRIPT>. This is as it should be. Older browsers, however (and there are still some out there), do not even recognize the <SCRIPT> and </SCRIPT> tags. This means that they ignore the tags themselves and treat all the JavaScript between them as HTML text to be displayed. Unless you take steps to prevent it, users of these old browsers see your JavaScript code formatted into big meaningless paragraphs and presented as web page content!

In order to prevent this, you enclose the body of your script within an HTML comment, using the format shown in Example 19-4.

Example 19–4: A Script Hidden from Old Browsers

```
1  <SCRIPT LANGUAGE="JavaScript">
2  <!-- Begin HTML comment that hides the script.
3       // JavaScript statements go here.
4
5
6  // End HTML comment that hides the script. -->
7  </SCRIPT>
```

Browsers that do not understand the <SCRIPT> and </SCRIPT> tags simply ignore them. Thus, lines 1 and 7 in Example 19-4 have no effect on these browsers. They'll ignore lines 2 through 6 as well, because the first four characters on line 2 begin an HTML comment and the last three characters on line 6 end that comment—everything in between is ignored by the HTML parser.

This script-hiding technique also works for browsers that *do* support JavaScript. Lines 1 and 7 indicate the beginning and ending of a script. As noted in Chapter 2, *Lexical Structure*, JavaScript-enabled web browsers recognize the HTML comment opening string <!--, but treat it as a single-line comment. Thus, a browser with JavaScript support treats line 2 as a single-line comment. Similarly, line 6 begins with the // single-line comment string, so that line is ignored by JavaScript-enabled browsers as well. This leaves lines 3 through 5, which are executed as JavaScript statements.

While it takes a little getting used to, this simple and elegant mix of HTML and JavaScript comments does exactly what we need: it prevents JavaScript code from being displayed by browsers that do not support JavaScript. Although a declining number of browsers require this type of commenting, it is still quite common to see it used in JavaScript code on the Internet. The comments need not be as verbose as in Example 19-4, of course. It is common to see scripts like this:

```
<SCRIPT LANGUAGE="JavaScript">
<!-- Begin hiding.
  document.write(new Date());
// End hiding. -->
</SCRIPT>
```

It is also common to strip the English text out of the comments altogether:

```
<SCRIPT LANGUAGE="JavaScript">
<!--
  document.write(new Date());
// -->
</SCRIPT>
```

This commenting technique has solved the problem of hiding our JavaScript code from browsers that can't run it. The next step in failing gracefully is to display a message to the user letting her know that the page cannot run.

19.3.2 *<NOSCRIPT>*

The <NOSCRIPT> and </NOSCRIPT> tags enclose an arbitrary block of HTML text that should be displayed by any browser that does not support JavaScript. These tags can be employed to let a user know that her browser cannot correctly display your pages that require JavaScript. For example:

```
<SCRIPT LANGUAGE="JavaScript1.1">
  // Your JavaScript code here.
</SCRIPT>
<NOSCRIPT>
<HR SIZE=4>
<H1>This Page Requires JavaScript 1.1</H1>
This page requires a browser that supports JavaScript 1.1.<P>
Your browser either does not support JavaScript, or it has JavaScript
support disabled. If you want to correctly view this page, please
upgrade your browser or enable JavaScript support.
<HR SIZE=4>
</NOSCRIPT>
```

There is one problem with the <NOSCRIPT> tag. It was introduced into HTML by Netscape with the release of Navigator 3. Thus, it is not supported in Navigator 2. Since Navigator 2 does not support <NOSCRIPT> and </NOSCRIPT>, it ignores the tags and displays the text that appears between them, even though it does support scripting. In the code shown above, this works out to our advantage, however, because we've specified that the code requires JavaScript 1.1 support.

20

LiveConnect: JavaScript and Java

As we saw in Chapter 14, *The Document Object Model*, as of JavaScript 1.1, Navigator and Internet Explorer both allow JavaScript programs to read and write the public fields and invoke the public methods of Java applets embedded in an HTML document. Internet Explorer treats an applet as a type of ActiveX control and uses its ActiveX Scripting technology to allow JavaScript programs to interact with the applet. This technology is not documented in this book, but you can learn more about it on the Microsoft web site. A good place to start is *http://www.microsoft.com/scripting*.

Navigator supports JavaScript interaction with Java applets through a technology known as LiveConnect. Since LiveConnect was designed specifically for the purpose of connecting JavaScript and Java, however, its capabilities go well beyond simply allowing JavaScript to interact with applets. This chapter explains how LiveConnect works and how you can use it in your programs. The bulk of the chapter is specific to Navigator, although Internet Explorer analogs to LiveConnect features are noted where such analogs exist.

To use LiveConnect effectively, you need to understand Java programming. This chapter assumes you have at least a basic familiarity with Java (see *Java in a Nutshell*, by David Flanagan, and *Exploring Java*, by Patrick Niemeyer and Joshua Peck, both published by O'Reilly).

20.1 Overview of LiveConnect

LiveConnect is the mechanism in Navigator that allows JavaScript and Java to work together. Using LiveConnect, all of the following are possible:

- A JavaScript program can interact with a Java applet, both by reading and writing public fields of the applet and by invoking public methods of the applet.

- A JavaScript program can interact with a Java-enabled Navigator plugin in the same way as with an applet.

- A JavaScript program can interact with the standard Java system classes that are built into the browser.

- An applet or a Java-enabled plugin can interact with JavaScript, reading and writing JavaScript object properties and array elements and invoking JavaScript functions.

The surprising thing about working with LiveConnect is how easy it is to accomplish these difficult things. LiveConnect automatically handles all the required communication and data type conversion that must take place to allow Java and JavaScript to work together. LiveConnect is an underlying communication framework that opens up all sorts of possibilities for communication among JavaScript programs, Java applets, and Java-enabled plugins. LiveConnect can be thought of as the glue that ties these things together, as Figure 20-1 illustrates.

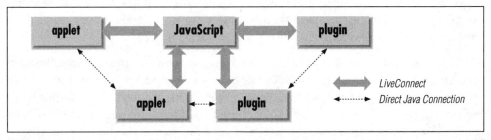

Figure 20–1: LiveConnect glues together JavaScript, applets, and plugins

20.2 LiveConnect Data Types

To understand how LiveConnect does its amazing job of connecting JavaScript to Java, you have to understand the five JavaScript data types that LiveConnect uses. (There is also a Java data type that LiveConnect uses to connect Java back to JavaScript; we'll learn about that Java class later in this chapter.) The following sections explain these JavaScript data types. Once we've explored these LiveConnect fundamentals, the following sections show how we can actually use LiveConnect to connect JavaScript to Java.

20.2.1 The JavaPackage Class

A *package* in Java is collection of related Java classes. The JavaPackage class is a JavaScript data type that represents a Java package. The properties of a JavaPackage are the classes that the package contains (classes are represented by the Java-Class class, which we'll see shortly), as well as any other packages that the package contains. There is a restriction on the JavaPackage class: you cannot use a JavaScript `for/in` loop to obtain a complete list of all packages and classes that a JavaPackage contains. This restriction is the result of an underlying restriction in the Java virtual machine.

All JavaPackage objects are contained within a parent JavaPackage; the Window property named `Packages` is a top-level JavaPackage that serves as the root of this package hierarchy. It has `java`, `sun`, and `netscape` properties, which are Java-Package objects that represent the various hierarchies of Java classes included with Navigator. For example, the JavaPackage `Packages.java` contains the JavaPackage `Packages.java.awt`. For convenience, every Window object also has `java`, `sun`, and `netscape` properties that are shortcuts to `Packages.java`, `Packages.sun`, and `Packages.netscape`. Thus, instead of typing `Packages.java.awt`, you can simply use `java.awt`.

To continue with the example, `java.awt` is a JavaPackage object that contains JavaClass objects, such as `java.awt.Button`, which represents the *java.awt.Button* class. But it also contains yet another JavaPackage object, `java.awt.image`, which represents the *java.awt.image* package in Java.

As you can see, the property naming scheme for the JavaPackage hierarchy mirrors the naming scheme for Java packages. Note, however, that there is one big difference between the JavaPackage class and the actual Java packages that it represents. Packages in Java are collections of classes, not collections of other packages. That is, *java.lang* is the name of a Java package, but *java* is not. So the JavaPackage object named `java` does not actually represent a package in Java but is simply a convenient placeholder in the package hierarchy for other JavaPackage objects that do represent real Java packages.

On most systems, Java classes are installed in files in a directory hierarchy that corresponds to their package name. For example, the *java.lang.String* class is stored in the file *java/lang/String.class*. Actually, this file is usually contained in a ZIP file, but the directory hierarchy is still there, encoded within the archive. Therefore, instead of thinking of a JavaPackage object as representing a Java package, you may find it clearer to think of it as representing a directory or subdirectory in the directory hierarchy of Java classes.

There are a couple of shortcomings of the JavaPackage class. There is no way for LiveConnect to tell in advance whether a property of a JavaPackage refers to a Java class or to another Java package, so JavaScript assumes that it is a class and tries to load a class. Thus, when you use an expression like java.awt, LiveConnect first looks for a class file *java/awt.class*. It may even search for this class over the network, causing the web server to log a "404 File Not Found" error. If LiveConnect does not find a class, it assumes that the property refers to a package, but it has no way to ascertain that the package actually exists and has real classes in it. This causes the second shortcoming: if you misspell a class name, LiveConnect happily treats it as a package name, rather than telling you that the class you are trying to use does not exist.

20.2.2 The JavaClass Class

The JavaClass class is a JavaScript data type that represents a Java class. A Java-Class object does not have any properties of its own—all of its properties represent (and have the same name as) the public static fields and methods of the represented Java class. These public static fields and methods are sometimes called *class fields* and *class methods* to indicate that they are associated with a class rather than an object instance. Unlike the JavaPackage class, JavaClass does allow the use of the for/in loop to enumerate its properties. Note that JavaClass objects do not have properties representing the instance fields and methods of a Java class—individual instances of a Java class are represented by the JavaObject class, which is documented shortly.

As we saw above, JavaClass objects are contained in JavaPackage objects. For example, java.lang is a JavaPackage that contains a System property. Thus, java.lang.System is a JavaClass object, representing the Java class *java.lang.System*. This JavaClass object, in turn, has properties such as out and in that represent static fields of the *java.lang.System* class. You can use JavaScript to refer to any of the standard Java system classes in this same way. The *java.lang.Double* class is named java.lang.Double (or Packages.java.lang.Double), for example, and the *java.awt.Button* class is java.awt.Button.

Another way to obtain a JavaClass object in JavaScript is to use the getClass() function. Given any JavaObject object, you can obtain a JavaClass object that represents the class of that Java object by passing the JavaObject to getClass().*

Once you have a JavaClass object, there are several things you can do with it. The JavaClass class implements the LiveConnect functionality that allows JavaScript programs to read and write the public static fields of Java classes and invoke the

---

* Don't confuse the JavaScript getClass() function, which returns a JavaClass object, with the Java getClass() method, which returns a *java.lang.Class* object.

public static methods of Java classes. For example, `java.lang.System` is a Java-Class. We can read the value of a static field of `java.lang.System` like this:

```
var java_console = java.lang.System.out;
```

Similarly, we might invoke a static method of `java.lang.System` with a line like this one:

```
var java_version = java.lang.System.getProperty("java.version");
```

Recall that Java is a typed language—all fields and method arguments have types. If you attempt to set a field or pass an argument of the wrong type, you cause a JavaScript error.

There is one more important feature of the JavaClass class. You can use JavaClass objects with the JavaScript `new` operator to create new instances of Java classes—i.e., to create JavaObject objects. The syntax for doing so is just as it is in JavaScript (and just as it is in Java):

```
var d = new java.lang.Double(1.23);
```

Finally, having created a JavaObject in this way, we can return to the `getClass()` function and show an example of its use:

```
var d = new java.lang.Double(1.23);    // Create a JavaObject.
var d_class = getClass(d);             // Obtain the JavaClass of the JavaObject.
if (d_class == java.lang.Double) ...;  // This comparison will be true.
```

When working with standard system classes like this, you can typically use the name of the system class directly rather than calling `getClass()`. The function is more useful in obtaining the class of a non-system object, such as an applet instance.

Instead of referring to a JavaClass with a cumbersome expression like `java.lang.Double`, you can define a variable that serves as a shortcut:

```
var Double = java.lang.Double;
```

This mimics the Java `import` statement and can improve the efficiency of your program, since LiveConnect does not have to look up the `lang` property of `java` and the `Double` property of `java.lang`.

20.2.3 The JavaObject Class

The JavaObject class is a JavaScript data type that represents a Java object. The JavaObject class is, in many ways, analogous to the JavaClass class. As with Java-Class, a JavaObject has no properties of its own—all of its properties represent (and have the same names as) the public instance fields and public instance methods of the Java object it represents. As with JavaClass, you can use a JavaScript for/in loop to enumerate all the properties of a JavaObject object. The JavaObject class implements the LiveConnect functionality that allows us to read and write the public instance fields and invoke the public methods of a Java object.

For example, if d is a JavaObject that represents an instance of the *java.lang.Double* class, we can invoke a method of that Java object with JavaScript code like this:

```
n = d.doubleValue();
```

Similarly, we saw above that the *java.lang.System* class has a static field *out*. This field refers to a Java object of class *java.io.PrintStream*. In JavaScript, we can refer to the corresponding JavaObject as:

```
java.lang.System.out
```

and we can invoke a method of this object like this:*

```
java.lang.System.out.println("Hello world!");
```

A JavaObject object also allows us to read and write the public instance fields of the Java object it represents. Neither the *java.lang.Double* class nor the *java.io.PrintStream* class used in the preceding examples has any public instance fields, however. But suppose we use JavaScript to create an instance of the *java.awt.Rectangle* class:

```
r = new java.awt.Rectangle();
```

Then we can read and write its public instance fields with JavaScript code like the following:

```
r.x = r.y = 0;
r.width = 4;
r.height = 5;
var perimeter = 2*r.width + 2*r.height;
```

The beauty of LiveConnect is that it allows a Java object, r, to be used just as if it were a JavaScript object. Some caution is required, however: r is a JavaObject and does not behave identically to regular JavaScript objects. The differences will be detailed later. Also, remember that unlike JavaScript, the fields of Java objects and the arguments of its methods are typed. If you do not specify JavaScript values of the correct types, you cause JavaScript errors.

---

* The output of this line of code doesn't appear in the web browser itself, but in the Java Console. Select **Show Java Console** in the **Options** menu to make the console visible.

20.2.4 The JavaArray Class

The final LiveConnect data type for JavaScript is the JavaArray class. As you might expect by now, instances of this class represent Java arrays and provide the Live-Connect functionality that allows JavaScript to read the elements of Java arrays. Like JavaScript arrays (and like Java arrays), a JavaArray object has a `length` property that specifies the number of elements it contains. The elements of a JavaArray object are read with the standard JavaScript `[]` array index operator. They can also be enumerated with a `for/in` loop. You can use JavaArray objects to access multi-dimensional arrays (actually arrays of arrays), just as in JavaScript or Java.

For example, suppose we create an instance of the *java.awt.Polygon* class:

```
p = new java.awt.Polygon();
```

The JavaObject p has properties `xpoints` and `ypoints` that are JavaArray objects representing Java arrays of integers. (To learn the names and types of these properties, look up the documentation for *java.awt.Polygon* in a Java reference manual.) We can use these JavaArray objects to randomly initialize the Java polygon with code like this:

```
for(var i = 0; i < p.xpoints.length; i++)
    p.xpoints[i] = Math.round(Math.random()*100);
for(var i = 0; i < p.ypoints.length; i++)
    p.ypoints[i] = Math.round(Math.random()*100);
```

20.2.5 Java Methods

The JavaClass and JavaObject classes allow us to invoke static methods and instance methods, respectively. In Navigator 3, Java methods were internally represented by a JavaMethod object. In Navigator 4, however, Java methods are simply native methods, just as the methods of built-in JavaScript objects like String and Date are.

When using Java methods, remember that they expect a fixed number of arguments of fixed types. If you pass the wrong number of arguments, or an argument of the wrong type, you cause a JavaScript error.

There is one shortcoming in the way LiveConnect handles Java methods. There may be multiple Java methods with the same name but with different argument types. Because the mapping of JavaScript types to Java types is not exact, it is possible that multiple Java methods may match a JavaScript method invocation. For example, if you pass two JavaScript numbers to a method, these could match an argument list of two integers or an argument list of two doubles. When this sort of ambiguity occurs, LiveConnect simply picks the first method it encounters in the class file. Since there is no general way to tell which method this will be, the only real solution is to avoid this ambiguous situation altogether.

20.3 LiveConnect Data Conversion

Java is a strongly typed language with a relatively large number of data types, while JavaScript is an untyped language with a relatively small number of types. Because of this major structural difference between the two languages, one of the central responsibilities of LiveConnect is data conversion. When JavaScript sets a Java class or instance field or passes an argument to a Java method, a JavaScript value must be converted to an equivalent Java value, and when JavaScript reads a Java class or instance field or obtains the return value of a Java method, that Java value must be converted into a compatible JavaScript value.*

Figure 20-2 and Figure 20-3 illustrate how data conversion is performed when JavaScript writes Java values and when it reads them, respectively.

Notice the following points about the data conversions illustrated in Figure 20-2:

- Figure 20-2 does not show all possible conversions between JavaScript types and Java types. This is because JavaScript-to-JavaScript type conversions can occur before the JavaScript-to-Java conversion takes place. For example, if you pass a JavaScript number to a Java method that expects a *java.lang.String* argument, JavaScript first converts that number to a JavaScript string, which can then be converted to a Java string.

- A JavaScript number can be converted to any of the primitive Java numeric types. The actual conversion performed depends, of course, on the type of the Java field being set or method argument being passed. Note that you can lose precision doing this, for example, when you pass a large number to a Java field of type `short` or when you pass a floating-point value to a Java integral type.

- A JavaScript number can also be converted to an instance of the Java class *java.lang.Double* but not to an instance of a related class, such as *java.lang.Integer* or *java.lang.Float*.

- JavaScript does not have any representation for character data, so a JavaScript number may also be converted to the Java primitive `char` type.

---

* In addition, data conversion must also happen when Java reads or writes a JavaScript field or invokes a JavaScript method. These conversions are done differently, however, and are described later in the chapter when we discuss how to use JavaScript from Java. For now, we're only considering the data conversion that happens when JavaScript code interacts with Java, not the other way around.

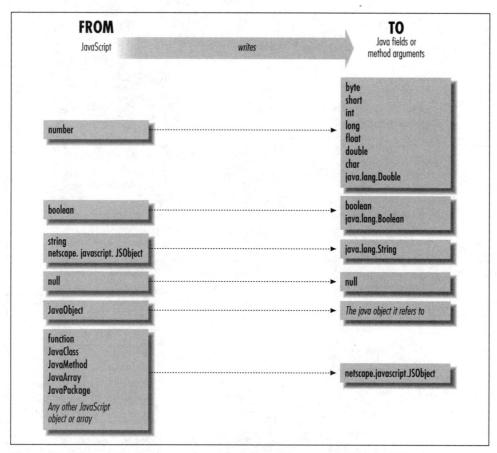

Figure 20-2: Data conversions performed when JavaScript writes Java values

- A JavaObject in JavaScript is "unwrapped" when passed to Java—it is converted to the Java object it represents. Note, however, that JavaClass objects in JavaScript are not converted to instances of *java.lang.Class*, as might be expected.

- JavaScript arrays are not converted to Java arrays.

Also notice these points about the conversions illustrated in Figure 20-3:

- Since JavaScript does not have a type for character data, the Java primitive char type is converted to a JavaScript number, not a string, as might be expected.

- A Java instance of *java.lang.Double, java.lang.Integer,* or a similar class is not converted to a JavaScript number. Like any Java object, it is converted to a JavaObject object in JavaScript.

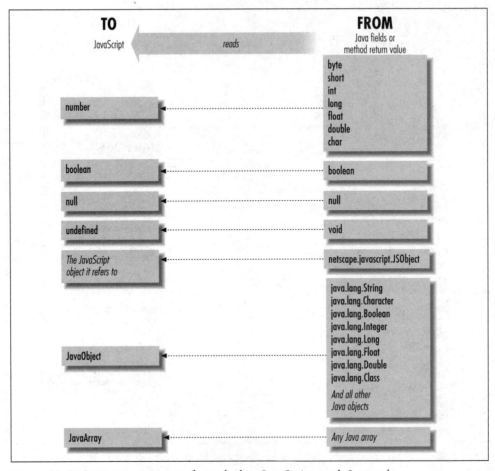

Figure 20–3: Data conversions performed when JavaScript reads Java values

- A Java string is an instance of *java.lang.String*, so like any other Java object, it is converted to a JavaObject object rather than to an actual JavaScript string.

- Any type of Java array is converted to a JavaArray object in JavaScript.

20.3.1 Wrapper Objects

Another important concept that you must grasp in order to fully understand Figure 20-2 and Figure 20-3 is the idea of "wrapper" objects. While conversions between most JavaScript and Java primitive types are possible, conversions between object types are not, in general, possible. This is why LiveConnect defines the JavaObject object in JavaScript—it represents a Java object that cannot be directly converted to a JavaScript object. In a sense, a JavaObject is a JavaScript wrapper around a Java object. When JavaScript reads a Java value (a field or the return value of a method), any Java objects are wrapped and JavaScript sees a JavaObject.

A similar thing happens when JavaScript writes a JavaScript object into a Java field or passes a JavaScript object to a Java method. There is no way to convert the JavaScript object to a Java object, so the object gets wrapped. The Java wrapper for a JavaScript object is the Java class *netscape.javascript.JSObject*.

Things get interesting when these wrapper objects are passed back. If JavaScript writes a JavaObject into a Java field or passes it to a Java method, LiveConnect first unwraps the object, converting the JavaObject back into the Java object that it represents. Similarly, if JavaScript reads a Java field or gets the return value of a Java method that is an instance of *netscape.javascript.JSObject*, that JSObject is also unwrapped to reveal and return the original JavaScript object.

20.3.2 LiveConnect Data Conversion in Navigator 3

In Navigator 3, there was a bug in the way that LiveConnect converted Java values to JavaScript values: the value of a primitive field of a Java object was incorrectly returned as a JavaScript object, rather than as a JavaScript primitive value. For example, if JavaScript read the value of a field of type int, LiveConnect in Navigator 3 converted that value to a Number object, rather than to a primitive numeric value. Similarly, LiveConnect converted the value of Java boolean fields to JavaScript Boolean objects, rather that primitive JavaScript boolean values. Note that this bug only occurred when querying the values of Java fields. It did not occur when LiveConnect converted the return value of a Java method.

Number and Boolean objects in JavaScript behave almost, but not exactly, the same as primitive number and boolean values. One important difference is that Number objects, like all JavaScript objects, use the + operator for string concatenation rather than addition. As a result, code like the following that uses LiveConnect in Navigator 3 can yield unexpected results:

```
var r = new java.awt.Rectangle(0,0,5,5);
var w = r.width;        // This is a Number object, not a primitive number.
var new_w = w + 1;      // Oops! new_w is now "51", not 6, as expected.
```

To work around this problem, you can explicitly call the valueOf() method to convert a Number object to its corresponding numeric value. For example:

```
var r = new java.awt.Rectangle(0,0,5,5);
var w = r.width.valueOf(); // Now we've got a primitive number.
var new_w = w + 1;         // This time, new_w is 6, as desired.
```

20.4 *JavaScript Conversion of JavaObjects*

Having worked your way through the previous dense data conversion section, you may be hoping that are done with the topic of data conversion. Unfortunately, there is more to be discussed on the topic of how JavaScript converts JavaObject objects to various JavaScript primitive types. Notice in Figure 20-3 that quite a few Java data types, including Java strings (instances of *java.lang.String*), are converted to JavaObject objects in JavaScript rather than being converted to actual JavaScript primitive types, such as strings. This means that when you use LiveConnect, you'll often be working with JavaObject objects.

Refer back to Table 11-1, which shows how various JavaScript data types are converted when used in various contexts. For example, when a number is used in a string context, it is converted to a string, and when an object is used in a boolean context, it is converted to the value `false` if it is `null` and `true` otherwise. These conversion rules don't apply to JavaObject objects, which are converted using their own rules as follows:

* When a JavaObject is used in a numeric context, it is converted to a number by invoking the `doubleValue()` method of the Java object it represents. If the Java object does not define this method, a JavaScript error occurs.

* When a JavaObject is used in a boolean context, it is converted to a boolean value by invoking the `booleanValue()` method of the Java object it represents. If the Java object does not define this method, a JavaScript error occurs.

* When a JavaObject is used in a string context, it is converted to a string value by invoking the `toString()` method of the Java object it represents. All Java objects define or inherit this method, so this conversion always succeeds.

* When a JavaObject is used in an object context, no conversion is necessary, since it is already a JavaScript object.

Because of these different conversion rules, and for other reasons as well, JavaObject objects behave differently than other JavaScript objects and there are some common pitfalls that you need to beware of. First, it is not uncommon to work with a JavaObject that represents an instance of a *java.lang.Double* or some other numeric object. In many ways, such a JavaObject behaves like a primitive number value, but be careful when using the + operator. When you use a JavaObject (or any JavaScript object) with +, you are specifying a string context, so the object is converted to a string for string concatenation instead of being converted to a number for addition.

When you want to explicitly convert a JavaScript object to a primitive value, you usually call its `valueOf()` method. Note that this does not work with JavaObject objects. As we discussed earlier, the JavaObject class defines no properties of its own; all of its properties represent fields and methods of the Java object it represents. This means that JavaObject objects don't support common JavaScript methods, such as `valueOf()`. In the case of our JavaObject-wrapped *java.lang.Double* object, you should call the Java `doubleValue()` method when you need to force the object into a primitive value.

Another difference between JavaObject objects and other JavaScript data types is that JavaObjects can only be used in a boolean context if they define a `boolean-Value()` method. Suppose `button` is a JavaScript variable that may contain `null` or may hold a JavaObject that represents an instance of the *java.awt.Button* class. If you want to check whether the variable contains `null`, you might write code like this, out of habit:

```
if (!button) { ... }
```

If `button` is `null`, this works fine. But if `button` actually contains a JavaObject representing a *java.awt.Button* instance, LiveConnect tries to invoke the `boolean-Value()` method. When it discovers that the *java.awt.Button* class doesn't define one, it causes a JavaScript error. The workaround in this case is to be explicit about what you are testing for, to avoid using the JavaObject in a boolean context:

```
if (button != null) { ... }
```

This is a good habit to get into, in any case, since it makes your code easier to read and understand.

20.5 Scripting Java with JavaScript

Now that we've discussed the JavaScript data types used by LiveConnect and the data conversions that go on when JavaScript reads and writes Java data values, we can begin to discuss some of the practical applications of LiveConnect. Bear in mind while reading this section that we have still only discussed half of LiveConnect—the half that allows JavaScript to work with Java. The portions of LiveConnect that allow a Java applet to use JavaScript are documented later.

20.5.1 Interacting with Applets

As we saw in Chapter 14, the Document object has an `applets[]` property—an array that contains one JavaObject object for each Java applet in the document. Each JavaObject object in this array represents the Java object of an applet, which is always an instance of some subclass of *java.applet.Applet*. Because LiveConnect exposes the Java object for each applet on a web page, you can freely read and write public fields of the applet and invoke public methods of the applet. Although Internet Explorer doesn't support LiveConnect, its ActiveX scripting technology allows you to read and write applet properties and invoke applet methods.

Example 20-1 shows some simple HTML that embeds an applet in a web page and includes buttons that start and stop the applet by using LiveConnect to invoke the applet's start() and stop() methods.

Example 20-1: Controlling an Applet with JavaScript

```
<!-- Here's the applet. -->
<APPLET NAME="animation" CODE="Animation.class" WIDTH=500 HEIGHT=200>
</APPLET>

<!-- And here are the buttons that start and stop it. -->
<FORM>
<INPUT TYPE=button VALUE="Start" onclick="document.animation.start()">
<INPUT TYPE=button VALUE="Stop" onclick="document.animation.stop()">
</FORM>
```

There are a couple of points to note about this example. First, the <APPLET> tag is given a NAME attribute; the value of that attribute becomes the name of a property in the document object. We've seen this technique before with the <FORM> and <IMG> tags; in this case it allows us to refer to an applet by name, such as docu-ment.animation, instead of by a number, such as document.applets[0].

The second point to note about this example is that it calls the start() and stop() methods of the applet. These are standard methods that all applets define; they are the methods that the browser itself calls to start and stop the applet. But you needn't limit yourself to calling the standard methods of the Java *Applet* class. If your applet defines methods of its own, you can call any of these as well.* If you were working with a full-featured animation applet, for example, you might define an HTML form to serve as a complete control panel for the animation, with **Fast-Forward** and **Rewind** buttons, an input field for specifying speed, and so on. The buttons in this control panel could then control the applet by invoking spe-cial-purpose methods, such as fast_forward(), provided by the applet.

It is also possible to write passive applets that take no action on their own but exist simply to serve your JavaScript code. An applet might define various utility functions for popping up dialog boxes that are more complex than those provided by the alert(), confirm(), and prompt() methods, for example.

---

* In fact, it is safer and more portable to call your own custom methods than to call the ones that are intended to be called by the browser.

20.5.2 Working with Plugins

Just as the `applets[]` array of the Document object contains JavaObjects that represent the applets embedded in a document with the `<APPLET>` tag, the `embeds[]` array of the Document object contains JavaObjects that represent data embedded in a web page with the `<EMBED>` tag. This is data that is meant to be displayed by a Navigator plugin.

Internet Explorer uses ActiveX controls to display embedded data and allows JavaScript programs to interact with these components through its ActiveX scripting technology. Although the underlying technology is very different from Live-Connect, the end results can be very similar. In fact, if a plugin for Navigator and an ActiveX control for Internet Explorer define the same API, the JavaScript code to interact with each of them may be the same, even though the interaction occurs through different mechanisms.

The JavaObject objects in the `embeds[]` array are all instances of some subclass of the *netscape.plugin.Plugin* class. Each Java-enabled plugin defines its own subclass of *netscape.plugin.Plugin* and creates an instance of that subclass for each piece of embedded data (each `<EMBED>` tag) that it displays. The purpose of a *netscape.plugin.Plugin* subclass is to define an API through which a Java applet or a JavaScript program can control the behavior of the plugin.

Because the objects in the `embeds[]` array are provided by plugins, the properties and methods of these objects depend on the particular plugins in use. In general, you'll have to read the vendor's documentation for any given plugin to determine how to control it through LiveConnect. If the plugin that is displaying the data is not Java-enabled, the corresponding entry in the `embeds[]` array contains a dummy JavaObject with no functionality.

Example 20-2 shows how you might use the LiveAudio plugin (bundled with Navigator 3 on most platforms) and LiveConnect to play a sound automatically when the user clicks a button or when the mouse passes over a hyperlink. The example relies upon the `play()` method of the *netscape.plugin.Plugin* instance provided by the LiveAudio plugin. This method and many others are detailed in the Live-Audio documentation.

Example 20-2: Controlling a Plugin from JavaScript

```
<!-- Here we embed some sounds in the browser, with attributes to -->
<!-- specify that they won't be played when first loaded. In this -->
<!-- example, we use sounds found locally on Windows 95 platforms. -->
<EMBED SRC="file:///C|/windows/media/Tada.wav" HIDDEN=true AUTOSTART=false>
<EMBED SRC="file:///C|/windows/media/Ding.wav" HIDDEN=true AUTOSTART=false>
<EMBED SRC="file:///C|/windows/media/The Microsoft Sound.wav"
       HIDDEN=true AUTOSTART=false>
```

Example 20-2: Controlling a Plugin from JavaScript (continued)

```
<!-- Here are some buttons that play those sounds. Note the use of the -->
<!-- embeds[] array and the play() method invoked through LiveConnect. -->
<FORM>
<INPUT TYPE=button VALUE="Play Sound #1" onClick="document.embeds[0].play()">
<INPUT TYPE=button VALUE="Play Sound #2" onClick="document.embeds[1].play()">
<INPUT TYPE=button VALUE="Play Sound #3" onClick="document.embeds[2].play()">
</FORM>


<!-- Here's a hypertext link that plays a sound when the user passes over. -->
<A HREF="" onMouseOver="document.embeds[0].play()">Click Me</A>
```

Although the objects in the embeds[] array are all instances of subclasses of *netscape.plugin.Plugin*, there is one method that all subclasses share. The isActive() method returns true if the specified Plugin object is still active and false if it is not. Generally, a plugin only becomes inactive if it is on a page that is no longer displayed. This situation can only arise when you store references to the embeds[] array of one window in JavaScript variables of another window.

20.5.3 Using the Java System Classes

All of the LiveConnect examples presented so far have made use of Java classes from the standard Sun Java libraries. There are not a whole lot of interesting things you can do with an instance of *java.lang.Double*, but we have seen some interesting uses of the *java.lang.System* class, for example.

LiveConnect gives us the capability to create new instances of Java classes, to set and query fields of classes and their instances, and to invoke methods of classes or instances. Using these capabilities, there are some interesting things we can do with the built-in, or system classes that are installed with Navigator. For example, as we'll see in Chapter 21, *JavaScript Security*, the new security model in Navigator 4 requires a signed script to invoke a Java method to request enhanced privileges that are not granted to unsigned scripts.

Note that the features described in this section have no analog in Internet Explorer. Although IE allows JavaScript programs to interact with applets, it only allows access to the one applet object, not to all of the Java system classes. Note, however, that if you need to use specific system classes, you can define special-purpose applet methods that perform the operations you need. By defining enough custom applet methods, you can simulate in IE most of the LiveConnect functionality available in Navigator.

LiveConnect does not give complete and unrestricted access to the Java system; in other words, there are some things we cannot do with LiveConnect. For example, LiveConnect does not give us the capability to define new Java classes or sub-classes from within JavaScript, nor does it give us the ability to create Java arrays.* In addition to these limitations, access to the standard Java classes is restricted for security reasons. An untrusted JavaScript program cannot use the *java.io.File* class, for example, because that would give it the power to read, write, and delete files on the host system—exactly the capabilities needed for creating Internet "viruses." Untrusted JavaScript code can only use Java in the ways that untrusted applets can. As we'll see in Chapter 21, however, users may decide to trust JavaScript code that has been digitally signed. Such signed JavaScript code may request special privileges that enable it to use classes such as *java.io.File.*

Example 20-3 shows JavaScript code that uses standard Java classes (the JavaScript code looks almost identical to Java code, in fact) to pop up a window and display some text. The result is shown in Figure 20-4.

Example 20-3: Scripting the Built-in Java Classes

```
var f = new java.awt.Frame("Hello World");
var ta = new java.awt.TextArea("hello, world", 5, 20);
f.add("Center", ta);
f.pack();
f.show();
```

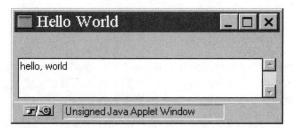

Figure 20-4: A Java window created from JavaScript

The code in Example 20-3 creates a very simple Java user interface. What is missing, however, is any form of event handling or user interaction. A program like the one shown here is restricted to doing output, since it doesn't include any way for JavaScript to be notified when the user interacts with the Java window.

It is possible, though complicated, to use JavaScript to define a Java user interface that responds to events. In Java 1.1 and later, notification of an event is performed by invoking a method of an *EventListener* object. As we'll see later in this chapter,

---

* JavaScript programs can create arrays indirectly using the Java 1.1 method `java.lang.reflect.Array.newInstance()`.

LiveConnect allows Java applets to execute arbitrary strings of JavaScript code. Therefore, it is possible to define a Java class that implements the appropriate *EventListener* interface and invokes a specified string of JavaScript code when it is notified that an event has occurred. If you create an applet with a method that allows you to create such *EventListener* objects, you can use JavaScript to piece together Java GUIs that include event handlers defined in JavaScript.

20.6 Using JavaScript from Java

Having explored how to control Java from JavaScript code, we now turn to the opposite problem: how to control JavaScript from Java code. This control is accomplished primarily through the *netscape.javascript.JSObject* class. Just as a JavaObject object is a JavaScript wrapper around a Java object, a JSObject object is a Java wrapper around a JavaScript object. Note that the features described here are available only in Navigator 3 and later. There is no comparable technology available in Internet Explorer.

20.6.1 The JSObject Class

All Java interactions with JavaScript are handled through an instance of the *netscape.javascript.JSObject* class. An instance of this class is a wrapper around a single JavaScript object. The class defines methods that allow you to read and write property values and array elements of the JavaScript object and to invoke methods of the object. Here is a synopsis of this class:

```
public final class JSObject extends Object {
    // Static method to obtain initial JSObject for applet's browser window
    public static JSObject getWindow(java.applet.Applet applet);
    public Object getMember(String name);            // Read object property.
    public Object getSlot(int index);                // Read array element.
    public void setMember(String name, Object value); // Set object property.
    public void setSlot(int index, Object value);     // Set array element.
    public void removeMember(String name);           // Delete property.
    public Object call(String methodName, Object args[]); // Invoke method.
    public Object eval(String s);                     // Evaluate string.
    public String toString();                         // Convert to string.
    protected void finalize();
}
```

Because all JavaScript objects appear in a hierarchy rooted in the current browser window, JSObject objects must also appear in a hierarchy. For a Java applet to interact with any JavaScript objects, it must first obtain a JSObject that represents the browser window (or frame) in which the applet appears. The JSObject class does not define a constructor method, so we cannot simply create an appropriate JSObject. Instead, we must call the static getWindow() method. When passed a reference to an applet, this method returns a JSObject that represents the browser window that contains the applet. Thus, every applet that interacts with JavaScript includes a line that looks something like this:

```
JSObject jsroot = JSObject.getWindow(this);  // "this" is the applet itself.
```

Having obtained a JSObject that refers to the root window of the JavaScript object hierarchy, you can use instance methods of the JSObject to read the values of properties of the JavaScript object that it represents. Most of these properties have values that are themselves JavaScript objects, so you can continue the process and read their properties as well. The JSObject `getMember()` method returns the value of a named property, while the `getSlot()` method returns the value of a numbered array element of the specified JavaScript object. You might use these methods as follows:

```
import netscape.javascript.JSObject;  // This must be at the top of the file.
    ...
JSObject jsroot = JSObject.getWindow(this);                 // self
JSObject document = (JSObject) jsroot.getMember("document"); // .document
JSObject applets = (JSObject) document.getMember("applets"); //    .applets
Applet applet0 = (Applet) applets.getSlot(0);               //       [0]
```

Note two things about this code fragment. First, `getMember()` and `getSlot()` both return a value of type Object, which generally must be cast to some more specific value, such as a JSObject. Second, the value read from slot 0 of the `applets` array can be cast to an Applet, rather than a JSObject. This is because the elements of the JavaScript `applets[]` array are JavaObject objects that represent Java Applet objects. When Java reads a JavaScript JavaObject, it unwraps that object and returns the Java object (in this case an Applet) that it contains. The data conversion that occurs through the JSObject interface is documented later in this section.

The JSObject class also supports methods for setting properties and array elements of JavaScript objects. `setMember()` and `setSlot()` are analogous to the `getMember()` and `getSlot()` methods. These methods set the value of a named property or a numbered array element to a specified value. Note, however, that the value to be set must be a Java object. This means that you can set JavaScript properties to values of types such as Applet, String, and JSObject, but you cannot set them to `boolean`, `int`, or `double` values. Instead of setting properties or array elements to primitive Java values, you must use corresponding Java classes, such as *Boolean*, *Integer*, and *Double*. Finally, the `removeMember()` method allows you to delete the value of a named property from a JavaScript object.

Besides reading and writing properties and array elements from JavaScript objects, the JSObject class also allows you to invoke methods of JavaScript objects. The JSObject `call()` method invokes a named method of the specified JavaScript

object and passes a specified array of Java objects as arguments to that method. As
we saw when setting JavaScript properties, it is not possible to pass primitive Java
values as arguments to a JavaScript method; instead you must use the corresponding Java object types. For example, you might use the `call()` method in Java
code like the following to open a new browser window:

```
public JSObject newwin(String url, String window_name)
{
    Object[] args = { url, window_name };
    JSObject win = JSObject.getWindow(this);
    return (JSObject) win.call("open", args);
}
```

The JSObject class has one more important method: `eval()`. This Java method
works just like the JavaScript function of the same name—it executes a string that
contains JavaScript code. You'll find that using `eval()` is often much easier than
using the various other methods of the JSObject class. Since all the code is passed
as a string, you can use string representations of the data types you want—you do
not have to convert Java primitive types to their corresponding object types. For
example, compare the following two lines of code that set properties of the main
browser window:

```
jsroot.setMember("i", new Integer(0));
jsroot.eval("self.i = 0");
```

The second line is obviously easier to understand. As another example, consider
the following use of `eval()` to write a particular frame being displayed in the
browser window:

```
JSObject jsroot = JSObject.getWindow(this);
jsroot.eval("parent.frames[1].document.write('Hello from Java!')");
```

To do the equivalent without the `eval()` method is a lot harder:

```
JSObject jsroot = JSObject.getWindow(this);
JSObject parent = (JSObject) jsroot.getMember("parent");
JSObject frames = (JSObject) parent.getMember("frames");
JSObject frame1 = (JSObject) frames.getSlot(1);
JSObject document = (JSObject) frame1.getMember("document");
Object[] args = { "Hello from Java!" };
document.call("write", args);
```

20.6.2 Using JSObjects in Applets

Example 20-4 shows the `init()` method of an applet that uses LiveConnect to
interact with JavaScript.

Example 20–4: Using JavaScript from an Applet Method

```
import netscape.javascript.*

public void init()
{
    // Get the JSObject representing the applet's browser window.
    JSObject win = JSObject.getWindow(this);

    // Run JavaScript with eval(). Careful with those nested quotes!
    win.eval("alert('The CPUHog applet is now running on your computer. " +
            "You may find that your system slows down a bit.');");
}
```

In order to use any applet, you must compile it and then embed it in an HTML file. When the applet interacts with JavaScript, special instructions are required for both of these steps.

20.6.2.1 Compiling applets that use the JSObject class

Any applet that interacts with JavaScript uses the *netscape.javascript.JSObject* class. To compile such an applet, therefore, your Java compiler must know where to find a definition of this class. Because the class is defined and shipped by Netscape and not by Sun, the *javac* compiler from Sun does not know about it. This section explains how to enable your compiler to find this required class. If you are not using the JDK™ from Sun, you may have to do something a little different—see the documentation from the vendor of your Java compiler or Java development environment.

To tell the JDK compiler where to find classes, you set the CLASSPATH environment variable. This environment variable specifies a list of directories and ZIP files that the compiler should search for class definitions (in addition to its standard directory of system classes). Navigator 4 stores its class definitions in a file named *java40.jar*.* The exact location of this file depends on the platform you are using and on how and where you installed the browser files. On a Unix system, the full path to this file depends on where you installed Navigator, but is typically something like this:

```
/usr/local/netscape/java/classes/java40.jar
```

On a Windows 95 system, the path also depends on where you chose to install Navigator, but it is usually something like this:

```
C:\Program Files\Netscape\Communicator\Program\Java\Classes\java40.jar
```

You may have to search a bit to locate this file on your system.

---

* In Navigator 3, this file was called *java_30* or some variation, such as *java_301*.

The *java40.jar* file, wherever it is located, is a ZIP file of all the Java classes Navigator needs. The *javac* compiler can extract classes from ZIP files, so you can tell the compiler where to find the *netscape.javascript.JSObject* class just by telling it where the ZIP file is. For a Unix system, set a path like this:

```
setenv CLASSPATH .:/usr/local/lib/netscape/java40
```

And for a Windows 95 system, set a path like this:

```
set CLASSPATH=.;C:\Program Files\Netscape\Communicator\Program\Java\Classes\Java40
```

20.6.2.2 *The MAYSCRIPT attribute*

There is an additional requirement for running an applet that interacts with JavaScript. As a security precaution, an applet is not allowed to use JavaScript unless the web page author (who may not be the applet author) explicitly gives the applet permission to do so. To give this permission, you must include the new MAYSCRIPT attribute in the applet's <APPLET> tag in the HTML file.

Example 20-4 showed a fragment of an applet that used JavaScript to display an alert dialog box. Once you have successfully compiled this applet, you might include it in an HTML file as follows:

```
<APPLET code="CPUHog.class" width=300 height=300 MAYSCRIPT></APPLET>
```

If you do not remember to include the MAYSCRIPT tag, the applet is not allowed to use the JSObject class.

20.6.2.3 *A complete example*

Example 20-5 shows a complete example of a Java class that uses LiveConnect and the JSObject class to communicate with JavaScript. The class is a subclass of *java.io.OutputStream*; it is used to allow a Java applet to write HTML text into a newly created web browser window. An applet might want to do this because it provides a way to display formatted text, which is difficult to do with Java itself.

Example 20–5: An OutputStream for Displaying HTML in a Browser Window

```
import netscape.javascript.JSObject;    // These are the classes we'll use.
import java.applet.Applet;
import java.io.OutputStream;

// An output stream that sends HTML text to a newly created web browser window.
public class HTMLOutputStream extends OutputStream
{
    JSObject main_window;       // The initial browser window
    JSObject window;            // The new window we create
    JSObject document;          // The document of that new window
    static int window_num = 0;  // Used to give each new window a unique name
```

Example 20–5: An OutputStream for Displaying HTML in a Browser Window *(continued)*

```
    // To create a new HTMLOutputStream, you must specify the applet that
    // will use it (this specifies a browser window) and the desired size
    // for the new window.
    public HTMLOutputStream(Applet applet, int width, int height)
    {
        // Get main browser window from the applet with JSObject.getWindow().
        main_window = JSObject.getWindow(applet);
        // Use JSObject.eval() to create a new window.
        window = (JSObject)
            main_window.eval("self.open('','" +
                            "'HTMLOutputStream" + window_num++ + "','" +
                            "'menubar,status,resizable,scrollbars," +
                            "width=" + width + ",height=" + height + "')");
        // Use JSObject.getMember() to get the document of this new window.
        document = (JSObject) window.getMember("document");
        // Then use JSObject.call() to open this document.
        document.call("open", null);
    }


    // This is the write() method required for all OutputStream subclasses.
    public void write(byte[] chars, int offset, int length)
    {
        // Create a string from the specified bytes.
        String s = new String(chars, 0, offset, length);
        // Store the string in an array for use with JSObject.call().
        Object[] args = { s };
        // Check to see if the window has been closed.
        boolean closed = ((Boolean)window.getMember("closed")).booleanValue();
        // If not, use JSObject.call() to invoke document.write().
        if (!closed) document.call("write", args);
    }
    // Here are two variants on the above method, also required.
    public void write(byte[] chars) { write(chars, 0, chars.length); }
    public void write(int c) { byte[] chars = {(byte)c}; write(chars, 0, 1); }


    // When the stream is closed, use JSObject.call() to call Document.close.
    public void close() { document.call("close", null); }


    // This method is unique to HTMLOutputStream. If the new window is
    // still open, use JSObject.call() to invoke Window.close() to close it.
    public void close_window()
    {
        boolean closed = ((Boolean)window.getMember("closed")).booleanValue();
        if (!closed) window.call("close", null);
    }
}
```

20.6.3 *Data Conversion*

At the beginning of this chapter, we discussed the rules by which values are converted when JavaScript reads and writes Java fields and invokes Java methods. Those rules explained how the JavaScript JavaObject, JavaArray, and JavaClass objects convert data; they apply only to the case of JavaScript manipulating Java. When Java manipulates JavaScript, the conversion is performed by the Java JSObject class and the conversion rules are different. Figure 20-5 and Figure 20-6 illustrate these conversions.

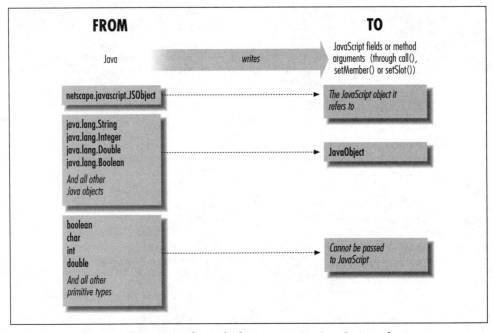

Figure 20-5: Data conversions performed when Java writes JavaScript values

The point to remember when studying these figures is that Java can only interact with JavaScript through the API provided by the JSObject class. Because Java is a strongly typed language, the methods defined by this class can only work with Java objects, not primitive values. For example, when you read the value of a JavaScript number, the `getMember()` method returns a *java.lang.Double* object, rather than a primitive `double` value.

When writing JavaScript functions that are invoked from Java, bear in mind that the arguments passed by Java are either JavaScript objects from unwrapped Java JSObjects or JavaObjects. LiveConnect simply does not allow Java to pass primitive values as method arguments. As we saw earlier in this chapter, JavaObject objects behave somewhat differently than other objects. For example, an instance of

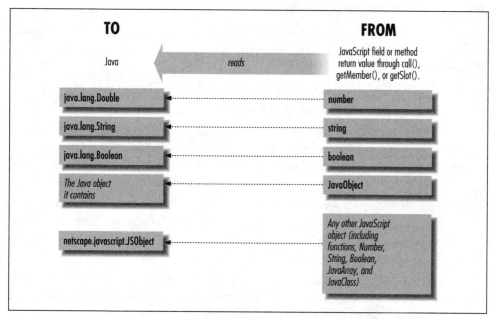

Figure 20–6: Data conversions performed when Java reads JavaScript values

java.lang.Double behaves differently than a primitive JavaScript number or even a JavaScript Number object. The same caution applies when you are working with JavaScript properties that have their values set by Java.

One way to avoid the whole issue of data conversion is to use the `eval()` method of the JSObject class whenever your Java code wants to communicate with JavaScript. In order to do this, your Java code must convert all method arguments or property values to string form. Then, the string to be evaluated can be passed unchanged to JavaScript, which can convert the string form of the data to the appropriate JavaScript data values.

20.7 Summary

LiveConnect allows JavaScript and Java to cooperate through two fairly separate and symmetrical systems. In JavaScript, the JavaPackage, JavaClass, JavaObject, and JavaArray objects all allow JavaScript to read and write Java properties and arrays and to invoke Java methods. In Java, the *netscape.javascript.JSObject* class allows a Java program to read and write properties of JavaScript objects and elements of JavaScript arrays, to invoke JavaScript functions, and to evaluate strings of JavaScript code. The following two sections summarize these two halves of LiveConnect.

20.7.1 JavaScript to Java

- The JavaClass, JavaObject, and JavaArray objects allow transparent communication between JavaScript and Java—they handle data conversion and all the tricky behind-the-scenes work.

- The data conversions performed when JavaScript reads and writes Java values are illustrated in Figure 20-2 and Figure 20-3.

- Most Java objects are converted to JavaScript JavaObject objects. JavaObject objects behave differently than other JavaScript objects and need to be handled with care. In particular, JavaObject objects are converted to numeric, boolean, and string values differently than other JavaScript objects are.

- You can use the JavaPackage objects referred to by the Window properties `Packages`, `java`, `sun`, and `netscape` to obtain a JavaClass object for any of the standard classes built in to Navigator. The JavaClass object allows you to read and write static properties and invoke static methods of a class.

- You can use the `new` operator on a JavaClass object to create a new Java object and a JavaScript JavaObject wrapper for it. You can use this JavaObject to read and write instance fields and invoke instance methods.

- The `getClass()` function allows you to obtain a JavaClass object that corresponds to the Java class of a JavaObject object.

- You can use the `document.applets[]` array and the JavaObject objects it contains to interact with applets. Manipulating the fields and methods of a custom applet allows a richer set of possibilities than simply scripting with the basic Java classes.

- The `document.embeds[]` array and the JavaObject objects it contains allow you to interact with the plugins that display embedded data in the document. You can control plugins through vendor-specific Java APIs.

- You can script Java directly from JavaScript simply by working with the predefined classes. It is possible but difficult to define Java event handlers that execute specified JavaScript code when triggered.

20.7.2 Java to JavaScript

- The *netscape.javascript.JSObject* class is the Java equivalent of the JavaScript JavaObject class. It handles data conversion and all the behind-the-scenes work to allow Java code to communicate with JavaScript.

- The data conversions performed when Java reads and writes JavaScript data are illustrated in Figure 20-5 and Figure 20-6.

- The getMember() and getSlot() methods of JSObject allow Java to read JavaScript object properties and array elements.

- The setMember() and setSlot() methods allow Java to set values of JavaScript object properties and array elements.

- The call() method of JSObject allows Java to invoke JavaScript functions.

- The eval() method of JSObject allows Java to pass an arbitrary string of JavaScript code to the JavaScript interpreter for execution. This method is often easier to use than the other JSObject methods.

- An applet that uses the JSObject class must import it with an import statement. To compile the applet, the CLASSPATH environment variable must be set to include the Java classes supplied by Netscape.

- To interact with JavaScript, an applet must be embedded in an HTML document with an <APPLET> tag that includes the MAYSCRIPT attribute.

21

JavaScript Security

Because of the wide-open nature of the Internet, security is an important issue. This is particularly true with the introduction of languages like Java and JavaScript because they allow executable content to be embedded in otherwise static web pages. Since loading a web page can cause arbitrary code to be executed on your computer, stringent security precautions are required to prevent malicious code from doing any damage to your data or your privacy. This chapter discusses Internet security issues related to JavaScript. Note that this chapter does *not* cover any of the many other issues involved in web security, such as the authentication and cryptographic technologies used to keep the contents of web documents and HTML forms private while they traverse the Web.

21.1 JavaScript and Security

JavaScript's first line of defense against malicious code is that the language simply doesn't support certain capabilities. For example, client-side JavaScript does not provide any way to write or delete files or directories on the client computer. With no File object and no file access functions, a JavaScript program cannot delete a user's data or plant viruses on the user's system.

Similarly, client-side JavaScript has no networking primitives of any type. A JavaScript program can load URLs and send HTML form data to web servers, CGI scripts, and email addresses, but it cannot establish a direct connection to any other hosts on the network. This means, for example, that a JavaScript program cannot use a client's machine as an attack platform from which to attempt to crack passwords on another machine. (This would be a particularly dangerous possibility if the JavaScript program had been loaded from the Internet through a firewall and could then attempt to break into the intranet protected by the firewall.)

While this intentional lack of features in client-side JavaScript provides a basic level of security against the most egregious attacks, other security issues remain. These are primarily privacy issues—JavaScript programs must not be allowed to export information about the user of a browser when that information is supposed to be private.

When you browse the Web, one of the pieces of information you are by default consenting to release about yourself is the web browser that you use. As a standard part of the HTTP protocol, a string identifying your browser, version, and vendor is sent with every request for a web page. This information is public, as is the IP address of your Internet connection, for example. Other information, however, should not be public: this includes your email address, which should not be released unless you choose to do so by sending an email message or authorizing an automated email message to be sent under your name.

Similarly, your browsing history (the record of which sites you've already visited) and the contents of your bookmarks list should remain private. Your browsing history and bookmarks say a lot about your interests; this is information that direct marketers and others pay good money for so that they can target sales pitches to you more effectively . You can be sure that if a web browser or JavaScript allowed this valuable private information to be stolen, someone would be stealing it every time you visited their site, and it would be on the market only nanoseconds later. Most web users would be uncomfortable knowing that any site they visited could find out that they were cat fanciers, for example, who were also interested in women's footwear and the Sierra Club.

Even assuming that we have no embarrassing fetishes to hide, there are plenty of good reasons to be concerned about data privacy. One such reason is a pragmatic concern about receiving electronic junk mail ("spam") and the like. Another is a very legitimate concern about keeping secrets. We don't want a JavaScript program loaded from the Internet and running in one web browser window to be able to start examining the contents of other browser windows that contain pages loaded from the company intranet behind the firewall.

When web pages contain only static HTML, Navigator, Internet Explorer, and other browsers already have the ability to establish secure communication channels on the Web, so that the information transferred back and forth between web server and web client remains private. But by turning static HTML into dynamic programs, JavaScript opens the door to unethical web pages that steal private information and send it (through secure or insecure channels) back to the web server. The remainder of this chapter explains how JavaScript defends itself against such abuses.

21.2 *Restricted or Privileged Features*

As I've already mentioned, the first line of defense against malicious scripts in client-side JavaScript is that the language simply omits certain capabilities. The second line of defense is that JavaScript imposes restrictions on certain features that it does support. For example, client-side JavaScript supports a `close()` method for the Window object, but it restricts this method so that a script can only close a window that was opened by a script from the same web server. In particular, a script cannot close a window that the user opened; if it tries to do so, the user is presented with a confirmation box asking if he really wants to close the window.

As we'll see later in the chapter, this `close()` restriction, and the other restrictions described below, are not hard-and-fast rules. Instead, it can be helpful to think of them as "privileged features." If a script has been granted an appropriate privilege, it can close a browser window without user confirmation, for example.

The following is a list of the security restrictions, or privileged features, in client-side JavaScript. For each restricted feature, the name of the privilege is listed as well. We'll see how a script can request these privileges later in the chapter:

- The array elements and properties of the History object cannot be read without the `UniversalBrowserRead` privilege. The array elements and properties contain a record of URLs that the browser has previously visited, which is private information.

- The `value` property of the FileUpload object cannot be set without the `UniversalFileRead` privilege. If this property could be set, an unprivileged script could set it to any desired filename and cause the form to upload the contents of any specified file (such as a password file) to the server.

- A script cannot submit a form (using the `submit()` method of the Form object, for example) to a `mailto:` or `news:` URL without the `UniversalSendMail` privilege or the user's explicit approval through a confirmation dialog. Such a form submission would contain the user's email address, which should not be made public without the user's permission.

- A JavaScript program cannot close a browser window without user confirmation unless it opened the window itself or it has the `UniversalBrowserWrite` privilege. This prevents malicious scripts from calling `self.close()` to close the user's browsing window, thereby causing the program to exit.

- A script without the `UniversalBrowserWrite` privilege cannot open a window that is smaller than 100 pixels on a side or cause a window to be resized to smaller than 100 pixels on a side. Similarly, such an unprivileged script cannot move a window off the screen, create a window that is larger than the screen, or create a window without a titlebar. This prevents scripts from opening windows that the user cannot see or could easily overlook; such windows could contain scripts that keep running after the user thinks they have stopped.

- A script cannot hide or show the menubar, status line, scrollbars, toolbar, location bar, directory bar, or personal bar of the browser without the `Universal-BrowserWrite` privilege. This prevents scripts from making annoying changes to the user's display preferences.

- Causing a window to display an `about:` URL, such as `about:cache`, requires the `UniversalBrowserRead` privilege. These URLs can expose system information, such as the contents of the browser's cache.

- A script cannot set any of the properties of an Event object without the `UniversalBrowserWrite` privilege. This prevents unprivileged scripts from spoofing events.

- The `UniversalBrowserWrite` privilege is required for a script to capture events that occur in documents or layers loaded from different sources than the script. This prevents unprivileged scripts from snooping on the user's input (such as the keystrokes that constitute a password entry) to other pages.

- A script cannot read user preferences with the `preference()` method without the `UniversalPreferencesRead` privilege. `preference()` is a new feature of Navigator 4; it is a method of the Navigator object.

- A script must have the `UniversalPreferencesWrite` privilege in order to use the `preference()` method to set user preferences.

21.3 The Same Origin Policy

There is one far-reaching security restriction in JavaScript that deserves its own section. This restriction is known as the "same origin" policy: a script can only read the properties of windows and documents that have the same origin (i.e., that were loaded from the same host, through the same port, and by the same protocol) as the script itself. A script with the `UniversalBrowserRead` privilege is allowed to read the properties of windows and documents with a different origin, and a script with the `UniversalBrowserWrite` privilege is allowed to write those properties. A script with both privileges, or with the combined `UniversalBrowserAccess` privilege, can both read and write the properties of windows and documents with a different origin.

The same origin policy does not actually apply to all properties of all objects in a window from a different origin. But it does apply to many of them, and in particular, it applies to practically all of the properties of the Document object. For all intents and purposes, you should consider all predefined properties of all client-side objects off limits to your unprivileged scripts that come from different origins. Note, however, that access to user-defined properties is not restricted in this way. Thus, if a web page wants to open itself up to scripts from other origins, it should copy the values of the desired properties to new, user-defined, and thereby unrestricted properties. For example, a web page might allow other pages to examine its hypertext links with code like the following:

```
document.mylinks = document.links;
```

The same origin policy is a fairly severe restriction, but it is necessary to prevent untrusted scripts from stealing proprietary information. Without this restriction, an untrusted script (perhaps a script loaded through a firewall into a browser on a secure corporate intranet) in one window could spy on the contents of other browser windows, which might contain private information.

Still, there are circumstances where the same origin policy is too restrictive. It poses particular problems for large web sites that use more than one server. For example, a script from *home.netscape.com* might legitimately want to read properties of a document loaded from *developer.netscape.com*, or scripts from *orders.acme.com* might need to read properties from documents on *catalog.acme.com*. To support large web sites of this sort, JavaScript 1.1 introduced the domain property of the Document object. By default, the domain property contains the hostname of the server from which the document was loaded. You can set this property, but only to a string that is a valid domain suffix of itself. Thus, if domain is originally the string "home.netscape.com", you can set it to the string "netscape.com", but not to "home.netscape" or "cape.com", and certainly not to "microsoft.com".

If two windows contain scripts that set domain to the same value, the same origin policy is relaxed for these two windows and each of the windows may read properties from the other. For example, cooperating scripts in documents loaded from *orders.acme.com* and *catalog.acme.com* might set their document.domain properties to "acme.com", thereby making the documents appear to have the same origin and enabling each document to read properties of the other.

21.4 The Data-Tainting Security Model

You may occasionally hear mention of the data-tainting security model. This security model was included experimentally in Navigator 3; it has been abandoned in favor of the privilege-based model of Navigator 4. In the data-tainting model, scripts had unrestricted access to all properties. However, properties that contained private or sensitive data were "tainted." This taint propagated, so any data derived from tainted properties was also tainted. The restriction that this model imposed was not on what properties could be read, but on what could be done with the resulting data. The key feature of the model was that tainted data could never leave the client: a form that contained tainted data could not be submitted, for example.

While theoretically quite interesting, the data-tainting model was an evolutionary dead end. It was never enabled by default and required some sophistication on the part of the end user to enable. Thus, it never came into common use and is not documented here. Data tainting has been superseded by signed scripts and the privilege-based model, which are described in the following section.

21.5 Signed Scripts and Privileges

In Internet Explorer 4, scripts are always unprivileged and it is impossible to escape the security restrictions described at the beginning of this chapter.* Navigator 4, however, supports a security model that allows digitally signed scripts to request privileges, and subject to user approval, to selectively lift various security restrictions.

A digital signature is a cryptographic device that allows you to securely establish the origin of a piece of signed data, such as a JavaScript program. A digital signature is unforgeable and it contains a cryptographic checksum for the signed data. This means that if you are presented with a file of JavaScript code that bears the digital signature of "David Flanagan," you know that some entity named David Flanagan signed the code, and you know that the code has not been modified since he signed it.

Signers do not have to be people; any entity or *principal*, such as a corporation, can attach a digital signature to a JavaScript program or other data. By signing a

---

* Internet Explorer 4's security model is based on the notion of "security zones." Sites within different zones are trusted at different levels and are granted different levels of privilege. Unfortunately, this security model does not allow fine-grained control over JavaScript and its security restrictions: it merely allows scripting to be enabled or disabled. IE 4 uses digital signatures to authenticate the origin of downloaded ActiveX controls, but it does not apply this AuthentiCode technology to JavaScript programs. So, while IE 4 does have a security model, it is not relevant to JavaScript programmers and is not discussed in this chapter.

JavaScript program, the signer acknowledges itself as the author (or owner or originator) of the program and accepts responsibility for the program's actions. If signed code behaves maliciously, the digital signature unambiguously establishes the identity of the responsible party. A digital signature on JavaScript code is, in effect, a guarantee that the signed code won't behave maliciously and can be trusted. Although the guarantee may not actually be backed by any legal or financial remedy, the signer is at least putting its good name on the line. If Netscape started distributing malicious programs bearing the corporate signature, that signature would not remain trusted for very long!

Note that a digital signature only establishes identity; it does not establish trust. If I download a JavaScript program that bears the digital signature of an entity named Chaos Computer Club or Viruses Unlimited, I know something about the origin of the program, but that does not mean that I trust the program. Trust decisions can only come from the end user. By establishing identity, digital signatures serve as an important piece of an overall security policy, but they are only one piece of the puzzle.

The complete security picture includes many policy decisions made by the user, which are statements about trust. For example, one possible policy is the following: "I don't trust any JavaScript code, unless it bears the digital signature of Netscape, O'Reilly & Associates, or David Flanagan." Trust is not a boolean, on-or-off quantity, however: there may be many different levels of trust. A more realistic statement of a user's security policy might be: "I trust Netscape and Microsoft halfway. Code bearing their digital signatures should be allowed to open browser windows of any size, close windows, and manipulate events, but it should not be allowed to read my browsing history, set my preferences, or send email in my name. On the other hand, I trust David Flanagan unconditionally and will allow code signed by him to do absolutely anything it wants."

In the Netscape security model, trust is measured by the set of privileges granted to a principal (the signing entity). For example, one entity might be allowed `UniversalBrowserWrite` privileges, but not `UniversalSendMail` privileges. A security policy consists of a list of all trusted entities and the set of privileges that each entity is to be granted.

Configuring such a security policy can be a lot of work; figuring it all out in advance is not something that can really be asked or expected of relatively naive browser users. Therefore, the Netscape security model does not simply grant privileges to signed code. Instead, it requires the code to request the privileges it desires. By doing so, the browser is able to present the user with a choice: "A JavaScript program signed by David Flanagan has requested permission to send email bearing your name. Do you trust David Flanagan enough to grant this privilege? Do you want your decision to apply to any future code signed by David Flanagan as well?" Choices like this are presented to the user through security dialogs, such as that pictured in Figure 21-1.

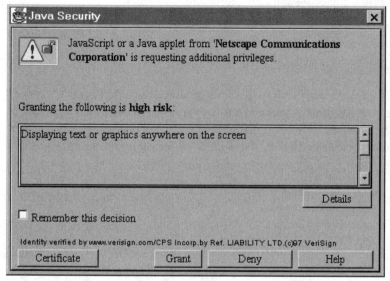

Figure 21–1: A security dialog queries the user about trust

By requiring scripts to request their privileges, Navigator 4 allows the user to build her security policy on a case-by-case basis. The user is presented with choices as necessary, and while these can be a little cumbersome the first time a signed program is run, the browser remembers the decisions the user has made, so the dialogs are only presented that first time the program is run.

To summarize, the Navigator security model begins with a set of restricted operations, such as sending email, that untrusted scripts are not allowed to perform. It uses digital signatures to securely establish the origin of a signed script and to verify that the script has not been tampered with or corrupted since it was signed. Signed scripts must request and be granted privileges before they can perform restricted operations. To grant a privilege, Navigator must know whether the end user trusts the signer enough to allow the privilege. To determine the level of trust, the browser asks the user, or consults a database of security policy trust decisions that the user has already made.

The following sections explain in more detail how you can sign your own JavaScript code and how your signed code can request additional privileges.

21.6 Signing Scripts

You can sign your JavaScript programs with a program from Netscape called *signtool*. This program is available for download from the Netscape web site at:

> *http://developer.netscape.com/software/signedobj/*

This section provides only a tutorial overview of code signing with *signtool*. Complete documentation for *signtool* is available at:

> *http://developer.netscape.com/library/documentation/signedobj/signtool/*

Because JavaScript programs typically consist of multiple included scripts, embedded scripts, and event handlers, signing a JavaScript program is actually a matter of generating a digital signature for each of the separate pieces of JavaScript code in the program. Every piece of code must be signed, or the program functions as if it were unsigned. *signtool* generates all the digital signatures that are necessary and stores them in a JAR file. This format is commonly used in Java programming; it is nothing more than a ZIP file with the addition of a metainformation directory that contains such information as a manifest of the archive contents, and auxiliary information such as digital signatures. Any JavaScript code included with the tag `<SCRIPT SRC=>` is placed in this JAR archive. Embedded scripts and event handlers may optionally be included in the JAR archive but also remain in their HTML files. Typically, it is only the digital signatures for these pieces of code that are stored in the archive.

21.6.1 Preparing Your Files for Signing

Before you can run *signtool* to sign the JavaScript code in an HTML file, you must prepare the HTML file for signing. As we've seen, digital signatures are collected into a JAR archive file. Within an HTML file, you specify the name of this archive with the `ARCHIVE` attribute of a `<SCRIPT>` tag. Most JavaScript programs use only a single archive file. These programs only need to specify the `ARCHIVE` attribute once; the specified JAR file is the default archive for the rest of the JavaScript code in the file. Thus, the first step in preparing your JavaScript program for signing is to add an `ARCHIVE` attribute to the first `<SCRIPT>` tag in the HTML file (or the first tag in each HTML file, if your program uses multiple files). Note that this first `<SCRIPT>` tag with the `ARCHIVE` attribute must be the first JavaScript code in the file—it must appear before any event handlers specified as HTML attributes, for example. In some cases, you may have to add an empty `<SCRIPT>` tag at the start of your file, just for the purpose of specifying the `ARCHIVE` attribute.

Files of JavaScript code that are included in an HTML file with the SRC attribute of a <SCRIPT> tag become part of the JAR archive itself. Both the file and its digital signature are placed in the archive and can be retrieved from it by name. Thus, for these included scripts, the only preparation you need to make is to specify an ARCHIVE attribute if it has not already been specified in an earlier <SCRIPT> tag.

Scripts that appear embedded in the HTML file are a different matter, however. These scripts do not exist in a separate file and thus do not have names. In order to associate digital signatures with these scripts, they must be given names. This is done with the ID attribute of the <SCRIPT> tag. Every embedded script must be given an ID attribute before the program can be signed. Note that the name assigned with the ID tag must be unique within the HTML file, and if the JAR archive stores digital signatures for multiple HTML pages, it must be unique across all those pages.

Event handlers of HTML elements are like embedded scripts in that they do not have names. For an event handler to be signed, the HTML element of which it is a part must be given a unique ID attribute as well. The same applies to JavaScript entities. Recall that a JavaScript entity is JavaScript code that appears in an attribute value within &{ and }; delimiters. Any HTML tag that contains such a JavaScript entity must also have a unique ID attribute. Finally, there is no general way to associate a name with javascript: URLs, so JavaScript code that appears in these URLs cannot be signed. Because *all* JavaScript code in a program must be signed, you cannot use javascript: URLs in signed programs.

Example 21-1 shows a simple JavaScript program prepared for signing with ARCHIVE and ID attributes.

Example 21-1: An HTML File Prepared for Signing

```
<!--
  This is an included script. Its contents will be placed in the JAR
  file. The ARCHIVE attribute specifies the name of the JAR file, and
  the SRC file specifies the name for the code within the archive, and
  also the name of the digital signature of that code.
-->
<SCRIPT ARCHIVE="history.jar" SRC="history.js"></SCRIPT>

<SCRIPT ID="s1">
/*
 * This is an inline script. It implicitly uses the ARCHIVE attribute
 * specified in the first SCRIPT tag. The ID tag specifies the name
 * under which the digital signature for this code will be stored.
 */
var history_window;
</SCRIPT>
```

Example 21–1: An HTML File Prepared for Signing (continued)

```
<FORM>
<!--
  These two buttons both have event handlers that contain JavaScript
  code, and must therefore be signed. The ID attributes specify the
  names under which the digital signatures of the code will be stored
  in the JAR file specified by a previous ARCHIVE attribute. Note that
  an ARCHIVE attribute can only be specified for a SCRIPT tag, so
  a SCRIPT tag must appear before any event handlers appear.
-->
<INPUT TYPE=BUTTON VALUE="Show History" ID="s2"
       onClick="history_window = openHistoryWindow();">
<INPUT TYPE=BUTTON VALUE="Hide History" ID="s3"
       onClick="history_window.close();">
</FORM>
```

21.6.2 Generating a Test Certificate

Before you can create a digital signature, you must have what is known as a "signing certificate." This certificate is some data signed by a trusted third party that certifies that you really are who you say you are. The need for certificates is best explained by analogy. If I walk into a grocery store and try to pay for my groceries with a check that I sign "Bill Gates", the clerk isn't going to accept the check unless I can produce a driver's license or some other form of photo identification (a "certificate") that proves that I am really Bill Gates and that the signature on the check matches the known signature of Bill Gates.

This is essentially what a signing certificate does as well. Technically, there is nothing to stop me from creating a bogus digital signature under the name "Bill Gates". But unless that signature is accompanied by a certificate that proves that I'm the real Bill Gates, no one is going to take my signature seriously. To get a certificate, you pay a company known as a certificate authority (CA), to issue you one (the best known CA is currently VeriSign). With the money you pay them, they do some investigation (such as getting a credit report on you or visiting your business offices), and once they are satisfied that you actually are who you claim to be, they certify this and issue you a small file that contains your name and other identifying information, signed with their digital signature. There is a bootstrapping problem here: if you don't trust my signature without a certificate, why do you trust the digital signature of the certificate authority that signed my certificate? The answer is that CAs have well-known digital signatures and widely distributed certificates. Every copy of Netscape 4 comes preconfigured with valid certificates for a number of public CAs, for example. Figure 21-2 shows a window displayed by Navigator 4 that contains the contents of such a certificate.

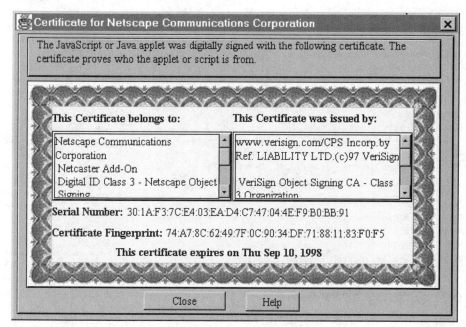

Figure 21–2: A graphical representation of a web site's certificate

If you are reading this chapter, you are probably just beginning to experiment with signed JavaScript programs, and you probably don't want to shell out money to get a certificate. Fortunately, *signtool* generates a test certificate for you that you can use while developing and testing your program. The test certificate generated by *signtool* is not certified by any CA. Instead, the certificate is self-signed; it bears your own digital signature. By analogy, imagine that the grocery clerk has just asked me to prove that I am really Bill Gates. A self-signed certificate is like my taking out a piece of paper and writing: "I hereby certify that I am really Bill Gates. Signed, Bill Gates". At this point, a smart grocery clerk would call the police and have me thrown out of the store!

So, while no sane end user will trust your self-signed certificate, it is still useful for developing software. To create one for yourself, use the -G option to *signtool*. You should also use the -d option to specify the directory that the certificate should be installed in. On Unix systems, this directory is `~/.netscape`. On Windows 95 systems, it is typically `c:\Program Files\Netscape\Users\default\`. Note that because *signtool* updates the key and certificate databases used by Navigator, you should quit Navigator before generating a key. Also, since keys and certificates are protected by passwords, you must use the Navigator **Security Info** window to give yourself a password before you can generate a key. Select the **Passwords** topic in the **Security Info** dialog to create a password. The following example shows a sample certificate being generated; the text entered by the user is in boldface:

```
oxymoron:163 % signtool -G davidflanagan -d ~/.netscape
using certificate directory: /home/david/.netscape

Enter certificate information. All fields are optional. Acceptable
characters are numbers, letters, spaces, and apostrophes.
certificate common name: David Flanagan
organization: O'Reilly
organization unit:
state or province: CA
country (must be exactly 2 characters): US
username: david
email address: enter email address
Enter Password or Pin for "Communicator Certificate DB": enter password
generated public/private key pair
certificate request generated
certificate has been signed
certificate "davidflanagan" added to database
Exported certificate to x509.raw and x509.cacert.
```

21.6.3 *Signing Your Code*

Now that you've prepared your HTML files for signing and have generated a test certificate, you can go ahead and use *signtool* to actually produce a JAR file containing the necessary digital signatures. To do this, follow these steps:

1. Create an empty directory.

2. Copy the HTML and JavaScript files you want signed to the new directory.

3. Invoke *signtool*. Specify that it is signing HTML and JavaScript files with the -J option. Specify the certificate to use for signing with the -k option. Use the name of the directory as the final argument on the command line.

4. After *signtool* finishes, the directory contains a JAR archive with whatever name you specified in the ARCHIVE attribute of the <SCRIPT> tag in your HTML files. *signtool* also creates a directory with the suffix *.arc*. This is an unpacked version of the *.jar* archive. While it provides a convenient way to examine the contents of the archive, this directory is not required and you can delete it.

Here's a transcript of the signing process on a Unix system:

```
oxymoron:174 % mkdir history
oxymoron:175 % cp history.html history.js history/
oxymoron:176 % signtool -J -k davidflanagan history
using key "davidflanagan"
using certificate directory: /home/david/.netscape

Generating inline signatures from HTML files in: history
Processing HTML file: history.html
```

```
(stashing a copy of history.js -> history.arc)
 entry: history.arc/inlineScripts/s1
 entry: history.arc/inlineScripts/s2
 entry: history.arc/inlineScripts/s3

signing: history/history.jar
Generating history/history.arc/META-INF/manifest.mf file..
--> history.js
adding history/history.arc/history.js to history/history.jar...
--> inlineScripts/s1
adding history/history.arc/inlineScripts/s1 to history/history.jar...
--> inlineScripts/s2
adding history/history.arc/inlineScripts/s2 to history/history.jar...
--> inlineScripts/s3
adding history/history.arc/inlineScripts/s3 to history/history.jar...
Generating zigbert.sf file..
Enter Password or Pin for "Communicator Certificate DB":enter password
adding history/history.arc/META-INF/manifest.mf to history/history.jar...
adding history/history.arc/META-INF/zigbert.sf to history/history.jar...
adding history/history.arc/META-INF/zigbert.rsa to history/history.jar...
jarfile "history/history.jar" signed successfully

oxymoron:177 % ls history
history.arc   history.html  history.jar   history.js
```

21.6.4 Scripts from Secure Servers

As an alternative to signing your JavaScript programs, you can serve them from a
secure server. Navigator treats all scripts loaded over a secure SSL connection as if
they were signed by the secure server itself. If your web site includes a secure
server, this may be an ideal solution for you.

21.6.5 Codebase Principals

Signing scripts can be a cumbersome process during program development. Because a digital signature includes a cryptographic checksum of the signed data,
your code must be resigned after any change (no matter how insignificant) you
make to it. This can significantly slow down your development and debugging
process.

As a way around this problem, Navigator 4 supports "codebase principals" as an
optional alternative to signed scripts. By default, only a digital signature or a
secure web server is sufficient to establish the entity, or principal, that is responsible for a given program. However, if you enable the codebase principals feature,
Navigator treats each codebase as a unique principal and allows you to assign

trust to JavaScript programs based upon their origin, rather than upon the secure identity of their originator. Each Internet domain is a unique codebase, and the local filesystem also constitutes a codebase. With codebase principals enabled, you can establish a security policy that states, for example, that you are willing to grant the `UniversalBrowserWrite` privilege to JavaScript code that comes from the server *www.davidflanagan.com*; and furthermore, that you are willing to grant any requested privilege to JavaScript code loaded through a `file:` URL from the local filesystem.

Trust is assigned to a codebase principal just as it is to a principal with a more secure identity: the user is asked to grant or deny privilege requests. Figure 21-3 shows a dialog asking the user to grant or deny privileges to code loaded from a codebase principal.

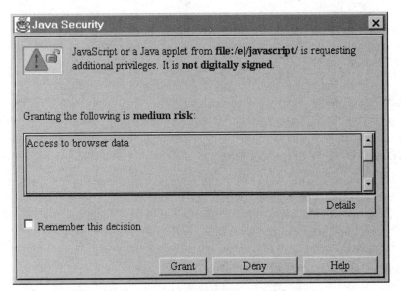

Figure 21–3: Establishing trust for an insecure codebase

Enabling codebase principals frees you from the requirement to sign your scripts after each change, but because it is insecure, this is not an option that you should leave enabled, and it is certainly not an option that you should ask your end users to enable. The reason that codebase principals are not secure, by the way, is that it is not difficult for sophisticated hackers to spoof Internet hosts. You should not trust JavaScript code based solely on its origin, because that origin can easily be faked.

With all that explanation and warning, you should not be surprised to learn that Navigator does not make it easy to enable codebase principals. In fact, doing so requires a manual edit to the Navigator preferences file. The location of this file depends on the operating system. On Windows 95 systems, for example, the file is typically:

```
c:\Program Files\Netscape\Users\default\prefs.js
```

It might also be:

```
c:\Program Files\Netscape\Users\username\prefs.js
```

On Unix systems, the preferences file is:

```
~/.netscape/preferences.js
```

Once you have located the preferences file, you enable codebase principals by adding this line of JavaScript code to it:

```
user_pref("signed.applets.codebase_principal_support", true);
```

Remember, codebase principals is a useful feature during development, but you should not leave it enabled all the time.

21.7 Requesting Privileges

Now that we've seen how to sign a script, we can move on and discuss how to write code that takes advantage of the privileges allowed to trusted, signed scripts. As we've seen, scripts must request any privileges they need in order to perform restricted operations. The Navigator privilege model is based on the Java security model and is also used to enable privileges for Java applets that run in Navigator. This means that privileges are actually managed by and requested through Java. Thus, to request a privilege, a JavaScript program must use LiveConnect to invoke a Java method. You request privileges by invoking the `enablePrivilege()` method of the `netscape.security.PrivilegeManager` Java class. You pass a string to this method that specifies the name of the privilege you would like to enable. For example:

```
netscape.security.PrivilegeManager.enablePrivilege("UniversalSendMail");
```

That's all there is to it. If the user grants the privilege, your program can proceed to perform restricted operations that unsigned or untrusted programs could not peform. Unfortunately, the `enablePrivilege()` method does not have a useful return value. If the user does not grant the privilege, the method does not return `false`. Instead, it throws an exception, which in Navigator 4 causes a messy-looking JavaScript error. Navigator 5 should support exception handling, so it will be possible to write programs that gracefully handle the denial of privileges.

The privileges that are useful to JavaScript programs were described in detail at the beginning of this chapter, as part of the discussion of security restrictions for unprivileged scripts. Briefly, the available privileges are:

UniversalBrowserRead

Allows a script to read properties of windows from different origins, to read properties and array elements of the History object, to extract information from special about: URLs, and to read the data property of the Event object passed to ondragdrop() event handlers.

UniversalBrowserWrite

Allows a script to write properties of windows from different origins, to set properties of the Event object, to capture events from windows or frames with different origins, to close windows, to open or resize very small or very large windows, and to move windows offscreen.

UniversalBrowserAccess

This privilege is a combination of UniversalBrowserRead and Universal-BrowserWrite. It allows all operations allowed by either of those privileges.

UniversalFileRead

Allows a script to set the value property of a FileUpload object, thereby enabling the script to transmit the contents of any file in the local filesystem to a CGI script on a web server.

UniversalPreferencesRead

Allows the use of the navigator.preference() method to query user preferences.

UniversalPreferencesWrite

Allows the use of the navigator.preference() method to set user preferences.

UniversalSendMail

Allows a script to call the submit() method of a Form object that sends form data to a mailto: or news: URL. Posting such a form sends email or posts a Usenet article under the user's name; it contains the user's email address.

21.7.1 *Privilege Duration*

One way to increase security is to limit vulnerability to security breaches or attacks by minimizing the amount of code that runs with augmented privileges. Thus, a privilege enabled with enablePrivilege() lasts only until the function that enabled it returns or until it is explicitly disabled with the corresponding dis-ablePrivilege() method. It is a good idea to segregate your privileged code into separate functions, so that privileges are only enabled while those functions are running.

21.7.2 Examining Browsing History

Example 21-2 shows the file *history.js*. It contains a method that opens a new window and displays the current window's browsing history in that new window. Because the browsing history is the user's private information, doing this requires the `UniversalBrowserRead` privilege, which is requested with the Java `enablePrivilege()` method.

Example 21-2: Requesting a Privilege

```
// This function requests the UniversalBrowserRead privilege to enable
// it to read the array elements of the History object.
function openHistoryWindow() {
    // Open a new window.
    var w = window.open("", "historyWindow",
                        "width=500,height=300,menubar,resizable");
    var d = w.document;

    // Request a privilege.
    netscape.security.PrivilegeManager.enablePrivilege("UniversalBrowserRead");

    // Output the browsing history of this window as links in the new window.
    for(var i = 0; i < history.length; i++) {
        d.write('<A TARGET="new" HREF="' + history[i] + '">');
        d.write(history[i]);
        d.writeln('</A>');
    }
    d.close();

    // Return the new window.
    return w;

    // The privilege is automatically disabled when this function returns.
}
```

21.8 Mixing Signed and Unsigned Scripts

Because all the scripts in all the windows of a web browser run in the same environment, any script can affect the operation of any other script—for example, by setting properties in another script's global object, or by replacing a function that a script calls on with some other implementation of that function. Because scripts can interact like this, the Navigator security model must be very careful when signed scripts are mixed with unsigned scripts, so that the untrusted unsigned scripts do not subvert the trusted scripts and gain access to privileges they should not have.

As I've said before, all JavaScript code in a HTML document must be signed or the browser behaves as if none of it were signed. Scripts can actually be signed by more than one signer, so the general rule is that Navigator determines the largest subset of signers that have signed *all* of the JavaScript code on the page. For example, if a page includes a file of JavaScript code signed by David Flanagan and Bill Gates and also has an embedded script and an event handler signed only by David Flanagan, the browser operates as if the code were signed by David Flanagan alone.

As another example, consider a web page exported by *www.davidflanagan.com* that contains two embedded scripts signed by David Flanagan and one event handler that the author forgot to sign. In this case, the only common identity shared by these pieces of JavaScript code is that they all have *www.davidflanagan.com* as their codebase. In a browser with codebase principals enabled, this program might still be granted privileges, if the user were a trusting sort. But in the typical situation, without codebase principals enabled, no principal could be established for the program, and the program would not even be allowed to request privileges from the user.

21.8.1 The Same Signer Policy

The previous section explained a basic rule for JavaScript code within a single web page: for the signature to be valid, all the JavaScript code on the page must be signed. The rules are not quite so strict for programs that use multiple windows or frames. Consider a program that displays two frames in the web browser window: one that contains signed scripts and one that contains unsigned scripts. Because these two windows have different signers, they effectively have different origins and fall under the "same origin" policy described at the beginning of this chapter. We might call this version of the policy the "same signer" policy.

What this means is that the scripts in one frame cannot read properties from the other frame. Of course, the signed scripts can simply request the `Universal-BrowserRead` privilege in order to get around this restriction. On the other hand, the unsigned scripts in the other frame cannot read or write any properties in the signed frame. This is a crucial restriction, because it prevents untrusted code from manipulating the functions, properties, or execution environment of trusted code and makes it impossible (hopefully) for the untrusted code to subvert the trusted code. While the same origin policy restricted scripts from reading many properties of windows and documents with a different origin, the same signer policy is even more strict: unsigned scripts in one window or frame can read only a small handful of simple read-only properties (such as `width`, `height`, and `closed`) of windows containing signed scripts.

21.8.2 The import and export Statements

The `import` and `export` statements of JavaScript 1.2 provide a way to selectively relax the same-signer policy. These statements were introduced in Chapter 6, *Statements*. A signed script in one window or frame can use the `export` statement to make one or more of its functions available for import into unsigned (or differently signed) scripts in other windows or frames. The `import` statement makes a function or functions exported by a signed script in another window or frame available to the unsigned scripts in the current frame.

For example, you might define a signed, privileged script in the <HEAD> section of a document that contains a frameset, and then use the `export` statement to export some of the privileged functions defined by that signed script. Unsigned scripts in the individual frames of the frameset could then `import` those privileged functions and use them as necessary.

Be careful when you `export` privileged functions. Make sure that there is no way that untrusted code can take advantage of the privileges granted to those functions and use them to serve malicious ends.

III

Reference

This part of the book is a complete reference to all of the objects, properties, functions, methods, and event handlers in client-side JavaScript and in the core JavaScript language. The first few pages of this part explain how to use this reference material and provide a table of contents for it.

JavaScript Reference

This section of the book is a complete reference for all JavaScript objects, properties, constants, arrays, functions, methods, and event handlers. It even includes documentation for two Java classes used by Navigator.

How to Find the Reference Page You Want

The reference section is arranged alphabetically, and all properties, methods, and event handlers are alphabetized by their full name, which includes the name of the object of which they are a part. For example, if you want to read about the `write()` method of the Document object, look up "Document.write", not just "write".

JavaScript defines some global variables, such as `navigator` and `Packages`, which, strictly speaking, are properties of the Window object. They are never used this way, however, and so these few "globals" are alphabetized without the "Window." prefix. Note, however, that other properties, methods, and event handlers of the Window object, such as `location`, `alert()`, and `onload()` *are* documented as part of the Window object. Thus you should look these up as "Window.location", "Window.alert()", and "Window.onload()".

Sometimes you may need to look up a method or property without knowing what object it is part of. Or you may not be able to find a reference page where you expect it. The table of contents that follows should help you with this. The left column lists the names of all objects, functions, properties, methods, and event handlers in JavaScript, while the right column gives the full name of the reference page on which documentation can be found. Note that some property, method, and event-handler names are used by more than one object. So, for example, if you look up the `toString()` method in the table, you find several reference pages that document different objects' implementations of that method.

Table of Contents

For	See
bold	String.bold
Boolean	Boolean
border	Image.border
borderWidths	Style.borderWidths
bottom	Layer.clip.bottom
btoa	Window.btoa
Button	Button, Event.button
call	JSObject.call
callee	Arguments.callee
caller	Arguments.caller, Function.caller
cancelBubble	Event.cancelBubble
captureEvents	Document.captureEvents, Layer.captureEvents, Window.captureEvents
ceil	Math.ceil
charAt	String.charAt
charCodeAt	String.charCodeAt
charset	Document.charset
Checkbox	Checkbox
checked	Checkbox.checked, Input.checked, Radio.checked
children	Document.children, HTMLElement.children
classes	Document.classes
className	HTMLElement.className
clear	Document.clear
clearInterval	Window.clearInterval
clearTimeout	clearTimeout, Window.clearTimeout
click	Input.click
clientInformation	Window.clientInformation
clientX	Event.clientX
clientY	Event.clientY
close	close, Document.close, Window.close
closed	closed, Window.closed
colorDepth	Screen.colorDepth
compile	RegExp.compile
complete	Image.complete
concat	Array.concat, String.concat
confirm	confirm, Window.confirm
constructor	Object.constructor
contains	HTMLElement.contains
contextual	Document.contextual
cookie	Document.cookie

For	See
cos	Math.cos
Crypto	Crypto, Window.crypto
ctrlKey	Event.ctrlKey
current	History.current
data	Event.data
Date	Date
defaultCharset	Document.defaultCharset
defaultChecked	Checkbox.defaultChecked, Input.defaultChecked, Radio.defaultChecked
defaultSelected	Option.defaultSelected
defaultStatus	defaultStatus, Window.defaultStatus
defaultValue	Input.defaultValue
description	MimeType.description, Plugin.description
disableExternalCapture	Window.disableExternalCapture
disablePrivilege	PrivilegeManager.disablePrivilege
Document	Document, document, HTMLElement.document, Layer.document, Window.document
domain	Document.domain
E	Math.E
Element	Element
elementFromPoint	Document.elementFromPoint
elements	Form.elements
embeds	Document.embeds
enabledPlugin	MimeType.enabledPlugin
enableExternalCapture	Window.enableExternalCapture
enablePrivilege	PrivilegeManager.enablePrivilege
encoding	Form.encoding
escape	escape
eval	eval, JSObject.eval, Object.eval
Event	Event, Window.event
exec	RegExp.exec
exp	Math.exp
expando	Document.expando
fgColor	Document.fgColor
filename	Plugin.filename
FileUpload	FileUpload
find	Window.find
fixed	String.fixed
floor	Math.floor
focus	focus, Input.focus, Window.focus

For	See
fontcolor	String.fontcolor
fontsize	String.fontsize
Form	Form, Input.form
forms	Document.forms
forward	History.forward, Window.forward
Frame	Frame
frames	frames, Window.frames
fromCharCode	String.fromCharCode
fromElement	Event.fromElement
Function	Function
getAttribute	HTMLElement.getAttribute
getClass	getClass
getDate	Date.getDate
getDay	Date.getDay
getFullYear	Date.getFullYear
getHours	Date.getHours
getMember	JSObject.getMember
getMilliseconds	Date.getMilliseconds
getMinutes	Date.getMinutes
getMonth	Date.getMonth
getSeconds	Date.getSeconds
getSelection	Document.getSelection
getSlot	JSObject.getSlot
getTime	Date.getTime
getTimezoneOffset	Date.getTimezoneOffset
getUTCDate	Date.getUTCDate
getUTCDay	Date.getUTCDay
getUTCFullYear	Date.getUTCFullYear
getUTCHours	Date.getUTCHours
getUTCMilliseconds	Date.getUTCMilliseconds
getUTCMinutes	Date.getUTCMinutes
getUTCMonth	Date.getUTCMonth
getUTCSeconds	Date.getUTCSeconds
getWindow	JSObject.getWindow
getYear	Date.getYear
global	RegExp.global
go	History.go
handleEvent	Document.handleEvent, HTMLElement.handleEvent, Layer.handleEvent, Window.handleEvent
hash	Link.hash, Location.hash

For	See
height	Document.height, Event.height, Image.height, Layer.clip.height, Screen.height
Hidden	Hidden, Layer.hidden
History	History, history, Window.history
home	Window.home
host	Link.host, Location.host
hostname	Link.hostname, Location.hostname
href	Link.href, Location.href
hspace	Image.hspace
HTMLElement	HTMLElement
id	HTMLElement.id
ids	Document.ids
ignoreCase	RegExp.ignoreCase
Image	Image
images	Document.images
index	Option.index
indexOf	String.indexOf
Infinity	Infinity
innerHeight	Window.innerHeight
innerHTML	HTMLElement.innerHTML
innerText	HTMLElement.innerText
innerWidth	Window.innerWidth
Input	Input, RegExp.input
insertAdjacentHTML	HTMLElement.insertAdjacentHTML
insertAdjacentText	HTMLElement.insertAdjacentText
isFinite	isFinite
isNaN	isNaN
italics	String.italics
java	java, Packages.java, Window.java
JavaArray	JavaArray
JavaClass	JavaClass
javaEnabled	Navigator.javaEnabled
JavaObject	JavaObject
JavaPackage	JavaPackage
join	Array.join
JSObject	JSObject
keyCode	Event.keyCode
lang	HTMLElement.lang
language	Navigator.language
lastIndex	RegExp.lastIndex

For	See
lastIndexOf	String.lastIndexOf
lastMatch	RegExp.lastMatch
lastModified	Document.lastModified
lastParen	RegExp.lastParen
Layer	Layer
layers	Document.layers, Layer.layers
layerX	Event.layerX
layerY	Event.layerY
left	Layer.clip.left, Layer.left
leftContext	RegExp.leftContext
length	Arguments.length, Array.length, Form.length, Function.length, History.length, Input.length, JavaArray.length, Plugin.length, Select.length, String.length, Window.length
Link	Link, String.link
linkColor	Document.linkColor
links	Document.links
LN10	Math.LN10
LN2	Math.LN2
load	Layer.load
location	Document.location, Location, location, Window.location
locationbar	Window.locationbar
log	Math.log
LOG10E	Math.LOG10E
LOG2E	Math.LOG2E
lowsrc	Image.lowsrc
margins	Style.margins
match	String.match
Math	Math, Window.Math
max	Math.max
MAX_VALUE	Number.MAX_VALUE
menubar	Window.menubar
method	Form.method
MimeType	MimeType
mimeTypes	Navigator.mimeTypes
min	Math.min
MIN_VALUE	Number.MIN_VALUE
modifiers	Event.modifiers
moveAbove	Layer.moveAbove
moveBelow	Layer.moveBelow
moveBy	Layer.moveBy, Window.moveBy

For	See
moveTo	Layer.moveTo, Window.moveTo
moveToAbsolute	Layer.moveToAbsolute
multiline	RegExp.multiline
name	Anchor.name, Form.name, Image.name, Input.name, Layer.name, name, Plugin.name, Window.name
NaN	NaN, Number.NaN
navigate	navigate, Window.navigate
Navigator	Navigator, navigator, Window.navigator
NEGATIVE_INFINITY	Number.NEGATIVE_INFINITY
netscape	netscape, Packages.netscape, Window.netscape
next	History.next
Number	Number
Object	Object
offscreenBuffering	Window.offscreenBuffering
offset	Layer.offset
offsetHeight	HTMLElement.offsetHeight
offsetLeft	HTMLElement.offsetLeft
offsetParent	HTMLElement.offsetParent
offsetTop	HTMLElement.offsetTop
offsetWidth	HTMLElement.offsetWidth
offsetX	Event.offsetX
offsetY	Event.offsetY
onabort	Image.onabort
onblur	Input.onblur, Window.onblur
onchange	FileUpload.onchange, Input.onchange, Select.onchange, Text.onchange, Textarea.onchange
onclick	Button.onclick, Checkbox.onclick, HTMLElement.onclick, Input.onclick, Link.onclick, Radio.onclick, Reset.onclick, Submit.onclick
ondblclick	HTMLElement.ondblclick
ondragdrop	Window.ondragdrop
onerror	Image.onerror, Window.onerror
onfocus	Input.onfocus, Window.onfocus
onHelp	HTMLElement.onHelp
onkeydown	HTMLElement.onkeydown
onkeypress	HTMLElement.onkeypress
onkeyup	HTMLElement.onkeyup
onload	Image.onload, Window.onload
onmousedown	HTMLElement.onmousedown
onmousemove	HTMLElement.onmousemove
onmouseout	HTMLElement.onmouseout, Link.onmouseout

For	See
onmouseover	HTMLElement.onmouseover, Link.onmouseover
onmouseup	HTMLElement.onmouseup
onmove	Window.onmove
onreset	Form.onreset
onresize	Window.onresize
onsubmit	Form.onsubmit
onunload	Window.onunload
open	Document.open, open, Window.open
opener	opener, Window.opener
Option	Option
options	Input.options, Select.options
outerHeight	Window.outerHeight
outerHTML	HTMLElement.outerHTML
outerText	HTMLElement.outerText
outerWidth	Window.outerWidth
Packages	Packages, Window.Packages
paddings	Style.paddings
pageX	Event.pageX, Layer.pageX
pageXOffset	Window.pageXOffset
pageY	Event.pageY, Layer.pageY
pageYOffset	Window.pageYOffset
parent	parent, Window.parent
parentElement	HTMLElement.parentElement
parentLayer	Layer.parentLayer
parentWindow	Document.parentWindow
parse	Date.parse
parseFloat	parseFloat
parseInt	parseInt
Password	Password
pathname	Link.pathname, Location.pathname
personalbar	Window.personalbar
PI	Math.PI
pixelDepth	Screen.pixelDepth
platform	Navigator.platform
Plugin	Plugin
plugins	Document.plugins, Navigator.plugins
pop	Array.pop
port	Link.port, Location.port
POSITIVE_INFINITY	Number.POSITIVE_INFINITY
pow	Math.pow

For	See
preference	Navigator.preference
previous	History.previous
print	Window.print
PrivilegeManager	PrivilegeManager
prompt	prompt, Window.prompt
protocol	Link.protocol, Location.protocol
prototype	Function.prototype
push	Array.push
Radio	Radio
random	Crypto.random, Math.random
readyState	Document.readyState
reason	Event.reason
referrer	Document.referrer
refresh	Navigator.plugins.refresh
RegExp	RegExp
releaseEvents	Document.releaseEvents, Layer.releaseEvents, Window.releaseEvents
reload	Location.reload
removeAttribute	HTMLElement.removeAttribute
removeMember	JSObject.removeMember
replace	Location.replace, String.replace
reset	Form.reset, Reset
resizeBy	Layer.resizeBy, Window.resizeBy
resizeTo	Layer.resizeTo, Window.resizeTo
returnValue	Event.returnValue
reverse	Array.reverse
right	Layer.clip.right
rightContext	RegExp.rightContext
round	Math.round
routeEvent	Document.routeEvent, Layer.routeEvent, Window.routeEvent
savePreferences	Navigator.savePreferences
Screen	Screen, window.Screen
screenX	Event.screenX, Window.screenX
screenY	Event.screenY, Window.screenY
scroll	scroll, Window.scroll
scrollbars	Window.scrollbars
scrollBy	Window.scrollBy
scrollIntoView	HTMLElement.scrollIntoView
scrollTo	Window.scrollTo
search	Link.search, Location.search, String.search

For	See
select	Input.select, Select
selected	Option.selected
selectedIndex	Input.selectedIndex, Select.selectedIndex
self	self, Window.self
setAttribute	HTMLElement.setAttribute
setDate	Date.setDate
setFullYear	Date.setFullYear
setHotkeys	Window.setHotkeys
setHours	Date.setHours
setInterval	Window.setInterval
setMember	JSObject.setMember
setMilliseconds	Date.setMilliseconds
setMinutes	Date.setMinutes
setMonth	Date.setMonth
setResizable	Window.setResizable
setSeconds	Date.setSeconds
setSlot	JSObject.setSlot
setTime	Date.setTime
setTimeout	setTimeout, Window.setTimeout
setUTCDate	Date.setUTCDate
setUTCFullYear	Date.setUTCFullYear
setUTCHours	Date.setUTCHours
setUTCMilliseconds	Date.setUTCMilliseconds
setUTCMinutes	Date.setUTCMinutes
setUTCMonth	Date.setUTCMonth
setUTCSeconds	Date.setUTCSeconds
setYear	Date.setYear
setZOptions	Window.setZOptions
shift	Array.shift
shiftKey	Event.shiftKey
siblingAbove	Layer.siblingAbove
siblingBelow	Layer.siblingBelow
signText	Crypto.signText
sin	Math.sin
slice	Array.slice, String.slice
small	String.small
sort	Array.sort
source	RegExp.source
sourceIndex	HTMLElement.sourceIndex
splice	Array.splice

For	See
split	String.split
sqrt	Math.sqrt
SQRT1_2	Math.SQRT1_2
SQRT2	Math.SQRT2
src	Image.src, Layer.src
srcElement	Event.srcElement
srcFilter	Event.srcFilter
status	status, Window.status
statusbar	Window.statusbar
stop	Window.stop
strike	String.strike
String	String
style	HTMLElement.style, Style
sub	String.sub
submit	Form.submit, Submit
substr	String.substr
substring	String.substring
suffixes	MimeType.suffixes
sun	Packages.sun, sun, Window.sun
sup	String.sup
systemLanguage	Navigator.systemLanguage
tagName	HTMLElement.tagName
tags	Document.tags
taint	taint
taintEnabled	Navigator.taintEnabled
tan	Math.tan
target	Event.target, Form.target, Link.target
test	RegExp.test
text	Anchor.text, Link.text, Option.text, Text
Textarea	Textarea
title	Document.title, HTMLElement.title
toElement	Event.toElement
toGMTString	Date.toGMTString
toLocaleString	Date.toLocaleString
toLowerCase	String.toLowerCase
toolbar	Window.toolbar
top	Layer.clip.top, Layer.top, top, Window.top
toString	Array.toString, Boolean.toString, Date.toString, Function.toString, JSObject.toString, Number.toString, Object.toString

For	See
toUpperCase	String.toUpperCase
toUTCString	Date.toUTCString
TYPE	Event.TYPE, Event.type, Input.type, MimeType.type, Select.type
unescape	unescape
unshift	Array.unshift
untaint	untaint
unwatch	Object.unwatch
URL	Document.URL, URL
userAgent	Navigator.userAgent
userLanguage	Navigator.userLanguage
UTC	Date.UTC
value	Button.value, Checkbox.value, FileUpload.value, Hidden.value, Input.value, Option.value, Password.value, Radio.value, Reset.value, Submit.value, Text.value, Textarea.value
valueOf	Date.valueOf, Object.valueOf
visibility	Layer.visibility
vlinkColor	Document.vlinkColor
vspace	Image.vspace
watch	Object.watch
which	Event.which
width	Document.width, Event.width, Image.width, Layer.clip.width, Screen.width
window	Layer.window, Window, window, Window.window
write	Document.write
writeln	Document.writeln
x	Anchor.x, Event.x, Layer.x, Link.x
y	Anchor.y, Event.y, Layer.y, Link.y
zIndex	Layer.zIndex

How to Read the Reference Pages

Once you've found the reference page you're looking for, you shouldn't have much difficulty obtaining the information you need from it. Still, however, you'll be able to make better use of this reference section if you understand how the reference pages are written and organized. The very first reference page is titled "Sample Entry"; it explains the structure of each reference page and tells you where to find various types of information within the pages. Do be sure to read this page before diving into the reference section.

Sample Entry — how to read these reference pages

Title and Description

Every reference entry begins with a title and one-line description like those above. The entries are alphabetized by title. The one-line description gives you a quick summary of the item documented in the entry; it can help you decide quickly if you've found the page you're looking for.

Availability

Because JavaScript has grown significantly between versions, you'll find a number of properties, methods, and objects documented here that are available only in JavaScript 1.1 (or later) or only in JavaScript 1.2 (or later), or, in some cases, only in Navigator or only in Internet Explorer. Because this availability information is so crucial, it is placed right at the beginning of each reference entry. You can assume that anything available in one version of JavaScript is also available in later versions.

The "Availability" section provides other information as well. For each entry, it specifies whether the item being documented is part of core JavaScript or client-side JavaScript. This section also specifies whether an existing item has been enhanced in a later version of the language and when an item has been deprecated. Deprecated items are no longer supported and may be removed from the language in future versions. Therefore, you should avoid using deprecated items in new JavaScript code.

Inherits From

As described in Chapter 8, *Objects*, JavaScript classes can inherit properties and methods from other classes. This is relatively common in client-side JavaScript. For example, the Link object inherits from the HTMLElement object, and the Button object inherits from the Input object which in turn inherits from the HTMLElement object. When this occurs, an "Inherits From" section appears in the reference entry. When you see this section, it should be a signal to you to look up the listed superclasses. For example, the Button class inherits its `form` property from Input. This means that you won't find a reference entry for `Button.form`; you'll have to look it up as `Input.form` instead.

Synopsis

The next section of every page is a synopsis of how you use the object, method, property, function, or event handler in your actual code. For example, the synopsis for the Form object is:

```
document.form_name
document.forms[form_number]
```

This synopsis shows two different ways of referring to a Form object. The italic font indicates text that is to be replaced with something else. *form_name* should be replaced with the name of a form, and *form_number* should be replaced with the index of the form in the `forms[]` array. Similarly, *document* should be replaced in these synopses with a reference to a Document object. By looking up the synopsis of the Document object, we discover that it also has two forms:

```
document
window.document
```

That is, you can replace *document* with the literal `document` or with *window*.document. If you choose the latter, you'll need to look up the synopsis of the Window object to find out how to refer to a Window—that is, what to replace *window* with.

Arguments

If the reference page describes a function or method that has arguments, the Synopsis is followed by an "Arguments" subsection that describes the arguments to the function or method. For some object types, such as the Date object, the Synopsis section is replaced by a "Constructor" section, which is also followed by an Arguments subsection.

arg1   The arguments are described in a list here. This is the description for argument *arg1*, for example.

arg2   And this is the description for argument *arg2*.

Returns

If a function or method has a return value, the Arguments subsection is followed by a "Returns" subsection that explains the return value of the function, method, or constructor.

Properties

If the reference page documents an object, the "Properties" section lists the properties the object supports and provides short explanations of each. Each property also has a complete reference page of its own. For example, the reference page for the Document object lists the `lastModified` property in this section and gives a brief explanation of it, but the property is fully documented in the `Document.lastModified` reference page. The property listing looks like this:

prop1   This is a summary of property `prop1`, including the type of the property, its purpose or meaning, and whether it is read-only or read/write.

prop2   This is the same for `prop2`.

Methods

The reference page for an object that defines methods includes a "Methods" section. It is just like the Properties section, except that it documents methods instead of properties.

Event Handlers

Some objects define event handlers in addition to properties and methods. They are listed and briefly described in this section.

HTML Syntax

A number of client-side JavaScript objects have analogs in HTML. The reference pages for these objects include a section that shows the annotated HTML syntax that is used to create one of the JavaScript objects. For example, the reference page for the Button form element has the following in its "HTML Syntax" section:

```
<INPUT
    TYPE="button"          Specifies that this is a button
    VALUE="label"          The text that is to appear within the button
                           Specifies the value property
    [ NAME="name" ]        A name that can later be used to refer to the button
                           Specifies the name property
    [ onClick="handler" ]  JavaScript statements to be executed when the button is clicked
  >
```

Description

Most reference entries contain a "Description" section, which is the basic description of whatever is being documented—the heart of the reference page. Unfortunately, on some of the more complex pages, you have to read through quite a bit of synopsis and syntax, and lists of properties, methods, and event handlers before you get to the description.

For some pages this section is no more than a short paragraph. On others, it may occupy a page or more. For some very simple methods, the Arguments and Returns sections document the method sufficiently by themselves, so the Description section is omitted.

Usage

Some pages have a "Usage" section in addition to the Description. When this section appears, be sure to pay attention. It describes common techniques for using the item, or it contains cautions that you should be aware of.

Example

Some pages follow the Description and Usage information with an example showing a typical usage. Most pages do not contain examples—you'll find those in first half of this book.

Bugs

When an item doesn't work quite right, this section describes the bugs.

See Also

Many reference pages conclude with cross-references to related reference pages that may be of interest. Sometimes reference pages also refer back to one of the main chapters of the book.

---

alert() — see Window.alert()

Anchor — the target of a hypertext link

Availability

Client-side JavaScript 1.2

Inherits From

HTMLElement

Synopsis

```
document.anchors[i]
document.anchors.length
```

Properties

Anchor inherits properties from HTMLElement and also defines or overrides the following:

name   The name of the anchor.

text   The text of the anchor.

x   The X-coordinate of the anchor.

y   The Y-coordinate of the anchor.

HTML Syntax

An Anchor object is created by any standard HTML <A> tag that contains a <NAME> attribute:

```
<A
   NAME="name"                        Links may refer to this anchor by this name.
>
text
</A>
```

Description

An anchor is a named location within an HTML document. Anchors are created with an <A> tag that has a NAME attribute specified. The Document object has an anchors[] array property that contains Anchor objects that represent each of the anchors in the document. This anchors[] array has existed since JavaScript 1.0, but the Anchor object was not implemented until JavaScript 1.2. Therefore, the elements of anchors[] were null until JavaScript 1.2.

Note that the <A> tag used to create anchors is also used to create hypertext links. Although hypertext links are often called anchors in HTML parlance, they are represented in JavaScript with the Link object, not with the Anchor object.

See Also

Document.anchors[], Link

Anchor.name — the name of an anchor

Availability

Client-side JavaScript 1.2

Synopsis

```
anchor.name
```

Description

The `name` property contains the name of an Anchor object. Its value is initially set by the `NAME` attribute of the `<A>` tag.

Anchor.text — the text of an anchor

Availability

Client-side Navigator 4

Synopsis

    anchor.text

Description

The `text` property specifies the plain text, if any, between the `<A>` and `</A>` tags of an anchor. Note that this property only works correctly if there are no intervening HTML tags between the `<A>` and `</A>` tags. If there are other HTML tags, the `text` property may only contain a portion of the anchor text.

`HTMLElement.innerText` provides the IE 4 equivalent of this Navigator-specific property.

Anchor.x — the X-coordinate of an anchor

Availability

Client-side Navigator 4

Synopsis

    anchor.x

Description

`x` specifies the X-coordinate of the anchor relative to the containing document, that is, the number of pixels between the anchor and the left edge of the document.

In IE 4, `HTMLElement.offsetLeft` is similar to, but not always the same as, `Anchor.x`.

Anchor.y — the Y-coordinate of an anchor

Availability

Client-side Navigator 4

Synopsis

    anchor.y

Description

`y` specifies the Y-coordinate of the anchor relative to the containing document, that is, the number of pixels between the anchor and the top edge of the document.

In IE 4, `HTMLElement.offsetTop` is similar to, but not always the same as, `Anchor.y`.

Applet — an applet embedded in a web page

Availability

Client-side JavaScript 1.1

Synopsis

```
document.applets[i]
document.appletName
```

Properties

The properties of an Applet object are the same as the public fields of the Java applet it represents.

Methods

The methods of an Applet object are the same as the public methods of the Java applet it represents.

Description

The Applet object represents a Java applet embedded in an HTML document. The properties of the Applet object represent the public fields of the applet, and the methods of the Applet object represent the public methods of the applet. LiveConnect technology in Navigator and ActiveX technology in Internet Explorer allow JavaScript programs to use the Applet object to read and write the fields and invoke the methods of the corresponding Java applet. See Chapter 20, *LiveConnect: JavaScript and Java*, for details.

Remember that Java is a strongly typed language. This means that each field of an applet has been declared to have a specific data type, and setting it to a value of some other type causes a runtime error. The same is true of applet methods: each argument has a specific type, and arguments cannot be omitted as they can be in JavaScript.

See Also

JavaObject, Chapter 20

Area — see Link

---

arguments[ ] — an array of function arguments

Availability

Core JavaScript 1.1; ECMA-262; only defined within a function body

Synopsis

```
arguments
```

Description

Within the body of a function, arguments refers to the Arguments object for the function. This object is an array containing all arguments passed to the function and also has several other properties of interest. The arguments identifier is essentially a local variable automatically declared and initialized within every function. It refers to an Arguments object only within the body of a function and is undefined in global code.

Be careful not to confuse `arguments` with the (deprecated) `Function.arguments` property.

See Also

Arguments, Chapter 7, *Functions*

Arguments — arguments and other properties of a function

Availability

Core JavaScript 1.1; ECMA-262; only defined within a function body

Synopsis

```
arguments
```

Elements

The Arguments object is an array. Its elements are the values that were passed as arguments to the function. Element 0 is the first argument, element 1 is the second argument, and so on. All values passed as arguments become array elements of the Arguments object, whether or not those arguments are given names in the function declaration.

Properties

`callee`   A reference to the function that is currently executing.

`caller`   A reference to the Arguments object of the function that called this one. Navigator 4 only.

`length`   The number of arguments passed to the function, and the number of array elements in the Arguments object.

Description

When a function is invoked, an Arguments object is created for it, and the local variable `arguments` is automatically initialized to refer to that Arguments object. The main purpose of the Arguments object is to provide a way to determine how many arguments were passed to the function and to refer to unnamed arguments. In addition to the array elements and `length` property, however, the `callee` and `caller` properties can also be useful in specialized situations.

Be careful not to confuse the Arguments object with the (deprecated) `Function.arguments` property.

See Also

Function, Chapter 7

Arguments.callee — the function that is currently running

Availability

Core JavaScript 1.2; ECMA-262; only defined within a function body

Synopsis

```
arguments.callee
```

Description

`arguments.callee` refers to the function that is currently running. It provides a way for an unnamed function to refer to itself.

Arguments.caller — the calling context

Availability

Core Navigator 4; only defined within a function body

Synopsis

```
arguments.caller
```

Description

The `caller` property of an Arguments object refers to the Arguments object of the calling function (or null if the function was invoked from the top level). You can use this property to generate stack traces, for example.

`arguments.caller` is supported by Navigator 4 but is not part of the ECMA-262 standard. Adding it to the language can create optimization difficulties, and for this reason the `caller` property may not be standardized.

Don't confuse `arguments.caller` with the deprecated `Function.caller` property.

Bugs

When a function is invoked from the top level, its `arguments.caller` property should be `null`. In Navigator 4, however, a bug causes `arguments.caller` to refer self-referentially to `arguments` at the top of the caller chain.

Arguments.length — the number of arguments passed to a function

Availability

Core JavaScript 1.1; ECMA-262; only defined within a function body

Synopsis

```
arguments.length
```

Description

The `length` property of the Arguments object specifies the size of the `arguments[]` array, and thereby specifies the number of arguments passed to the current function.

Note that this property specifies the number of arguments actually passed, not the number expected. See `Function.length` and `Function.arity` for the number of declared arguments.

See Also

Function.arity, Function.length

Array — built-in support for arrays

Availability

Core JavaScript 1.1; enhanced by ECMA-262; enhanced in Navigator 4. Array functionality is available in JavaScript 1.0, but the Array object itself is not supported by Navigator 2.

Constructor

```
new Array()
new Array(size)
new Array(element0, element1, ..., elementn)
```

Arguments

size   The desired number of elements in the array. The returned array has its length field set to *size*.

element0, ...elementn

An argument list of two or more arbitrary values. When the Array() constructor is invoked with these arguments, the newly created array is initialized with the specified argument values as its elements and its length field set to the number of arguments.

Returns

The newly created and initialized array. When Array() is invoked with no arguments, the returned array has a length field of 0.

Properties

length   A read/write integer specifying the number of elements in the array, or, when the array does not have contiguous elements, a number one larger than the index of the last element in the array.

Methods

concat()   Concatenate elements to an array.

join()   Convert all array elements to strings and concatenate them.

pop()   Remove an item from the end of an array.

push()   Push an item onto the end of an array.

reverse()   Reverse, in place, the order of the elements of an array.

shift()   Shift an element off the beginning of an array.

slice()   Return a subarray slice of an array.

`sort()`	Sort, in place, the elements of an array.
`splice()`	Insert, delete, or replace array elements.
`toString()`	Convert an array to a string.
`unshift()`	Insert elements at the beginning of an array.

Description

Arrays are a basic syntactic feature of JavaScript. All JavaScript objects, regardless of their type, may be used as arrays. The dual nature of arrays and objects is discussed in Chapter 9, *Arrays*, along with full details on the JavaScript syntax for reading and setting array elements.

Array is a special object type, added in JavaScript 1.1, which, along with the usual array capabilities that all JavaScript objects have, also provides additional array functionality: a constructor function for initializing arrays; an automatically updated `length` field that stores the size of the array; and `join()`, `reverse()`, and `sort()` methods that manipulate the elements of an array. Additional methods were added by ECMA-262 and by Navigator 4.

See Also

Object, Chapter 9

Array.concat() — concatenate arrays

Availability

Core JavaScript 1.2

Synopsis

```
array.concat(value,...)
```

Arguments

value, ...   Any number of values to be concatenated with *array*.

Returns

A new array, which is formed by concatenating each of the specified arguments to *array*.

Description

`concat()` creates and returns a new array that is the result of concatenating each of its arguments to *array*. It does not modify *array*. If any of the arguments to `concat()` is itself an array, the elements of that array are concatenated, rather than the array itself.

Example

```
var a = [1,2,3];
a.concat(4, 5)          // Returns [1,2,3,4,5]
a.concat([4,5]);        // Returns [1,2,3,4,5]
a.concat([4,5],[6,7])   // Returns [1,2,3,4,5,6,7]
a.concat(4, [5,[6,7]])  // Returns [1,2,3,4,5,[6,7]]
```

See Also
Array.join( ), Array.push( ), Array.splice( )

Array.join( ) — concatenate array elements to form a string

Availability
Core JavaScript 1.1; ECMA-262

Synopsis
```
array.join()
array.join(separator)
```

Arguments
separator   An optional character or string used to separate one element of the array from the next in the returned string. If this argument is omitted, the empty string is used.

Returns
The string that results from converting each element of *array* to a string and then concatenating them together, with the *separator* string between elements.

Description
join( ) converts each of the elements of an array to a string and then concatenates those strings, inserting the specified *separator* string between the elements. It returns the resulting string.

Usage
You can perform the opposite direction—split a string up into array elements—with the split( ) method of the String object.

Example
```
a = new Array(1, 2, 3, "testing");
s = a.join("+");   // s is the string "1+2+3+testing".
```

See Also
String.split( )

Array.length — the size of an array

Availability
Core JavaScript 1.1, Internet Explorer 3; ECMA-262

Synopsis
```
array.length
```

Description

The length property of an array is always one larger than the highest element defined in the array. For traditional "dense" arrays that have contiguous elements and begin with element 0, the length property specifies the number of elements in the array.

The length property of an array is initialized when the array is created with the Array() constructor method. Adding new elements to an array updates the length, if necessary:

```
a = new Array();                      // a.length initialized to 0
b = new Array(10);                    // b.length initialized to 10
c = new Array("one", "two", "three"); // c.length initialized to 3
c[3] = "four";                        // c.length updated to 4
c[10] = "blastoff";                   // c.length becomes 11
```

Note that all JavaScript objects can be used as arrays, but only those created with the Array() constructor have an automatically created and updated length property.

You can set the value of the length property to change the size of an array. If you set length to be smaller than its previous value, the array is truncated and elements at the end are lost. If you set length to be larger than its previous value, the array becomes bigger and the new elements added at the end of the array have the special JavaScript undefined value.

Usage

The Array() constructor and length field were added to JavaScript in Navigator 3. Some Navigator 2 programs attempt to simulate a length field by setting it in the array constructor methods they write. Note, however, that the length field is not automatically updated as elements are added to the array, nor can it grow or shrink the array when its value is set.

Array.pop() — remove and return the last element of an array

Availability

Core Navigator 4

Synopsis

```
array.pop()
```

Returns

The last element of *array*.

Description

pop() deletes the last element of *array*, decrements the array length, and returns the value of the element that it deleted.

Example

pop(), and its companion method push(), provide the functionality of a first-in, last-out (FILO) stack. For example:

```
var stack = [];          // stack: []
stack.push(1, 2);        // stack: [1,2]        Returns 2
stack.pop();             // stack: [1]          Returns 2
stack.push([4,5]);       // stack: [1,[4,5]]    Returns [4,5]
stack.pop()              // stack: [1]          Returns [4,5]
stack.pop();             // stack: []           Returns 1
```

See Also

Array.push()

Array.push() — append elements to an array

Availability

Core Navigator 4

Synopsis

```
array.push(value, ...)
```

Arguments

value, ...   One or more values to be appended to the end of *array*.

Returns

The last value appended.

Description

push() appends its arguments, in order, to the end of *array*. It modifies *array* directly, rather than creating a new array.

push(), and its companion method pop(), use arrays to provide the functionality of a first in, last out (FILO) stack. See Array.pop() for an example.

See Also

Array.pop()

Array.reverse() — reverse the elements of an array

Availability

Core JavaScript 1.1; ECMA-262

Synopsis

```
array.reverse()
```

Description

The reverse() method of an Array object reverses the order of the elements of an array. It does this "in place"—it rearranges the elements of the specified *array*, without creating a new array. If there are multiple references to *array*, the new order of the array elements is visible through all references.

Example

```
a = new Array(1, 2, 3);     // a[0] == 1, a[2] == 3;
a.reverse();      // Now a[0] == 3, a[2] == 1;
```

Array.shift() — shift array elements down

Availability

Core Navigator 4

Synopsis

```
array.shift()
```

Returns

The former first element of the array.

Description

shift() removes and returns the first element of *array*, shifting all subsequent elements down one place to occupy the newly vacant space at the start of the array. Note that shift() does not create a new array; instead, it modifies *array* directly.

shift() is similar to Array.pop(), except it operates on the beginning of an array rather than the end. shift() is often used in conjunction with unshift().

Example

```
var a = [1, [2,3], 4]
a.shift();            // Returns 1;      a = [[2,3], 4]
a.shift();            // Returns [2,3];  a = [4]
```

See Also

Array.pop(), Array.unshift()

Array.slice() — return a portion of an array

Availability

Core JavaScript 1.2

Synopsis

```
array.slice(start, end)
```

Arguments

start   The array index at which the slice is to begin. If negative, this argument specifies a position measured from the end of the array. That is, −1 indicates the last element, −2 indicates the second from last element, and so on.

end   The array index immediately after the end of the slice. If not specified, the slice includes all array elements from the *start* to the end of the array. If this argument is negative, it specifies an array element measured from the end of the array.

Returns

A new array that contains the elements in the specified slice of *array*.

Description

slice() returns a slice, or subarray, of *array*. The returned array contains the element specified by *start*, and contains all subsequent elements up to, but not including, the element specified by *end*. If *end* is not specified, the returned array contains all elements from the *start* to the end of *array*.

Note that slice() does not modify the array. If you want to actually remove a slice of an array, use Array.splice().

Example

```
var a = [1,2,3,4,5];
a.slice(0,3);    // Returns [1,2,3]
a.slice(3);      // Returns [4,5]
a.slice(1,-1);   // Returns [2,3,4]
a.slice(-3,-2);  // Returns [3]. Buggy in IE 4: returns [1,2,3]
```

Bugs

start cannot be a negative number in Internet Explorer 4.

See Also

Array.splice()

Array.sort() — sort the elements of an array

Availability

Core JavaScript 1.1; ECMA-262

Synopsis

```
array.sort()
array.sort(orderfunc)
```

Arguments

orderfunc   An optional function used to specify the sorting order.

Description

The sort() method sorts the elements of *array* in place—no copy of the array is made. If sort() is called with no arguments, the elements of the array are arranged in alphabetical order (more precisely, the order determined by the character encoding). To do this, elements are first converted to strings, if necessary, so that they can be compared.

If you want to sort the array elements in some other order, you must supply a comparison function that compares two values and returns a number indicating their relative order. The comparison function should take two arguments, a and b, and should return:

- A value less than zero, if, according to your sort criteria, *a* is "less than" *b* and should appear before *b* in the sorted array.

- Zero, if *a* and *b* are equivalent for the purposes of this sort.

- A value greater than zero, if *a* is "greater than" *b* for the purposes of the sort.

Example

The following code shows how you might write a comparison function to sort an array of numbers in numerical, rather than alphabetical order:

```
// An ordering function for a numerical sort
function numberorder(a, b) { return a - b; }

a = new Array(33, 4, 1111, 222);
a.sort();                // Alphabetical sort: 1111, 222, 33, 4
a.sort(numberorder);     // Numerical sort: 4, 33, 222, 1111
```

Array.splice() — insert, remove, or replace array elements

Availability

Core Navigator 4

Synopsis

```
array.splice(start, deleteCount, value, ...)
```

Arguments

start   The array element at which the insertion and/or deletion is to begin.

deleteCount The number of elements, starting with and including *start*, to be deleted from *array*. This argument is optional; if not specified, splice() deletes all elements from *start* to the end of the array.

value,...   Zero or more values to be inserted into *array*, beginning at the index specified by *start*.

Returns

An array containing the elements, if any, deleted from *array*. Note, however, that due to a bug, the return value is not always an array in Navigator 4.

Description

splice() deletes zero or more array elements starting with and including the element *start* and replaces them with zero or more values specified in the argument list. Array elements that appear after the insertion or deletion are moved as necessary so that they remain contiguous with the rest of the array. Note that, unlike the similarly named slice(), splice() modifies *array* directly.

Example

The operation of `splice()` is most easily understood through an example:

```
var a = [1,2,3,4,5,6,7,8]
a.splice(4);    // Returns [5,6,7,8]. a is [1,2,3,4]
a.splice(1,2);  // Returns [2,3]. a is [1,4]
a.splice(1,1);  // Should return [4]. Nav4 returns 4. a is [1]
```

Bugs

`splice()` is supposed to return an array of deleted elements in all cases. However, in Navigator 4, when a single element is deleted, it returns the element, rather than an array containing the element. If no elements are deleted, Navigator 4 returns nothing, instead of returning an empty array as it should.

See Also

Array.slice()

Array.toString() — convert an array to a string

Availability

Core JavaScript 1.1; ECMA-262

Synopsis

```
array.toString()
```

Returns

A string representation of *array*.

Description

The `toString()` method of an array converts an array to a string and returns the string. When an array is used in a string context, JavaScript automatically converts it to a string by calling this method. On some occasions, however, you may want to call `toString()` explicitly.

`toString()` converts an array to a string by first converting each of the array elements to strings (by calling their `toString()` methods). Once each element is converted to a string, it outputs them in a comma-separated list. In Navigator 4, in JavaScript code with a LANGUAGE attribute explicitly specified as "JavaScript1.2", `toString()` returns its list of comma-separated array elements within square brackets. This behavior is not compatible with ECMA-262, however.

Array.unshift() — insert elements at the beginning of an array

Availability

Core Navigator 4

Synopsis

```
array.unshift(value, ...)
```

Arguments

value, ...   One or more values that are to be inserted at the start of *array*.

Returns

The new length of the array.

Description

unshift() inserts its arguments at the beginning of *array*, shifting the existing elements to higher indexes to make room. The first argument to shift() becomes the new element 0 of the array, the second argument, if any, becomes the new element 1, and so on. Note that unshift() does not create a new array; it modifies *array* directly.

Example

unshift() is often used in conjunction with shift(). For example:

```
var a = [];           // a:[]
a.unshift(1);         // a:[1]           Returns: 1
a.unshift(22);        // a:[22,1]        Returns: 2
a.shift();            // a:[1]           Returns: 22
a.unshift(33,[4,5]);  // a:[33,[4,5],1]  Returns: 3
```

See Also

Array.shift()

---

blur() — see Window.blur()

Boolean — support for boolean values

Availability

Core JavaScript 1.1; ECMA-262

Constructor

```
new Boolean(value)        Constructor function
Boolean(value)            Conversion function
```

Arguments

value   The value to be held by the Boolean object or to be converted to a boolean value.

Returns

When invoked as a constructor with the `new` operator, `Boolean()` converts its argument to a boolean value and returns a Boolean object that contains that value. When invoked as a function, without the `new` operator, `Boolean()` simply converts its argument to a primitive boolean value and returns that value.

The values 0, NaN, `null`, the empty string `""`, and the undefined value are all converted to `false`. All other values, including the string "false", are converted to `true`.

Methods

`toString()`   Return "true" or "false", depending on the boolean value represented by the Boolean object.

Description

Boolean values are a fundamental data type in JavaScript. The Boolean object is an object wrapper around the boolean value. This Boolean object type exists primarily to provide a `toString()` method to convert boolean values to strings. When the `toString()` method is invoked to convert a boolean value to a string (and it is often invoked implicitly by JavaScript) JavaScript internally converts the boolean value to a transient Boolean object, on which the method can be invoked.

See Also

Object

Boolean.toString() — convert a boolean value to a string

Availability

Core JavaScript 1.1; ECMA-262

Synopsis

```
b.toString()
```

Returns

The string "true" or "false", depending on the value of the primitive boolean value or Boolean object *b*.

Button — a graphical pushbutton

Availability

Client-side JavaScript 1.0; enhanced in JavaScript 1.1

Inherits From

Input, HTMLElement

Synopsis

```
form.button_name
form.elements[i]
```

Properties

Button inherits properties from Input and HTMLElement and also defines or overrides the following:

value   A read-only String property, specified by the HTML `VALUE` attribute, which specifies the value displayed in the Button element.

Methods

Button inherits methods from Input and HTMLElement.

Event Handlers

Button inherits event handlers from Input and HTMLElement and also defines or overrides the following:

onclick   Invoked when the button is clicked.

HTML Syntax

A Button element is created with a standard HTML `<INPUT>` tag:

```
<FORM>
    . . .
  <INPUT
    TYPE="button"          Specifies that this is a button
    VALUE="label"          The text that is to appear within the button
                           Specifies the value property
    [ NAME="name" ]        A name that can later be used to refer to the button
                           Specifies the name property
    [ onClick="handler" ]  JavaScript statements to be executed when the button
                           is clicked
  >
    . . .
</FORM>
```

Description

The Button element represents a graphical push button in a form within an HTML document. The `value` property contains the text that is displayed by the button. The `name` property is a name by which the button may be referred to. The `onClick` event handler is invoked when the user clicks on the button.

Usage

Use a Button element whenever you want to allow the user to trigger some action on your web page. You can sometimes use a Link object for the same purpose, but unless the desired action is to follow a hypertext link, a Button is a better choice than a Link, because it makes it more explicit to the user that there is something to be triggered.

Note that the Submit and Reset elements are types of Buttons that submit a form and reset a form's values. Often these default actions are sufficient for a form, and you do not need to create any other types of buttons.

Example

```
<FORM name="form1">
    <INPUT type="button"
        name="press_me_button"
        value="Press Me"
        onClick="username = prompt('What is your name?','')"
    >
</FORM>
```

See Also

Form, HTMLElement, Input, Reset, Submit

Button.onclick — the handler invoked when a Button is clicked

Availability

Client-side JavaScript 1.0

Synopsis

```
<INPUT TYPE="button" VALUE="button-text" onClick="handler">
button.onclick
```

Description

The onclick property of a Button object refers to an event handler function that is invoked when the user clicks on the button. See HTMLElement.onclick for complete details. Note, however, that Button.onclick has been supported since JavaScript 1.0, unlike the generalized HTMLElement.onclick handler.

See Also

HTMLElement.onclick, Chapter 15, *Events and Event Handling*

Button.value — the text that appears in a Button

Availability

Client-side JavaScript 1.0

Synopsis

```
button.value
```

Description

value is a read-only string property of the Button object. It contains the text that appears in the button. The value of this property is specified by the VALUE attribute of the HTML <INPUT> tag that creates the button.

Checkbox — a graphical checkbox

Availability

Client-side JavaScript 1.0; enhanced in JavaScript 1.1

Inherits From

Input, HTMLElement

Synopsis

A single Checkbox element with a unique name may be referenced in either of these ways:

```
form.checkbox_name
form.elements[i]
```

When a form contains a group of checkboxes with the same name, they are placed in an array and may be referenced as follows:

```
form.checkbox_name[j]
form.checkbox_name.length
```

Properties

Checkbox inherits properties from Input and HTMLElement and also defines or overrides the following:

checked   A read/write boolean value that specifies whether the button is checked or not.

defaultChecked

          A read-only boolean that specifies the initial state of the checkbox. May be specified with the HTML CHECKED attribute.

value   A read/write string, initially set by the HTML VALUE attribute, which specifies the value returned by the Checkbox if it is selected when the form is submitted.

Methods

Checkbox inherits the methods of Input and HTMLElement.

Event Handlers

Checkbox inherits event handlers from Input and HTMLElement and also defines or overrides the following:

onclick   Invoked when the checkbox is clicked.

HTML Syntax

A Checkbox element is created with a standard HTML <INPUT> tag. Multiple Checkbox elements are often created in groups by specifying multiple <INPUT> tags that have the same NAME attribute.

```
<FORM>
   . . .
  <INPUT
    TYPE="checkbox"            Specifies that this is a checkbox
    [ NAME="name" ]            A name that can later be used to refer to this checkbox
                               or to the group of checkboxes with this name
                               Specifies the name property
    [ VALUE="value" ]          The value returned when this checkbox is selected
                               Specifies the value property
    [ CHECKED ]                Specifies that the checkbox is initially checked
                               Specifies the defaultChecked property
    [ onClick="handler" ]      JavaScript statements to be executed
   >                           when the checkbox is clicked
 label                         The HTML text that should appear next to the checkbox
   . . .
</FORM>
```

Description

The Checkbox element represents a single graphical checkbox in an HTML form. Note that the text that appears next to the checkbox is not part of the Checkbox element itself and must be specified externally to the Checkbox's HTML <INPUT> tag.

The onClick event handler allows you to specify JavaScript code to be executed when the Checkbox is checked or unchecked.

You can examine the checked property to determine the state of the Checkbox, and you can also set this property to check or uncheck the Checkbox. Note that setting checked changes the graphical appearance of the Checkbox but does not invoke the onClick event handler.

It is good programming style to specify the NAME attribute for a Checkbox; this is mandatory if the checkbox is part of a form that submits data to a CGI script running on a web server. Specifying a NAME attribute sets the name property and also allows you to refer to the Checkbox by name (instead of as a member of the form elements array) in your JavaScript code, which makes the code more modular and portable.

For example, if the NAME attribute of a checkbox in form f is "opts", f.opts refers to the Checkbox element. Checkbox elements are often used in related groups, however, and each member of the group is given the same NAME attribute (the shared name defines the members of the group). In this case, JavaScript places each Checkbox element in the group in an array, and the array is given the shared name. If, for example, each of a group of Checkboxes in form f has its NAME attribute set to "opts", f.opts is an array of Checkbox elements, and f.opts.length is the number of elements in the array.

Unfortunately, in Navigator 2, there is a bug in how Checkbox elements in a group are assigned to an array. See the Bugs section of this reference page for details.

You can set the VALUE attribute or the value property of a Checkbox to specify the string that is passed to the server if the Checkbox is checked when the form is submitted. For a single checkbox, used alone, the default value of "on" is usually adequate. When multiple checkboxes with the same name are used, each should specify a distinct value so that a list of values from selected checkboxes can be passed to the server.

Usage

Checkbox elements can be used to present the user with one or more options. This element type is suitable for presenting non-mutually exclusive choices. Use the Radio element for mutually exclusive lists of options.

Bugs

As described above, when a group of Checkbox elements share the same NAME attribute, JavaScript assigns them to an array bearing that name. Unfortunately, there is a bug in this process in Navigator 2: if the Checkbox elements do not have event handlers specified with the onClick attribute, they are assigned to the array in reverse order. This is counterintuitive and is incompatible with Navigator 3, in which the bug has been fixed.

The workaround is always to assign an event handler, if only a dummy one, to your Checkbox elements that are manipulated with JavaScript. You can do this by including onClick="0" in the <INPUT> tag for each Checkbox element you define. With this workaround, you can ensure that the elements are assigned to the array in the same order in Navigator 2 and Navigator 3.

See Also

Form, HTMLElement, Input, Radio

Checkbox.checked — whether a Checkbox is checked

Availability

Client-side JavaScript 1.0

Synopsis

```
checkbox.checked
```

Description

checked is a read/write boolean property of the Checkbox object. If the Checkbox is checked, the checked property is true. If the Checkbox is not checked, checked is false.

If you set checked to true, the Checkbox appears checked. Similarly, if you set this property to false, the Checkbox appears unchecked. Note that setting the checked property does not cause the Checkbox's onClick event handler to be invoked.

Checkbox.defaultChecked — the initial state of a Checkbox

Availability

Client-side JavaScript 1.0

Synopsis

```
checkbox.defaultChecked
```

Description

defaultChecked is a read-only boolean property of the Checkbox object. It is true if the Checkbox is initially checked—if the CHECKED attribute appears in the Checkbox's HTML <INPUT> tag. If this attribute does not appear, the Checkbox is initially unchecked, and defaultChecked is false.

Checkbox.onclick — the handler invoked when a Checkbox is selected

Availability

Client-side JavaScript 1.0

Synopsis

```
<INPUT TYPE="checkbox" onClick="handler">
checkbox.onclick
```

Description

The onclick property of a Checkbox object refers to an event handler function that is invoked when the user clicks on the Checkbox. See HTMLElement.onclick for complete details. Note, however, that Checkbox.onclick has been supported since JavaScript 1.0, unlike the generalized HTMLElement.onclick handler.

See Also

HTMLElement.onclick, Chapter 15

Checkbox.value — the value returned when a form is submitted

Availability

Client-side JavaScript 1.0

Synopsis

```
checkbox.value
```

Description

value is a read/write string property of the Checkbox object. It specifies the text that is passed to the web server if the Checkbox is checked when the form is submitted. The initial value of value is specified by the VALUE attribute of the Checkbox's HTML <INPUT> tag. If no VALUE attribute is specified, the default value string is "on".

Note that the value field does not specify whether or not the Checkbox is selected; the checked property specifies the current state of the Checkbox.

When defining a group of related checkboxes that share the same name in a form that is submitted to the server, it is important that each be given a distinct value attribute.

clearTimeout() — see Window.clearTimeout()

close() — see Window.close()

closed — see Window.closed

confirm() — see Window.confirm()

Crypto — cryptography-related resources

Availability

Client-side Navigator 4.04 and later

Synopsis

```
crypto
```

Functions

```
crypto.random()
```
> Generate a random string of bytes.

```
crypto.signText()
```
> Ask the user to attach his digital signature to an arbitrary string of text.

Description

The Crypto object was added to Navigator 4 in Version 4.04. It is referred to by the `crypto` property of each Window object. It defines the `signText()` method that can be used to ask the user to attach his digital signature to an arbitrary string of text. The `random()` method returns a random string of bytes.

Crypto.random() — generate random byte strings

Availability

Client-side Navigator 4.04 and later

Synopsis

```
crypto.random(numbytes)
```

Arguments

numbytes   The number of bytes of cryptographic-grade pseudo-random data to be generated.

Returns

A string containing *numbytes* characters, where each character is a random byte of data.

Description

`Crypto.random()` is a pseudo-random number generator suitable for use in cryptographic applications. Rather than returning a random number like `Math.random()` does, it returns a string of random bytes.

See Also

Math.random()

Crypto.signText() — ask the user to digitally sign text

Availability

Client-side Navigator 4.04 and later

Synopsis

```
crypto.signText(text, CASelection, allowedCA, ...)
```

Arguments

`text`   The text to be signed.

`CASelection` A string that specifies how the certificate to be used for the signature is to be selected. If this argument is "ask", the user is presented with a choice of all available certificates (or, if any `allowedCA` arguments are specified, the user is presented with a list of all certificates signed by one of those specified CAs).

                  If `CASelection` is "auto", `signText()` automatically selects a certificate signed by one of the CAs listed in the remaining arguments to this method.

`allowedCA...`

                  Zero or more strings, each specifying the distinguished name (DN) of a Certificate Authority (CA) trusted by the server that is using the signed text. If any `allowedCA` arguments are specified, the digital signature is generated using a certificate issued by one of the specified CAs. If the user does not have a certificate from one of the specified CAs, the signature cannot be generated, and `signText()` returns an error code.

Returns

If no errors occur, `signText()` returns a string of base-64 encoded binary data representing a PKCS #7 signed object. If this value is stored in a Hidden element and transmitted to a server via form submission, the server can decode it and verify the signature using the Netscape Signature Verification Tool.

`signText()` may also return one of three possible string error codes defined as follows:

`error:noMatchingCert`

                  The user does not have any certificates, or does not have a certificate issued by one of the specified `allowedCA` arguments.

```
error:userCancel
```
The user refused to sign the text and clicked the **Cancel** button in the dialog displayed by signText().

```
error:internalError
```
An internal error (such as out-of-memory) prevented the text from being signed.

Description

signText() displays a dialog box containing *text* and asking the user to guarantee that text by placing his digital signature on it. The user can sign the text by clicking the **Ok** button of the dialog box, or can refuse to sign the text by clicking the **Cancel** button.

If the *CASelection* argument is "ask", the dialog box also contains a list of suitable certificates that the user can use to generate the signature. If this argument is "auto", signText() automatically searches for and chooses a suitable certificate.

These first two required arguments are followed by zero or more names of Certificate Authorities that your application trusts. These arguments specify which certificates can be used to generate a digital signature that will be considered valid by the service verifying the signature.

If no errors occur, signText() returns a string of base-64 encoded binary data. This string can be stored in a form and transmitted to a server, where it can be decoded and the signature can be verified.

Date — manipulate dates and times

Availability

Core JavaScript 1.0; enhanced by ECMA-262

Constructor

```
new Date();
new Date(milliseconds)
new Date(datestring);
new Date(year, month, day, hours, minutes, seconds, ms)
```

With no arguments, the Date() constructor creates a Date object set to the current date and time. When one numeric argument is passed, it is taken as the internal numeric representation of the date in milliseconds, as returned by the getTime() method. When one string argument is passed, it is a string representation of a date, in the format accepted by the Date.parse() method. Otherwise, the constructor is passed between two and seven arguments that specify the individual fields of the date and time. All but the year and month fields are optional. Note that these date and time fields are specified using local time, not UTC time.

Date() can also be called as a function, without the new operator. The ECMA-262 standard specifies that when called as a function it should behave exactly as it does when used as a constructor. In Navigator 3 and 4, however, calling Date() as a function returns a string representation of the specified date rather than an actual Date object.

Arguments

milliseconds
> The number of milliseconds between the desired date and midnight GMT on January 1, 1970. For example, passing the argument 5000 would create a date that represents five seconds past midnight on 1/1/70.

datestring
> A single argument that specifies the date and, optionally, the time as a String. The string should be in a format accepted by `Date.parse()`.

year
> The year, in four-digit format. For example, specify 2001 for the year 2001.

month
> The month, specified as an integer from 0 (January) to 11 (December).

day
> The day of the month, specified as an integer from 1 to 31. Note that this argument uses 1 as its lowest value, while other arguments use 0 as their lowest value. This argument is optional.

hours
> The hour, specified as an integer from 0 (midnight) to 23 (11 p.m.). This argument is optional.

minutes
> The minutes in the hour, specified as an integer from 0 to 59. This argument is optional.

seconds
> The seconds in the minute, specified as an integer from 0 to 59. This argument is optional.

ms
> The milliseconds in the second, specified as an integer from 0 to 999. This argument is optional, and prior to JavaScript 1.2, it is ignored.

Methods

Once a Date object is created by using `Date()` as a constructor in any of the forms shown above, any of the following methods can be used to operate on the Date object. Note that unlike most JavaScript objects, the Date object has no properties that can be read and written directly; instead, all access to date and time fields is done through these methods:

`getDate()`   Return the day of the month of a Date object.

`getDay()`   Return the day of the week of a Date object.

`getFullYear()`
> Return the year of the date in full four-digit form.

`getHours()`   Return the hours field of a Date object.

`getMilliseconds()`
> Return the milliseconds field of a Date object.

`getMinutes()`
> Return the minutes field of a Date object.

`getMonth()`   Return the month field of a Date object.

`getSeconds( )`
> Return the seconds field of a Date object.

`getTime( )`   Return the internal, millisecond representation of a Date object.

`getTimezoneOffset( )`
> Return the time zone difference, in minutes, between this date and GMT.

`getUTCDate( )`
> Return the day of the month, in universal time.

`getUTCDay( )`   Return the day of the week, in universal time.

`getUTCFullYear( )`
> Return the full four-digit year, in universal time.

`getUTCHours( )`
> Return the hours field, in universal time.

`getUTCMilliseconds( )`
> Return the milliseconds field, in universal time.

`getUTCMinutes( )`
> Return the minutes field, in universal time.

`getUTCMonth( )`
> Return the month field, in universal time.

`getUTCSeconds( )`
> Return the seconds field, in universal time.

`getYear( )`   Return the year field of a Date object. Deprecated in favor of `getFullYear( )`.

`setDate( )`   Set the day of the month field of a Date object.

`setFullYear( )`
> Set the year field to a full four-digit year.

`setHours( )`   Set the hour field of a Date object.

`setMilliseconds( )`
> Set the milliseconds field of a Date object.

`setMinutes( )`
> Set the minutes field of a Date object.

`setMonth( )`   Set the month field of a Date object.

`setSeconds( )`
> Set the seconds field of a Date object.

`setTime( )`   Set the fields of a Date object using the millisecond format.

`setUTCDate( )`
> Set the day of the month field, in universal time.

`setUTCFullYear()`
> Set the year field to a full four-digit year, using universal time.

`setUTCHours()`
> Set the hour field, in universal time.

`setUTCMilliseconds()`
> Set the milliseconds field, in universal time.

`setUTCMinutes()`
> Set the minutes field, in universal time.

`setUTCMonth()`
> Set the month field, in universal time.

`setUTCSeconds()`
> Set the seconds field, in universal time.

`setYear()`   Set the year field of a Date object. Deprecated in favor of `setFullYear()`.

`toGMTString()`
> Convert a Date to a string, using the GMT time zone.

`toLocaleString()`
> Convert a Date to a string, using the local time zone.

`toString()`   Convert a Date to a string.

`toUTCString()`
> Convert a Date to a string, using universal time.

`valueOf()`   Convert a Date to its internal millisecond format.

Static Methods

In addition to the many instance methods listed above, the Date object also defines two static methods. These methods are invoked through the `Date()` constructor itself, not through individual Date objects:

`Date.parse()`
> Convert a string representation of a date to the internal millisecond representation.

`Date.UTC()`   Convert a numeric date and time specification to millisecond representation.

Description

The Date object is a data type built into the JavaScript language. Date objects are created with the `new Date()` syntax shown in the preceding Constructor section.

Once a Date object is created, there are a number of methods that allow you to operate on it. Most of the methods simply allow you to get and set the year, month, day, hour, minute, and second fields of the object. ECMA-262 and JavaScript 1.2 add a full set of methods that allow you to set and retrieve these fields using UTC (universal, or GMT) time. The `toUTC-String()` and `toLocaleString()` methods convert dates to human-readable strings. `get-Time()` and `setTime()` convert to and from the internal representation of the Date object—the number of milliseconds since midnight (GMT) on January 1, 1970. In this standard millisecond format, a date and time are represented by a single integer, which makes date arithmetic particularly easy.

Most of the Date object methods are invoked through an instance of the Date object. For example:

```
d = new Date();  // Get today's date and time
document.write('Today is: " + d.toLocaleString());  // and print it out.
```

Bugs

In Navigator 2, the Date object has quite a few bugs and is almost unusable.

Example

A common use of the Date object is to subtract the millisecond representations of the current time from some other time to determine the difference between the two times. The following example shows two such uses:

```
<SCRIPT language="JavaScript">
today = new Date();      // Make a note of today's date.
christmas = new Date();  // Get a date with the current year.
christmas.setMonth(11);  // Set the month to December...
christmas.setDate(25);   // and the day to the 25th.

// If Christmas hasn't already passed, compute the number of
// milliseconds between now and Christmas, then convert this
// to a number of days and print a message.
if (today.getTime() < christmas.getTime()) {
    difference = christmas.getTime() - today.getTime();
    difference = Math.floor(difference / (1000 * 60 * 60 * 24));
    document.write('Only ' + difference + ' days until Christmas!<P>');
}
</SCRIPT>
```

... rest of HTML document here ...

```
<SCRIPT language="JavaScript">
// Here we use Date objects for timing. We divide by 1000
// to convert milliseconds to seconds. We could divide
// further to convert to minutes, hours or days.
now = new Date();
document.write('<P>It took ' +
    (now.getTime()-today.getTime())/1000 +
    'seconds to load this page.');
</SCRIPT>
```

See Also

Date.parse( ), Date.UTC( )

Date.getDate( ) — return the day of the month

Availability

Core JavaScript 1.0; ECMA-262

Synopsis

```
date.getDate()
```

Returns

The day of the month of the specified Date object *date*. Return values are between 1 and 31.

Date.getDay( ) — return the day of the week

Availability

Core JavaScript 1.0; ECMA-262

Synopsis

```
date.getDay()
```

Returns

The day of the week of the specified Date object *date*. Return values are between 0 (Sunday) and 6 (Saturday).

Date.getFullYear( ) — return the year (local time)

Availability

Core JavaScript 1.2; ECMA-262

Synopsis

```
date.getFullYear()
```

Returns

The year that results when *date* is expressed in local time. The return value is a full four-digit year, including the century, not a two-digit abbreviation.

Date.getHours( ) — return the hours field of a Date

Availability

Core JavaScript 1.0; ECMA-262

Synopsis

```
date.getHours()
```

Returns

The hours field of the specified Date object *date*. Return values are between 0 (midnight) and 23 (11 p.m.).

Date.getMilliseconds() — return the milliseconds field of a Date

Availability

Core JavaScript 1.2; ECMA-262

Synopsis

```
date.getMilliseconds()
```

Returns

The milliseconds field, expressed in local time, of *date*.

Date.getMinutes() — return the minutes field of a Date

Availability

Core JavaScript 1.0; ECMA-262

Synopsis

```
date.getMinutes()
```

Returns

The minutes field of the specified Date object *date*. Return values are between 0 and 59.

Date.getMonth() — return the month of a Date

Availability

Core JavaScript 1.0; ECMA-262

Synopsis

```
date.getMonth()
```

Returns

The month field of the specified Date object *date*. Return values are between 0 (January) and 11 (December).

Date.getSeconds() — return the seconds field of a Date

Availability

Core JavaScript 1.0; ECMA-262

Synopsis

```
date.getSeconds()
```

Returns

The seconds field of the specified Date object `date`. Return values are between 0 and 59.

Date.getTime() — return a Date in milliseconds

Availability

Core JavaScript 1.0; ECMA-262

Synopsis

```
date.getTime()
```

Returns

The millisecond representation of the specified Date object `date`; that is, the number of milliseconds between midnight (GMT) on 1/1/1970 and the date and time specified by `date`.

Usage

`getTime()` converts a date and time to a single integer. This is useful when you want to compare two Date objects or to determine the time elapsed between two dates.

`Date.parse()` and `Date.UTC()` allow you to convert a date and time specification to millisecond representation without going through the overhead of first creating a Date object.

See Also

Date, Date.parse(), Date.setTime(), Date.UTC()

Date.getTimezoneOffset() — determine the offset from GMT

Availability

Core JavaScript 1.0; ECMA-262

Synopsis

```
date.getTimezoneOffset()
```

Returns

The difference, in minutes, between Greenwich Mean Time (GMT) and local time.

Description

`getTimezoneOffset()` returns the number of minutes difference between the GMT or UTC time zone and the local time zone. In effect, this function tells you what time zone the JavaScript code is running in. The return value is measured in minutes, rather than hours, because some countries have time zones that are not at even one-hour intervals.

`getTimezoneOffset()` is invoked through a Date object. Note, however, that it doesn't actually reference the Date object, and so it ought to be an independent function instead of a method.

Date.getUTCDate() — return the day of the month (universal time)

Availability

Core JavaScript 1.2; ECMA-262

Synopsis

```
date.getUTCDate()
```

Returns

The day of the month (a value between 1 and 31) that results when *date* is expressed in universal time.

Date.getUTCDay() — return the day of the week (universal time)

Availability

Core JavaScript 1.2; ECMA-262

Synopsis

```
date.getUTCDay()
```

Returns

The day of the week that results when *date* is expressed in universal time. Return values are between 0 (Sunday) and 6 (Saturday).

Date.getUTCFullYear() — return the year (universal time)

Availability

Core JavaScript 1.2; ECMA-262

Synopsis

```
date.getUTCFullYear()
```

Returns

The year that results when *date* is expressed in universal time. The return value is a full four-digit year, not a two-digit abbreviation.

Date.getUTCHours() — return the hours field of a Date (universal time)

Availability

Core JavaScript 1.2; ECMA-262

Synopsis

```
date.getUTCHours()
```

Returns

The hours field, expressed in universal time, of *date*. The return value is an integer between 0 (midnight) and 23 (11 p.m.).

Date.getUTCMilliseconds() — return the milliseconds field of a Date (universal time)

Availability

Core JavaScript 1.2; ECMA-262

Synopsis

```
date.getUTCMilliseconds()
```

Returns

The milliseconds field, expressed in universal time, of *date*.

Date.getUTCMinutes() — return the minutes field of a Date (universal time)

Availability

Core JavaScript 1.2; ECMA-262

Synopsis

```
date.getUTCMinutes()
```

Returns

The minutes field, expressed in universal time, of *date*. The return value is an integer between 0 and 59.

Date.getUTCMonth() — return the month of the year (universal time)

Availability

Core JavaScript 1.2; ECMA-262

Synopsis

```
date.getUTCMonth()
```

Returns

The month of the year that results when *date* is expressed in universal time. The return value is an integer between 0 (January) and 11 (December). Note that the Date object represents the first day of the month as 1, but represents the first month of the year as 0.

Date.getUTCSeconds() — return the seconds field of a Date (universal time)

Availability

Core JavaScript 1.2; ECMA-262

Synopsis

```
date.getUTCSeconds()
```

Returns

The seconds field, expressed in universal time, of *date*. The return value is an integer between 0 and 59.

Date.getYear() — return the year field of a Date

Availability

Core JavaScript 1.0; ECMA-262; deprecated in JavaScript 1.2 in favor of getFullYear()

Synopsis

```
date.getYear()
```

Returns

The year field of the specified Date object *date*.

Description

getYear() returns the year field of a specified Date object. In Navigator 2 and 3, the return value of this method is the year minus 1900 for dates between the years 1900 and 1999. For example, if *date* represents a date in 1997, the return value is 97. For dates prior to 1900 or after 1999, getYear() returns the year itself in Navigator 2 and 3. For example, if *date* represents a date in the year 2000, the method returns 2000 on Navigator platforms.

Internet Explorer 3 always returns the year minus 1900, however, so getYear() on this platform returns 85 to represent 1985, 100 to represent the year 2000, and 110 to represent 2010. IE 3 cannot represent years prior to 1970, so these return values are never negative numbers.

To work around these strange and incompatible return values, you should replace getYear() with a function like the following:

```
// Returns correct year for any year after 1000
function getFullYear(d)
```

```
{
    var y = d.getYear();
    if (y < 1000) y += 1900;
    return y;
}
```

Bugs

The disparity in return values between dates in the twentieth and twenty-first centuries in Navigator is bizarre, and, if not carefully taken into account, may be the source of millennium bugs in your code. The incompatibility between platforms makes this method especially annoying to use.

Date.parse() — parse a date/time string

Availability

Core JavaScript 1.0; ECMA-262

Synopsis

```
Date.parse(date)
```

Arguments

date   A string containing the date and time to be parsed.

Returns

The number of milliseconds between the specified date and time and midnight, January 1, 1970, GMT.

Description

Date.parse() is a static method of Date. It is always invoked as Date.parse(), not as date.parse().

Date.parse() takes a single string argument. It parses the date contained in this string and returns it in millisecond format, which can be used directly, used to create a new Date object, or used to set the date in an existing Date object with Date.setTime().

The date formats understood by Date.parse() are implementation dependent. All implementations, however, should understand the IETF standard date format used in email and other Internet communications. Dates in this format look like this:

```
Wed, 8 May 1996 17:41:46 -0400
```

This is the format written by the Date.toGMTString() method. Date.parse() can also parse dates in this format from which the day of the week, the time zone, the seconds, or the complete time specification have been omitted. It also understands the GMT time zone and the standard abbreviations for the time zones of the United States.

Bugs

In Navigator 2, prior to Version 2.0.2, this function cannot correctly parse time zone information.

See Also

Date, Date.setTime( ), Date.toGMTString( ), Date.UTC( )

Date.setDate( ) — set the day of the month

Availability

Core JavaScript 1.0; ECMA-262

Synopsis

```
date.setDate(day_of_month)
```

Arguments

day_of_month

A number between 1 and 31 that is set as the day of the month in the Date object *date*.

Returns

In JavaScript 1.2, this method returns the internal millisecond representation of the adjusted date, as mandated by ECMA-262. Prior to JavaScript 1.2, it returns nothing.

Date.setFullYear( ) — set the year

Availability

Core JavaScript 1.2; ECMA-262

Synopsis

```
date.setFullYear(year)
```

Arguments

year   The year, expressed in local time, to be set in *date*. This argument should be a full year including the century, such as 1999, and not an abbreviation such as 99.

Returns

The internal millisecond representation of the adjusted date.

Date.setHours() — set the hours field of a Date

Availability

Core JavaScript 1.0; ECMA-262

Synopsis

```
date.setHours(hours)
```

Arguments

hours   An integer between 0 (midnight) and 23 (11 p.m.) that is set as the hours value for the Date object *date*.

Returns

In JavaScript 1.2, this method returns the internal millisecond representation of the adjusted date, as mandated by ECMA-262. Prior to JavaScript 1.2, it returns nothing.

Date.setMilliseconds() — set the milliseconds field of a Date

Availability

Core JavaScript 1.2; ECMA-262

Synopsis

```
date.setMilliseconds(millis)
```

Arguments

millis   The milliseconds field, expressed in local time, to be set in *date*. This argument should be an integer between 0 and 999.

Returns

The internal millisecond representation of the adjusted date.

Date.setMinutes() — set the minutes field of a Date

Availability

Core JavaScript 1.0; ECMA-262

Synopsis

```
date.setMinutes(minutes)
```

Arguments

minutes   An integer between 0 and 59 that is set as the minutes value in the Date object *date*.

Returns

In JavaScript 1.2, this method returns the internal millisecond representation of the adjusted date, as mandated by ECMA-262. Prior to JavaScript 1.2, it returns nothing.

Date.setMonth() — set the month field of a Date

Availability

Core JavaScript 1.0; ECMA-262

Synopsis

```
date.setMonth(month)
```

Arguments

month   An integer between 0 (January) and 11 (December) that is set as the month value for the Date object *date*.

Returns

In JavaScript 1.2, this method returns the internal millisecond representation of the adjusted date, as mandated by ECMA-262. Prior to JavaScript 1.2, it returns nothing.

Date.setSeconds() — set the seconds field of a Date

Availability

Core JavaScript 1.0; ECMA-262

Synopsis

```
date.setSeconds(seconds)
```

Arguments

seconds   An integer between 0 and 59 that is set as the seconds value for the Date object *date*.

Returns

In JavaScript 1.2, this method returns the internal millisecond representation of the adjusted date, as mandated by ECMA-262. Prior to JavaScript 1.2, it returns nothing.

Date.setTime() — set a Date in milliseconds

Availability

Core JavaScript 1.0; ECMA-262

Synopsis

```
date.setTime(milliseconds)
```

Arguments

milliseconds

> The number of milliseconds between the desired date and time and midnight GMT on January 1, 1970. Representing a date in this millisecond format makes it independent of time zone.

Date.setUTCDate() — set the day of the month (universal time)

Availability

Core JavaScript 1.2; ECMA-262

Synopsis

`date.setUTCDate(day_of_month)`

Arguments

day_of_month

> The day of the month, expressed in universal time, to be set in *date*. This argument should be an integer between 1 and 31.

Returns

The internal millisecond representation of the adjusted date.

Date.setUTCFullYear() — set the year (universal time)

Availability

Core JavaScript 1.2; ECMA-262

Synopsis

`date.setUTCFullYear(year)`

Arguments

year

> The year, expressed in universal time, to be set in *date*. This argument should be a full year including the century, such as 1999, and not an abbreviation such as 99.

Returns

The internal millisecond representation of the adjusted date.

Date.setUTCHours() — set the hours field of a Date (universal time)

Availability

Core JavaScript 1.2; ECMA-262

Synopsis

date.setUTCHours(*hours*)

Arguments

hours   The hours field, expressed in universal time, to be set in *date*. This argument should be an integer between 0 (midnight) and 23 (11 p.m.).

Returns

The internal millisecond representation of the adjusted date.

Date.setUTCMilliseconds() — set the milliseconds field of a Date (universal time)

Availability

Core JavaScript 1.2; ECMA-262

Synopsis

date.setUTCMilliseconds(*millis*)

Arguments

millis   The milliseconds field, expressed in universal time, to be set in *date*. This argument should be an integer between 0 and 999.

Returns

The internal millisecond representation of the adjusted date.

Date.setUTCMinutes() — set the minutes field of a Date (universal time)

Availability

Core JavaScript 1.2; ECMA-262

Synopsis

date.setUTCMinutes(*minutes*)

Arguments

minutes   The minutes field, expressed in universal time, to be set in *date*. This argument should be an integer between 0 and 59.

Returns

The internal millisecond representation of the adjusted date.

Date.setUTCMonth() — set the month (universal time)

Availability

Core JavaScript 1.2; ECMA-262

Synopsis

```
date.setUTCMonth(month)
```

Arguments

month   The month, expressed in universal time, to be set in *date*. This argument should be an integer between 0 (January) and 11 (December). Note that months are numbered beginning with 0, while days within the month (see Date.setUTCDate()) are numbered beginning with 1.

Returns

The internal millisecond representation of the adjusted date.

Date.setUTCSeconds() — set the seconds field of a Date (universal time)

Availability

Core JavaScript 1.2; ECMA-262

Synopsis

```
date.setUTCSeconds(seconds)
```

Arguments

seconds   The seconds field, expressed in universal time, to be set in *date*. This argument should be an integer between 0 and 59.

Returns

The internal millisecond representation of the adjusted date.

Date.setYear() — set the year field of a Date

Availability

Core JavaScript 1.0; ECMA-262; deprecated in JavaScript 1.2 in favor of setFullYear()

Synopsis

```
date.setYear(year)
```

Arguments

year   An integer that is set as the year value for the Date object *date*. Usually, you should use a four-digit format for year specifications. For example, specify 2001 for the year 2001. For years within the 20th century, you can also subtract 1900 and specify the date in two-digit format. For example, you could specify 97 for the year 1997.

Returns

In JavaScript 1.2, this method returns the internal millisecond representation of the adjusted date, as mandated by ECMA-262. Prior to JavaScript 1.2, it returns nothing.

Date.toGMTString() — convert a date to a universal time string

Availability

Core JavaScript 1.0; ECMA-262; deprecated in JavaScript 1.2 in favor of `toUTCString()`

Synopsis

```
date.toGMTString()
```

Returns

A string representation of the date and time specified by the Date object *date*. The date is converted from the local time zone to the GMT time zone before being converted to a string.

Description

`toGMTString()` converts a date to a string using the GMT time zone. The format of the returned string is implementation dependent, but usually it appears something like this:

```
Tue, 02 Apr 1996 02:04:57 GMT
```

See Also

Date, Date.parse( ), Date.toLocaleString( ), Date.toUTCString()

Date.toLocaleString() — convert a Date to a string

Availability

Core JavaScript 1.0; ECMA-262

Synopsis

```
date.toLocaleString()
```

Returns

A string representation of the date and time specified by the Date object *date*. The date and time are represented in the local time zone.

Usage

`toLocaleString()` converts a date to a string, using the local time zone. This method also uses local conventions for date and time formatting, so the format may vary widely from platform to platform, and also from country to country. `toLocaleString()` returns a string formatted in what is likely the user's preferred date and time format. Because the format may vary widely, this method is not useful when the date string must be passed to a CGI script or otherwise machine processed.

Use `Date.toGMTString()` to convert a date to a string using the GMT time zone and a more standard format.

See Also

Date, Date.parse( ), Date.toGMTString( ), Date.toUTCString( )

Date.toString() — convert a date to a string

Availability

Core JavaScript 1.0; ECMA-262

Synopsis

```
date.toString()
```

Returns

A human-readable string representation of *date*, expressed in the local time zone.

Description

`toString( )` returns a human-readable, implementation-dependent string representation of *date*. Unlike `toUTCString( )`, `toString( )` expresses the date in the local time zone. Unlike `toLocaleString( )`, `toString( )` may not represent the date and time using locale-specific formatting.

Date.toUTCString() — convert a date to a string (universal time)

Availability

Core JavaScript 1.2; ECMA-262

Synopsis

```
date.toUTCString()
```

Returns

A human-readable string representation, expressed in universal time, of *date*.

Description

`toUTCString( )` is exactly the same as the `Date.toGMTString( )` method but is preferred over that method because its name is more precise.

Date.UTC() — convert a date specification to milliseconds

Availability

Core JavaScript 1.0; ECMA-262

Synopsis

```
Date.UTC(year, month, day, hours, minutes, seconds, ms);
```

Arguments

year   The year in four-digit format or in two-digit format for years between 1900 and 1999.

month   The month, specified as an integer from 0 (January) to 11 (December).

day   The day of the month, specified as an integer from 1 to 31. Note that this argument uses 1 as its lowest value, while other arguments use 0 as their lowest value.

hours   The hour, specified as an integer from 0 (midnight) to 23 (11 p.m.). This argument may be omitted if *minutes* and *seconds* are also omitted.

minutes   The minutes in the hour, specified as an integer from 0 to 59. This argument may be omitted if *seconds* is also omitted.

seconds   The seconds in the minute, specified as an integer from 0 to 59. This argument may be omitted.

ms   The number of milliseconds. This argument may be omitted. This argument is ignored prior to JavaScript 1.2.

Returns

The number of milliseconds between midnight on January 1, 1970, UTC, and the time specified (also in UTC) by the arguments.

Description

Date.UTC() is static method; it is invoked through the Date() constructor, not through an individual Date object.

The arguments to Date.UTC() specify a date and time and are understood to be in UTC (Universal Coordinated Time)—they are in the GMT time zone. The specified UTC time is converted to the millisecond format, which can be used by the Date() constructor method and by the Date.setTime() method.

Usage

The Date() constructor method can accept date and time arguments identical to those that Date.UTC() accepts. The difference is that the Date() constructor assumes local time, while Date.UTC() assumes universal time (GMT). To create a Date object using a UTC time specification, you can use code like this:

```
d = new Date(Date.UTC(1996, 4, 8, 16, 30));
```

Bugs

In Navigator 2, Date.UTC() does not compute the correct number of milliseconds.

See Also

Date, Date.parse(), Date.setTime()

Date.valueOf() — convert a date to a number

Availability

Core JavaScript 1.1; ECMA-262

Synopsis

```
date.valueOf()
```

Returns

A numeric representation of *date*. The value returned is the same number of milliseconds as returned by Date.getTime().

---

defaultStatus — see Window.defaultStatus

---

document — see Window.document

Document — represents an HTML document

Availability

Client-side JavaScript 1.0; enhanced in JavaScript 1.1, and in Navigator 4 and Internet Explorer 4

Inherits From

HTMLElement

Synopsis

```
window.document
document
```

Properties

Document inherits properties from HTMLElement, and also defines the following. Navigator 4 and Internet Explorer 4 both define a number of incompatible Document properties that are used mostly for DHTML; they are listed separately after these properties:

alinkColor   A string that specifies the color of activated links. May be set in the document <HEAD> or through the ALINK attribute of <BODY>.

anchors[]   An array of Anchor objects, one for each hypertext target in the document.

applets[]   An array of Java objects, one for each <APPLET> that appears in the document. JavaScript 1.1 and higher.

bgColor   A string that specifies the background color of the document. Initially set through the BGCOLOR attribute of <BODY>.

cookie   A string that is the value of a cookie associated with this document.

domain   A string that specifies the Internet domain the document is from. Used for security purposes. JavaScript 1.1 and higher.

embeds[ ]   An array of Java objects, one for each <EMBED> tag that appears in the document. JavaScript 1.1 and higher.

fgColor   A string that specifies the color of document text. May be set in the document <HEAD> or through the TEXT attribute of <BODY>.

forms[ ]   An array of Form objects, one for each <FORM> that appears in the document.

images[ ]   An array of Image objects, one for each image embedded in the document with the <IMG> tag. JavaScript 1.1 and higher.

lastModified
               A read-only string that specifies the date of the most recent change to the document (as reported by the web server).

linkColor   A string that specifies the color of unvisited links in the document. May be set in the document <HEAD> or through the LINK attribute of <BODY>.

links[ ]   An array of Link objects, one for each hypertext link in the the document.

location   A synonym for the URL property. Not the same as the Location object *window*.location.

plugins[ ]   A synonym for the embeds[ ] array. JavaScript 1.1 and higher.

referrer   A read-only string that specifies the URL of the document that contained the link that referred to the current document.

title   A read-only string that specifies the <TITLE> of the document.

URL   A read-only string that specifies the URL of the document.

vlinkColor   A string that specifies the color of visited links. May be set in the document <HEAD> or through the VLINK attribute of <BODY>.

Navigator 4 Properties

classes   A property used to define CSS style classes from JavaScript.

height   The height, in pixels, of the document.

ids   A property used to define CSS styles for individual document elements.

layers[ ]   An array of all Layer objects contained within the document.

tags   A property used to define CSS styles for HTML tags.

width   The width, in pixels, of the document.

Internet Explorer 4 Properties

activeElement
               The element in the document that has input focus.

all[]   An array of all elements within the document.

charset   The character set of the document.

children[]   An array of all elements that are direct children of the document.

defaultCharset
                 The default character set of the document.

expando   Disallow new property creation; helps with debugging.

parentWindow
                 The window that contains the document.

readyState   The loading status of a document.

Methods

Document inherits methods from HTMLElement and also defines the following. Navigator 4 and IE 4 both define a number of incompatible Document methods that are used mostly for DHTML; they are listed separately after these properties:

clear( )   A method that erases the contents of the document. This method is deprecated in JavaScript 1.1.

close( )   A method that closes a document stream opened with the open( ) method.

open( )   A method that opens a stream to which document contents may be written.

write( )   A method that inserts the specified string or strings into the document currently being parsed or into a document stream opened with open( ).

writeln( )   A method identical to write( ), except that it appends a newline character to the output.

Navigator 4 Methods

captureEvents( )
                 Request events of specified types.

contextual( )
                 Define contextual CSS styles.

getSelection( )
                 Return the currently selected document text.

releaseEvents
                 Stop capturing specified event types.

routeEvent( )
                 Route a captured event to the next interested element. See Window.routeEvent( ).

Internet Explorer 4 Methods

elementFromPoint( )
                 Return the element located at a given (X-coordinate, Y-coordinate) point.

Event Handlers

The <BODY> tag has onLoad and onUnload attributes. Technically, however, the onload and onunload event handlers belong to the Window object rather than the Document object. See Window.onload and Window.onunload.

HTML Syntax

The Document object obtains values for a number of its properties from attributes of the HTML <BODY> tag. Also, the HTML contents of a document appear between the <BODY> and </BODY> tags:

```
<BODY
    [ BACKGROUND="imageURL" ]      A background image for the document
    [ BGCOLOR="color" ]            A background color for the document
    [ TEXT="color" ]               The foreground color for the document's text
    [ LINK="color" ]               The color for unvisited links
    [ ALINK="color" ]              The color for activated links
    [ VLINK="color" ]              The color for visited links
    [ onLoad="handler" ]           JavaScript to run when the document is loaded
    [ onUnload="handler" ]         JavaScript to run when the document is unloaded
>
HTML document contents go here.
</BODY>
```

Description

The Document object represents the HTML document displayed in a browser window or frame (or layer, in Navigator 4). The properties of this object provide details about many aspects of the document, from the colors of the text, background, and anchors, to the date on which the document was last modified. The Document object also contains a number of arrays that describe the contents of the document. The links[] array contains one Link object for each hypertext link in the document. Similarly, the applets[] array contains one object for each Java applet embedded in the document, and the forms[] array contains one Form object for each HTML form that appears in the document.

The write() method of the Document object is especially notable. When invoked in scripts that are run while the document is loading, you can call document.write() to insert dynamically generated HTML text into the document.

With the advent of the Document Object Model (DOM) and DHTML, the Document object has acquired a number of properties and methods that are specific to either Navigator 4 or IE 4. Because these properties and methods are not portable, they are listed separately in the Properties and Methods sections of this reference page.

See Chapter 14, *The Document Object Model*, for an overview of the Document object and of many of the JavaScript objects to which it refers. See Chapter 17, *Dynamic HTML*, for an overview of DHTML.

See Also

Form, Window, Chapter 14

Document.activeElement — which input element has the focus

Availability

Client-side Internet Explorer 4

Synopsis

```
document.activeElement
```

Description

`activeElement` is a read-only property that refers to the input element within the document that is currently active (i.e., has the input focus).

Document.alinkColor — the color of activated links

Availability

Client-side JavaScript 1.0

Synopsis

```
document.alinkColor
```

Description

`alinkColor` is a string property that specifies the color of activated links in *document*. Browsers may display this color between the times that the user presses and releases the mouse button over the link.

The activated link color can be specified through the `ALINK` attribute in the `<BODY>` HTML tag, and the `alinkColor` property contains the specified value. The color may also be specified by assigning a value to `alinkColor` directly, but this may be done only in the `<HEAD>` of the document, before the `<BODY>` tag is parsed.

Colors are specified either as one of the standard color names recognized by JavaScript or as red, green, and blue color values, expressed as a string of six hexadecimal digits in the form `"RRGGBB"`.

See Also

Document.bgColor, Document.fgColor, Document.linkColor, Document.vlinkColor

---

Document.all[ ] — all HTML elements in a document

Availability

Client-side Internet Explorer 4

Synopsis

```
document.all[i]
document.all.item(name)
document.all.tags(tagname)
```

Description

`all[]` is a versatile array that contains all the HTML elements in a document. `all[]` contains the elements in source order, and you can extract them directly from the array if you know their exact numeric position within the array. It is more common, however, to use the `all.item()` method to extract a named element or to use the `all.tags()` method to extract an array of elements of a certain type.

`all.item()` is passed an element name and returns the HTML element that has that name as the value of its `NAME` or `ID` attribute. If more than one element has that name, this method returns an array of those elements.

`all.tags()` is passed a tag name and returns an array of HTML elements of the specified type.

See Also

HTMLElement

Document.anchors[] — the Anchors in a document

Availability

Client-side JavaScript 1.0; array elements are `null` prior to JavaScript 1.2

Synopsis

```
document.anchors
document.anchors.length
```

Description

The `anchors` property is an array of Anchor objects, one for each anchor that appears in `document`. An anchor is a named position within the document that can serve as the target of a hypertext link. The `anchors[]` array has `anchors.length` elements, numbered from zero to `anchors.length-1`.

Prior to JavaScript 1.2, the Anchor object was unimplemented, and the elements of `anchors[]` were all `null`.

Do not confuse anchors with hypertext links, which are represented in JavaScript by the Link objects in the `Document.links[]` array.

See Also

Anchor, Document.links[], Link

Document.applets[] — the applets in a document

Availability

Client-side JavaScript 1.1

Synopsis

```
document.applets
document.applets.length
```

Description

The `applets[]` property of the Document object is an array of Applet objects, one for each applet that appears in the document. You can use the Applet object to read and write all public variables in the applet, and you can invoke all of the applet's public methods.

If an <APPLET> tag has a `NAME` attribute, the applet may also be referred to by using the name as a property of `document` or as an index into the `applets` array. Thus, if the first applet in a document has `NAME="animator"`, you can refer to it in any of these three ways:

```
document.applets[0]
document.animator
document.applets["animator"]
```

See Also

Applet, Chapter 20

Document.bgColor — the document background color

Availability

Client-side JavaScript 1.0

Synopsis

```
document.bgColor
```

Description

`bgColor` is a string property that specifies the background color of *document*.

The document text color can be set through the `BGCOLOR` attribute in the <BODY> HTML tag, and the `bgColor` property contains the specified value. The background color may also be specified by assigning a value to `bgColor` directly. Unlike the other color properties, `bgColor` can be set at any time.

Colors are specified either as one of the standard color names recognized by JavaScript or as red, green, and blue color values, expressed as a string of six hexadecimal digits in the form `"RRGGBB"`.

Usage

When setting one color property for a Document, you should probably set the other color properties to match. Be careful when specifying color values; it is far easier to end up with a garish web page than it is to choose a palette of harmonious colors. In general, the default colors are a safe choice and may also reflect the end user's color preferences.

Note that the background of a document may also be set to an image with the `BACKGROUND` attribute of the HTML <BODY> tag.

See Also

Document.alinkColor, Document.fgColor, Document.linkColor, Document.vlinkColor

Document.captureEvents() — see Window.captureEvents()

Document.charset — the character set in use

Availability

Client-side Internet Explorer 4

Synopsis

```
document.charset
```

Description

`charset` specifies the character set currently in use for the document.

Document.children — the child elements of the document

Availability

Client-side Internet Explorer 4

Synopsis

```
document.children
```

Description

`children` is an array that contains the HTML elements, in source order, that are direct children of the *document*. Note that this is different than the `all[]` array that contains all elements in the document, regardless of their position in the containment hierarchy.

Document.classes — define style classes

Availability

Client-side Navigator 4

Synopsis

```
document.classes.className.tagName
```

Description

`classes` is an associative array that contains associative arrays that contain Style objects. You can use this property to specify styles that apply to all tags of type *tagName* that have a CLASS attribute of *className*. If *tagName* is `all`, the styles apply to any tags that have their CLASS attribute set to *className*.

For example, the following line specifies that all <P> tags with CLASS="quote" should be italicized:

```
document.classes.quote.P.fontStyle = "italic";
```

Note that styles can only be specified in the <HEAD> of a document. Also note that both *className* and *tagName* are case-insensitive.

See Also
Chapter 17

Document.clear() — clear a document

Availability
Client-side JavaScript 1.0; deprecated

Synopsis
```
document.clear()
```

Description
The clear() method of the Document object is deprecated and should not be used. To clear a document, you should simply open a new one with Document.open().

See Also
Document.close(), Document.open(), Document.write()

Document.close() — close an output stream

Availability
Client-side JavaScript 1.0

Synopsis
```
document.close()
```

Description
This method displays any output to *document* that has been written but not yet displayed, and closes the output stream to *document*. When generating complete HTML pages with Document.write(), you should invoke Document.close() when you reach the end of the page.

After *document*.close() has been called, if any further output is written to *document* (e.g., with *document*.write()), the document is implicitly cleared and reopened, erasing all the output that was written prior to calling the close() method.

See Also
Document.open(), Document.write()

Document.contextual() — define a contextual style

Availability
Client-side Navigator 4

Synopsis

```
document.contextual(style1, style2, ...)
```

Arguments

style1   A style object expressed with the `tags` or `classes` properties of the Document object.

style2... One or more additional style objects.

Returns

A style object that represents *style2* in the context of *style1*.

Description

The `contextual()` method returns a Style object that you can use to specify contextual styles that occur when tags of one type appear within tags (or classes) of another type. For example, you could use `contextual()` as follows to specify that bold text that appears within a <H1> heading should be red:

```
document.contextual(document.tags.H1, document.tags.B).color = "red";
```

Note that style specifications must appear in the <HEAD> of the document, before any text has been output.

See Also

Document.classes, Document.ids, Document.tags, Chapter 17

Document.cookie — the cookie(s) of the document

Availability

Client-side JavaScript 1.0

Synopsis

```
document.cookie
```

Description

`cookie` is a string property that allows you to read, create, modify, and delete the cookie or cookies that apply to the current document. A *cookie* is a small amount of named data stored by the web browser. It serves to give web browsers a "memory," so that they can use data input on one page in another page or recall user preferences across web browsing sessions. Cookie data is automatically transmitted between web browser and web server when appropriate, so that CGI scripts on the server end can read and write cookie values. Client-side JavaScript code can also read and write cookies with this property.

The `Document.cookie` property does not behave like a normal read/write property. You may both read and write the value of of `Document.cookie`, but the value you read from this property is, in general, not the same as the value you write. For complete details on the use of this particularly complex property, see Chapter 18, *Saving State with Cookies*.

Usage

Cookies are intended for infrequent storage of small amounts of data. They are not intended as a general-purpose communication or programming mechanism, so use them in moderation. Note that web browsers are not required to retain the value of more than 20 cookies per web server (for the entire server, not just for your site on the server), nor to retain a cookie *name/value* pair of more than 4 kilobytes in length.

See Also

Chapter 18

Document.defaultCharset — the default character set of a document

Availability

Client-side Internet Explorer 4

Synopsis

```
document.defaultCharset
```

Description

`defaultCharset` specifies the default character set of the document.

Document.domain — the security domain of a document

Availability

Client-side JavaScript 1.1

Synopsis

```
document.domain
```

Description

For security reasons, an unsigned script running in one window is not allowed to read properties of another window unless that window comes from the same web server as the host. This causes problems for large web sites that use multiple servers. For example, a script on the host *www.oreilly.com* might want to be able to share properties with a script from the host *search.oreilly.com*.

The `domain` property helps to address this problem. Initially, this string property contains the hostname of the web server from which the document was loaded. You can set this property, but only in a very restricted way: it can only be set to a domain suffix of itself. For example, a script loaded from *search.oreilly.com* could set its own `domain` property to "oreilly.com". If a script from *www.oreilly.com* is running in another window, and it also sets its `domain` property to "oreilly.com", these two scripts can share properties, even though they did not originate on the same server.

Note, however, that a script from *search.oreilly.com* can't set its `domain` property to "search.oreilly". And, importantly, a script from *snoop.spam.com* cannot set its `domain` to "oreilly.com" to determine, for example, what search keywords you use.

See Also

Chapter 21, *JavaScript Security*

Document.elementFromPoint() — determine which HTML element is at a given point

Availability

Client-side Internet Explorer 4

Synopsis

```
document.elementFromPoint(x, y)
```

Arguments

x   The X-coordinate.

y   The Y-coordinate.

Returns

The HTML element that appears at point (*x*, *y*) in `document`.

Document.embeds[] — the objects embedded in a document

Availability

Client-side JavaScript 1.1

Synopsis

```
document.embeds[i]
document.embeds.length
document.embed-name
```

Description

The `embeds` property of the Document object is an array of objects that represent data embedded in the document with the `<EMBED>` tag. The objects in the `embeds[]` array do not refer to the embedded data directly, but refer instead to the object that displays that data. In Navigator, this is a JavaObject representing the plugin that displays the data. In IE, this is an object that represents the ActiveX control that displays the data.

In either case, you can use the objects in the `embeds[]` array to interact with embedded data. The way you do this, however, is specific to the type of embedded data and the plug-in or ActiveX control that is used to display it. Consult the developer's documentation for the plugin or ActiveX control to learn whether it can be scripted from JavaScript and, if so, what the supported APIs are.

`Document.plugins[]` is a synonym for `Document.embeds[]`. Do not confuse it with `Navigator.plugins[]`.

See Also

JavaObject, Chapter 20

Document.expando — disallow new property creation

Availability

Client-side Internet Explorer 4

Synopsis

```
document.expando
```

Description

The `expando` property, if set to `false`, prevents client-side objects from being expanded. That is, it causes a runtime error if a program attempts to set the value of a nonexistent property of a client-side object. Setting `expando` to `false` can sometimes help to catch bugs caused by property misspellings, which can otherwise be difficult to detect. This property can be particularly helpful for programmers who are switching to JavaScript after becoming accustomed to case-insensitive languages.

Although `expando` only works in IE 4, it can be set safely (if ineffectively) in Navigator.

Document.fgColor — the default text color

Availability

Client-side JavaScript 1.0

Synopsis

```
document.fgColor
```

Description

`fgColor` is a string property that specifies the default color of text in `document`. This default color is used for all text in the document except hypertext links and text with an alternate color specified through the `COLOR` attribute of the HTML `<FONT>` tag.

The document text color can be set through the `TEXT` attribute in the `<BODY>` HTML tag, and the `fgColor` property contains the specified value. The default color may also be specified by assigning a value to `fgColor` directly, but this may only be done in the `<HEAD>` of the document, before the `<BODY>` tag is parsed.

Colors are specified either as one of the standard color names recognized by JavaScript or as red, green, and blue color values, expressed as a string of six hexadecimal digits in the form `"RRGGBB"`.

See Also

Document.alinkColor, Document.bgColor, Document.linkColor, Document.vlinkColor

Document.forms[ ] — the Forms in a document

Availability

Client-side JavaScript 1.0

Synopsis

```
document.forms
document.forms.length
```

Description

The forms property is an array of Form objects, one for each HTML form that appears in *document*. The forms[] array has forms.length elements, numbered from zero to forms.length-1.

See Also

Form, Chapter 16, *Forms and Form Elements*

Document.getSelection( ) — return the selected text

Availability

Client-side Navigator 4

Synopsis

```
document.getSelection()
```

Returns

The text, if any, that is currently selected within the document. This returned text has HTML formatting tags removed.

Document.handleEvent( ) — see Window.handleEvent( )

Document.height — the height of a document

Availability

Client-side Navigator 4

Synopsis

```
document.height
```

Description

height contains the height, in pixels, of the document.

Document.ids — define styles for individual tags

Availability

Client-side Navigator 4

Synopsis

```
document.ids.elementName
```

Description

The `ids` property of the document object refers to an associative array of Style objects. By giving any HTML element a unique name with the `ID` attribute, you can define styles specific to that element by setting properties on the Style object specified by the *elementName* property of `ids`.

For example, if we give an element a unique name like this:

```
<P ID="p23">
```

Then we can set styles for that particular element like this:

```
document.ids.p23.color = "blue";
```

Note that any style definitions must appear in the `<HEAD>` of the document. Also note that the *elementName* property is case-insensitive.

See Also

Chapter 17

Document.images[ ] — the images embedded in a document

Availability

Client-side JavaScript 1.1

Synopsis

```
document.images[i]
document.images.length
document.image-name
```

Description

The `images` property of the Document object is an array of Image objects, one for each image that is embedded in the document with the HTML `<IMG>` tag.

If the `NAME` attribute is specified in the `<IMG>` tag for an Image, a reference to that image is also stored in a property of the Document object. This property has the same name as the image. So, if an image has a `NAME="toggle"` attribute, you can refer to the image with `document.toggle`.

See Also

Image

Document.lastModified — the modification date of a document

Availability

Client-side JavaScript 1.0

Synopsis

```
document.lastModified
```

Description

lastModified is a read-only string property that contains the date and time at which *document* was most recently modified. This data is derived from HTTP header data sent by the web server. The web server generally obtains the last-modified date by examining the modification date of the file itself.

Web servers are not required to provide last-modified dates for the documents they serve. When a web server does not provide a last modification date, JavaScript assumes 0, which translates to a date of midnight, January 1, 1970, GMT. The example below shows how you can test for this case.

Example

It is a good idea to let readers know how recent the information you provide on the Web is. You can include an automatic timestamp in your documents by placing the following script at the end of each HTML file. Doing this means you do not need to update the modification time by hand each time you make a change to the file. Note that this script tests that the supplied date is valid before displaying it:

```
<SCRIPT>
if (Date.parse(document.lastModified) != 0)
    document.write('<P><HR><SMALL><I>Last modified: '
                   + document.lastModified
                   + '</I></SMALL>');

</SCRIPT>
```

See Also

Document.location, Document.referrer, Document.title

Document.layers[] — the layers contained in a document

Availability

Client-side Navigator 4

Synopsis

```
document.layers
document.layers.length
```

Description

The layers property of a Document object is an array of Layer objects which represent the layers contained within a document. Each Layer object contains its own subdocument, accessible through the document property of the Layer object.

See Also

Layer, Layer.document

Document.linkColor — the color of unfollowed links

Availability

Client-side JavaScript 1.0

Synopsis

```
document.linkColor
```

Description

linkColor is a string property that specifies the color of unvisited links in *document*. All hypertext links in the document are displayed in this color, except for those that have already been followed or visited.

The link color can be specified through the LINK attribute in the <BODY> HTML tag, and the linkColor property contains the specified value. The color may also be specified by assigning a value to linkColor directly, but this may only be done in the <HEAD> of the document, before the <BODY> tag is parsed.

Colors are specified either as one of the standard color names recognized by JavaScript or as red, green, and blue color values, expressed as a string of six hexadecimal digits in the form "*RRGGBB*".

See Also

Document.alinkColor, Document.bgColor, Document.fgColor, Document.vlinkColor,

Document.links[] — the Link objects in a document

Availability

Client-side JavaScript 1.0

Synopsis

```
document.links
document.links.length
```

Description

The links property is an array of Link objects, one for each hypertext link that appears in *document*. The links[] array has links.length elements, numbered from zero to links.length-1.

See Also

Link

Document.location — the URL of the current document

Availability

Client-side JavaScript 1.0; deprecated in JavaScript 1.1 in favor of `Document.URL`

Synopsis

```
document.location
```

Description

In JavaScript 1.0, `location` is a read-only string property that contains the complete URL of the current *document*. The `document.location` property of a document is usually equal to the `location.href` of the window that contains it. These two properties are not always equal, however, because `Document.location` may be modified through URL redirection—`Window.location` contains the requested URL, and `Document.location` specifies the actual URL of the retrieved document.

In JavaScript 1.1, `Document.location` is no longer a string; instead, it is a reference to the same Location object to which `Window.location` refers. In JavaScript 1.1, `Document.location` is deprecated, and the new JavaScript 1.1 property `Document.URL` takes its place.

See Also

Document.URL, Window.location

Document.open() — begin a new document

Availability

Client-side JavaScript 1.0

Synopsis

```
document.open()
document.open(mimetype)
```

Arguments

mimetype   An optional string argument that specifies the type of data to be written to and displayed in *document*. The value of this argument should be one of the standard MIME types that the browser understands ("text/html", "text/plain", "image/gif", "image/jpeg", "image/x-bitmap" for Navigator) or some other MIME type that can be handled by an installed plugin. If this argument is omitted, it is taken to be "text/html". This argument is ignored by IE 3, which always assumes a document of type "text/html".

Description

The `document.open()` method opens a stream to *document*, so that subsequent *document*`.write()` calls can append data to the document. The optional *mimetype* argument specifies the type of data to be written and tells the browser how to interpret that data.

If there is any existing document displayed when the `open()` method is called, it is automatically cleared by the call to `open()` or by the first call to `write()` or `writeln()`.

After opening a document with `open()` and writing data to it with `write()`, you should complete the document by calling `close()`.

Usage

You usually call `Document.open()` with no argument to open an HTML document. Occasionally, a "text/plain" document is useful, for example, for a pop-up window of debugging messages.

See Also

Document.close(), Document.write()

Document.parentWindow — the window of a document

Availability

Client-side Internet Explorer 4

Synopsis

```
document.parentWindow
```

Description

The `parentWindow` property of a document refers to the Window object that contains the document. This property is only available in IE 4. Since IE 4 does not support layers, all documents are contained within windows (or frames).

Document.plugins[] — the objects embedded in a document

Availability

Client-side JavaScript 1.1

Synopsis

```
document.plugins[i]
document.plugins.length
document.embedded-object-name
```

Description

The `plugins` property of the Document object is a synonym for the `embeds` property. Both properties refer to an array of objects that represent the plugin or ActiveX control being used to display embedded data in a document.

The `embeds` property is the preferred way to access this array, since it avoids confusion with the `Navigator.plugins[]` array. See Document.embeds[] for full details.

See Also

Document.embeds[ ]

Document.readyState — the loading status of a document

Availability

Client-side Internet Explorer 4

Synopsis

```
document.readyState
```

Description

The `readyState` property specifies the loading status of a document. It has one of the following four string values:

`uninitialized`
       The document has not started loading.

`loading`   The document is loading.

`interactive` The document has loaded sufficiently for the user to interact with it.

`complete`   The document is completely loaded.

Document.referrer — the URL of the linked-from document

Availability

Client-side JavaScript 1.0; non-functional in Internet Explorer 3

Synopsis

```
document.referrer
```

Description

`referrer` is a read-only string property that contains the URL of the document, if any, from which the current *document* was reached. For example, if the user follows a link in document A to document B, the `Document.referrer` property in document B contains the URL of document A. On the other hand, if the user types the URL of document B directly and does not follow any link to get there, the `Document.referrer` property for document B is an empty string.

See Also

Document.lastModified, Document.location, Document.title

Document.releaseEvents() — see Window.releaseEvents( )

Document.routeEvent() — see Window.routeEvent( )

Document.tags — define styles for HTML tags

Availability
Client-side Navigator 4

Synopsis
```
document.tags.tagname
```

Description
The `tags` property of the document object refers to an associative array of Style objects. You can define CSS styles that apply to all tags of type *tagname* by setting properties of the *tagname* property of `tags`.

For example, to specify that all <H1> elements should be blue, you could use a line like the following:

```
document.tags.H1.color = "blue";
```

Note that any style definitions must appear in the <HEAD> of the document. Also note that the *tagname* property is case-insensitive.

See Also
Chapter 17

Document.title — the title of a document

Availability
Client-side JavaScript 1.0

Synopsis
```
document.title
```

Description
`title` is a read-only string property that specifies the title of the current *document*. The title is any text that appears between <TITLE> and </TITLE> tags in the <HEAD> of the document.

See Also
Document.lastModified, Document.location, Document.referrer

Document. URL — the URL of the current document

Availability

Client-side JavaScript 1.1

Synopsis

```
document.URL
```

Description

URL is a read-only string property that contains the complete URL of the current *document*.

document.URL is usually equal to *window*.location.href for the *window* that contains *document*. These two are not always equal, however, because the Document.URL property may be modified through URL redirection—Window.location contains the requested URL, and Document.URL specifies the actual URL where it was found.

Usage

Some web authors like to include the URL of a document somewhere within the document, so that, for example, if the document is cut-and-pasted to a file or printed out, there is still a reference to its location online. The following script, when appended to a document, auto-matically adds the document's URL:

```
<SCRIPT>
document.write('<P><HR><SMALL><I>URL: ' + document.URL
    + '</I></SMALL>');
</SCRIPT>
```

See Also

Document.lastModified, Document.location, Document.referrer, Document.title, Window.location

Document.vlinkColor — the color of visited links

Availability

Client-side JavaScript 1.0

Synopsis

```
document.vlinkColor
```

Description

vlinkColor is a string property that specifies the color of visited links in *document*. This color is displayed for links that reference URLs the user has already visited.

The visited link color can be specified through the VLINK attribute in the <BODY> HTML tag, and the vlinkColor property contains the specified value. The color may also be specified by assigning a value to vlinkColor directly, but this may only be done in the <HEAD> of the document, before the <BODY> tag is parsed.

Colors are specified either as one of the standard color names recognized by JavaScript or as red, green, and blue color values, expressed as a string of six hexadecimal digits in the form "*RRGGBB*".

See Also

Document.alinkColor, Document.bgColor, Document.fgColor, Document.linkColor

Document.width — the width of a document

Availability

Client-side Navigator 4

Synopsis

```
document.width
```

Description

width contains the width, in pixels, of the document.

Document.write() — append data to a document

Availability

Client-side JavaScript 1.0

Synopsis

```
document.write(value,...)
```

Arguments

value   An arbitrary JavaScript value to be appended to *document*. If the value
           is not a string, it is converted to one before being appended.

. . .   Any number (zero or higher) of additional values to be appended (in
           order) to *document*.

Description

document.write() appends each of its arguments, in order, to *document*. Any arguments
that are not strings are converted to strings before they are written to the end of the document.

Document.write() is usually used in one of two ways. First, it is invoked on the current
document within a <SCRIPT> tag or within a function that is executed while the document
is still being parsed. In this case, the write() method writes its HTML output as if that output appeared literally in the file, at the location of the code that invoked the method.

Second, Document.write() is commonly used to generate dynamically the contents of a
document for a window other than the current window. In this case, the target document is
never in the process of being parsed, and so the output cannot appear "in place" as it does
in the case just described. In order for write() to output text into a document, that document must be open. You can open a document by explicitly calling the Document.open()
method, if you choose. In most cases this is unnecessary, however, because when write()
is invoked on a document that is closed, it implicitly opens the document. When a document is opened, any contents that previously appeared in that document are discarded and
replaced with a blank document.

Once a document is open, Document.write() can append any amount of output to the
end of the document. When a new document has been completely generated by this

technique, the document should be closed by calling Document.close(). Note that although the call to open() is usually optional, the call to close() is never optional.

The results of calling Document.write() may not be immediately visible in the targeted web browser window or frame. This is because a web browser may buffer up data to output in larger chunks. Calling Document.close() is the only way to explicitly force all buffered output to be "flushed" and displayed in the browser window.

See Also

Document.close( ), Document.open( ), Document.writeln( ), Chapter 14

Document.writeln( ) — append data and a newline to a document

Availability

Client-side JavaScript 1.0

Synopsis

```
document.writeln(value,...)
```

Arguments

value

> An arbitrary JavaScript value that is to be appended to *document*. If the value is not a string, it is converted to one before being appended.

. . .

> Any number (zero or higher) of additional values to be appended (in order) to *document*.

Description

Document.writeln() behaves just like Document.write() except that after appending all of its arguments to *document*, it also appends a newline character. See Document.write() for more information on this method.

Newline characters are not usually displayed in HTML documents, so in general, it is only useful to use Document.writeln() when writing text to appear in a <PRE> environment, or when writing to a document opened with a mime type of "text/plain".

See Also

Document.close( ), Document.open( ), Document.write( )

Element — see Input

escape( ) — encode a string for transmission

Availability

Core JavaScript 1.0; ECMA-262; Unicode support in Internet Explorer 4

Synopsis

```
escape(s)
```

Arguments

s   The string that is to be "escaped" or encoded.

Returns

An encoded copy of s.

Description

escape() is a global function in client-side JavaScript. It creates and returns a new string that contains an encoded version of s. The string s itself is not modified.

The string is encoded as follows: all spaces, punctuation, accented characters, and any other characters that are not ASCII letters or numbers are converted to the form %xx, where xx is two hexadecimal digits that represent the ISO-8859-1 (Latin-1) encoding of the character. For example, the ! character has the Latin-1 encoding of 33, which is 21 hexadecimal, so escape() replaces this character with the sequence %21. Thus the expression:

```
escape("Hello World!");
```

yields the string:

```
Hello%20World%21
```

The purpose of the escape() encoding is to ensure that the string is portable to all computers and transmittable across all networks, regardless of the character encodings the computers or networks support (as long as they support ASCII).

The encoding performed by escape() is like the URL encoding used to encode query strings and other portions of a URL that might include spaces, punctuation, or characters outside of the standard ASCII character set. The only difference is that in the URL encoding, spaces are replaced with a '+' character, while escape() replaces spaces with the %20 sequence.

IE 4 supports two-byte Unicode characters, and on the IE 4 platform, escape() encodes two-byte characters using the format %uxxxx.

Use the unescape() function to decode a string encoded with escape().

A common use of escape() is to encode cookie values, which have restrictions on the punctuation characters they may contain. See Document.cookie.

See Also

Document.cookie, String, unescape()

eval( ) — execute JavaScript code from a string

Availability

Core JavaScript 1.0; ECMA-262

Synopsis

```
eval(code)
```

Arguments

code   A string that contains the JavaScript expression to be evaluated or the statements to be executed.

Returns

The value of the evaluated *code*, if any.

Description

eval() is a global method of core JavaScript that evaluates a string containing JavaScript code. If *code* contains an expression, eval evaluates the expression and returns its value. If *code* contains a JavaScript statement or statements, eval() executes those statements and returns the value, if any, returned by the last statement.

eval() provides a very powerful capability to the JavaScript language, but its use is infrequent in real-world programs. Obvious uses are to write programs that act as recursive JavaScript interpreters, and to write programs that dynamically generate and evaluate JavaScript code.

In Navigator 3, eval() is also available as an object method. See Object.eval().

Bugs

eval() crashes Navigator 2 on 16-bit Windows (Windows 3.1) platforms.

See Also

Object.eval()

Event — details about an event

Availability

Client-side JavaScript; incompatible versions are supported by Navigator 4 and Internet Explorer 4

Synopsis

```
function handler(event) { ... }        Event handler argument in Navigator 4
window.event                           Window property in IE 4
```

Navigator 4 Properties

data   URLs of dragged-and-dropped objects.

height   The new height after a resize event.

layerX   The layer-relative X-coordinate of the event.

layerY   The layer-relative Y-coordinate of the event.

modifiers   The modifier keys that were held down.

pageX   The document-relative X-coordinate of the event.

pageY   The document-relative Y-coordinate of the event.

screenX   The screen-relative X-coordinate of the event.

screenY   The screen-relative Y-coordinate of the event.

target   The element that generated the event.

type   The type of the event.

TYPE   Various event type bitmasks.

which   Which key or mouse button was used.

width   The new width after a resize event.

x   The layer-relative X-coordinate of the event.

y   The layer-relative Y-coordinate of the event.

Internet Explorer 4 Properties

altKey   Whether the **ALT** key was down.

button   The mouse button that was pressed.

cancelBubble
                Set to prevent the event from propagating further.

clientX   The document-relative X-coordinate of the event.

clientY   The document-relative Y-coordinate of the event.

ctrlKey   Whether the **CTRL** key was down.

fromElement   The element the mouse is moving out of.

keyCode   The character code of the key pressed.

offsetX   The container-relative X-coordinate of the event.

offsetY   The container-relative Y-coordinate of the event.

reason   Status code for data transfer events.

returnValue   Set to specify event handler return value.

screenX	The screen-relative X-coordinate of the event.
screenY	The screen-relative Y-coordinate of the event.
shiftKey	Whether the **SHIFT** key was held down.
srcElement	The element that generated the event.
srcFilter	The filter object for a filter change event.
toElement	The element that the mouse is moving into.
type	The type of the event.
x	Event position relative to a dynamically positioned container.
y	Event position relative to a dynamically positioned container.

Description

The Event object provides details about an event that has occurred. Unfortunately, those details are not standardized, and Navigator 4 and IE 4 define Event objects that are almost entirely incompatible. Besides having different properties, Navigator 4 and IE 4 provide access to Event objects in different ways. In Navigator, an Event object is passed as an argument to every event handler. For event handlers defined by HTML attributes, the name of the event argument is event. In IE, the Event object of the most recent event is instead stored in the event property of the Window object.

See Also

Chapter 15

Event.altKey — whether the ALT key was pressed during an event

Availability

Client-side Internet Explorer 4

Synopsis

```
event.altKey
```

Description

altKey is a boolean value that specifies whether the **ALT** key was held down when the event occurred.

See Also

Event.ctrlKey, Event.modifiers, Event.shiftKey

Event.button — which mouse button was pressed

Availability

Client-side Internet Explorer 4

Synopsis

```
event.button
```

Description

For mouse events, button specifies which mouse button was pressed. The integers 1, 2, and 3 specify the left, middle, and right buttons.

See Also

Event.which

Event.cancelBubble — stop event propagation

Availability

Client-side Internet Explorer 4

Synopsis

```
event.cancelBubble
```

Description

If an event handler wants to stop an event from being propagated up to containing objects, it should set cancelBubble to true.

Event.clientX — the X-coordinate, within a page, of the event

Availability

Client-side Internet Explorer 4

Synopsis

```
event.clientX
```

Description

clientX specifies the X-coordinate, relative to the web browser page, at which the event occurred.

See Also

Event.pageX, Event.screenX, Event.x

Event.clientY — the Y-coordinate, within a page, of the event

Availability

Client-side Internet Explorer 4

Synopsis

```
event.clientY
```

Description

clientY specifies the Y-coordinate, relative to the web browser page, at which the event occurred.

See Also

Event.pageY, Event.screenY, Event.y

Event.ctrlKey — whether the CTRL key was pressed during an event

Availability

Client-side Internet Explorer 4

Synopsis

```
event.ctrlKey
```

Description

ctrlKey is a boolean value that specifies whether the **CTRL** key was held down when the event occurred.

See Also

Event.altKey, Event.modifiers, Event.shiftKey

Event.data — data from a DragDrop event

Availability

Client-side Navigator 4; requires UniversalBrowserWrite privilege to set; requires UniversalBrowserRead privilege to read

Synopsis

```
event.data
```

Description

The data property of the Event object is used only for events of type "dragdrop". It refers to an array of strings, each of which is a URL that represents a dropped object. For security reasons, only trusted scripts with the UniversalBrowserRead privilege can read this property.

Event.fromElement — the object the mouse is moving from

Availability

Client-side Internet Explorer 4

Synopsis

```
event.fromElement
```

Description

For mouseover and mouseout events, fromElement refers to the object from which the mouse pointer is moving.

See Also

Event.toElement

Event.height — the new height of a resized window or frame

Availability

Client-side Navigator 4

Synopsis

```
event.height
```

Description

The height property is set only in events of type "resize". It specifies the new height of the window or frame that was resized.

Event.keyCode — the Unicode encoding of the key typed

Availability

Client-side Internet Explorer 4

Synopsis

```
event.keyCode
```

Description

For keyboard events, keyCode specifies the Unicode character code generated by the key that was struck.

See Also

Event.which

Event.layerX — the X-coordinate, within a layer, of the event

Availability

Client-side Navigator 4

Synopsis

```
event.layerX
```

Description

`layerX` specifies the X-coordinate, relative to the enclosing layer, at which an event occurred.

Event.layerY — the Y-coordinate, within a layer, of the event

Availability

Client-side Navigator 4

Synopsis

```
event.layerY
```

Description

`layerY` specifies the Y-coordinate, relative to the enclosing layer, at which an event occurred.

Event.modifiers — which keyboard modifier keys are held down

Availability

Client-side Navigator 4

Synopsis

```
event.modifiers
```

Description

`modifiers` specifies which keyboard modifier keys were held down when the event occurred. This numeric value is a bitmask consisting of any of the values `Event.ALT_MASK`, `Event.CONTROL_MASK`, `Event.META_MASK`, or `Event.SHIFT_MASK`.

See Also

Event.altKey, Event.ctrlKey, Event.shiftKey

Event.offsetX — the X-coordinate of the event, relative to the container

Availability

Client-side Internet Explorer 4

Synopsis

`event.offsetX`

Description

`offsetX` specifies the X position at which the event occurred, within the coordinate system of the container of the event's source element (see `Event.srcElement`).

See Also

Event.clientX, Event.screenX, Event.srcElement

Event.offsetY — the Y-coordinate of the event, relative to the container

Availability

Client-side Internet Explorer 4

Synopsis

`event.offsetY`

Description

`offsetY` specifies the Y position at which the event occurred, within the coordinate system of the container of the event's source element (see `Event.srcElement`).

See Also

Event.clientY, Event.screenY, Event.srcElement

Event.pageX — the X-coordinate, within a page, of the event

Availability

Client-side Navigator 4

Synopsis

`event.pageX`

Description

`pageX` specifies the X-coordinate, relative to the web browser page, at which the event occurred. Note that this coordinate is relative to the top-level page, not to any enclosing layers.

See Also

Event.clientX, Event.x

Event.pageY — the Y-coordinate, within a page, of the event

Availability

Client-side Navigator 4

Synopsis

```
event.pageY
```

Description

pageY specifies the Y-coordinate, relative to the web browser page, at which the event occurred. Note that this coordinate is relative to the top-level page, not to any enclosing layers.

See Also

Event.clientY, Event.y

Event.reason — data transfer status

Availability

Client-side Internet Explorer 4

Synopsis

```
event.reason
```

Description

For the datasetcomplete event, reason contains a code that specifies the status of the data transfer. A value of 0 indicates successful transfer. A value of 1 indicates that the transfer was aborted. A value of 2 indicates that an error occurred during data transfer.

Event.returnValue — specify a return value for the event handler

Availability

Client-side Internet Explorer 4

Synopsis

```
event.returnValue
```

Description

If returnValue is set, its value takes precedence over the value actually returned by an event handler. Set this property to false to cancel the default action of the source element on which the event occurred.

Event.screenX — the screen X-coordinate of the event

Availability

Client-side JavaScript 1.2

Synopsis

```
event.screenX
```

Description

screenX specifies the X-coordinate, relative to the screen, at which the event occurred. Note that, unlike most Event properties, screenX is supported by, and has the same meaning in, both Navigator 4 and Internet Explorer 4.

Event.screenY — the screen Y-coordinate of the event

Availability

Client-side JavaScript 1.2

Synopsis

```
event.screenY
```

Description

screenY specifies the Y-coordinate, relative to the screen, at which the event occurred. Note that, unlike most Event properties, screenY is supported by, and has the same meaning in, both Navigator 4 and Internet Explorer 4.

Event.shiftKey — whether the SHIFT key was pressed during an event

Availability

Client-side Internet Explorer 4

Synopsis

```
event.shiftKey
```

Description

shiftKey is a boolean value that specifies whether the **SHIFT** key was held down when the event occurred.

See Also

Event.altKey, Event.ctrlKey, Event.modifiers

Event.srcElement — the object on which the event occurred

Availability

Client-side Internet Explorer 4

Synopsis

```
event.srcElement
```

Description

srcElement is a reference to the Window, Document, or HTMLElement object that generated the event.

See Also

Event.target

Event.srcFilter — the filter that changed

Availability

Client-side Internet Explorer 4

Synopsis

```
event.srcFilter
```

Description

For filterchange events, srcFilter specifies the filter that changed.

Event.target — the object on which the event occurred

Availability

Client-side Navigator 4

Synopsis

```
event.target
```

Description

target specifies the Window, Document, Layer, or HTMLElement object on which the event occurred.

See Also

Event.srcElement

Event.toElement — the object to which the mouse is moving

Availability

Client-side Internet Explorer 4

Synopsis

```
event.toElement
```

Description

For mouseover and mouseout events, `toElement` refers to the object into which the mouse pointer is moving.

See Also

Event.fromElement

Event.TYPE — static event type constants for bitmasks

Availability

Client-side Navigator 4

Synopsis

```
Event.TYPE
```

Description

The Event class defines bitmask constants for each of the supported event types. These static properties are used to form the bitmasks that are passed to `captureEvents()` and `releaseEvents()`. The following list gives the available constants:

`Event.ABORT`	`Event.KEYDOWN`	`Event.MOUSEUP`
`Event.BLUR`	`Event.KEYPRESS`	`Event.MOVE`
`Event.CHANGE`	`Event.KEYUP`	`Event.RESET`
`Event.CLICK`	`Event.LOAD`	`Event.RESIZE`
`Event.DBLCLICK`	`Event.MOUSEDOWN`	`Event.SELECT`
`Event.DRAGDROP`	`Event.MOUSEMOVE`	`Event.SUBMIT`
`Event.ERROR`	`Event.MOUSEOUT`	`Event.UNLOAD`
`Event.FOCUS`	`Event.MOUSEOVER`	

See Also

Window.captureEvents(), Window.releaseEvents()

Event.type — the type of the event

Availability

Client-side JavaScript 1.2

Synopsis

```
event.type
```

Description

`type` is a string property that specifies the type of the event. Its value is the name of the event handler, minus the "on" prefix. So, when the `onclick()` event handler is invoked, the `type` property of the Event object is "click".

The following list gives the event types supported by Navigator 4:

```
abort      error        mousedown    reset
blur       focus        mousemove    resize
change     keydown      mouseout     select
click      keypress     mouseover    submit
dblclick   keyup        mouseup      unload
dragdrop   load         move
```

The following list gives the event types supported by Internet Explorer 4:

```
abort            datasetcomplete   keypress          resize
afterupdate      dblclick          keyup             rowenter
beforeunload     dragstart         load              rowexit
beforeupdate     error             mousedown         scroll
blur             errorupdate       mousemove         select
bounce           filterchange      mouseout          selectstart
change           finish            mouseover         start
click            focus             mouseup           submit
dataavailable    help              readystatechange  unload
datasetchanged   keydown           reset
```

Event.which — which key or mouse button was clicked

Availability

Client-side Navigator 4

Synopsis

```
event.which
```

Description

For keyboard and mouse events, which specifies which key or mouse button was pressed or released. For keyboard events, this property contains the character encoding of the key that was pressed. For mouse events, it contains 1, 2, or 3, indicating the left, middle, or right buttons.

See Also

Event.button, Event.keyCode

Event.width — the new width of a resized window or frame

Availability

Client-side Navigator 4

Synopsis

```
event.width
```

Description

The `width` property is set only in events of type "resize". It specifies the new width of the window or frame that was resized.

Event.x — the X-coordinate of the event within a positioned element

Availability

Client-side JavaScript 1.2

Synopsis

```
event.x
```

Description

x specifies the X-coordinate at which the event occurred. In Navigator 4, this property is a synonym for `layerX`, and specifies the position relative to the containing layer (if any). In Internet Explorer 4, this property specifies the X position relative to the innermost containing element that is dynamically positioned using CSS-P.

Event.y — the Y-coordinate of the event within a positioned element

Availability

Client-side JavaScript 1.2

Synopsis

```
event.y
```

Description

y specifies the Y-coordinate at which the event occurred. In Navigator 4, this property is a synonym for `layerY`, and specifies the position relative to the containing layer (if any). In Internet Explorer 4, this property specifies the Y position relative to the innermost containing element that is dynamically positioned using CSS-P.

FileUpload — a file upload field for form input

Availability

Client-side JavaScript 1.0

Inherits From

Input, HTMLElement

Synopsis

```
form.name
form.elements[i]
```

Properties

FileUpload inherits properties from Input and HTMLElement and defines or overrides the following:

value A read-only string that specifies the value contained in the input field (which is also the value sent to the server when the form is submitted). In Navigator 2, this field is always blank. In Navigator 3, any filename specified by the user may be read, but the property still may not be set.

Methods

FileUpload inherits methods from Input and HTMLElement.

Event Handlers

FileUpload inherits event handlers from Input and HTMLElement and defines or overrides the following:

onchange Invoked when the user changes the value in the FileUpload element and moves the keyboard focus elsewhere. This event handler is not invoked for every keystroke in the FileUpload element, but only when the user completes an edit.

HTML Syntax

A FileUpload element is created with a standard HTML <INPUT> tag:

```
<FORM ENCTYPE="multipart/form-data"
        METHOD=post>                     Required attributes
    ...
  <INPUT
    TYPE"file"                           Specifies that this is a FileUpload element
    [ NAME="name" ]                      A name that can later be used to refer to this element
                                         Specifies the name property
    [ SIZE=integer ]                     How many characters wide the element is
    [ MAXLENGTH=integer ]                Maximum allowed number of input characters
    [ onBlur="handler" ]                 The onblur() event handler
    [ onChange="handler" ]               The onchange() event handler
    [ onFocus="handler" ]                The onfocus() event handler
  >
    ...
```

Description

The FileUpload element represents a file upload input element in a form. In many respects, this input element is much like the Text element. On the screen, it appears like a text input field, with the addition of a **Browse** button that opens a directory browser. Entering a filename into a FileUpload element (either directly or through the browser) causes Netscape to submit the contents of that file along with the form. For this to work, the form must use "multipart/form-data" encoding and the POST method.

The FileUpload element does not have a `defaultValue` property and does not recognize the `VALUE` HTML attribute to specify an initial value for the input field. Similarly, the `value` property of the FileUpload element is read-only. Only the user may enter a filename; JavaScript may not enter text into the FileUpload field in any way. This is to prevent malicious JavaScript programs from uploading arbitrary files (such as password files) off the user's machine.

See Also

Form, HTMLElement, Input, Text

FileUpload.onchange — the handler invoked when input value changes

Availability

Client-side JavaScript 1.0

Synopsis

```
<INPUT TYPE=file onChange="handler"...>
fileupload.onchange
```

Description

The `onchange` property of a FileUpload element specifies an event handler function that is invoked when the user changes the value in the input field (either by typing directly or using the **Browse** button) and then moves input focus elsewhere. This handler is intended to process a complete change to the input value, and therefore is not invoked on a keystroke-by-keystroke basis.

The initial value of this property is a function that contains the semicolon-separated JavaScript statements specified by the `onChange` attribute of the HTML tag that defined the object. When an event handler function is defined by an HTML attribute, it is executed in the scope of *element* rather than in the scope of the containing window.

In Navigator 4, the `onchange` handler function is passed an Event object as an argument. In IE 4, no argument is passed, but the applicable Event object is available as the `event` property of the Window object that contains the *element*.

See Also

Input.onchange, Chapter 15

FileUpload.value — the filename selected by the user

Availability

Client-side JavaScript 1.1

Synopsis

```
fileupload.value
```

Description

value is a read-only string property of the FileUpload object. It specifies the filename entered by the user into the FileUpload object. The user may enter a filename either by typing it directly or by using the directory browser associated with the FileUpload object.

To prevent malicious programs from uploading arbitrary files from the client, this property may not be set by JavaScript code. Similarly, the VALUE attribute of the <INPUT> tag does not specify a default value for this property.

---

focus() — see Window.focus()

Form — an HTML input form

Availability

Client-side JavaScript 1.0

Inherits From

HTMLElement

Synopsis

```
document.form_name
document.forms[form_number]
```

Properties

Form inherits properties from HTMLElement and also defines or overrides the following:

action
: A read/write string specifying the URL to which the form will be submitted. Initially specified by the ACTION attribute.

elements[]
: An array of input elements that appear in the form. Each element is a Button, Checkbox, Hidden, Password, Radio, Reset, Select, Submit, Text, or Textarea object.

elements.length
: The number of items in the elements[] array.

encoding
: A read/write string that specifies the encoding method used for form data. Initially specified by the ENCTYPE attribute. The default encoding of "application/x-www-form-urlencoded" is almost always appropriate.

length
: The number of elements in the form. Equivalent to elements.length.

method
: A read/write string that specifies the technique for submitting the form. It should have the value "get" or "post". Initially specified by the METHOD attribute.

name
: The name of the form. Specified by the NAME attribute.

target
: A read/write string that specifies the name of the frame or window in which the results of submitting a form should be displayed. Initially specified by the TARGET attribute. The special names "_top", "_parent", "_self", and "_blank" are also supported for the target property and the TARGET attribute.

Methods

Form inherits methods from HTMLElement and also defines the following:

reset()   Reset each of the input elements of the form to their default values.

submit()   Submit the form.

Event Handlers

Form inherits event handlers from HTMLElement, and also defines the following:

onreset   Invoked just before the elements of the form are reset. Specified in HTML by
               the onReset attribute.

onsubmit   Invoked just before the form is submitted. Specified in HTML by the onSub-
               mit attribute. This event handler allows form entries to be validated before
               being submitted.

HTML Syntax

A Form object is created with a standard HTML <FORM> tag. The form contains any input
elements created with the <INPUT>, <SELECT>, and <TEXTAREA> tags between <FORM> and
</FORM>.

```
<FORM
    [ NAME="form_name" ]          Used to name the form in JavaScript
    [ TARGET="window_name" ]      The name of the window for responses
    [ ACTION="url" ]              The URL to which the form is submitted
    [ METHOD=(GET|POST) ]         The method of form submission
    [ ENCTYPE="encoding" ]        How the form data is encoded
    [ onReset="handler" ]         A handler invoked when form is reset
    [ onSubmit="handler" ]        A handler invoked when form is submitted
>
Form text and input elements go here.
</FORM>
```

Description

The Form object represents an HTML <FORM> in a document. Each form in a document is
represented as an element of the Document.forms[] array. Named forms are also represented by the *form_name* property of their document, where *form_name* is the name specified in the NAME attribute of the <FORM> tag.

The elements of a form (buttons, input fields, checkboxes, and so on) are collected in the
Form.elements[] array. Named elements, like named forms, can also be referenced
directly by name—the element name is used as a property name of the Form object. Thus,
to refer to a Text object element named phone within a form named questionnaire, you
might use the JavaScript expression:

```
document.questionnaire.phone
```

See the descriptions of the Form properties and methods for more information about this
object.

See Also

Button, Checkbox, FileUpload, Hidden, Input, Password, Radio, Reset, Select, Submit, Text, Textarea, Chapter 16

Form.action — the URL for form submission

Availability

Client-side JavaScript 1.0; read-only in Internet Explorer 3

Synopsis

```
form.action
```

Description

`action` is a read/write string property of the Form object. It specifies the URL to which the form data is sent when the form is submitted. The initial value of this property is specified by the `ACTION` attribute of the `<FORM>` HTML tag. Usually, this URL specifies the address as a CGI script, although it can also be a `mailto:` or `news:` address.

You can set this property in IE 3, but doing so has no effect on how the form is submitted.

Form.elements[] — the input elements of the form

Availability

Client-side JavaScript 1.0

Synopsis

```
form.elements[i]
form.elements.length
```

Description

`form.elements` is an array of the form input objects in `form`. The array has `elements.length` items in it. These items may be of any of the form input element types: Button, Checkbox, Hidden, Password, Radio, Reset, Select, Submit, Text, and Textarea. These form input objects appear in the array in the same order that they appear in the HTML source code for the form.

Usage

If an item in the `form.elements[]` array has been given a name with the `NAME="name"` attribute of its HTML `<INPUT>` tag, that item's name becomes a property of `form`, and this property refers to the item. Thus, it is possible to refer to input objects by name instead of by number:

```
form.name
```

Usually, referring to elements by name is easier, and it is therefore a good idea to specify the `NAME` attribute for all form elements.

See Also

Button, Checkbox, Form, Hidden, Input, Password, Radio, Reset, Select, Submit, Text, Textarea

Form.encoding — the encoding of form data

Availability

Client-side JavaScript 1.0; read-only in Internet Explorer 3

Synopsis

```
form.encoding
```

Description

`encoding` is a read/write string property of the Form object. It specifies how form data is encoded for transmission when the form is submitted. The initial value of this property is specified by the `ENCTYPE` attribute of the `<FORM>` tag. The default value is "application/x-www-form-urlencoded", which is sufficient for almost all purposes. Other values may sometimes be necessary. For example, a value of "text/plain" is convenient when the form is being submitted by email to a `mailto:` URL. See *CGI Programming on the World Wide Web*, by Shishir Gundavaram (O'Reilly), for further information.

You can set this property in IE 3, but doing so has no effect on how the form is encoded.

Form.length — the number of elements in a form

Availability

Client-side JavaScript 1.0

Synopsis

```
form.length
```

Description

The `length` property of *form* specifies the number of form elements contained in the form. It is the same as *form*.`elements`.`length`.

Form.method — the submission method for the form

Availability

Client-side JavaScript 1.0; read-only in Internet Explorer 3

Synopsis

```
form.method
```

Description

`method` is a read/write string property of the Form object. It specifies the method by which form data is submitted. The initial value of this property is specified by the `METHOD` attribute of the `<FORM>` tag. The two legal values are `GET` and `POST`.

The `GET` method is the default. It is usually used for form submissions such as database queries that do not have side effects. With this method, the encoded form data is appended to the URL specified by the `Form.action` property. CGI scripts receiving a form submitted by this method generally read the form data from the `QUERY_STRING` environment variable.

The `POST` method is appropriate for form submissions, such as additions to databases, that have side effects. With this method, encoded form data is sent in the HTTP request body and is available to CGI scripts that read from the standard input stream.

You can set this property in IE 3, but doing so has no effect on how the form is submitted.

Form.name — the name of a form

Availability
Client-side JavaScript 1.0

Synopsis
```
form.name
```

Description
The `name` property specifies the name of the form. The initial value of this read/write string property is the value of the `NAME` attribute of the `<FORM>` tag.

Form.onreset — the handler invoked when a form is reset

Availability
Client-side JavaScript 1.1

Synopsis
```
<FORM ... onReset="handler" ... >
form.onreset
```

Description
The `onreset` property of a Form object specifies an event handler function that is invoked when the user clicks on a **Reset** button in the form or when the `Form.reset()` method is called.

The initial value of this property is a function that contains the semicolon-separated JavaScript statements specified by the `onReset` attribute of the HTML `<FORM>` tag. When an event handler function is defined by an HTML attribute, it is executed in the scope of *element* rather than the scope of the containing window.

In Navigator 4, the `onreset` handler function is passed an Event object as an argument. In IE 4, no argument is passed, but the applicable Event object is available as the `event` property of the Window object that contains the *element*.

If the `onreset` handler returns `false`, the elements of the form are not reset.

Example
You could use the following event handler to ask the user to confirm that they really want to reset the form:

```
<FORM ...
    onReset="return confirm('Really erase all entered data?')"
>
```

See Also
Form.onsubmit, Form.reset( ), Chapter 15

Form.onsubmit — invoked when a form is submitted

Availability
Client-side JavaScript 1.0

Synopsis
```
<FORM ... onSubmit="handler" ... >
form.onsubmit
```

Description
The onsubmit property of a Form object specifies an event handler function that is invoked when the user submits a form by clicking on a **Submit** button in the form. Note that this event handler is not invoked when the Form.submit( ) method is called.

The initial value of this property is a function that contains the semicolon-separated JavaScript statements specified by the onSubmit attribute of the HTML <FORM> tag. When an event handler function is defined by an HTML attribute, it is executed in the scope of *element* rather than the scope of the containing window.

In Navigator 4, the onsubmit handler function is passed an Event object as an argument. In IE 4, no argument is passed, but the applicable Event object is available as the event property of the Window object that contains the *element*.

If the onsubmit handler returns false, the elements of the form are not submitted. If the handler returns any other value or returns nothing, the form is submitted normally. Because the onsubmit handler can cancel form submission, it is ideal for performing form data validation.

See Also
Form.submit( ), Chapter 15

Form.reset( ) — reset the elements of a form

Availability
Client-side JavaScript 1.1

Synopsis
```
form.reset( )
```

Description

The reset() method resets the specified form, restoring each element of the form to its default value, exactly as if a **Reset** button had been pressed by the user. The form's onreset() event handler is first invoked and may prevent the reset from occurring by returning the value false.

Form.submit() — submit a form

Availability

Client-side JavaScript 1.0

Synopsis

```
form.submit()
```

Description

The submit() method submits the specified *form*, almost as if a **Submit** button had been pressed by the user. The form is submitted as specified by the action, method, and encoding properties of *form* (or the ACTION, METHOD, and ENCTYPE attributes of the <FORM> tag), and the results are displayed in the window or frame specified by the target property or the TARGET attribute.

The one important difference between the submit() method and form submission by the user is that the onsubmit() event handler is not invoked when submit() is called. If you use onsubmit() to perform input validation, for example, you'll have to do that validation explicitly before calling submit().

Usage

It is more common to use a **Submit** button to allow the user to submit the form than it is to call the submit() method yourself.

Form.target — the window for form results

Availability

Client-side JavaScript 1.0; read-only in Internet Explorer 3

Synopsis

```
form.target
```

Description

target is a read/write string property of the Form object. It specifies the name of the frame or window in which the results of the submission of *form* should be displayed. The initial value of this property is specified by the TARGET attribute of the <FORM> tag. If unset, the default is for form submission results to appear in the same window as the form.

Note that the value of target is the *name* of a frame or window, not the actual frame or window itself. The name of a frame is specified by the NAME attribute of the <FRAME> tag. The name of a window is specified when the window is created with a call to the Window.open() method. If target specifies the name of a window that does not exist, Navigator automatically opens a new window to display the results of form submission, and any future forms with the same target name use the same newly created window.

Four special target names are supported. The target named "_blank" specifies that a new, empty browser window should be created and used to display the results of the form submission. The target "_self" is the default; it specifies that the form submission results should be displayed in the same frame or window as the form itself. The target "_parent" specifies that the results should be displayed in the parent frame of the frame that contains the form. Finally, the "_top" target specifies that the results should be displayed in the topmost frame—in other words, all frames should be removed, and the results should occupy the entire browser window.

You can set this property in IE 3, but doing so has no effect on the actual target of the form.

See Also
Link.target

Frame — a type of Window object

Availability
Client-side JavaScript 1.0

Synopsis
```
window.frames[i]
window.frames.length
frames[i]
frames.length
```

Description
Though the Frame object is sometimes referred to, there is, strictly speaking, no such object. All frames within a browser window are instances of the Window object, and they contain the same properties and support the same methods and event handlers as the Window object does. See the Window object, and its properties, methods, and event handlers for details.

There are a few practical differences between Window objects that represent top-level browser windows and those that represent frames within a browser window, however:

- When the defaultStatus property is set for a frame, the specified status message is only visible when the mouse is within that frame.

- The top and parent properties of a top-level browser window always refer to the top-level window itself. These properties are really useful only for frames.

- The close() method is not useful for Window objects that are frames.

See Also
Window

frames[] — see Window.frames[]

Function — a JavaScript function

Availability

Core JavaScript 1.0; enhanced in JavaScript 1.1 and 1.2

Synopsis

```
function functionname(argument_name_list)    Function definition statement
{
     body
}
function (argument_name_list) { body }       Unnamed function literal; JavaScript 1.2
functionname(argument_value_list)            Function invocation
```

Constructor

```
new Function(argument_names, body)           JavaScript 1.1 and later
```

Arguments

`argument_names`

> Any number of string arguments, each naming one argument of the Function object being created.

`body`

> A string that specifies the body of the function. It may contain any number of JavaScript statements, separated with semicolons.

Properties

`arguments[]` An array of arguments that were passed to the function. Deprecated.

`arity`   The number of named arguments specified when the function was declared.

`caller`   A reference to the Function object that invoked this one, or `null` if the function is invoked at the top level. Deprecated.

`length`   The number of named arguments specified when the function was declared.

`prototype` An object which, for a constructor function, defines properties and methods shared by all objects created with that constructor function.

Methods

`apply()`   Invoke a function as a method of a specified object, passing a specified array of arguments.

`toString()` Return a string representation of the function.

Description

A function is a fundamental data type in JavaScript. Chapter 7 explains how to define and use functions, and Chapter 8 covers the related topics of methods, constructors, and the `prototype` property of functions. See those chapters for complete details.

In JavaScript 1.1, a function is automatically given a local variable, named *arguments*, that refers to an Arguments object. This object is an array of the values passed as arguments to the function and also defines other useful properties. See the Arguments reference page for details.

See Also

Arguments, Chapter 7, Chapter 8

Function.apply() — invoke a function as a method of an object

Availability

Core Navigator 4

Synopsis

```
function.apply(thisobj, args)
```

Arguments

thisobj   The object to which *function* is to be applied. In the body of the function, *thisobj* becomes the value of the this keyword.

args   An array of values to be passed as arguments to *function*.

Returns

Whatever value is returned by the invocation of *function*.

Description

apply() invokes the specified *function* as if it were a method of *thisobj*, passing it the arguments contained in the *args* array. It returns the value returned by the function invocation.

Function.arguments[] — arguments passed to a function

Availability

Core JavaScript 1.0; ECMA-262; deprecated in favor of the Arguments object

Synopsis

```
function.arguments[i]
function.arguments.length
```

Description

The arguments property of a Function object is an array of the arguments that are passed to a function. arguments.length specifies the number of elements in the array. JavaScript allows any number and any type of arguments to be passed to a function, and the arguments[] array allows you to write functions that can gracefully accept a variable number of arguments.

Note that the arguments property of a function is only defined while the function is executing, within the body of the function. Also note that this property has been deprecated in favor of the Arguments object.

See Also

Arguments

Function.arity — the number of declared arguments

Availability

Core Navigator 4, with `LANGUAGE="JavaScript1.2"`

Synopsis

    function.arity

Description

The `arity` property specifies the number of named arguments that were declared when a function was defined. It is a synonym for the `Function.length` property but has a name that is less likely to be confused with the `Arguments.length` property.

Note that the `arity` property is only defined in Navigator 4, and only when `LAN-GUAGE="JavaScript1.2"` is explicitly specified in the <SCRIPT> tag.

See Also

Arguments.length, Function.length

Function.caller — the function that called this one

Availability

Core JavaScript 1.0

Synopsis

    function.caller

Description

The `caller` property of a Function object is a reference to the function that invoked the current one. If the function was invoked from the top level of a JavaScript program, `caller` is `null`. This property may only be used from within the function (i.e., the `caller` property is only defined for a function while that function is executing).

In Navigator 4, the `Arguments.caller` property provides similar information. Note that `Function.caller` is not part of the ECMA-262 standard.

See Also

Arguments

Function.length — the number of declared arguments

Availability

Core JavaScript 1.1; ECMA-262

Synopsis

```
function.length
```

Description

The `length` property of a function specifies the number of named arguments declared when the function was defined. The function may actually be invoked with more than or fewer than this number of arguments.

Bugs

This property does not work correctly in Navigator 4.

See Also

Arguments.length, Function.arity

Function.prototype — the prototype for a class of objects

Availability

Core JavaScript 1.1

Synopsis

```
function.prototype
```

Description

The `prototype` property of a function is used when the function is used as a constructor. It refers to an object that serves as the prototype for an entire class of objects. Any object created by the constructor inherits all properties of the object referred to by the `prototype` property.

See Chapter 8 for a full discussion of constructor functions, the `prototype` property, and the definition of classes in JavaScript.

Bugs

Navigator 3 requires a constructor to be used once before anything can be assigned to its prototype object.

See Also

Chapter 8

Function.toString() — convert a function to a string

Availability

Core JavaScript 1.0; ECMA-262

Synopsis

```
function.toString()
```

Returns

A string that represents the function.

Description

The toString() method of the Function object converts a function to a string in an implementation-dependent way. In Navigator, this method returns a string of valid JavaScript code—code that includes the function keyword, argument list, the complete body of the function, and so on.

getClass() — return the JavaClass of a JavaObject

Availability

Client-side Navigator 3

Synopsis

```
getClass(javaobj)
```

Arguments

javaobj   A JavaObject object.

Returns

The JavaClass object of javaobj.

Description

getClass() is a function that takes a JavaObject object (javaobj) as an argument. It returns the JavaClass object of that JavaObject. That is, it returns the JavaClass object that represents the Java class of the Java object represented by the specified JavaObject.

Usage

Don't confuse the JavaScript getClass() function with the *getClass* method of all Java objects. Similarly, don't confuse the JavaScript JavaClass object with the Java *java.lang.Class* class.

Consider the Java rectangle object created with the following line:

```
var r = new java.awt.Rectangle();
```

r is a JavaScript variable that holds a JavaObject object. Calling the JavaScript function get-Class() returns a JavaClass object that represents the *java.awt.Rectangle* class:

```
var c = getClass(r);
```

You can see that this is so by comparing this JavaClass object to java.awt.Rectangle:

```
if (c == java.awt.Rectangle) ...
```

The Java getClass() method is invoked differently and performs an entirely different function:

```
c = r.getClass();
```

After executing the above line of code, c is a JavaObject that represents a *java.lang.Class* object. This *java.lang.Class* object is a Java object that is a Java representation of the *java.awt.Rectangle* class. See your Java documentation for details on what you can do with the *java.lang.Class* class.

To summarize, you can see that the following expression always evaluates to true, for any JavaObject o:

```
(getClass(o.getClass()) == java.lang.Class)
```

See Also

java, JavaArray, JavaClass, JavaObject, JavaPackage, Packages, Chapter 20

Hidden — hidden data for client/server communication

Availability

Client-side JavaScript 1.0; enhanced in JavaScript 1.1

Inherits From

Input, HTMLElement

Synopsis

```
form.name
form.elements[i]
```

Properties

Hidden inherits properties from Input and HTMLElement and defines or overrides the following:

value A read/write string, initially set by the HTML VALUE attribute, which specifies arbitrary data to be transmitted to the server when the form is submitted. This data is never visible to the user.

HTML Syntax

A Hidden element is created with a standard HTML <INPUT> tag:

```
<FORM>
    ...
  <INPUT
     TYPE="hidden"              Specifies that this is a Hidden element
     [ NAME="name" ]            A name that can later be used to refer to this element
                                Specifies the name property
```

```
    [ VALUE="value" ]      The value transmitted when the form is submitted
                           Specifies the initial value of the value property

 >
     . . .
 </FORM>
```

Description

The Hidden element is an invisible form element that allows arbitrary data to be transmitted to the server when the form is submitted. You can use a Hidden element when you want to transmit information besides the user's input data to the server.

When an HTML document is generated on the fly by a server, another use of Hidden form elements is to transmit data from the server to the client for later processing by JavaScript on the user's side. For example, the server might transmit raw data to the client in a compact, machine-readable form by specifying the data in the VALUE attribute of a Hidden element or elements. On the client side, a JavaScript program (transmitted along with the data or in another frame) could read the value property of the Hidden element or elements and process, format, and display that data in a less compact, human-readable (and perhaps user-configurable) format.

Hidden elements can also be useful for communication between CGI scripts, even without the intervention of JavaScript on the client side. In this usage, one CGI script generates a dynamic HTML page containing hidden data, which is then submitted back to a second CGI script. This hidden data can communicate state information, such as the results of submission of a previous form.

Cookies can also be used to transmit data from client to server. An important difference between hidden form elements and cookies, however, is that cookies are persistent on the client side.

See Also

Document.cookie, Form, HTMLElement, Input

Hidden.value — arbitrary data submitted with a form

Availability

Client-side JavaScript 1.0

Synopsis

```
hidden.value
```

Description

value is a read/write string property of the Hidden object. It specifies arbitrary data that is passed to the web server when the form containing the Hidden object is submitted. The initial value of value is specified by the VALUE attribute of the <INPUT> tag that defines the Hidden object. See Hidden for a description of how this property can be used.

history — see Window.history

History — the URL history of the browser

Availability

Client-side JavaScript 1.0; additional features available in Navigator 4 with the `Universal-BrowserRead` privilege

Synopsis

```
window.history
frame.history
history
```

Properties

current   A string that specifies the URL of the current document. Available in Navigator 4 with the `UniversalBrowserRead` privilege.

length   The number of URLs saved in the History object.

next   A string that specifies the URL of the document after the current one in the history list. Available in Navigator 4 with the `UniversalBrowserRead` privilege.

previous   A string that specifies the URL of the document before the current one in the history list. Available in Navigator 4 with the `UniversalBrowserRead` privilege.

Methods

back()   Go backwards to a previously visited URL.

forward() Go forward to a previously visited URL.

go()   Go to a previously visited URL.

toString() Return an HTML-formatted table containing the window's browsing history. Available in Navigator 4 with the `UniversalBrowserRead` privilege.

Description

The History object is a read-only array of strings that specify the URLs that have been previously visited by the browser. The contents of this array are equivalent to the URLs listed in Navigator's **Go** menu. For security and privacy reasons, the contents of the array are not available without the `UniversalBrowserRead` privilege.

Without the `UniversalBrowserRead` privilege, and in browsers that do not support the Navigator 4 security model, scripts can only use the History object in a restricted way. They can use the `length` property to determine the number of entries on the History object's URL list, and they can use the `back()`, `forward()`, and `go()` methods to cause the browser to revisit any of the URLs in the array, but they cannot make the browser read, directly or indirectly, the URLs stored in the array.

In Navigator 4, for signed scripts with `UniversalBrowserRead`, the elements of the array are available and may be read but not changed. Also, the `current`, `next`, and `previous` properties are available. These properties are strings that specify the URL of the current document and the URLs of the documents that precede and follow it in the history array. Finally, the `UniversalBrowserRead` privilege makes the `toString()` method of the History object functional. This method returns a string of HTML text. When this string is formatted by a browser (i.e., written with `document.write()`), it displays the browser history as a table of URLs, each with an appropriate hyperlink.

Example

Untrusted scripts and scripts running in browsers other than Navigator 4 can use the `back()`, `forward()`, and `go()` methods of the History object. The following line performs the same action as clicking the **Back** button:

```
history.back();
```

The following performs the same action as clicking the **Back** button twice:

```
history.go(-2);
```

With the `UniversalBrowserRead` privilege, you can access the history object as an array and read URLs directly. The first URL displayed by the current window is:

```
history[0]
```

The last URL displayed by that window is:

```
history[history.length-1]
```

The currently displayed URL is:

```
history.current
```

And the URLs of the documents before and after that one in the history array are:

```
history.previous
history.next
```

See Also

Location, Chapter 21

History.back() — return to the previous URL

Availability

Client-side JavaScript 1.0

Synopsis

```
history.back()
```

Description

back() causes the window or frame to which the History object belongs to revisit the URL (if any) that was visited immediately before the current one. Calling this method has the same effect as a user's click on the Navigator **Back** button. It is also equivalent to:

```
history.go(-1);
```

History.current — the URL of the currently displayed document

Availability

Client-side Navigator 4; requires UniversalBrowserRead

Synopsis

```
history.current
```

Description

The current property of the History object is a read-only string that contains the URL of the current document.

History.forward() — visit the next URL

Availability

Client-side JavaScript 1.0

Synopsis

```
history.forward()
```

Description

forward() causes the window or frame to which the History object belongs to revisit the URL (if any) that was visited immediately after the current one. Calling this method has the same effect as a user's click on the Navigator **Forward** button. It is also equivalent to:

```
history.go(1);
```

Note that if the user has not used the **Back** button or the **Go** menu to move backwards through the history, and if JavaScript has not invoked the History.back() or History.go() methods, the forward() method has no effect because the browser is already at the end of its list of URLs and there is no URL to go forward to.

History.go() — revisit a URL

Availability

Client-side JavaScript 1.0; enhanced in JavaScript 1.1

Synopsis

```
history.go(relative_position)
history.go(target_string)
```

Arguments

`relative_position`

> The relative position in the History list of the URL to be visited. In IE 3, this argument must be 1, 0, or −1.

`target_string`

> A substring of the URL to be visited. This version of the `go()` method was added in JavaScript 1.1.

Description

The first form of the `History.go()` method takes an integer argument and causes the browser to visit the URL that is the specified number of positions distant in the history list maintained by the History object. Positive arguments move the browser forward through the list, and negative arguments move it backwards. Thus, calling `history.go(-1)` is equivalent to calling `history.back()` and, in Navigator, produces the same effect as a user's click on the **Back** button. Similarly, `history.go(3)` revisits the same URL that would be visited by calling `history.forward()` three times. Calling `go()` with an argument of 0 causes the current page to be reloaded (although in Navigator 3, the `Location.reload()` provides a better way of doing this). This form of the method is buggy in multiframe documents in Navigator 3, and in Internet Explorer it can only be called with the values 1, 0, and −1.

The second form of the `History.go()` method was implemented in JavaScript 1.1. It takes a string argument and causes the browser to revisit the first (i.e., most recently visited) URL that contains the specified string.

History.length — the number of elements in the history array

Availability

Client-side Navigator 2, Internet Explorer 4

Synopsis

```
history.length
```

Description

The History object is an array of URLs. Like all arrays, it has a `length` property that specifies the number of elements in the array. Although the elements of this array can only be read in Navigator 4 by signed scripts with the UniversalBrowserRead privilege, the `length` property of the array has been available since Navigator 2 and is also available in IE 4. In IE 3, the `length` property always returns 0.

History.next — the URL of the next document in the history array

Availability

Client-side Navigator 4; requires `UniversalBrowserRead`

Synopsis

```
history.next
```

Description

The `next` property of the History object is a read-only string that contains the URL of the document after the current one in the history array. It can only be read by trusted scripts that have the `UniversalBrowserRead` privilege.

History.previous — the URL of the previous document in the history array

Availability

Client-side Navigator 4; requires `UniversalBrowserRead`

Synopsis

```
history.previous
```

Description

The `previous` property of the History object is a read-only string that contains the URL of the document before the current one in the history array. It can only be read by trusted scripts that have the `UniversalBrowserRead` privilege.

HTMLElement — the superclass of all HTML elements

Availability

Client-side JavaScript 1.2

Synopsis

HTMLElement is the superclass of all classes that represent HTML elements. Therefore, HTMLElement objects are used in many contexts in client-side JavaScript and are available in all of the following ways:

```
document.images[i]
document.links[i]
document.anchors[i]
document.forms[i]
document.forms[i].elements[j]
document.elementName
document.formName.elementName
document.all[i]
```

Internet Explorer 4 Properties

`all[]`	An array of all elements contained by this element.
`children[]`	The elements that are direct children of this element.
`className`	The value of the CLASS attribute.
`document`	A reference to the containing Document object.
`id`	The value of the ID attribute.
`innerHTML`	HTML text within the element.
`innerText`	Plain text within the element.
`lang`	The value of the LANG attribute.
`offsetHeight`	
	The height of the element.
`offsetLeft`	The X-coordinate of the element.
`offsetParent`	
	The containing element relative to which `offsetLeft` and `offsetTop` are measured.
`offsetTop`	The Y-coordinate of the element.
`offsetWidth`	The width of the element.
`outerHTML`	The HTML text of the element, including its start and end tags.
`outerText`	The plain text that constitutes the document, including its start and end tags.
`parentElement`	
	The element that is the direct parent of this one.
`sourceIndex`	The index of the element in Document.all[].
`style`	The inline CSS style attributes for this element.
`tagName`	The name of the HTML tag that created this element.
`title`	The value of the TITLE attribute.

Navigator 4 Methods

`handleEvent()`
Pass an Event object to the appropriate event handler.

Internet Explorer 4 Methods

`contains()`	Determine whether the element contains a specified element.
`getAttribute`	
	Get the value of a named attribute.
`insertAdjacentHTML()`	
	Insert HTML text into the document near this element.

`insertAdjacentText()`
      Insert plain text into the document near this element.

`removeAttribute()`
      Delete an attribute and its value from the element.

`scrollIntoView()`
      Scroll the document so the element is visible at the top or bottom of the window.

`setAttribute`
      Set the value of an attribute of the element.

Event Handlers

`onclick`   Invoked when the user clicks on the element.

`ondblclick`   Invoked when the user double-clicks on the element.

`onhelp`   Invoked when the user requests help. IE 4 only.

`onkeydown`   Invoked when the user presses a key.

`onkeypress`   Invoked when the user presses and releases a key.

`onkeyup`   Invoked when the user releases a key.

`onmousedown` Invoked when the user presses a mouse button.

`onmousemove` Invoked when the user moves the mouse.

`onmouseout`   Invoked when the user moves the mouse off the element.

`onmouseover` Invoked when the user moves the mouse over an element.

`onmouseup`   Invoked when the user releases a mouse button.

Description

HTMLElement is the superclass of all JavaScript classes that represent HTML elements: Anchor, Form, Image, Input, Link, and so on. The IE 4 document object model exposes all HTML elements in a document and defines quite a few properties and methods that are inherited by all those elements. In addition, HTMLElement defines a number of event handlers that are implemented in both IE 4 and Navigator 4.

See Also

Anchor, Form, Image, Input, Link, Chapter 14, Chapter 15

HTMLElement.all[ ] — all elements contained within an element

Availability

Client-side Internet Explorer 4

Synopsis

```
element.all[]
```

Description

The `all[]` array of an element contains the complete list of elements contained within *element*, in source order. This property behaves exactly like the `Document.all[]` property.

See Also

Document.all[]

HTMLElement.children[] — the direct children of an element

Availability

Client-side Internet Explorer 4

Synopsis

```
element.children[]
```

Description

The `children[]` array contains the elements contained directly within *element*.

HTMLElement.className — the value of the CLASS attribute

Availability

Client-side Internet Explorer 4; DOM draft

Synopsis

```
element.className
```

Description

The `className` property is a read/write string that specifies the value of the CLASS attribute of an element. This property is used in conjunction with cascading style sheets.

HTMLElement.contains() — whether one element is contained in another

Availability

Client-side Internet Explorer 4

Synopsis

```
element.contains(target)
```

Arguments

target   An HTMLElement object.

Returns

true if *element* contains *target*, or false if it does not.

HTMLElement.document — the Document object that contains an element

Availability

Client-side Internet Explorer 4

Synopsis

```
element.document
```

Description

In IE 4 DHTML, the document property refers to the Document object that contains the element.

HTMLElement.getAttribute() — get an attribute value

Availability

Client-side Internet Explorer 4

Synopsis

```
element.getAttribute(name)
```

Arguments

name   The name of the attribute.

Returns

The value of the named attribute of *element*, or null if *element* does not have an attribute named *name*.

HTMLElement.handleEvent() — see Window.handleEvent()

HTMLElement.id — the value of the ID attribute

Availability

Client-side Internet Explorer 4; DOM draft

Synopsis

```
element.id
```

Description

The id property is a read/write string that specifies the value of the ID attribute of an element. This property is used to assign a unique name to an element.

HTMLElement.innerHTML — the HTML text contained within the element

Availability

Client-side Internet Explorer 4

Synopsis

```
element.innerHTML
```

Description

In IE 4 DHTML, `innerHTML` is a read/write string property that specifies the HTML text that is contained within the `element`, not including the opening and closing tags of `element` itself. Setting this property replaces the content of `element` with the specified HTML text. Note that you cannot set this property while the document is loading.

HTMLElement.innerText — the text within the element

Availability

Client-side Internet Explorer 4

Synopsis

```
element.innerText
```

Description

In IE 4 DHTML, `innerText` is a read/write string property that specifies the plain text contained within the `element`, not including the opening and closing tags of `element` itself. Setting this property replaces the content of `element` with unparsed plain text. Note that you cannot set this property while the document is loading.

HTMLElement.insertAdjacentHTML() — insert HTML text around an element

Availability

Client-side Internet Explorer 4

Synopsis

```
element.insertAdjacentHTML(where, text)
```

Arguments

where   A string specifying where the text is to be inserted. The value "BeforeBegin" specifies that *text* is to be inserted before the start tag of *element*. "AfterBegin" specifies that *text* is to be inserted immediately after the start tag of *element*. "BeforeEnd" specifies that *text* is to be inserted immediately before the end tag of *element*. "AfterEnd" specifies that *text* is to be inserted immediately after the end tag of *element*.

text   The HTML text to insert.

Description

insertAdjacentHTML() inserts the HTML *text* at a position within or next to *element*, as specified by the argument *where*.

HTMLElement.insertAdjacentText() — insert plain text before or after an element

Availability

Client-side Internet Explorer 4

Synopsis

```
element.insertAdjacentText(where, text)
```

Arguments

where   A string that specifies where the text is to be inserted. The value
                  "BeforeBegin" specifies that *text* is to be inserted before the start tag of
                  element. "AfterBegin" specifies that *text* is to be inserted immediately
                  after the start tag of *element*. "BeforeEnd" specifies that *text* is to be
                  inserted immediately before the end tag of *element*. "AfterEnd" specifies that *text* is to be inserted immediately after the end tag of *element*.

text   The plain text to insert.

Description

insertAdjacentText() inserts the plain text *text* at a position within or next to *element*, as specified by the argument *where*.

HTMLElement.lang — the value of the LANG attribute

Availability

Client-side Internet Explorer 4; DOM draft

Synopsis

```
element.lang
```

Description

The lang property is a read/write string that specifies the value of the LANG HTML attribute of the *element*.

HTMLElement.offsetHeight — the height of the element

Availability

Client-side Internet Explorer 4

Synopsis

```
element.offsetHeight
```

Description

In IE 4 DHTML, the offsetHeight property specifies the height, in pixels, of the element and all of its content.

HTMLElement.offsetLeft — the X-coordinate of the element

Availability

Client-side Internet Explorer 4

Synopsis

```
element.offsetLeft
```

Description

In IE 4 DHTML, the offsetLeft property specifies the X-coordinate of *element*. This X-coordinate is relative to the container element specified by the offsetParent property.

HTMLElement.offsetParent — defines the coordinate system of the element

Availability

Client-side Internet Explorer 4

Synopsis

```
element.offsetParent
```

Description

In IE 4 DHMTL, offsetParent specifies the container element that defines the coordinate system in which offsetLeft and offsetTop are measured. For most elements, offsetParent is the Document object that contains them. However, if an element has a dynamically positioned container, the dynamically positioned element is the offsetParent. Similarly, table cells are positioned relative to the row in which they are contained.

HTMLElement.offsetTop — the Y-coordinate of the element

Availability

Client-side Internet Explorer 4

Synopsis

```
element.offsetTop
```

Description

In IE 4 DHTML, the `offsetTop` property specifies the Y-coordinate of `element`. This Y coordinate is relative to the container element specified by the `offsetParent` property.

HTMLElement.offsetWidth — the width of the element

Availability

Client-side Internet Explorer 4

Synopsis

```
element.offsetWidth
```

Description

In IE 4 DHTML, the `offsetWidth` property specifies the width, in pixels, of the element and all of its content.

HTMLElement.onclick — the handler invoked when the user clicks on an element

Availability

Client-side JavaScript 1.2; HTML 4.0

Synopsis

```
<ELEMENT onClick="handler" ... >
element.onclick
```

Description

The `onclick` property of an HTMLElement object specifies an event handler function that is invoked when the user clicks on the `element`. Note that `onclick` is different than `onmousedown`. A click event does not occur unless a mousedown event and the subsequent mouseup event both occur over the same `element`.

The initial value of this property is a function that contains the JavaScript statements specified by the `onClick` attribute of the HTML tag that defined the object. When an event handler function is defined by an HTML attribute, it is executed in the scope of `element` rather than in the scope of the containing window.

In Navigator 4, the `onclick` handler function is passed an Event object as an argument. In IE 4, no argument is passed, but the applicable Event object is available as the `event` property of the Window object that contains the `element`.

In Navigator 4, the `Event.which` property specifies which mouse button was pressed. In IE 4, the `Event.button` property specifies the button number.

See Also

Event, Input.onclick, Chapter 15

HTMLElement.ondblclick — the handler invoked when the user double-clicks on an element

Availability

Client-side JavaScript 1.2; HTML 4.0

Synopsis

```
<ELEMENT onDblClick="handler" ... >
element.ondblclick
```

Description

The `ondblclick` property of an HTMLElement object specifies an event handler function that is invoked when the user double-clicks on the *element*.

The initial value of this property is a function that contains the JavaScript statements specified by the `onDblClick` attribute of the HTML tag that defined the object. When an event handler function is defined by an HTML attribute, it is executed in the scope of *element* rather than in the scope of the containing window.

In Navigator 4, the `ondblclick` handler function is passed an Event object as an argument. In IE 4, no argument is passed, but the applicable Event object is available as the `event` property of the Window object that contains the *element*.

See Also

Event, Chapter 15

HTMLElement.onhelp — the handler invoked when the user presses F1

Availability

Client-side Internet Explorer 4

Synopsis

```
<ELEMENT onHelp="handler" ... >
element.onhelp
```

Description

The `onhelp` property of *element* specifies an event handler function that is invoked when the user presses the **F1** key while *element* has the keyboard focus.

The initial value of this property is a function that contains the JavaScript statements specified by the `onHelp` attribute of the HTML <BODY> or <FRAMESET> tag that defined the window. When an event handler function is defined by an HTML attribute, it is executed in the scope of *element* rather than in the scope of the containing window.

After the `onhelp` handler function is invoked, Internet Explorer 4 displays the built-in help window.

HTMLElement.onkeydown — the handler invoked when the user presses a key

Availability

Client-side JavaScript 1.2; HTML 4.0

Synopsis

```
<ELEMENT onKeyDown="handler" ... >
element.onkeydown
```

Description

The `onkeydown` property of an HTMLElement object specifies an event handler function that is invoked when the user presses a key over the *element*.

The initial value of this property is a function that contains the JavaScript statements specified by the `onKeyDown` attribute of the HTML tag that defined the object. When an event handler function is defined by an HTML attribute, it is executed in the scope of *element* rather than the scope of the containing window.

In Navigator 4, the `onkeydown` handler function is passed an Event object as an argument. In IE 4, no argument is passed, but the applicable Event object is available as the `event` property of the Window object that contains the *element*.

The character code of the key pressed is contained in the `which` property of the Event object in Navigator 4, and in the `keyCode` property of the Event object in IE 4. You can convert this keycode to a string with `String.fromCharCode()`. The modifier keys in effect can be determined from the `Event.modifiers` property in Navigator 4, or with `Event.shiftKey()` and related methods in IE 4.

In Navigator 4, you can cancel processing of the keystroke by returning `false` from this handler. In IE 4, you cancel processing by setting `Event.returnValue` to `false`. In IE 4, this handler may return an alternate keycode which is used in place of the key actually pressed by the user.

You can often use the `onkeypress` event handler instead of the `onkeydown` and `onkeyup` handlers.

See Also

Event, HTMLElement.onkeypress, Chapter 15

HTMLElement.onkeypress — the handler invoked when the user presses a key

Availability

Client-side JavaScript 1.2; HTML 4.0

Synopsis

```
<ELEMENT onKeyPress="handler" ... >
element.onkeypress
```

Description

The `onkeypress` property of an HTMLElement object specifies an event handler function that is invoked when the user presses a key over the *element*. A keypress event is generated after a key down event and before the corresponding key up event. The keypress and key down events are similar. Unless you care about receiving individual key up events, you should use `onkeypress` instead of `onkeydown`.

The initial value of this property is a function that contains the JavaScript statements specified by the `onKeyPress` attribute of the HTML tag that defined the object. When an event handler function is defined by an HTML attribute, it is executed in the scope of *element* rather than in the scope of the containing window.

In Navigator 4, the `onkeypress` handler function is passed an Event object as an argument. In IE 4, no argument is passed, but the applicable Event object is available as the `event` property of the Window object that contains the *element*.

The character code of the key pressed is contained in the `which` property of the Event object in Navigator 4 and in the `keyCode` property of the Event object in IE 4. You can convert this keycode to a string with `String.fromCharCode()`. The modifier keys in effect can be determined from the `Event.modifiers` property in Navigator 4, or with `Event.shiftKey()` and related methods in IE 4.

In Navigator 4, you can cancel processing of the keystroke by returning `false` from this handler. In IE 4, you cancel processing by setting `Event.returnValue` to `false`. In IE 4, this handler may return an alternate keycode that is used in place of the key actually pressed by the user.

See Also

Event, Chapter 15

HTMLElement.onkeyup — the handler invoked when the user releases a key

Availability

Client-side JavaScript 1.2; HTML 4.0

Synopsis

```
<ELEMENT onKeyUp="handler" ... >
element.onkeyup
```

Description

The `onkeyup` property of an HTMLElement object specifies an event handler function that is invoked when the user releases a key over the *element*.

The initial value of this property is a function that contains the JavaScript statements specified by the `onKeyUp` attribute of the HTML tag that defined the object. When an event handler function is defined by an HTML attribute, it is executed in the scope of *element* rather than in the scope of the containing window.

In Navigator 4, the `onkeyup` handler function is passed an Event object as an argument. In IE 4, no argument is passed, but the applicable Event object is available as the `event` property of the Window object that contains the *element*.

See Also

Event, HTMLElement.onkeydown, Chapter 15

HTMLElement.onmousedown — the handler invoked when the user presses a mouse button

Availability

Client-side JavaScript 1.2; HTML 4.0

Synopsis

```
<ELEMENT onMouseDown="handler" ... >
element.onmousedown
```

Description

The onmousedown property of an HTMLElement object specifies an event handler function that is invoked when the user presses a mouse button over *element*.

The initial value of this property is a function that contains the JavaScript statements specified by the onMouseDown attribute of the HTML tag that defined the object. When an event handler function is defined by an HTML attribute, it is executed in the scope of *element* rather than in the scope of the containing window.

In Navigator 4, the onmousedown handler function is passed an Event object as an argument. In IE 4, no argument is passed, but the applicable Event object is available as the event property of the Window object that contains the *element*.

In Navigator 4, the Event.which property specifies which mouse button was pressed. In IE 4, the Event.button property specifies the button number.

See Also

Event, HTMLElement.onclick, Chapter 15

HTMLElement.onmousemove — the handler invoked when the mouse moves within an element

Availability

Client-side JavaScript 1.2; HTML 4.0

Synopsis

```
<ELEMENT onMouseMove="handler" ... >
element.onmousemove
```

Description

The onmousemove property of an HTMLElement object specifies an event handler function that is invoked when the user moves the mouse pointer within the *element*.

The initial value of this property is a function that contains the JavaScript statements specified by the onMouseMove attribute of the HTML tag that defined the object. When an event handler function is defined by an HTML attribute, it is executed in the scope of *element* rather than in the scope of the containing window.

In Navigator 4, the onmousemove handler function is passed an Event object as an argument. In IE 4, no argument is passed, but the applicable Event object is available as the event property of the Window object that contains the *element*.

If you define an onmousemove event handler, mouse motion events are generated and reported in huge quantities when the mouse is moved within *element*. Keep this in mind when writing the function to be invoked by the event handler.

In Navigator 4, you cannot define this event handler on individual elements; instead, you must explicitly register your interest in mouse motion events by capturing them with the captureEvents() method of a Window, Document, or Layer object.

See Also

Event, Window.captureEvents(), Chapter 15

HTMLElement.onmouseout — the handler invoked when mouse moves out of an element

Availability

Client-side JavaScript 1.2; HTML 4.0

Synopsis

```
<ELEMENT onMouseOut="handler" ... >
element.onmouseout
```

Description

The onmouseout property of an HTMLElement object specifies an event handler function that is invoked when the user moves the mouse pointer out of the *element*.

The initial value of this property is a function that contains the JavaScript statements specified by the onMouseOut attribute of the HTML tag that defined the object. When an event handler function is defined by an HTML attribute, it is executed in the scope of *element* rather than in the scope of the containing window.

In Navigator 4, the onmouseout handler function is passed an Event object as an argument. In IE 4, no argument is passed, but the applicable Event object is available as the event property of the Window object that contains the *element*.

See Also

Event, Link.onmouseout, Chapter 15

HTMLElement.onmouseover — the handler invoked when the mouse moves over an element

Availability

Client-side JavaScript 1.2; HTML 4.0

Synopsis

```
<ELEMENT onMouseOver="handler" ... >
element.onmouseover
```

Description

The onmouseover property of an HTMLElement object specifies an event handler function that is invoked when the user moves the mouse pointer over the *element*.

The initial value of this property is a function that contains the JavaScript statements specified by the onMouseOver attribute of the HTML tag that defined the object. When an event handler function is defined by an HTML attribute, it is executed in the scope of *element* rather than in the scope of the containing window.

In Navigator 4, the onmouseover handler function is passed an Event object as an argument. In IE 4, no argument is passed, but the applicable Event object is available as the event property of the Window object that contains the *element*.

See Also

Event, Link.onmouseover, Chapter 15

HTMLElement.onmouseup — the handler invoked when the user releases a mouse button

Availability

Client-side JavaScript 1.2; HTML 4.0

Synopsis

```
<ELEMENT onMouseUp="handler" ... >
element.onmouseup
```

Description

The onmouseup property of an HTMLElement object specifies an event handler function that is invoked when the user releases a mouse button over the *element*.

The initial value of this property is a function that contains the JavaScript statements specified by the onMouseUp attribute of the HTML tag that defined the object. When an event handler function is defined by an HTML attribute, it is executed in the scope of *element* rather than in the scope of the containing window.

In Navigator 4, the onmouseup handler function is passed an Event object as an argument. In IE 4, no argument is passed, but the applicable Event object is available as the event property of the Window object that contains the *element*.

In Navigator 4, the Event.which property specifies which mouse button was pressed. In IE 4, the Event.button property specifies the button number.

See Also

Event, HTMLElement.onclick, Chapter 15

HTMLElement.outerHTML — the HTML of an element

Availability

Client-side Internet Explorer 4

Synopsis

```
element.outerHTML
```

Description

In IE 4 DHTML, outerHTML is a read/write property that specifies the HTML text of an element, including its start and end tags. Setting this property to a string of HTML text completely replaces element and its contents. Note that you cannot set this property while the document is loading.

HTMLElement.outerText — the text of an element

Availability

Client-side Internet Explorer 4

Synopsis

```
element.outerText
```

Description

In IE 4 DHTML, outerText is a read/write property that specifies the plain text of an element, including its start and end tags. Setting this property completely replaces element and its contents with the specified plain text. Note that you cannot set this property while the document is loading.

HTMLElement.parentElement — the container of an element

Availability

Client-side Internet Explorer 4

Synopsis

```
element.parentElement
```

Description

In IE 4 DHTML, parentElement is a read-only property that specifies the element that directly contains element.

HTMLElement.removeAttribute() — delete an attribute

Availability

Client-side Internet Explorer 4

Synopsis

```
element.removeAttribute(name)
```

Arguments

name   The name of the attribute to be deleted.

Returns

true on success; false on failure.

Description

removeAttribute() deletes the attribute *name* from *element*. If *element* does not have an attribute named *name*, this method returns false.

HTMLElement.scrollIntoView() — make an element visible

Availability

Client-side Internet Explorer 4

Synopsis

```
element.scrollIntoView(top)
```

Arguments

top   An optional boolean argument that specifies whether the element should be scrolled to the top or bottom of the screen. If true or omitted, *element* appears at the top of the screen. If false, *element* appears at the bottom of the screen.

Description

scrollIntoView() scrolls the document containing *element* so that the top of *element* is aligned with the top of the display area, or so that the bottom of *element* is aligned with the bottom of the display area.

HTMLElement.setAttribute() — set the value of an attribute

Availability

Client-side Internet Explorer 4

Synopsis

```
element.setAttribute(name, value)
```

Arguments

name   The name of the attribute to set.

value   The value to set it to.

Description

setAttribute() sets the attribute *name* of *element* to *value*.

HTMLElement.sourceIndex — the index of the element in Document.all[]

Availability

Client-side Internet Explorer 4

Synopsis

element.sourceIndex

Description

In IE 4 DHTML, sourceIndex specifies the index of *element* in the all[] array of the Document object that contains it.

HTMLElement.style — the inline CSS style of the element

Availability

Client-side Internet Explorer 4; DOM draft

Synopsis

element.style

Description

The style property specifies the CSS Style object for *element*. Setting the properties of this Style object changes the display style of *element*.

HTMLElement.tagName — the tag type of an element

Availability

Client-side Internet Explorer 4; DOM draft

Synopsis

element.tagName

Description

tagName is a read-only string property that specifies the name of the HTML tag that defined *element*.

HTMLElement.title — tool tip for an element

Availability

Client-side Internet Explorer 4; DOM draft

Synopsis

    element.title

Description

title is a read/write string property that specifies the value of the TITLE attribute of the tag that defined *element*. Most browsers use this string as the contents of a "tool tip" for the element.

Image — an image embedded in an HTML document

Availability

Client-side JavaScript 1.1

Inherits From

HTMLElement

Synopsis

    document.images[*i*]
    document.images.length
    document.*image-name*

Constructor

    new Image(*width*, *height*);

Arguments

width, height
> An optionally specified width and height for the image.

Properties

Image inherits properties from HTMLElement and defines or overrides the following:

border
> A read-only integer that specifies the width, in pixels, of the border around an image. Its value is set by the BORDER attribute.

complete
> A read-only boolean that specifies whether the image is completely loaded yet.

height
> A read-only integer that specifies the height, in pixels, of the image. Its value is set by the HEIGHT attribute.

hspace
> A read-only integer that specifies the amount of extra horizontal space, in pixels, inserted on the left and right of the image. Its value is set by the HSPACE attribute.

lowsrc
> A read/write string that specifies the URL of an alternate image, suitable for display at low resolutions. Its initial value is set by the LOWSRC attribute.

name
> A read-only string, specified by the HTML NAME attribute, that specifies the name of the image. When an image is given an name with the NAME attribute, a reference to the image is placed in the *image-name* property in addition to being placed in the document.images[ ] array.

src   A read/write string that specifies the URL of the image to be displayed. Its
                    initial value is set by the SRC attribute. Setting this property causes a new
                    image to be loaded and displayed.

vspace   A read-only integer that specifies the amount of extra vertical space, in pix-
                    els, inserted above and below the image. Its value is set by the VSPACE
                    attribute.

width   A read-only integer that specifies the width, in pixels, of the image. Its value
                    is set by the WIDTH attribute.

Event Handlers

Image inherits event handlers from HTMLElement and also defines the following:

onabort   Invoked if the user aborts the download of an image.

onerror   Invoked if an error occurs while downloading the image.

onload   Invoked when the image successfully finishes loading.

HTML Syntax

The Image object is created with a standard HTML <IMG> tag. Some <IMG> attributes have
been omitted from the following syntax because they are not used by or accessible from
JavaScript:

```
<IMG SRC="url"                          The image to display
     WIDTH=pixels                       The width of the image
     HEIGHT=pixels                      The height of the image
     [ NAME="image_name" ]              A property name for the image
     [ LOWSRC="url" ]                   Alternate low-resolution image
     [ BORDER=pixels ]                  Width of image border
     [ HSPACE=pixels ]                  Extra horizontal space around image
     [ VSPACE=pixels ]                  Extra vertical space around image
     [ onLoad=handler ]                 Invoked when image fully loaded
     [ onError=handler ]                Invoked if error in loading
     [ onAbort=handler ]                Invoked if user aborts load
>
```

Description

The Image objects in the document.images[] array represent the images embedded in an
HTML document using the <IMG> tag. Most of the properties of this object are read-only.
The src and lowsrc properties are exceptions, however; they may be set dynamically.
When you set the src property, the browser loads the image specified by the new value of
the src property or by the lowsrc property, if specified, for low-resolution monitors. Note
that if you want to use the lowsrc property, you must set it *before* you set the src property
because setting the src property starts the download of the new image.

You can create Image objects dynamically in your JavaScript code using the Image() constructor function. Note that this constructor method does not have an argument to specify
the image to be loaded. As with images created from HTML, you tell Navigator to load an
image by setting the src property of any images you create explicitly. There is no way to
display an Image object in the web browser. All you can do is force the Image object to

download an image by setting the `src` property. This is useful, however, because it loads an image into the browser's cache. Later, if that same image URL is specified for one of the images in the `images[]` array, it is preloaded and displays quickly. You might do this with lines like the following:

```
document.images[2].src = preloaded_image.src;
document.toggle_image.src = toggle_off.src;
```

Usage

Setting the `src` property of an Image object can be a way to implement simple animations in your web pages. It is also an excellent technique for changing the graphics on a page as the user interacts with the page. For example, you might create your own submit button using an image and a hypertext link. The button would start out with a disabled graphic and remain that way until the user had correctly entered all the required information into the form, at which point the graphic would change, and the user would be able to submit the form.

Image.border — the border width of an image

Availability

Client-side JavaScript 1.1

Synopsis

```
image.border
```

Description

The `border` property of the Image object is a read-only integer that specifies the width, in pixels, of the border the browser places around images that are hypertext links. The value of this property is specified by the `BORDER` attribute of the `<IMG>` HTML tag.

Image.complete — whether an image load is complete

Availability

Client-side JavaScript 1.1

Synopsis

```
image.complete
```

Description

The `complete` property is a read-only boolean value that specifies whether an image is completely loaded or, more accurately, whether the browser has completed its attempt to load the image. If an error occurs during loading, or if the load is aborted, the `complete` property is still set to `true`.

See Also

Image.onabort, Image.onerror, Image.onload

Image.height — the height of an image

Availability

Client-side JavaScript 1.1

Synopsis

```
image.height
```

Description

The `height` property of the Image object is a read-only integer that specifies the height of *image*. It is set by the `HEIGHT` attribute of the `<IMG>` HTML tag.

The `HEIGHT` attribute is optional in HTML, but including it greatly improves the layout time of your pages. Also, because of a bug in Navigator 2, all images in a page that contains JavaScript must have `WIDTH` and `HEIGHT` attributes specified (even though the Image object is not available in that browser).

Image.hspace — the horizontal padding for an image

Availability

Client-side JavaScript 1.1

Synopsis

```
image.hspace
```

Description

The `hspace` property of the Image object is a read-only integer that specifies the number of extra blank pixels that appear to the left and right of the image in the browser window. The value of this property is specified by the `HSPACE` attribute of the `<IMG>` tag.

Image.lowsrc — an alternate image for low-resolution displays

Availability

Client-side JavaScript 1.1

Synopsis

```
image.lowsrc
```

Description

The `lowsrc` property of the Image object is a read/write string that specifies the URL of an alternate image (usually a smaller one) to display when the user's browser is running on a low-resolution monitor. The initial value is specified by the `LOWSRC` attribute of the `<IMG>` tag.

Setting this property has no immediate effect. If the `src` property is set, however, a new image is loaded, and on low-resolution systems, the current value of the `lowsrc` property is used instead of the newly updated value of `src`.

Image.name — the name of an image

Availability

Client-side JavaScript 1.1

Synopsis

```
image.name
```

Description

name is a read-only string property of the Image object. Its value is specified by the NAME attribute of the HTML <IMG> tag that creates the Image object. Image objects created with the Image() constructor function cannot have names assigned.

Usage

Images created in an HTML document with the <IMG> tag are listed in the document.images[] array in JavaScript. If an image is given a name, the image is also stored in a property with that name in the document object. For example, an image with the attribute:

```
NAME="toggle_button"
```

could be referred to as:

```
document.toggle_button
```

Image.onabort — the handler invoked when the user aborts image loading

Availability

Client-side JavaScript 1.1

Synopsis

```
<IMG ... onAbort="handler" ... >
image.onabort
```

Description

The onabort property of an Image object specifies an event handler function that is invoked when the user aborts the loading of an image (for example, by clicking the **Stop** button).

The initial value of this property is a function that contains the JavaScript statements specified by the onAbort attribute of the <IMG> tag that defined the Image object. When an event handler function is defined by an HTML attribute, it is executed in the scope of *element* rather than in the scope of the containing window.

In Navigator 4, the onabort handler function is passed an Event object as an argument. In IE 4, no argument is passed, but the applicable Event object is available as the event property of the Window object that contains the *element*.

Image.onerror — the handler invoked when an error occurs during image loading

Availability

Client-side JavaScript 1.1

Synopsis

```
<IMG ... onError="handler" ... >
image.onerror
```

Description

The `onerror` property of an Image object specifies an event handler function that is invoked when an error occurs during the loading of an image.

The initial value of this property is a function that contains the JavaScript statements specified by the `onError` attribute of the `<IMG>` tag that defined the Image object. When an event handler function is defined by an HTML attribute, it is executed in the scope of `element` rather than in the scope of the containing window.

In Navigator 4, the `onerror` handler function is passed an Event object as an argument. In IE 4, no argument is passed, but the applicable Event object is available as the `event` property of the Window object that contains the `element`.

Image.onload — the handler invoked when an image finishes loading

Availability

Client-side JavaScript 1.1

Synopsis

```
<IMG ... onLoad="handler" ... >
image.onload
```

Description

The `onload` property of an Image object specifies an event handler function that is invoked when an image loads successfully.

The initial value of this property is a function that contains the JavaScript statements specified by the `onLoad` attribute of the `<IMG>` tag that defined the Image object. When an event handler function is defined by an HTML attribute, it is executed in the scope of `element` rather than in the scope of the containing window.

In Navigator 4, the `onload` handler function is passed an Event object as an argument. In IE 4, no argument is passed, but the applicable Event object is available as the `event` property of the Window object that contains the `element`.

Image.src — the URL of the embedded image

Availability

Client-side JavaScript 1.1

Synopsis

```
image.src
```

Description

The `src` property of the Image object is a read/write string that specifies the URL of the image to be displayed by the browser. The initial value of this property is specified by the `SRC` attribute of the <IMG> tag.

When you set this property to the URL of a new image, the browser loads and displays that new image (or, on low-resolution systems, the image specified by the `lowsrc` property). This is very useful for updating the graphical appearance of your web pages in response to user actions, and can also be used to perform simple animation.

Image.vspace — the vertical padding for an image

Availability

Client-side JavaScript 1.1

Synopsis

```
image.vspace
```

Description

The `vspace` property of the Image object is a read-only integer that specifies the number of extra blank pixels that appear above and below the image in the browser window. The value of this property is specified by the `VSPACE` attribute of the <IMG> tag.

Image.width — the width of an image

Availability

Client-side JavaScript 1.1

Synopsis

```
image.width
```

Description

The `width` property of the Image object is a read-only integer that specifies the width of *image*. It is set by the `WIDTH` attribute of the <IMG> HTML tag.

The `WIDTH` attribute is optional in HTML, but including it greatly improves the layout time of your pages. Also, because of a bug in Navigator 2, all images in a page that contains JavaScript must have `WIDTH` and `HEIGHT` attributes specified (even though the Image object is not available in that browser).

Infinity — a numeric constant that represents infinity

Availability

Core Internet Explorer 4; ECMA-262; not supported by Navigator 4

Synopsis

```
Infinity
```

Description

`Infinity` is a core JavaScript constant containing the special numeric value representing positive infinity.

See Also

isFinite( ), NaN, Number.POSITIVE_INFINITY

Input — an input element in an HTML form

Availability

Client-side JavaScript 1.0; enhanced in JavaScript 1.1

Inherits From

HTMLElement

Synopsis

```
form.elements[i]
form.name
```

Properties

Input inherits properties from HTMLElement and defines or overrides the following:

checked
  A read/write boolean that indicates the selection state of form elements that can appear checked or unchecked.

defaultChecked
  A read-only boolean that specifies the default state of a form element that can be checked. This value is specified by the `CHECKED` attribute of the HTML tag that creates the element, and its value is used when the form is reset.

defaultValue
  A read-only string that specifies the default value for a form element. For elements that display text, this property specifies the initial value displayed and the value displayed after the form is reset. This property corresponds to the HTML `VALUE` attribute.

form
  A read-only reference to the Form object that contains this element.

length
  For the Select form element, this property specifies the number of options or choices (each represented by an Option object) that are contained within the `options[]` array of the element.

name   A read-only string, specified by the HTML NAME attribute, that specifies the name of this element. This name may be used to refer to the element, as shown in the synopsis above.

options[]   For the Select form element, this array contains Option objects that represent the options or choices displayed by the Select object. The number of elements in the array is specified by the length property of the Select element.

selectedIndex
                    For the Select form element, this integer specifies which of the options displayed by the Select object is currently selected. In JavaScript 1.1, this property is read/write. In JavaScript 1.0, it is read-only.

type   A read-only string property, available as of Navigator 3, that specifies the type of the form element.

value   A string property that specifies the value to be sent to the server for this element when the form that contains it is submitted.

Methods

Input inherits methods from HTMLElement and defines or overrides the following:

blur()   Remove keyboard focus from the element.

click()   Simulate a mouseclick on the form element.

focus()   Give keyboard focus to the element.

select()   For form elements that display editable text, select the text that appears in the element.

Event Handlers

Input inherits event handlers from HTMLElement and defines or overrides the following:

onblur   Invoked when the user takes keyboard focus away from the element.

onchange   For form elements that are not buttons, this event handler is invoked when the user enters or selects a new value.

onclick   For form elements that are buttons, this event handler is invoked when the user clicks or selects the button.

onfocus   Invoked when the user gives keyboard focus to the element.

Description

Form elements are stored in the elements[] array of the Form object. The contents of this array are Input objects, which represent the individual buttons, input fields, and other controls that appear within the form. Many types of input elements are created with the <INPUT> tag; others are created with the <SELECT> and <OPTION> tags and the <TEXTAREA> tag. The various form input elements share quite a few properties, methods, and event handlers, which are described on this reference page. Specific behaviors for specific types of form elements are described on their own pages.

The Input object defines many shared properties, methods, and event handlers, but not all of them are shared by all types of form elements. For example, the Button object triggers the `onclick` event handler but not the `onchange` handler, while the Text object triggers `onchange` but not `onclick`. The following figure shows all of the form elements and the properties associated with them.

ELEMENT	checked	defaultChecked	defaultValue	form	length	name	options	selectedIndex	type	value	blur()	click()	focus()	select()	onblur	onchange	onclick	onfocus
Button				•		•			•	•	•	•	•		•		•	•
Checkbox	•	•		•		•			•	•	•	•	•		•		•	•
Radio	•	•		•		•			•	•	•	•	•		•		•	•
Reset				•		•			•	•	•	•	•		•		•	•
Submit				•		•			•	•	•	•	•		•		•	•
Text			•	•		•			•	•	•		•	•	•	•		•
Textarea			•	•		•			•	•	•		•	•	•	•		•
Password			•	•		•			•	•	•		•	•	•	•		•
FileUpload			•	•		•			•	•	•		•	•	•			•
Select				•	•	•	•	•	•		•		•		•	•		•
Hidden				•		•			•	•								

There are two broad categories of form elements. The first is the buttons: Button, Checkbox, Radio, Reset, and Submit. These elements have an `onclick` event handler but not an `onchange` handler. Similarly, they respond to the `click()` method but not to the `select()` method. The second category contains those elements that display text: Text, Textarea, Password, and FileUpload. These elements have an `onchange` event handler rather than an `onclick` handler, and they respond to the `select()` method but not to the `click()` method.

The Select element is a special case. It is created with the `<SELECT>` tag and is less like the `<INPUT>` elements than the other form elements. Although the Select element is technically represented by a different object type, it is still convenient to consider it an Input object.

Bugs

Because of differences in windowing systems, the behavior of form elements differs slightly between platforms, particularly in early releases of Navigator. For example, on Unix platforms, which run the X Window System, only the text-entry form elements participate in keyboard navigation, so the button elements and the Select element do not respond to the `blur()` and `focus()` methods, nor do they invoke the `onblur` and `onfocus` event handlers.

See Also

Button, Checkbox, FileUpload, Form, Hidden, Password, Radio, Reset, Select, Submit, Text, Textarea, Chapter 16

Input.blur() — remove keyboard focus from a form element

Availability

Client-side JavaScript 1.0

Synopsis

```
input.blur()
```

Description

The `blur()` method of a form element removes keyboard focus from that element without invoking the `onblur` event handler; it is essentially the opposite of the `focus()` method. The `blur()` method does not transfer keyboard focus anywhere, however, so the only time that it is actually useful to call this method is directly before you plan to transfer keyboard focus elsewhere with the `focus()` method, when you don't want the `onblur` event handler to be triggered. That is, by removing focus explicitly from the element, you won't be notified when it is removed implicitly by a `focus()` call on another element.

All form elements other than Hidden support the `blur()` method. Unfortunately, not all platforms support keyboard navigation equally well. In Navigator 2 and 3 for Unix platforms, the `blur()` method is only functional for those form elements that display text: Text, Textarea, Password, and FileUpload.

Input.checked — whether a Checkbox or Radio element is checked

Availability

Client-side JavaScript 1.0

Synopsis

```
input.checked
```

Description

The `checked` property is a read/write boolean that specifies whether a Checkbox or Radio form element is currently checked or not. You can set the state of these button elements by setting the value of this property. This property is not used by other form elements.

See Also

Checkbox, Radio

Input.click() — simulate a mouseclick on a form element

Availability

Client-side JavaScript 1.0

Synopsis

```
input.click()
```

Description

The `click()` method of a form element simulates a mouseclick on the form element but does not invoke the `onclick` event handler of the element.

The `click()` method is not often useful. Because it does not invoke the `onclick` event handler, it is not useful to call this method on Button elements—they don't have any behavior other than that defined by the `onclick` handler. Calling `click()` on a Submit or Reset element submits or resets a form, but this can be more directly achieved with the `submit()` and `reset()` method of the Form object itself.

Input.defaultChecked — a Checkbox or Radio element's default status

Availability

Client-side JavaScript 1.0

Synopsis

```
input.defaultChecked
```

Description

The `defaultChecked` property is a read-only boolean value that specifies whether a Checkbox or Radio element is checked by default. This property has no meaning for other form elements. `defaultChecked` corresponds to the `CHECKED` attribute in the HTML `<INPUT>` tag that created the form element. If `CHECKED` was present, `defaultChecked` is `true`. Otherwise, `defaultChecked` is `false`.

The `defaultChecked` property is used to restore the Checkbox or Radio element to its default value when the form is reset.

See Also

Checkbox, Radio

Input.defaultValue — the default text displayed in an element

Availability

Client-side JavaScript 1.0

Synopsis

```
input.defaultValue
```

Description

The `defaultValue` property of a form element specifies the initial text that appears in the form element and the value that is restored to that element when the form is reset. This property is only used by the Text, Textarea, and Password elements. For security reasons, it is not used by the FileUpload element. For Checkbox and Radio elements, the equivalent property is `defaultChecked`.

See Also

Password, Text, Textarea

Input.focus() — give keyboard focus to a form element

Availability

Client-side JavaScript 1.0

Synopsis

```
input.focus()
```

Description

The focus() method of a form element transfers keyboard focus to that element without calling the onfocus event handler. That is, it makes the element the active one with respect to keyboard navigation and keyboard input. Thus, if you call focus() for a Text element, any text the user types appears in that text element. Or, if you call focus() for a Button element, the user can invoke that button from the keyboard.

All form elements except the Hidden element support the focus() method. Unfortunately, not all platforms support keyboard navigation equally well. In Unix versions of Navigator, focus() is only functional for those form elements that display text: Text, Textarea, Password, and FileUpload.

Input.form — the Form containing the element

Availability

Client-side JavaScript 1.0

Synopsis

```
input.form
```

Description

The form property of an input element is a read-only reference to the Form object that contains the element.

The form property allows the event handlers of one form element to easily refer to sibling elements in the same form. When an event handler is invoked, the this keyword refers to the form element for which it was invoked. Thus, an event handler can use the expression this.form to refer to the form that contains it. From there, it can refer to sibling elements by name, or it can use the elements[] array of the Form object to refer to them by number.

See Also

Form

Input.length — see Select.length

Input.name — the name of a form element

Availability

Client-side JavaScript 1.0

Synopsis

    input.name

Description

name is a read-only string property of every form element. The value of this property is set by the NAME attributes of the HTML <INPUT> tag that defines the form element.

The name of a form element is used for two purposes. First, it is used when the form is submitted. Data for each element in the form is usually submitted in the format:

    name=value

where *name* and *value* are encoded as necessary for transmission. If a name is not specified for a form element, the data for that element cannot be submitted to a web server.

The second use of the name property is to refer to a form element in JavaScript code. The name of an element becomes a property of the form that contains the element. The value of this property is a reference to the element. For example, if address is a form that contains a text input element with the name zip, address.zip refers to that text input element.

With Radio and Checkbox form elements, it is common to define more than one related object, each of which have the same name property. In this case, data is submitted to the server with this format:

    name=value1,value2,...,valuen

Similarly, in JavaScript, each of the elements that shares a name becomes an element of an array with that name. Thus, if four Checkbox objects in the form order share the name options, they are available in JavaScript as elements of the array order.options[ ].

Bugs

In Navigator 2, when multiple form elements are given the same name and placed in an array, they are only placed in the array in the expected source order if they all define an event handler, even a dummy event handler that does nothing. If none of the elements defines event handlers, the elements are inserted into the array in reverse order. If some define event handlers and others don't, the order is less predictable. In cases where array order actually matters, the workaround to this bug is to define dummy event handlers as needed.

Input.onblur — the handler invoked when a form element loses focus

Availability

Client-side JavaScript 1.0

Synopsis

```
<INPUT TYPE=type onBlur="handler">
input.onblur
```

Description

The `onblur` property of an Input object specifies an event handler function that is invoked when the user transfers keyboard focus away from that input element. Calling `blur()` to remove focus from an element does not invoke `onblur` for that object. Note, however, that calling `focus()` to transfer focus to some other element causes the `onblur` event handler to be invoked for whatever element currently has the focus.

The initial value of this property is a function that contains the semicolon-separated JavaScript statements specified by the `onBlur` attribute of the HTML tag that defined the object. When an event handler function is defined by an HTML attribute, it is executed in the scope of *element* rather than in the scope of the containing window.

In Navigator 4, the `onblur` handler function is passed an Event object as an argument. In IE 4, no argument is passed, but the applicable Event object is available as the `event` property of the Window object that contains the *element.*

The `onblur` event handler is available for all form elements except the Hidden element. In Navigator on Unix platforms, however, it is only invoked for the text-entry elements: Text, Textarea, Password, and FileUpload. Note that in JavaScript 1.1, the Window object also defines an `onblur` event handler.

See Also

Window.onblur, Chapter 15

Input.onchange — the handler invoked when a form element's value changes

Availability

Client-side JavaScript 1.0

Synopsis

```
<INPUT TYPE=type onChange="handler">
input.onchange
```

Description

The `onchange` property of an Input object specifies an event handler function that is invoked when the user changes the value displayed by a form element. Such a change may be an edit to the text displayed in Text, Textarea, Password, or FileUpload elements, or the selection or deselection of an option in a Select element. Note that this event handler is only invoked when the user makes such a change—it is not invoked if a JavaScript program changes the value displayed by an element.

Also note that the `onchange` handler is not invoked every time the user enters or deletes a character in a text-entry form element. `onchange` is not intended for that type of character-by-character event handling. Instead, `onchange` is invoked when the user's edit is complete. The browser assumes that the edit is complete when keyboard focus is moved to some other element—for example, when the user clicks on the next element in the form. See `HTMLElement.onkeypress` for character-by-character event notification.

The `onchange` event handler is not used by the Hidden element or by any of the button elements. Those elements—Button, Checkbox, Radio, Reset, and Submit—use the `onclick` event handler instead.

The initial value of this property is a function that contains the semicolon-separated JavaScript statements specified by the `onChange` attribute of the HTML tag that defined the object. When an event handler function is defined by an HTML attribute, it is executed in the scope of *element* rather than in the scope of the containing window.

In Navigator 4, the `onchange` handler function is passed an Event object as an argument. In IE 4, no argument is passed, but the applicable Event object is available as the `event` property of the Window object that contains the *element*.

See Also

HTMLElement.onkeypress, Chapter 15

Input.onclick — the handler invoked when a form element is clicked

Availability

Client-side JavaScript 1.0; enhanced in JavaScript 1.1

Synopsis

```
<INPUT TYPE=type onClick="handler">
input.onclick
```

Description

The `onclick` property of an Input object specifies an event handler function that is invoked when the user clicks on the input element. It is not invoked when the `click()` method is called for the element.

Only form elements that are buttons invoke the `onclick` event handler. These are the Button, Checkbox, Radio, Reset, and Submit elements. Other form elements use the `onchange` event handler instead of `onclick`.

The initial value of the `onclick` property is a function containing the semicolon-separated JavaScript statements specified by the `onClick` attribute of the HTML tag that defined the object. When an event handler function is defined by an HTML attribute, it is executed in the scope of *element* rather than in the scope of the containing window.

In Navigator 4, the `onclick` handler function is passed an Event object as an argument. In IE 4, no argument is passed, but the applicable Event object is available as the `event` property of the Window object that contains the *element*.

Note that the Reset and Submit elements perform a default action when clicked: they reset and submit, respectively, the form that contains them. You can use the `onclick` event handlers of each of these elements to perform actions in addition to these default actions. In JavaScript 1.1, you can also prevent these default actions from occurring by returning `false`. That is, if the `onclick` handler of a **Reset** button returns `false`, the form is not reset, and if the `onclick` handler of a **Submit** button returns `false`, the form is not submitted. Note that you do similar things with the `onsubmit` and `onreset` event handlers of the Form object itself.

Finally, note that the Link object also defines an `onclick` event handler.

See Also

Link.onclick, Chapter 15

Input.onfocus — the handler invoked when a form element gains focus

Availability

Client-side JavaScript 1.0

Synopsis

```
<INPUT TYPE=type onFocus="handler">
input.onfocus
```

Description

The `onfocus` property of an Input object specifies an event handler function that is invoked when the user transfers keyboard focus to that input element. Calling `focus()` to set focus to an element does not invoke `onfocus` for that object.

The initial value of this property is a function that contains the semicolon-separated JavaScript statements specified by the `onFocus` attribute of the HTML tag that defined the object. When an event handler function is defined by an HTML attribute, it is executed in the scope of *element* rather than in the scope of the containing window.

In Navigator 4, the `onfocus` handler function is passed an Event object as an argument. In IE 4, no argument is passed, but the applicable Event object is available as the `event` property of the Window object that contains the *element*.

The `onfocus` event handler is available for all form elements except the Hidden element. In Navigator on Unix platforms, however, it is only invoked for the text-entry elements: Text, Textarea, Password, and FileUpload. Note that in JavaScript 1.1, the Window object also defines an `onfocus` event handler.

See Also

Window.onfocus, Chapter 15

Input.options[] — see Select.options[]

Input.select() — select the text in a form element

Availability

Client-side JavaScript 1.0

Synopsis

```
input.select()
```

Description

The `select()` method selects the text displayed in a Text, Textarea, Password, or File-Upload element. The effects of selecting text may vary from platform to platform, but typically, invoking this method produces the same result as the user dragging the mouse across all the text in the specified Text object. On most platforms, this produces the following effects:

- The text is highlighted, often displayed with colors reversed.

- If the text remains selected the next time the user types a character, the selected text is deleted and replaced with the newly typed character.

- The text becomes available for cut-and-paste.

The user can usually deselect text by clicking in the Text object or by moving the cursor. Once deselected, the user can add and delete individual characters without replacing the entire text value.

Input.selectedIndex — see Select.selectedIndex

Input.type — the type of a form element

Availability

Client-side JavaScript 1.1

Synopsis

    input.type

Description

`type` is a read-only string property of all form elements. It specifies the type of the form element. The value of this property for each possible form element is given in the following table.

Note that the Select element has two possible `type` values, depending on whether it allows single or multiple selection. Also note that unlike other input element properties, `type` is not available in JavaScript 1.0.

Object Type	HTML Tag	type Property
Button	`<INPUT TYPE=button>`	"button"
Checkbox	`<INPUT TYPE=checkbox>`	"checkbox"
FileUpload	`<INPUT TYPE=file>`	"file"
Hidden	`<INPUT TYPE=hidden>`	"hidden"
Password	`<INPUT TYPE=password>`	"password"
Radio	`<INPUT TYPE=radio>`	"radio"
Reset	`<INPUT TYPE=reset>`	"reset"
Select	`<SELECT>`	"select-one"
Select	`<SELECT MULTIPLE>`	"select-multiple"
Submit	`<INPUT TYPE=submit>`	"submit"

Object Type	HTML Tag	type Property
Text	`<INPUT TYPE=text>`	"text"
Textarea	`<TEXTAREA>`	"textarea"

Input.value — the value displayed or submitted by a form element

Availability

Client-side Navigator 2; buggy in Internet Explorer 3

Synopsis

```
input.value
```

Description

`value` is a read/write string property of all form elements. It specifies the value that is displayed by the form element and/or submitted for the element when the form is submitted. The `value` property of the Text element, for example, is the user's input, which is also the value submitted with the form. For the Checkbox object, on the other hand, the `value` property specifies a string that is not displayed but is submitted with the form if the Checkbox element is checked when the form is submitted.

The initial value of the `value` property is specified by the `VALUE` attribute of the HTML tag that defines the form element.

For Button, Submit, and Reset objects, the `value` property specifies the text to appear within the button. On some platforms, changing the `value` property of these elements actually changes the text displayed by the buttons on-screen. This does not work on all platforms, however, and is not an advisable technique. Changing the label of a button may change the size of the button, causing it to overlap and obscure other portions of the document.

The Select element has a `value` property, like all form elements, but does not use it. Instead, the value submitted by this element is specified by the `value` property of the Option objects it contains.

For security reasons, the `value` property of the FileUpload element is read-only.

isFinite( ) — determine whether a number is finite

Availability

Core JavaScript 1.2; ECMA-262

Synopsis

```
isFinite(n)
```

Arguments

n   The number to be tested.

Returns

true if the *n* is a finite number or false if *n* is NaN (not a number) or positive or negative infinity.

See Also

Infinity, isNaN(), NaN, Number.NaN, Number.NEGATIVE_INFINITY, Number.POSITIVE_INFINITY

---

isNaN() — check for not-a-number

Availability

Core JavaScript 1.1; ECMA-262

Synopsis

```
isNaN(x)
```

Arguments

x   The value to be tested.

Returns

true if *x* is the reserved value NaN (not-a-number); false if *x* is a legal number, string, or any other type.

Description

isNaN() tests its argument to determine whether it is the reserved value NaN, which represents an illegal number (such as the result of division by zero). This function is required, because comparing a NaN with any value, including itself, always returns false, so it is not possible to test for NaN with the == operator.

A common use of isNaN() is to test the results of parseFloat() and parseInt() to determine if they represent legal numbers. You can also use isNanN() to check for arithmetic errors, such as division by zero.

See Also

isFinite(), NaN, Number.NaN, parseFloat(), parseInt()

---

java — the java.* package

Availability

Client-side Navigator 3

Synopsis

```
java
```

Description

`java` is a global property of the Window object and is usually used without reference to any particular window. It is a synonym for `Packages.java`, and contains a read-only reference to a JavaPackage object that represents the top node of the *java.** package name hierarchy. The `java` Package contains, for example, a `lang` property, which is a reference to the JavaPackage object for the *java.lang* package.

See Also

JavaPackage, Packages.java

JavaArray — JavaScript representation of a Java array

Availability

Client-side Navigator 3

Synopsis

```
javaarray.length        The length of the array.
javaarray[index]        Read or write an array element.
```

Properties

`length`   A read-only integer that specifies the number of elements in the Java array represented by the JavaArray object.

Description

The JavaArray object is a JavaScript representation of a Java array, and it allows JavaScript code to read and write the elements of the array using familiar JavaScript array syntax. In addition, the JavaArray object has a `length` field that specifies the number of elements in the Java array.

When reading and writing values from array elements, data conversion between JavaScript and Java representations is automatically handled by the system. See Chapter 20 for full details.

Usage

Note that Java arrays differ from JavaScript arrays in a couple of important aspects. First, Java arrays have a fixed length that is specified when they are created. For this reason, the JavaArray `length` field is read-only. The second difference is that Java arrays are *typed* (i.e., their elements must all be of the same type of data). Attempting to set an array element to a value of the wrong type results in a JavaScript error.

Example

`java.awt.Polygon` is a JavaClass object. We can create a JavaObject representing an instance of the class like this:

```
p = new java.awt.Polygon();
```

This object p has properties `xpoints` and `ypoints`, which are JavaArray objects representing Java arrays of integers. We could initialize the contents of these arrays with JavaScript code like the following:

```
for(int i = 0; i < p.xpoints.length; i++)
    p.xpoints[i] = Math.round(Math.random()*100);
for(int i = 0; i < p.ypoints.length; i++)
    p.ypoints[i] = Math.round(Math.random()*100);
```

See Also

getClass( ), java, JavaClass, JavaObject, JavaPackage, Packages, Chapter 20

JavaArray.length — the number of elements in a Java array

Availability

Client-side Navigator 3

Synopsis

```
javaarray.length
```

Description

The `length` property of the JavaArray object is a read-only integer that specifies the number of elements in the Java array represented by the JavaArray object. This property is read-only because arrays in Java have a fixed length.

See Also

getClass( ), java, JavaArray, JavaClass, JavaObject, JavaPackage, Packages, Chapter 20

JavaClass — JavaScript representation of a Java class

Availability

Client-side Navigator 3

Synopsis

```
javaclass.static_member          Read or write a static Java field or method.
new javaclass(...)               Create a new Java object.
```

Properties

Each JavaClass object contains properties that have the same names as the public static fields and methods of the Java class it represents. These properties allow you to read and write the static fields of the class and invoke the static methods of the class. Each JavaClass object has different properties; you can use a `for/in` loop to enumerate them for any given JavaClass object.

Description

The JavaClass object is a JavaScript representation of a Java class. The properties of a JavaClass object represent the public static fields and methods (sometimes called class fields and class methods) of the represented class. Note that the JavaClass object does not have properties representing the *instance* fields of a Java class—individual instances of a Java class are represented by the JavaObject object.

The JavaClass object implements the LiveConnect functionality that allows JavaScript programs to read and write the static variables of Java classes using normal JavaScript syntax.

The JavaClass object also provides the functionality that allows JavaScript to invoke the static methods of a Java class.

Besides allowing JavaScript to read and write Java variable and method values, the Java-Class object also allows JavaScript programs to create Java objects (represented by a JavaObject object) by using the `new` keyword and invoking the constructor method of a JavaClass.

The data conversion required for communication between JavaScript and Java through the JavaClass object is handled automatically by LiveConnect. See Chapter 20 for full details.

Usage

Bear in mind that Java is a *typed* language. This means that each of the fields of an object has a specific data type, and you can set it only to values of that type. Attempting to set a field to a value that is not of the correct type results in a JavaScript error. Attempting to invoke a method with arguments of the wrong type also causes an error.

Example

`java.lang.System` is a JavaClass object that represents the *java.lang.System* class in Java. You can read a static field of this class with code like the following:

```
var java_console = java.lang.System.out;
```

You can invoke a static method of this class with a line like this one:

```
var version = java.lang.System.getProperty("java.version");
```

Finally, the JavaClass object also allows you to create new Java objects like this:

```
var java_date = new java.lang.Date();
```

See Also

getClass( ), java, JavaArray, JavaObject, JavaPackage, Packages, Chapter 20

JavaObject — JavaScript representation of a Java object

Availability

Client-side Navigator 3

Synopsis

`javaobject.member`   *Read or write an instance field or method.*

Properties

Each JavaObject object contains properties that have the same names as the public instance fields and methods (but not the static or class fields and methods) of the Java object it represents. These properties allow you to read and write the value of public fields and invoke the public methods. The properties of a given JavaObject object obviously depend on the type of Java object it represents. You can use the `for/in` loop to enumerate the properties of any given JavaObject.

Description

The JavaObject object is a JavaScript representation of a Java object. The properties of a JavaObject object represent the public instance fields and public instance methods defined for the Java object. (The class or static fields and methods of the object are represented by the JavaClass object.)

The JavaObject object implements the LiveConnect functionality that allows JavaScript programs to read and write the public instance fields of a Java object, using normal JavaScript syntax. The JavaObject also provides the functionality that allows JavaScript to invoke the methods of a Java object. Data conversion between JavaScript and Java representations is handled automatically by LiveConnect. See Chapter 20 for full details.

Usage

Bear in mind that Java is a *typed* language. This means that each of the fields of an object has a specific data type, and you can set it only to values of that type. For example, the width field of a java.awt.Rectangle object is an integer field, and attempting to set it to a string causes a JavaScript error to occur.

Example

java.awt.Rectangle is a JavaClass that represents the *java.awt.Rectangle* class. We can create a JavaObject that represents an instance of this class like this:

```
var r = new java.awt.Rectangle(0,0,4,5);
```

And then we can read the public instance variables of this JavaObject r with code like this:

```
var perimeter = 2*r.width + 2*r.height;
```

We can also set the value of public instance variables of r using JavaScript syntax:

```
r.width = perimeter/4;
r.height = perimeter/4;
```

See Also

getClass( ), java, JavaArray, JavaClass, JavaPackage, Packages, Chapter 20

JavaPackage — JavaScript representation of a Java package

Availability

Client-side Navigator 3

Synopsis

```
package.package_name        Refers to another JavaPackage
package.class_name          Refers to a JavaClass object
```

Properties

The properties of a JavaPackage object are the names of the JavaPackage objects and JavaClass objects that it contains. These properties are different for each individual JavaPackage. Note that it is not possible to use the JavaScript for/in loop to iterate over the list of property names of a Package object. Consult a Java reference manual to determine the packages and classes contained within any given package.

Description

The JavaPackage object is a JavaScript representation of a Java package. A package in Java is a collection of related classes. In JavaScript, a JavaPackage can contain classes (represented by the JavaClass object), and it can also contain other JavaPackage objects.

For example, the JavaPackage object named `java` has properties named `lang` and `net`, among others, that are references to other JavaPackage objects, which represent the *java.lang* and *java.net* packages. The `java.awt` JavaPackage contains properties named `Frame` and `Button`, which are both references to JavaClass objects and represent the classes *java.awt.Frame* and *java.awt.Button*. The `java.awt` JavaPackage object also contains a property named `image`, which is a reference to yet another JavaPackage object, this one representing the *java.awt.image* package.

As you can see, the property naming scheme for the JavaPackage hierarchy mirrors the naming scheme for Java packages. Note that there is one big difference between the Java-Package object and actual Java packages. Packages in Java are collections of classes, not collections of other packages. So the JavaPackage object named `java` does not actually represent a package in Java, but is simply a convenient placeholder for other JavaPackages that do represent *java.lang*, *java.net*, *java.io*, and other core Java packages.

In the above discussion, we've been referring to a JavaPackage object named `java`, but we haven't said where this `java` object comes from (i.e., what `java` is a property of). The `java` JavaPackage object is actually a property of every Window object, which makes it a "global" variable in client-side JavaScript. Since every JavaScript expression is evaluated in the context of one window or another, you can always just use `java` and know that you are referring to the JavaPackage object you want.

There are other global JavaPackage objects as well. The `sun` JavaPackage refers to Java packages from Sun Microsystems, which have names beginning with "sun." Similarly, the `netscape` JavaPackage refers to Java packages from Netscape. Finally, the `Packages` property is a JavaPackage object that contains references to each of these `java`, `sun`, and `netscape` JavaPackages. Thus, you can use `Packages.java` as a synonym for `java` when you want to be more explicit about just what it is that you are referring to (or when you already have a local variable named `java`).

It is not possible to use the `for/in` loop to determine the names of the packages and classes contained within a JavaPackage. You must have this information in advance. You can find it in any Java reference manual or by examining the Java class hierarchy yourself.

See Chapter 20 for further details on working with Java packages, classes, and objects.

See Also

java, JavaArray, JavaClass, JavaObject, netscape, Packages, sun, Chapter 20

JSObject — Java representation of a JavaScript object

Availability

A Java class in the *netscape.javascript* package included with Navigator 3 and later

Synopsis

```
public final class netscape.javascript.JSObject extends Object
```

Methods

call()   Invoke a method of the JavaScript object.

eval()   Evaluate a string of JavaScript code in the context of the JavaScript object.

getMember()   Get the value of a property of the JavaScript object.

getSlot()   Get the value of an array element of the JavaScript object.

getWindow()   Get a "root" JSObject that represents the JavaScript Window object of the web browser.

removeMember()
                Delete a property from the JavaScript object.

setMember()   Set the value of a property of the JavaScript object.

setSlot()   Set the value of an array element of the JavaScript object.

toString()   Invoke the JavaScript toString() method of the JavaScript object, and return its result.

Description

The JSObject is a Java class, not a JavaScript object; it cannot be used in your JavaScript programs. Instead, the JSObject is used by Java applets that wish to communicate with JavaScript by reading and writing JavaScript properties and array elements, by invoking JavaScript methods, and by evaluating and executing arbitrary strings of JavaScript code. Obviously, since JSObject is a Java class, you must understand Java programming in order to use it.

A Java applet that wishes to use the JSObject class must obtain an initial JSObject instance that represents the web browser window in which the applet is running. The JSObject class does not define a constructor method, so the only way to obtain this initial instance is by invoking the static getWindow() method and passing it the *java.applet.Applet* instance that represents the applet. This static method returns a "root" JSObject instance, and you can use the getMember() and getSlot() methods to obtain any other JSObjects that the applet requires.

Note that if an applet uses the JSObject class, it must have the MAYSCRIPT attribute set in its <APPLET> tag, or it is not allowed to manipulate JavaScript from Java. Also, an applet that uses the JSObject class should import the class with a line like the following:

```
import netscape.javascript.JSObject;
```

To compile an applet that uses JSObject, the compiler must be able to locate that class. Depending on the vendor of your compiler, this is usually done by setting your CLASSPATH environment variable. The actual class file for the JSObject class is found in the Java class JAR file (e.g., *java40.jar, java_30*) that is part of the Navigator distribution.

Full details on programming with the JSObject can be found in Chapter 20.

See Also
Chapter 20

JSObject.call() — invoke a method of a JavaScript object

Availability
A Java method in the *netscape.javascript* package included with Navigator 3 and later

Synopsis
```
public Object call(String methodName, Object args[])
```

Arguments

methodName   The name of the JavaScript method to be invoked.

args[]   An array of Java objects to be passed as arguments to the method.

Returns
A Java object that represents the return value of the JavaScript method.

Description
The call() method of the Java JSObject class invokes a named method of the JavaScript object represented by the JSObject. Arguments are passed to the method as an array of Java objects, and the return value of the JavaScript method is returned as a Java object. Chapter 20 describes the data conversion performed to convert the method arguments from Java objects to JavaScript values and to convert the method return value from a JavaScript value to a Java object.

JSObject.eval() — evaluate a string of JavaScript code

Availability
A Java method in the *netscape.javascript* package included with Navigator 3 and later

Synopsis
```
public Object eval(String s)
```

Arguments

s   A string that contains arbitrary JavaScript statements separated by semi-colons.

Returns
The JavaScript value of the last expression evaluated in *s*, converted to a Java object.

Description
The eval() method of the Java JSObject class evaluates the JavaScript code contained in the String *s* in the context of the JavaScript object specified by the JSObject. The eval() method of the Java JSObject class behaves much like the JavaScript global eval() function.

The argument *s* may contain any number of JavaScript statements separated by semicolons; these statements are executed in the order in which they appear. The return value of eval() is the value of the last statement or expression evaluated in *s*.

JSObject.getMember() — read a property of a JavaScript object

Availability

A Java method in the *netscape.javascript* package included with Navigator 3 and later

Synopsis

```
public Object getMember(String name)
```

Arguments

name   The name of the property to be read.

Returns

A Java Object that contains the value of the named property of the specified JSObject.

Description

The getMember() method of the Java JSObject class reads and returns to Java the value of a named property of a JavaScript object. The return value may be another JSObject object, or a Double, Boolean, or String object, but it is returned as a generic Object, which you must cast as necessary.

JSObject.getSlot() — read an array element of a JavaScript object

Availability

A Java method in the *netscape.javascript* package included with Navigator 3 and later

Synopsis

```
public Object getSlot(int index)
```

Arguments

index   The index of the array element to be read.

Returns

The value of the array element at the specified *index* of a JavaScript object.

Description

The getSlot() method of the Java JSObject class reads and returns to Java the value of an array element at the specified *index* of a JavaScript object. The return value may be another JSObject object, or a Double, Boolean, or String object, but it is returned as a generic Object, which you must cast as necessary.

JSObject.getWindow() — return initial JSObject for browser window

Availability

A static Java method in the *netscape.javascript* package included with Navigator 3 and later

Synopsis

```
public static JSObject getWindow(java.applet.Applet applet);
```

Arguments

applet   An Applet object running in the web browser window for which a
                JSObject is to be obtained.

Returns

A JSObject that represents the JavaScript Window object for the web browser window
that contains the specified applet.

Description

The getWindow() method is the first JSObject method that any Java applet calls. JSObject
does not define a constructor, and the static getWindow() method provides the only way to
obtain an initial "root" JSObject from which other JSObjects may be obtained.

JSObject.removeMember() — delete a property of a JavaScript object

Availability

A Java method in the *netscape.javascript* package included with Navigator 3 and later

Synopsis

```
public void removeMember(String name)
```

Arguments

name   The name of the property to be deleted from the JSObject.

Description

The removeMember() method of the Java JSObject class deletes a named property from the
JavaScript object represented by the JSObject.

JSObject.setMember() — set a property of a JavaScript object

Availability

A Java method in the *netscape.javascript* package included with Navigator 3 and later

Synopsis

```
public void setMember(String name, Object value)
```

Arguments

name   The name of the property to be set in the JSObject.

value   The value to which the named property should be set.

Description

The setMember() method of the Java JSObject class sets the value of a named property of a JavaScript object from Java. The specified *value* may be any Java Object. Primitive Java values may not be passed to this method. In JavaScript, the specified *value* is accessible as a JavaObject object.

JSObject.setSlot() — set an array element of a JavaScript object

Availability

A Java method in the *netscape.javascript* package included with Navigator 3 and later

Synopsis

```
public void setSlot(int index, Object value)
```

Arguments

index   The index of the array element to be set in the JSObject.

value   The value to which the specified array element should be set.

Description

The setSlot() method of the Java JSObject class sets the value of a numbered array element of a JavaScript object from Java. The specified *value* may be any Java Object. Primitive Java values may not be passed to this method. In JavaScript, the specified *value* is accessible as a JavaObject object.

JSObject.toString() — return the string value of a JavaScript object

Availability

A Java method in the *netscape.javascript* package included with Navigator 3 and later

Synopsis

```
public String toString()
```

Returns

The string returned by invoking the toString() method of the JavaScript object represented by the specified Java JSObject.

Description

The toString() method of the Java JSObject class invokes the JavaScript toString() method of the JavaScript object represented by a JSObject and returns the result of that method.

Layer — an independent layer in a DHTML document

Availability

Client-side Navigator 4

Synopsis

```
document.layers[i]
```

Constructor

```
new Layer(width, parent)
```

Arguments

width
: The width of the new layer, in pixels.

parent
: The Layer or Window that should be the parent of this newly created layer. This argument is optional; if omitted, the new layer is a child of the current window.

Notes

The Layer() constructor creates a new Layer object and returns it. You can set its size, position, and other attributes with the various Layer properties and methods described in the following lists. In particular, you must set the hidden property to false to make the new layer visible. See the src property and load() methods in particular for ways to set the content of a layer. Alternatively, you can dynamically generate content for the layer by writing to its document property.

Note that you can only call the Layer() constructor once the current document and all of its layers have finished loading.

Properties

above
: The layer above this one.

background
: The background image of the layer.

below
: The layer below this one.

bgColor
: The background color of the layer.

clip.bottom
: The bottom of the layer's clipping area.

clip.height
: The height of the layer's clipping area.

clip.left
: The left edge of the layer's clipping area.

clip.right
: The right edge of the layer's clipping area

clip.top
: The top of the layer's clipping area.

clip.width
: The width of the layer's clipping area.

document
: The Document object of a layer.

hidden	Whether a layer is hidden.
layers[]	An array of nested layers.
left	The X-coordinate, relative to the containing layer.
name	The name of the layer.
pageX	The X-coordinate, relative to the top-level document.
pageY	The Y-coordinate, relative to the top-level document.
parentLayer	The containing layer.
siblingAbove	
	The sibling layer that is above this one.
siblingBelow	
	The sibling layer that is below this one.
src	The source URL of a layer's contents.
top	The Y-coordinate, relative to the containing layer.
visibility	Visibility state of the layer.
window	The Window object that contains the layer.
x	The X-coordinate, relative to the containing layer.
y	The Y-coordinate, relative to the containing layer.
zIndex	The layer's position in the stacking order.

Methods

captureEvents()	
	Specify event types to be captured.
handleEvent()	
	Dispatch an event to the appropriate handler.
load()	Load a new URL and resize.
moveAbove()	Move this layer above another.
moveBelow()	Move this layer below another.
moveBy()	Move the layer to a relative position.
moveTo()	Move the layer to a position relative to its containing layer.
moveToAbsolute()	
	Move the layer to a position relative to the page.
offset()	A synonym for moveBy().
releaseEvents()	
	Stop capturing specified event types.

resizeBy()   Resize the layer by the specified amounts.

resizeTo()   Resize the layer to the specified size.

routeEvent()
               Route an event to the next interested handler.

HTML Syntax

A Layer object can be created with the Navigator-specific <LAYER> tag in HTML:

```
<LAYER
    [ ID="layername" ]                    Layer name
    [ LEFT=x ]                            Position relative to containing layer
    [ TOP=y ]
    [ PAGEX=x ]                           Position relative to toplevel document
    [ PAGEY=y ]
    [ WIDTH=w ]                           Size of layer
    [ HEIGHT=h ]
    [ SRC="url" ]                         URL of layer contents
    [ CLIP="x,y,w,h" ]                    Clipping rectangle for layer
    [ CLIP="w,h" ]                        Alternate syntax: x,y default to 0
    [ ZINDEX=z ]                          Stacking order
    [ ABOVE="layername" ]                 Alternative ways of specifying stacking
    [ BELOW="layername" ]
    [ VISIBILITY=vis ]                    "show", "hide", or "inherit"
    [ BGCOLOR=color ]                     Background color of layer
    [ BACKGROUND="url" ]                  Background image of layer
    [ onMouseOver="handler" ]             Invoked when mouse enters layer
    [ onMouseOut="handler" ]              Invoked when mouse leaves layer
    [ onFocus="handler" ]                 Invoked when layer gets focus
    [ onBlur="handler" ]                  Invoked when layer loses focus
    [ onLoad="handler" ]                  Invoked when layer's contents are loaded
>
```

Description

The Layer object is Navigator 4's technique for supporting dynamically positionable HTML elements. A Layer object can be created in three ways: with the <LAYER> tag, with the Layer() constructor, or, most portably, by using CSS-P style attributes on HTML elements, as explained in Chapter 17.

See Also

Window, Chapter 17

Layer.above — the layer above this one

Availability

Client-side Navigator 4

Synopsis

```
layer.above
```

Description

The `above` property refers to the Layer object immediately above `layer` in the stacking order. If there is no such layer, `above` is `null`.

See Also

Layer.below, Layer.zIndex

Layer.background — the background image of a Layer

Availability

Client-side Navigator 4

Synopsis

```
layer.background
```

Description

The `background` property of a Layer refers to an Image object that specifies the image displayed in the background of the layer. The initial value of this property is specified by the `BACKGROUND` attribute of the `LAYER` tag. You can change the image displayed in the background of the layer by setting the `background.src` property. If set to `null`, no image is displayed, and the background color (specified by `bgColor`) is displayed instead.

Layer.below — the layer below this one.

Availability

Client-side Navigator 4

Synopsis

```
layer.below
```

Description

The `below` property refers to the Layer object immediately below `layer` in the stacking order. If there is no such layer, `below` is `null`.

See Also

Layer.above, Layer.zIndex

Layer.bgColor — the background color of a layer

Availability

Client-side Navigator 4

Synopsis

```
layer.bgColor
```

Description

bgColor is a read/write string property that specifies the background color of *layer*. The initial value of this property is specified by the BGCOLOR attribute of the <LAYER> tag.

Note that Layer.background takes precedence over Layer.bgColor, so the color specified by this property only appears if the background.src property of *layer* is null.

Colors may be specified by name, or in the form #*rrggbb*, where *rr*, *gg*, and *bb* are two hexadecimal digits that specify the levels of red, green, and blue in the color. Colors may also be specified as an integer literal of the form 0x*rrggbb*.

Layer.captureEvents() — see Window.captureEvents()

Layer.clip.bottom — the bottom of the layer's clipping region

Availability

Client-side Navigator 4

Synopsis

```
layer.clip.bottom
```

Description

The clip.bottom property of the Layer object specifies the Y-coordinate of the bottom edge of the layer's clipping area. This value is relative to Layer.top.

Layer.clip.height — the height of the layer's clipping region

Availability

Client-side Navigator 4

Synopsis

```
layer.clip.height
```

Description

The clip.height property of the Layer object specifies the height of the layer's clipping area. This value is relative to Layer.clip.top; setting it also sets the value of Layer.clip.bottom.

Layer.clip.left — the left of the layer's clipping region

Availability

Client-side Navigator 4

Synopsis

```
layer.clip.left
```

Description

The `clip.left` property of the Layer object specifies the X-coordinate of the left edge of the layer's clipping area. This value is relative to `Layer.left`.

Layer.clip.right — the right of the layer's clipping region

Availability

Client-side Navigator 4

Synopsis

```
layer.clip.right
```

Description

The `clip.right` property of the Layer object specifies the X-coordinate of the right edge of the layer's clipping area. This value is relative to `Layer.right`.

Layer.clip.top — the top of the layer's clipping region

Availability

Client-side Navigator 4

Synopsis

```
layer.clip.top
```

Description

The `clip.top` property of the Layer object specifies the Y-coordinate of the top edge of the layer's clipping area. This value is relative to `Layer.top`.

Layer.clip.width — the width of the layer's clipping region

Availability

Client-side Navigator 4

Synopsis

```
layer.clip.width
```

Description

The `clip.width` property of the Layer object specifies the width of the layer's clipping area. This value is relative to `Layer.clip.left`; setting it also sets the value of `Layer.clip.right`.

Layer.document — the Document object of a Layer

Availability

Client-side Navigator 4

Synopsis

```
layer.document
```

Description

The `document` property of a Layer object contains a read-only reference to the Document object contained within that layer.

Layer.handleEvent( ) — see Window.handleEvent( )

Layer.hidden — whether a layer is hidden

Availability

Client-side Navigator 4; deprecated; use Layer.visibility instead

Synopsis

```
layer.hidden
```

Description

`hidden` specifies whether a layer is hidden (`true`) or visible (`false`). Setting this property to `true` hides the layer, and setting it to `false` makes the layer visible.

See Also

Layer.visibility

Layer.layers[ ] — the layers contained within a layer

Availability

Client-side Navigator 4; deprecated; use `Layer.document.layers` instead

Synopsis

```
layer.layers[]
layer.layers.length
```

Description

`layers[]` is an array that contains any child Layer objects of *layer*. It is the same as the `document.layers[]` array of a layer.

Layer.left — the X-coordinate of a layer

Availability

Client-side Navigator 4

Synopsis

```
layer.left
```

Description

The `left` property is a read/write integer that specifies the X-coordinate, relative to the containing layer or document, of *layer*. Setting this property moves the layer to the left or right. `left` is a synonym for `x`.

Layer.load() — change layer contents and width

Availability

Client-side Navigator 4

Synopsis

```
layer.load(src, width)
```

Arguments

src   A string that specifies the URL of the document to be loaded into *layer*.

width   An integer that specifies a new width, in pixels, for *layer*.

Description

`load()` loads a new document into *layer* and specifies a *width* at which the lines of that document are wrapped.

Note, however, that `load()` does not work while the current document is still being parsed. For this reason, you should not call `load()` in a top-level script; instead, call it in an event handler or a function that is itself called from an event handler.

See Also

Layer.src

Layer.moveAbove() — move one layer above another

Availability

Client-side Navigator 4

Synopsis

```
layer.moveAbove(target)
```

Arguments

target   The reference Layer object above which *layer* is to be placed.

Description

moveAbove() changes the stacking order so that *layer* appears on top of *target*. *layer* becomes a sibling of *target* if it is not already one. *layer* is given the same *zIndex* as *target* and is placed after *target* in the layers[] array of the containing document.

Layer.moveBelow() — move one layer below another

Availability

Client-side Navigator 4

Synopsis

```
layer.moveBelow(target)
```

Arguments

target   The reference Layer object below which *layer* is to be placed.

Description

moveBelow() changes the stacking order so that *layer* appears beneath *target*. *layer* becomes a sibling of *target* if it is not already one. *layer* is given the same *zIndex* as *target* and is placed before *target* in the layers[] array of the containing document.

Layer.moveBy() — move a Layer to a relative position

Availability

Client-side Navigator 4

Synopsis

```
layer.moveBy(dx, dy)
```

Arguments

dx   The number of pixels to move the layer to the right (may be negative).

dy   The number of pixels to move the layer down (may be negative).

Description

moveBy() moves *layer dx* pixels to the right and *dy* pixels down from its current position.

Layer.moveTo() — move a Layer

Availability

Client-side Navigator 4

Synopsis

```
layer.moveTo(x, y)
```

Arguments

x	The desired X-coordinate of the layer.
y	The desired Y-coordinate of the layer.

Description

moveTo() moves the upper-left corner of *layer* to the coordinates specified by *x* and *y*. Note that these coordinates are expressed relative to the containing layer or document.

Layer.moveToAbsolute() — move a Layer to page coordinates

Availability

Client-side Navigator 4

Synopsis

```
layer.moveToAbsolute(x, y)
```

Arguments

x	The desired X-coordinate of the layer.
y	The desired Y-coordinate of the layer.

Description

moveToAbsolute() moves the upper-left corner of *layer* to the document coordinates specified by *x* and *y*. Note that these coordinates are expressed relative to the page or top-level document, not relative to any containing layers.

Layer.name — the name of a Layer

Availability

client-side Navigator 4

Synopsis

```
layer.name
```

Description

name is a read/write string that specifies the name of a layer. The initial value of this property is specified by the NAME or ID attributes of the HTML tag used to create the layer. This initial value is also used as the name of the Document property that refers to the Layer object.

Layer.offset() — move a Layer to a relative position

Availability

Client-side Navigator 4; deprecated; use Layer.moveBy() instead

Synopsis

```
layer.offset(dx, dy)
```

Arguments

dx   The number of pixels to move the layer to the right (may be negative).

dy   The number of pixels to move the layer down (may be negative).

Description

offset() moves a layer relative to its current position. offset() is a synonym for moveBy().

Layer.pageX — the X-coordinate of a layer, relative to the page

Availability

Client-side Navigator 4

Synopsis

```
layer.pageX
```

Description

The pageX property is a read/write integer that specifies the X-coordinate, relative to the top-level document, of *layer*. Note that this coordinate is relative to the top-level page, not relative to any containing layer.

Layer.pageY — the Y-coordinate of a layer, relative to the page

Availability

Client-side Navigator 4

Synopsis

```
layer.pageY
```

Description

The `pageY` property is a read/write integer that specifies the Y-coordinate, relative to the top-level document, of *layer*. Note that this coordinate is relative to the top-level page, not relative to any containing layer.

Layer.parentLayer — the parent of the Layer

Availability

Client-side Navigator 4

Synopsis

    layer.parentLayer

Description

`parentLayer` is a read-only reference to the Layer or Window object that contains (is the parent of) *layer*.

Layer.releaseEvents( ) — see Window.releaseEvents( )

Layer.resizeBy( ) — resize a Layer by a relative amount

Availability

Client-side Navigator 4

Synopsis

    layer.resizeBy(dw, dh)

Arguments

dw   The number of pixels by which to increase the width of the window (may be negative).

dh   The number of pixels by which to increase the height of the window (may be negative).

Description

`resizeBy()` resizes *layer* by incrementing its `clip.width` and `clip.height` properties by *dw* and *dh*. It does not cause the contents of the layer to be reformatted, so making a layer smaller may cause layer contents to be clipped.

Layer.resizeTo( ) — resize a Layer

Availability

Client-side Navigator 4

Synopsis

```
layer.resizeTo(width, height)
```

Arguments

`width`   The desired width of the layer.

`height`   The desired height of the layer.

Description

`resizeTo( )` resizes *layer* by setting its `clip.width` and `clip.height` properties to *width* and *height*. It does not cause the contents of the layer to be reformatted, so making a layer smaller may cause layer contents to be clipped.

Layer.routeEvent( ) — see Window.routeEvent( )

Layer.siblingAbove — the sibling layer above this one

Availability

Client-side Navigator 4

Synopsis

```
layer.siblingAbove
```

Description

The `siblingAbove` property refers to the sibling Layer object (i.e., a child of the same parent Layer) immediately above *layer* in the stacking order. If there is no such layer, `siblingAbove` is `null`.

See Also

Layer.above, Layer.siblingBelow, Layer.zIndex

Layer.siblingBelow — the sibling layer below this one

Availability

Client-side Navigator 4

Synopsis

```
layer.siblingBelow
```

Description

The `siblingBelow` property refers to the sibling Layer object (i.e., a child of the same parent Layer) immediately below *layer* in the stacking order. If there is no such layer, `siblingBelow` is `null`.

See Also
Layer.below, Layer.siblingAbove, Layer.zIndex

Layer.src — the source URL of a Layer's content

Availability
Client-side Navigator 4

Synopsis
```
layer.src
```

Description
src is a read/write string that specifies the URL, if any, of the contents of a layer. Setting this property to a new URL causes the browser to read the contents of that URL and display them in the browser. Note, however, that this does not work while the current document is still being parsed. For this reason, you should not set src in a top-level script; instead, set it in an event handler or a function called from an event handler.

See Also
Layer.load( )

Layer.top — the Y-coordinate of a layer

Availability
Client-side Navigator 4

Synopsis
```
layer.top
```

Description
The top property is a read/write integer that specifies the Y-coordinate, relative to the containing layer or document, of *layer*. Setting this property moves the layer up or down. top is a synonym for y.

Layer.visibility — whether a layer is visible

Availability
Client-side Navigator 4

Synopsis
```
layer.visibility
```

Description
The visibility property is a read/write string that specifies the visibility of *layer*. There are three possible legal values: "show" specifies that the layer should be visible; "hide" specifies that the layer should not be visible; "inherit" specifies that the layer should inherit the visibility of its parent layer.

Layer.window — the window that contains a layer

Availability

Client-side Navigator 4

Synopsis

```
layer.window
```

Description

The `window` property of a Layer refers to the Window object that contains the layer, regardless of how deeply nested the layer is within other layers.

Layer.x — the X-coordinate of a layer

Availability

Client-side Navigator 4

Synopsis

```
layer.x
```

Description

x is the X-coordinate of the layer, relative to the containing layer or document. Setting this property moves the layer. x is a synonym for the `left` property.

Layer.y — the Y-coordinate of a layer

Availability

Client-side Navigator 4

Synopsis

```
layer.y
```

Description

y is the Y-coordinate of a layer, relative to the containing layer or document. Setting this property moves the layer. y is a synonym for the `top` property.

Layer.zIndex — stacking order of a layer

Availability

Client-side Navigator 4

Synopsis

```
layer.zIndex
```

Description

The zIndex property of a Layer specifies the position of the layer in the z-order, or stacking order, of layers. When two layers overlap, the one with the higher zIndex appears on top and obscures the one with the lower zIndex. If two sibling layers have the same zIndex, the one that appears later in the layers[] array of the containing document is displayed later and overlaps any that appears earlier.

zIndex is a read/write property. Setting this property changes the stacking order, and causes layers to be redisplayed in the new order. Setting this property may cause the layers[] array of the containing document to be reordered.

Link — a hypertext link

Availability

Client-side JavaScript 1.0; enhanced in JavaScript 1.1

Inherits From

HTMLElement

Synopsis

```
document.links[]
document.links.length
```

Properties

Link inherits properties from HTMLElement and also defines or overrides the following:

hash   A read/write string that specifies the hash portion of the HREF URL, including the leading hash (#) mark. This portion specifies the name of an anchor within the object referred to by the URL.

host   A read/write string that specifies the combination of the hostname and port portions of the HREF URL.

hostname   A read/write string that specifies the hostname portion of the HREF URL.

href   A read/write string that specifies the complete URL specified by the HREF property.

pathname   A read/write string that specifies the path portion of the HREF URL.

port   A read/write string that specifies the port portion of the HREF URL.

protocol   A read/write string that specifies the protocol portion of the HREF URL, including the trailing colon.

search   A read/write string that specifies the search or query portion of the HREF URL, including the leading question mark.

target   A read/write string property that specifies the name of a Window object (i.e., a frame or a top-level browser window) in which the HREF URL should be displayed.

text   The plain text that appears between the <A> and </A> tags that created the
                Link object.

x   The X-coordinate of the Link within its Document.

y   The Y-coordinate of the Link within its Document.

Methods

Link inherits the methods of HTMLElement.

Event Handlers

Link inherits the event handlers of HTMLElement and defines special behavior for the following three:

onclick   Invoked when the user clicks on the link. In JavaScript 1.1, this event han-
                dler may prevent the link from being followed by returning false. On Win-
                dows platforms in Navigator 3, this event handler does not work for links
                created with the <AREA> tag.

onmouseout   Invoked when the user moves the mouse off the link. Available in JavaScript
                1.1 and later.

onmouseover   Invoked when the user moves the mouse over the link. The status prop-
                erty of the current window may be set here. May return true to tell the
                browser not to display the URL of the Link.

HTML Syntax

A Link object is created with standard <A> and </A> tags. The HREF attribute is required for
all Link objects. If the NAME attribute is also specified, an Anchor object is also created:

```
<A HREF="url"                            The destination of the link
    [ NAME="anchor_tag" ]                Creates an Anchor object
    [ TARGET="window_name" ]             Where the new document should be displayed
    [ onClick="handler" ]                Invoked when link is clicked
    [ onMouseOver="handler" ]            Invoked when mouse is over link
    [ onMouseOut="handler" ]             Invoked when mouse leaves link
>
link text or image                       The visible part of the link
</A>
```

In JavaScript 1.1 and later, a Link object is also created by each <AREA> tag within a client-
side image map. This is also standard HTML:

```
<MAP NAME="map_name">
    <AREA SHAPE="area_shape"
        COORDS=coordinates
        HREF="url"                       The destination of the link
        [ TARGET="window_name" ]         Where the new document should be displayed
        [ onClick="handler" ]            Invoked when area is clicked
```

```
               [ onMouseOver="handler" ]        Invoked when mouse is over area
               [ onMouseOut="handler"  ]        Invoked when mouse leaves area
    >
        . . .
    </MAP>
```

Description

The Link object represents a hypertext link or a clickable area of a client-side image map in an HTML document. All links created with the <A> (and, in Navigator 3, the <AREA>) tag are represented by Link objects and stored in the links[] array of the Document object. Note that links created by both the <A> and <AREA> tags are stored in the same array—there is no distinction between them.

The destination of a hypertext link is a URL, of course, and many of the properties of the Link object specify the contents of that URL. The Link object is similar to the Location object, which also has a full set of URL properties. In the case of the Location object, these properties describe the URL of the currently displayed document.

In addition to its properties, the Link object has three event handlers. The onmouseover(), onclick(), and onmouseout() event handlers specify code to be executed when the mouse passes over the hypertext link, clicks on it, and moves off or out of the link's region of the screen.

See Also

Anchor, Location

Link.hash — the anchor specification of a Link

Availability

Client-side JavaScript 1.0

Synopsis

```
Link.hash
```

Description

hash is a read/write string property of the Link object. It specifies the anchor portion of the Link's URL, including the leading hash (#) mark. For example, the hash property of the following (fictitious) URL is "#result":

http://www.oreilly.com:1234/catalog/search.html?JavaScript#result

This anchor portion of a URL refers to a named position within the data referenced by the Link. In HTML files, positions are named with anchors created with the <A NAME="anchor_name"> tag.

Link.host — the hostname and port portions of a Link

Availability

Client-side JavaScript 1.0

Synopsis

```
Link.host
```

Description

host is a read/write string property of the Link object. It specifies the hostname and port portions of a Link's URL. For example, the host of the following (fictitious) URL is "www.oreilly.com:1234":

> *http://www.oreilly.com:1234/catalog/search.html?JavaScript#result*

Link.hostname — the hostname portion of a Link

Availability

Client-side JavaScript 1.0

Synopsis

```
Link.hostname
```

Description

hostname is a read/write string property of the Link object. It specifies the hostname portion of a Link's URL. For example, the hostname of the following (fictitious) URL is "www.oreilly.com":

> *http://www.oreilly.com:1234/catalog/search.html?JavaScript#result*

Link.href — the complete URL of a Link

Availability

Client-side JavaScript 1.0

Synopsis

```
Link.href
```

Description

href is a read/write string property of the Link object. It specifies the complete text of the Link's URL, unlike other Link URL properties which specify only portions of the URL.

Link.onclick — the handler invoked when a Link is clicked

Availability

Client-side JavaScript 1.0; enhanced in JavaScript 1.1

Synopsis

```
<A ... onClick="handler" ... >
<AREA ... onClick="handler" ... >
link.onclick
```

Description

The `onclick` property of a Link object specifies an event handler function that is invoked when the user clicks on the link. The initial value of this property is a function that contains the JavaScript statements specified by the `onClick` attribute of the `<A>` or `<AREA>` tag that defined the Link object. When an event handler function is defined in this way by an HTML attribute, it is executed in the scope of *element* rather than in the scope of the containing window.

The `onclick` event handler is invoked before the browser follows the clicked hypertext link. This allows you to set the `href`, `target`, and other properties of the link dynamically (using the `this` keyword to refer to the clicked link). You may also use `Window.alert()`, `Window.confirm()`, and `Window.prompt()` from this event handler.

In JavaScript 1.1, you may prevent the browser from following the link by returning `false`. If you return `true`, or any other value, or nothing, the browser follows the link as soon as `onclick` returns. You might stop the browser from following a link if you use the `Window.confirm()` method to ask the user if they really want to follow the link and the user chooses the **Cancel** button, for example. In general, if you want a link that performs some action but does not cause a new URL to be displayed, it is better to use the `onclick` event handler of a Button object instead of the `onclick` handler of a Link object.

Note that while the `onclick` event handler returns `false` to tell the browser not to perform its default action (following a link), the `onmouseover` event handler must return `true` to tell the browser not to take its default action (displaying the URL of the link). This incompatibility exists for historical reasons. The standard for Form and form element event handlers is to return `false` to prevent the browser from performing a default action.

In Navigator 4, the `onclick` handler function is passed an Event object as an argument. In IE 4, no argument is passed, but the applicable Event object is available as the `event` property of the Window object that contains the hypertext link.

Bugs

In Navigator 3, the `onclick` event handler of the `<AREA>` does not work on Windows platforms. A workaround is to specify a `javascript:` URL as the value of the `HREF` attribute of the `<AREA>` tag.

See Also

Chapter 15

Link.onmouseout — the handler invoked when the mouse leaves a link

Availability

Client-side JavaScript 1.1

Synopsis

```
<A ... onMouseOut="handler" ... >
<AREA ... onMouseOut="handler" ... >
link.onmouseout
```

Description

The `onmouseout` property of a Link object specifies an event handler function that is invoked when the user moves the mouse off a hypertext link. The initial value of this property is a function that contains the JavaScript statements specified by the `onMouseOut` attribute of the `<A>` or `<AREA>` tag that defined the Link object. When an event handler function is defined in this way by an HTML attribute, it is executed in the scope of *element* rather than in the scope of the containing window.

In Navigator 4, the `onmouseout` handler function is passed an Event object as an argument. In IE 4, no argument is passed, but the applicable Event object is available as the `event` property of the Window object that contains the hypertext link.

See Also

Chapter 15

Link.onmouseover — the handler invoked when the mouse goes over a link

Availability

Client-side JavaScript 1.0

Synopsis

```
<A ... onMouseOver="handler" ... >
<AREA ... onMouseOver="handler" ... >
link.onmouseover
```

Description

The `onmouseover` property of a Link object specifies an event handler function that is invoked when the user moves the mouse over a hypertext link. The initial value of this property is a function that contains the JavaScript statements specified by the `onMouseOver` attribute of the `<A>` or `<AREA>` tag that defined the Link object. When an event handler function is defined in this way by an HTML attribute, it is executed in the scope of *element* rather than in the scope of the containing window.

By default, the browser displays the URL that a hypertext link refers to in the status line whenever the mouse goes over the link. The `onmouseover` event handler is invoked before the URL is displayed. If the handler returns `true`, the browser does not display the URL. Thus, an event-handler function that returns `true` can display a custom message in the status line by setting the `Window.status` property to any desired value itself.

Note that while this event handler returns `true` to tell the browser not to perform its default action (displaying the URL of a link), the `onclick` event handler of the Link object must return `false` to tell the browser not to take its default action (following the link). This incompatibility exists for historical reasons. The standard for Form and form element event handlers is to return `false` to prevent the browser from performing a default action.

In Navigator 4, the `onmouseover` handler function is passed an Event object as an argument. In IE 4, no argument is passed, but the applicable Event object is available as the `event` property of the Window object that contains the hypertext link.

See Also

Chapter 15

Link.pathname — the path portion of a Link

Availability

Client-side JavaScript 1.0

Synopsis

```
Link.pathname
```

Description

`pathname` is a read/write string property of the Link object. It specifies the pathname portion of a Link's URL. For example, the `pathname` of the following (fictitious) URL is "/catalog/search.html":

http://www.oreilly.com:1234/catalog/search.html?JavaScript#result

---

Link.port — the port portion of a Link

Availability

Client-side JavaScript 1.0

Synopsis

```
Link.port
```

Description

`port` is a read/write string property of the Link object. It specifies the port portion of a Link's URL. For example, the `port` of the following (fictitious) URL is "1234":

http://www.oreilly.com:1234/catalog/search.html?JavaScript#result

---

Link.protocol — the protocol portion of a Link

Availability

Client-side JavaScript 1.0

Synopsis

```
Link.protocol
```

Description

`protocol` is a read/write string property of the Location and the Link objects. It specifies the protocol portion of a Link's URL, including the trailing colon. For example, the `proto-col` of the following (fictitious) URL is "http:":

http://www.oreilly.com:1234/catalog/search.html?JavaScript#result

---

Link.search — the query portion of a Link

Availability

Client-side JavaScript 1.0

Synopsis

```
Link.search
```

Description

The `search` is a read/write string property of the Link object. It specifies the query portion of a Link's URL, including the leading question mark. For example, the `search` of the following (fictitious) URL is "?query=JavaScript&matches=66":

http://www.oreilly.com:1234/search.html?query=JavaScript&matches=66#result

---

Link.target — the target window of a hypertext link

Availability

Client-side JavaScript 1.0

Synopsis

```
link.target
```

Description

`target` is a read/write string property of the Link object. It specifies the name of the frame or window in which the URL referred to by the Link object should be displayed. The initial value of this property is specified by the `TARGET` attribute of the <A> tag that creates the Link object. If this attribute is unset, the default is for the window containing the Link to be used, so that following a hypertext link overwrites the document that contains the link.

Note that the value of *target* is the *name* of a frame or window, not an actual JavaScript reference to the frame or window itself. The name of a frame is specified by the `NAME` attribute of the <FRAME> tag. The name of a window is specified when the window is created with a call to the `Window.open()` method. If `target` specifies the name of a window that does not exist, Navigator automatically opens a new window to display the URL, and any future links with the same `target` name use that freshly created window.

Four special target names are supported. The target named "_blank" specifies that a new, empty browser window should be created and used to display the new URL. The target "_self" is the default; it specifies that the new URL should be displayed in the same frame or window as the link. The target "_parent" specifies that the results should be displayed in the parent frame of the frame that contains the link. Finally, the "_top" target specifies that the new URL should be displayed in the topmost frame—in other words, all frames should be removed, and the new URL should occupy the entire browser window.

See Also

Form.target

Link.text — the text of a link

Availability

Client-side Navigator 4

Synopsis

```
link.text
```

Description

The text property specifies the plain text, if any, between the `<A>` and `</A>` tags of a link. Note that this property only works correctly if there are no intervening HTML tags between the `<A>` and `</A>` tags. If there are other HTML tags, the text property may only contain a portion of the link text.

`HTMLElement.innerText` provides the IE 4 equivalent of this Navigator-specific property.

Link.x — the X-coordinate of a link

Availability

Client-side Navigator 4

Synopsis

```
link.x
```

Description

x specifies the X-coordinate of the link, relative to the containing document. That is, x specifies the number of pixels between the link and the left edge of the document.

In IE 4, `HTMLElement.offsetLeft` is similar to, but not always the same as, `Link.x`.

Link.y — the Y-coordinate of a link

Availability

Client-side Navigator 4

Synopsis

```
link.y
```

Description

y specifies the Y-coordinate of the link, relative to the containing document. That is, y specifies the number of pixels between the link and the top edge of the document.

In IE 4, `HTMLElement.offsetTop` is similar to, but not always the same as, `Link.y`.

location — see Window.location

Location — represents and controls browser location

Availability

Client-side JavaScript 1.0; enhanced in JavaScript 1.1

Synopsis

```
location
window.location
```

Properties

The properties of a Location object refer to the various portions of a URL, which has the following general format:

```
protocol://hostname:port/pathname?search#hash
```

See the URL object for further details on these URL properties:

hash   The hash portion of the URL, including the leading hash (#) mark. This portion specifies the name of an anchor within a single HTML file.

host   A combination of the hostname and port portions of the URL.

hostname   The hostname portion of the URL.

href   The complete URL.

pathname   The path portion of the URL.

port   The port portion of the URL.

protocol   The protocol portion of the URL, including the trailing colon.

search   The search or query portion of the URL, including the leading question mark.

Methods

reload()   Reload the current document from the cache or the server. This method was added in JavaScript 1.1.

replace()   Replace the current document with a new one, without generating a new entry in the browser's session history. This method was added in JavaScript 1.1.

Description

The Location object is stored in the `location` property of the Window object, and represents the web address (the "location") of the document currently displayed in that window. The `href` property contains the complete URL of that document, and the other properties of the Location object each describe a portion of that URL. These properties are much like the URL properties of the Link object.

While the Link object represents a hyperlink in a document, the Location object represents the URL, or location, currently displayed by the browser. But the Location object does more than that: it also *controls* the location displayed by the browser. If you assign a string containing a URL to the Location object or to its `href` property, the web browser responds by loading the newly specified URL and displaying the document it refers to.

Instead of setting `location` or `location.href` to replace the current URL with a completely new one, you can also modify just a portion of the current URL by assigning strings to the other properties of the Location object. Doing this creates a new URL, with one new portion, which the browser loads and displays. For example, if you set the `hash` property of the Location object you can cause the browser to move to a named location within the current document. In Navigator 2, the browser reloads the entire document to accomplish this; this bug is fixed in Navigator 3. Similarly, if you set the `search` property, you can cause the browser to reload the current URL with a new query string appended. If the URL refers to a CGI script, the document resulting from the new query string may be quite different from the original document.

In addition to its URL properties, the Location object also defines two methods. The `reload()` method reloads the current document, and the `replace()` method loads a new document without creating a new history entry for it—the new document replaces the current one in the browser's history list.

See Also

Link, Window.location

Location.hash — the anchor specification of the current URL

Availability

Client-side JavaScript 1.0

Synopsis

    Location.hash

Description

`hash` is a read/write string property of the Location object. It specifies the anchor portion of the current URL, including the leading hash (#) mark. For example, the `hash` property of the following (fictitious) location is "#result":

http://www.oreilly.com:1234/catalog/search.html?JavaScript#result

Location.host — the hostname and port portions of the current URL

Availability

Client-side JavaScript 1.0

Synopsis

```
Location.host
```

Description

host is a read/write string property of the Location object. It specifies the hostname and port portions of the current URL. For example, the host of the following (fictitious) location is "www.oreilly.com:1234":

http://www.oreilly.com:1234/catalog/search.html?JavaScript#result

---

Location.hostname — the hostname portion of the current URL

Availability

Client-side JavaScript 1.0

Synopsis

```
Location.hostname
```

Description

hostname is a read/write string property of the Location object. It specifies the hostname portion of the current URL. For example, the hostname of the following (fictitious) location is "www.oreilly.com":

http://www.oreilly.com:1234/catalog/search.html?JavaScript#result

---

Location.href — the complete currently displayed URL

Availability

Client-side JavaScript 1.0

Synopsis

```
Location.href
```

Description

href is a read/write string property of the Location object. It specifies the complete text of the URL of the currently displayed document, unlike other Location properties, which specify only portions of the URL.

Location.pathname — the path portion of the current URL

Availability

Client-side JavaScript 1.0

Synopsis

```
Location.pathname
```

Description

`pathname` is a read/write string property of the Location object. It specifies the path portion of the current URL. For example, the `pathname` of the following (fictitious) location is "/catalog/search.html":

> *http://www.oreilly.com:1234/catalog/search.html?JavaScript#result*

Location.port — the port portion of the current URL

Availability

Client-side JavaScript 1.0

Synopsis

```
Location.port
```

Description

`port` is a read/write string property of the Location object. It specifies the port portion of the current URL. For example, the `port` of the following (fictitious) location is "1234":

> *http://www.oreilly.com:1234/catalog/search.html?JavaScript#result*

Location.protocol — the protocol portion of the current URL

Availability

Client-side JavaScript 1.0

Synopsis

```
Location.protocol
```

Description

`protocol` is a read/write string property of the Location and the Link objects. It specifies the protocol portion of a Location, including the trailing colon. For example, the `protocol` of the following (fictitious) location is "http:":

> *http://www.oreilly.com:1234/catalog/search.html?JavaScript#result*

Location.reload() — reload the current document

Availability

Client-side JavaScript 1.1

Synopsis

```
location.reload()
location.reload(force)
```

Arguments

force   A boolean argument that specifies whether the document should be reloaded, even if the server reports that it has not been modified since it was last loaded. If this argument is omitted, or if it is false, the method only reloads the full page if it has changed since last loaded.

Description

The reload() method of the Location object reloads the document that is currently displayed in the window of the Location object. When called with no arguments, or with the argument false, it uses the If-Modified-Since HTTP header to determine whether the document has changed on the web server. If the document has changed, reload reloads the document from the server, and if not, it reloads the document from the cache. This is the same action that occurs when the user clicks on Navigator's **Reload** button.

When reload() is called with the argument true, it always bypasses the cache and reloads the document from the server, regardless of the last-modified time of the document. This is the same action that occurs when the user shift-clicks on Navigator's **Reload** button.

Location.replace() — replace one displayed document with another

Availability

Client-side JavaScript 1.1

Synopsis

```
location.replace(url)
```

Arguments

url   A string that specifies the URL of the new document that is to replace the current one.

Description

The replace() method of the Location object loads and displays a new document. Loading a document in this way is different than simply setting *location* or *location*.href in one important respect: the replace() method does not generate a new entry in the History object. When you use replace(), the new URL overwrites the current entry in the History object. After calling replace(), that is, the browser's **Back** button does not return you to the previous URL; it returns you to the URL before that one.

Usage

When you are working with multiple frames and/or JavaScript generated documents, you sometimes end up with quite a few temporary documents. If there are more than just a few of these documents, it becomes annoying to the user to back out of your web site with the **Back** button. If you use the `replace()` method to load these documents, however, you can prevent this problem.

See Also

History

Location.search — the query portion of the current URL

Availability

Client-side JavaScript 1.0

Synopsis

```
Location.search
```

Description

The `search` is a read/write string property of the Location object. It specifies the query portion of the current URL, including the leading question mark. For example, the `search` of the following (fictitious) location is "?query=JavaScript&matches=66":

http://www.oreilly.com:1234/search.html?query=JavaScript&matches=66#result

---

Math — a placeholder for mathematical functions and constants

Availability

Core JavaScript 1.0; ECMA-262

Synopsis

```
Math.constant
Math.function()
```

Constants

Math.E   The constant *e*, the base of the natural logarithm.

Math.LN10   The natural logarithm of 10.

Math.LN2   The natural logarithm of 2.

Math.LOG10E   The base-10 logarithm of *e*.

Math.LOG2E   The base-2 logarithm of *e*.

Math.PI   The constant π.

```
Math.SQRT1_2
```
>   1 divided by the square root of 2.

```
Math.SQRT2    The square root of 2.
```

Static Functions

```
Math.abs()    Compute an absolute value.

Math.acos()   Compute an arc cosine.

Math.asin()   Compute an arc sine.

Math.atan()   Compute an arc tangent.

Math.atan2()
```
>   Compute the angle from the X-axis to a point.

```
Math.ceil()   Round a number up.

Math.cos()    Compute a cosine.

Math.exp()    Compute an exponent of e.

Math.floor()
```
>   Round a number down.

```
Math.log()    Compute a natural logarithm.

Math.max()    Return the larger of two numbers.

Math.min()    Return the smaller of two numbers.

Math.pow()    Compute $x^y$.

Math.random()
```
>   Compute a random number.

```
Math.round()
```
>   Round to the nearest integer.

```
Math.sin()    Compute a sine.

Math.sqrt()   Compute a square root.

Math.tan()    Compute a tangent.
```

Description

Math is a placeholder object that contains mathematical functions and constants. These functions and constants are conveniently grouped by this Math object and are invoked with syntax like this:

```
y = Math.sin(x);
area = radius * radius * Math.PI;
```

Math is not a class of objects like Date and String are. Math is simply an object that contains references to mathematical constants and functions. These functions happen to be invoked through the Math object, but they do not operate on that object, as methods would.

See Also
Number

Math.abs() — compute an absolute value

Availability
Core JavaScript 1.0; ECMA-262

Synopsis
```
Math.abs(x)
```

Arguments
x   Any number.

Returns
The absolute value of x.

Math.acos() — compute an arc cosine

Availability
Core JavaScript 1.0; ECMA-262

Synopsis
```
Math.acos(x)
```

Arguments
x   A number between −1.0 and 1.0.

Returns
The arc cosine, or inverse cosine, of the specified value x. This return value is between 0 and π radians.

Math.asin() — compute an arc sine

Availability
Core JavaScript 1.0; ECMA-262

Synopsis
```
Math.asin(x)
```

Arguments
x   A number between −1.0 and 1.0.

Returns

The arc sine of the specified value x. This return value is between $-\pi/2$ and $\pi/2$ radians.

Math.atan() — compute an arc tangent

Availability

Core JavaScript 1.0; ECMA-262

Synopsis

```
Math.atan(x)
```

Arguments

x   Any number.

Returns

The arc tangent of the specified value x. This return value is between $-\pi/2$ and $\pi/2$ radians.

Math.atan2() — compute the angle from the X-axis to a point

Availability

Core JavaScript 1.0; ECMA-262

Synopsis

```
Math.atan2(x, y)
```

Arguments

x   The X-coordinate of the point.

y   The Y-coordinate of the point.

Returns

The counterclockwise angle, measured in radians, between the positive X-axis and the point (x, y).

Description

The Math.atan2() function performs half of the conversion between Cartesian coordinates and polar coordinates. It computes and returns the angle θ of an (x, y) point.

This function is named Math.atan2() because it performs a similar computation to Math.atan(). Math.atan2() is passed separate x and y arguments, and Math.atan() is passed the ratio of those two arguments.

Math.ceil() — round a number up

Availability

Core JavaScript 1.0; ECMA-262

Synopsis

```
Math.ceil(x)
```

Arguments

x   Any numeric value or expression.

Returns

The closest integer greater than or equal to *x*.

Description

Math.ceil() computes the ceiling function—i.e., it returns the closest integer value that is greater than or equal to the function argument. Math.ceil() differs from Math.round() in that it always rounds up, rather than rounding up or down to the closest integer. Also note that Math.ceil() does not round negative numbers to larger negative numbers; it rounds them up towards zero.

Example

```
a = Math.ceil(1.99);    // Result is 2.0
b = Math.ceil(1.01);    // Result is 2.0
c = Math.ceil(1.0);     // Result is 1.0
d = Math.ceil(-1.99);   // Result is -1.0
```

Math.cos() — compute a cosine

Availability

Core JavaScript 1.0; ECMA-262

Synopsis

```
Math.cos(x)
```

Arguments

x   An angle, measured in radians. To convert degrees to radians, multiply by 0.017453293 ($2\pi/360$).

Returns

The cosine of the specified value *x*. This return value is between –1.0 and 1.0.

Math.E — the mathematical constant *e*

Availability

Core JavaScript 1.0; ECMA-262

Synopsis

```
Math.E
```

Description

`Math.E` is the mathematical constant *e*, the base of the natural logarithms, with a value of approximately 2.71828.

Math.exp() — compute e^x

Availability

Core JavaScript 1.0; ECMA-262

Synopsis

```
Math.exp(x)
```

Arguments

x   A numeric value or expression to be used as the exponent.

Returns

e^x, *e* raised to the power of the specified exponent *x*, where *e* is the base of the natural logarithms, approximately 2.71828.

Math.floor() — round a number down

Availability

Core JavaScript 1.0; ECMA-262

Synopsis

```
Math.floor(x)
```

Arguments

x   Any numeric value or expression.

Returns

The closest integer less than or equal to *x*.

Description

`Math.floor()` computes the floor function—i.e., it returns the nearest integer value that is less than or equal to the function argument. `Math.floor()` rounds a floating-point value down to the closest integer. This differs from `Math.round()`, which rounds up or down to the nearest integer. Also note that `Math.floor()` rounds negative numbers to be more negative, not closer to zero.

Example

```
a = Math.floor(1.99);    // Result is 1.0
b = Math.floor(1.01);    // Result is 1.0
c = Math.floor(1.0);     // Result is 1.0
d = Math.floor(-1.01);   // Result is -2.0
```

Math.LN10 — the mathematical constant $\log_e 10$

Availability

Core JavaScript 1.0; ECMA-262

Synopsis

```
Math.LN10
```

Description

Math.LN10 is $\log_e 10$, the natural logarithm of 10, which has a value of approximately 2.3025850929940459011.

Math.LN2 — the mathematical constant $\log_e 2$

Availability

Core JavaScript 1.0; ECMA-262

Synopsis

```
Math.LN2
```

Description

Math.LN2 is $\log_e 2$, the natural logarithm of 2, which has a value of approximately 0.69314718055994528623.

Math.log() — compute a natural logarithm

Availability

Core JavaScript 1.0; ECMA-262

Synopsis

```
Math.log(x)
```

Arguments

x   Any numeric value or expression greater than zero.

Returns

The natural logarithm of *x*.

Description

Math.log() computes $\log_e x$, the natural logarithm of its argument. The argument must be greater than zero.

Usage

You can compute the base-10 and base-2 logarithms of a number with the following formulas:

$$\log_{10} x = \log_{10} e \cdot \log_e x$$
$$\log_2 x = \log_2 e \cdot \log_e x$$

These formulas translate into the following JavaScript functions:

```
function log10(x) { return Math.LOG10E * Math.log(x); }
function log2(x) { return  Math.LOG2E * Math.log(x); }
```

Math.LOG10E — the mathematical constant $\log_{10} e$

Availability

Core JavaScript 1.0; ECMA-262

Synopsis

```
Math.LOG10E
```

Description

Math.LOG10E is $\log_{10} e$, the base-10 logarithm of the constant *e*. It has a value of approximately 0.43429448190325181667.

Math.LOG2E — the mathematical constant $\log_2 e$

Availability

Core JavaScript 1.0; ECMA-262

Synopsis

```
Math.LOG2E
```

Description

Math.LOG2E is $\log_2 e$, the base-2 logarithm of the constant *e*. It has a value of approximately 1.442695040888963387.

Math.max() — return the larger of two values

Availability

Core JavaScript 1.0; ECMA-262

Synopsis

```
Math.max(a, b)
```

Arguments

a, b   Any two numeric values or expressions.

Returns

The larger of the two values a and b.

Math.min() — return the smaller of two values

Availability

Core JavaScript 1.0; ECMA-262

Synopsis

```
Math.min(a, b)
```

Arguments

a, b   Any two numeric values or expressions.

Returns

The smaller of the two values a and b.

Math.PI — the mathematical constant π

Availability

Core JavaScript 1.0; ECMA-262

Synopsis

```
Math.PI
```

Description

Math.PI is the constant π or pi, the ratio of the circumference of a circle to its diameter. It has a value of approximately 3.14159265358979.

Math.pow() — compute x^y

Availability

Core JavaScript 1.0; ECMA-262

Synopsis

```
Math.pow(x, y)
```

Arguments

x   The number to be raised to a power.

y   The power that *x* is to be raised to.

Returns

x to the power of y, x^y

Usage

Any values of *x* and *y* may be passed to `Math.pow()`. However, if the result is an imaginary or complex number, `Math.pow()` returns NaN. In practice, this means that if *x* is negative, *y* should be a positive or negative integer. Also, bear in mind that large exponents can easily cause floating-point overflow and return a value of infinity.

See Also

Math, Math.exp()

Math.random() — return a pseudo-random number

Availability

Core JavaScript 1.1; ECMA-262

Synopsis

```
Math.random()
```

Returns

A pseudo-random number between 0.0 and 1.0.

Math.round() — round to the nearest integer

Availability

Core JavaScript 1.0; ECMA-262

Synopsis

```
Math.round(x)
```

Arguments

x   Any number.

Returns

The integer closest to *x*.

Description

`Math.round()` rounds its argument up or down to the nearest integer. It rounds .5 up. For example, it rounds 2.5 to 3, and rounds –2.5 to –2.

Math.sin() — compute a sine

Availability

Core JavaScript 1.0; ECMA-262

Synopsis

```
Math.sin(x)
```

Arguments

x   An angle, in radians. To convert degrees to radians, multiply by 0.017453293 ($2\pi/360$).

Returns

The sine of x.

Math.sqrt() — compute a square root

Availability

Core JavaScript 1.0; ECMA-262

Synopsis

```
Math.sqrt(x)
```

Arguments

x   Any numeric value or expression greater than or equal to zero.

Returns

The square root of x. Returns NaN if x is less than zero.

Usage

You can compute roots other than the square root of a number with Math.pow(). For example:

```
function cube_rt(x) { return Math.pow(x,1/3); }
```

Math.SQRT1_2 — the mathematical constant $1/\sqrt{2}$

Availability

Core JavaScript 1.0; ECMA-262

Synopsis

```
Math.SQRT1_2
```

Description

Math.SQRT1_2 is $1/\sqrt{2}$, the reciprocal of the square root of 2. It has a value of approximately 0.7071067811865476.

Math.SQRT2 — the mathematical constant $\sqrt{2}$

Availability

Core JavaScript 1.0; ECMA-262

Synopsis

```
Math.SQRT2
```

Description

Math.SQRT2 is the constant $\sqrt{2}$, the square root of 2. It has a value of approximately 1.414213562373095.

Math.tan() — compute a tangent

Availability

Core JavaScript 1.0; ECMA-262

Synopsis

```
Math.tan(x)
```

Arguments

x   An angle, measured in radians. To convert degrees to radians, multiply by 0.017453293 ($2\pi/360$).

Returns

The tangent of the specified angle x.

MimeType — represents a MIME data type

Availability

Client-side Navigator 3

Synopsis

```
navigator.mimeTypes[i]
navigator.mimeTypes["type"]
navigator.mimeTypes.length
```

Properties

description A read-only string that provides an English description of the content and encoding of the type.

enabledPlugin
>   A reference to the Plugin object that supports this MIME type, or null, if no installed and enabled plugin supports it.

suffixes
>   A read-only string that specifies a comma-separated list of the common file-name extensions associated with this MIME type.

type
>   A read-only string that indicates the name of the MIME data type, such as "text/html" or "video/mpeg".

Description

The MimeType object represents a MIME type (i.e., a data format) supported by Navigator. The format may be supported directly by the browser, or through an external helper application or a plugin for embedded data.

Usage

The navigator.mimeTypes[] array may be indexed numerically or with the name of the desired MIME type (which is the value of the type property). To check which MIME types are supported by Navigator, you can loop through each element in the array numerically. Or, if you just want to check whether a specific type is supported, you can write code like the following:

```
var show_movie = (navigator.mimeTypes["video/mpeg"] != null);
```

See Also

Navigator, Plugin

MimeType.description — a description of a MIME type

Availability

Client-side Navigator 3

Synopsis

```
mimetype.description
```

Description

The description property of a MimeType object is a human-readable description (in English) of the data type described by the MimeType. This description is more explicit and understandable than the name property.

MimeType.enabledPlugin — the plugin that handles the MIME type

Availability

Client-side Navigator 3

Synopsis

```
mimetype.enabledPlugin
```

Description

The `enabledPlugin` property is a reference to a Plugin object that represents the installed and enabled plugin that handles the specified MIME type. If the MIME type is not handled by any plugins, the value of this property is `null`.

Usage

The `navigator.mimeType[]` array tells you whether a given MIME type is supported by the browser in some fashion. The `enabledPlugin` property of the MimeType object, however, tells you whether a particular supported type is supported with a plugin or not (MIME types can also be supported with helper applications, or directly by the browser). If a MIME type is supported by a plugin, data of that type can be embedded in a web page with the `<EMBED>` tag.

MimeType.suffixes — common file suffixes for a MIME type

Availability

Client-side Navigator 3

Synopsis

```
mimetype.suffixes
```

Description

The `suffixes` property of a MimeType object is a read-only string that contains a comma-separated list of filename suffixes (not including the '.' character) that are commonly used with files of the specified MIME type. For example, the suffixes for the `text/html` MIME type are "html, htm".

MimeType.type — the name of a MIME type

Availability

Client-side Navigator 3

Synopsis

```
mimetype.type
```

Description

The `type` property of a MimeType object is a read-only string that specifies the name of the MIME type. This is a unique string such as "text/html" or "image/jpeg" that distinguishes this MIME type from all others. It describes the general type of data and the data format used.

The value of the `type` property can also be used as an index to access the elements of the `navigator.mimeTypes[]` array.

name — see Window.name

NaN — the not-a-number constant

Availability

Core Internet Explorer 4; ECMA-262; not supported by Navigator 4

Synopsis

    NaN

Description

NaN is a core JavaScript constant containing the special numeric not-a-number value.

See Also

Infinity, isNaN( ), Number.NaN

---

navigate( ) — see Window.navigate( )

---

navigator — a reference to the Navigator object

Availability

Client-side JavaScript 1.0

Synopsis

    navigator

Description

The navigator property contains a read-only reference to a Navigator object, which provides version and configuration information about the web browser. See the Navigator object for details.

All windows have a navigator property that refers to a Navigator object, and all Navigator objects contain the same values. Therefore, the Navigator object is usually referred to simply as navigator without an explicit window reference.

The property name navigator obviously refers to the Navigator browser. Nevertheless, this property is portable. IE 4 defines a property name clientInformation that refers to the same object as navigator. Although clientInformation is a more descriptive and less vendor-specific name, it is not supported by Navigator and is not portable.

See Also

Navigator, Window

Navigator — information about the browser in use

Availability

Client-side JavaScript 1.0; enhanced in JavaScript 1.1 and 1.2

Synopsis

```
navigator
```

Properties

`navigator.appCodeName`
> The code name of the browser.

`navigator.appName`
> The name of the browser.

`navigator.appVersion`
> Version information for the browser.

`navigator.language`
> The default language of the browser. Navigator 4 only.

`navigator.mimeTypes[ ]`
> An array of MimeType objects describing the MIME types recognized and supported by the browser. Added in JavaScript 1.1. This array is always empty in IE.

`navigator.platform`
> A string that specifies the platform on which the browser is running.

`navigator.plugins[ ]`
> An array of Plugin objects describing the installed plugins. Added in JavaScript 1.1. This array is always empty in IE.

`navigator.systemLanguage`
> The system-level language code. IE 4 only.

`navigator.userAgent`
> The string passed by the browser as the user-agent header in HTTP requests.

`navigator.userLanguage`
> The language code for the user's language. IE 4 only.

Functions

`navigator.javaEnabled( )`
> Test whether Java is supported and enabled in the current browser. Added in JavaScript 1.1.

`navigator.plugins.refresh( )`
> Check for newly installed plugins, enter them in the `plugins[]` array, and optionally reload documents using those plugins. Added in Navigator 3.

`navigator.preference()`
> Query or set user preferences. Navigator 4 only.

`navigator.savePreferences()`
> Save user preferences. Navigator 4 only.

`navigator.taintEnabled()`
> Test whether the data-tainting security model is supported and enabled in the current browser. Added in JavaScript 1.1. Deprecated in Navigator 4.

Description

The Navigator object contains properties that describe the web browser in use. You can use its properties to perform platform-specific customization. The name of this object obviously refers to the Netscape Navigator browser, but other browsers that implement JavaScript support this object as well.

There is only a single instance of the Navigator object, which you can reference through the `navigator` property of any Window object. Because of the implicit window reference, you can always refer to the Navigator object simply as `navigator`.

See Also

MimeType, Plugin

Navigator.appCodeName — the code name of the browser

Availability

Client-side JavaScript 1.0

Synopsis

```
navigator.appCodeName
```

Description

`navigator.appCodeName` is a read-only string property that specifies the code name of the browser. In Navigator 2, 3, and 4, this is "Mozilla". For compatibility, this property is "Mozilla" in IE 3 and IE 4 as well.

Navigator.appName — the application name of the browser

Availability

Client-side JavaScript 1.0

Synopsis

```
navigator.appName
```

Description

`navigator.appName` is a read-only string property that specifies the name of the browser. For Navigator, the value of this property is "Netscape". In IE, the value of this property is "Microsoft Internet Explorer".

Navigator.appVersion — the platform and version of the browser

Availability

Client-side JavaScript 1.0

Synopsis

```
navigator.appVersion
```

Description

`navigator.appVersion` is a read-only string property that specifies platform and version information for the browser in some implementation-specific format. For Navigator, this property has the following format:

```
version (platform; encryption[; detail])
```

version is the version number; "4.04", for example. *platform* is a general indication of the platform. For example, "Win16" indicates a 16-bit version of Windows, "Win95" indicates Windows 95, and "X11" indicates a Unix platform running the X Window System. *encryption* is either "U", indicating a domestic U.S. release of Navigator with strong encryption, or "I", indicating an international release with weakened encryption capabilities (to comply with U.S. government export control laws on cryptographic technologies.) Finally, the optional *detail* may provide additional information about the platform. On my platform, for example, it is the string "Linux 1.2.13 i486".

In IE 4 running on Windows 95, this property has a value like "4.0 (compatible; MSIE 4.01; Windows 95)". IE 3 reports a version number of "2.0". This is to be compatible with Navigator 2, which it most closely resembles. The remainder of the string does contain complete IE version information, however.

Note that both Navigator and Internet Explorer return a version number as the first part of `navigator.appVersion`. This means that you can pass this property to `parseInt()` or to `parseFloat()`.

Navigator.javaEnabled() — test whether Java is available

Availability

Client-side JavaScript 1.1

Synopsis

```
navigator.javaEnabled()
```

Returns

`true` if Java is supported by and enabled on the current browser; `false` otherwise.

Description

You can use `navigator.javaEnabled()` to check whether the current browser supports Java and can therefore display applets.

Navigator.language — the default language of the browser

Availability

Client-side Navigator 4

Synopsis

```
navigator.language
```

Description

Navigator 4 is available in different versions that support different languages. `naviga-tor.language` specifies the default language of the current version. The value of this property is a standard two-letter language code such as "en" for English or "fr" for French. Or it is a five-letter string that indicates a language and a regional variant, such as "fr_CA" for French, as spoken in Canada.

Note that IE 4 does not support this property, but provides two different language-related properties of the Navigator object instead.

See Also

Navigator.systemLanguage, Navigator.userLanguage

Navigator.mimeTypes[ ] — an array of supported MIME types

Availability

Client-side JavaScript 1.1; always empty in Internet Explorer 4

Synopsis

```
navigator.mimeTypes[]
navigator.mimeTypes.length
```

Description

`navigator.mimeTypes` is an array of MimeType objects, each of which represents one of the MIME types (e.g., "text/html" and "image/gif") supported by the browser. The `mime-Types[]` array is defined by IE 4, but is always empty because IE 4 does not support the MimeType object.

See Also

Navigator.plugins[], MimeType, Plugin

Navigator.platform — the operating system the browser is running under

Availability

Client-side JavaScript 1.2

Synopsis

```
navigator.platform
```

Description

navigator.platform contains a string that specifies the operating system/hardware platform the browser is running under. Typical values are "Win32", "Win16", "MacPPC", and so on.

Navigator.plugins[ ] — an array of installed plugins

Availability

Client-side JavaScript 1.1; always empty in Internet Explorer 4

Synopsis

```
navigator.plugins[]
navigator.plugins.length
```

Description

navigator.plugins is an array of Plugin objects, each of which represents one plugin that has been installed along with the browser. The Plugin object provides information about the plugin, including a list of MIME types it supports. A *plugin* is the Netscape name for a software package that can be invoked by Navigator to display specific data types within the browser window.

The plugins[] array is defined by IE 4, but is always empty because IE 4 does not support plugins or the Plugin object.

See Also

Navigator.mimeTypes[ ], MimeType, Plugin

Navigator.plugins.refresh() — make newly installed plugins available

Availability

Client-side Navigator 3

Synopsis

```
navigator.plugins.refresh([reload])
```

Arguments

reload   An optional boolean argument that, if true, specifies that refresh() should reload any pages that contain <EMBED> tags and use plugins. If this argument is omitted, it defaults to false.

Description

The refresh() method causes Navigator to check whether any new plugins have been installed. If so, the plugins[] array is updated ("refreshed") to include the newly installed plugins. If the reload argument is specified and is true, Navigator also reloads any currently displayed documents that contain <EMBED> tags and use plugins.

Note the unusual synopsis for this method. `refresh()` is a method of the `plugins[]` array, not of the Navigator object. For almost all purposes, however, it is simpler to consider it a method of the Navigator object, which is why it is grouped here with the methods and properties of that object.

Navigator.preference() — set or retrieve user preferences

Availability

Client-side Navigator 4; requires `UniversalPreferencesRead` privilege to query preferences; requires `UniversalPreferencesWrite` privilege to set preference values

Synopsis

```
navigator.preference(prefname)
navigator.preference(prefname, value)
```

Arguments

prefname   The name of the preference to be queried or set.

value   The value to which the named preference is to be set.

Returns

If only one argument is passed to `preference()`, it returns the value of the named user preference. If a name and a value are passed, `preference()` sets the user preference and does not return anything.

Description

`navigator.preference()` queries or sets the user preference named *prefname*. If a second argument, *value*, is passed, the named preference is set to that value. If no *value* argument is provided, `preference()` returns the value of the named user preference.

Navigator supports a long list of user preferences; complete documentation of the names and values of these preferences is beyond the scope of this book. You can find a comprehensive list in the document at *http://developer.netscape.com/docs/manuals/deploymt/ jsprefs.htm*. You can also learn a lot about supported preferences by studying the file in which Navigator stores user preference values. On Unix systems, this file is typically *~/.netscape/preferences.js*. On Windows 95, you can find preference values in a file like *C:\Program Files\Netscape\Users\<name>\prefs.js*.

Note that most preferences settings are best left to the user. You should not modify them unless you know *exactly* what you are doing. Note also that only trusted scripts are allowed to read or modify preference settings.

Navigator.savePreferences() — save the user's preferences

Availability

Client-side Navigator 4; requires `UniversalPreferencesWrite` privilege

Synopsis

```
navigator.savePreferences()
```

Description

`navigator.savePreferences()` saves the current state of the user's preferences to disk. This is also done automatically when Navigator exits.

See Also

Navigator.preference()

Navigator.systemLanguage — the default language of the underlying system

Availability

Client-side Internet Explorer 4

Synopsis

```
navigator.systemLanguage
```

Description

`navigator.systemLanguage` is a read-only property that specifies the default language of the operating system. This property is available only in IE 4; its value uses the same standard codes used by `navigator.language`.

See Also

Navigator.language, Navigator.userLanguage

Navigator.taintEnabled() — test whether data tainting is enabled

Availability

Client-side JavaScript 1.1; deprecated

Synopsis

```
navigator.taintEnabled()
```

Returns

`true` if, and only if, the data-tainting security model is supported by and enabled on the current browser; `false` if the data-tainting security model is not in effect.

Description

Data tainting was an experimental security model in Navigator 3. It is no longer supported, and the `taintEnabled()` method is deprecated. IE 4 defines this method for compatibility, but it always returns `false`.

Navigator.userAgent — the HTTP user-agent value

Availability

Client-side JavaScript 1.0

Synopsis

```
navigator.userAgent
```

Description

`navigator.userAgent` is a read-only string property that specifies the value the browser uses for the user-agent header in HTTP requests. Typically, this is the value of `navigator.appCodeName` followed by a slash and the value of `navigator.appVersion`. For example:

```
Mozilla/4.0 (compatible; MSIE 4.01; Windows 95)
```

Navigator.userLanguage — the language of the current user

Availability

Client-side Internet Explorer 4

Synopsis

```
navigator.userLanguage
```

Description

`navigator.userLanguage` is a read-only property that specifies the preferred language of the user. This property is available only in IE 4; its value uses the same standard codes used by `navigator.language`.

See Also

Navigator.language, Navigator.systemLanguage

netscape — the Java netscape.* package

Availability

Client-side Navigator 3

Synopsis

```
netscape
```

Description

`netscape` is a global property of the Window object; it is usually used without reference to any particular window. It is a synonym for `Packages.netscape` and contains a read-only reference to a JavaPackage object that represents the top node of the *netscape.** package name hierarchy. The `netscape` Package contains, for example, a `javascript` property that is a reference to the Package object for the *netscape.javascript* package.

See Also

JavaPackage, Packages.netscape

Number — support for numbers

Availability

Core JavaScript 1.1; ECMA-262

Synopsis

```
Number.constant
```

Constructor

```
new Number(value)
Number(value)
```

Arguments

value   The numeric value of the Number object being created, or a value to be converted to a number.

Returns

When Number() is used with the new operator as a constructor, it returns a newly constructed Number object. When Number() is invoked as a function without the new operator, it converts its argument to a primitive numeric value and returns that value (or NaN if the conversion failed).

Constants

Number.MAX_VALUE
>The largest representable number.

Number.MIN_VALUE
>The smallest representable number.

Number.NaN   Not-a-number value.

Number.NEGATIVE_INFINITY
>Negative infinite value; returned on overflow.

Number.POSITIVE_INFINITY
>Infinite value; returned on overflow.

Methods

toString()   Convert a number to a string, using a specified radix (base).

Description

Numbers are a basic, primitive data type in JavaScript. In JavaScript 1.1, however, JavaScript also supports the Number object, which represents a primitive numeric value. JavaScript automatically converts between the primitive and object forms as necessary. In JavaScript 1.1, you can explicitly create a Number object with the Number() constructor, although there is rarely any need to do so.

The `Number()` constructor can also be used without the `new` operator, as a conversion function. When invoked in this way, it attempts to convert its argument to a number and returns the primitive numeric value (or NaN) that results from the conversion.

The `Number()` constructor is most commonly used as a placeholder for five useful numeric constants: the largest and smallest representable numbers; positive and negative infinity; and the special not-a-number value. Note that these values are properties of the `Number()` constructor function itself, not of individual number objects. For example, you use the `MAX_VALUE` property as follows:

```
biggest = Number.MAX_VALUE
```

but *not* like this:

```
n = new Number(2);
biggest = n.MAX_VALUE
```

By contrast, the `toString()` method of the Number object is a method of each Number object, not of the `Number()` constructor function. As noted above, JavaScript automatically converts from primitive numeric values to Number objects whenever necessary. This means that we can use the `toString()` method with a variable that holds a number, even though that value is not actually an object:

```
value = 1234;
binary_value = n.toString(2);
```

See Also

Infinity, Math, NaN

Number.MAX_VALUE — the maximum numeric value

Availability

Core JavaScript 1.1; ECMA-262

Synopsis

```
Number.MAX_VALUE
```

Description

`Number.MAX_VALUE` is the largest number representable in JavaScript. Its value is approximately 1.79E+308.

Number.MIN_VALUE — the minimum numeric value

Availability

Core JavaScript 1.1; ECMA-262

Synopsis

```
Number.MIN_VALUE
```

Description

`Number.MIN_VALUE` is the smallest (closest to zero, not most negative) number representable in JavaScript. Its value is approximately 2.22E-308.

Number.NaN — the special not-a-number value

Availability

Core JavaScript 1.1; ECMA-262

Synopsis

```
Number.NaN
```

Description

`Number.NaN` is a special value that indicates that the result of some mathematical operation (such as taking the square root of a negative number) is not-a-number. `parseInt()` and `parseFloat()` return this value when they cannot parse the specified string, and you might use `Number.NaN` in a similar way to indicate an error condition for some function that normally returns a valid number.

JavaScript prints the `Number.NaN` value as `NaN`. Note that the `NaN` value always compares unequal to any other number, including `NaN` itself. Thus, you cannot check for the Not-a-Number value by comparing to `Number.NaN`. Use the `isNaN()` function instead.

See Also

isNaN(), NaN

Number.NEGATIVE_INFINITY — negative infinity

Availability

Core JavaScript 1.1; ECMA-262

Synopsis

```
Number.NEGATIVE_INFINITY
```

Description

`Number.NEGATIVE_INFINITY` is a special numeric value that is returned when an arithmetic operation or mathematical function generates a negative value greater than the largest representable number in JavaScript (i.e., more negative than `-Number.MAX_VALUE`).

JavaScript displays the `NEGATIVE_INFINITY` value as `-Infinity`. This value behaves mathematically like infinity; for example, anything multiplied by infinity is infinity and anything divided by infinity is zero.

See Also

Infinity, isFinite( )

Number.POSITIVE_INFINITY — infinity

Availability

Core JavaScript 1.1; ECMA-262

Synopsis

```
Number.POSITIVE_INFINITY
```

Description

`Number.POSITIVE_INFINITY` is a special numeric value that is returned when an arithmetic operation or mathematical function generates a value greater than the largest representable number in JavaScript (i.e., greater than `Number.MAX_VALUE`).

JavaScript displays the `POSITIVE_INFINITY` value as `Infinity`. This value behaves mathematically like infinity; for example, anything multiplied by infinity is infinity and anything divided by infinity is zero.

Note that when numbers "underflow," or become less than `Number.MIN_VALUE`, JavaScript converts them to zero.

See Also

Infinity, isFinite( )

Number.toString() — convert a number to a string

Availability

Core JavaScript 1.1; ECMA-262

Synopsis

```
number.toString(radix)
```

Arguments

radix   In Navigator 3, this optional argument specifies the base that should be used to convert the number. It should be an integer between 2 and 36. If no value is specified, base 10 is used. In IE 4 and ECMA-262, this argument is ignored.

Returns

The string representation of the number (in the specified *radix* in Navigator 3).

Description

The `toString()` method of the Number object converts a Number to a string. In Internet Explorer and ECMA-262, this method always uses base 10. In Navigator 3, however, an optional argument allows a radix between 2 and 36 to be specified.

Object — a superclass that contains features of all JavaScript objects

Availability

Core JavaScript 1.0; ECMA-262; enhanced in JavaScript 1.1 and Navigator 4

Constructor

```
new Object();
new Object(value);
```

Arguments

value   In JavaScript 1.1, this optional argument specifies a primitive JavaScript value—a number, boolean, or string—that is to be converted to an object.

Returns

If no *value* argument is passed, this constructor returns a newly created object, which has no properties defined. If a primitive *value* argument is specified, the constructor creates and returns a Number, Boolean, or String object wrapper for the primitive value.

Properties

constructor   A read-only reference to the JavaScript function that was the constructor for the object. Added in JavaScript 1.1.

Methods

assign()   A method that, if defined, is used to implement the JavaScript assignment operator (=). Navigator only. Deprecated.

eval()   Evaluate a string of JavaScript code in the context of the given object. Navigator 3. Deprecated. Use the global eval() function instead.

toString()   A method that, if defined, is used to convert an object to a string.

unwatch()   Stop a watchpoint. Navigator 4.

valueOf()   Return the primitive value of the object, if any. For objects of type Object, this method simply returns the object itself. For other object types, such as Number and Boolean, this method returns the primitive value associated with the object. This method was added in JavaScript 1.1

watch()   Define a watchpoint: execute a specified function when the value of a named property is changed. Navigator 4.

Description

The Object class is a built-in data type of the JavaScript language. It serves as the superclass for all other JavaScript objects; therefore, methods and behavior of the Object class are inherited by all other objects. The basic behavior of objects in JavaScript is explained in Chapter 8.

Note that the toString() and valueOf() methods listed above are unusual in that they are not predefined. Instead, these are methods that you can define for any object and that are invoked by the JavaScript system at appropriate times to convert the object to a string or a primitive value.

See Also

Array, Boolean, Function, Function.prototype, Number, String, Chapter 8

Object.assign() — overload the assignment operator

Availability

Core Navigator 3; deprecated in favor of `Object.watch()`

Synopsis

```
object.assign(value)
```

Arguments

value   The value to be assigned. The `assign()` method should, in some fashion, assign *value* to the object.

Description

The `assign()` method is not one you usually call explicitly in your JavaScript code. Instead you define this method for certain objects, and the system invokes the method automatically when a value is assigned to that object.

If an object o has an `assign()` method defined, the assignment:

```
o = value;
```

is translated to the following function call:

```
o.assign(value);
```

The `assign()` method should be written to expect a single argument, which is always the value of the right-hand side of an assignment operator. When invoked, the object refers to the left-hand side of the assignment. The body of the method should assign, in some appropriate fashion, the *value* to the object.

Note that `assign()` is supported by Navigator only and is non-portable. In Navigator 4, `assign()` is deprecated in favor of `watch()` (which is also non-portable).

Object.constructor — an object's constructor function

Availability

Core JavaScript 1.1; ECMA-262

Synopsis

```
object.constructor
```

Description

The `constructor` property of any object is a read-only reference to the function that was used as the constructor for that object. For example, if you create an array a with the `Array()` constructor, `a.constructor` is an `Array`:

```
a = new Array(1,2,3);    // Create an object.
a.constructor == Array   // Evaluates to true.
```

One common use of the `constructor` property is to determine the type of unknown objects. Given an unknown value, you can use the `typeof` operator to determine whether it is a primitive value or an object. If it is an object, you can use the `constructor` property to determine what type of object it is. For example, the following function determines whether a given value is an array:

```
function isArray(x) {
    return ((typeof x == "object") && (x.constructor == Array));
}
```

Note, however, that this technique is not possible with all object types. In Navigator 3, there is no `Window()` constructor, for example, and Window objects have their `constructor` property set to `Object`.

Object.eval() — evaluate JavaScript code in a string

Availability

Core Navigator 3; deprecated in Navigator 4

Synopsis

```
object.eval(code)
```

Arguments

code   A string that contains the JavaScript expression to be evaluated or the statements to be executed.

Returns

The value of the evaluated *code*, if any.

Description

`eval()` executes the JavaScript code in its string argument *code*. It behaves much like the global function `eval()` but evaluates *code* in the scope of *object* instead of in the global scope.

`eval()` has been available as a global function since JavaScript 1.0. In Navigator 3, it was generalized to be a method of all objects. EMCA-262 did not adopt `Object.eval()`, however, and it was deprecated in Navigator 4. `Object.eval()` was actually removed from early versions of Navigator 4, then restored in Navigator 4.02 for backwards compatibility.

In Navigator 4.02 and later, you can replace:

```
object.eval(s)
```

with:

```
with (object) eval(s)
```

See Also
eval()

Object.toString() — define an object's string representation

Availability
Core JavaScript 1.0; ECMA-262

Synopsis
```
object.toString()
```

Returns
A string representing the object.

Description

The toString() method is not one you often call explicitly in your JavaScript programs. Instead, you define this method in your objects, and the system calls it whenever it needs to convert your object to a string.

The JavaScript system invokes the toString() method to convert an object to a string whenever the object is used in a string context. For example, if an object is converted to a string when it is passed to a function that expects a string argument:

```
alert(my_object);
```

Similarly, objects are converted to strings when they are concatenated to strings with the + operator:

```
alert('My object is: ' + my_object);
```

The toString() method is invoked without arguments and should return a string. To be useful, the string you return should be based, in some way, on the value of the object for which the method was invoked.

When you define a custom class in JavaScript, it is good practice to define a toString() method for the class. If you do not, the object inherits the default toString() method from the Object class. This default method returns a string of the form:

```
[object class]
```

where *class* is the class of the object: a value such as "Object", "String", "Number", "Function", "Window", "Document", and so on.

Usage

The `toString()` method can be quite useful when you are debugging JavaScript programs—it allows you to print objects and see their value. For this reason alone, it is a good idea to define a `toString()` method for every object class you create.

The string returned by `toString()` can be as complex as you like, and this method need not be restricted to use in debugging, of course. For example, a `toString()` method could be defined to return HTML-formatted text as `History.toString()` does. If the wording and formatting are chosen appropriately, you could use `document.write()` to output a string representation of an object directly into an HTML document!

Although the `toString()` method is usually invoked automatically by the system, there are times when you may invoke it yourself. For example, you might want to do an explicit conversion of an object to a string in a situation where JavaScript does not do it automatically for you:

```
y = Math.sqrt(x);
ystr = y.toString();
```

Note in this example that numbers have a built-in `toString()` method that you can use to force a conversion.

In other circumstances, you might choose to use a `toString()` call even in a context where JavaScript would do the conversion automatically. Using `toString()` explicitly can help to make your code clearer:

```
alert(my_obj.toString());
```

It does not generally make sense to define a `toString()` method for only a single object, so you usually assign this method to a prototype object so that it is available to all objects in a class of objects.

Object.unwatch() — remove a watchpoint

Availability

Core Navigator 4

Synopsis

```
object.unwatch(propname)
```

Arguments

propname   The property of *object* that is no longer to be "watched."

Description

Calling `unwatch()` for an *object* and property name *propname* removes any watchpoint handler function previously registered for that property of that object with `watch()`.

Object.valueOf() — the primitive value of the specified object

Availability

Core JavaScript 1.1; ECMA-262

Synopsis

```
object.valueOf(typehint);
```

Arguments

typehint   An optional string argument that provides a hint about the desired type for the returned value. When Navigator 4 invokes the `valueOf()` method of an object, in some circumstances it passes one of the strings "boolean", "string", "number", or even "object" to provide guidance about what kind of value the object should be converted to. Note that this argument is not part of the ECMA-262 standard and is not passed by IE or by Navigator 2 or 3.

Returns

The primitive value associated with the *object*, if any. Otherwise, returns the object itself.

Description

The `valueOf()` method of an object returns the primitive value associated with that object, if there is one. For objects of type Object and for the client-side JavaScript objects, there is no primitive value, and this method simply returns the object itself.

For objects of type Number, however, `valueOf()` returns the primitive numeric value represented by the object. Similarly, it returns the primitive boolean value associated with a Boolean object and the string associated with a String object.

It is rarely necessary to invoke the `valueOf()` method yourself. JavaScript does this automatically whenever an object is used where a primitive value is expected. In fact, because of this automatic invocation of the `valueOf()` method, it is difficult to even distinguish between primitive values and their corresponding objects. The `typeof` operator shows you the difference between strings and String objects for example, but in practical terms, you can use them equivalently in your JavaScript code.

The `valueOf()` methods of the Number, Boolean, and String objects convert these wrapper objects to the primitive values they represent. The `Object()` constructor performs the opposite operation when invoked with a number, boolean, or string argument: it wraps the primitive value in an appropriate object wrapper. JavaScript performs this primitive-to-object conversion for you in almost all circumstances, so it is rarely necessary to invoke the `Object()` constructor in this way.

In some circumstances, you may want to define a custom `valueOf()` method for your own objects. For example, you might define a JavaScript object type to represent complex numbers (a real number plus an imaginary number). As part of this object type, you'd probably define methods for performing complex addition, multiplication, and so on. But you might also want the ability to treat your complex numbers like ordinary real numbers by discarding the imaginary part. You might do something like the following:

```
Complex.prototype.valueOf = new Function("return this.real");
```

With this `valueOf()` method defined for your Complex object type, you could then do things like pass one of your complex number objects to `Math.sqrt()`, which would compute the square root of the real portion of the complex number.

Furthermore, if you were working exclusively with Navigator 4, you could make use of the *typehint* argument it passes to `valueOf()` to implement a method that returned different primitive values when a complex number object was used in different circumstances. For example, you could write a `valueOf()` method that would convert a complex object to a number by returning its real part, and to a boolean value by checking to see if either the real or imaginary parts were non-zero.

See Also

Object.toString()

Object.watch() — set a watchpoint

Availability

Core Navigator 4

Synopsis

```
object.watch(propname, handler)
```

Arguments

propname   The name of the property that is to be "watched."

handler   The function to be invoked when a value is assigned to the specified property *propname* of *object*.

Description

Calling the `watch()` method of an *object* allows you to specify a *handler* function that is invoked whenever any value is assigned to the property named *propname*.

handler is a function that is passed three arguments: the first argument is the name of the property that was changed, the second argument is the current value of that property, and the third argument is the proposed new value of the property. The return value of this *handler* function becomes the new value of the property. Thus, for example, a handler function can prevent a property from being changed by always returning its second argument.

Although `watch()` can be used to create read-only properties and other special property behaviors, it is not portable, and is therefore most useful when used for debugging purposes only.

open() — see Window.open( )

opener — see Window.opener

Option — an option in a Select box

Availability

Client-side JavaScript 1.0; enhanced in JavaScript 1.1

Inherits From

HTMLElement

Synopsis

```
select.options[i]
```

Constructor

In JavaScript 1.1, Option objects can be created dynamically with the Option() constructor:

```
new Option(text, value, defaultSelected, selected)
```

Arguments

text   An optional string argument that specifies the text property of the Option object.

value   An optional string argument that specifies the value property of the Option object.

defaultSelected

              An optional boolean argument that specifies the defaultSelected property of the Option object.

selected   An optional boolean argument that specifies the selected property of the Option object.

Properties

Option inherits the properties of HTMLElement and also defines the following:

defaultSelected

              A read-only boolean that specifies whether this option is selected by default. Set by the SELECTED attribute.

index   A read-only integer that specifies the index of this option within the array of options.

selected   A read/write boolean that specifies whether this option is currently selected. Its initial value is specified by the SELECTED attribute.

text   The text that describes the option. It is the plain text (not formatted HTML text) that follows the <OPTION> tag. In JavaScript 1.1, this property is read/write. Prior to 1.1, it is read-only.

value   A read/write string that specifies the value to be passed to the server if this
                   option is selected when the form is submitted. The initial value is specified
                   by the VALUE attribute.

HTML Syntax

An Option object is created by an <OPTION> tag within a <SELECT>, which is within a
<FORM>. Multiple <OPTION> tags typically appear within the <SELECT>.

```
<FORM ...>
  <SELECT  ...>
    <OPTION
        [ VALUE="value" ]          The value returned when the form is submitted
        [ SELECTED ] >             Specifies whether this option is initially selected
    plain_text_label               The text to display for this option
    [ </OPTION> ]
        ...
  </SELECT>
        ...
</FORM>
```

Description

The Option object describes a single option displayed within a Select object. The properties
of this object specify whether it is selected by default, whether is is currently selected, what
position it has in the options[ ] array of its containing Select object, what text it displays,
and what value it passes to the server if it is selected when the containing form is submitted.

Note that although the text displayed by this option is specified outside of the <OPTION>
tag, it must be plain, unformatted text without any HTML tags so that it can be properly displayed in list boxes and drop-down menus that do not support HTML formatting.

In JavaScript 1.1, you can dynamically create new Option objects for display in a Select
object with the Option() constructor. Once a new Option object is created, it can be
appended to the list of options in a Select object s by assigning it to s.options[op-
tions.length]. See Select.options[ ] for details.

See Also

Select, Select.options[]

Option.defaultSelected — whether an object is selected by default

Availability

Client-side JavaScript 1.0

Synopsis

option.defaultSelected

Description

The `defaultSelected` property is a read-only boolean that specifies whether the Option *option* is initially selected when the Select object that contains it is created. The Reset object uses this property to reset a Select object to its initial state, and you can use it to achieve the same effect in your code.

Option.index — the position of the option

Availability

Client-side JavaScript 1.0

Synopsis

    option.index

Description

The `index` property specifies the position or index of the Option object *option* within the `options[]` array of the Select object that contains it. The first Option object in the array is at index 0 and has its `index` property set to 0. The second Option has an `index` of 1, and so on.

Option.selected — whether the option is selected

Availability

Client-side JavaScript 1.0

Synopsis

    option.selected

Description

The `selected` property is a read/write boolean value that specifies whether a Option object within a Select object is currently selected. You can use this property to test whether a given option is selected. You can also use it to select (by setting it to `true`) or deselect (by setting it to `false`) a given option. Note that when you select or deselect an option in this way the `Select.onchange()` event handler is not invoked.

Usage

To determine the selected options in a Select object, you can loop through the `Select.options[]` array testing the `selected` property of each item. When multiple selections are not allowed (i.e., when the `MULTIPLE` attribute does not appear in the `<SELECT>` tag), however, it is much easier to simply check the `selectedIndex` property of the Select object.

See Also

Select, Select.selectedIndex

Option.text — the label for an option

Availability

Client-side JavaScript 1.0; read/write in JavaScript 1.1

Synopsis

```
option.text
```

Description

The `text` property is a string that specifies the text that appears to the user for the Option object *option*. The initial value of this property is whatever plain text (without HTML tags) appears after the `<OPTION>` tag and before the next `<OPTION>`, `</OPTION>`, or `</SELECT>` tag.

In JavaScript 1.0, the `text` property is read-only. In JavaScript 1.1, it is read/write. By setting a new value for this property, you can change the text that appears for the option within its Select object. Note that if you plan to use this technique, you should ensure that changing the option label does not make the Select object wider, or if the object must become wider, that no information to the right of the Select object becomes obscured when it grows.

Option.value — the value returned when the form is submitted

Availability

Client-side JavaScript 1.0

Synopsis

```
option.value
```

Description

`value` is a read/write string property of the Option object. It specifies the text that is passed to the web server if the *option* is selected when the form is submitted. The initial value of `value` is specified by the `VALUE` attribute of the `<OPTION>` tag. If the form is submitted to a server (as opposed to simply used by JavaScript on the client side), each Option object within a Select object should have a distinct `value`.

Packages — packages of Java classes

Availability

Client-side Navigator 3

Synopsis

```
Packages
```

Properties

`java`   A reference to a JavaPackage object that represents the top node of the *java.** package hierarchy.

netscape   A reference to a JavaPackage object that represents the top node of the *netscape.** package hierarchy.

sun   A reference to a JavaPackage object that represents the top node of the *sun.** package hierarchy.

Description

Packages is defined as a property of all Window objects. It refers to the top-level JavaPackage object: the JavaPackage that contains all other JavaPackage objects.

A JavaPackage object in JavaScript is an object that contains references to other JavaPackage objects and to JavaClass objects. Each JavaPackage object represents a node in the tree of package names. The Packages property refers to a JavaPackage object that is the root of this package name hierarchy.

The Packages JavaPackage object always contains three properties—java, sun, and netscape—which refer to other JavaPackage objects representing the *java.**, *sun.**, and *netscape.** Java packages. If other Java packages are installed in the browser and fall outside of these three standard package hierarchies, the JavaPackage object contains other properties that refer to those other package hierarchies.

Usage

The Window object also contains "global" properties named java, netscape, and sun, all of which are synonyms for the properties of the Packages object. So instead of writing Packages.java.lang.Math, for example, you can just write java.lang.Math.

See Also

JavaClass, JavaObject, JavaPackage

Packages.java — the root of the core Java language packages

Availability

Client-side Navigator 3

Synopsis

```
Packages.java
java
```

Description

The java property of the Packages object is a JavaPackage that contains each of the packages that comprise the core Java class library. These are packages such as *java.lang*, *java.io*, and *java.applet*. java is a shortcut for Packages.java.

See Also

java, JavaPackage

Packages.netscape — the root of the Java packages from Netscape

Availability

Client-side Navigator 3

Synopsis

```
Packages.netscape
netscape
```

Description

The `netscape` property of the `Packages` object is a JavaPackage that contains each of the packages that comprise the *netscape.** class library from Netscape. The packages in this class library include *netscape.javascript*, for example. `netscape` is a shortcut for `Packages.netscape`.

See Also

JavaPackage, netscape

Packages.sun — the root of the Java packages from Sun Microsystems

Availability

Client-side Navigator 3

Synopsis

```
Packages.sun
sun
```

Description

The `sun` property of the `Packages` object is a JavaPackage that contains each of the packages that comprise the *sun.** class library from Sun Microsystems. These packages are shipped with Sun's Java implementation but are not an official part of the Java language, so using these packages may make your programs less portable. `sun` is a shortcut for `Packages.sun`.

See Also

JavaPackage, sun

---

parent — see Window.parent

---

parseFloat( ) — convert a string to a number

Availability

Core JavaScript 1.0; enhanced in JavaScript 1.1; ECMA-262

Synopsis

```
parseFloat(s)
```

Arguments

s   The string to be parsed and converted to a number.

Returns

The parsed number, or NaN, if s does not begin with a valid number. In JavaScript 1.0, parseFloat() returns 0 instead of NaN when s cannot be parsed as a number.

Description

parseFloat() parses and returns the first number that occurs in s. Parsing stops, and the value is returned, when parseFloat() encounters a character in s that is not a valid part of the number. If s does not begin with a number that parseFloat() can parse, the function returns NaN, a special value that represents not-a-number. You can test for the NaN value with the isNaN() function.

NaN is not supported in JavaScript 1.0, so in that version of the language, parseFloat() returns 0 when it cannot parse s. This means that in JavaScript 1.0, if the return value of parseFloat() is 0, you must perform additional tests on s to determine whether it really represents the number zero or does not represent a number at all.

See Also

isNaN(), parseInt()

---

parseInt() — convert a string to an integer

Availability

Core JavaScript 1.0; enhanced in JavaScript 1.1; ECMA-262

Synopsis

```
parseInt(s)
parseInt(s, radix)
```

Arguments

s   The string to be parsed.

radix   An optional integer argument that represents the radix (i.e., base) of the number to be parsed.

Returns

The parsed number, or NaN, if s does not begin with a valid integer. In JavaScript 1.0, parseInt() returns 0 instead of NaN when it cannot parse s.

Description

parseInt() parses and returns the first number that occurs in s. Parsing stops, and the value is returned, when parseInt() encounters a character in s that is not a valid numeral for the specified radix. If s does not begin with a number that parseInt() can parse, the function returns NaN, a reserved value that represents not-a-number. You can test for the NaN value with the isNaN() function.

In JavaScript 1.0, NaN is not supported, and parseInt() returns 0 instead of NaN when it cannot parse *s*. In this version of the language, parseInt() cannot distinguish between a malformed string value and a legal value 0.

The *radix* argument specifies the base of the number to be parsed. Specifying 10 makes the parseInt() parse a decimal number. The value 8 specifies that an octal number (using digits 0 through 7) is to be parsed. The value 16 specifies a hexadecimal value, using digits 0 through 9 and letters A through F. *radix* can be any value between 2 and 36.

If *radix* is 0, or if it is not specified, parseInt() tries to determine the radix of the number from *s*. If *s* begins with 0x, parseInt() parses the remainder of *s* as a hexadecimal number. If *s* begins with a 0, parseInt() parses the number in octal. Otherwise, if *s* begins with a digit from 1 through 9, parseInt() parses it as a decimal number.

See Also

isNaN(), parseFloat()

Password — a text input field for sensitive data

Availability

Client-side JavaScript 1.0; enhanced in JavaScript 1.1

Inherits From

Input, HTMLElement

Synopsis

```
form.name
form.elements[i]
```

Properties

Password inherits properties from Input and HTMLElement and defines or overrides the following:

value   The value displayed by the Password element. Unlike the value property of other input elements, this one is subject to security restrictions and bugs.

Methods

Password inherits methods from Input and HTMLElement.

Event Handlers

Password inherits methods from Input and HTMLElement.

HTML Syntax

A Password element is created with a standard HTML <INPUT> tag:

```
<FORM>
    ...
    <INPUT
```

```
        TYPE="password"              Specifies that this is a Password element
        [ NAME="name" ]              A name that can later be used to refer to this element
                                     Specifies the name property
        [ VALUE="default" ]          The default value transmitted when the form is submitted
        [ SIZE=integer ]             How many characters wide the element is
    >

        . . .
    </FORM>
```

Description

The Password element is a text input field intended for input of sensitive data, such as passwords. As the user types characters, only asterisks appear, so that the input value cannot be read by a bystander looking over the user's shoulder. As a further security precaution, there are limitations on how JavaScript can read and write the value property of a Password element. See Text and Input for more information.

See Also

Input, Text

Password.value — user input to the Password object

Availability

Client-side JavaScript 1.0; modified in JavaScript 1.2

Synopsis

```
password.value
```

Description

The value property of the Password object is a string that specifies the password entered by the user and is the value sent over the Net when the form is submitted. The initial value of this property is specified by the VALUE attribute of the <INPUT> element that defined the Password object.

Because of the sensitive nature of password input, security restrictions protect the value property. In JavaScript 1.0 and 1.1, you can read the initial value of this property (specified by the VALUE attribute) and you can read a value set by JavaScript, but you cannot read a value entered by the user. If the user enters a value into a Password element, JavaScript reads that value as a string of asterisks, just as it is displayed on the screen. This restriction has been lifted in JavaScript 1.2, and JavaScript programs can read user input to a Password element.

value is a read/write property, and JavaScript programs can set it. However, setting value has no effect on the string displayed within the Password element and has no effect on the value that is sent over the network when the form is submitted. For this reason, the value property of the Password element is effectively, if not actually, read-only.

Plugin — describes an installed plugin

Availability

Client-side Navigator 3

Synopsis

```
navigator.plugins[i]
navigator.plugins['name']
```

Properties

description   A read-only string that contains a human-readable description of the plugin, specified by the plugin itself. This property may specify a full product name, information about the vendor and version, and so on.

filename   A read-only string that specifies the name of the disk file that contains the plugin code.

length   The number of MIME types supported by the plugin. MimeType objects describing these types are array elements of the Plugin object.

name   A read-only string that specifies the name of the plugin. This is generally a much shorter string than description. The value of this property may be used as an index into the navigator.plugins[] array.

Elements

The array elements of the Plugin object are MimeType objects that specify the data formats supported by the plugin.

Description

A *plugin* is a software module that can be invoked by Navigator to display specialized types of embedded data within the browser window. In Navigator 3, plugins are represented by the Plugin object. This object is somewhat unusual in that it has both regular object properties and array elements. The properties of the Plugin object provide various pieces of information about the plugin, and its array elements are MimeType objects that specify the embedded data formats that the plugin supports.

Plugin objects are obtained from the plugins[] array of the Navigator object. navigator.plugins[] may be indexed numerically when you want to loop through the complete list of installed plugins, looking for one that meets your needs (for example, one that supports the MIME type of the data you want to embed in your web page). This array can also be indexed by plugin name, however. That is, if you want to check whether a specific plugin is installed in the user's browser, you might use code like this:

```
document.write( navigator.plugins("Shockwave") ?
                "<EMBED SRC="movie.dir' HEIGHT=100 WIDTH=100>" :
                "You don't have the Shockwave plugin!" );
```

The name used as an array index with this technique is the same name that appears as the value of the name property of the Plugin.

Don't confuse the fact that Plugin objects are stored in an array of the Navigator object with the fact that each Plugin object is itself an array of MimeType objects. Because there are two arrays involved, you may end up with code that looks like these lines:

```
navigator.plugins[i][j]         // The jth MIME type of the ith plugin
navigator.plugins["LiveAudio"][0] // 1st MIME type of LiveAudio plugin
```

Finally, note that while the array elements of a Plugin object specify the MIME types supported by that plugin, you can also determine which plugin supports a given MIME type with the `enabledPlugin` property of the MimeType object.

See Also

Navigator, MimeType, MimeType.enabledPlugin

Plugin.description — English description of a plugin

Availability

Client-side Navigator 3

Synopsis

```
plugin.description
```

Description

The `description` property of a Plugin object is a read-only string that contains a human-readable English description of the specified plugin. The text of this description is provided by the creators of the plugin and may contain vendor and version information as well as a brief description of the function of the plugin.

Plugin.filename — the filename of the plugin program

Availability

Client-side Navigator 3

Synopsis

```
plugin.filename
```

Description

The `filename` property of the Plugin object is a read-only string that specifies the name of the file on disk that contains the plugin program itself. This name may vary from platform to platform. The `name` property is more useful than `filename` for identifying a plugin.

Plugin.length — the number of MIME types supported

Availability

Client-side Navigator 3

Synopsis

```
plugin.length
```

Description

Each Plugin object contains MimeType array elements that specify the data formats supported by the plugin. As with all arrays, the `length` property specifies the number of elements in the array.

Plugin.name — the name of a plugin

Availability

Client-side Navigator 3

Synopsis

```
plugin.name
```

Description

The `name` property of a Plugin object is a read-only string that specifies the name of the plugin. Each plugin should have a name that uniquely identifies it.

The value of the `name` property can also be used as an index into the `navigator.plugins[]` array. You can use this fact to determine easily whether a particular named plugin is installed in the current browser:

```
var sw_installed = (navigator.plugins["Shockwave"] != null);
```

Note that some plugins may support a configurable list of MIME types. Once you have determined that a desired plugin is installed, you may also need to consult the `Plugin.mimeTypes[]` array to be sure that the plugin can display the type of data you want it to.

PrivilegeManager — Java class used by signed scripts

Availability

Client-side Navigator 4

Synopsis

```
netscape.security.PrivilegeManager
```

Methods

`disablePrivilege()`
> Disables a privilege enabled by `enablePrivilege()`.

`enablePrivilege()`
> Enable a named privilege.

Description

netscape.security.PrivilegeManager is a Java class used by signed scripts to request or relinquish extended security privileges. See Chapter 21 for details.

See Also

Chapter 21

PrivilegeManager.disablePrivilege() — disable a privilege

Availability

Client-side Navigator 4

Synopsis

```
netscape.security.PrivilegeManager.disablePrivilege(privilege)
```

Arguments

privilege   A string that specifies the privilege to be disabled. This is usually one of
the standard system privileges, such as "UniversalBrowserRead" or "UniversalBrowserWrite".

Description

disablePrivilege() is a static Java method of the *netscape.security.PrivilegeMan-
ager* Java class. A signed script can call this method to disable an extended privilege.

See Also

Chapter 21

PrivilegeManager.enablePrivilege() — enable a privilege

Availability

Client-side Navigator 4

Synopsis

```
netscape.security.PrivilegeManager.enablePrivilege(privilege)
```

Arguments

privilege   A string that specifies the privilege to be enabled. This is usually one of
the standard system privileges, such as "UniversalBrowserRead" or "UniversalBrowserWrite".

Description

enablePrivilege() is a static Java method of the *netscape.security.PrivilegeMan-
ager* Java class. A signed script can call this method to temporarily enable an extended
privilege. The privilege remains enabled until the current method returns or until the script
calls the corresponding disablePrivilege() method.

See Also

Chapter 21

prompt() — see Window.prompt()

Radio — a graphical radio button

Availability

Client-side JavaScript 1.0; enhanced in JavaScript 1.1

Inherits From

Input, HTMLElement

Synopsis

The Radio button element is usually used in groups of mutually exclusive options that have the same name. To reference one Radio element within a group, use this syntax:

```
form.radio_name[j]
form.radio_name.length
```

Properties

Radio inherits properties from Input and HTMLElement, and defines or overrides the following:

checked   A read/write boolean value that specifies whether the button is checked or not.

defaultChecked
            A read-only boolean that specifies the initial state of the radio button. May be specified with the HTML CHECKED attribute.

value   A read/write string, initially set by the HTML VALUE attribute, that specifies the value returned by the Radio button if it is selected when the form is submitted.

Methods

Radio inherits methods from Input and HTMLElement.

Event Handlers

Radio inherits event handlers from Input and HTMLElement and defines or overrides the following:

onclick   Invoked when the radio button is clicked.

HTML Syntax

A Radio element is created with a standard HTML <INPUT> tag. Radio elements are created in groups by specifying multiple <INPUT> tags that have the same NAME attribute.

```
<FORM>
    ...
  <INPUT
    TYPE="radio"              Specifies that this is a radio button
```

```
    [ NAME="name" ]                 A name that can later be used to refer to this button...
                                    ...or to the group of buttons with this name
                                    Specifies the name property
    [ VALUE="value" ]               The value returned when this button is selected
                                    Specifies the value property
    [ CHECKED ]                     Specifies that the button is initially checked
                                    Specifies the defaultChecked property
    [ onClick="handler" ]           JavaScript statements to be executed when the button
                                    is clicked
  >
label                               The HTML text that should appear next to the button
  ...
</FORM>
```

Description

The Radio element represents a single graphical radio button in an HTML form. A radio button is one button in a group of buttons that represent mutually exclusive choices. When one button is selected, the previously selected button becomes deselected. The onClick event handler allows you to specify JavaScript code to be executed when the button is selected.

You can examine the checked property to determine the state of the button, and you can also set this property to select or deselect the button. Note that setting checked changes the graphical appearance of the button but does not invoke the onClick event handler. The initial value of the checked property and the value of the defaultChecked property are determined by the CHECKED attribute. Only one Radio element in a group may contain this attribute—it sets the checked and defaultChecked properties true for that element and false for all other Radio buttons in the group. If none of the elements has the CHECKED attribute, the first one in the group is checked (and defaultChecked) by default.

Note that the text that appears next to a Radio button is not part of the Radio element itself and must be specified externally to the Radio's HTML <INPUT> tag.

Radio elements are used in groups of mutually exclusive options. A mutually exclusive group is defined as the set of all Radio elements within a form that have the same name. If the shared name of a group of Radio elements in form f is opts, f.opts is an array of Radio elements and f.opts.length is the number of elements in the array.

You can set the VALUE attribute or the value property of a Radio element to specify the string that is passed to the server if the Radio element is checked when the form is submitted. Each Radio element in a group should specify a distinct value so that a script on the server can determine which one was checked when the form was submitted.

Usage

Radio elements can be used to present the user with a list of multiple, mutually exclusive, options. Use the Checkbox element to present a single option or to present a list of options that are not mutually exclusive.

Bugs

As described in the HTML Syntax section, when a group of Radio elements share the same NAME attribute, JavaScript assigns them to an array that bears that name. Unfortunately, there is a bug in this process in Navigator 2: if the Radio elements do not have event handlers specified with the onClick attribute, they are assigned to the array in reverse order. The workaround is to always assign an event handler, if only a dummy one, to all of your Radio elements that are manipulated with JavaScript.

See Also

Checkbox, Form, Input

Radio.checked — whether a Radio button is selected

Availability

Client-side JavaScript 1.0

Synopsis

```
radio.checked
```

Description

checked is a read/write boolean property of the Radio object. If the Radio button is checked, the checked property is true. If the Radio button is not checked, checked is false.

If you set checked to true, the Radio button becomes selected, and the previously selected button becomes deselected. Note, however, that setting the checked property of a radio button to false has no effect, because at least one button must always be selected; you cannot deselect a radio button except by selecting some other button.

Note that setting the checked property does not cause the Radio's onClick event handler to be invoked. If you want to invoke that event handler, you must do so explicitly.

Radio.defaultChecked — initial state of a Radio button

Availability

Client-side JavaScript 1.0

Synopsis

```
radio.defaultChecked
```

Description

defaultChecked is a read-only boolean property of the Radio object. It is true if the Radio button is initially selected—if the CHECKED attribute appears in the Radio's HTML <INPUT> tag. If this tag does not appear, the Radio button is initially deselected, and defaultChecked is false.

Radio.onclick — the handler invoked when a Radio button is selected

Availability

Client-side JavaScript 1.0

Synopsis

```
<INPUT TYPE="radio" onClick="handler" ... >
radio.onclick
```

Description

The `onclick` property of a Radio object refers to an event handler function that is invoked when the user clicks on the checkbox. See `HTMLElement.onclick` for complete details. Note, however, that `Radio.onclick` has been supported since JavaScript 1.0, unlike the generalized `HTMLElement.onclick` handler.

See Also

HTMLElement.onclick, Chapter 15

Radio.value — value returned when the form is submitted

Availability

Client-side JavaScript 1.0

Synopsis

```
radio.value
```

Description

`value` is a read/write string property of the Radio object. It specifies the text that is passed to the web server if the radio button is checked when the form is submitted. The initial value of `value` is specified by the `VALUE` attribute of the Radio's HTML `<INPUT>` tag. If the form is submitted to a server (as opposed to simply used by JavaScript on the client side) each radio button in a group must have a distinct `value`.

Note that the `value` field does not specify whether or not the radio button is currently selected; the `checked` property specifies the current state of the Radio object.

RegExp — regular expressions for pattern matching

Availability

Core JavaScript 1.2

Literal Syntax

```
/pattern/attributes
```

Constructor

```
new RegExp(pattern, attributes)
```

Arguments

pattern   A string that specifies the pattern of the regular expression.

attributes   An optional string containing one or both of the global "g" attribute and the case-insensitive "i" attribute.

Instance Properties

global   Whether the RegExp has the g attribute.

ignoreCase   Whether the RegExp has the i attribute.

lastIndex   The character position of the last match; used for finding multiple matches in a string.

source   The source text of the regular expression.

Static Properties

RegExp.$*n*   The text that matched the *n*th subexpression.

RegExp.input or RegExp.$_
        The text to match against, if no other text is supplied.

RegExp.lastMatch or RegExp["$&"]
        The matching text from the last successful match.

RegExp.lastParen or RegExp["$+"]
        The text that matched the last subexpression.

RegExp.leftContext or RegExp["$`"]
        The text to the left of the matched text.

RegExp.multiline or RegExp["$*"]
        Whether pattern matching is done in multiline mode.

RegExp.rightContext or RegExp["$'"]
        The text to the right of the matched text.

Methods

compile()   Define a new pattern and attributes for a RegExp object.

exec()   Powerful, general-purpose pattern matching.

test()   Test whether a string contains a pattern.

Description

The RegExp object represents a regular expression, a powerful tool for performing pattern matching on strings. See Chapter 10, *Pattern Matching with Regular Expressions*, for complete details on regular expression syntax and use.

See Also

Chapter 10

RegExp.$n — the text that matched a subexpression

Availability

Core JavaScript 1.2

Synopsis

`RegExp.$1`	*Text matching first subexpression*
`RegExp.$2`	*Text matching second subexpression*
...	
`RegExp.$9`	*Text matching ninth subexpression*
`RegExp["$+"]`	*See RegExp.lastParen*
`RegExp["$&"]`	*See RegExp.lastMatch*
`RegExp["$`"]`	*See RegExp.leftContext*
`RegExp["$'"]`	*See RegExp.rightContext*
`RegExp["$*"]`	*See RegExp.multiline*
`RegExp.$_`	*See RegExp.input*

Description

`RegExp.$1` through `RegExp.$9` are static properties of the `RegExp()` constructor. These read-only properties hold the text that matched the first through the ninth parenthesized subexpressions of the last successful match performed by any of the RegExp or String pattern matching methods. If the regular expression contained fewer than nine parenthesized subexpressions, not all the properties are used. If it contained more than nine subexpressions, the values of all after the first nine are not stored.

Note that the text that matched the various subexpressions is also part of the arrays returned by `String.match()` and `RegExp.exec()`, so you do not often need to use these properties directly.

The various other static RegExp properties that begin with $ are synonyms for other properties. See their descriptions under those properties.

RegExp.compile() — change a regular expression

Availability

Core JavaScript 1.2

Synopsis

`regexp.compile(newpattern, attributes)`

Arguments

newpattern   A string that specifies the new pattern to be used by *regexp*.

attributes   An optional string that specifies the new attributes for *regexp*. If specified, it should be "g", "i", or "gi". If this attribute is omitted, *regexp* has neither the g nor the i attribute.

Returns

A reference to *regexp*.

Description

`compile()` changes the pattern that a RegExp object matches and the attributes it uses to perform the match. Instead of creating a new RegExp object for each pattern you want to match, the `compile()` method allows you to change the pattern of an existing object. This may be slightly more efficient than creating a new object.

RegExp.exec() — general-purpose pattern matching

Availability

Core JavaScript 1.2; buggy in Internet Explorer 4

Synopsis

```
regexp.exec(string)
regexp(string)
```

Arguments

string   The string to be searched. If not specified, `RegExp.input` is searched.

Returns

An array containing the results of the match, or `null` if no match was found.

Description

`exec()` is the most powerful of all the RegExp and String pattern matching methods. It is a general-purpose method that is somewhat more complex to use than `RegExp.test()`, `String.search()`, `String.replace()`, and `String.match()`. Note that a RegExp object itself can be invoked as a function; doing so is exactly the same as invoking the `exec()` method of the RegExp object.

`exec()` searches *string* for text that matches *regexp*. If *string* is not specified, it searches the string in `RegExp.input`. If it finds a match, it returns an array of results. Element 0 of this array is the matched text. Element 1 is the text that matched the first parenthesized subexpression, if any, within *regexp*. Element 2 contains the text that matched the second subexpression, and so on. The array `length` property specifies the number of elements in the array, as usual. In addition to the array elements and the `length` property, the value returned by `exec()` also has two other properties. The `index` property specifies the character position of the first character of the matched text. The `input` property refers to *string*. This returned array is the same as the array that is returned by the `String.match()` method, when invoked on a non-global RegExp object.

When `exec()` is invoked on a non-global pattern, it performs the search and returns the result described above. When *regexp* is a global regular expression, however, `exec()` behaves in a slightly more complex way. It begins searching *string* at the character position specified by the `lastIndex` property of *regexp*. When it finds a match, it sets `lastIndex` to the position of the first character after the match. This means that you can invoke the `exec()` repeatedly in order to loop through all matches in a string. When `exec()` cannot find any more matches, it returns `null` and resets `lastIndex` to zero. If you begin searching a new string immediately after successfully finding a match, you have to manually reset `lastIndex`.

Note that `exec()` always includes full details of every match in the array it returns, whether or not *regexp* is a global pattern. This is where `exec()` differs from `String.match()`, which returns much less information when used with global patterns. In fact, calling the `exec()` method repeatedly in a loop is the only way to obtain complete pattern matching information for a global pattern.

Like all RegExp and String pattern matching methods, `exec()` sets `leftContext`, `rightContext`, `$1`, and other static properties of RegExp when it finds a match. Note, however, that the array returned by `exec()` contains equivalent information, and you never need to use these static properties when working with `exec()`.

Example

You can use `exec()` in a loop to find all matches within a string. For example:

```
var pattern = /\bJava\w*\b/g;
var text = "JavaScript is more fun than Java or JavaBeans!";
var result;
while((result = pattern.exec(text)) != null) {
    alert("Matched '" + result[0] + "' at position " + result.index);
}
```

Bugs

In Internet Explorer 4, `exec()` does not properly set or use the `lastIndex` property, so it cannot be used with global patterns in the kind of loop shown in the example above. Also, the *string* argument may not be omitted in IE 4; `exec()` does not make use of `RegExp.input` in that browser. Finally, RegExp objects cannot be invoked directly as functions in IE 4.

See Also

RegExp.lastIndex, RegExp.test(), String.match(), String.replace(), String.search(), Chapter 10

RegExp.global — whether a regular expression matches globally

Availability

Core JavaScript 1.2; not implemented in Internet Explorer 4

Synopsis

```
regexp.global
```

Description

`global` is a read-only boolean instance property of RegExp objects. It specifies whether a particular regular expression is global—whether it was created with the g attribute.

RegExp.ignoreCase — whether a regular expression is case-insensitive

Availability

Core JavaScript 1.2; not implemented in Internet Explorer 4

Synopsis

```
regexp.ignoreCase
```

Description

`ignoreCase` is a read-only boolean instance property of RegExp objects. It specifies whether a particular regular expression is case-insensitive—whether it was created with the `i` attribute.

RegExp.input — input buffer for pattern matching

Availability

Core JavaScript 1.2; with special client-side behavior; non-functional in Internet Explorer 4

Synopsis

```
RegExp.input
RegExp.$_
```

Description

The static property `RegExp.input` specifies the text to be used for pattern matching when no string is passed to `RegExp.exec()` or `RegExp.test()`. `RegExp.input` is a read/write property, so you can set it at any time.

`RegExp.$_` is a synonym for `RegExp.input`, and its name may be a convenient shortcut for Perl programmers. Its use is discouraged.

In client-side JavaScript, `RegExp.input` is automatically set before certain event handlers are called, and automatically reset to the empty string when those event handlers return. This is a convenience for event handlers that use regular expression pattern matching to perform input validation or other operations. In Navigator 4, the event handlers of the Text and TextArea objects (but not the Password or FileUpload objects) set `RegExp.input` to the current value of the user's input. The event handlers of the Select object set `RegExp.input` to the text of the selected option. The `onclick()` handler of the Link object sets `RegExp.input` to the text of the hyperlink. Curiously, however, the `onmouseover()` and `onmouseout()` handlers set `RegExp.input` to the text of the URL to which the Link refers.

Bugs

The `RegExp.input` property exists in IE 4 but behaves completely differently than it does in Navigator 4. In IE 4, the various RegExp and String pattern matching methods set `RegExp.input` to whatever string was just searched, but `RegExp.test()` and `RegExp.exec()` never use the value of this property. In IE 4, it is an error to call either of those methods with no string argument. Client-side event handlers do not set the `RegExp.input` property in IE 4. The `RegExp.$_` synonym is not supported in IE 4.

See Also

RegExp.exec( ), RegExp.multiline, RegExp.test( )

RegExp.lastIndex — the character position after the last match

Availability

Core JavaScript 1.2; not implemented in Internet Explorer 4

Synopsis

```
regexp.lastIndex
```

Description

lastIndex is a read/write instance property of RegExp objects. For global regular expressions, it contains an integer that specifies the character position immediately following the last match found by the RegExp.exec( ) and RegExp.test( ) methods. These methods use this property as the starting point for the next search they conduct. This allows you to call those methods repeatedly, to loop through all matches in a string. Note that lastIndex is not used by RegExp objects that do not have the g attribute and do not represent global patterns.

This property is read/write, so you can set it at any time. exec( ) and test( ) automatically reset lastIndex to 0 when they fail to find a match (or another match). If you begin to search a new string after a successful match of some other string, you have to explicitly set this property to 0.

Bugs

This property is not implemented in IE 4. This means that it is not possible to use RegExp.exec( ) with a global regular expression in IE 4 to loop automatically through all matches in a string. In IE 4, the array returned by RegExp.exec( ) includes a lastIndex property that specifies the first position after the matched text. If necessary, you can use this with a method such as String.substring( ) to break a string up into pieces which can be searched individually.

See Also

RegExp.exec( ), RegExp.test( )

RegExp.lastMatch — the text of the last successful pattern match

Availability

Core JavaScript 1.2; not implemented in Internet Explorer 4

Synopsis

```
RegExp.lastMatch
RegExp["$&"]
```

Description

RegExp.lastMatch is a read-only static property of the RegExp() constructor. It specifies the text of the last successful match performed by any of the RegExp or String pattern matching methods.

RegExp["$&"] is a synonym for RegExp.lastMatch, and may occasionally be a useful shortcut for experienced Perl programmers. Its use is discouraged.

Note that the value of RegExp.lastMatch can be easily obtained from the value returned by String.match() and RegExp.exec(). Therefore, this property is not often needed. This is fortunate since neither RegExp.lastMatch nor RegExp["$&"] is implemented in IE 4.

RegExp.lastParen — the text that matched the last subexpression

Availability

Core JavaScript 1.2; not implemented in Internet Explorer 4

Synopsis

```
RegExp.lastParen
RegExp["$+"]
```

Description

RegExp.lastParen is a read-only static property of the RegExp() constructor. It specifies the text that matched the last parenthesized subexpression in the last successful match performed by any of the RegExp or String pattern matching methods.

RegExp["$+"] is a synonym for RegExp.lastParen, and may occasionally be a useful shortcut for experienced Perl programmers. Its use is discouraged.

Note that the value of RegExp.lastParen can be easily obtained from the value returned by String.match() and RegExp.exec(). Therefore, this property is not often needed. This is fortunate because neither RegExp.lastParen nor RegExp["$+"] is implemented in IE 4.

RegExp.leftContext — the text before the last match

Availability

Core JavaScript 1.2; not implemented in Internet Explorer 4

Synopsis

```
RegExp.leftContext
RegExp["$`"]
```

Description

RegExp.leftContext is a read-only static property of the RegExp() constructor. It specifies the text that precedes the matched substring in the last successful match performed by any of the RegExp or String pattern matching methods.

RegExp["$`"] is a synonym for RegExp.leftContext, and may occasionally be a useful shortcut for experienced Perl programmers. Its use is discouraged.

Note that the value of RegExp.leftContext can be easily obtained from the value returned by String.match() and RegExp.exec(). Therefore, this property is not often needed. This is fortunate since neither RegExp.leftContext nor RegExp["$`"] is implemented in IE 4.

RegExp.multiline — whether matches are performed in multiline mode

Availability

Core JavaScript 1.2 with special client-side behavior; not implemented in Internet Explorer 4

Synopsis

```
RegExp.multiline
RegExp["$*"]
```

Description

`RegExp.multiline` is a static property of the `RegExp()` constructor. It specifies whether pattern matching is to be performed in multiline mode or not. When this property is `true`, the `^` and `$` patterns match not only the beginning and end of a string, but also the beginning and end of a line within the string. `RegExp.multiline` is a read/write property, so you can set it at any time.

`RegExp["$*"]` is a synonym for `RegExp.multiline`, and may occasionally be a useful shortcut for Perl programmers. Its use is discouraged.

In Navigator 4, `RegExp.multiline` is automatically set to `true` immediately before any event handlers of the TextArea or Link objects are called, and is automatically reset to `false` immediately after those handlers return. The property is also automatically set to `false` immediately before any event handlers of the Text or Select objects are called. Although this is supposed to be convenient for event handlers that use regular expressions for input validation, it means that you cannot set `RegExp.multiline` to `true` and expect it to retain that value throughout your program. Instead, you often have to explicitly set it to `true` every time you want to perform a match in multiline mode.

Bugs

Neither the `RegExp.multiline` property nor its `RegExp["$*"]` synonym is implemented in IE 4. IE 4 does not allow pattern matching to be performed in multiline mode.

See Also

RegExp.input()

RegExp.rightContext — the text after the last match

Availability

Core JavaScript 1.2; not implemented in Internet Explorer 4

Synopsis

```
RegExp.rightContext
RegExp["$'"]
```

Description

`RegExp.rightContext` is a read-only static property of the `RegExp()` constructor. It specifies the text that follows the matched substring of the last successful match performed by any of the RegExp or String pattern matching methods.

`RegExp["$'"]` is a synonym for `RegExp.rightContext`, and may occasionally be a useful shortcut for experienced Perl programmers. Its use is discouraged.

Note that the value of `RegExp.rightContext` can be obtained from the value returned by `String.match()` and `RegExp.exec()`. Therefore, this property is not often needed. This is fortunate since neither `RegExp.rightContext` nor `RegExp["$'"]` is implemented in IE 4.

RegExp.source — the text of the regular expression

Availability

Core JavaScript 1.2

Synopsis

```
regexp.source
```

Description

`source` is a read-only string instance property of RegExp objects. It contains the text of the RegExp pattern. This text does not include the delimiting slashes used in regular expression literals, and it does not include the g and i attributes.

RegExp.test() — test whether a string contains a match

Availability

Core JavaScript 1.2

Synopsis

```
regexp.test(string)
```

Arguments

string   The string to be tested. If omitted, `RegExp.input` is tested instead.

Returns

`true` if *string* contains text that matches *regexp*; `false` otherwise.

Description

`test()` tests *string* to see if it contains text that matches *regexp*. If so, it returns `true`; otherwise, it returns `false`. If *string* is omitted, `test` tests the string stored in RegExp.input.

If `test()` finds a match, it sets `RegExp.leftContext`, `RegExp.rightContext`, `RegExp.$1`, and various other static properties of the RegExp class to provide more information about the match.

When *regexp* is a global pattern (i.e., a regular expression with the g attribute), `test()` begins searching *string* at the character position specified by the `lastIndex` property of *regexp*. If `test()` finds a match for a global pattern, it sets `lastIndex` to the character position immediately after the match it found. What this means is that when you are working with global regular expressions, you can call `test()` repeatedly on the same string to find all matches. In practice, it is unusual to use `test()` with global patterns. If you are interested in finding all matches for a pattern, you typically use `RegExp.exec()` to obtain more information about each match.

Example

```
var pattern = /java/i;
pattern.test("JavaScript");   // Returns true
pattern.test("ECMAScript");   // Returns false
```

Bugs

In IE 4, test() does not properly set or use the lastIndex property, so it cannot be used with global patterns to loop through a string testing for multiple matches. Also, the *string* argument may not be omitted in IE 4; test() does not make use of RegExp.input in that browser.

See Also

RegExp.exec( ), RegExp.lastIndex, String.match( ), String.replace( ), String.substring( ), Chapter 10

Reset — a button to reset a form's values

Inherits From

Input, HTMLElement

Availability

Client-side JavaScript 1.0; enhanced in JavaScript 1.1

Synopsis

```
form.name
form.elements[i]
```

Properties

Reset inherits properties from Input and HTMLElement and defines or overrides the following:

value   A read-only string, set by the HTML VALUE attribute, that specifies the text to appear in the button. If no VALUE is specified, then (in Navigator) the button is labelled "Reset" by default.

Methods

Reset inherits the methods of Input and HTMLElement.

Event Handlers

Reset inherits the event handlers of Input and HTMLElement and defines or overrides the following:

onclick   Invoked when the **Reset** button is clicked.

HTML Syntax

A Reset element is created with a standard HTML <INPUT> tag:

```
<FORM>
   ...
  <INPUT
    TYPE="reset"              Specifies that this is a Reset button
    [ VALUE="label" ]         The text that is to appear within the button
                              Specifies the value property
    [ NAME="name" ]           A name that can later be used to refer to the button
                              Specifies the name property
    [ onClick="handler" ]     JavaScript statements to be executed when the button
                              is clicked
  >
   ...
</FORM>
```

Description

The Reset element has the same properties and methods as the Button element, but has a more specialized purpose. When a Reset element is clicked on, all input elements in the form that contains it have their values reset to their initial default values. (For most elements, this means to the value specified by the HTML VALUE attribute.) If no initial value was specified, a click on the **Reset** button clears any user input from those elements.

Usage

If no VALUE attribute is specified for a Reset element, it is labelled "Reset". In some forms, it may be better to label the button "Clear Form" or "Defaults".

In JavaScript 1.1, you can simulate the action of a **Reset** button with the reset() method of the Form object. Also in JavaScript 1.1, the onreset event handler of the Form object is invoked before the form is reset. This event handler can cancel the reset by returning false.

See Also

Button, HTMLElement, Input, Form

Reset.onclick — the handler invoked when a Reset button is clicked

Availability

Client-side JavaScript 1.0; enhanced in JavaScript 1.1

Synopsis

```
<INPUT TYPE="reset" onClick="handler" ... >
reset.onclick
```

Description

The `onclick` property of a Reset object refers to an event handler function that is invoked when the user clicks on the **Reset** button. See `HTMLElement.onclick` for complete details. Note, however, that `Reset.onclick` has been supported since JavaScript 1.0, unlike the generalized `HTMLElement.onclick` handler.

The **Reset** button has the special function of resetting all form elements to their default value. The `onclick` event handler may add any additional functionality to the **Reset** button. In JavaScript 1.1, the `onclick` handler may return `false` to prevent the Reset object from resetting the form. (For example, the `onclick` handler could use `confirm()` to ask the user to confirm the reset and return `false` if it was not confirmed.)

See Also

Form.onreset, Form.reset(), HTMLElement, HTMLElement.onclick, Input

---

Reset.value — the label of a Reset button

Availability

Client-side JavaScript 1.0

Synopsis

```
reset.value
```

Description

The `value` property is a read-only string that specifies the text that appears within the Reset button. It is specified by the `VALUE` attribute of the `<INPUT>` tag that created the button. If no `VALUE` attribute is specified, the default `value` is "Reset".

Screen — provides information about the display

Availability

Client-side JavaScript 1.2

Synopsis

```
screen
```

Properties

`screen.availHeight`
> The available height of the screen.

`screen.availLeft`
> The first available pixel on the left.

`screen.availTop`
> The first available pixel on the top.

`screen.availWidth`
> The available width of the screen.

```
screen.colorDepth
```
>   The depth of the browser's color palette.

```
screen.height
```
>   The total height of the screen, in pixels.

```
screen.pixelDepth
```
>   The bits-per-pixel value for the screen.

```
screen.width
```
>   The total width of the screen, in pixels.

Description

The `screen` property of every Window refers to a Screen object. The static properties of this global object contain information about the screen on which the browser is displayed. JavaScript programs can use this information to optimize their output to match the user's display capabilities. For example, a program could choose between large and small images based on the display size, and it could choose between 16-bit color images and 8-bit color images based on the screen's color depth. A JavaScript program can also use the information about the size of the screen in order to center new browser windows on the screen.

See Also

Window.screen

Screen.availHeight — the available height of the screen

Availability

Client-side JavaScript 1.2

Synopsis

```
screen.availHeight
```

Description

`screen.availHeight` specifies the available height, in pixels, of the screen on which the web browser is displayed. On operating systems such as Windows, this available height does not include vertical space allocated to semipermanent features, such as the task bar at the bottom of the screen.

Screen.availLeft — the first available horizontal pixel

Availability

Client-side Navigator 4

Synopsis

```
screen.availLeft
```

Description

`screen.availLeft` specifies the leftmost X-coordinate that is not allocated to a semipermanent display feature, such as an application shortcut bar or Windows 95 task bar.

Screen.availTop — the first available vertical pixel

Availability

Client-side Navigator 4

Synopsis

```
screen.availTop
```

Description

`screen.availTop` specifies the topmost Y-coordinate that is not allocated to a semipermanent display feature, such as an application shortcut bar or the Windows 95 task bar.

Screen.availWidth — the available width of the screen

Availability

Client-side JavaScript 1.2

Synopsis

```
screen.availWidth
```

Description

`screen.availWidth` specifies the available width, in pixels, of the screen on which the web browser is displayed. On operating systems such as Windows, this available width does not include horizontal space allocated to semipermanent features, such as application shortcut bars.

Screen.colorDepth — the depth of the web browser's color palette

Availability

Client-side JavaScript 1.2

Synopsis

```
screen.colorDepth
```

Description

`colorDepth` specifies the base-2 logarithm of the number of colors allocated by the web browser and available for the display of images. For example, if a browser preallocates 128 colors, `screen.colorDepth` would be 7. On systems that do not allocate color palettes, this value is the same as the number of bits-per-pixel for the screen.

In IE 4, `colorDepth` specifies the color depth of the screen, in bits-per-pixel, rather than the depth of a preallocated color palette. The `screen.pixelDepth` property provides this value in Navigator.

Screen.height — the height of the screen

Availability
Client-side JavaScript 1.2

Synopsis
```
screen.height
```

Description
`screen.height` specifies the height, in pixels, of the screen on which the web browser is displayed.

Screen.pixelDepth — the color depth of the screen

Availability
Client-side Navigator 4

Synopsis
```
screen.pixelDepth
```

Description
`screen.pixelDepth` specifies the color depth, in bits-per-pixel, of the screen on which the web browser is displayed.

Screen.width — the width of the screen

Availability
Client-side JavaScript 1.2

Synopsis
```
screen.width
```

Description
`screen.width` specifies the width, in pixels, of the screen on which the web browser is displayed.

---

scroll( ) — see Window.scroll( )

Select — a graphical selection list

Availability
Client-side JavaScript 1.0; enhanced in JavaScript 1.1

Inherits From
Input, HTMLElement

Synopsis

```
form.element_name
form.elements[i]
```

Properties

Select inherits properties from Input and HTMLElement and defines or overrides the following:

length   A read-only integer that specifies the number of elements in the options[ ] array (i.e., the number of options that appear in the Select element).

options   An array of Option objects, each of which describes one of the options displayed within the Select element.

selectedIndex
          A read-only (read/write in Navigator 3) integer that specifies the index of the selected option within the Select element. If the Select element has its MULTIPLE attribute set and allows multiple selections, this property only specifies the index of the first selected item or −1 if none are selected.

type   A read-only string that specifies the type of this form element. For Select elements, it has the value "select-one" or "select-multiple". Available in Navigator 3 and later.

Methods

Select inherits the methods of Input and HTMLElement.

Event Handlers

Select inherits event handlers from Input and HTMLElement and defines or overrides the following:

onchange Invoked when the user selects or deselects an item.

HTML Syntax

A Select element is created with a standard HTML <SELECT> tag. Options to appear within the Select element are created with the <OPTION> tag:

```
<FORM>
    . . .
<SELECT
    NAME="name"                 A name that identifies this element; specifies name property
    [ SIZE=integer ]            Number of visible options in Select element
    [ MULTIPLE ]                Multiple options may be selected, if present.
    [ onChange="handler" ]      Invoked when the selection changes
>
<OPTION VALUE="value1" [SELECTED]> option_label1
<OPTION VALUE="value2" [SELECTED]> option_label2
Other options here
</SELECT>
    . . .
</FORM>
```

Description

The Select element represents a graphical list of choices from which the user may select. If the MULTIPLE attribute is present in the HTML definition of the element, the user may select any number of options from the list. If that attribute is not present, the user may select only one option, and options have a radio button behavior—selecting one deselects whichever was previously selected.

The options in a Select element may be displayed in two distinct ways. If the SIZE attribute has a value greater than 1, or if the MULTIPLE attribute is present, they are displayed in a list box which is SIZE lines high in the browser window. If SIZE is smaller than the number of options, the list box includes a scrollbar so that all the options are accessible. On the other hand, if SIZE is specified as 1 and MULTIPLE is not specified, the currently selected option is displayed on a single line and the list of other options is made available through a drop-down menu. The first presentation style displays the options clearly but requires more space in the browser window. The second style requires minimal space but does not display alternative options as explicitly.

The options[] property of the Select element is the most interesting. This is the array of Option objects that describe the choices presented by the Select element. The length property specifies the length of this array (as does options.length). See the documentation of the Option object for details.

In JavaScript 1.1, the options displayed by the Select element may be dynamically modified. You can change the text displayed by an Option object simply by setting its text property. You can change the number of options displayed by the Select element by setting the options.length property. And you can create new options for display with the Option() constructor function. See Select.options[] and Option for details.

Note that the Select object is a kind of Input object and inherits from Input, despite the fact that Select objects are not created with HTML <INPUT> tags.

See Also

Form, HTMLElement, Input, Option

Select.length — the number of options in a Select object

Availability

Client-side JavaScript 1.0

Synopsis

```
select.length
```

Description

The length property of a *select* object is a read-only integer that specifies the number of elements in the *select*.options[] array. *select*.length refers to the same value as *select*.options.length.

Select.onchange — the handler invoked when the selection changes

Availability

Client-side JavaScript 1.0

Synopsis

```
<SELECT ... onChange="handler" ... >
select.onchange
```

Description

The `onchange` property of a Select object refers to an event handler function that is invoked when the user selects or deselects an option. See `Input.onchange` for further details on this event handler.

Bugs

In the Windows versions of Navigator 2, when the Select object is displayed in its drop-down menu form, the `onchange()` event handler is not invoked immediately after a choice is made; it is not invoked until the user clicks somewhere else on the page. This bug has been fixed in Navigator 3.

See Also

Input.onchange, Option

Select.options[] — the choices in a Select object

Availability

Client-side JavaScript 1.0; enhanced in JavaScript 1.1

Synopsis

```
select.options[i]
select.options.length
```

Description

The `options[]` property contains an array of Option objects, each of which describes one of the selection options presented within the Select object *select*. The `options.length` property specifies the number of elements in the array, as does the *select*`.length` property. See the Option object for further details.

In JavaScript 1.1, you can modify the options displayed in a Select object in any of the following ways:

- If you set `options.length` to 0, all options in the Select object are cleared.

- If you set `options.length` to a value less than the current value, the number of options in the Select object is decreased and those at the end of the array disappear.

- If you set an element in the `options[]` array to `null`, that option is removed from the Select object and the elements above it in the array are moved down, changing their indices, to occupy the new space in the array.

- If you create a new Option object with the Option() constructor (see the Option reference entry), you can add that option to the end of list of options in the Select object by assigning the newly created option to a position at the end of the options[] array. To do this, set options[options.length].

See Also

Option

Select.selectedIndex — the selected option

Availability

Client-side JavaScript 1.0; writeable in JavaScript 1.1

Synopsis

```
select.selectedIndex
```

Description

The selectedIndex property of the Select object is an integer that specifies the index of the selected option within the Select object. If no option is selected, selectedIndex is –1. If more than one option is selected, selectedIndex specifies the index of the first one only.

In JavaScript 1.0, selectedIndex is a read-only property. In JavaScript 1.1, it is read/write: by setting the value of this property, you cause the specified option to become selected. You also cause all other options to become deselected, even if the Select object has the MULTIPLE attribute specified. When doing list-box style selection (instead of drop-down menu selection) you can deselect all options by setting selectedIndex to –1. Note that changing the selection in this way does not trigger the onchange() event handler.

Usage

When the MULTIPLE attribute is specified and selection of multiple options is allowed, the selectedIndex property is not very useful. In this case, to determine which options are selected, you should loop through the options[] array of the Select object and check the selected property of each Option object.

See Also

Option

Select.type — type of form element

Availability

Client-side JavaScript 1.1

Synopsis

```
select.type
```

Description

`type` is a read-only string property shared by all form elements; it specifies the type of the element. The Select object is unusual in that there are two possible values for the `type` property. If the Select object allows only a single selection (i.e., if the MULTIPLE attribute does not appear in the object's HTML definition), the value of the `type` property is "select-one". If the MULTIPLE attribute does appear, the value of the `type` attribute is "select-multiple".

See Also

Input.type,

---

self — see Window.self

---

setTimeout( ) — see Window.setTimeout( )

---

status — see Window.status

String — support for strings

Availability

Core JavaScript 1.0; enhanced in JavaScript 1.1, 1.2; ECMA-262

Constructor

```
new String(value)        JavaScript 1.1
```

Arguments

`value`   The initial value of the String object being created. This argument is converted to a string, if necessary.

Returns

A newly created String object that holds the string `value`, or the string representation of `value`.

Properties

`length`   The number of characters in the string.

Array Access

In Navigator 4, strings can be treated as if they were arrays. Each element of a string is the character at that position. So, for example, instead of writing `s.charAt(3)`, you could write `s[3]`. Note, however, that this behavior is not specified by ECMA-262 and is not portable.

Methods

anchor()   Return a copy of the string, in an <A NAME=> environment.

big()   Return a copy of the string, in a <BIG> environment.

blink()   Return a copy of the string, in a <BLINK> environment.

bold()   Return a copy of the string, in a <B> environment.

charAt()   Extract the character at a given position from a string.

charCodeAt()
                Return the encoding of the character at a given position in a string.

concat()   Concatenate one or more values to a string.

fixed()   Return a copy of the string, in a <TT> environment.

fontcolor()   Return a copy of the string, in a <FONT COLOR=> environment.

fontsize()   Return a copy of the string, in a <FONT SIZE=> environment.

indexOf()   Search the string for a character or substring.

italics()   Return a copy of the string, in a <I> environment.

lastIndexOf()
                Search the string backwards for a character or substring.

link()   Return a copy of the string, in a <A HREF=> environment.

match()   Perform pattern matching with a regular expression.

replace()   Perform a search-and-replace operation with a regular expression.

search()   Search a string for a substring that matches a regular expression.

slice()   Return a slice or substring of a string.

small()   Return a copy of the string, in a <SMALL> environment.

split()   Split a string into an array of strings, breaking at a specified delimiter string or regular expression.

strike()   Return a copy of the string, in a <STRIKE> environment.

sub()   Return a copy of the string, in a <SUB> environment.

substring()   Extract a substring of a string.

substr()   Extract a substring of a string. A variant of substring().

sup()   Return a copy of the string, in a <SUP> environment.

toLowerCase()
                Return a copy of the string, with all characters converted to lowercase.

toUpperCase()
                Return a copy of the string, with all characters converted to uppercase.

Static Methods

```
String.fromCharCode()
```
Create a new string using the character codes passed as arguments.

Description

Strings are a basic data type in JavaScript. The String object type exists to provide methods for operating on string values. The `length` property of a String object specifies the number of characters in the string. The String class defines a number of methods, many of which simply make a copy of the string with HTML tags added before and after. Other methods, however, perform more interesting functions: extracting a character or a substring from the string or searching for a character or a substring, for example.

Example

A number of the String methods are used for creating HTML:

```
link_text = "My Home Page".bold();
document.write(link_text.link("http://www.djf.com/~david"));
```

The code above embeds the following string into the HTML document that is currently being parsed:

```
<A HREF="http://www.djf.com/~david"><B>My Home Page</B></A>
```

Other methods of the String object perform more interesting functions. The following code, for example, extracts the third through fifth characters of a string and converts them to uppercase letters:

```
s.substring(2,5).toUpperCase();
```

See Also

Chapter 3, *Data Types and Values*

String.anchor() — add an HTML anchor to a string

Availability

Core JavaScript 1.0

Synopsis

```
string.anchor(name)
```

Arguments

name   The value of the NAME attribute of the HTML <A> tag—the name of the anchor to be created.

Returns

A copy of *string*, enclosed within <A NAME="*name*"> and </A> HTML tags.

String.big() — make a string <BIG>

Availability

Core JavaScript 1.0

Synopsis

```
string.big()
```

Returns

A copy of *string*, enclosed within <BIG> and </BIG> HTML tags.

String.blink() — make a string <BLINK>

Availability

Core JavaScript 1.0

Synopsis

```
string.blink()
```

Returns

A copy of *string*, enclosed within <BLINK> and </BLINK> HTML tags.

String.bold() — make a string bold with <B>

Availability

Core JavaScript 1.0

Synopsis

```
string.bold()
```

Returns

A copy of *string*, enclosed within <B> and </B> HTML tags.

String.charAt() — get the *n*th character from a string

Availability

Core JavaScript 1.0; ECMA-262

Synopsis

```
string.charAt(n)
```

Arguments

n   The index of the character that should be returned from *string*.

Returns

The *n*th character of *string*.

Description

String.charAt( ) returns the *n*th character of the string *string*. The first character of the string is numbered 0. If *n* is not between 0 and *string.length*–1, this method returns an empty string. Note that JavaScript does not have a character data type that is distinct from the string type, so the returned character is a string of length 1.

See Also

String.charCodeAt( ), String.indexOf( ), String.lastIndexOf( )

String.charCodeAt( ) — get the *n*th character code from a string

Availability

Core JavaScript 1.2; ECMA-262

Synopsis

    string.charCodeAt(*n*)

Arguments

n   The index of the character whose encoding is to be returned.

Returns

The Unicode encoding of the *n*th character within *string*. This return value is a 16-bit integer between 0 and 65535.

Description

charCodeAt( ) is like charAt( ) except that it returns the character encoding at a specific location, rather than returning a substring that contains the character itself.

See String.fromCharCode( ) for a way to create a string from Unicode encodings.

Bugs

Navigator 4 does not have full support for 16-bit Unicode characters and strings.

See Also

String.charAt( ), String.fromCharCode( )

String.concat() — concatenate strings

Availability

Core JavaScript 1.2

Synopsis

```
string.concat(value, ...)
```

Arguments

`value, ...`   One or more values to be concatenated to `string`.

Returns

A new string that results from concatenating each of the arguments to `string`.

Description

`concat()` converts each of its arguments to a string (if necessary) and appends them, in order, to the end of `string`. It returns the resulting concatenation. Note that `string` itself is not modified.

`String.concat()` is an analog to `Array.concat()`. Note that it is often easier to use the + operator to perform string concatenation.

See Also

Array.concat()

String.fixed() — make a string fixed-width with < TT >

Availability

Core JavaScript 1.0

Synopsis

```
string.fixed()
```

Returns

A copy of `string`, enclosed within <TT> and </TT> HTML tags.

String.fontcolor() — set a string's color with <FONT>

Availability

Core JavaScript 1.0

Synopsis

```
string.fontcolor(color)
```

Arguments

color   A string that specifies the color name or value to be used as the value of the COLOR attribute in the <FONT> HTML tag.

Returns

A copy of *string*, contained within <FONT COLOR="*color*"> and </FONT> HTML tags.

String.fontsize() — set a string's font size with <FONT>

Availability

Core JavaScript 1.0

Synopsis

```
string.fontsize(size)
```

Arguments

size   An integer between 1 and 7 or a string that starts with a "+" or "–" sign followed by a digit between 1 and 7. If an integer is specified, it is an absolute font size specification. If a string beginning with "+" or "–" is specified, it is a font size specification that is relative to the <BASEFONT> font size.

Returns

A copy of *string*, contained within <FONT SIZE="*size*"> and </FONT> HTML tags.

String.fromCharCode() — create a string from character encodings

Availability

Core JavaScript 1.2; ECMA-262

Synopsis

```
String.fromCharCode(c1, c2, ...)
```

Arguments

c1, c2, ...

       Zero or more integers that specify the Unicode encodings of the characters in the string to be created.

Returns

A new string containing the specified characters.

Description

This static method provides a way to create a string by specifying the individual numeric Unicode encodings of its characters. Note that as a static method, fromCharCode() is a property of the String() constructor, and is not a method of strings or String objects.

String.charCodeAt() is a companion instance method that provides a way to obtain the encodings of the individual characters of a string.

Example

```
// Create the string "hello"
var s = String.fromCharCode(104, 101, 108, 108, 111);
```

Bugs

Navigator 4 does not have full support for 16-bit Unicode characters and strings.

See Also

String.charCodeAt( )

String.indexOf( ) — search a string

Availability

Core JavaScript 1.0; ECMA-262

Synopsis

```
string.indexOf(substring)
string.indexOf(substring, start)
```

Arguments

substring   The substring that is to be searched for within *string*.

start   An optional integer argument that specifies the position within *string* at which the search is to start. Legal values are 0 (the position of the first character in the string) to *string*.length-1 (the position of the last character in the string). If this argument is omitted, the search begins at the first character of the string.

Returns

The position of the first occurrence of *substring* within *string* that appears after the *start* position, if any, or -1 if no such occurrence is found.

Description

String.indexOf( ) searches the string *string* from beginning to end to see if it contains an occurrence of *substring*. The search begins at position *start* within *string*, or at the beginning of *string*, if *start* is not specified. If an occurrence of *substring* is found, String.indexOf( ) returns the position of the first character of the first occurrence of *substring* within *string*. Character positions within *string* are numbered starting with zero.

If no occurrence of *substring* is found within *string*, String.indexOf( ) returns -1.

Bugs

In Navigator 2 and 3, if *start* is greater than the length of *string*, indexOf( ) returns the empty string, rather than -1.

See Also

String.charAt( ), String.lastIndexOf( ), String.substring( )

String.italics( ) — make a string italic with <I>

Availability

Core JavaScript 1.0

Synopsis

```
string.italics()
```

Returns

A copy of *string*, enclosed within <I> and </I> HTML tags.

String.lastIndexOf( ) — search a string backwards

Availability

Core JavaScript 1.0; ECMA-262

Synopsis

```
string.lastIndexOf(substring)
string.lastIndexOf(substring, start)
```

Arguments

substring   The substring that is to be searched for within *string*.

start   An optional integer argument that specifies the position within *string* where the search is to start. Legal values are 0 (the position of the first character in the string) to *string*.length−1 (the position of the last character in the string). If this argument is omitted, the search begins at the last character of the string.

Returns

The position of the last occurrence of *substring* within *string* that appears before the *start* position, if any, or −1 if no such occurrence is found within *string*.

Description

String.lastIndexOf( ) searches the string from end to beginning to see if it contains an occurrence of *substring*. The search begins at position *start* within *string*, or at the end of *string* if *start* is not specified. If an occurrence of *substring* is found, String.lastIndexOf( ) returns the position of the first character of that occurrence. Since this method searches from end to beginning of the string, the first occurrence found is the last one in the string that occurs before the *start* position.

If no occurrence of *substring* is found, String.lastIndexOf( ) returns −1.

Note that although String.lastIndexOf( ) searches *string* from end to beginning, it still numbers character positions within *string* from the beginning. The first character of the string has position 0, and the last has position *string*.length−1.

See Also

String.charAt( ), String.indexOf( ), String.substring( )

String.length — the length of a string

Availability

Core JavaScript 1.0; ECMA-262

Synopsis

```
string.length
```

Description

The `String.length` property is a read-only integer that indicates the number of characters in the specified *string*. For any string *s*, the index of the last character is `s.length-1`.

String.link( ) — add a hypertext link to a string

Availability

Core JavaScript 1.0

Synopsis

```
string.link(href)
```

Arguments

href   The URL target of the hypertext link that is to be added to the string. This string argument specifies the value of the `HREF` attribute of the `<A>` HTML tag.

Returns

A copy of *string*, enclosed within `<A HREF="href">` and `</A>` HTML tags.

String.match( ) — find one or more regular expression matches

Availability

Core JavaScript 1.2

Synopsis

```
string.match(regexp)
```

Arguments

regexp   The RegExp object that specifies the pattern to be matched.

Returns

An array containing the results of the match. The contents of the array depend on whether *regexp* is a global RegExp with the g attribute. Details on this return value are given below.

Description

match() searches *string* for one or more matches of *regexp*. The behavior of this method depends significantly on whether *regexp* has the g attribute or not.

If *regexp* does not have the g attribute, match() searches *string* for a single match. If no match is found, match() returns null. Otherwise, it returns an array containing information about the match that it found. Element 0 of the array contains the matched text. The remaining elements contain the text that matched any parenthesized subexpressions within the array. In addition to these normal array elements, the returned array also has two object properties. The index property of the array specifies the character position within *string* of the start of the matched text. The input property of the returned array is a reference to *string*.

If *regexp* has the g flag, match() does a global search, searching *string* for all matching substrings. It returns null if no match is found, and it returns an array if one or more matches are found. The contents of this returned array are quite different for global matches, however. In this case, the array elements contain each of the matched substrings within *string*. The returned array does not have index or input properties in this case. Note that for global matches, match() does not provide information about parenthesized subexpressions in this case, nor does it specify where within *string* each match occurred. If you need to obtain this information for a global search, you can use RegExp.exec().

If replace() performs any replacements, it sets RegExp.leftContext, RegExp.rightContext, RegExp.$1 and various other static properties of the RegExp class to provide more information about the last replacement it made.

If match() finds any matches, it sets RegExp.leftContext, RegExp.rightContext, RegExp.$1 and various other static properties of the RegExp class to provide more information about the last match it found.

Example

The following global match finds all numbers within a string:

```
"1 plus 2 equals 3".match(/\d+/g)  // Returns ["1", "2", "3"]
```

The following non-global match uses a more complex regular expression with several parenthesized subexpressions. It matches a URL, and its subexpressions match the protocol, host, and path portions of the URL:

```
var url = /(\w+):\/\/([\w.]+)\/(\S*)/;
var text = "Visit my home page at http://www.isp.com/~david";
var result = text.match(url);
if (result != null) {
    var fullurl = result[0];    // Contains "http://www.isp.com/~david"
    var protocol = result[1];   // Contains "http"
    var host = result[2];       // Contains "www.isp.com"
    var path = result[3];       // Contains "~david"
}
```

See Also

RegExp, RegExp.exec( ), RegExp.test( ), String.replace( ), String.search( ), Chapter 10

String.replace( ) — replace substring(s) matching a regular expression

Availability

Core JavaScript 1.2

Synopsis

```
string.replace(regexp, replacement)
```

Arguments

regexp   The RegExp object that specifies the pattern to be replaced.

replacement   A string that specifies the replacement text. The dollar sign ($) has spe-
                 cial meaning within this replacement string, as described in the Descrip-
                 tion section.

Returns

A new string, with the first matches, or all matches, of *regexp* replaced with *replacement*.

Description

`replace( )` performs a search-and-replace operation on *string*. It searches *string* for substrings that match *regexp* and replaces them with *replacement*. If *regexp* has the global g
attribute specified, `replace( )` replaces all matching substrings. Otherwise, it replaces only
the first matching substring.

The $ character has special meaning within the *replacement* string. As shown in the fol-
lowing table, it indicates that a string derived from the pattern match is to be used in the
replacement. Note that if you want a dollar sign to appear literally in the *replacement*
string, you must escape it with backslashes: "\\$".

Characters	Replacement
$1, $2, ... $9	The text that matched the first through ninth parenthesized subexpression within *regexp*.
$+	The text that matched the last-parenthesized subexpression within *regexp*.
$&	The substring that matched *regexp*.
$`	The text to the left of the matched string.
$'	The string to the right of the matched text.
\\$	A literal dollar sign.

If `replace( )` performs any replacements, it sets `RegExp.leftContext`, `RegExp.rightCon-
text`, `RegExp.$1` and various other static properties of the **RegExp** class to provide more
information about the last replacement it made.

Example

To ensure that the capitalization of the word "JavaScript" is correct:

```
text.replace(/javascript/i, "JavaScript");
```

To convert a single name from "Doe, John" format to "John Doe" format:

```
name.replace(/(\w+)\s*,\s*(\w+)/, "$2 $1");
```

To replace all straight quotes with curly quotes:

```
text.replace(/"([^"]*)"/g, "``$1''");
```

See Also

RegExp, RegExp.exec(), RegExp.test(), String.match(), String.search(), Chapter 10

String.search() — search for a regular expression

Availability

Core JavaScript 1.2

Synopsis

```
string.search(regexp)
```

Arguments

regexp   The RegExp object to be searched for in *string*.

Returns

The position of the start of the first substring of *string* that matches *regexp*, or −1 if no match was found.

Description

search() looks for a substring matching *regexp* within *string* and returns the position of the first character of the matching substring, or −1 if no match was found.

search() does not do global matches; it always returns the position of the first match regardless of whether *regexp* has the g modifier set.

If search() finds a match for *regexp*, it sets RegExp.leftContext, RegExp.rightContext, RegExp.$1 and various other static properties of the RegExp class to provide more information about the match.

Example

```
var s = "JavaScript is fun";
s.search(/script/i)  // Returns 4
s.search(/a(.)a/)     // Returns 1, sets RegExp.$1 to "v"
```

See Also

RegExp, RegExp.exec( ), RegExp.test( ), String.match( ), String.replace( ), Chapter 10

String.slice() — extract a substring

Availability

Core JavaScript 1.2

Synopsis

```
string.slice(start, end)
```

Arguments

start   The string index where the slice is to begin. If negative, this argument specifies a position measured from the end of the string. That is, −1 indicates the last character, −2 indicates the second from last character, and so on.

end   The string index immediately after the end of the slice. If not specified, the slice includes all characters from *start* to the end of the string. If this argument is negative, it specifies a position measured from the end of the string.

Returns

A new string that contains all the characters of *string* from and including *start* and up to but not including *end*.

Description

slice( ) returns a string containing a slice, or substring, of *string*. It does not modify *string*.

The String methods slice( ), substring( ), and substr( ) all return specified portions of a string. slice( ) is more flexible than substring( ) because it allows negative argument values. slice( ) differs from substr( ) in that it specifies a substring with two character positions, while substr( ) uses one position and a length. Note also that String.slice( ) is an analog of Array.slice( ).

Example

```
var s = "abcdefg";
s.slice(0,4)     // Returns "abcd"
s.slice(2,4)     // Returns "cd"
s.slice(4)       // Returns "efg"
s.slice(3,-1)    // Returns "def"
s.slice(3,-2)    // Returns "de"
s.slice(-3,-1)   // Returns "ef" in Navigator, "abcdef" in IE 4
```

Bugs

Negative values for *start* do not work in Internet Explorer 4. Instead of specifying a character position measured from the end of the string, they specify character position 0.

See Also

Array.slice( ), String.substring( )

String.small() — make a string <SMALL>

Availability

Core JavaScript 1.0

Synopsis

```
string.small()
```

Returns

A copy of *string*, enclosed within <SMALL> and </SMALL> HTML tags.

String.split() — break a string into an array of strings

Availability

Core JavaScript 1.1; ECMA-262

Synopsis

```
string.split(delimiter);
```

Arguments

delimiter   The character, string, or, in JavaScript 1.2, the regular expression at which the *string* splits. If no delimiter is specified, the returned array has only one element, the string itself. If the delimiter is the empty string, *string* is split between every character.

Returns

An array of strings, created by splitting *string* into substrings at the boundaries specified by *delimiter*.

Description

The split( ) method creates and returns an array of substrings of the specified string. These substrings are created by splitting the string at every occurrence of the specified *delimiter*. The delimiter character or characters are not part of the returned substrings.

If no *delimiter* is specified, the string is not split at all, and the returned array contains only a single, unbroken string element. If the empty string is specified as the *delimiter*, each character in *string* becomes a separate element in the returned array.

In JavaScript 1.2, you can pass a regular expression as a delimiter. This allows more complex delimiters, such as /\S+/, which specifies a delimiter of one or more characters of whitespace.

Note that the `String.split()` method is the inverse of the `Array.join()` method.

Example

The `split()` method is most useful when you are working with highly structured strings. For example:

```
s = "1,2,3,4,5"
a = s.split(",");
```

Another common use of the `split()` method is to parse commands and similar strings by breaking them down into words delimited by spaces:

```
words = sentence.split(' ');
```

In JavaScript 1.2, this can be improved upon by using a regular expression as a delimiter:

```
words = sentence.split(/\s+/);
```

See Also

Array.join( ), RegExp, Chapter 10

String.strike() — strike out a string with <STRIKE>

Availability

Core JavaScript 1.0

Synopsis

```
string.strike()
```

Returns

A copy of *string*, enclosed within <STRIKE> and </STRIKE> HTML tags.

String.sub() — make a string a subscript with <SUB>

Availability

Core JavaScript 1.0

Synopsis

```
string.sub()
```

Returns

A copy of *string*, enclosed within _{and} HTML tags.

String.substr() — extract a substring

Availability

Core JavaScript 1.2

Synopsis

```
string.substr(start, length)
```

Arguments

start The start position of the substring. If this argument is negative, it specifies a position measured from the end of the string: –1 specifies the last character, –2 specifies the second-to-last character, and so on.

length The number of characters in the substring. If this argument is omitted, the returned substring includes all characters from the starting position to the end of the string.

Returns

A copy of the portion of *string* starting at and including the character specified by *start* and continuing for *length* characters, or to the end of the string, if *length* is not specified.

Description

substr() extracts and returns a substring of *string*. It does not modify *string*.

Note that substr() specifies the desired substring with a character position and a length. This provides a useful alternative to String.substring() and String.splice(), which specify a substring with two character positions.

Example

```
var s = "abcdefg";
s.substr(2,2);    // Returns "cd"
s.substr(3);      // Returns "defg"
s.substr(-3,2);   // Returns "ef" in Navigator and "ab" in IE 4
```

Bugs

Negative values for *start* do not work in Internet Explorer 4. Instead of specifying a character position measured from the end of the string, they specify character position 0.

See Also

String.slice( ), String.substring( )

String.substring() — return a substring of a string

Availability

Core JavaScript 1.0; ECMA-262

Synopsis

```
string.substring(from, to)
```

Arguments

from   An integer that specifies the position within *string* of the first character of the desired substring. *from* must be between 0 and `string.length-1`.

to   An optional integer that is one greater than the position within *string* of the last character of the desired substring. *to* must be between 1 and `string.length`.

Returns

A new string, of length `to-from`, which contains a substring of *string*. The new string contains characters copied from positions *from* to *to-1* of *string*.

Description

`String.substring()` returns the specified substring of *string*. If *from* equals *to*, `String.substring()` returns an empty (length 0) string. If *from* is greater than *to*, this method first swaps the two arguments before proceeding.

Usage

`String.substring()` can be a confusing function to use. It is important to remember that the character at position *from* is included in the substring, but that the character at position *to* is not included in the substring. One notable feature of assigning the arguments this way is that the length of the returned substring is always equal to *to-from*.

Often it is more convenient to extract a substring of a string by specifying the start character and the desired length of the substring. In JavaScript 1.2 you can use `String.substr()` to do this. JavaScript 1.2 also provides `String.slice()`, which is sometimes a more convenient method than `substring()`.

See Also

String.charAt( ), String.indexOf( ), String.lastIndexOf( ), String.slice( ), String.substr( )

String.sup() — make a string a superscript with <SUP>

Availability

Core JavaScript 1.0

Synopsis

```
string.sup()
```

Returns

A copy of *string*, enclosed within `<SUP>` and `</SUP>` HTML tags.

String.toLowerCase() — convert a string to lowercase

Availability

Core JavaScript 1.0; ECMA-262

Synopsis

```
string.toLowerCase()
```

Returns

A copy of *string*, with all uppercase letters converted to lowercase.

String.toUpperCase() — convert a string to uppercase

Availability

Core JavaScript 1.0; ECMA-262

Synopsis

```
string.toUpperCase()
```

Returns

A copy of *string*, with all lowercase letters converted to uppercase.

Style — cascading style sheet attributes

Availability

Client-side JavaScript 1.2

Synopsis

Navigator

```
document.classes.className.tagName
document.ids.elementName
document.tags.tagName
document.contextual(...)
```

Internet Explorer

```
htmlElement.style
```

Properties

The Style object has properties corresponding to each of the CSS attributes supported by the browser.

Navigator Methods

`borderWidths()`
            Specify all four border width properties.

`margins()`   Specify all four margin properties.

`paddings()`   Specify all four padding properties.

Description

The properties of the Style object correspond to the attributes of a cascading style sheet (CSS) and specify values for those attributes. Although both Navigator 4 and IE 4 support CSS and the Style object, they define entirely different ways to refer to Style objects. See Chapter 17 for details.

The properties of the Style object correspond directly to the CSS attributes supported by the browser. For compatibility with JavaScript syntax, however, hyphenated CSS attribute names are written with mixed capitalization with the hyphen removed. So, for example, the CSS `color` attribute is represented by the `color` property of the Style object, while the CSS `background-color` attribute is represented by the `backgroundColor` property of the Style object.

The CSS standard defines a large number of attributes, and the emerging CSS-2 standard defines an even larger number. A complete discussion of CSS attributes, their values, and their effects on document style is beyond the scope of this book. Therefore, complete coverage of the properties of the Style object is also beyond the scope of this book. However, the following lists give the Style properties documented by Netscape and by Microsoft. New properties will undoubtedly be added to these lists as the browsers improve their support for CSS and as the CSS-2 standard is finalized. Note that in addition to the properties listed below, the Navigator 4 Style object also defines three convenience methods, `border-Widths()`, `margins()`, and `paddings()`, which are documented in separate reference entries.

The following list gives Style properties for Navigator 4:

backgroundColor	clear	listStyleType	paddingTop
backgroundImage	color	marginBottom	textAlign
borderBottomWidth	display	marginLeft	textDecoration
borderColor	fontFamily	marginRight	textIndent
borderLeftWidth	fontSize	marginTop	textTransform
borderRightWidth	fontStyle	paddingBottom	whiteSpace
borderStyle	fontWeight	paddingLeft	
borderTopWidth	lineHeight	paddingRight	

The following list gives Style properties for Internet Explorer 4:

background	borderWidth	overflow
background-Attachment	clear	paddingBottom
backgroundColor	clip	paddingLeft

```
backgroundImage          color              paddingRight
backgroundPosition       cssText            paddingTop
backgroundPositionX      cursor             pageBreakAfter
backgroundPositionY      display            pageBreakBefore
backgroundRepeat         filter             pixelHeight
border                   font               pixelLeft
borderBottom             fontFamily         pixelTop
borderBottomColor        fontSize           pixelWidth
borderBottomStyle        fontStyle          posHeight
borderBottomWidth        fontVariant        position
borderColor              fontWeight         posLeft
borderLeft               height             posTop
borderLeftColor          left               posWidth
borderLeftStyle          letterSpacing      styleFloat
borderLeftWidth          lineHeight         textAlign
borderRight              listStyle          textDecoration
borderRightColor         listStyleImage     textIndent
borderRightStyle         listStylePosition  textTransform
borderRightWidth         listStyleType      top
borderStyle              margin             verticalAlign
borderTop                marginBottom       visibility
borderTopColor           marginLeft         width
borderTopStyle           marginRight        zIndex
borderTopWidth           marginTop
```

See Also

Chapter 17

Style.borderWidths() — set all border width properties

Availability

Client-side Navigator 4

Synopsis

```
style.borderWidths(top, right, bottom, left)
```

Arguments

top   A string specifying the `borderTopWidth` property.

right   A string specifying the `borderRightWidth` property.

bottom   A string specifying the `borderBottomWidth` property.

left   A string specifying the `borderLeftWidth` property.

Description

`borderWidths()` is a convenience method that sets the values of all four border width properties of *style*.

Style.margins() — set all margin properties

Availability

Client-side Navigator 4

Synopsis

```
style.margins(top, right, bottom, left)
```

Arguments

`top`	A string specifying the `marginTop` property.
`right`	A string specifying the `marginRight` property.
`bottom`	A string specifying the `marginBottom` property.
`left`	A string specifying the `marginLeft` property.

Description

`margins()` is a convenience method that sets the values of all four margin properties of *style*.

Style.paddings() — set all padding properties

Availability

Client-side Navigator 4

Synopsis

```
style.paddings(top, right, bottom, left)
```

Arguments

`top`	A string specifying the `paddingTop` property.
`right`	A string specifying the `paddingRight` property.
`bottom`	A string specifying the `paddingBottom` property.
`left`	A string specifying the `paddingLeft` property.

Description

`paddings()` is a convenience method that sets the values of all four padding properties of *style*.

Submit — a button to submit a form

Availability
Client-side JavaScript 1.0; enhanced in JavaScript 1.1

Inherits From
Input, HTMLElement

Synopsis
```
form.name
form.elements[i]
form.elements['name']
```

Properties
Submit inherits properties from Input and HTMLElement and defines or overrides the following:

value   A read-only string, set by the HTML VALUE attribute, that specifies the text to appear in the button. If no VALUE is specified, (in Navigator) the button is labelled "Submit Query" by default.

Methods
Submit inherits the methods from Input and HTMLElement.

Event Handlers
Submit inherits event handlers from Input and HTMLElement and defines or overrides the following:

onclick   Invoked when the **Submit** button is clicked.

HTML Syntax
A Submit object is created with a standard HTML <INPUT> tag:

```
<FORM>
    ...
  <INPUT
    TYPE="submit"              Specifies that this is a Submit button
    [ VALUE="label" ]          The text that is to appear within the button
                               Specifies the value property
    [ NAME="name" ]            A name that can later be used to refer to the button
                               Specifies the name property
    [ onClick="handler" ]      JavaScript statements to be executed when the button is clicked
  >
    ...
</FORM>
```

Description

The Submit element has the same properties and methods as the Button object, but has a more specialized purpose. When a **Submit** button is clicked, it submits the data in the form that contains the button to the server specified by the form's ACTION attribute and loads the resulting HTML page sent back by that server. In JavaScript 1.1, the exception is that the form is not submitted if either of the Submit.onclick or Form.onsubmit event handlers return false.

Note that in JavaScript 1.1 the Form.submit() method provides an alternative way to submit a form.

If no VALUE attribute is specified for a Submit object, it is typically labelled "Submit Query". In some forms, it may make more sense to label the button "Submit" or "Done" or "Send".

See Also

Button, Form.onsubmit, Form.submit( ), HTMLElement, Input

Submit.onclick — invoked when a Submit button is clicked

Availability

Client-side JavaScript 1.0; enhanced in JavaScript 1.1

Synopsis

```
<INPUT TYPE="submit" onClick="handler" ... >
submit.onclick
```

Description

The onclick property of a Submit object refers to an event handler function that is invoked when the user clicks on the **Submit** button. See HTMLElement.onclick for complete details. Note, however, that Submit.onclick has been supported since JavaScript 1.0, unlike the generalized HTMLElement.onclick handler.

The **Submit** button has the special function of submitting the form to a server. The onclick event handler may add any additional functionality to the **Submit** button. In JavaScript 1.1 the onclick handler may return false to prevent the Submit object from submitting the form. (For example, the onclick handler could perform form validation and return false if required fields in the form were not filled in.)

See Also

Form.onsubmit, Form.submit( ), HTMLElement.onclick

Submit.value — the label of a Submit button

Availability

Client-side JavaScript 1.0

Synopsis

```
submit.value
```

Description

The `value` property is a read-only string that specifies the text that appears within the **Submit** button. It is specified by the `VALUE` attribute of the `<INPUT>` tag that created the button. If no `VALUE` attribute is specified, the default `value` (for English-language browsers) is Submit Query.

---

sun — the sun.* Java package

Availability

Client-side Navigator 3

Synopsis

```
sun
```

Description

`sun` is a synonym for `Packages.sun`, and contains a reference to a JavaPackage object that represents the top node of the *sun.*Java package name hierarchy.

See Also

JavaPackage, Packages.sun

---

taint() — taint a value or window

Availability

Available experimentally in client-side Navigator 3; deprecated in Navigator 4

Synopsis

```
taint()
taint(value)
```

Arguments

value   The value for which a tainted copy is to be made. If this argument is not specified, `taint()` adds taint to the current window instead.

Returns

A tainted copy of *value*, if it is a primitive data type, or a tainted reference to *value*, if it is an object type.

Description

Data tainting was a security model available on an experimental basis in Navigator 3. The experiment proved unsuccessful and it was removed in Navigator 4. `taint()` is a deprecated function used in conjunction with that model. Data tainting is not documented in this book.

Text — a graphical text input field

Availability

Client-side JavaScript 1.0; enhanced in JavaScript 1.1

Inherits From

Input, HTMLElement

Synopsis

```
form.name
form.elements[i]
```

Properties

Text inherits properties from Input and HTMLElement and defines or overrides the following:

value   A read/write string that specifies the value contained in the input field (which is also the value sent to the server when the form is submitted). The initial value of this property is specified by the VALUE attribute.

Methods

Text inherits the methods of Input and HTMLElement.

Event Handlers

Text inherits the event handlers of Input and HTMLElement and defines or overrides the following:

onchange   Invoked when the user changes the value in the Text element and moves the keyboard focus elsewhere. This event handler is not invoked for every keystroke in the Text element, but only when the user completes an edit.

HTML Syntax

A Text element is created with a standard HTML <INPUT> tag:

```
<FORM>
    ...
  <INPUT
    TYPE="text"                   Specifies that this is a Text element
    [ NAME="name" ]               A name that can later be used to refer to this element
                                  Specifies the name property
    [ VALUE="default" ]           The default value transmitted when the form is submitted
                                  Specifies the defaultValue property
    [ SIZE=integer ]              How many characters wide the element is
    [ MAXLENGTH=integer ]         Maximum allowed number of input characters
    [ onChange="handler" ]        The onchange() event handler
  >
    ...
</FORM>
```

Description

The Text element represents a text input field in a form. The SIZE attribute specifies the width, in characters, of the input field as it appears on the screen, and the MAXLENGTH attribute specifies the maximum number of characters the user is allowed to enter.

Besides these HTML attributes, value is the main property of interest for the Text element. You can read this property to obtain the user's input, or you can set it to display arbitrary (unformatted) text in the input field.

Usage

Use the Password element instead of the Text element when the value you are asking the user to enter is sensitive information, such as a password that should not be displayed openly on the screen. Use a Textarea element to allow the user to enter multiple lines of text.

When a form contains only one Text or Password element, the form is automatically submitted if the user strikes the **Return** key in that Text or Password element. In many forms, this is a useful shortcut. In some, however, it can be confusing if the user strikes **Return** and submits the form before entering input into other form elements such as Checkboxes and Radio buttons. You can sometimes minimize this confusion by placing Text elements with their default submission action at the bottom of the form.

See Also

Form, Input, Password, Textarea

Text.onchange — the handler invoked when input value changes

Availability

Client-side JavaScript 1.0

Synopsis

```
<INPUT TYPE=text onChange="handler" ... >
text.onchange
```

Description

The onchange property of a Text element refers to an event handler function that is invoked when the user changes the value in the input field and then "commits" those changes by moving keyboard focus elsewhere (i.e., by clicking the mouse elsewhere or by typing the **Tab** or **Return** keys).

Note that the onchange event handler is *not* invoked when the value property of a Text object is set by JavaScript. Also, note that this handler is intended to process a complete change to the input value, and therefore is not invoked on a keystroke-by-keystroke basis. See HTMLElement.onkeypress for information on receiving notification of every key press event.

See Input.onchange for complete details about the onchange event handler.

See Also

HTMLElement.onkeypress, Input.onchange

Text.value — user input to the Text object

Availability

Client-side JavaScript 1.0

Synopsis

```
text.value
```

Description

value is a read/write string property of the Text object. The initial value of value is specified by the VALUE attribute of the <INPUT> tag that defines the Text object. When the user types characters into the Text object, the value property is updated to match the user's input. If you set the value property explicitly, the string you specify is displayed in the Text object. This value property contains the string that is sent to the server when the form is submitted.

Textarea — a multiline text input area

Availability

Client-side JavaScript 1.0; enhanced in JavaScript 1.1

Inherits From

Input, HTMLElement

Synopsis

```
form.name
form.elements[i]
```

Properties

Textarea inherits the properties of Input and HTMLElement and defines or overrides the following:

value   A read/write string that specifies the value contained in the Textarea (which is also the value sent to the server when the form is submitted). The initial value of this property is the same as the defaultValue property.

Methods

Textarea inherits the methods of Input and HTMLElement.

Event Handlers

Textarea inherits the event handlers of Input and HTMLElement and defines or overrides the following:

onchange   Invoked when the user changes the value in the Textarea element and moves the keyboard focus elsewhere. This event handler is not invoked for every keystroke in the Textarea element, but only when the user completes an edit.

HTML Syntax

A Textarea element is created with standard HTML <TEXTAREA> and </TEXTAREA> tags:

```
<FORM>
    . . .
   <TEXTAREA
     [ NAME="name" ]                        A name that can be used to refer to this element
     [ ROWS=integer ]                       How many lines tall the element is
     [ COLS=integer ]                       How many characters wide the element is
     [ WRAP=off|virtual|physical ]          How word wrapping is handled
     [ onChange="handler" ]                 The onchange() event handler
   >
     plain_text                             The initial text; specifies defaultValue
   </TEXTAREA>
    . . .
</FORM>
```

Description

The Textarea element represents a text input field in a form. The NAME attribute specifies a name for the element. This is mandatory if the form is to be submitted, and it also provides a convenient way to refer to the Textarea element from JavaScript code. The COLS attribute specifies the width, in characters, of the element as it appears on the screen, and the ROWS attribute specifies the height, in lines of text, of the element. The WRAP attribute specifies how long lines should be handled: the value off specifies that they should be left as is; the value virtual specifies that they should be displayed with line breaks but transmitted without; and the value physical specifies that they should be displayed and transmitted with line breaks inserted.

Besides these HTML attributes, value is the main property of interest for the Textarea element. You can read this property to obtain the user's input, or you can set it to display arbitrary (unformatted) text in the Textarea. The initial value of the value property (and the permanent value of the defaultValue property) is the text that appears between the <TEXTAREA> and </TEXTAREA> tags.

Note that the Textarea object is a kind of Input object and inherits from Input, despite the fact that Textarea objects are not created with HTML <INPUT> tags.

Usage

If you need only a single line of input text, use the Text element. If the text to be input is sensitive information, such as a password, use the Password element.

See Also

Form, HTMLElement, Input, Password, Text

Textarea.onchange — the handler invoked when input value changes

Availability

Client-side JavaScript 1.0

Synopsis

```
<TEXTAREA onchange="handler" ... >
    . . .
</TEXTAREA>
textarea.onchange
```

Description

The `onchange` property of a Textarea element refers to an event handler function that is invoked when the user changes the value in the text area and then "commits" those changes by moving keyboard focus elsewhere.

Note that the `onchange` event handler is *not* invoked when the `value` property of a Text object is set by JavaScript. Also, note that this handler is intended to process a complete change to the input value, and therefore is not invoked on a keystroke-by-keystroke basis. See `HTMLElement.onkeypress` for information on receiving notification of every key press event.

See `Input.onchange` for complete details about the `onchange` event handler.

See Also

HTMLElement.onkeypress, Input.onchange

Textarea.value — user input to the Textarea object

Availability

Client-side JavaScript 1.0

Synopsis

```
textarea.value
```

Description

`value` is a read/write string property of the Textarea object. The initial value of `value` is the same as the `defaultValue` property—the plain text (i.e., without any HTML tags) that appears between the `<TEXTAREA>` and `</TEXTAREA>` tags. When the user types characters into the Textarea object, the `value` property is updated to match the user's input. If you set the `value` property explicitly, the string you specify is displayed in the Textarea object. This `value` property contains the string that is sent to the server when the form is submitted.

Bugs

In Navigator 2, the Textarea object required the use of platform-specific newline characters or newline sequences. Thus, appending the "\n" character (newline character for Unix) to the `value` property of a Textarea object would not actually start a new line on Windows platforms (which use a sequence of "\r\n" to delimit lines), for example. As of Navigator 3, this problem has been resolved—any newline character or sequence is automatically mapped to the correct platform-specific sequence.

To work around the bug on Navigator 2 platforms, you'll need a variable that contains the platform-specific newline sequence. One easy way to obtain such a newline variable is to create your Textarea element with a default value which consists of a single blank line. Then you can copy the `defaultValue` property of this element; it contains the newline sequence required on the current platform.

top — see Window.top

unescape() — decode an escaped string

Availability

Core JavaScript 1.0; ECMA-262; Unicode support in Internet Explorer 4

Synopsis

```
unescape(s)
```

Arguments

s   The string that is to be decoded or "unescaped."

Returns

A decoded copy of s.

Description

The `unescape()` function is a built-in part of JavaScript; it is not a method of any object.

`unescape()` decodes a string encoded with `escape()`. It creates and returns a decoded copy of s. It decodes s by finding and replacing character sequences of the form %*xx*, where *xx* is two hexadecimal digits. Each such sequence is replaced by the single character represented by the hexadecimal digits in the Latin-1 encoding.

Thus, `unescape()` decodes the string:

```
Hello%20World%21
```

to:

```
Hello World!
```

In IE 4, `unescape()` can decode Unicode characters encoded in the format %u*xxxx*.

See `escape()` for more information on this encoding and decoding technique.

See Also

escape(), String

untaint() — untaint a value or window

Availability

Available experimentally in client-side Navigator 3; deprecated in Navigator 4.

Synopsis

```
untaint()
untaint(value)
```

Arguments

value   The value for which a non-tainted copy is to be made. If this argument is not specified, untaint() removes taint from the current window instead.

Returns

An untainted copy of value, if it is a primitive data type, or an untainted reference to value, if it is an object type.

Description

Data tainting was a security model available on an experimental basis in Navigator 3. The experiment proved unsuccessful, and it was removed in Navigator 4. untaint() is a deprecated function used in conjunction with that model. Data tainting is not documented in this book.

URL — see Link, Location, or Document.URL

---

window — see Window.window

Window — a web browser window or frame

Availability

Client-side JavaScript 1.0; enhanced in JavaScript 1.1 and 1.2

Synopsis

```
self
window
window.frames[i]
```

Properties

The Window object defines the following properties. Non-portable, browser-specific properties are listed separately after this list:

closed   A read-only boolean that specifies whether a window has been closed. Added in JavaScript 1.1.

defaultStatus
            A read/write string that specifies the default message to appear in the status line.

document   A reference to the Document object contained in the window.

frames[]   An array of frames contained by this window.

history   A reference to the History object for this window.

length   The number of elements in the frames[] array. Same as frames.length. Read-only.

location   A reference to the Location object for this window.

Math   A reference to an object holding various mathematical functions and constants.

name   A string that contains the name of the window. The name is optionally specified when the window is created with the open() method. Read-only in JavaScript 1.0; read/write in JavaScript 1.1.

navigator   A reference to the Navigator object that applies to this and all other windows.

offscreenBuffering
              Specifies the type of buffering performed by the browser.

opener   A read/write property that refers to the Window object that called open() to create this window. Available in JavaScript 1.1 and later.

parent   A reference to the parent window or frame of the current window. Only useful when the current window is a frame rather than a top-level window.

screen   A reference to the Screen object of the window.

self   A reference to the window itself. A synonym of window.

status   A read/write string that specifies the current contents of the status line.

top   A reference to the top-level window that contains the current window. Only useful when the current window is a frame rather than a top-level window.

window   A reference to the window itself. A synonym of self.

Navigator Properties

crypto   A reference to the Crypto object that contains cryptographic methods.

innerHeight   The height of the document display area of the window.

innerWidth   The width of the document display area of the window.

java   A reference to the JavaPackage object that is the top of the package name hierarchy for the core *java.** packages that comprise the Java language.

locationbar   Controls the visibility of the location bar.

menubar   Controls the visibility of the menubar.

netscape   A reference to the JavaPackage object which is the top of the Java package name hierarchy for the *netscape.** Java packages from Netscape.

outerHeight   The full height of the window.

outerWidth   The full width of the window.

Packages   A reference to a JavaPackage object that represents the top of the Java package name hierarchy.

pageXOffset   The horizontal scrolling position.

pageYOffset   The vertical scrolling position.

personalbar   Controls the visibility of the "personal bar."

screenX   The X-coordinate of the window on the screen.

screenY   The Y-coordinate of the window on the screen.

scrollbars   Controls the visibility of the scrollbars.

statusbar   Controls the visibility of the status line.

sun   A reference to the JavaPackage object which is the top of the Java package name hierarchy for the *sun.** Java packages from Sun Microsystems.

toolbar   Controls the visibility of the toolbar.

Internet Explorer Properties

clientInformation

A more appropriate name for the navigator property.

event   A reference to the Event object of the most recent event.

Methods

The Window object has the following portable methods. Non-portable, browser-specific methods are listed separately after this list:

alert( )   Display a simple message in a dialog box.

blur( )   Take keyboard focus from the top-level browser window; this sends the window to the background on most platforms.

clearInterval

Cancel periodic execution of code.

clearTimeout( )

Cancel a pending timeout operation.

close( )   Close a window.

confirm( )   Ask a yes-or-no question with a dialog box.

focus( )   Give the top-level browser window keyboard focus; this brings the window to the front on most platforms.

moveBy( )   Move the window by a relative amount.

moveTo( )	Move the window to an absolute position.
open( )	Create and open a new window.
prompt( )	Ask for simple string input with a dialog box.
resizeBy( )	Resize the window by a specified amount.
resizeTo( )	Resize the window to a specified size.
scroll( )	Scroll the document displayed in the window.
scrollBy	Scroll the window by a specified amount.
scrollTo( )	Scroll the window to a specified position.

setInterval( )
Execute code at periodic intervals.

setTimeout( )
Execute code after a specified amount of time elapses.

Navigator Methods

atob( )	Decode base-64 encoded data.
back( )	Behave as if the user clicked the **Back** button.
btoa( )	Encode binary data into a base-64 ASCII string.

captureEvents( )
Specify event types to be routed directly to the window.

disableExternalCapture( )
Disable capturing of events from other windows.

enableExternalCapture( )
Enable capturing of events from other windows.

find( )	Simulate a click on the browser's **Find** button.
forward( )	Simulate a click on the browser's **Forward** button.
handleEvent	Invoke the appropriate event handler for a given Event object.
home( )	Display the browser's home page.
print( )	Simulate a click on the browser's **Print** button.

releaseEvents( )
Specify types of events that are no longer to be captured.

routeEvent( )
Pass an Event to the appropriate handler of the next interested object.

setHotkeys( )
Turn keyboard shortcuts on or off.

`setResizable()`
> Specify whether the user can resize the window.

`setZOptions()`
> Specify window stacking behavior.

`stop()`   Simulate a click on the browser's **Stop** button.

Internet Explorer Methods

`navigate()`   Load and display the specified URL.

Event Handlers

`onblur`   Invoked when the window loses focus.

`ondragdrop`   Invoked when the user drops an object on the browser. Navigator 4 only.

`onerror`   Invoked when a JavaScript error occurs.

`onfocus`   Invoked when the window gains focus.

`onload`   Invoked when the document (or frameset) is fully loaded.

`onmove`   Invoked when the window is moved. Navigator 4 only.

`onresize`   Invoked when the window is resized.

`onunload`   Invoked when the browser leaves the current document or frameset.

Description

The Window object represents a browser window or frame. It is documented in detail in Chapter 13, *Windows and Frames*.

In client-side JavaScript, the Window serves as the "global object", and all expressions are evaluated in the context of the current Window object. This means that no special syntax is required to refer to the current window, and you can use the properties of that window object as if they were global variables. For example, you can write `document` rather than `window.document`. Similarly, you can use the methods of the current window object as if they were functions: `alert()` instead of `window.alert()`.

The Window object does have `window` and `self` properties that refer to the window object itself. You can use these when you want to make the current window reference explicit rather than implicit. In addition to these two properties, the `parent` and `top` properties and the `frames[]` array refer to other Window objects related to the current one.

To refer to a frame within a window, use:

```
frames[i] or self.frames[i]          Frames of current window
window.frames[i]                     Frames of specified window
```

To refer to the parent window (or frame) of a frame, use:

```
parent or self.parent                Parent of current window
window.parent                        Parent of specified window
```

To refer to the top-level browser window from any frame contained within it, use:

`top` *or* `self.top`	*Top window of current frame*
`window.top`	*Top window of specified frame*

New top-level browser windows are created with the `Window.open()` method. When you call this method, save the return value of the `open()` call in a variable, and use that variable to reference the new window. In JavaScript 1.1, the `opener` property of the new window is a reference back to the window that opened it.

In general, the methods of the Window object manipulate the browser window or frame in some way. The `alert()`, `confirm()` and `prompt()` methods are notable: they interact with the user through simple dialog boxes.

See Chapter 13 for an in-depth overview of the Window object, and see the individual reference pages for complete details on all the Window properties, methods, and event handlers.

See Also

Document, Chapter 13

Window.alert() — display a message in a dialog box

Availability

Client-side JavaScript 1.0

Synopsis

```
window.alert(message)
```

Arguments

message   The plain text (not HTML) string to display in a dialog box popped up over *window*.

Description

The `alert()` method displays the specified *message* to the user in a dialog box. The dialog box contains an **Ok** button that the user can click to dismiss the dialog box.

On Windows platforms, the dialog box displayed by `alert()` is modal, and JavaScript execution pauses until the user dismisses it. In Navigator on Unix platforms, however, the `alert()` dialog box is non-modal, and execution continues uninterrupted.

Usage

Perhaps the most common use of the `alert()` method is to display error messages when the user's input to some form element is invalid in some way. The alert dialog can inform the user of the problem and explain what needs to be corrected to avoid the problem in the future. The appearance of the `alert()` dialog box is platform-dependent, but generally it contains graphics that indicate an error, warning, or alert message of some kind. While `alert()` can display any desired message, the alert graphics of the dialog mean that this method is not appropriate for simple informational messages like: "Welcome to my home page" or "You are the 177th visitor this week!"

Note that the *message* displayed in the dialog is a string of plain text, not formatted HTML. You can use the newline character "\n" in your strings to break your message across multiple lines. You can also do some very rudimentary formatting using spaces and can approximate horizontal rules with underscore characters, but the results you achieve depend greatly on the font used in the dialog, and are thus system-dependent.

In Navigator, the message displayed is prefaced with "JavaScript Alert:". The alert box in IE does not indicate that the message comes from a JavaScript program; this has been raised as a possible security concern.

See Also

Window.confirm( ), Window.prompt( )

Window.atob( ) — decode base-64 encoded data

Availability

Client-side Navigator 4

Synopsis

```
window.atob(str64)
```

Arguments

str64   An ASCII string of base-64 encoded data to be decoded.

Returns

A string of binary data.

Description

`atob( )` decodes a base-64 encoded string and returns the decoded value as a string. Each character of the string represents one byte of binary data. This data can be retrieved with `String.charCodeAt( )`.

See Also

String.charCodeAt( ), Window.btoa( )

Window.back( ) — go back to previous document

Availability

Client-side Navigator 4

Synopsis

```
window.back()
```

Description

Calling `back( )` makes the browser display the document previously displayed in *window*, exactly as if the user had clicked on the window's **Back** button.

Note that for framed documents, there may be differences between the behavior of `Window.back( )` and `History.back( )`.

Window.blur() — remove keyboard focus from a top-level window

Availability

Client-side JavaScript 1.1

Synopsis

```
window.blur()
```

Description

The blur() method removes keyboard focus from the top-level browser window specified by the Window object. If the Window object is a frame, keyboard focus is given to the top-level window that contains that frame. On most platforms, a top-level window is sent to the background (to the bottom of the window stack) when it has focus taken from it.

See Also

Window.focus()

Window.btoa() — encode binary data using base-64 ASCII encoding

Availability

Client-side Navigator 4

Synopsis

```
window.btoa(data)
```

Arguments

data   A string of binary data to be encoded. Each character of this string contains one byte of data.

Returns

A new string containing the base-64 encoded version of *data*.

Description

btoa() encodes a string of binary *data* using base-64 encoding and returns the encoded string. Each character of *data* represents one byte of binary data, and *data* should really be considered an array of bytes rather than a string of characters. The base-64 encoded string returned by btoa() contains only valid ASCII characters.

Note that binary data can be encoded into a string with String.fromCharCode().

See Also

String.fromCharCode(), Window.atob()

Window.captureEvents() — specify event types to be captured

Availability

Client-side Navigator 4

Synopsis

```
window.captureEvents(eventmask)
document.captureEvents(eventmask)
layer.captureEvents(eventmask)
```

Arguments

eventmask   An integer that specifies the type of events that the window, document, or layer should capture. This value should be one of the static event type constants defined by the Event class, or should be a group of event type constants combined with the bitwise-OR (|) or addition operators.

Description

captureEvents() is a method of the Window, Document, and Layer classes. Its purpose is the same for all three: in the Navigator 4 event model, it specifies that all events of a given type or types occurring within the specified *window*, *document*, or *layer* should be passed to the window, document, or layer instead of to the object on which they actually occurred.

The type of the events to be captured is specified by *eventmask*, a bitmask comprised of static constants defined by the Event class. See Event.*TYPE* for a full list of these bitmask constants.

See Also

Window.handleEvent(), Window.releaseEvents(), Window.routeEvent(), Event.TYPE, Chapter 15

Window.clearInterval() — stop periodically executing code

Availability

Client-side JavaScript 1.2

Synopsis

```
window.clearInterval(intervalId)
```

Arguments

intervalId   The value returned by the corresponding call to setInterval().

Description

clearInterval() stops the repeated execution of code that was started by a call to set-Interval(). The *intervalId* argument must be the value that was returned by a call to setInterval().

See Also

Window.setInterval( )

Window.clearTimeout( ) — cancel deferred execution

Availability

Client-side JavaScript 1.0

Synopsis

```
window.clearTimeout(timeoutId)
```

Arguments

timeoutId   A value returned by setTimeout() that identifies the timeout to be canceled.

Description

The clearTimeout() method cancels the execution of code that has been deferred with the setTimeout() method. The *timeoutId* argument is a value returned by the call to setTimeout() and identifies which (of possibly more than one) block of deferred code to cancel.

See Also

Window.setTimeout( )

Window.clientInformation — synonym for Window.navigator

Availability

Client-side Internet Explorer 4

Synopsis

```
window.clientInformation
clientInformation
```

Description

The clientInformation property is an IE 4 synonym for the navigator property. Both refer to a Navigator object.

Despite the fact that clientInformation has a better name and is less Navigator-specific than navigator, it is not supported by Navigator and is therefore not portable.

See Also

navigator, Navigator

Window.close() — close a browser window

Availability

Client-side JavaScript 1.0

Synopsis

```
window.close()
```

Description

The `close()` method closes the top-level browser window specified by *window*. A window can close itself by calling `self.close()` or simply `close()`.

In JavaScript 1.1, only windows that are opened by JavaScript can be closed by JavaScript. This prevents malicious scripts from causing the user's browser to exit.

There is no meaningful way to close a frame within a window. Thus, the `close()` method should only be invoked for Window objects that represent top-level browser windows, not those that represent frames.

See Also

Window.closed, Window.open( ), Window.opener

Window.closed — whether a window has been closed

Availability

Client-side JavaScript 1.1

Synopsis

```
window.closed
```

Description

The `closed` property of the Window object is a read-only boolean value that specifies whether the window has been closed. When a browser window closes, the Window object that represents it does not simply disappear. The Window object continues to exist, but its `closed` property is set to `true`.

Usage

Once a window has been closed, you should not attempt to use or manipulate it in any way. If your code needs to use a window that may be closed without your program's knowledge, you should always be sure to test the `closed` property before using the Window object.

See Also

Window.close( ), Window.open( ), Window.opener

Window.confirm( ) — ask a yes-or-no question

Availability

Client-side JavaScript 1.0

Synopsis

```
window.confirm(question)
```

Arguments

question   The plain text (not HTML) string to be displayed in the dialog. It should generally express a question you want the user to answer.

Returns

true if the user clicks the **OK** button, or false if the user clicks the **Cancel** button.

Description

The confirm( ) method displays the specified *question* in a dialog box that pops up over *window*. The appearance of the dialog is platform-dependent, but it generally contains graphics that indicate that the user is being asked a question. The dialog contains **OK** and **Cancel** buttons that the user can use to answer the question. If the user clicks the **OK** button, confirm( ) returns true. If the user clicks **Cancel**, confirm( ) returns false.

The dialog box that is displayed by the confirm( ) method is *modal*—that is, it blocks all user input to the main browser window until the user dismisses the dialog by clicking on the **OK** or **Cancel** buttons. Since this method returns a value depending on the user's response to the dialog, JavaScript execution pauses in the call to confirm( ), and subsequent statements are not executed until the user responds to the dialog.

Usage

Note that the *question* displayed in the dialog is a string of plain text, not formatted HTML. You can use the newline character, "\n", in your strings to break your question across multiple lines. You can also do some very rudimentary formatting using spaces and you can approximate horizontal rules with underscore characters, but the results you achieve depend greatly on the font used in the dialog and are thus system-dependent.

Also, there is no way to change the labels that appear in the buttons of the dialog box (to make them read **Yes** and **No**, for example). Therefore, you should take care to phrase your question or message in such a way that **OK** and **Cancel** are suitable responses.

See Also

Window.alert( ), Window.prompt( )

Window.crypto — reference to the Crypto object

Availability

Client-side Navigator 4.04 and later

Synopsis

```
window.crypto
```

Description

`crypto` is a read-only reference to the Crypto object associated with the window. See Crypto for details.

See Also

Crypto

Window.defaultStatus — the default status line text

Availability

Client-side JavaScript 1.0

Synopsis

```
window.defaultStatus
```

Description

`defaultStatus` is a read/write string property that specifies default text to appear in the window's status line. In Navigator, the status line is used to display the browser's progress while loading a file and to display the destination of hypertext links that the mouse is over. While it is not displaying any of these transient messages, the status line is, by default, blank. However, you can set the `defaultStatus` property to specify a default message to be displayed when the status line is not otherwise in use, and you can read the `default-Status` property to determine what the default message is. The text you specify may be temporarily overwritten with other messages, such as those that are displayed when the user moves the mouse over a hypertext link, but the `defaultStatus` message is always redisplayed when the transient message is erased.

If you set `defaultStatus` for a Window object that is a frame, the message you specify is visible whenever the mouse is within that frame (whether or not that frame has focus). When you specify `defaultStatus` for a top-level window that contains no frames, your message is always visible when the window is visible. If you specify `defaultStatus` for a top-level window that contains frames, your message is only visible when the mouse is over the borders that separate the frames. Thus, in order to guarantee visibility of a message in a framed document, you should set `defaultStatus` for all frames in the document.

Usage

`defaultStatus` is used to display semipermanent messages in the status line. To display transient messages, use the `status` property.

See Also

Window.status

Window.disableExternalCapture( ) — disable cross-server event capturing

Availability

Client-side Navigator 4; requires `UniversalBrowserWrite` privilege

Synopsis

```
window.disableExternalCapture()
```

Description

`disableExternalCapture( )` is the opposite of `Window.enableExternalCapture( )`. It prevents a script from capturing events that occur in a window, document, or layer loaded from a different server than the script.

See Also

Window.captureEvents( ), Window.enableExternalCapture( ), Chapter 15

Window.document — the Document of the Window

Availability

Client-side JavaScript 1.0

Synopsis

```
window.document
```

Description

The `document` property contains a read-only reference to the Document object that describes the document contained in *window*, which can be any top-level window or frame. See the Document object for further details.

Window.enableExternalCapture( ) — enable cross-server event capturing

Availability

Client-side Navigator 4; requires `UniversalBrowserWrite` privilege

Synopsis

```
window.enableExternalCapture()
```

Description

For security reasons, scripts cannot by default capture events that occur in content loaded from a different server than the script was loaded from. (This means that scripts cannot eavesdrop on other scripts and, for example, detect the keystrokes of a password.) However, a trusted script that has the `UniversalBrowserWrite` privilege may call `enableExternalCapture( )` to allow it to capture events that occur in windows, documents, or layers that were loaded from a different server than the trusted script.

See Also

Window.captureEvents( ), Window.disableExternalCapture( ), Chapter 15

Window.event — describes the most recent event

Availability

Client-side Internet Explorer 4

Synopsis

```
window.event
```

Description

The event property refers to an Event object that contains the details of the most recent event to occur within *window*.

In the Navigator 4 event model, an Event object describing the event is passed as an argument to every event handler. In IE 4, however, no Event object is passed, and event handlers must obtain information about the event from the event property of the Window object.

See Also

Chapter 15

Window.find( ) — search the document

Availability

Client-side Navigator 4

Synopsis

```
window.find()
window.find(target,
caseSensitive,
backwards)
```

Arguments

target
: The string to search for in the *window*. If omitted, find( ) displays a search dialog box to prompt the user to enter a search string.

caseSensitive
: A boolean that specifies whether the search should be case-sensitive or not. If omitted, false is assumed, and the search is case-insensitive.

backwards
: A boolean that specifies whether the search should be done backwards or not. If omitted, the default value is false, which specifies a forward search.

Returns

true if the search string is found, false otherwise.

Description

find() searches the document displayed in *window* for a specified *target* string. If invoked with no arguments, find() pops up a dialog box to prompt the user to enter a search string, exactly as if the user had clicked on the browser's **Find** button.

If find() finds the specified string in the document, it highlights it and returns true. If it does not find the specified string, it returns false.

If *backwards* is omitted or false, find() searches forward, either from the first character following the current selection, or from the beginning of the document, if there is no current selection. Because find() selects text it finds, multiple calls to find() progress through all matches in the document. If the *backwards* argument is true, find searches backwards, either beginning at the first character before the current selection, or beginning at the end of the document, if there is no current selection.

Window.focus() — give keyboard focus to a top-level window

Availability

Client-side JavaScript 1.1

Synopsis

```
window.focus()
```

Description

The focus() method gives keyboard focus to the top-level browser window specified by the Window object. If the Window object is a frame, keyboard focus is given to the frame and to the top-level window that contains that frame. On most platforms, a top-level window is brought forward to the top of the window stack when it is given focus.

See Also

Window.blur()

Window.forward() — go forward to next document

Availability

Client-side Navigator 4

Synopsis

```
window.forward()
```

Description

Calling forward() makes the browser display the next document in *window*, exactly as if the user had clicked on the window's **Forward** button.

Note that for framed documents, there may be differences between the behavior of Window.forward() and History.forward().

Window.frames[] — list of frames within a window

Availability

Client-side JavaScript 1.0

Synopsis

```
window.frames[i]
window.frames.length
```

Description

The frames property is an array of references to Window objects, one for each frame contained within the specified *window*. The frames.length property contains the number of elements in the frames[] array, as does the *window*.length property. Note that frames referenced by the frames[] array may themselves contain frames and may have a frames[] array of their own.

Window.handleEvent() — pass an event to the appropriate handler

Availability

Client-side Navigator 4

Synopsis

```
window.handleEvent(event)
document.handleEvent(event)
layer.handleEvent(event)
htmlElement.handleEvent(event)
```

Arguments

event   An Event object to be handled.

Returns

Whatever value is returned by the event handler that is invoked to handle *event*.

Description

handleEvent() is a method of the Window, Document, and Layer classes, and of all HTML elements that support event handlers. When invoked on any object *o*, it determines the type of its *event* argument and passes that Event object to the appropriate handler of *o*.

See Also

Window.routeEvent(), Chapter 15

Window.history — the History of the Window

Availability

Client-side JavaScript 1.0

Synopsis

```
window.history
```

Description

The `history` property contains a read-only reference to the History object of *window*, which may be any top-level window or frame. See the History object for further details.

Window.home() — display the home page

Availability

Client-side Navigator 4

Synopsis

```
window.home()
```

Description

Calling `home()` makes the browser display its own configured home page, as if the user had clicked the browser's **Home** button.

Window.innerHeight — the height of the document display area

Availability

Client-side Navigator 4; `UniversalBrowserWrite` privilege required to set to less than 100 pixels

Synopsis

```
window.innerHeight
```

Description

`innerHeight` is a read/write property that specifies the height, in pixels, of the document display area of *window*. This height does not include the height of the menubar, toolbars, scrollbars, and so on.

Window.innerWidth — the width of the document display area

Availability

Client-side Navigator 4; `UniversalBrowserWrite` privilege required to set to less than 100 pixels

Synopsis

```
window.innerWidth
```

Description

innerWidth is a read/write property that specifies the width, in pixels, of the document display area of *window*. This height does not include the width of the scrollbars, window decorations, and so on.

Window.java — see java

Window.length — the number of frames in the window

Availability

Client-side JavaScript 1.0

Synopsis

```
window.length
```

Description

The length property specifies the number of frames contained in *window*, which may be any top-level window or frame. length also specifies the number of elements in the *window*.frames[ ] array.

Window.location — the URL of the window

Availability

Client-side JavaScript 1.0

Synopsis

```
window.location
```

Description

The location property contains a reference to the Location object of *window*. This object specifies the URL of the currently loaded document. See the Location object for further details.

Assigning a string containing a URL to the location property causes the browser to load and display the contents of that URL.

Window.locationbar — the visibility of the browser's location bar

Availability

Client-side Navigator 4; UniversalBrowserWrite privilege required to change visibility

Synopsis

```
window.locationbar.visibility
```

Description

`locationbar` is a read-only property that refers to a Bar object representing the location bar of the browser. The `visibility` property of the Bar object allows you to determine whether the location bar is currently displayed in *window*. Signed scripts with the `UniversalBrowserWrite` privilege can use this property to show or hide the location bar.

Window.Math — see Math

Window.menubar — the visibility of the browser's menubar

Availability

Client-side Navigator 4; `UniversalBrowserWrite` privilege required to change visibility

Synopsis

```
window.menubar.visibility
```

Description

`menubar` is a read-only property that refers to a Bar object representing the menubar of the browser. The `visibility` property of the Bar object allows you to determine whether the menubar is currently displayed in *window*. Signed scripts with the `UniversalBrowserWrite` privilege can use this property to show or hide the menubar.

Window.moveBy() — move a window to a relative position

Availability

Client-side JavaScript 1.2; Navigator 4 requires `UniversalBrowserWrite` privilege to move the window off-screen

Synopsis

```
window.moveBy(dx, dy)
```

Arguments

dx   The number of pixels to move the window to the right.

y   The number of pixels to move the window down.

Description

`moveBy()` moves the *window* to the relative position specified by *dx* and *dy*. In Navigator, the `UniversalBrowserWrite` privilege is required to move the window partially or fully off screen.

Window.moveTo() — move a window to an absolute position

Availability

Client-side JavaScript 1.2; Navigator 4 requires `UniversalBrowserWrite` privilege to move the window off-screen

Synopsis

```
window.moveTo(x, y)
```

Arguments

x   The X-coordinate of the new window position.

y   The Y-coordinate of the new window position.

Description

`moveTo()` moves the `window` so that its upper-left corner is at the position specified by *x* and *y*. In Navigator, the `UniversalBrowserWrite` privilege is required to move the window partially or fully off screen.

Window.name — the name of a window

Availability

Client-side JavaScript 1.0; read/write in JavaScript 1.1

Synopsis

```
window.name
```

Description

The *name* property is a string that specifies the name of *window*. This property is read-only in JavaScript 1.0 and is read/write in JavaScript 1.1. The name of a top-level window is initially specified by the *name* argument of the `Window.open()` method. The name of a frame is initially specified by the `NAME` attribute of the `<FRAME>` HTML tag.

The name of a top-level window or frame may be used as the value of a `TARGET` attribute of an `<A>` or `<FORM>` tag. Using the `TARGET` attribute in this way specifies that the hyperlinked document or the results of form submission should be displayed in the named window.

The initial window opened by Navigator, and any windows opened with the **New Web Browser** menu item initially have no name (i.e., name `==""`), and so these windows cannot be addressed with a `TARGET` attribute from a separate top-level window. In JavaScript 1.1, you can set the *name* attribute to remedy this situation.

See Also

Form.target, Link.target

Window.navigate() — load a new URL

Availability

Client-side Internet Explorer 3

Synopsis

```
window.navigate(url)
```

Arguments

url   A string that specifies the URL to be loaded and displayed.

Description

The `Window.navigate()` method of Internet Explorer loads the specified *url* into the specified *window* ("navigates to" the *url*).

`navigate()` is not supported by Navigator. The same function can be accomplished both in Navigator and IE by simply assigning the desired *url* to the `location` property of the desired *window*.

See Also

Location, Window.location

Window.navigator — see navigator and Navigator

Window.netscape — see netscape

Window.offscreenBuffering — whether window updates are buffered

Availability

Client-side JavaScript 1.2

Synopsis

```
window.offscreenBuffering
```

Description

The `offscreenBuffering` property specifies whether updates to *window* are done into an offscreen buffer before being transferred to the window. This kind of double buffering can reduce flicker during DHTML animations, but it requires extra memory and CPU time.

The default value of this property is "auto", which specifies that the browser decides when it is appropriate to perform buffering and when it is not necessary. Setting this property to `true` forces the browser to perform buffering, and setting it to `false` turns off buffering altogether.

Window.onblur — the handler invoked when the window loses keyboard focus

Availability

Client-side JavaScript 1.1

Synopsis

```
<BODY onBlur="handler" ... >
<FRAMESET onBlur="handler" ... >
window.onblur
```

Description

The `onblur` property of a Window specifies an event handler function that is invoked when the window loses keyboard focus.

The initial value of this property is a function that contains the semicolon-separated JavaScript statements specified by the `onBlur` attribute of the `<BODY>` or `<FRAMESET>` tags.

In Navigator 4, the `onblur` handler function is passed an Event object as an argument. In IE 4, no argument is passed, but the applicable Event object is available as the `event` property of the Window object that contains the *element*.

Usage

If your web page does some sort of animation, you might use the `onblur()` event handler to stop the animation when the window doesn't have the input focus, on the theory that if the window doesn't have the focus, the user probably can't see it or isn't paying attention to it.

See Also

Window.blur(), Window.focus(), Window.onfocus

Window.ondragdrop — the handler invoked when the user drops items in the window

Availability

Client-side Navigator 4

Synopsis

```
<BODY onDragDrop="handler" ... >
<FRAMESET onDragDrop="handler" ... >
window.ondragdrop
```

Description

The `ondragdrop` property of the Window object specifies an event handler function that is invoked when the user uses system drag-and-drop capabilities to drop an object or objects on the window.

The initial value of this property is a function that contains the JavaScript statements specified by the `onDragDrop` attribute of the HTML `<BODY>` or `<FRAMESET>` tag that defined the window. When an event handler function is defined by an HTML attribute, it is executed in the scope of *element* rather than in the scope of the containing window.

The `ondragdrop` handler function is passed an Event object as an argument. The `data` property of this object is an array of strings containing the URLs of the dropped objects. Note, however, that the `UniversalBrowserRead` privilege is required to read this `data` property.

Window.onerror — the handler invoked when a JavaScript error occurs

Availability

Client-side JavaScript 1.1

Synopsis

You register an `onerror` event handler like this:

```
window.onerror=handler-func
```

The browser invokes the handler like this:

```
window.onerror(message, url, line)
```

Arguments

`message`   A string that specifies the error message for the error that occurred.

`url`   A string that specifies the URL of the document in which the error occurred.

`line`   A number that specifies the line number at which the error occurred.

Returns

`true` if the handler has handled the error and JavaScript should take no further action. `false` if JavaScript should post the default error message dialog box for this error.

Description

The `onerror` property of the Window object specifies an error handler function that is invoked when a JavaScript error occurs in code executing in that window. By default, JavaScript displays an error dialog box when an error occurs. You can customize error handling by providing your own `onerror` event handler.

You define an `onerror` event handler for a window by setting the `onerror` property of a Window object to an appropriate function. Note that unlike other event handlers in JavaScript, the `onerror` handler cannot be defined in an HTML tag.

When the `onerror` handler is invoked, it is passed three arguments: the first is a string specifying the error message; the second is a string specifying the URL of the document in which the error occurred; and the third is a number that specifies the line number at which the error occurred. An error handling function may do anything it wants with these arguments: it may display its own error dialog or may log the error in some way, for example. When the error handling function is done, it should return `true` if it has completely handled the error and wants JavaScript to take no further action. Or, it should return `false` if it has merely noted or logged the error in some fashion and still wants JavaScript to display the error message in its default dialog box.

Note that while this event handler returns `true` to tell the browser to take no further action, most Form and form element event handlers return `false` to prevent the browser from performing some action, such as submitting a form. This inconsistency can be confusing.

You can turn off error handling entirely for a window by setting the `onerror` property of the window to a function that returns `true` and does nothing else. You can restore the default error-handling behavior (the dialog box) by setting `onerror` to a function that returns `false` and does nothing else.

Window.onfocus — the handler invoked when a window is given focus

Availability

Client-side JavaScript 1.1

Synopsis

```
<BODY onFocus="handler" ... >
<FRAMESET onFocus="handler" ... >
window.onfocus
```

Description

The `onfocus` property of a Window specifies an event handler function that is invoked when the window is given keyboard focus.

The initial value of this property is a function that contains the semicolon-separated JavaScript statements specified by the `onFocus` attribute of the <BODY> or <FRAMESET> tags.

In Navigator 4, the `onfocus` handler function is passed an Event object as an argument. In IE 4, no argument is passed, but the applicable Event object is available as the `event` property of the Window object that contains the *element*.

Usage

If your web page does some sort of animation, you might use the `onfocus` event handler to start the animation and the `onblur` handler to stop it, so that it only runs while the user is paying attention to the window.

See Also

Window.blur( ), Window.focus( ), Window.onblur

Window.onload — the handler invoked when a document finishes loading

Availability

Client-side JavaScript 1.0

Synopsis

```
<BODY onLoad="handler" ... >
<FRAMESET onLoad="handler" ... >
window.onload
```

Description

The `onload` property of a Window specifies an event handler function that is invoked when a document or frameset is completely loaded into its window or frame.

The initial value of this property is a function that contains the semicolon-separated JavaScript statements specified by the `onLoad` attribute of the `<BODY>` or `<FRAMESET>` tags.

When the `onload` event handler is invoked, you can be certain that the document has fully loaded, and therefore that all scripts within the document have executed, all functions within scripts are defined, and all forms and other document elements have been parsed and are available through the Document object.

Usage

If any of your document's event handlers depend on the document being fully loaded, you should be sure to check that it is loaded before executing those handlers. If the network connection were to stall out after a button appeared in the document but before the parts of the document that the button relied on were loaded, when the user clicked the button she would get unintended behavior or an error message. One good way to verify that the document is loaded is to use the `onload` handler to set a variable, `loaded`, for example, to `true`, and to check the value of this variable before doing anything that depends on the complete document being loaded.

Bugs

JavaScript is supposed to guarantee that the `onload` handler for each frame in a window is invoked before the `onload` handler for the window itself. Unfortunately, Navigator 2 does not always do this. Thus in a framed document, you may need to check that each of your individual frames has fully loaded.

See Also

Window.onunload

Window.onmove — the handler invoked when a window is moved

Availability

Client-side Navigator 4; not supported on Navigator 4 Unix platforms

Synopsis

```
<BODY onMove="handler" ... >
<FRAMESET onMove="handler" ... >
window.onmove
```

Description

The `onmove` property of the Window object specifies an event handler function that is invoked when the user moves a top-level window to a new position on the screen.

The initial value of this property is a function that contains the JavaScript statements specified by the `onMove` attribute of the HTML `<BODY>` or `<FRAMESET>` tag that defined the window. When an event handler function is defined by an HTML attribute, it is executed in the scope of *element* rather than in the scope of the containing window.

The `onmove` handler function is passed an Event object as an argument. The properties of this object contain information about the new position of the window.

Window.onresize — the handler invoked when a window is resized

Availability

Client-side JavaScript 1.2

Synopsis

```
<BODY onResize="handler" ... >
<FRAMESET onResize="handler" ... >
window.onresize
```

Description

The `onresize` property of the Window object specifies an event handler function that is invoked when the user changes the size of the window or frame.

The initial value of this property is a function that contains the JavaScript statements specified by the `onResize` attribute of the HTML `<BODY>` or `<FRAMESET>` tag that defined the window. When an event handler function is defined by an HTML attribute, it is executed in the scope of *element* rather than in the scope of the containing window.

In Navigator 4, the `onresize` handler function is passed an Event object as an argument. In IE 4, no argument is passed, but the applicable Event object is available as the `event` property of the Window object that contains the *element*.

In Navigator 4, the new size of the window is available from the `width` and `height` properties of the Event object.

Window.onunload — the handler invoked when the browser leaves a page

Availability

Client-side JavaScript 1.0

Synopsis

```
<BODY onUnload="handler" ... >
<FRAMESET onUnload="handler" ... >
window.onunload
```

Description

The `onunload` property of a Window specifies an event handler function that is invoked when the browser "unloads" a document or frameset in preparation for loading a new one.

The initial value of this property is a function that contains the semicolon-separated JavaScript statements specified by the `onUnload` attribute of the `<BODY>` or `<FRAMESET>` tags.

The `onunload` event handler provides the opportunity to perform any necessary cleanup of the browser state before a new document is loaded.

When the browser leaves a site using frames, the `onunload` handler for each frame is invoked before the `onunload` handler of the browser itself.

The `onunload()` handler is invoked when the user has instructed the browser to leave the current page and move somewhere else. Therefore, it is almost never appropriate to delay the loading of the desired new page by popping up dialog boxes (with `Window.confirm()` or `Window.prompt()` for example) from an `onunload` event handler.

See Also

Window.onload

Window.open() — open a new browser window or locate a named window

Availability

Client-side JavaScript 1.0; enhanced in JavaScript 1.1

Synopsis

```
window.open(url, name, features, replace)
```

Arguments

url
An optional string that specifies the URL to be displayed in the new window. If this argument is omitted, or if the empty string is specified, the new window does not display a document.

name
An optional string of alphanumeric and underscore characters that specifies a name for the new window. This name can be used as the value of the TARGET attribute of <A> and <FORM> HTML tags. If this argument names a window that already exists, the open() method does not create a new window, but simply returns a reference to the named window. In this case, the *features* argument is ignored.

features
A string that specifies which features of a standard browser window are to appear in the new window. The format of this string is specified below. This argument is optional; if it is not specified, the new window has all standard features.

replace
An optional boolean argument that specifies whether the *url* that is loaded into the new page should create a new entry in the window's browsing history or replace the current entry in the browsing history. If this argument is `true`, no new history entry is created. This argument was added in JavaScript 1.1. Note that it doesn't make much sense to use this argument for newly created windows; it is intended for use when changing the contents of an existing window.

Returns

A reference to a Window object, which may be a newly created or an already existing one, depending on the *name* argument.

Description

The open() method looks up an already existing window or opens a new browser window. If the *name* argument specifies the name of an existing window, a reference to that window is returned. The returned window displays the URL specified by *url*, but the *fea-*

tures argument is ignored. This is the only way in JavaScript to obtain a reference to a window which is known only by name.

If the *name* argument is not specified, or if no window with that name already exists, the open() method creates a new browser window. The created window displays the URL specified by *url* and has the name specified by *name* and the size and controls specified by *features* (the format of this argument is described below). If *url* is the empty string, open() opens a blank window.

The *name* argument specifies a name for the new window. This name may only contain alphanumeric characters and the underscore character. It may be used as the value of the TARGET attribute of an <A> or <FORM> tag in HTML to force documents to be displayed in the window.

In JavaScript 1.1, when you use Window.open() to load a new document into a named window, you can pass the *replace* argument to specify whether the new document has its own entry in the window's browsing history or whether it replaces the history entry of the current document. If *replace* is true, the new document replaces the old. If this argument is false is or not specified, the new document has its own entry in the Window's browsing history. This argument provides functionality much like that of the Location.replace() method.

Don't confuse this Window.open() method with the document.open() method; the two perform very different functions. For clarity in your code, you may want to use window.open() instead of open(). In event handlers defined as HTML attributes, open() is usually interpreted as document.open(), so in this case you must use window.open().

Window Features

The *features* argument is a comma-separated list of features to appear in the window. If this optional argument is empty or not specified, all features are present in the window. On the other hand, if *features* specifies any one feature, any features that do not appear in the list do not appear in the window. The string should not contain any spaces or other whitespace. Each element in the list has the format:

    feature[=value]

For most features, the *value* is yes or no. For these features, the equals sign and the *value* may be omitted—if the feature appears, yes is assumed, and if it doesn't, no is assumed. For the width and height features, the *value* is required and must specify a size in pixels.

The available features and their meanings are listed below:

alwaysLowered

> Specifies that the window should always remain at the bottom of the stack. Navigator 4 only. Requires UniversalBrowserWrite privilege.

alwaysRaised

> Specifies that the window should always appear at the top of the stack. Navigator 4 only. Requires UniversalBrowserWrite privilege.

channelmode   Specifies whether the window should appear in channel mode. IE 4 only

dependent	If set to "no", specifies that the new window should not be a dependent child of the current window. Navigator 4 only.
directories	Directory buttons, such as "What's New" and "What's Cool" in Netscape.
fullscreen	Specifies whether the window should appear in full screen mode. IE 4 only.
height	Specifies the height, in pixels, of the window's document display area.
hotkeys	Disable most keyboard shortcuts for windows with no menubar. Navigator 4 only. Requires `UniversalBrowserWrite` privilege.
innerHeight	Specifies the height, in pixels, of the window's document display area. Navigator 4 only.
innerWidth	Specifies the width, in pixels, of the window's document display area. Navigator 4 only.
left	The X-coordinate, in pixels, of the window. IE 4 only. In Navigator, use `screenX`.
location	The input field for entering URLs directly into the browser.
menubar	The menubar.
outerHeight	Specifies the total height, in pixels, of the window. Navigator 4 only.
innerWidth	Specifies the total width, in pixels, of the window. Navigator 4 only.
resizable	If this feature is not present or is set to `no`, the window does not have resize handles around its border. (Depending on the platform, the user may still have ways to resize the window.) Note that a common bug is to misspell this feature as "resizeable," with an extra "e."
screenX	The X-coordinate, in pixels, of the window. Navigator 4 only. Use `left` in IE 4.
screenY	The Y-coordinate, in pixels, of the window. Navigator 4 only. Use `top` in IE 4.
scrollbars	This feature enables horizontal and vertical scrollbars when they are necessary.
status	The status line.
toolbar	The browser toolbar, with **Back** and **Forward** buttons, etc.
top	The Y-coordinate, in pixels, of the window. IE 4 only. Use `screenY` in Navigator.
width	Specifies the width, in pixels, of the window's document display area.
z-lock	Specifies that the window should not be raised in the stacking order when activated. Navigator 4 only. Requires `UniversalBrowserWrite` privilege.

Bugs

In Navigator 2 on Unix and Macintosh platforms, the *url* argument is ineffective. The solution is to call `open()` once to create the window, and then call it again to set the URL, or better still, use the `location` property of the new (blank) window to load the desired URL.

See Also

Location.replace( ), Window.close( ), Window.opener

Window.opener — the window that opened this one

Availability

Client-side JavaScript 1.1

Synopsis

```
window.opener
```

Description

The `opener` property is a read/write reference to the Window object that contained the script that called `open()` to open this top-level browser window. This property is only valid for Window objects that represent top-level windows, not those that represent frames.

The `opener` property is useful so that a newly created window can refer to variables and functions defined in the window that created it.

Window.outerHeight — the height of the window area

Availability

Client-side Navigator 4; `UniversalBrowserWrite` privilege required to set to less than 100 pixels

Synopsis

```
window.outerHeight
```

Description

`outerHeight` is a read/write property that specifies the height, in pixels, of *window*. This height includes the height of the menubar, toolbars, scrollbars, window borders, and so on.

Window.outerWidth — the width of the window

Availability

Client-side Navigator 4; `UniversalBrowserWrite` privilege required to set to less than 100 pixels

Synopsis

```
window.outerWidth
```

Description

`outerWidth` is a read/write property that specifies the width, in pixels, of *window*. This includes the width of the window borders, scrollbars, and so on.

Window.Packages — see Packages

Window.pageXOffset — the current horizontal scroll position

Availability

Client-side Navigator 4

Synopsis

```
window.pageXOffset
```

Description

`pageXOffset` is a read-only integer that specifies the number of pixels that the current document has been scrolled to the right.

See Also

Window.scrollBy( ), Window.scrollTo( )

Window.pageYOffset — the current vertical scroll position

Availability

Client-side Navigator 4

Synopsis

```
window.pageYOffset
```

Description

`pageYOffset` is a read-only integer that specifies the number of pixels that the current document has been scrolled down. A value of 0 means that the top of the document is visible at the top of the window.

See Also

Window.scrollBy( ), Window.scrollTo( )

Window.parent — the parent of a frame

Availability

Client-side JavaScript 1.0

Synopsis

```
window.parent
```

Description

The `parent` property is a read-only reference to the Window object that contains *window*. If *window* specifies a top-level window, `parent` refers to the window itself. If *window* is a frame, the `parent` property refers to the top-level window or frame that contains *window*.

Usage

The `parent` property is generally useful for frames rather than for top-level windows. With a function like the following, you can use the property to determine whether a given Window object is a top-level window or a frame:

```
function is_toplevel(w) { return (w.parent == w); }
```

See Also

Window.top

Window.personalbar — the visibility of the browser's personal bar

Availability

Client-side Navigator 4; `UniversalBrowserWrite` privilege required to change visibility

Synopsis

```
window.personalbar.visibility
```

Description

`personalbar` is a read-only property that refers to a Bar object representing the personal bar of the browser. The `visibility` property of the Bar object allows you to determine whether the personal bar is currently displayed in *window*. Signed scripts with the `UniversalBrowserWrite` privilege can use this property to show or hide the personal bar.

Window.print() — print the document

Availability

Client-side Navigator 4

Synopsis

```
window.print()
```

Description

Calling `print()` prints the current document, exactly as if the user had clicked the browser's **Print** button.

Window.prompt() — get string input in a dialog

Availability

Client-side JavaScript 1.0

Synopsis

```
window.prompt(message, default)
```

Arguments

message   The plain text (not HTML) string to be displayed in the dialog. It should ask the user to enter the information you want.

default   A string that is displayed as the default input in the dialog. Pass the empty string ("") to make prompt() display an empty input box.

Returns

The string entered by the user, or the empty string if the user did not enter a string, or null if the user clicked **Cancel**.

Description

The prompt() method displays the specified *message* in a dialog box that also contains a text input field and **OK**, **Clear**, and **Cancel** buttons. Platform-dependent graphics in the dialog help to indicate to the user that her input is desired.

If the user clicks the **Cancel** button, prompt() returns null. If the user clicks the **Clear** button, prompt() erases any current text in the input field. If the user clicks the **OK** button, prompt() returns the value currently displayed in the input field.

The dialog box that is displayed by the prompt() method is *modal*—that is, it blocks all user input to the main browser window until the user dismisses the dialog by clicking on the **OK** or **Cancel** buttons. Since this method returns a value depending on the user's response to the dialog, JavaScript execution pauses in the call to prompt(), and subsequent statements are not executed until the user responds to the dialog.

See Also

Window.alert(), Window.confirm()

Window.releaseEvents() — stop capturing events

Availability

Client-side Navigator 4

Synopsis

```
window.releaseEvents(eventmask)
document.releaseEvents(eventmask)
layer.releaseEvents(eventmask)
```

Arguments

eventmask   An integer that specifies the type of events that the window, document, or layer should stop capturing. This value should be one of the static event type constants defined by the Event class, or should be a group of event type constants combined with the bitwise-OR (|) or addition operator.

Description

The `releaseEvents()` method of the Window, Document, and Layer objects performs the opposite action of the `captureEvents()` method of those classes. In the Navigator 4 event model, `releaseEvents()` specifies that the *window*, *document*, or *layer* should no longer capture events of the types specified by *eventmask*. See Event.*TYPE* for a list of the constants that can be used in the *eventmask* argument.

See Also

Window.captureEvents( ), Window.handleEvent( ), Window.routeEvent( ), Event.TYPE, Chapter 15

Window.resizeBy() — resize a window by a relative amount.

Availability

Client-side JavaScript 1.2; Navigator 4 requires `UniversalBrowserWrite` privilege to set either width or height to less than 100 pixels

Synopsis

```
window.resizeBy(dh, dw)
```

Arguments

dw   The number of pixels by which to increase the width of the window.

dh   The number of pixels by which to increase the height of the window.

Description

`resizeBy()` resizes *window* by the relative amounts specified by *dh* and *dw*. In Navigator, the `UniversalBrowserWrite` privilege is required if these changes would produce a window with either a width or height of less than 100 pixels.

Window.resizeTo() — resize a window

Availability

Client-side JavaScript 1.2; Navigator 4 requires `UniversalBrowserWrite` privilege to set either width or height to less than 100 pixels

Synopsis

```
window.resizeTo(width, height)
```

Arguments

width   The desired width for the window.

height   The desired height for the window.

Description

resizeTo() resizes *window* so that it is *width* pixels wide and *height* pixels high. In Navigator, the UniversalBrowserWrite privilege is required if either *width* or *height* is less than 100 pixels.

Window.routeEvent() — pass a captured event to the next handler

Availability

Client-side Navigator 4

Synopsis

```
window.routeEvent(event)
document.routeEvent(event)
layer.routeEvent(event)
```

Arguments

event   The captured Event object to be routed to the next event handler.

Returns

Whatever value was returned by the handler to which the *event* was routed.

Description

routeEvent() is a method of the Window, Document, and Layer classes, and it behaves the same for all three. When a captured Event object, *event*, is passed to an event handler of *window, document,* or *layer,* that handler may choose to pass the event on to the next interested event handler, if any. If the window, document, or layer contains some other window (frame), document, or layer that has also used captureEvents() to register interest in events of that type, the event is routed to the appropriate handler on that window, document, or layer object.

On the other hand, if there is no containing window, document, or layer object that has expressed interest in the event, routeEvent() passes the *event* object to the appropriate event handler of the object on which the event originated. The combination of captureEvents() and routeEvent() forms the basis of Navigator's "trickle-down" event model.

See Also

Window.captureEvents(), Window.handleEvent(), Window.releaseEvents(), Chapter 15

Window.screen — information about the screen

Availability

Client-side JavaScript 1.2

Synopsis

```
screen
window.screen
```

Description

The `screen` property refers to the Screen object that is shared by all windows in a browser. This Screen object contains properties that specify information about the screen: the number of available pixels and the number of available colors.

See Also

Screen

Window.screenX — the X-coordinate of a window on the screen

Availability

Client-side Navigator 4

Synopsis

```
window.screenX
```

Description

`screenX` specifies the X-coordinate of the upper-left corner of *window* on the screen. If *window* is a frame, this property specifies the X-coordinate of the top-level window that contains the frame.

Window.screenY — the Y-coordinate of a window on the screen

Availability

Client-side Navigator 4

Synopsis

```
window.screenY
```

Description

`screenY` specifies the Y-coordinate of the upper-left corner of *window* on the screen. If *window* is a frame, this property specifies the Y-coordinate of the top-level window that contains the frame.

Window.scroll() — scroll a document in a window

Availability

Client-side JavaScript 1.1; deprecated in JavaScript 1.2 in favor of `scrollTo()`

Synopsis

```
window.scroll(x, y)
```

Arguments

x   The X-coordinate to scroll to.

y   The Y-coordinate to scroll to.

Description

The `scroll()` method moves the window's document within the window, so that the specified *x* and *y* coordinates of the document appear in the upper-left corner of the window.

The X-coordinate increases to the right, and the Y-coordinate increases down the page. Thus, `scroll(0,0)` always places the top-left corner of the document in the top-left corner of the window.

In JavaScript 1.2, the `scrollTo()` and `scrollBy()` methods are preferred over `scroll()`.

Window.scrollbars — the visibility of the browser's scroll bars

Availability

Client-side Navigator 4; `UniversalBrowserWrite` privilege required to change visibility

Synopsis

```
window.scrollbars.visibility
```

Description

`scrollbars` is a read-only property that refers to a Bar object representing the scrollbars of the browser. The `visibility` property of the Bar object allows you to determine whether the scrollbars are currently displayed in *window*. Signed scripts with the `Universal-BrowserWrite` privilege can use this property to show or hide the scrollbars.

Window.scrollBy() — scroll the document by a relative amount

Availability

Client-side JavaScript 1.2

Synopsis

```
window.scrollBy(dx, dy)
```

Arguments

dx   The number of pixels to scroll the document to the right.

dy   The number of pixels to scroll the document down.

Description

scrollBy() scrolls the document displayed in window by the relative amounts specified by *dx* and *dy*.

Window.scrollTo() — scroll the document

Availability

Client-side JavaScript 1.2

Synopsis

```
window.scrollTo(x, y)
```

Arguments

x   The document X-coordinate that is to appear at the left edge of the window's document display area.

y   The document Y-coordinate that is to appear at the top of the window's document display area.

Description

scrollTo() scrolls the document displayed within *window*, so that the point in the document specified by the *x* and *y* coordinates is displayed in the upper-left hand corner, if possible.

scrollTo() is preferred over the JavaScript 1.1 Window.scroll() method, which does the same thing but has an inadequately descriptive name.

Window.self — the window itself

Availability

Client-side JavaScript 1.0

Synopsis

```
window.self
```

Description

The self property contains a reference to the Window object specified by *window*; *window*.self is identical to *window*. Because a reference to the current top-level window or frame is implicit in all JavaScript expressions, you can simply use self to refer to the current window.

Usage

The `self` property provides a way to explicitly refer to the current window or frame when necessary (for example, when passing the current window to a function). The `self` property is also sometimes useful for code clarity. Using `self.name` to refer to the name of the current window or frame is less ambiguous than simply using `name`, for example.

The `window` property is a synonym for the `self` property.

See Also

Window.window

Window.setHotkeys() — allow or disallow keyboard shortcuts

Availability

Client-side Navigator 4; requires `UniversalBrowserWrite` privilege

Synopsis

```
window.setHotkeys(enabled)
```

Arguments

`enabled`   A boolean argument that specifies whether keyboard shortcuts in a window without a menubar should be enabled (`true`) or not (`false`).

Description

`setHotkeys()` specifies whether the user is allowed to issue browser commands from the keyboard in a window without a menubar. It is akin to the `hotkeys` option that can be passed to `Window.open()`.

See Also

Window.open()

Window.setInterval() — periodically execute specified code

Availability

Client-side JavaScript 1.2; Internet Explorer 4 supports only one of the two forms of this method

Synopsis

```
window.setInterval(code, interval)
window.setInterval(func, interval, args...)
```

Arguments

`code`   A string of JavaScript code to be periodically executed. If this string contains multiple statements, they must be separated from each other by semicolons.

func   A JavaScript function to be periodically executed. This form of the
                method is not available in IE 4.

interval   An integer that specifies the interval, in milliseconds, between invoca-
                tions of *code* or *func*.

args...   Any number of arbitrary values to be passed as arguments to each invo-
                cation of *func*.

Returns

A value that can be passed to `Window.clearInterval()` to cancel the periodic execution of *code* or *func*.

Description

`setInterval()` causes the JavaScript statements specified in the string *code* to be executed
repeatedly, at intervals of *interval* milliseconds.

In Navigator 4, but not IE 4, a function may be passed as the first argument instead of a
string. In this form of `setInterval()`, the specified function, *func*, is invoked repeatedly,
at intervals of *interval* milliseconds. Any additional argument values, *args*, passed to
`setInterval()` are passed as arguments to each invocation of `func()`.

In both forms, `setInterval()` returns a value that can later be passed to `Window.clear-
Interval()` to stop *code* or *func* from being repeatedly executed.

`setInterval()` is related to `setTimeout()`. Use `setTimeout()` when you want to defer
the execution of code, but do not want it to be executed repeatedly.

See Also

Window.clearInterval(), Window.setTimeout()

Window.setResizable() — allow or disallow window resizing

Availability

Client-side Navigator 4; requires `UniversalBrowserWrite` privilege

Synopsis

`window.setResizable(resizable)`

Arguments

resizable   A boolean argument that specifies whether the window should be resiz-
                able (`true`) or not (`false`).

Description

`setResizable()` specifies whether the user is allowed to resize the window. It is akin to
the `resizable` option that can be passed to `Window.open()`. Note that the windowing systems on some platforms may not honor this method.

See Also

Window.open( )

Window.setTimeout() — defer execution of code

Availability

Client-side JavaScript 1.0

Synopsis

```
window.setTimeout(code, delay)
```

Arguments

code   A string that contains the JavaScript code to be executed after the *delay* has elapsed.

delay   The amount of time, in milliseconds, before the JavaScript statements in the string *code* should be executed.

Returns

An opaque value ("timeout id") that can be passed to the clearTimeout( ) method to cancel the execution of *code*.

Description

The setTimeout( ) method defers the execution of the JavaScript statements in the string *code* for *delay* milliseconds. Once the specified number of milliseconds has elapsed, the statements in *code* are executed normally. Note that they are executed only once. To execute code repeatedly, *code* must itself contain a call to setTimeout( ) to register itself to be executed again. In JavaScript 1.2, you can use Window.setInterval( ) to register code that is executed at periodic intervals.

The statements in the string *code* are executed in the context of *window*; i.e., *window* is the current window for those statements. If more than one statement appears in *code*, the statements must be separated from each other with semicolons.

Bugs

Repeated use of setTimeout( ) can cause memory leaks in Navigator 2.

See Also

Window.clearTimeout( ), Window.setInterval( )

Window.setZOptions() — control window stacking

Availability

Client-side Navigator 4; requires UniversalBrowserWrite privilege

Synopsis

```
window.setZOptions(option)
```

Arguments

`option`   The stacking option for the window.

Description

`setZOptions()` specifies the stacking behavior for `window`. `option` should be one of the following four values:

`"alwaysRaised"`
: The window should always be on top, even when other windows are active.

`"alwaysLowered"`
: The window should always be on the bottom, even when it is active.

`"z-lock"`   The window remains "locked" in the stacking order, and does not rise to the top when it becomes active.

`""` (the empty string)
: When none of the above three options are specified, the window is given normal stacking behavior, and is raised and lowered like a normal window.

Note that these options can also be set in a call to `Window.open()`.

Note that the windowing systems on various platforms differ in their capabilities. Therefore, these stacking behaviors may vary between platforms, and may not be available on all platforms.

See Also

Window.open()

Window.status — specify a transient status-line message

Availability

Client-side JavaScript 1.0

Synopsis

```
window.status
```

Description

`status` is a read/write string property that specifies a transient message to appear in the window's status line. The message generally appears only for a limited amount of time—until it is overwritten by another message, or until the user moves the mouse to some other area of the window, for example. When a message specified with `status` is erased, the status line returns to its default blank state, or to the default message specified by the `defaultStatus` property.

Although only top-level windows have a status line, the `status` property of frames may also be set. Doing so displays the specified message in the top-level window's status line. Transient messages set by frames are visible regardless of which frame currently has focus or which frame the mouse is in. This differs from the behavior of the `defaultStatus` property.

Usage

`status` is used to display transient messages in the status line. To display semipermanent messages, use the `defaultStatus` property.

In general, setting the `status` property is only useful from event handlers and in code fragments deferred with the `Window.setTimeout()` method. If you set `status` directly from a script, the message is not visible to the user. It is not displayed right away, and when it is displayed, it is likely to be immediately overwritten by a browser message such as "Document: done".

If you want to set the `status` property in the `onMouseOver()` event handler of a hypertext link, you must return `true` from that event handler. This is because the default action when the mouse goes over a link is to display the URL of that link, thereby overwriting any status message set by the event handler. By returning `true` from the event handler, you cancel this default action and leave your own `status` message displayed (until the mouse moves off the link).

See Also

Window.defaultStatus

Window.statusbar — the visibility of the browser's status line

Availability

Client-side Navigator 4; `UniversalBrowserWrite` privilege required to change visibility

Synopsis

```
window.statusbar.visibility
```

Description

`statusbar` is a read-only property that refers to a Bar object representing the "status bar" or "status line" of the browser. The `visibility` property of the Bar object allows you to determine whether the status line is currently displayed in `window`. Signed scripts with the `UniversalBrowserWrite` privilege can use this property to show or hide the status line.

Window.stop() — stop loading the document

Availability

Client-side Navigator 4

Synopsis

```
window.stop()
```

Description

Calling `stop()` stops the browser from loading the current document, exactly as if the user had clicked the browser's **Stop** button.

Window.sun — see sun

Window.toolbar — the visibility of the browser's toolbar

Availability

Client-side Navigator 4; `UniversalBrowserWrite` privilege required to change visibility

Synopsis

```
window.toolbar.visibility
```

Description

`toolbar` is a read-only property that refers to a Bar object representing the toolbar of the browser. The `visibility` property of the Bar object allows you to determine whether the toolbar is currently displayed in *window*. Signed scripts with the `UniversalBrowserWrite` privilege can use this property to show or hide the toolbar.

Window.top — the window of a frame

Availability

Client-side JavaScript 1.0

Synopsis

```
window.top
```

Description

The `top` property is a read-only reference to the Window object that is the top-level window that contains *window*. If *window* is a top-level window itself, the `top` property simply contains a reference to *window*. If *window* is a frame, the `top` property contains a reference to the top-level window that contains the frame. Note that the `top` property refers to a top-level window even if *window* refers to a frame contained within another frame (which may itself be contained within a frame, and so on). Compare this with the `Window.parent` property.

Usage

Certain operations, such as setting the `status` and `defaultStatus` properties, are only useful when performed on a top-level window. When JavaScript code running in a frame needs to operate on its top-level window, it can use the `top` property. For example, it could display a message in the message line as follows:

```
top.defaultStatus = 'Welcome to my Home Page!';
```

See Also

Window.parent

Window.window — the window itself

Availability

Client-side JavaScript 1.0

Synopsis

```
window.window
```

Description

The `window` property is identical to the `self` property; it contains a reference to the Window object specified by *window*. That is, *window*.`window` is identical to *window* itself. Because a reference to the current top-level window or frame is implicit in all JavaScript expressions, you can simply use `window` to refer to the current window.

Usage

The `window` property (and its synonym, `self`) provides a way to explicitly refer to the current window or frame when necessary, or when convenient for code clarity. To open a new window in an event handler, for example, it is necessary to use `window.open()`, because `open()` by itself would be confused with the `Document.open()` method.

See Also

Window.self

Index

Numbers

√2 constant, 614
√2/2 constant, 613

Symbols

& (bitwise and) operator, 77
  && (logical and) operator, 75
  &{} for entities, 220
' (apostrophe), 39
* (asterisk)
  multiplication operator, 68
  in regular expressions, 169
@ (at sign) for conditional comments, 350
\ (backslash), 39
  \n in regular expressions, 170–171
  literals in regular expressions, 166
! (bang)
  logical not operator, 77
  != (inequality) operator, 72
  !== (non-identity) operator, 73
[] (brackets)
  accessing array elements, 45, 85, 98, 155
  accessing object properties, 145
  regular expression character classes, 167
^ (caret)
  anchor character, 172
  bitwise exclusive or operator, 78
  negating character class elements, 167
: (colon) for labels, 99
, (comma) operator, 84, 98
, (comma), trailing in array literals, 47

{} (curly braces)
  delimiting statement blocks, 88, 103
  in regular expressions, 169
$ (dollar sign)
  anchor character, 172
  $` property (RegExp), 180
  $1, $2, . . . properties (RegExp), 179
. (dot) operator, 84, 127
" (double quote), 38
= (equal sign)
  assignment operator, 78
  combined with operations, 79
  == (equality) operator, 70–71
  === (identity) operator, 48, 72
> (greater than sign)
  greater than operator, 73–74
  >= (greater than or equal) operator, 73
  >> (shift right with sign) operator, 78
  >>> (shift right zero fill) operator, 78
– (hyphen)
  negation operator, 68
  subtraction operator, 68
  whitespace, newline characters, 39
–– (decrement) operator, 69
< (less than)
  less than operator, 73–74
  <!-- --> (comment tags), 30, 352–353
  <= (less than or equal) operator, 73–74
  << (shift left) operator, 78
() (parentheses), 42, 44, 67, 86, 112
  in regular expressions, 169, 171
% (modulo) operator, 68

About the Author

David Flanagan is an author, consulting computer programmer, user interface designer, and trainer. His previous books with O'Reilly & Associates include the bestselling *Java in a Nutshell, Java Examples in a Nutshell, X Toolkit Intrinsics Reference Manual,* and *X Volume 6C, Motif Tools: Streamlined GUI Design and Programming with the Xmt Library.* David has a degree in computer science and engineering from the Massachusetts Institute of Technology.

Colophon

Our look is the result of reader comments, our own experimentation, and feedback from distribution channels. Distinctive covers complement our distinctive approach to technical topics, breathing personality and life into potentially dry subjects.

The animal on the cover of *JavaScript: The Definitive Guide* is a Javan rhinoceros. All five species of rhinoceros are distinguished by their large size, thick, armor-like skin, three-toed feet, and single or double snout horn. The Javan rhinoceros, along with the Sumatran rhinoceros, is one of two forest-dwelling species. The Javan rhinoceros is similar in appearance to the Indian rhinoceros, but smaller and with certain distinguishing characteristics, primarily skin texture.

Rhinoceroses are often depicted standing up to their snouts in water or mud. In fact, they can frequently be found just like that. When not resting in a river, rhinos will dig deep pits in which to wallow. Both of these resting places provide a couple of advantages. First, they give the animal relief from the tropical heat and protection from blood-sucking flies. (The mud that the wallow leaves on the skin of the rhinoceros provides some protection from flies, also.) Second, mud wallows and river water help support the considerable weight of these huge animals, thereby relieving the strain on their legs and back.

Folklore has long held that the horn of the rhinoceros possesses magical and aphrodisiacal powers, and that humans who gain possession of the horns will gain those powers, also. This is one of the reasons why rhinoceroses are a prime target of poachers. All species of rhinoceros are in danger, and the Javan rhino is the most precarious. There are fewer than 100 of these animals still living. At one time Javan rhinoceroses could be found throughout southeastern Asia, but they are now believed to exist only in Indonesia and Vietnam.

Edie Freedman designed the cover of this book, using a 19th-century engraving from the Dover Pictorial Archive. The cover layout was produced by Kathleen Wilson with QuarkXPress 3.3 using the ITC Garamond font. Whenever possible, our books use RepKover™, a durable and flexible lay-flat binding. If the page count exceeds RepKover's limit, perfect binding is used.

The inside layout was designed by Nancy Priest and Mary Jane Walsh. Text was prepared in SGML using the DocBook 2.1 DTD. The print version of this book was created by translating the SGML source into a set of gtroff macros using a filter developed at ORA by Norman Walsh. Steve Talbott designed and wrote the underlying macro set on the basis of the GNU troff -gs macros; Lenny Muellner adapted them to SGML and implemented the book design. The GNU groff text formatter version 1.09 was used to generate PostScript output. The text and heading fonts are ITC Garamond Light and Garamond Book; the constant-width font used in this book is Letter Gothic. The illustrations that appeared in earlier editions of this book were created in Macromedia Freehand 5.0 by Chris Reilley. For this third edition, Rob Romano created and updated figures using Macromedia Freehand 7.0. This colophon was written by Clairemarie Fisher O'Leary.

More Titles from O'Reilly

Web Programming

CGI Programming on the World Wide Web

By Shishir Gundavaram
1st Edition March 1996
450 pages, ISBN 1-56592-168-2

This book offers a comprehensive explanation of CGI and related techniques for people who hold on to the dream of providing their own information servers on the Web. It starts at the beginning, explaining the value of CGI and how it works, then moves swiftly into the subtle details of programming.

Dynamic HTML: The Definitive Reference

By Danny Goodman
1st Edition July 1998
1088 pages, ISBN 1-56592-494-0

Dynamic HTML: The Definitive Reference is an indispensable compendium for Web content developers. It contains complete reference material for all of the HTML tags, CSS style attributes, browser document objects, and JavaScript objects supported by the various standards and the latest versions of Netscape Navigator and Microsoft Internet Explorer.

Frontier: The Definitive Guide

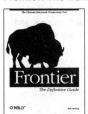

By Matt Neuburg
1st Edition February 1998
618 pages, 1-56592-383-9

This definitive guide is the first book devoted exclusively to teaching and documenting Userland Frontier, a powerful scripting environment for web site management and system level scripting. Packed with examples, advice, tricks, and tips, *Frontier: The Definitive Guide* teaches you Frontier from the ground up. Learn how to automate repetitive processes, control remote computers across a network, beef up your web site by generating hundreds of related web pages automatically, and more. Covers Frontier 4.2.3 for the Macintosh.

Learning VBScript

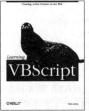

By Paul Lomax
1st Edition July 1997
616 pages, includes CD-ROM
ISBN 1-56592-247-6

This definitive guide shows web developers how to take full advantage of client-side scripting with the VBScript language. In addition to basic language features, it covers the Internet Explorer object model and discusses techniques for client-side scripting, like adding ActiveX controls to a web page or validating data before sending to the server. Includes CD-ROM with over 170 code samples.

Web Client Programming with Perl

By Clinton Wong
1st Edition March 1997
228 pages, ISBN 1-56592-214-X

Web Client Programming with Perl shows you how to extend scripting skills to the Web. This book teaches you the basics of how browsers communicate with servers and how to write your own customized web clients to automate common tasks. It is intended for those who are motivated to develop software that offers a more flexible and dynamic response than a standard web browser.

Web Authoring and Design

Designing with JavaScript

By Nick Heinle
1st Edition September 1997
256 pages, Includes CD-ROM
ISBN 1-56592-300-6

Written by the author of the "JavaScript Tip of the Week" web site, this new Web Review Studio book focuses on the most useful and applicable scripts for making truly interactive, engaging web sites. You'll not only have quick access to the scripts you need, you'll finally understand why the scripts work, how to alter the scripts to get the effects you want, and, ultimately, how to write your own groundbreaking scripts from scratch.

Web Authoring and Design

Information Architecture for the World Wide Web

By Louis Rosenfeld & Peter Morville
1st Edition January 1998
226 pages, ISBN 1-56592-282-4

Learn how to merge aesthetics and mechanics to design web sites that "work." This book shows how to apply principles of architecture and library science to design cohesive web sites and intranets that are easy to use, manage, and expand. Covers building complex sites, hierarchy design and organization, and techniques to make your site easier to search. For webmasters, designers, and administrators.

HTML: The Definitive Guide, 3rd Edition

By Chuck Musciano & Bill Kennedy
3rd Edition August 1998
576 pages, ISBN 1-56592-492-4

This complete guide is chock full of examples, sample code, and practical, hands-on advice to help you create truly effective web pages and master advanced features. Learn how to insert images and other multimedia elements, create useful links and searchable documents, use Netscape extensions, design great forms, and lots more. The third edition covers HTML 4.0, Netscape 4.5, and Internet Explorer 4.0, plus all the common extensions.

Web Navigation: Designing the User Experience

By Jennifer Fleming
1st Edition September 1998
288 pages, Includes CD-ROM
ISBN 1-56592-351-0

This book takes the first in-depth look at designing Web site navigation through design strategies to help you uncover solutions that work for your site and audience. It focuses on designing by purpose, with chapters on entertainment, shopping, identity, learning, information, and community sites. Comes with a CD-ROM that containing software demos and a "netography" of related Web resources.

Photoshop for the Web

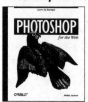

By Mikkel Aaland
1st Edition April 1998
238 pages, ISBN 1-56592-350-2

Photoshop for the Web shows you how to use the world's most popular imaging software to create Web graphics and images that look great and download blazingly fast. The book is crammed full of step-by-step examples and real-world solutions from some of the country's hottest Web producers, including *HotWired*, c*l*net, *Discovery Online*, *Second Story*, *SFGate*, and more than 20 others.

Web Server Administration

Building Your Own WebSite™

By Susan B. Peck & Stephen Arrants
1st Edition July 1996
514 pages, Includes CD-ROM,
ISBN 1-56592-232-8

This is a hands-on reference for Windows® 95 and Windows NT™ users who want to host a site on the Web or on a corporate intranet. This step-by-step guide will have you creating live web pages in minutes. You'll also learn how to connect your web to information in other Windows applications, such as word processing documents and databases. The book is packed with examples and tutorials on every aspect of web management, and it includes the highly acclaimed WebSite™ 1.1 server software on CD-ROM.

Stopping SPAM

By Alan Schwartz & Simson Garfinkel
1st Edition October 1998
204 pages, ISBN 1-56592-388-X

This book describes spam—unwanted email messages and inappropriate news articles—and explains what you and your Internet service providers and administrators can do to prevent it, trace it, stop it, and even outlaw it. Contains a wealth of advice, technical tools, and additional technical and community resources.

O'REILLY®

TO ORDER: **800-998-9938** • **order@oreilly.com** • *http://www.oreilly.com/*
OUR PRODUCTS ARE AVAILABLE AT A BOOKSTORE OR SOFTWARE STORE NEAR YOU.
FOR INFORMATION: **800-998-9938** • **707-829-0515** • **info@oreilly.com**

Web Server Administration

Writing Apache Modules with Perl and C

By Lincoln Stein & Doug MacEachern
1st Edition March 1999 (est.)
700 pages (est.), ISBN 1-56592-567-X

This guide to Web programming teaches
you how to extend the capabilities of the
Apache Web server. It explains the design
of Apache, mod_perl, and the Apache API,
then demonstrates how to use them to
rewrite CGI scripts, filter HTML documents
on the server-side, enhance server log functionality, convert file
formats on the fly, and more.

Web Security & Commerce

By Simson Garfinkel
with Gene Spafford
1st Edition June 1997
506 pages, ISBN 1-56592-269-7

Learn how to minimize the risks of the
Web with this comprehensive guide. It
covers browser vulnerabilities, privacy
concerns, issues with Java, JavaScript,
ActiveX, and plug-ins, digital certificates,
cryptography, web server security, blocking software, censorship
technology, and relevant civil and criminal issues.

Web Performance Tuning

By Patrick Killelea
1st Edition October 1998
374 pages, ISBN 1-56592-379-0

Web Performance Tuning hits the ground
running and gives concrete advice for
improving crippled Web performance right
away. For anyone who has waited too long
for a Web page to display or watched
servers slow to a crawl, this book includes
tips on tuning the server software, operating system, network, and
the Web browser itself.

Apache: The Definitive Guide

By Ben Laurie & Peter Laurie
1st Edition March 1997
274 pages, includes CD-ROM
ISBN 1-56592-250-6

Despite all the media attention to Netscape,
Apache is far and away the most widely
used web server platform in the world.
This book, written and reviewed by key
members of the Apache Group, is the only
complete guide on the market today that describes how to obtain,
set up, and secure the Apache software. Includes CD-ROM with
Apache sources and demo sites discussed in the book.

Building Your Own Web Conferences™

By Susan B. Peck & Beverly Murray Scherf
1st Edition March 1997
270 pages, Includes CD-ROM
ISBN 1-56592-279-4

Building Your Own Web Conferences is
a complete guide for Windows® 95 and
NT™ users on how to set up and manage
dynamic virtual communities that improve
workgroup collaboration and keep visitors
coming back to your site. The second in O'Reilly's "Build Your
Own..." series, this book comes with O'Reilly's state-of-the-art
WebBoard™ 2.0 software on CD-ROM.

How to stay in touch with O'Reilly

1. Visit Our Award-Winning Web Site

http://www.oreilly.com/

★ "Top 100 Sites on the Web" —*PC Magazine*
★ "Top 5% Web sites" —*Point Communications*
★ "3-Star site" —*The McKinley Group*

Our web site contains a library of comprehensive product information (including book excerpts and tables of contents), downloadable software, background articles, interviews with technology leaders, links to relevant sites, book cover art, and more. File us in your Bookmarks or Hotlist!

2. Join Our Email Mailing Lists

New Product Releases
To receive automatic email with brief descriptions of all new O'Reilly products as they are released, send email to:
listproc@online.oreilly.com
Put the following information in the first line of your message (*not* in the Subject field):
subscribe oreilly-news

O'Reilly Events
If you'd also like us to send information about trade show events, special promotions, and other O'Reilly events, send email to:
listproc@online.oreilly.com
Put the following information in the first line of your message (*not* in the Subject field):
subscribe oreilly-events

3. Get Examples from Our Books via FTP

There are two ways to access an archive of example files from our books:

Regular FTP
- ftp to:
  ftp.oreilly.com
  (login: anonymous
  password: your email address)
- Point your web browser to:
  ftp://ftp.oreilly.com/

FTPMAIL
- Send an email message to:
  ftpmail@online.oreilly.com
  (Write "help" in the message body)

4. Contact Us via Email

order@oreilly.com
To place a book or software order online. Good for North American and international customers.

subscriptions@oreilly.com
To place an order for any of our newsletters or periodicals.

books@oreilly.com
General questions about any of our books.

software@oreilly.com
For general questions and product information about our software. Check out O'Reilly Software Online at **http://software.oreilly.com/** for software and technical support information. Registered O'Reilly software users send your questions to: **website-support@oreilly.com**

cs@oreilly.com
For answers to problems regarding your order or our products.

booktech@oreilly.com
For book content technical questions or corrections.

proposals@oreilly.com
To submit new book or software proposals to our editors and product managers.

international@oreilly.com
For information about our international distributors or translation queries. For a list of our distributors outside of North America check out:
http://www.oreilly.com/www/order/country.html

O'Reilly & Associates, Inc.
101 Morris Street, Sebastopol, CA 95472 USA
TEL 707-829-0515 or 800-998-9938
(6am to 5pm PST)
FAX 707-829-0104

O'REILLY®

Titles from O'Reilly

International Distributors

UK, EUROPE, MIDDLE EAST AND NORTHERN AFRICA (EXCEPT FRANCE, GERMANY, SWITZERLAND, & AUSTRIA)

INQUIRIES
International Thomson Publishing Europe
Berkshire House
168-173 High Holborn
London WC1V 7AA
United Kingdom
Tel: 44-1-71-497-1422
Fax: 44-1-71-497-1426

ORDERS
International Thomson Publishing Services, Ltd.
Cheriton House, North Way
Andover, Hampshire SP10 5BE
United Kingdom
Tel: 44-1-264-342-832 (UK)
Tel: 44-1-264-342-806 (outside UK)
Fax: 44-1-264-364-418 (UK)
Fax: 44-1-264-342-761 (outside UK)
Email: itpint@itps.co.uk

FRANCE
GEODIF
61, Bd Saint-Germain
75240 Paris Cedex 05, France
Tel: 33-1-44-41-46-16 (French books)
Tel: 33-1-44-41-11-87 (English books)
Fax: 33-1-44-41-11-44
Email: distribution@eyrolles.com

ORDERS
SODIS
128, av.du Mal de Lattre de Tassigny
77403 Lagny Cédex, France
Tel: 33-1-60-07-82-00
Fax: 33-1-64-30-32-27

INQUIRIES
Éditions O'Reilly
18 rue Séguier
75006 Paris, France
Tel: 33-1-40-51-52-30
Fax: 33-1-40-51-52-31
Email: france@editions-oreilly.fr

GERMANY, SWITZERLAND, AUSTRIA

INQUIRIES
O'Reilly Verlag
Balthasarstr. 81
D-50670 Köln, Germany
Tel: 49-221-973160-0
Fax: 49-221-973160-8
Email: anfragen@oreilly.de

ORDERS
International Thomson Publishing
Königswinterer Straße 418
53227 Bonn, Germany
Tel: 49-228-970240
Fax: 49-228-441342
Email: order@oreilly.de

CANADA (FRENCH LANGUAGE BOOKS)
Les Éditions Flammarion ltée
375, Avenue Laurier Ouest
Montréal (Québec) H2V 2K3
Tel: 00-1-514-277-8807
Fax: 00-1-514-278-2085
Email: info@flammarion.qc.ca

HONG KONG
City Discount Subscription Service, Ltd.
Unit D, 3rd Floor, Yan's Tower
27 Wong Chuk Hang Road
Aberdeen, Hong Kong
Tel: 852-2580-3539
Fax: 852-2580-6463
Email: citydis@ppn.com.hk

KOREA
Hanbit Media, Inc.
Sonyoung Bldg. 202
Yeksam-dong 736-36
Kangnam-ku
Seoul, Korea
Tel: 822-554-9610
Fax: 822-556-0363
Email: hant93@chollian.dacom.co.kr

SINGAPORE, MALAYSIA, THAILAND
Addison-Wesley Longman Singapore Pte., Ltd.
25 First Lok Yang Road
Singapore 629734
Tel: 65-268-2666
Fax: 65-268-7023
Email: Daniel.Loh@awl.com.sg

PHILIPPINES
Mutual Books, Inc.
429-D Shaw Boulevard
Mandaluyong City, Metro
Manila, Philippines
Tel: 632-725-7538
Fax: 632-721-3056
Email: mbikikog@mnl.sequel.net

TAIWAN
O'Reilly Taiwan
No. 3, Lane 131
Hang-Chow South Road
Section 1, Taipei, Taiwan
Tel: 886-2-23968990
Fax: 886-2-23968916
Email: benh@oreilly.com

CHINA
China National Publishing
Industry Trading Corporation
504 AnHuiLi, AnDingMenWai
P.O. Box 782
Beijing 100011, China P.R.
Tel: 86-10-6424-0483
Fax: 86-10-6421-4540
Email: frederic@oreilly.com

INDIA
Computer Bookshop (India) Pvt. Ltd.
190 Dr. D.N. Road, Fort
Bombay 400 001 India
Tel: 91-22-207-0989
Fax: 91-22-262-3551
Email: cbsbom@giasbm01.vsnl.net.in

JAPAN
O'Reilly Japan, Inc.
Kiyoshige Building 2F
12-Bancho, Sanei-cho
Shinjuku-ku
Tokyo 160-0008 Japan
Tel: 81-3-3356-5227
Fax: 81-3-3356-5261
Email: japan@oreilly.com

ALL OTHER ASIAN COUNTRIES
O'Reilly & Associates, Inc.
101 Morris Street
Sebastopol, CA 95472 USA
Tel: 707-829-0515
Fax: 707-829-0104
Email: order@oreilly.com

AUSTRALIA
WoodsLane Pty., Ltd.
7/5 Vuko Place
Warriewood NSW 2102
Australia
Tel: 61-2-9970-5111
Fax: 61-2-9970-5002
Email: info@woodslane.com.au

NEW ZEALAND
Woodslane New Zealand, Ltd.
21 Cooks Street (P.O. Box 575)
Waganui, New Zealand
Tel: 64-6-347-6543
Fax: 64-6-345-4840
Email: info@woodslane.com.au

SOUTH AFRICA
International Thomson South Africa
Building 18, Constantia Park
138 Sixteenth Road
(P.O. Box 2459)
Halfway House, 1685 South Africa
Tel: 27-11-805-4819
Fax: 27-11-805-3648

LATIN AMERICA
McGraw-Hill Interamericana
Editores, S.A. de C.V.
Cedro No. 512
Col. Atlampa
06450, Mexico, D.F.
Tel: 52-5-547-6777
Fax: 52-5-547-3336
Email: mcgraw-hill@infosel.net.mx